PEREGRINE BOOKS

THE LIFE OF HENRY JAMES

VOL. 2

'The greatest literary biography of our time' – A. L. Rowse

Since 1953, when the first part was published, Leon Edel's life of Henry James has been the subject of increasing critical acclaim. It now appears in Penguins in a 'definitive edition' of two volumes.

Volume Two carries on the story from 1889 until the death of the 'Master' in 1916. James had settled in England, latterly at Lamb House, Rye, and his reputation as one of the leading literary figures of his generation was assured. After a brief dalliance with the theatre which, although unsuccessful, profoundly influenced his later writing, his output of novels and stories continued, and this period saw the publication of *The Spoils of Poynton*, *The Turn of the Screw*, *The Ambassadors* and *The Golden Bowl*. Like Orwell and T. S. Eliot, Henry James was reluctant to open his life to biographers, but Professor Edel, in what amounts to an object-lesson in the art of biography, has masterfully uncovered the life of a man whose contribution, by precept and practice, to English literature was enormous.

*

Leon Edel is a fellow of the Royal Society of Literature, a member of the American Academy of Arts and Letters, a past president of P.E.N. (U.S.) and, after occupying the Henry James Chair of English and American Letters at New York University, he was named to the Citizens' Chair of English at the University of Hawaii, which he now holds.

LEON EDEL

•

THE LIFE OF
HENRY JAMES

•

Volume 2

PENGUIN BOOKS

Penguin Books Ltd, Harmondsworth, Middlesex, England
Penguin Books, 625 Madison Avenue, New York, New York 10022, U.S.A.
Penguin Books Australia Ltd, Ringwood, Victoria, Australia
Penguin Books Canada Ltd, 2801 John Street, Markham, Ontario, Canada L3R 1B4
Penguin Books (N.Z.) Ltd, 182–190 Wairau Road, Auckland 10, New Zealand

—

First published in 3 volumes (*The Middle Years 1884–94*; *The Treacherous Years 1895–1900*;
The Master 1901–16) by Rupert Hart-Davis Ltd 1963, 1969, 1972
First published in this edition in Penguin Books 1977
Copyright © Leon Edel, 1963, 1969, 1972, 1977

—

Made and printed in Great Britain by
Hazell Watson & Viney Ltd,
Aylesbury, Bucks
Set in Linotype Pilgrim

Contents

CONTENTS

CONTENTS

CONTENTS

BOOK ONE
THE DRAMATIC YEARS
1890-95

Part One
Theatricals

I

A Chastening Necessity

HENRY JAMES'S beloved Aunt Kate – Catherine Walsh – his mother's sister, died early in 1889. She had been a second mother to the James children and a 'third person' in that lively and troubled household – almost -a second wife to the elder Henry James. The account of her funeral in New York, from William, made vivid to Henry 'for almost the first time that the dear old Aunt's place on earth is vacant forever'. Kate Walsh had imprinted on Henry James the idea of a man attended by two strong women. He used the name of Kate often in his work, usually to portray a woman of will and determination.

The aunt left a substantial estate, but mainly to the women of the Walsh family and only token gifts to the James children. Henry James had no expectations of inheritance; but at this time he was seriously re-examining his professional and financial position. He continued to give his sister his inheritance from his father, that is, his share of the Syracuse rents which yielded him $100 a month. Alice spent little and put aside this money for her brother's future use, in the confident belief he would survive her. The question which troubled the novelist most was not his earning power; he did very well, given his modest reputation; but he felt that he could not keep up the pace of the previous five years during which he had run three large serials through the magazines, while producing articles and reviews at the same time. The work gave him a sufficient income; but when the serials appeared in book form they did not sell. He looked with envy at novelists who earned massive royalties; their works were constantly in the market. He usually received a handsome advance of around $1,200 for the book version of a novel, but his royalties did not often cover this sum, so that he was nearly always in debt to his publishers. He was vividly reminded of this when *The Tragic Muse* had run its long course in the *Atlantic*. The Macmillans told him they doubted whether the book would sell and this time offered him only £70 in advance instead of the usual £250. The letter James wrote to Macmillan is perhaps unique in publishing history in its imperious tone – that of a man deeply disturbed that his reputation could not obtain more money-credit. 'In spite of what you tell me of the poor success of my recent books,' he told Macmillan, 'I still do desire to get a larger sum, and have determined to take what steps I can in this direction.' He went on:

These steps I know will carry me away from you, but it comes over me that that is after all better, even with a due and grateful recognition of the readiness you express to go on with me, unprofitable as I am. I say it is 'better' because I had far rather that in those circumstances you should *not* go on with me. I would rather not be published at all than be published and not pay – other people at least. The latter alternative makes me uncomfortable and the former makes me, of the two, feel least like a failure; the failure that, at this time of day, it is too humiliating to consent to be without trying, at least, as they say in America, to 'know more about it'. Unless I can put the matter on a more remunerative footing all round I shall give up my English 'market' – heaven save the market! – and confine myself to my American. But I must experiment a bit first – and to experiment is of course to say farewell to you. Farewell, then, my dear Macmillan, with great regret – but with the sustaining cheer of all the links in the chain that remain still unbroken. Yours ever HENRY JAMES

For the first time in his long career as a writer he now turned to a literary agent, the well-known firm of H. P. Watt. Watt negotiated a contract by which James surrendered all his rights in *The Tragic Muse* for five years to Macmillan in return for the £250 he wanted. James was mollified; but he had had his warning. He announced this would be his last long fiction. From now on he would write only short stories and articles; he would free himself from the slavery of the monthly deadline; and this would leave him time for a sustained 'assault' on the stage.

I

James might have been more cautious had he not at this moment received overtures from the theatre. They came in unexpected form. Edward Compton, a young actor-manager, who had been playing classical comedies in the provinces for a decade, asked James to turn his 1877 novel, *The American*, into a play. He saw in the role of Christopher Newman a vivid part for himself, and in Claire de Cintré a suitable role for his wife, the American actress Virginia Bateman. A long meditation in James's notebooks shows how he weighed this offer.

I had practically given up my old, valued, long cherished dream of doing something for the stage, for fame's sake, and art's, and fortune's: overcome by the vulgarity, the brutality, the baseness of the condition of the English-speaking theatre today. But after an interval, a long one, the vision has revived, on a new and a very much humbler basis, and especially under the lash of necessity. Of art or fame *il est maintenant fort peu question*: I simply *must* try, and try seriously, to produce half a dozen – a dozen, five dozen – plays for the sake of my pocket, my material future. Of how little money the novel makes for me I needn't discourse here. The theatre has sought me out – in the person of the good, the yet unseen, Compton. I have listened and considered and reflected, and the matter is transposed to a minor key.

What profit he might make would mean

real freedom for one's general artistic life: it all hangs together (time, leisure, independence for 'real literature', and, in addition, a great deal of experience of *tout un côté de la vie*). Therefore my plan is to try with a settled resolution – that is, with a full determination to return repeatedly to the charge, overriding, annihilating, despising the boundless discouragements, disgusts, *écœurements*. One should *use* such things – grind them to powder.

And then, settling down to a review of the story of *The American*, Henry wrote : 'Oh, how it [the play] must not be too good and how very bad it must be!' Which may explain why he exclaimed '*À moi, Scribe; à moi, Sardou; à moi, Dennery!*' These masters of the 'well-made play' in France were to be his guide and example. They had written splendid 'sure-fire' dramas; James had seen their works and seen the crowds flocking to their theatres. There was never, from the first, any doubt in his mind that the theatre would be for him a kind of artistic slumming expedition : it would offer its amusement but also financial rewards; it would be a compromise – an exciting gamble.

James confided to Robert Louis Stevenson

I propose, for a longish period, to do nothing but short lengths. I want to leave a multitude of pictures of my time, projecting my small circular frame upon as many different spots as possible and going in for number as well as quality, so that the number may constitute a total having a certain value as observation and testimony.

A year and a half later, confessing to Stevenson that he had begun experimenting with the theatre, he wrote : 'Don't be hard on me – simplifying and chastening necessity has laid its brutal hand on me and I have had to try to make somehow or other the money I don't make by literature. My books don't sell, and it looks as if my plays might. Therefore I am going with a brazen front to write half a dozen.'

2

The 1890s ushered in this new life for Henry James. He emerged from his study in De Vere Gardens to besiege the theatre; and this confrontation induced a state of malaise and often acute anxiety. By nature he was a retiring writer, whose desk was a private citadel; he never talked about work in progress until the book was ready to be given to the world. He negotiated directly with publishers and editors, and had been accustomed, until recently, to prompt publication. The world of the theatre seemed to him the exact opposite : everything was done in a glare of publicity and with interminable delay. If he so much as had a talk with a manager, the theatrical gossip-columns immediately knew of it. There seemed to be an incessant public chatter in which actors and actresses joined. James found this irritating. He shrank from it; he sought to avoid it. Much as he liked going to the theatre, he hated the stage itself : hated it, yet was fascinated by it. Moreover he had a curious story-book conception of it, not a little like a young stage-struck person : this was based on his study of the traditions of the Maison de Molière and his own nights in the Rue de Richelieu, going back to the early 1870s; and upon his long friendship with Mrs Kemble and her talk of the theatre in her day. He would speak of the stage as a 'straitjacket' for any self-respecting man of letters. He felt himself encased in it even before he approached the theatre.

During the next five years, from 1890 to the beginning of 1895, James devoted himself to the writing of plays. His artist-self enjoyed planning scenarios and reading them to actors and actresses; he found it exciting to match stage-folk with his characters. He discovered, however, that the theatre was a place where nothing seemed to happen. Actor-managers 'talk of years as we talk of months', he ruefully said. If a play failed, they could always pull out some classic or revive an old success while they planned their next venture. They seemed little interested in art or literature. What interested them was whether the 'vehicle' would fill the theatre. These were the realities James had to face – these and the conditions he had described through his character Gabriel Nash – the hasty dinners swallowed in restaurants, the lines of cabs at the theatre-doors, the race with the clock to release the audience.

Fancy putting the exquisite before such a tribunal as that! There's not even a question of it. The dramatist wouldn't if he could, and in nine cases out of ten he couldn't if he would. He has to make the basest concessions. What can you do with a character, with an idea, with a feeling, between dinner and the suburban trains? You can give a gross rough sketch of them, but how little you touch them, how bald you leave them! What crudity compared with what the novelist does!

A would-be dramatist, approaching the stage with so acute a sense of its shortcomings and material difficulties, was hardly in a frame of mind to attack it with the required defences – resourcefulness, patience, resilience, and a capacity to endure discouragement. Henry James had perhaps intuitively realized that it would be better to begin with a modest company, and discover in the provinces some of the secrets of this 'most unholy trade'. Edward Compton wanted to establish himself in a theatre in London. He gave James a £250 advance to dramatize *The American*, and early in 1890 the novelist – having disposed of *The Tragic Muse* – set himself to his task. His correspondence is filled with mysterious allusions; he cultivates secrecy; he adjures William to silence. His sister's private journal, however, mirrors his activities. They seem to have filled her sick-room with a lively sense of stage personalities and of adventure. 'My zeal in the affair is only matched by my indifference,' he writes to Stevenson. He was certainly far from indifferent. In the same letter he could write: 'I find the *form* opens out before me as if it were a kingdom to conquer.' Then he remembers that it is, by his standards, a paltry kingdom 'of ignorant brutes of managers and dense *cabotins* of actors'. All the same, he feels as if he had at last found his form, 'my real one – that for which pale fiction is an ineffectual substitute'. Realizing that this contradicted what he had just said, he adds:

God grant this unholy truth may not abide with me more than two or three years – time to dig out eight or ten rounded masterpieces and make withal enough money to enable me to retire in peace and plenty for the unmolested business of a *little* supreme writing, as distinct from gouging – which is the form above-mentioned.

It is useless to seek consistency in James's utterances about the stage. He apologizes right and left; he is also enjoying himself enormously. And he writes very strange plays – this master of drama within the novel-form. The simplest explanation lies precisely in the ambiguities expressed in his letters. To come into the open and into the life of practical action – as distinct from the life of imaginative action – was so foreign to James's nature that he seemed doomed to failure. No citadel can be assaulted by contempt for the conditions of the assault; no original creativity is possible when it is mixed with so much diffidence and disgust.

3

The American took shape rapidly. By 6 February 1890 James had sent the second act to Compton; at this moment he was calling the play *The Californian*. He told himself: 'Perhaps the best formula for the fabrication of a dramatic piece *telle qu'il nous faut en faire*, in the actual conditions, if we are to do anything at all is: Action which is never dialogue and dialogue which is always action.'

'I have written a big (and awfully good) four-act play, by which I hope to make my fortune,' he confided to Henrietta Reubell. And he told his sister he had met 'exactly the immediate, actual, intense British conditions, both subjective and objective'. The play would run two and three-quarter hours. He feared, however, the mediocrity of the provincial troupe. He was to receive a ten-per-cent royalty on gross receipts. And he dreamed of £80 a week during the provincial run and £350 a month when the play came to London. These were castles in the air and they were encouraged by a lively young man, a friend of Howells, who had come to London from America as agent for a New York publishing house. His name was Wolcott Balestier, and his energy, his exuberance, his business ability, captivated James. Balestier was twenty-nine. He had a way of living in a dream of greatness – of large contracts, vast enterprises. Balestier recognized that the impending international copyright agreement would end years of piracy in America. With sound business sense he set out to make arrangements with English writers for legal publication of their works. Small wonder that his dreams were infectious and that he was greeted by the writing world in England with open arms. He was the harbinger of a new era: a bringer of royalties from beyond the sea. He established an office at No. 2 Dean's Yard, overlooked by the towers of the Abbey and overlooking a portion of Westminster School, where the boys played Association football in the winter afternoons. Here amid the chiming of Abbey bells this young American combined the picturesque with the commercial. He had no sense of difficulty and no awe of greatness. James consulted him in all his theatrical affairs. He was one of the first of the group of young acolytes that now began to form around 'the Master', the young men of literature and of publishing who could offer him solace and comfort – and affection.

4

Fenimore, lonely on her Florentine hill-top after the death of Lizzie and the departure of Boott and Duveneck, was also planning a change. Much as she liked the Italian climate, and the city to which Henry James had introduced her almost ten years before, she felt that she had to find a new home. Her thought was that she would go back to England; and there are sufficient indications that in her fancy she wanted to be closer to the man who was much in her thoughts and who came to Italy only at long intervals.

The process of leaving the Villa Brichieri was difficult. She had become embedded in the place, almost morbidly, one might say, for in a tale she wrote about Bellosguardo her widowed heroine prefers death to leaving her villa and wastes away for no other visible reason than her grief and her memories. Fenimore was of stronger fibre. She went through her ordeal of getting her belongings together. James told Boott that it took her 'upwards of two months of incessant personal labour, night and day, to get out of a Brichieri bed or two', but 'the rupture of our last tie with that consecrated spot has really taken place'. Fenimore came first to England and in the autumn of 1889 spent a month at Richmond. She was joined by her sister, and the two left for a winter's tour of the Mediterranean – to Corfu and the Holy Land – which furnished Fenimore copy for some travel articles in *Harper's*. Early the following spring, however, she returned to England and fixed upon Cheltenham as her new abode. She preferred it to London, for she had started work on another novel. But she would again be near to James. He, however, once his play was in Compton's hands, decided – it seemed almost perverse – to leave for Italy. From Venice he wrote to Francis Boott, then in England to 'see Fenimore without fail – at 4 Promenade Terrace, Cheltenham'. Boott went, for James told him 'your visit was a great pleasure to her – and I should doubtless have heard in the same sense from Fenimore if I had heard at all. But I have scarcely had news of her since I came abroad.' He himself paid a visit on his return, for Miss Woolson's copy of *The Tragic Muse* is signed and dated 'Cheltenham, September 15, 1890'.

That James should have gone to Italy that summer while awaiting production of his play was not altogether strange : but it may have seemed so to Fenimore. He was not in the habit of journeying directly into the Italian heat. Nevertheless in the middle of May we find him at Milan, whence he writes to William about Howells's new novel, *A Hazard of New Fortunes*, finding in it much 'life and truth of observation and feeling'. 'His abundance and facility are my constant wonder and envy – or rather not, perhaps, envy, inasmuch as he has purchased them by throwing the whole question of form, style and composition overboard into the deep sea – from which, on my side, I am perpetually trying to fish them up.' He could write, however, a sincere letter to Howells praising this large work of his, telling him 'You are *less* big than Zola, but you are ever so much less clumsy and more really various.'

James went to Genoa, Pisa, Lucca, then hurried to Florence for emergency dental care. Dr W. W. Baldwin found the novelist nursing his jaw in an hotel and insisted on his coming to stay with him in the Via Palestro. He paid two sad visits to Bellosguardo, and in early June proceeded to Venice to the Barbaro. The palace was 'cool, melancholy, empty, delicious'. The Curtises decided to go to Oberammergau to see the 1890 Passion Play, and persuaded James to accompany them. The play struck him as 'primitive' and he disliked the way in which it was commercialized. Returning from this excursion he made a little tour of small Tuscan towns with Dr Baldwin in the suffocating summer heat and then stayed at Vallombrosa, near the Countess Peruzzi, (Edith Story), enjoying the mountain coolness. Mrs Gardner had rented the Barbaro from the Curtises for the rest of the summer, and he promised her a visit before returning to England. He was preparing to descend from his Miltonic altitude, when an urgent telegram came from Alice and he promptly left for London. He had gone abroad in the comparative security that he could linger until late summer, since Alice seemed comfortable in Leamington, and Katharine Loring had once again come out from America to be with her. The sudden summons, however, meant a new breakdown; and James decided that Alice had been immured too long in the provinces. With Miss Loring's help he had her moved

to London, to the South Kensington Hotel. In due course he found
rooms in Argyle Road, Campden Hill, about ten minutes from De
Vere Gardens. Alice's journal records that Dr Baldwin had come
from Florence and was staying in De Vere Gardens with her brother.
'Can she die?' James and Miss Loring had asked Baldwin (whom
apparently Alice refused to see – she had developed great hostility
toward physicians). Baldwin answered, 'They sometimes do.' Alice
recorded this in her journal with an increasing mixture of self-pity
and a mockery of death. For she had learned that she was doomed.
There came a moment when a doctor had to be summoned, and he
found a tumour of the breast. Some months later she allowed Baldwin to examine her when he was again in England. He diagnosed
cancer, and predicted to James the form it would take. Miss Loring
from now on remained with Alice. A silent and as yet remote death-
watch had begun, and one which Alice herself kept – oscillating
between moments of fear and of courage, mingling these with her
devotion to Parnell and the Irish, and the record of her brother's
theatricals. Her journal entries are exclamatory and astringent, shot
through again and again with felicities of the style which she shared
with Henry and William James.

<h2 style="text-align:center">5</h2>

James now began to discover how difficult the writing of a play
could be – even for one as experienced in dialogue as he was. Editors
might complain of length, but they never presumed, in those days
at least, to suggest alterations. With *The American*, which went into
rehearsal that autumn, he found himself doing a great deal of car-
pentry. A scene did not sound right: it had to be rewritten. Actors
objected to certain lines. Speeches needed to be made more colloquial. He submitted grudgingly to the first managerial cuts and kept
dashing into the provinces through rain and damp to meet the touring company wherever it might be. After a while he found himself
showing the actors how he thought certain 'bits' should be played:
he called on all his memories of the French theatre. Most important
of all was the task of teaching the tall and handsome Edward Compton how to talk 'American'. The typescript sent to the Lord Chamberlain's Office for the licensing of the play was the copy used by
Compton; written into it, in James's hand, are the American pro-
nunciations, the guiding principle of which seems to have been to

speak everything 'a little from the nose'. In making his compromises with the stage James was not above caricature.

Southport, near Liverpool, was selected for the out-of-town opening. There was a large winter population and a comfortable theatre, the Winter Gardens. Here on New Year's Day 1891 James arrived in a state of feverish excitement. Balestier joined him. 'My dear Suzerain of the Drama,' he had written with his usual extravagance, 'if you will let me "assist" at the first performance of the first play of our first dramatist this is to intimate that nothing short of legal proceedings to restrain my liberty can prevent my being present.' Also to Southport came William Archer, the drama-critic, who was helping to launch Ibsen in England and who presently would be collaborating with Shaw in his earliest plays. Archer had been urging English novelists to take the theatre seriously; and his arrival at Southport, after writing to James for permission to come, indicated that at least one important notice of the production would be written. James urged him to wait for a more finished play – to see it after its try-outs. But Archer was serious and hard-working. He refused to be put off.

The first night took place on 3 January 1891 and James spent a nervous day writing letters to all his friends, asking them to pray for him, explaining to Urbain Mengin that it was 'the thirst for gold that is pushing me along this dishonourable path', telling William he was in a state of 'abject, lonely, fear'. The hour finally came. James, watching the play from the right wing, found the audience appreciative and enjoyed its laughter. He enjoyed also, for the first time in his life, being dragged in front of an applauding house, and giving himself up, as he said, to a series of simpering bows, while from the 'gas-flaring indistinguishable dimness' came the pleasant sounds of acclaim. Compton pressed his hand. So far as Southport was concerned 'the stake was won'.

In a preface he was to write to Balestier's posthumous tales James alludes to this episode as

a wet winter night in a windy Lancashire town – a formidable 'first night' at a troubled provincial theatre to which he had made a long and loyal pilgrimage for purposes of 'support' at a grotesquely nervous hour – such an occasion comes back to me, vividly, with the very quality of the support afforded, lavish and eager and shrewd; with the pleasantness of the little commemorative inn-supper, half-histrionic and wholly confident, and with the dragged-out drollery of the sequel next day, our sociable, amused participation in a collective theatrical fitting, effected in pottering Sunday trains, besprinkled with refreshment-room impressions and terminating, that night, at an all but inaccessible Birmingham, in independent repose and relaxed criticism.

Next day James left the strolling players to pay a visit, but he told no one where he was going, save Miss Loring. He journeyed from Birmingham to Cheltenham, to spend the day and rehearse his minor provincial triumph to Miss Woolson. A month later he wrote to his brother: 'You can form no idea of how a provincial success is confined to the provinces.'

2

A London Début

HENRY JAMES had been given a lively taste of what it meant to be a strolling player. His sallies into the provinces, his continuing rehearsals and his constant amendment of scenes, provided him with a liberal education in theatricals. 'The authorship in any sense worthy of the name of a play,' he now explained to William, 'only *begins* when it is written, and I see that one's creation of it doesn't terminate till one has gone with it every inch of the way to the rise of the curtain.' The evening at Southport had been in reality a larger rehearsal: the curtain would rise only after *The American* was brought to London. Still William Archer offered high praise – the play was 'full of alert and telling dialogue' and showed 'a keen eye for stage effect'. Compton performed it on an average once a week while touring. *The American* was his one gamble in the 'modern'.

Balestier wrote to Howells: 'The most delightful feature of the success of the piece is its effect on James. He is like a runner ready to run a race. He has the air of one just setting out – a youngster with an oldster's grip and mastery: surely the most enviable of situations.' William sensed Henry's excitement in his letters. 'It is an extreme delight to see you in your old and sedate age going in for experiences as keen and uproarious as this, and I do most devoutly hope, now that you've made your plunge, that you'll keep at it and become a Dumas *fils*.'

James saw the play at its second performance at the Theatre

Royal, Wolverhampton, and a few days later at the Memorial Theatre, Stratford-on-Avon, where he was noticed in the audience and took a bow. He saw it once again in Leamington on 16 January where he was still rehearsing some of the scenes. 'I show 'em how to do it – and even then they don't know,' he told Miss Reubell.

Edward Compton had taken a long lease of the old Opera Comique Theatre in the Strand, where the early Gilbert and Sullivan operas had been performed. He invested a substantial sum in renovation; he installed 'the latest sanitary arrangements', and added two new stone staircases. He could not, however, alter the theatre's basic design, including a long subterranean passage to the stalls, which playgoers found rather discouraging. While waiting for his London first night James began to write a second play, and presently a third. His second was a comedy called *Mrs Vibert*; later the title was changed to *Tenants*. He had long ago read a tale in the *Revue des Deux Mondes* called 'Flavien: Scènes de la vie contemporaine' – a little melodrama which had in it all the ingredients of James's early tales: a General, a ward, the General's mistress, the sons of the general and of the mistress (really half-brothers) who fight a duel. He transferred the setting to England, and out of these stock situations he now manufactured a trite comedy, substituting fisticuffs for the duel. John Hare, an enterprising actor-manager, asked James to submit a play and was offered *Mrs Vibert*. A search began for possible interpreters. The novelist fixed his attention on Geneviève Ward, who had had a career on the operatic stage in New York and later in the theatre, and W. H. Vernon who had been her leading man in a number of productions. There were letters and telegrams, tea-hour readings, aided and abetted by James's friend Mrs Hugh Bell, herself the author of a number of closet-dramas. In his characteristic manner of this time James wrote to Mrs Bell that the third act of his *Mrs Vibert* was 'a pure *movement*, intensely interesting and suspense-producing, lasting forty minutes and subtly calculated to capture the Genevan and Vernonese mind'. He also said he had abridged his second act 'as effectually and bloodily as the most barbarous dramatic butchers could desire'. The images of the butcher's shop were to increase the longer James aspired to the theatre. He was to exclaim later of one of his efforts: 'Oh, the mutilated, brutally simplified, massacred little play.' Mrs Ward decided against the part and James turned to the celebrated tragedienne, Helena Modjeska. She, in turn, told him she could only see Geneviève Ward in the role. Hare speedily lost interest in the comedy and James set it aside.

That winter he wrote still another comedy, during six weeks spent in Paris. This was based on a recent tale, *The Solution*, which had gone back to the days of his adventures in the saddle and his Roman sightseeing with Mrs Wister and Mrs Mason. It was the story of a diplomat who is persuaded that he has compromised a young woman by taking her on an unchaperoned walk. James transferred the scene once more to England. In the hands of Oscar Wilde this could have become an amusing drawing-room farce. *Disengaged*, however, was a series of unmotivated entries and exits. He thought of the comedy as suitable for Ada Rehan, the Irish-American actress who had made a great hit on the London stage in classical comedy under the management of the New York stage veteran, Augustin Daly. Daly took an option on the play on the strength of James's literary reputation. For the next year and a half the novelist-playwright waited for this comedy to be produced. What held it up was that Daly was building a theatre in London. *Disengaged* was scheduled to be one of the 'attractions' of the new house.

This was James's situation as a dramatist by the time he began rehearsals for the London production of *The American*.

I

During one of his calls on Geneviève Ward – on 12 January 1891 – he encountered a young woman of considerable charm, with extraordinarily large clear blue eyes, which looked straight into his, and more 'personality' than he had found among most of the actresses in London. She was indeed an actress, and an American. Her name was Elizabeth Robins. She was 27, and had been on the stage for almost a decade. She had played small parts in New York, worked with James O'Neill, (the father of Eugene), and later been attached to the company at the Boston Museum. She had toured up and down the United States with the Booth-Barrett company playing minor Shakespearean roles and had then gone abroad. During a visit to Norway she had heard the name of Ibsen. Now, in London, she was appearing in *A Doll's House* before scandalized Victorian audiences. The battle for Ibsen had begun, and in this young woman the Norwegian had a vigorous and intelligent interpreter. She had a certain ease and quiet in her relations with people; she knew the value of few words, and the charm of being attentive. This was why she had been able to impress into her service Oscar Wilde and Beerbohm Tree, when she had decided not to return to trouping in America. What James thought of her on that day we do not know, but Miss Robins's diary leaves no doubt of her impression.

Delightful experience. He tells me about his play *The American*. We talk Ibsen and he is coming to see me in *Doll's House*. I like this man better I think than any *male* American I have met abroad. He is delightfully *grave* and without the Yankee traveller's thin pretence of cosmopolitanism. This meeting is a ray of sunshine in a dark day.

On 27 January, at a matinée of *A Doll's House* which he attended with Geneviève Ward, he watched Miss Robins; it was the first Ibsen play he had seen. Later that spring he saw her in *Hedda Gabler*; it was 'the talk of the town,' he wrote to Miss Reubell, 'with the most interesting English-speaking actress (or rather the *only* one,) that I have seen for many a day – Elizabeth Robins, an American of course. *Le cœur ne vous en dit-il pas?*' And to Mrs Gardner he said: 'She is slightly uncanny, but distinguished and individual.' James took Compton to see her perform and it was settled that they would invite her to play Claire de Cintré in *The American*, a role Mrs Compton had taken in the provinces but which she was relinquishing in London because she was pregnant.

What James could not have known was that Miss Robins's gift lay precisely in the playing of Heddas and Noras; although she had an adequate bag of tricks as an experienced actress, she was constitutionally incapable of creating so shrinking a flower as Claire – a woman all renunciation and passivity. The casting may have seemed wise at the time: and doubtless James had reason to believe that Miss Robins's gifts were less specialized. Nevertheless the role offered her could not have suited her less and she was to have great difficulty with it. Several other changes were made in the cast. Kate Bateman, Mrs Compton's older sister, came out of retirement to play the Marquise, and a young and vivacious French actress, Adrienne Dairolles, was given the part of Noémie.

New scenery was built; the furniture was imported from Paris; much attention was paid to the costumes. However the critics were to be puzzled over the fact that Henry dressed his American in a long chocolate-coloured coat with sky-blue trimmings, and buttons 'as large as cheese-plates'. The costume reminded them of a travelling showman; they knew that American millionaires dressed in much better taste. There was a strong element of travesty in Compton's appearance; and in his romantic story James could not – on the stage – draw the line between his comedy and his pathos, between outright farce and the high comedy of his original. The London rehearsals proved more strenuous than those in the provinces; and Miss Robins has left us an account of Henry's charm behind the scenes and his consideration for the actors. Sandwiches and other delicacies were brought down to rehearsals from De Vere Gardens by his servants. 'No other playwright, in my tolerably wide experience,' she wrote, 'ever thought of feeding his company.'

2

In the spring of 1891, when he had all but completed recasting *The American*, James had a bout of influenza. It left him weak and dispirited. He had always wanted to pay a longer visit to Ireland than his brief stay in Cork in 1882 and this seemed an opportune time; he would be within easy call of Alice and at the same time would take a respite from his theatrical chores and write some short stories. He went at the end of June to Kingstown, six miles from Dublin, and settled in the Royal Marine Hotel. Here he wrote *The Private Life*, and his little tale of *The Chaperon*, another of his stories of how a lady can breach the laws of society and then, with society's own amused consent, be re-accepted. The irony of the tale was that instead of the daughter being chaperoned by the mother, it is the mother who is chaperoned after a series of indiscretions – and reescorted into society – by the daughter. The dramatist Arthur Pinero, on reading this tale, pointed out that it had all the elements of an amusing stage play. The novelist promptly made notes to that end. A fragment of a scenario, dictated by him almost fifteen years later, is all that survives.

In Ireland he found 'peace and obscurity and leisure' and he recovered rapidly from his illness. In mid-July he wrote a gossipy letter to Francis Boott, mentioning among other things that Fenimore was moving from Cheltenham to Oxford 'for a year, a very right and good place for her. She believes she is then – after a year again – going to Italy to spend the rest of her life. But *chi lo sa?* I haven't either seen or heard of her "Bellosguardo story", but shall demand of her to send it to me.' This was the tale called *Dorothy* which had reflected Fenimore's difficulty in uprooting herself from the Villa Brichieri.

On 20 July James wrote one of his continuing series of letters to Lowell, who was dying. These are filled with the warmth of an old and sympathetic friendship. James described the Irish coast, the blueness of sea and greenness of shore, the graceful Wicklow mountains and hills of Howth and Killeny.

The very waves have a brogue as they break – and they broke Bray Head, the fine southernmost limit of the bay, long ago. But let me not have the air of inflicting upon you that deadliest of all things a scenery-letter, when my foremost wish is to throw myself into *your* environment. I have, somehow, a vision of you which makes my heart ache a good deal – and makes me brush from my eye the tear in which old London pictures – other pictures – are reflected. Your non-arrival – this spring – made me for the first time in my life willing to say that I 'realised' a situation. I seemed to see that you were tied down by pain and weakness, that you were suffering often and suffering much. I don't like to ask for fear of a yes, and I don't like not to ask for fear of your noticing my silence. In point of fact I *have* asked ...

And James went on to speak nostalgically of his lonely walks in London.

But, my dear Lowell, I don't write to rehearse to you your own incommodities. I have walked across the Park alone this summer and when I have had to go to Paddington I have slackened my step – oh so vainly – in Radnor Place, in the hope that from the little afternoon sittingroom you would call me in.

This was James's last letter to his friend. Lowell probably received it and read it a few days before he died, on 12 August 1891. 'It is a loss, and a pain, and a dear friend the less,' James wrote to du Maurier a few days after he had the news (he was now back in De Vere Gardens). 'And it seems a brutal negation of all his vitality – juvenility – almost, as it were, his *promise*.' Before the year was out he was to compose his long memorial essay, published in the *Atlantic*, in which he reviewed Lowell's career and his own fond memories of him. Once again he began in his high elegiac tone with certain reverberant sentences:

After a man's long work is over and the sound of his voice is still, those in whose regard he has held a high place find his image strangely simplified and summarized. The hand of death, in passing over it, has smoothed the folds, made it more typical and general. The figure retained by the memory is compressed and intensified; accidents have dropped away from it and shades have ceased to count : it stands, sharply, for a few estimated and cherished things, rather than, nebulously, for a swarm of possibilities. We cut the silhouette, in a word, out of the confusion of life, we save and fix the outline, and it is with his eye on this profiled distinction that the critic speaks.

The words had about them the sense of solemn obsequies and of the limitations of immortality. This was Henry James's public – and private – funeral oration for his friend.

3

No part of the production of *The American* is more vivid than the record of it in Alice James's journal – the joy with which, from the four walls of her sick-room, she allowed her imagination to soar to the footlights in the Strand. In his letters to William, Henry came to speak of his play and Alice as his two invalids. For his sister the episode was 'so shot through with the threads of golden comedy that we grew fat with laughter'. Six days before the opening night William James suddenly appeared in London after a rapid autumn crossing. He had come to say good-bye to Alice. He spent as many hours as he could with his sister; and he was at Henry's first night, and the intimate supper which Henry gave afterwards. The guests were the Comptons, Miss Robins, William Heinemann the publisher, and Wolcott Balestier. Heinemann had recently met James; and it was he who had set up a small acting-edition of *The American*, just enough copies for the cast and the author, in the hope of publishing the play if it should be a success.

The first night on 26 September 1891 in the refurbished London theatre was a dubious success, but distinctly a social one. Robert Lincoln, the American Minister, was in a box, and the stage journals spoke of the presence of various American 'millionaires'. Grace Norton was in London, and so – with William – Cambridge, Massachusetts was thoroughly represented. And Fenimore, by this time settled in Oxford, came to London for the occasion and met William for the first and only time. It is possible to see the opening through her eyes :

I put on my best, and we looked well enough, but were nothing to the others! Pink satin, blue satin, jewels of all sorts, splendour on all sides of us. The house was packed to the top, and the applause was great. When the performance was ended, and the actors had been called out, there arose loud cries of 'Author, author!' After some delays, Henry James appeared before the curtain and acknowledged the applause. He looked very well – quiet and dignified, yet pleasant; he only stayed a moment. The critics have since then written acres about the play. It has been warmly praised; attacked; abused; highly commended etc.

To read the critics today is to see quite clearly what was wrong with *The American*. The writing was often obscure; the play was more melodramatic than the novel. Miss Robins's Claire tended to be frantic and nervous. One critic said she imported into the play 'the hysterical manners of Ibsen's morbid heroines'. The comedy Christopher Newman was not altogether liked. His chocolate-coloured coat was the subject of much satiric reference; the critic of the *Era* remarked: 'We are as anxious as the critics of the newest school to hail the advent on our stage of literary men, but it is on condition that they bring their literature with them.'

The critics who were eager to see novelists working on the stage – men like William Archer – spoke in muted terms. Yet they too had to admit that James had sacrificed too much of the originality of his novel for mere melodrama. A. B. Walkley, admiring the amount of busy action exclaimed: 'What, Mr James? All this "between dinner and the suburban trains?"' It was probably Walkley, one of the most literate of drama-critics, who twitted James also in an anonymous review for his 'stage American, with the local colour laid on with a trowel, and strong accent, a fearful and wonderful coat and a recurrent catch-word'. Compton definitely had the accent, and for the rest 'a great deal of ugly overcoat'.

The production was lagging when the Prince of Wales decided that he wanted to see it. Compton asked James to 'dress' up a couple of boxes with 'smart people'. The novelist told Alice, 'I'd do anything for the good Compton, but it will make me charitable to the end of my days.' The visit of royalty had its desired effect; the play's run was prolonged. James and Compton decided to give it a further 'lift' and resorted to the unusual procedure of inviting the critics to a 'second edition' on the fiftieth night – James having taken a number of the critical suggestions and revised certain of the scenes. The critics were flattered and found the play improved. Miss Robins's acting was pronounced less 'somnambulistic'; however Compton had not been persuaded to doff his garment and he still sprinkled his dialogue with the tag-line – 'That's what I want t'see.' The play eked out seventy nights. Henry felt it was 'humiliating' to be beholden to royalty for part of his run; nevertheless that run had now been 'honourable'. He took solace in this fact. The revenue had been negligible.

Ten days after the closing James was summoned to Dresden where Wolcott Balestier had gone on publishing business. The young American had typhoid and James arrived in time to stand at his graveside, with Balestier's mother and sisters. 'The young Balestier, the effective and the indispensable, is dead! swept away like a cobweb, of which gossamer substance he seems to have been himself compounded, simply spirit and energy, with the slightest of fleshly wrapping.' This was Alice's comment in her journal – a tribute of the dying to the dead.

3

A Divine Cessation

ALICE JAMES announced her impending death by cable to William James. She dictated it to Henry on 5 March 1892: 'Tenderest love to all. Farewell. Am going soon. Alice.'

She had then but a few hours to live. During those hours she also dictated to Katharine Loring the ultimate passage in her journal:

I am being ground slowly on the grim grindstone of physical pain and on two nights I had almost asked for K's lethal dose, but one steps hesitantly along such unaccustomed ways and endures from second to second. I feel sure that it can't be possible but what the bewildered little hammer that keeps me going will very shortly see the decency of ending his distracted career. However this may be, physical pain, however great, ends in itself and falls away like dry husks from the mind, whilst moral discords and nervous horrors sear the soul.

That sentence bothered her; during her last night Alice tried to improve it. 'Oh, the wonderful moment when I felt myself floated for the first time, into the deep sea of divine *cessation*,' she dictated, 'and saw all the dear old mysteries and miracles vanish into vapour.' She was alluding to the fact that she had fainted away the previous evening, and felt as if she were dying. She came to just as Henry was being sent for; afterwards she was 'perfectly clear and humorous' with him about it. She wanted to talk, but could not, with her spasms of coughing.

On one of her last nights she had a dream which she told Katharine Loring. She saw a boat in which were Lizzie Boott and their common friend Annie Dixwell, who had died some time before Lizzie. They were putting out into a tumbled sea, seeming to pass from under the shadow of a cloud, and looking back at Alice. This 'impressed and agitated her much,' James wrote to Francis Boott.

The climax of her long years of invalidism came suddenly. She had been weaker at the end of February and had been given doses of morphine to assuage her pain. At William's suggestion Dr Lloyd Tuckey, an eminent psychiatrist, had been called in and used hypnotism as a further aid. At the beginning of March Alice contracted a cold; her doctors later speculated that a second tumour, perhaps in or near the lung – as Baldwin had predicted – exacerbated her condition. James, coming to see her on 5 March, was struck by the supreme deathlike emaciation that had come over her within forty-eight hours. Hypnotism helped to hold nervousness in arrest; and Katharine Loring was taught by Tuckey how to use it. It was on this day, a Saturday, that Alice dictated her farewell cable. Henry himself sent the final word the next day. The 'divine cessation' had come.

On the last page of Alice's journal, in Katharine Loring's hand, is a postscript: 'The dictation of March 4th was rushing about in her brain all day, and although she was very weak and it tired her much to dictate, she could not get her head quiet until she had it written; then she was relieved and I finished Miss Woolson's story of "Dorothy" to her.' The last story Alice listened to was Fenimore's Bellosguardo story – the story of the lingering death of a woman who does not want to live.

I

This was the first time that Henry James watched someone through the hours of death – and someone close to him. His mother had died suddenly, when he had been away from home; his father had been dead when he arrived after crossing the Atlantic. He looked on now with the helpless hurt and suffering that other great novelists have recorded; and it was both as brother and as novelist that he set down the final scene of his sister's undramatic life for their Cambridge brother. 'Alice died at exactly four o'clock on Sunday afternoon (about the same hour of the same day as mother), and it is now Tuesday morning,' he began, and then followed a painful step-by-step account. On Saturday, when Alice had taken on the look of death, the pain diminished, and 'left her consciously and oh longingly, close to the end'. Katharine and James sought to create an intense stillness around her. They hoped that in these circumstances she might sleep. In the later afternoon the novelist left her bedside for a while; Tuckey saw her during the evening and came back later still. James wanted to stay the night on Campden Hill, but Miss Loring thought this was pointless. There was nothing he could do. Alice said a few barely audible things to him, above all 'that she *couldn't*, oh, she COULDN'T, and begged it mightn't be exacted of her, live *another* day'. Then she sank into a gentle sleep. 'From that sleep she never woke – but after an hour or two it changed its character and became a loud, deep breathing – almost stertorous.' This was her condition when James reached the house again on Sunday morning at nine. From that hour until four he, Katharine and the nurse sat beside Alice's bed. Tuckey came in the morning at 11.30 expecting to find her dead; when Katharine described his patient's condition he said there was nothing he could further do.

Alice wished for death, yet she died reluctantly. Her automatic breathing continued for seven hours with no look of pain on her face, only more and more the look of death.

They were infinitely pathetic and, to me, most unspeakable hours. They would have been intolerable if it had not been so evident that all the hideous burden of suffering consciousness was utterly gone. As it is, they were the most appealing and pitiful thing I ever saw. But I have seen, happily, but little death immediately. Toward the end, for about an hour, the breathing became a constant sort of smothered whistle in the lung. The pulse flickered, came and went, ceased and revived a little again, and then with all perceptible action of the heart, altogether ceased to be sensible for some time before the breathing ceased.

An hour before the end there came a 'blessed change'. She began to breathe without effort, gently, peacefully and naturally, like a child. This lasted an hour, and then her breathing seemed to become intermittent, 'her face then seemed in a strange, dim, touching way to become clearer'. James went to the window to let in a little more of the afternoon light. 'It was a bright, kind, soundless Sunday.' When he came back she had drawn, he told William, 'the last breath'. Then the novelist, to be more precise, crossed out the word 'last' and made the sentence read 'she had drawn the breath that was not succeeded by another'.

Alice had asked to be cremated with the simplest possible ceremony. Her body lay in her room, on the bed in which she died, from that Sunday evening until Wednesday. During that time Henry spent many hours beside her. 'She looks most beautiful and noble – with *all* of the august expression that you can imagine – and with less, than before, of the almost ghastly emaciation of those last days.' Her ashes, by her wish, were to be sent to Cambridge and interred beside the graves of her parents.

At 11.45 on Wednesday morning, 9 March 1892, Henry, Katharine Loring, the nurse, and an old Cambridge friend who lived in England, Annie Ashburner Richards, took the train to Woking at Waterloo station. The hearse and the horses had been put on the train in a special car. At Woking they had a couple of miles' drive. There was a short simple service, 'read by an inoffensive, sweet-voiced young clergyman'. For an hour and a half Henry and his companions waited in a room next to the chapel till the cremation was completed. On his way back from Waterloo the novelist stopped at the Reform Club and wrote half a dozen sentences to William, describing the scene. 'It is the last, the last forever. I shall feel very lonely in England at first. But enough.'

2

In the days that followed, answering letters of condolence, he spoke of the release which had come to his sister. He rejoiced that this sudden illness had put an end to her lingering invalidism; and he mourned her as 'a rare and remarkable being'. One of the first to whom James wrote was Francis Boott. To him he spoke of his 'great sorrow', because 'even with everything that made life an unspeakable weariness to her, she contributed constantly, infinitely to the interest, the consolation, as it were, in disappointment and depression, of my own existence'.

Alice left an estate valued at $80,000. This she divided among her three brothers and Katharine Loring. Henry, William and Katharine received $20,000 each. Robertson was left a smaller amount and her silver. Her reason was that the younger brother's wife and children had large expectations, whereas William and Henry had none. Robertson James protested at this discrimination, and Henry announced that he was willing to transfer $5,000 from his inheritance, since he felt Katharine Loring could hardly be asked to do so, and that William, with four children, should not be asked to part with any share of what he was receiving. Henry and William both agreed that in this division of her estate Alice had 'most justly' placed Miss Loring 'on the footing of a brother'.

Alice's journal remained in Miss Loring's possession. Some time later, by agreement with William, four copies were printed, for the three brothers and herself. When Henry received his copy he expressed great alarm. The journal was filled with much minor gossip retailed by him to Alice to entertain her; it reflected, for all its fervent Irishness and stout Americanism, the state of mind of an invalid confined within four walls. He feared very much that the journal, if disseminated, would have the effect of his fictitious *Reverberator*. 'I have been immensely impressed with the thing as a revelation of a moral and personal picture,' Henry wrote to William.

It is heroic in its individuality, its independence – its face-to-face with the universe for-and-by herself – and the beauty and eloquence with which she often expresses this, let alone the rich irony and humour, constitute a new claim for the family renown. This last element – her style, her power to write – are indeed to me a delight.

At Henry's insistence the diary was not published during his lifetime.

In Dante William found a passage which both he and Henry agreed could fittingly be inscribed upon her grave. In 1892, when William was in Italy, a marble urn was executed with these words on it, 'ed essa da martiro e da essilio venne a questa pace'.

Three years after Alice's death Henry found himself riding one evening in London, in a four-wheeler, on his way to dine with Lord Lovelace. As he rattled through the cold clear night there came to him – he was unable to say why or how – the thought of a story he might write about 'the existence of a peculiar intense and interesting affection between a brother and sister'. As he recorded this in his notebook he spoke of 'two lives, two beings, and *one* experience'. The story would contain 'the idea of some unspeakable intensity of feeling, of tenderness, of sacred compunction, as it were, in relation to the *past*, the parents, the beloved mother, the beloved father – of those who have suffered before them and for them'.

On this evening Lord Lovelace showed Henry James the long-suppressed letters of Byron and Augusta Leigh, Byron's half-sister. The novelist later mused on the coincidence : that he should have himself thought of a tale of brotherly and sisterly love, on the very night that he was to be shown this evidence, although his tale would have been without 'the nefarious – abnormal – character' of the Byron-Leigh relation. His subject, he felt, would present

the image of a deep participating devotion ... The brother suffers, has the experience, is carried along by fate, etc.; and the sister understands, perceives, shares, with every pulse of her being. He has nothing to tell her – she *knows*; it's identity of sensation, of vibration. It's for *her*, the Pain of Sympathy : that would be the subject, the formula.

The note contains no mention of Alice, and James never wrote the story. Perhaps because he had long before, and for many years, lived it.

4

The Wheel of Time

HENRY ADAMS, sojourning in London early in 1892, saw Henry James as 'a figure in the same wallpaper'. But then, for Adams, life had taken on a sameness after Clover's death. E. S. Nadal, who had looked at James in so circumstantial a fashion when he was in Bolton Street, returning now to London after a decade, left his card at De Vere Gardens. James promptly replied 'Welcome back to old England,' and invited him to lunch. 'I found him in a handsome apartment in Kensington,' the former legation secretary wrote. 'He had a butler of a most respectable appearance, and he had a dachshund bitch with a beautiful countenance. He sat with the dachshund in his lap much of the time.'

Somehow they got to the subject of sex and began to compare European and American women. Nadal argued that American women had less 'sex' than European women, 'that in many American women it was negative, and in European women positive, and that many American girls looked like effeminate boys'. In his reminiscences, however, he does not tell us what James thought; unless indeed the novelist said nothing. He merely records one rejoinder as James stroked the head of his dog : 'She's got sex, if you like, and she's quite intelligent enough to be shocked by this conversation.'

He candidly told Nadal that his books were not selling. He seemed 'tired' of English society. He told him that he would never again enter an English country house for a staying visit. He expressed horror at the American women-tourists increasingly invading Europe with their Baedekers. And the James, who in the 1870s had amazed Nadal and Hoppin by his exploits as a diner-out, now astonished his old acquaintance by confessing that he dined at home, usually alone in his apartment. 'Don't you find that dull?' Nadal asked. 'No, I don't mind it,' James replied. Nadal thought it a mistake that the novelist should be allowing himself so large a measure of loneliness when he had his clubs. 'He didn't seem as happy as he used to be, and I could have wished him back in his old lodgings at No. 3 Bolton Street, "the half of my old number," without the very respectable butler, and looked after by the tall, slender, dark, rather pretty "person" with the sensitive risibilities.'

They talked also of *The American*. Nadal told him he had heard that, in spite of the critical notices, the play had been liked by the gallery. James said he believed this was true. Nadal observed :

He was not dramatic, certainly not theatrical. His talent was critical and narrative. In this attempt, he was moving in a direction away from, rather than toward, his true gift, the introvertive monologue in which he delighted, such as I used to hear from him in our nocturnal walks about the London streets. But then monologue would not have given him a nice apartment and a combination valet and butler. The nice flat and the butler in a swallow-tail coat were perhaps the result of living in England.

And Nadal added : 'He liked to have a look of success.'

I

William James, on seeing Henry in De Vere Gardens in 1889 after their long separation, had written home to his wife :

Harry is as nice and simple and amiable as he can be. He has covered himself, like some marine crustacean, with all sorts of material growths, rich sea-weeds and rigid barnacles and things, and lives hidden in the midst of his strange heavy alien manners and customs; but these are all

but 'protective resemblances', under which the same dear old, good, innocent and at bottom very powerless-feeling Harry remains, caring for little
but his writing, and full of dutifulness and affection for all gentle things.

The passage has often been quoted as if it were an objective picture of Henry James, rather than a characteristic (and slightly de-
preciatory) view by an older brother who had always tended to be
condescending to his younger rival. 'Powerless-feeling', to be sure,
whenever Henry was in William's presence; and William's picture
of his 'dear old, good, innocent' Harry is essentially that of the
'angel' of long ago. William, on his side, had particular reasons for
feeling powerful at this moment. He had just published his *Principles
of Psychology*. He was coming into belated success at the very
moment when Henry, celebrated and respected in the literary world,
was beginning to question the meaning of the fame that had come
to him a dozen years before. Henry had never been more ambitious,
and indeed never more powerful, than at this moment. Between the
time of William's description and the death of Alice – between 1889
and 1892 – he had brought out a long novel and a volume of tales
and had written many articles. During the year of Alice's death he
published ten tales and four articles. Not a month elapsed without
his being in one or another of the leading magazines on either side
of the Atlantic. And in the year following Alice's death – 1893 – he
surpassed all his previous records of publication by bringing out five
books, three volumes of tales and two of essays. Three of these books
appeared in one month, June 1893, *Picture and Text*, his essays on
art; *Essays in London*, largely a series of tributes and memorials of
his recently dead friends, and *The Private Life*. In addition, there now
lay on his desk the scripts of four comedies and that of *The American*.

Henry James had a full sense of the power he wielded in literary
circles. But he also had a sense of an encroaching loneliness as
familiar figures in his life continued to drop away: Mrs Procter and
Browning, the young Balestier, the beloved Lowell. In the autumn
of 1892 he was invited to the Abbey to still another funeral, walking
with his fellow men of letters at the interment of the Bard, the seemingly indestructible figure of Alfred Lord Tennyson. 'It was a lovely
day, the Abbey looked beautiful, everyone was there, but something
– I don't know what – of real impressiveness – was wanting.' There
were 'too many Masters of Balliol, too many Deans and Alfred

Austins'. James sent a copy of the Order of Service to Fenimore in Oxford.

A more personal loss was recorded by the novelist a month later, when he learned that his loyal friend Theodore Child had died in the East. Child had been the secret Boswell of his talks with the naturalists. He had published James in his little Paris newspaper. He had known him ever since the summer of 1876 at Etretat. Now he was gone, 'prematurely and lamentedly'. He had died in Persia, near Ispahan, and been buried in a lonely grave at Tulfa.

There were not only deaths but unexpected breaks with the past. For old times' sake James had kept up a correspondence with his Newport friend, Thomas Sergeant Perry, and had regularly sent him his books. Some impulse, some sense of his own failure in the American literary world, where he had wholly ceased to publish, had prompted Perry to send Henry a 'most offensive and impertinent' letter in which he expressed disapproval of his expatriation. 'It was too idiotic to notice and it was almost impertinent enough to return and it set the seal upon the conviction I have always privately had that he is a singularly poor creature,' Henry told William, and he decided to have nothing further to do with this 'singular helpless mediocrity'. This explains the large gap which now occurred in their otherwise voluminous correspondence. The friendship was resumed in late middle age.

2

Old figures in the crowded life of Henry James were disappearing; new ones were on his horizon – a generation of attractive young men, gifted and appreciative, only too willing to be acolytes and beginning to call him 'Master'. They had grown up with his books and they sought him out. They were young and full of promise; there was something touching in their worship of him, and in the affection his work seemed to inspire in them. One of James's heroes of this period 'observed the young now more than he had ever done; observed them that is, as the young'. Balestier had been one of the first; others came rapidly. One of the most sentimental of these attachments was formed with a gifted young man from New England, William Morton Fullerton, who arrived in London to work as a newspaperman. He had a poetic sense and a style already deeply influenced by James's. He was what might be called *un homme de cœur*: a romantic journalist full of the world and of its promise, and happy to give James his confidences. The novelist encouraged him, listened to him, sought his company. A native of Norwich, Connecticut, Fullerton was about 25 when he obtained a position on *The Times* in London. He was invited often to De Vere Gardens. Presently *The Times* sent him to Paris to work with Blowitz. Fullerton was to make the rest of his career in the French capital and he replaced Theodore Child in the regular round of James's Parisian visits. How influenced Fullerton was may be judged by the fact that he continued to write for *The Times* in 'kilometric sentences', after the manner of the later James; and Henry used to tease him at his using Jamesian phrases in his letters. Fullerton later gallicized himself by leaving English journalism and writing for the *Figaro*. He lived into modern times and became a friend, in the new century, of Edith Wharton. American soldiers, arriving in Paris after its liberation in the Second World War, found him a hardy octogenarian, among his books and papers in the Rue du Mont-Thabor. Henry James's letters to Fullerton testify to a genial camaraderie between journalist and man of letters, Fullerton being as it were on the border between the two. 'With your margin of youth and your close text of Talent,' James once wrote to him, envying him his years and his immersion in the wide world. He was a kind of boon-companion, someone with whom James did not need to be formal.

There was also Jonathan Sturges, a young graduate of Princeton. Sturges, a New Yorker, had been badly crippled in childhood by poliomyelitis; from the waist up he was a good-looking, broad-shouldered young man, with finely distinctive features. He liked best to go riding in Hyde Park in an open hansom, to conceal his infirmities. He inspired in James a great tenderness; it was almost as if, having had an invalid sister to care for all these years, he now had found a substitute. Later, Sturges would pay prolonged visits to James and provide much sociable and literary gossip. Through James he met Miss Reubell in Paris and frequented her salon; he became a friend of Whistler's as well. He wrote a certain number of stories and translated a group of Maupassant's tales which were published with a preface by James. In London he usually lived at Long's Hotel, where he was much sought after socially during periods of comparative health.

Another new friend was Henry Harland, author of certain popular novels in New York under the pen-name of Sydney Luska, and later editor of the *Yellow Book*. Harland brought Aubrey Beardsley to meet the novelist; he induced him to publish certain of his tales in that hard-bound journal of the late aestheticism. A still more interesting though passing figure was Henry Bennett Brewster, who attracted James by his achieved cosmopolitanism. 'Know Brewster? Why I invented Brewster – ten years ago,' Henry wrote to an inquiring friend in Rome in 1899. For Brewster was a character out of Henry James. His ancestors had come to the United States on the *Mayflower*; he numbered among them two Yankee clergymen and one minute-man. His father had been a physician. Handsome, bearded, with clear sharp eyes, Brewster had grown up in Europe with a mastery of several tongues and several literatures and a penchant for meditative writing. He wrote a book called *The Theory of Anarchy and of Law*, and a work *L'Âme Païenne* which had many admirers. He was much described in the memoirs of Ethel Smyth, whose lover he became, and his sophistication and 'Europeanization' led James to devote certain sentences to him in his *Notes of a Son and Brother*. In these he recalls that this master of three tongues, who was 'scarce American at all', had depreciated *The Marble Faun*. But then 'homely superstition had no hold on him', and he viewed Hawthorne only from his continentalized vision; there would have been small use in James's trying to make him see what was 'exquisite' in Hawthorne's Roman story. James and Brewster were to dine whenever they met, in London or abroad; and the novelist was to cherish his memory, after he died at a comparatively early age: 'I am haunted by the tragic image of our fine and inscrutable Brewster, who hadn't really half done with the exquisite mystification he somehow made of life – or perhaps received from it!' James felt him to have been 'such a strange handsome questioning cosmopolite ghost'.

They came, these younger men, into James's life, and some survived to create the legend of the Master. We catch their reflection in his tales of the literary life. In these, whether it is that of *The Death of the Lion* or of *The Figure in the Carpet*, there is always a young acolyte, a youthful spirit touched by the art of the great writer. One of the first of these was written during James's 50th year. He called it *The Middle Years* and it was the one new tale he published during 1893 – as if it had to stand alone as a kind of half-century manifesto. In this story a middle-aged writer has had a serious illness and fears he may die before he has his 'second chance', his opportunity for a 'later manner'. 'It had taken too much of life to produce too little of his art. At such a rate a first existence was too short.' He meets a young doctor who is prepared to abandon everything to take care of him, so powerfully has he been affected by the novelist's books. And Dencombe, dying, realizes that perhaps the most important thing is not whether there is to be another chance, a second existence: the important thing was to have created work which could arouse a response, make someone vibrate – 'It *is* glory – to have been tested, to have had our little quality and cast our little spell. The thing is to have made somebody care.'

These new young men surrounding James cared; they cared deeply. The world might ignore him; but James knew that so long as certain readers experienced his work as profoundly as this his personal *gloire* was assured. Thus he could end his doleful tale with the noble words of the artist: 'We work in the dark – we do what we can – we give what we have. Our doubt is our passion and our passion is our task. The rest is the madness of art.' He was coming to realize at this moment that the greatest art is not that which creates a sensation or a success – as his new friend Rudyard Kipling was doing at this moment. True art, by some strange process of human relation, inspires in others an interest, a depth of feeling, an attachment. The touching tale, fruit of these troubled months, ends in philosophic resignation. 'It's frustration that doesn't count,' says the great writer. The wise young acolyte-doctor replies: 'Frustration's only life.'

3

There is another revealing tale written a year earlier – in 1892 (when James was 49). It is called *The Wheel of Time*. In it we may discover a passage in which the hero muses (also at 49) on his lost youth.

He regretted it, he missed it, he tried to beckon it back; but the differences in London made him feel that it had gone forever. There might perhaps be some compensation in being fifty, some turn of the dim telescope, some view from the brow of the hill; it was a round, gross, stupid number, which probably would make one pompous, make one think one's self venerable. Meanwhile, at any rate, it was odious to be forty-nine.

The author of these lines now spins a variation on a story he had written when he was 36, and which he had then called *The Diary of a Man of Fifty*. At 36 one could imagine oneself 50 without too much pain; at 49 he made his character – 49! The hero of *The Diary of a Man of Fifty* tried to persuade a young man to do as he had done – turn his back on the daughter of the woman about whom he had been unsure; the young man did not heed his advice and married happily. In *The Wheel of Time* the ageing Maurice Glanvil is shown first in his twenties, when he turns his back on the plain but charming Fanny Knocker, in spite of her great fortune. He goes off to the Continent and contracts a bohemian marriage. His wife dies leaving him a daughter who grows up to be very plain. Then at 49 he meets Fanny Knocker again. She is now the widowed Mrs Tregent and in middle age her early charm has blossomed into beauty. Moreover she has a handsome son – who repeats the history of the hero, by turning his back on Glanvil's plain daughter, in spite of Mrs Tregent's efforts to bring about the marriage. Her revenge is double, in spite of herself.

There is, however, a deeper discovery made by Maurice: he discovers that he has really been the one passion in the life of Fanny Knocker Tregent – and this passage gives us pause. For the date on which the tale was set down in the notebook, 18 May 1892 – a month after Henry James became 49 – was also the day on which he had paid a visit to Constance Fenimore Woolson at Oxford. Maurice, in the tale, discussing the past with Mrs Tregent at one point provokes her to tears, and his discovery makes him feel 'humiliated' for an hour, but after that 'his pleasure was almost as great as his wonder'. And he meditates:

She had striven, she had accepted, she had conformed; but she had thought of him every day of her life. She had taken up duties and performed them, she had banished every weakness and practised every virtue; but the still hidden flame had never been quenched. His image had interposed, his reality had remained, and she had never denied herself the sweetness of hoping that she would see him again and that she should know him. She had never raised a little finger for it, but fortune had answered her prayer. Women were capable of these mysteries of sentiment, these intensities of fidelity, and there were moments in which Maurice Glanvil's heart beat strangely before a vision really so sublime. He seemed to understand now by what miracle Fanny Knocker had been beautified – the miracle of heroic docilities and accepted pangs and vanquished egotisms. It had never come in a night, but it had come by living for others. She was living for others still; it was impossible for him to see anything else at last than that she was living for him. The time of passion was over, but the time of service was long.

At 49 Henry James, like his wandering heroes, was still trying to fathom the heart of woman; still trying to unravel the mystery – to understand whether all his sureness of 35 about fickle womankind had been a mistake. He had finally come to understand Christina Light. But had he understood himself? The 'intensities of fidelity', the remark about 'living for others' : he was to say this of his mother in his autobiographies. But he seemed at this moment to be speaking of Constance Fenimore Woolson, as he had said it in his essay about her describing her long-suffering heroines.

4

Had Henry James reached some crisis in his long relation with Fenimore? We know that he went to see her ten days after Alice's funeral. On the day after his sister's cremation he wrote to Francis Boott : 'Our poor Fenimore, at Oxford, which she likes, has had a painful illness – an affection of the head, brought on by trying *false drums* (a new invention) in her ears. But she is better, though her hearing isn't. I go to see her next week.' He went to see her on 17 March and was there the entire day. How often he went again we do not know. But there is a further record of his spending a day at Oxford on 18 May 1892, a month after his 49th birthday. That Alice's death brought about some kind of change in Fenimore's attitude seems possible, and is suggested in the novel she was writing at this time. In this work (*Horace Chase*) the heroine has an invalid sister who plays a dominating role in her life. Alice had played such a role in Henry's life; and we may speculate that the question which now arose between them was whether Henry – now that Alice was gone – should not be more attentive to Fenimore. Fenimore's essential data in the novel are sufficiently eloquent : the heroine, although married to the elderly and wealthy Horace Chase, loves a younger man who is not interested in her, but for whom she is prepared to leave her husband. We cannot help thinking of plain Fanny Knocker and elderly, plain, deaf, devoted Constance Fenimore. The speculation might be gratuitous, were it not for a solitary paragraph which spilled out of Fenimore's pen a few months after James published *The Wheel of Time*. This was almost a year after Alice's death. In writing a letter to her nephew, Samuel Mather, Miss Woolson discussed her plan to return to Italy, as she had done once before upon completion of her novel. 'You will see in all this,' she wrote, 'I am giving up being near my kind friend Mr James.' She went on :

I don't know what made me tell you and Will that last message of his sister to me, that touched me so much. But I suppose it was simply the relief of having some of my own family to talk to, after being so long alone. I felt that I could say anything to you, without having to think whether it was safe or not, wise or not, prudent or not. – But Mr James will come to Italy every year, And perhaps we can write that play after all.

'Safe or not, wise or not, prudent or not' – these cautious words offer wide margin for speculation; and while this paragraph gives us no details, it tells us of the importance Fenimore had attached to being near Henry James, indeed it once again explains her presence in England when she preferred Italy. Her words suggest that some kind of truce, some *modus vivendi*, has been reached : almost, one might say, like an 'arrangement' after a separation or a divorce, an adjustment to circumstance – the annual visit. For the rest – what Alice's message was, we do not know. It might have been praise for the Bellosguardo story; it might have been something more significant, some comment on the relationship between Henry and Fenimore, perhaps a sisterly wish that they would marry. We remember that Fenimore's Bellosguardo story was read to Alice during her last hours. All we know is that the invalid sister in *Horace Chase* expresses herself with great freedom on the heroine's relations with her husband and the man she really loves. As for the talk of collaboration on a play, it can only leave us wondering. This is the only time in James's long career that the question of collaboration comes up – save that at this very time it becomes also the title of one of his tales. He was, in all his writing years, an arch-solitary of literature. He took no guidance; he consulted no one – although he talked freely enough about the problems of the market-place. He would have regarded collaboration as an abandoning of sovereign ground, the most sacred ground of his life.

We must recognize, however, that the proposed collaboration was in the writing of a play – and within the medium of the stage James might have been willing. Given the nature of the relationship, one must also consider that since James could not 'collaborate' with Fenimore in the one way in which she would have liked him to, that is in the realm of the affections, he had proposed a union in their art. Was the play begun? It is doubtful whether we shall ever know – the destructive hand of the novelist, the burning of the papers, seems to have been thorough. The play may never have gone beyond the stage of conversation.

The tale entitled *Collaboration* was in some ways prophetic of the sinister meaning the friendly word would take on during the Second World War. It is one of James's trifling and artful anecdotes. A young French poet and a young German composer fall in love with each other's work and set out to write an opera together. In doing this the Frenchman rejects his French fiancée, whose father fell in the Franco-Prussian war and whose mother can tolerate no alliance of any kind with a member of the race that invaded France. The brother of the German musician, who has been supporting him, also cannot tolerate collaboration with a member of the former enemy. The two artists are left alone, and the narrator can only proclaim the supremacy of art over nationalism, as Henry had proclaimed it when he told William he was tired of the 'international' theme. The deeper implication, if we wish to read it, is that of the love of the two men for each other, disguised in the love of each other's work. They take up life together – and the fiancée is spurned. She is spurned, as the woman was spurned in *The Diary of a Man of Fifty*, or as Fanny Knocker was spurned, or Maurice's ugly daughter. If the spurning was a mistake – as these various personages wonder or believe – the mistake is made and will be made again. James could not conceive of it otherwise. And however much he might appreciate and admire Fenimore's devotion to him, there was nothing he could give in return save a certain tenderness and consideration – and the pledge of a yearly visit! Things would have to go on pretty much as before. Whatever his affections might be, his career, his complicated relations with the older generation of his friends and the new young friends, were his way of life. He had never been ready to sacrifice any part of this for Fenimore. And he was probably only too glad to make Italy more than ever into a place of annual pilgrimage.

5

In Siena

In the spring of 1892, when Henry James had accustomed himself
to the absence of Alice, he set out for Italy. His theatrical ventures
were at a standstill. Augustin Daly had one of his comedies, and
James was waiting to hear from him; *The American* was being
played in the provinces by the Compton Comedy Company once or
twice a week. There was nothing to retain him in London; and with
the Season about to begin, this was an ideal time for flight. His friend
Paul Bourget had married during the previous year, and gone to Italy
on a prolonged honeymoon. He was now at Siena and the newly-
weds beckoned to James. And then Mrs Gardner had once again
rented the Palazzo Barbaro for the summer from the Curtises; she
signalled that she expected him to pay the visit he had been obliged
to cancel the previous summer.

He could leave London at will. There would be no more summoning telegrams, no more continuing letters and conferences with Miss
Loring. 'Alice's death has only left my life more *regular* – more an
affair of little slow contracted literary habits and small decorous
London observances,' James wrote to Grace Norton. He might have
added that it had left him with a wide margin of personal freedom.

He reached Siena on 5 June, going there straight from London,
with none of his usual pauses. He put up at the Grand Hôtel de
Sienne, where the Bourgets were staying. He found his French disciple stout, red, robust, *mieux assis* and rather beefy, like Balzac. He
was charmed by Bourget's wife, the former Minnie David. She was
slim, petite, fragile, 'a beautiful child', ministering to Bourget 'like
a little quivering pathetic priestess on a bas-relief'. James as usual
engaged a large cool drawing-room in which he worked, and a bedroom. Towards noon the writers would have their *déjeuner* together;
then they would retire to their rooms. Bourget was finishing a novel;
James was working at a series of tales. At six they would sally forth,
dine, walk in the Lizza, eat ices, hang over the Castello and enjoy
the medievalism of the ancient Tuscan town. James knew it well,
but he had never paid so enjoyable a visit to it and never at this time
of the year. The Italian summer 'broke in great verdurous waves at
the foot of our far-seeing ramparts' – corn and wheat and mulberries,

linked to 'cachottes' by vines, which seemed to him 'like joyous bathers – girls in the water – dipping up and down while they give each other their hands'. On balmy moonlight evenings he found the place a 'revel of history vivified'. It was a pleasure, moreover, to look at things in the company of the fragile and charming Minnie; 'to study the beautiful in her society'. As for Bourget, James had long ago formed his opinion of him. He thought him one of the most civilized of conversationalists – and despised his novels. Moreover he sooner or later told him what he thought of them. Bourget possessed a certain delicacy of perception and an admirable prose instrument; his fiction was narrow, deterministic, mechanistic; it was Zola's naturalism with a little superficial psychology added. If Bourget had absorbed James's theories of fiction, he lacked his humane grasp. The two were strangely dissimilar : Bourget moved rapidly into a kind of rigidity that left him old before his time; whereas James became increasingly tolerant of the world and of himself. Their meeting in Siena was a kind of midway point, during which they appeared briefly to move side by side. They were bound, however, in opposite directions. Two or three years earlier, James, reading Bourget's *Mensonges*, had expressed to his friends his keen disappointment in the turn his protégé was taking. And to Bourget himself he had said, quite bluntly :

I absolutely don't like this work. It's a pity – such a pity – she's a whore! – your manner of wishing to incarnate yourself each time in a prostitute – and to see men only as little hysterical, angry types who beat women with whom they sleep (and who deceive for them either husbands or lovers), or who try, like your detestable poet, to disfigure them. I speak with no false delicacy or hypocrisy; but your out-and-out eroticism displeases me as well as this exposition of dirty linens and dirty towels. In a word, all this is far from being life as I feel it, as I see it, as I know it, as I wish to know it.

In this letter (23 February 1888, written in French) James attacked Bourget for trying to describe the physical-erotic too minutely – 'the number of embraces, their quality, the exact place they occur, the manner in which they occur and a thousand other particularities more intensely personal and less producible in broad daylight than anything else in the world. What do we know moreover and how can we speak in all this for any one but one's self?' And he added 'the acts of love appear to me to constitute a special part of our being whose essential character lends itself to action and not to reflection.

It would never occur to me to want to know what goes on in their bedroom, in their bed, between a man and a woman.'

Such candour was possible only between friends; and if Bourget demurred it was because he, on his side, could see life only in his sado-masochistic way. James cared more for Bourget's essays and felt there were 'exquisite' pages in his *Sensations d'Italie*. William James met the Bourgets in America and chided Henry for making friends with so unworthy an individual. On that occasion Henry replied:

Oh yes, you are right in saying that in a manner he has got more out of me than I out of him – and yet you are wrong. I have got out of him that I know him as if I had made him – his nature, his culture, his race, his type, his *mœurs*, his mixture – whereas he knows (as a consequence of his own attitude) next to nothing about me. An individual so capable as I am of the uncanniest self-effacement in the active exercise of the passion of observation, always exposes himself a little to *looking* like a dupe – and he doesn't care a hang. And yet I *like* Bourget and have an affection for him; he has a great deal of individual charm, sensibility, generosity; and the sides by which he *dis*pleases are those of his race and the, in so many ways, abominable *milieu* in which his life has mainly been passed.

Differences vanished when the two authors were together. One day in June they drove to San Gemignano, 'a long, lovely day of the teeming Tuscan land, a garden of beauty and romance', and James saw the little old half-ruined city with its beautiful tower, perched on its hill-top, with sweet old chimes still ringing and 'the breath of the middle ages still in its streets'. He encountered four American women there, and learned that one of them was a journalist who discovered later what two prize subjects she had missed. She sent a card after them asking for interviews. On 3 July they saw the Palio from a balcony of the Marchese Chigi's palace. They also visited the *archivio* in the Palazzo Piccolomini; and James studied closely the Sienese School of painters. Each day had its adventures; and in the middle of their stay there arrived another Gallo-Roman, this one even more a mixture of the two than Bourget. This was Count Primoli, whom James had met on that memorable day when he had taken Maupassant to dine at Greenwich.

Early in July, when the heat became intense, the Bourgets left for the mountains, and Henry turned towards Venice and the summoning Mrs Gardner.

6

The Two Queens

MRS GARDNER, in a palace on the Grand Canal, was quite as much at home as in any of the domiciles she had created, in Beacon Street, in Brookline, or indeed ultimately in Boston's Fenway. *C'est mon plaisir* ... And it was her pleasure, for the second summer in succession, to occupy the Palazzo Barbaro, to create within it the 'court' with which she liked to surround herself. Awaiting her in Venice were seven gilded and painted armchairs acquired at the Borghese sale that spring, said to have been presented by the Doge of Venice to Pope Paul V. In London she had purchased a magnificent ruby, and had acquired a Madonna and Child supposedly by Filippino Lippi, (but later attributed by Bernard Berenson to an unidentified pupil of the painter), also a canvas by Rossetti. During this year she purchased the last of her series of strings of pearls. In Paris, on her way to Venice, she had acquired her first piece of Gothic carving, a panel representing Joan of Arc; and her first fine tapestry. She had not yet had the idea of creating her composite palace in the Fenway, but the heterogeneous items were being assembled. When James arrived, he found her thoroughly at home in Venice: the Palazzo was filled with guests. To his delight she placed a bed in the library, where, like his heroine Milly Theale much later, he awoke every day to find himself staring at the medallions and arabesques of the ceiling. Here the servant, Tita, coming in on diffident tiptoe, brought him his hot water in a large coffee-urn. He was surrounded by comfortable pink chairs and had a lemon-coloured sofa, and the shutters were clean and wrapped in white paper. A scorching sirocco was blowing; inside the palace, however, he was cool. The novelist revelled in the grandeur and the loveliness of the city – and Queen Isabella's game of modern life carried on within the frame of the past. He had always enjoyed it – and as for dreams of power and glory, he had but to walk across marble floors and great spaces to feel as if he were a Doge himself – conferring favours on a great lady.

The great lady – diminutive, tightly corseted, bejewelled and be-pearled – was 'of an energy,' he wrote to Miss Reubell, using, as he often did, the French form in English. James had informal as well as formal glimpses of the queenly Mrs Gardner. 'Dear Donna Isabella, I don't know where this will find you, but I hope it will find you with your hair not quite "up" – neither up nor down, as it were, in a gauze dressing-gown on a seagreen (so different from pea-green) chair, beneath a glorious gilded ceiling, receiving the matutinal tea from a Venetian slave.' And later in the letter: 'Don't tell me that you are *not* seated there in the attitude and costume which it was apparently my sole privilege to admire – I mean only *my* not my *only* privilege.' His fellow-guests included a young painter, Joseph Lindon Smith, and Alfred Q. Collins, whom James described as 'robust but not restrained', and sundry others – people were always coming and going. There was much music and much floating in gondolas. 'It is the essence of midsummer, but I buy five-franc alpaca jackets and feel so Venetian that you might almost own me,' he wrote to Mrs Curtis. 'She showed me yesterday, at Carrer's, her seven glorious chairs (the loveliest I ever saw) but they are not a symbol of her attitude – she never sits down.'

The more permanent and more reticent American Queen of the Grand Canal, she of Ca'Alvisi, was at Asolo. Even as Isabella Stewart spoke of her descent from the Stuart kings, so Katherine de Kay Bronson had come to identify herself with a queen whose name was also Katherine – Caterina Cornaro, who had been Queen of Cyprus, Jerusalem and Armenia, and who in 1489 had taken possession of Asolo, in the mountains behind Venice, and held court there in her ancient stone house, La Mura. Caterina had been art-loving and charitable; and Mrs Bronson, too, had had her poet, in Robert Browning, and her far-flung charities in Venetia. Of these James had written to her, 'Dearest Lady, I hope things are comfortable with you and the beggars of Venice haven't yet reduced you to their own condition.' In contrast with the rather short, half-shy yet dynamic Isabella Gardner, Queen Kate of Asolo was a soft, benevolent woman, with blue eyes and chestnut-brown hair drawn back from a round face. Discreet and of a mild temperament, she felt no threat to her sovereignty in the Boston Queen's temporary *villegiatura* on the Canal. Instead there was a noble exchange of salutations, a fine respect for each other's domains and queenship.

The two Queens corresponded, as Queens might. 'Dearest Lady Isabel,' wrote Mrs Bronson to Mrs Gardner. Her letters became increasingly affectionate, 'Dearest Charmeuse'. She offered counsel, out of her long residence abroad – and as women might exchange recipes, so Kate gave to Isabella the lore she had gathered from visiting royalty in Venice on the care of pearls; and her own lore on the care of lapdogs.

'I am glad to hear that our dear friend Henry James is with you,' came the word from the tower-house in Asolo. 'Tell him I wrote to him at Siena the other day and have just despatched a card to the director of the hotel to forward that valuable missive to the Barbaro. I hope he will be able to come here, and that you will find it agreeable to be here at the same time.'

Fond as James was of Mrs Bronson ('You have the sweet inventions of the heart,' he told her), he was not fond of Asolo. Its conditions of life were too primitive. 'I believe I am to go to Asolo for a day or two next week,' he wrote to Mrs Curtis, 'and I confess that I have a dread of exchanging this marble hall for the top of a stable.' This was perhaps a little strong, but James was underlining to Mrs Curtis the comforts of her *palazzo*. La Mura had originally been a part of the rampart of Asolo, and was set into one of its eighteen towers. Highly romantic and picturesque, and inspiring to Robert Browning, it did not correspond to James's ideal of Venetian splendour. He was reluctant to leave his pink chairs, his lemon sofa, and the lagoons. The expedition, however, was a success. Donna Isabella accompanied her famous courtier on a journey which she remembered as 'so romantic, so Italian'. James's recollection was also nostalgic. He spoke of 'the loggia, the mountains, the sunsets, the mornings, the evenings, the drives' and he wrote to Mrs Bronson that his return with Mrs Gardner, 'in the fragrant Italian eve, is one of the most poetical impressions of my life'.

That summer – 1892 – William James, on sabbatical leave, brought his family abroad for the first time – four children, two of them infants, and his wife. His two elder boys seemed like younger versions of himself and his novelist brother. Henry had memories only of little Harry, aged two or three, seen when he was last in America. After Billy had come Peggy and the baby, Alex. There had been another son, who died of whooping cough. William's family had thus duplicated that of his father – there would have been four boys and a girl. The family had gone straight to Switzerland, where the elder Henry James had taken his children in 1855 and later in 1859. Now William was at Lausanne. From Venice James with his sense of family loyalty, announced he would join them. But when

the time came he would gladly have remained in the amusing entourage of Mrs Gardner, to watch her play her grand game at the
Barbaro. The pleasures of a palatial existence had not yet palled.
Early in August he remarked, 'When I haven't a cousin in Venice, I
have a brother in Switzerland,' and took a train for Lausanne. He
had not seen William's wife, Alice, since the time of his father's
death. He put up at the Hôtel Richemont, expecting to join an intimate family group and to enjoy, for the first time, the full extent of
his unclehood. William, however, had not kept Henry informed of
his plans, and two days after the novelist arrived, he departed on a
walking tour in the Engadine. Henry always made William nervous;
and their reunions were nearly always marked by William's sudden
flight after the warmth of their first few hours together. The novelist
discovered his young nephews had been parcelled out in *pensions*
with Swiss pastors, and Alice with the two younger children was
staying in a Vaudois *pension*. 'Sufficient unto the day are the
nephews thereof,' he wrote to Mrs Gardner. 'I have been here since
yesterday noon, intently occupied in realizing that I am an uncle.'
But he felt let down and superfluous. He had quit the shining softness
of Venice for the Swiss mountains out a sense of duty, and found a
scattered family that took casual heed of him, as if they had not
been separated for years. It reminded him with sudden sharpness
of his own itinerant childhood days in Europe, when he and William had felt so acutely that they were 'hotel children' handed over
to substitute parents – couriers, tutors, governesses – while the father
and mother went sightseeing. One evening James went to Ouchy, to
pay a call on Henrietta Reubell, who was spending the summer there,
and his notebook records that 'the conversation had run a little upon
the way Americans drag their children about Europe'.

He remained for ten days. During this time he did what he could
in his avuncular role. He wrote a formal letter to little Harry James:
'Will you please say to M. Ceresole, with all my compliments, that
your uncle and brother, with your mother's consent, are coming to
pay you this little visit – if he doesn't disapprove.' Then he picked
up Billy at his *pension* and they arrived by boat, after luncheon,
landing at Vevey, where Daisy Miller had flourished several years
earlier. When the time came to leave he told his nephews that if they
wished to embrace and it bothered them to do so in his presence, he
would turn his back. This he promptly did, after adding that his
nephews must not think it unmanly to express their natural affec-

tions. Billy, who grew up to be a portrait-painter and Henry's favourite nephew, was to remember the extreme gravity and politeness of the massive uncle.

From Lausanne, in mid-August, the novelist-uncle journeyed to Paris. At the end of the month he was back in De Vere Gardens.

7

Mrs Kemble

'THE year's end is a terrible time,' wrote Henry James to Miss Reubell, on 1 January 1893, 'and the year's beginning is a worse.' In a bare three and a half months he would be 50: and how 'terrible' a time it was he found out shortly after he had clinked hot punch with London friends to see the year in. His plan was to return to Italy in mid-January. He had made a series of revisions in his comedy for Augustin Daly, and at Daly's request had strengthened the leading lady's part. There seemed no likelihood of immediate production. 'I think I *must* call on you to appreciate the heroic self-control with which I forbear to ask you *when* there is a calculable possibility of the play's being produced.' Daly was vague; and James could write tales in Italy as easily as in London. But he did not get away as he had planned. First he caught a cold; and when this seemed at an end he was reminded, in the most acute fashion possible, of his personal wheel of time. He had his first attack of gout. 'It is an atrocious complaint,' he told Miss Reubell in mid-January, when he had expected to be on his way south. 'I am still very lame and it will be several more days before I can put on a Christian shoe.'

On the evening of the day he wrote this, Mrs Kemble, while being helped to bed by her maid, gave a little sigh and fell dead. On 20 January, still hobbling, and with a shoe slit so that he could put it on, James made his way to Kensal Green to say farewell to one of the oldest and most cherished of his London friends. He had known her since their meetings in Rome in the 1870s, when she had appeared in purples and mauves and possessed in her voice the manner, the style and grandeur of the Kembles. The day of the funeral was soft, and, as he said, 'kind'. The number of mourners was limited. At 84 Mrs Kemble had long outlived her contemporaries. She was laid in the same earth as her father, under a mountain of flowers. Returning to De Vere Gardens, James wrote one of his elegiac letters to Mrs Wister, in far-off Philadelphia, to bring home to Mrs Kemble's daughter the scene he had just witnessed. 'It was all bright, somehow, and public and slightly pompous.' He spoke of the good fortune of Mrs Kemble's instantaneous death; and he described the aspect of her maid standing by the graveside, 'with a very white face and her hands full of flowers'. Then he wrote: 'I am conscious of a strange bareness and a kind of evening chill, as it were, in the air, as of some great object that had filled it for long and left an emptiness – from displacement – to all the senses.' Mrs Kemble had wanted to go, he said, and 'she went when she could, at last, without a pang. She was very touching in her infirmity all these last months – and yet with her wonderful air of smouldering embers under ashes, she leaves a great image – a great memory.'

On the day of the funeral George Bentley, who had published Mrs Kemble's various books, asked James to write a tribute in the magazine *Temple Bar*. James replied, 'She ought to have rested in some fold of the Alps – which she adored – and which she in a manner resembled! I feel a great responsibility in speaking of her.' He had hoped to get away to Italy, where his brother and his family were wintering in Florence. Once again he postponed his departure.

The article, which was published almost immediately, is one of the most vivid of his series of memorials. He had seen her when he was a boy, in a park in New York, on horseback; later he had heard her read Shakespeare in London, in St John's Wood; and then he had known her in Rome, in Philadelphia, in London. She could take him back to the 1820s – the time of Jeffrey Aspern – and to the time when she had written the famous journal of her experiences of slavery on a Georgia plantation. He described her 'robust and ironic interest in life' and the far-away past to which she gave continuity. She had sat to Sir Thomas Lawrence for her portrait; and Sir Thomas had been in love with Sir Joshua's 'tragic Muse' – Mrs Kemble's aunt, Mrs Siddons. She had breakfasted with Sir Walter Scott and sung with Tom Moore; she had seen Edmund Kean and Mademoiselle Mars on the stage. She had 'felt, observed, imagined, reflected, reasoned, gathered in her passage the abiding impressions, the sense and suggestions of things'.

James sought to sketch 'the grand line and mass of her personality', to bring Mrs Kemble back to a new generation, and he filled his essay with examples of her talk. When someone told her that she was a clever woman, she had answered, 'How dare you call me any-thing so commonplace.' She used to say, 'If my servants can live with me a week they can live with me forever; but the first week sometimes kills them.' In Switzerland the guides used to call her '*la dame qui va chantant par les montagnes*'. Her talk had been filled with 'the ghosts of a dead society'. She never read or allowed newspapers in her home. She had detested the stage, to which she had been dedicated when young; but if she left her profession, she could not get rid of her instincts, 'which kept her dramatic long after she ceased to be theatrical'. James remembered taking her to a comedy and her saying: 'Yes, they're funny; but they don't begin to know how funny they might be.' With his tribute to Lowell of the previous year, the memorial to Frances Anne Kemble belongs to James's fine art of painting portraits in prose; and when, later, he brought out his *Essays in London* that volume seemed indeed to be an extended series of obituaries. To these he added the one on Brown-ing. He included also his admirable essay on Flaubert's letters – this too a kind of memorial.

'A prouder nature never affronted the long humiliation of life,' James wrote, and he also said that the death of the actress seemed like the end of some reign, the fall of some empire. In his own life this was decidedly true. Mrs Kemble was the last and the most im-portant of the three old dowagers of his London life. She had reigned for many years, giving him love and tenderness and the support of her grand and assertive manner. Now all that remained to him were a few letters, in her shaky hand, which he saved, and her travelling clock which she left him, and which ticked away the hours on his table – and his crowded memories of old occasions, meetings in Switzerland, the little tour in France, and above all her London fire-side, where she had talked from an inexhaustible fund of experi-ence and anecdote. From Mrs Kemble had come more *données* for novels and tales than from anyone else, as James's notebooks testify. She exemplified for him the various – and the copious – in life. Her photograph, an aged and wrinkled, worldly-wise female, hung ever after in his study.

8

Tale of a Tiger-Cat

WHILE he was still recovering from his gout, James received a letter from Morton Fullerton inquiring about a tale by Vernon Lee which was supposed to have satirized the novelist. The story was *Lady Tal*, and it appeared in a volume of what Miss Lee termed *Polite Stories*, bearing the generic title *Vanitas*. James answered he had heard that 'the said Vernon has done something to me'. He did not know what she had done and was determined not to find out, so that he wouldn't have to bother – 'I don't *care* to care,' he said.

Henry James had indeed been satirized and quite pointedly by his Florentine friend. What seemed to have rankled had been his interest during her writing of *Miss Brown* nine years before, and the coldness with which he had received the book. In her tale she depicted an American writer named Jervase Marion, a 'psychological' novelist, 'an inmate of the world of Henry James and a kind of Henry James'. Having clearly labelled him, she went on to describe his mannerisms and his speech. Marion encounters in Venice the striking Lady Tal, who is writing a novel. Given to fathoming people, he has difficulty in fathoming her; he interests himself in her work so that he may find out more about her. There were many remarks in the tale which James (if he had read it) would have found cruel and unkind, not least the statement that he was 'not at home' in England, and that he had 'expatriated himself, leaving brothers, sisters, friends of child-hood' and 'condemned himself to live in a world of acquaintances'.

James had originally urged William to call on Vernon Lee in Florence. Now he wrote warning him that he should 'draw it mild with her on the question of friendship. She's a tiger-cat!' There was a 'great second-rate element in her first-rateness'. He told William he had not read her story and knew of it only by hearsay. Nevertheless he considered that she had indulged in a piece of 'treachery to private relations'. She had done this sort of thing to others, and it was 'markedly "saucy"' and a 'particularly impudent and black-guardly sort of thing to do to a friend and one who has treated her with such particular consideration as I have'.

His warning came too late. William had already dined in the Via Garibaldi. Far from following Henry's advice, William wrote to Vernon Lee that he had read the story, found the portrait 'clever enough' and not exactly malicious. However, to use a friend for 'copy' implied on her part 'such a strangely *objective* way of taking human beings, and such a detachment from the sympathetic considerations which usually govern human intercourse, that you will not be surprised to learn that seeing the book has quite quenched my desire to pay you another visit'.

Vernon Lee was penitent. William wrote to her a week later; 'A woman in tears is something that I can never stand out against! Your note wipes away the affront as far as I am concerned, only you must never, *never*, NEVER, do such a thing again in any future book! It is too serious a matter.' When Henry learned of William's *démarches* on his behalf, he expressed himself as 'partly amused and partly disconcerted'. He would have preferred indifference. 'I don't find her note at all convincing; – she is doubtless sorry to be disapproved of in high quarters.' Henry was convinced that what she had done was 'absolutely deliberate, and her humility, which is easy and inexpensive, after the fact, doesn't alter her absolutely impertinent nature'.

From then on Henry 'cut' Vernon Lee. An attempt by a mutual friend to bring the two together in 1900 proved unsuccessful. The novelist said he regretted to have failed 'of sight and profit of one of the most intelligent persons it had ever been my fortune to know'. The use of the 'had ever been' was eloquent – and final. Vernon Lee had committed, as far as Henry was concerned, an unpardonable sin : she had taken a portrait from life, one filled with observation and understanding, and had not exposed it to the process of art. Even his own portrait of Miss Peabody, in *The Bostonians*, which had turned out to be a likeness, had been re-imagined; and it had been done without malice. Vernon Lee had indeed sinned twice. She had invaded James's privacy; moreover, she had committed an artistic sin. There could be no forgiving. But James too had been at fault. He had shown a well-intentioned friendliness and interest in a young woman; yet it had been an egotistical interest and it had not reckoned with the effect it might have on her. James had once again been the victim of his inability (when he dropped his usual aloof manner before certain women) to recognize that his intentions might be misinterpreted.

In the end, however, Vernon Lee seems to have accepted James's criticism. 'I feel every day more and more than I don't know enough of life to write a novel I should care to read.' And she added, in a letter to her mother, 'Life is too serious to be misrepresented as in *Miss Brown*.'

9

In the Market-Place

AT the beginning of 1893 James's situation in the theatre was as follows: *The American* had been revised and turned into a comedy; the gloom of the last act had been dissipated by having Valentin de Bellegarde recover instead of die after the duel. The play continued to be given in this form in the provinces. *Tenants*, written for John Hare, was for the moment on the shelf. *Mrs Jasper*, Daly's play, was scheduled for production at the end of the year. He had sketched out a second play for Ada Rehan, which would later become the tale *Covering End*. He had three other scenarios either on paper or in his head, for he spoke of them later that summer. He had spent now almost three years trying to launch himself as a dramatist: the best he could say was that he had had an 'honourable' run of a single play in London.

He lingered in De Vere Gardens after writing his article on Mrs Kemble, and went to Paris towards the end of March. He had planned to go to Florence, to be with William and his family; it now looked, however, as if William was coming north. When Henry inquired why he was abandoning the city at the best time of the year, his brother answered: 'I don't wonder that it seems strange to you. *Your* view of Italy is that of the tourist; and that is really the only way to *enjoy* any place. Ours is that of the resident in whom the sweet decay breathed in for six months has produced a sort of physiological craving for a change to robuster air.' Henry may have winced at being called a 'tourist' by the teasing William: he felt that he had long ago 'taken possession' of that country. However he took his brother at his word and settled in the Hôtel Westminster, to work at another play, and enjoy the Parisian spring. He visited Daudet and found him more of an invalid than ever; they dined together twice, and on one of these occasions Henry encountered in his home Maurice Barrès, whom he had met in Florence. Lucien, Daudet's younger son, late in life, said he 'seemed to remember' seeing also James and the young Proust at table in the Daudet dining-room in the Rue de Bellechasse at this time.

A further attack of gout limited James's activities for a few days, and Morton Fullerton came with some regularity to see him at his hotel. When he recovered he dined and went to art exhibitions with Miss Reubell, had lunch with Jusserand, and encountered some of the 'babyish decadents'. On one occasion he went to tea with the Whistlers, installed now 'in their queer little garden-house of the Rue du Bac, where the only furniture is the paint on the walls and the smile on the lady's broad face'. He remembered the place well: he would use it in *The Ambassadors*. One afternoon James spent talking with Henry Harland at a café in the Champs Elysées; he liked him and pitied him, feeling that Harland's literary ambition was much greater than his literary faculty.

On 4 May he went to Lucerne and put up at the Hôtel National, to be near his brother. William's sabbatical year was running to its end, and James had seen little of the nephews. The family was about five miles away, on the lakeside; Mrs James was in Munich, but returned during Henry's stay. His relatives were numerous in Europe that summer; he ticked them off to Mrs Wister – one brother, three sisters-in-law and eight nephews and nieces. His stay at Lucerne was not prolonged. Theatrical affairs were summoning him to London – the opening of Daly's new theatre and the production of *The Second Mrs Tanqueray*, in which Elizabeth Robins had yielded the main role to the then almost unknown Mrs Patrick Campbell. James was invited to the opening night.

Sitting in his hotel-room in Lucerne he wrote:

Among the delays, the disappointments, the *déboires* of the horrid theatric trade nothing is so soothing as to remember that literature sits patient at my door, and that I have only to lift the latch to let in the exquisite little form that is, after all, nearest to my heart and with which I am so far from having done. I let it in and the old brave hours come back; I live them over again – I add another little block to the small literary monument that it has been given to me to erect.

He was destined during this year, however, not to lift the latch. He had published ten tales during 1892; during 1893 *The Middle Years* appeared, and that was all. The greater part of his 50th year was spent in the market-place.

He was back in time to see Mrs Patrick Campbell win a great triumph at the opening of *The Second Mrs Tanqueray*. On the following morning he wrote to Arthur Pinero: 'I was held, as in a strong hand, by your play.' What was more, the production convinced him that George Alexander was a manager for whom a serious drama might be written. James sought a meeting with him and told him he was prepared to outline three subjects. This he did on 2 July in a letter written from Ramsgate. The first was a romantic costume play about a young man destined for the priesthood, one act of which James had completed and sent to Alexander; the second was a sketch of 'a three-act comedy, pure and simple', and the third was 'a three-act contemporary play, less purely a comedy, but on a subject very beautiful to my sense' – probably his plan to dramatize *The Chaperon*.

Alexander liked the play about the young priest. The actor had a fine pair of legs and was always partial to costume. James settled down at Ramsgate to the writing of his drama, first labelled *The Hero* and later called *Guy Domville*. It was based on an anecdote of a member of an old Venetian family who had become a monk, 'and who was taken almost forcibly out of his convent and brought back into the world in order to keep the family from becoming extinct'. No theme could have been closer to James at this moment. The monk forced into the world from his cloister was in the same position as Henry James, forcing himself into the market-place from the literature 'patient at my door'. Thus was formed, at this moment, a curious partnership in the theatre – that of the 50-year-old James, exasperated by his unsuccessful efforts to get himself produced on the London stage, and the actor-manager of the St James's, who was the talk of London because of *Mrs Tanqueray*.

George Alexander was 35 and all 'theatre'. Henry Irving had once remarked to him at a rehearsal, 'Now Alexander, not quite so much Piccadilly.' The actor-manager *was* Piccadilly to his finger-tips. A dandy, his dress was a matter for *Punch* cartoons: he had the best-creased trousers in London in an era when they were worn baggy. He was variously described as a hard-headed business man and a 'tailor's dummy'. He lacked the larger imagination and compensated for this by a kind of furious efficiency. His theatre was a model of good management. There was an air of 'competence' about everything he did. He was all profile and elegance. He was careful to surround himself with good actors – but none that would show him to poor advantage.

He was having trouble with the fiery temperament of Mrs Pat at this time, and their quarrels, on stage and off, are a part of the theatrical history of the 1890s.

From the first James had no doubt that he was dealing with a cool businessman. This was clear from his terms. Like Daly, he offered to pay £5 a night; however he placed a ceiling of £3,000 on royalties, with the full rights in the play to go to him after the ceiling was reached. 'I should be obliged to you if you can put the case to me more dazzlingly, another way,' Henry James replied. He consulted an American friend, Isaac Austen Henderson, a former New York newspaper publisher and amateur of the arts, who urged him to insist on £10 a performance. The novelist finally settled for £7 for London and America and £5 elsewhere and for a ten-year period. He brought Alexander the completed play that autumn, knowing that he would have to wait until *Mrs Tanqueray* had run its full course. Alexander had to meet at least one other commitment – a play by Henry Arthur Jones.

The novelist visited Whitby in September and stayed in Lowell's old rooms. There were memories of his friend on every side. He was consoled by the company of George du Maurier. Late in September he returned to London and met Zola, who was in England for a brief visit. They had lunch and talked of Bourget's disappointing novels; they agreed that Bourget had been neglecting his literary reputation in Paris and was travelling too much abroad. He was at this moment on a tour of the United States. James observed that the Bourgets, in their 'complete and cautious absence from Paris', seemed in reality to be running away from themselves and the problem of settling down. He found Zola 'very sane and common and inexperienced'. To Stevenson he wrote: 'Nothing, literally nothing, has ever happened to him but to write the Rougon-Macquart'.

10

Rehearsal

AUGUSTIN DALY had long been a manager, and a famous one, in New York. A 'man of the theatre' in the old sense, he had been a drama-reviewer in his youth, and later an adapter of plays from French or German into American settings. During his lifetime he fashioned more than ninety such 'vehicles'. He had now built his theatre in London, and while his reputation rested largely on his staging of comedies of manners, in which Miss Rehan brilliantly played, he had welcomed the opportunity to do a new play by an American novelist of James's eminence. The original script of *Mrs Jasper* had seemed to him weak, and earlier in the year James had made many revisions at his suggestion. Daly was hardly a literary figure, but he knew what he wanted; and what he wanted above all was a strong part for Miss Rehan. James, aware of this, had yielded ground on almost every proposal save one: this was that he give Miss Rehan some rhymed couplets at the end of the play in the classical manner. The novelist had never been a writer of verse. Daly did not insist.

The script, however, must have been rather carelessly read by Daly, and even by Miss Rehan. For when they finally took it in hand it became clear to them that they had an amateurish unactable play. Entrances and exits were handled with an awkwardness that could have created laughter in the theatre. The characters had occasional funny lines; yet they never came to life even as caricatures. The play was mechanical and contrived.

With Daly as his producer and with Miss Rehan's gift for artificial comedy, James was letting a splendid opportunity in the theatre slip through his fingers. His tales of the late 1870s had shown that he could write Miss Rehan's kind of comedy; and it was probably this which had given the manager and the actress complete faith in the novelist's ability to supply them with a workable play. James relied for his humour on 'tag' lines, and a certain amount of verbal repetition. Daly, in asking for changes, said that the play's faults were 'fundamental'. The principal one was the slenderness of the theme – the young man who believes he has compromised a young lady. James conceded that the lack of action in his original version was 'vainly dissimulated by a superabundance of movement'. This was especially true of the last act. But he repaired the play half-heartedly, and seemed to expect the actors to supply what he failed to provide.

Daly had publicly announced the work when he opened his new theatre, and James had gone over the models of the stage sets. The Daly account-books record payments made in preparation for the production. Daly's season, however, ran into difficulties. The London audiences were attached to certain playhouses and had not yet accustomed themselves to the existence of his new establishment.

James believed that with the losses Daly had suffered, his play would be a distinct asset for the new season. He explained to William that

my play, inconceivable as it appears, is the only 'novelty' with which he (Daly) seems to have armed himself for his campaign in his new and beautiful theatre. If I 'save' him, it will be so much wind in my sails – and if I don't, the explanation will be, largely, not dishonourable to me. But I long for the reality, the ingenuity and the combined amusement and disgust of rehearsals.

Late in October Daly re-read the play, with more misgivings than ever, and asked for further cuts and revisions. 'I will go over the copy,' James replied, 'and be as heroic as I can.' Six days later James reported 'utter failure'. He assured Daly, however, that he would leave himself quite 'open to impressions' during the rehearsals. In November Daly announced the production of the play for January and promised rehearsals early in December. The manager was unhappy over the new title, *Disengaged*. It did not say enough to the public. He wanted to get Miss Rehan's role into it. James bombarded him with more titles, and *Mrs Jasper's Way* was finally selected.

In the production of *The American* James had been a participant from the first; now, however, he had to wait for signals from the managerial office. Daly had his own methods of work established by long usage. One or two readings of the play seem to have taken place privately in Daly's office, and the first James heard of these was in a letter from the manager on 3 December informing him that the comedy still lacked 'story'. Since James had conceded this point long ago, it seemed to him late in the day to have it brought up again. 'I am very sorry, not a little alarmed,' he wrote to Daly; and it was agreed that they would hold their first rehearsal on 6 December. To Elizabeth Robins the dramatist confided that 'they have begun, or are just beginning, I believe, some intensely private preliminaries at Daly's – which make me very uneasy'.

What happened at the rehearsal we shall never know, for we must depend on Henry James's rather coloured version. He arrived expecting to be allowed to read the play to the actors and to explain its fine points to them, as dramatists did in France. 'I was not given a single second's opportunity of having the least contact or word with any member of the company,' he complained afterwards. It was all 'a ghastly and disgraceful farce'. The actors read their parts 'stammer-ingly' (he also called it a 'mumbled' reading) and vanished at the end of the third act. James described Miss Rehan as looking 'white, hag-gard, ill, almost in anguish'. He could not bring himself to speak to her.

The next morning James wrote to Daly withdrawing the comedy. He said that his play might not contain 'the elements of success', but that at 'my stage of relationship to the theatre I am much too ner-vous a subject not to accept as *determining*, in regard to my own action, any sound of alarm, or of essential scepticism, however abrupt, on the part of a manager'. It was clear to him that Daly was no longer interested; at the same time James could not for a moment 'profess that the scene I witnessed on your stage' had thrown any light on the play. He had only derived an intenser impression 'of the quick brevity of the three acts and their closeness and crispness of texture'. Daly replied that he was as disappointed as Henry 'at the unexpected results' of the several readings. He had been 'from the first attracted (and perhaps blinded) by the literary merits of the piece'. The rehearsals, 'however crude they may have seemed to you, convinced me that the lack of situation and dramatic climax could not be overcome by the smartest wit however much it might be accentuated by expression or enforced by the actor's art'.

Writing to William, the novelist said Daly had arranged this read-ing in order to induce him to withdraw the play. 'He is an utter cad and Ada Rehan is the same. They simply kicked me between them (and all in one "rehearsal") out of the theatre. How can one rehearse with people who are dying to get rid of you?' It was true that Daly wished to get rid of the play. The correspondence between the man-ager and James, however, does not substantiate the novelist's charge that Daly deliberately provoked withdrawal of *Mrs Jasper's Way*.

'At the rehearsal you attended,' Daly wrote,

there was no pretence on my part, or that of the actors, to give you any-thing approaching a performance. The players merely gave you a reading of their lines, and an indication of their movements and positions on the scene – from a view of which I had hoped you might have gathered, as I had already, that something was needed (beside accentuation and ex-pression) to make a success of the work.

As instance of his own good faith he reminded James of scenery under construction and costumes ordered in Paris by Miss Rehan.

James's reply was a long and bitter recapitulation of the entire history of the negotiations. He complained that he had never had an opportunity to discuss the role of Mrs Jasper with Miss Rehan, and that Daly had not adequately demonstrated to him its shortcomings. He took a parting shot at both Daly's unsuccessful season and his actress by expressing 'the regret that the actress who had been willing to act the parts I have, for the most part, seen her act this winter, should not have been moved even to *study* that of the heroine of my comedy'.

The play, and the possibility of being produced by Daly, loomed much larger in Henry's life than in that of the manager; and there is no doubt that the 'rehearsal' would have had much more meaning for Daly than for the nervous author. Faced with an experienced manager and a highly competent company, Henry James had offered a trivial and inadequate piece of work. He had counted passively on the actors. On a deeper level it might be said that James worked in the theatre 'against the grain'. His own resistances could not be overcome. The text of the play bears witness against him.

Part Two
The Altar of the Dead

II

A Venetian Christmas

'MR JAMES will come to Italy every year. And perhaps we will write that play after all.' Fenimore packed her trunks at 15 Beaumont Street in Oxford. There were more trunks than ever. She sent the heavy ones by sea to Venice and a heavy box of books. Among the books were the volumes Henry had inscribed and given to her, including his latest work, *Essays in London*, the works of Turgenev in French, which she had had bound in dark green; and her own novels, some of which she had had rebound in morocco. She had finished the serial of *Horace Chase* and planned that summer to revise it for book publication. It was June when she was ready to leave. In London she paused for some visits to the dentist. And then early one morning at her hotel she awoke with a high fever. A doctor was sent for at 4 a.m. and she was ill with influenza for some days. When she finally left for the Continent she felt weak; and she was deeply depressed.

She had no thought of returning to Florence, much as she loved that city. There had been too much heartache in leaving Bellosguardo. But she longed for Venice. She had spent happy weeks there almost a dozen years before. Arriving in late June, gliding through the canals, it seemed as if she could recover some of her old happiness. She found rooms in the Casa Biondetti, not far from the Salute. She had five windows on the Canal and she spent hours looking at the water-traffic. She had a drawing-room, a small dining-room, two bedrooms and a one-room penthouse, where there was always the sea-breeze and a splendid view. The woman of the house cooked for her.

Fenimore, however, wanted a furnished apartment rather than mere lodgings, and began an active search almost immediately. It was part of her Venetian adventure, to travel by gondola to various palaces and smaller houses, in search of a place she could make into a home. She met the Curtises – probably through Henry James – and on 14 July he spoke of her in a letter to Mrs Curtis: 'I am very sorry indeed Miss Woolson has trouble in finding a house. But I had an idea she wanted – I think she does want – to abide for a winter experimentally, first, in a *quartière mobigliato*.' On 19 September he wrote to the same correspondent: 'I shall do my best to prove to Miss Woolson that Venice is better than Cooperstown. I am very glad to hear that she has at last a roof of her own. The having it, I am sure, will do much to anchor her.' In October he wrote to Francis Boott and announced he would go to Italy – to Tuscany – in the spring.

I shall take Venetia by the way and pay a visit to our excellent friend Fenimore. She has taken, for the winter, General de Horsey's Casa Semitecolo, near the Palazzo Dario, and I believe is materially comfortable; especially as she loves Venice, for which small blame to her! But I figure her as extremely exhausted (as she always is at such times), with her writing and re-writing of her last novel – a great success, I believe, in relation to the particular public (a very wide American one) that she addresses. She is to have, I trust, a winter of bookless peace.

I

Fenimore had not altogether made up her mind to stay on in Venice. There were times when she thought, as James said, of returning to ancestral Cooperstown in New York; but she used to wonder whether – after a villa in Florence and a palace in Venice – she would not find life a little humdrum in America. She was certain she would find it more expensive. General de Horsey, who never stayed in Venice in the winter, was delighted to have Miss Woolson as his tenant. He leased her two floors on an eight-months' lease at $40 a month; Fenimore had two drawing-rooms, a winter bedroom on the side opposite the Canal looking down into a little *calle*, a summer bedroom on the Canal, a dining-room, kitchen and three servants' rooms. The furniture was excellent. She sent for furnishings she had left in Florence – the Brichieri chair Mrs Browning had sat in, which Boott had acquired; her high desk – she always wrote standing up, sometimes for hours on end – and linens.

Her deafness tended to make her a *solitaire*. She found it easier to decline invitations than to accept them. And while the Americans in Venice were friendly, she spent much time alone. That summer she had rapidly established her routine of work. Her maid called her at 4.30 when the dawn was on the Venetian waters. She would write until 9.30. Then her cook would bring her breakfast. With the shutters closed to keep out the heat, she would continue to work until about 4. Her gondola would now take her to the Lido. She liked a late afternoon dip in the warm Adriatic waters; and she would let herself float endlessly on the little waves. Refreshed, she would return for dinner at 7.30. The evenings were always spent looking at the lights and listening to music. Mrs Bronson was kind and hospitable; and Fenimore became very good friends with her daughter, Edith.

By early winter she was installed in the Semitecolo. There, with her Pomeranian, whom she named Otello and called affectionately Tello, she gave herself over to the lonely life she had always led. She began a series of visits to various islands and lagoons and took copious notes. These have survived; they are a succession of minute details:

September 3rd, six p.m. Warm, still, not at all hot, autumnal. The water of a pearl and dove colour. Dove-coloured clouds gathering in the west. The beautiful line of the Euganean Hills like dark blue velvet. The sun comes out below the clouds behind S. Giorgio in Alga, lighting it up in profile with its trees and meadows. The sun in *rays*. One fishing boat. The two piles inky black. I saw the Dolomites or Venetian Alps for the first time at the time of this sunset, after three months in Venice! In September the islands all begin to look nearer and clearer.

October 10th, six p.m. Sun gone down, and the whole west salmon colour and gold. Euganean Hills and all the Alps violet velvet. Low tide and men with legs bare searching for things in the seaweed and islands. Vast plains of seaweed.

Dec. 3rd. White snow on the mountains; vaguely seen against dove or slate-coloured sky and dove-coloured mist. Like crayon drawing.

She compiled for Mrs Bronson a list of islands which during the centuries had been swallowed up by the sea. She often visited San Niccolò di Lido, once with Mr Curtis, where there was a fort and a cemetery with English and German graves. She had always walked in cemeteries, a habit begun in the American South, where she had visited and written about those of the Civil War. There were notes also on many islands, visited patiently, day after day, during December. She seemed to be content with a cataloguing of these scraps of land and what the play of light and the fishing-boats did to them in the way of constantly changing their background. Thus her notes on San Michele, Cemetery Island.

The old brown gondola rowed by the cemetery monk.
The Mass of the Dead which I saw.
The appearance of the cemetery on All Souls' Day.
Pink walls. Cypresses (?) near the church. Campanile of cemetery church,
  pink bricks with white corners.
White marble top story with round topped windows.
White dome with a red circle.

She told herself she would begin a new novel with the new year.
In the spring Henry James would pay his promised visit.

2

Towards Christmas she seems to have made up her mind that she
might take root in the place, for she began to look at unfurnished
apartments, often with Edith Bronson for company. She liked Venetian society; it was small and not very demanding; she found it rather
lazy, if sometimes 'exclusive'. Its members did not trouble themselves to pursue strangers. 'I have never been so kindly received as
here; but there are few young people. It is essentially a society of
older persons,' wrote this woman of 53. She had just looked at a
magnificent apartment in the Palazzo Pesaro, on the Grand Canal,
below the Rialto – ten or twelve superb high-ceilinged rooms with
great balconies on the Canal, all in perfect order, owned by the
Duchess of Bevilacqua, available for $400 a year. But how did one
heat such a place in winter? – especially with those high ceilings?
And where would she find enough furniture?

On Christmas Eve it was so warm that Fenimore had no use for
her fur cloak. She went to the Lido in her gondola and walked for
two hours on the Adriatic beach. Otello chased up and down the
sand. For a while she sat on the grassy embankment of the Fort San
Niccolò, after asking permission of the military guard. The sea and
sky were blue, and the long line of the Alps was visible with more
distinctness than she had ever noticed before. Never one for imaginative imagery, she observed that 'the snow peaks looked like pink ice
cream'. She also remarked that the large tree at San Niccolò was a
sycamore; and she wrote down the inscription on one of the graves
in the cemetery

  ... dopo 45 anni vita laboriosa ed onesta, affranto dalle sventure, per
troppo delicate sentire, finiva di vivere, agosto 1887 ...

In her notebook, on a somewhat more imaginative plane, she reflected that the pink-flushed peaks were riding through immeasurable space – 'they are the outer edge of our star, they cut the air as they fly. They are the rim of the world.' And then a strange note of melancholy : 'I should like to turn into a peak when I die; to be a beautiful purple mountain, which would please the tired, sad eyes of thousands of human beings for ages.'

That same day she wrote to an old friend and the melancholy feeling returned :

I have taught myself to be calm and philosophic, and I feel perfectly sure that the next existence will make clear all the mysteries and riddles of this. In the meantime, one can do one's duty or try to do it. But if at any time you should hear that I have gone, I want you to know beforehand that my end was peace, and even joy at the release ... Now I am going out again for another walk through the beautiful Piazza.

3

In London, in De Vere Gardens, Henry James spent a lonely Christmas, rejoicing in his solitude. A few evenings earlier, calling on Elizabeth Robins, he stayed past midnight, and apparently talked at length of his difficulties in the theatre. Miss Robins wrote to her and James's friend, Mrs Bell : 'James stayed till after one in the morning and I'm dead beat.' She added : 'H. J. was ghastly depressing.' The episode with Daly had shaken him severely; he persevered, however, in the hope that he would fare better with Alexander. Just before Christmas he made certain new cuts and revisions in the *Guy Domville* script. 'Alexander's preparations of my other play are going on sedulously as to which situation and circumstances are all essentially different' – different from those surrounding his Daly play, he explained to William.

On the day after Christmas, sitting by his fire, in a still empty London, he gave himself over to reverie. 'Vague, dim forms of imperfect conceptions seem to brush across one's face with a blur of suggestion, a flutter of impalpable wings,' he wrote. He began to sketch a new play. Calm though London was, in the season of peace, James's mind seemed to be filled with violence. He drew up an outline for a play of Ibsen-like intensity in which he devised a climax more terrible than any he had ever set down before. There would be a dying woman, who would exact a pledge from her husband that he should never remarry so long as their child was alive; and this would be an open invitation to another woman to do away with this human obstacle. The wife dies. The 'Bad Heroine' is 'fearfully in love with my Hero'. There is also a 'Good Heroine', whom he loves.

Then, somehow, *this* is what I saw half an hour ago, as I sat in the flickering firelight of the winter dusk. The women have a talk – I won't answer, nor *attempt* to, now, here, of course, for links and liaisons – the women have a talk in which the good girl learns with *dismay* that it is the life of the child that keeps her from her lover. The effect of this revelation upon her is not, to the bad girl's sense, what she expected from it. She rebels, she protests, she is far from willing to give him up. Then my young lady takes a decision – she determines to poison the child – on the calculation that suspicion will fall on the rival. She does so – and on the theory of *motive* – suspicion does fall on the wretched girl.

This was an amalgam of a thriller and Ibsen : and probably James was already seeing Miss Robins in the role of the Hedda-like 'Bad Heroine'. Later he would amend his form of violence; in *The Other House* the child is drowned rather than poisoned. The fantasy was strange and unusual in a man whose novels record little violence. 'As I so barbarously and roughly jot the story down,' James wrote, 'I seem to feel in it the stuff of a play, of the particular limited style and category that can only be dreamed of for E[dward] C[ompton].'

After Christmas, and until the new year, he attacked a large mass of correspondence. He wrote a long letter to William describing the Daly episode, and discussing the visit of the Bourgets in America. 'London has been very still, very empty and of an air extraordinarily soft and clear. I have passed no more selfishly complacent Christmas – in the cheerful void left by the almost universal social flight to the country.' He told William he was working 'heroically' at the drama. However, he found it difficult to engage in ventures which produced for the time being no income. He had begun, however, now that Alice was dead, to receive the rents from Syracuse which he had made over to her during her lifetime : and these, little more than $100 a month, gave him – after twenty-five years in which he had lived by his pen – a certain margin. Nevertheless his habits were expensive; and he worked still as one who had to earn his living. He would do so to the end.

The Daly episode had been, he told William, 'a horrid experience', but nothing that one might not expect 'in the vulgar theatrical world'. However, he was not giving up the theatre.

I mean to wage this war ferociously for one year more – 1894 – and then (unless the victory and the spoils have not by that become more proportionate than hitherto to the humiliations and vulgarities and disgusts, all the dishonour and chronic insult incurred) to 'chuck' the whole intolerable experiment and return to more elevated and more independent courses. The whole odiousness of the thing lies in the connection between the drama and the theatre. The one is admirable in its interest and difficulty, the other loathsome in its conditions.

'I have come,' he told William, 'to *hate* the whole theatrical subject.'

On the last day of 1893 he wrote a letter to Venice, to Mrs Bronson. As in his other letters, he described the Christmas quiet that had descended on London, and the peaceful days he had spent. 'I like the dusky London holiday-making, and the shopfronts flaring in the damp afternoons.' Elsewhere in this letter he asked : 'Do you see anything of my old friend Miss Woolson? I am very fond of her and should be glad if there was any way in which you could be kind to her.'

12

Miss Woolson

IN the early morning hours of 24 January 1894 – a little after one o'clock – two men walking in the *calle* beside the Casa Semitecolo noticed, in the dark, a white mass on the cobbles. One of the men thrust at it with his stick and evoked a startling unearthly moan. The frightened men began to shout. Lights appeared, and servants : a nurse came running out of the building. Miss Woolson was carried back into the Casa. She had been ill with a new bout of influenza and had had a high fever. A few minutes before the men came upon her, she had sent her nurse to get something from one of the drawing-rooms. While the nurse was gone, she had apparently opened the second-storey window of her bedroom and thrown herself – or as her relatives claimed, fallen – into the little street.

The grand-niece of James Fenimore Cooper was placed on her

bed. She lay peacefully, with no sign of pain and little sign of life. The doctor was summoned. She was, however, beyond recall. By the time the wintry dawn broke over the little canals and the lagoons, and over the Alps she had so recently contemplated, the solitary, shut-in life of Constance Fenimore Woolson had come to an end.

The American consul was promptly informed and cables were dispatched to Miss Woolson's sister, Clara Benedict, in New York. A cousin, Grace Carter, who was in Munich, was summoned. Miss Woolson had died on a Wednesday; on Thursday the 25th the cousin arrived and took charge. From the nurse she gathered that Fenimore had spoken of wanting to be buried in Rome. The servants were dismissed and the Casa locked up under consular seal to await the arrival of the sister. Miss Carter accompanied the body to Rome, where John Hay, friend of Fenimore, happened to be on a holiday. He took charge of the final arrangements.

I

Henry James received the tidings of Miss Woolson's death from Mrs Benedict in a cable from New York. She asked him whether he might find it possible to leave for Venice. Shocked and mystified, he assumed that Miss Woolson, like Lizzie Boott, had died of natural causes; an exchange of telegrams with Dr Baldwin in Florence and word from John Hay gave him the facts about the funeral in Rome, which had been set for Wednesday, the 31st, but no other details. He accordingly went, on the Saturday afternoon, to Cook's and made his travel-plans. On returning to De Vere Gardens, he found a note from Constance Fletcher, who lived in the Palazzo Capello in Venice, and who was at that moment in London. She enclosed a clipping from a Venetian newspaper which gave a circumstantial account of the manner in which Miss Woolson had met her end.

It was now that James experienced the full shock and horror of the occurrence. He had always known of Fenimore's tendency to melancholy; he had recognized the solitude of her life; he had done what he could, when he was with her, to mitigate it. That she should have resorted to this extreme to release herself from her loneliness baffled him, and he searched his memories in his despair to discover clues that might help. By the next day, Sunday, he had made up his mind that he could not face the ordeal of her funeral. Before the 'horror and pity' of the news, he wrote to John Hay,

I have utterly collapsed. I have let everything go, and last night I wired to Miss Carter that my dismal journey was impossible to me. I have, this morning, looked it more in the face, but I can't attempt it. I shall wire you tomorrow morning – one can do nothing here today; but meanwhile I must repeat to you that with the dreadful *image* before me I feel a real personal indebtedness to you in the assurance I have of your beneficent action and tenderness – in regard to offices that you will scarcely know how to make soothing and pitying enough.

He went on to say that

Miss Woolson was so valued and close a friend of mine and had been for so many years that I feel an intense nearness of participation in every circumstance of her tragic end and in every detail of the sequel. But it is just this nearness of emotion that has made – since yesterday – the immediate horrified rush to personally *meet* these things impossible to me.

Difficult as it is to speculate on the motives of James's decision, one thing is clear : he had been quite resigned to going to Rome when he had thought Fenimore had died of natural causes. From the moment that he learned she had taken her own life– as *The Times* finally reported the next day – he had been sickened and overwhelmed, not only by grief and, as he said, horror and pity, but also – as his later words and works were to show – by a feeling that in some way he too had some responsibility for her last act. To Miss Carter he wrote 'unquestionably she had become actively insane under the influence of her illness and her fever'. What struck him now, with full force, was the pathetic ordeal of this middle-aged, deaf woman, who worked so hard and led so cloistered an existence. 'What a picture of lonely unassisted suffering!' he wrote to Hay. 'It is too horrible for thought.'

He wrote to Mrs Bronson much in the same vein. He had been determined to go to Italy even though Dr Baldwin had tried to dissuade him; but it had been when he heard, 'for the first time, of the unimagined and terrible manner of her death' that he had lost heart. 'So I have been kept away from you,' he told Mrs Bronson,

and I can't, while the freshness of such a misery as it all must have been, is in the air, feel anything but that Venice is not a place I want immediately to see. I had known Miss Woolson for many years and was extremely attached to her – she was the gentlest and tenderest of women, and full of intelligence and sympathy.

His decision not to go to Rome was apparently an instinctive act of self-protection: it came out of the confusion of feeling which he experienced at this moment. In recent months he had mourned the passing of many who were close to him; he could have faced the dead Fenimore if she had died as his sister had died. It was the brutality, the violence, the stark horror, the mystery, the seeming madness of Fenimore's last act which struck him – and that he should have been so mistaken in a person for whom he had shown so much affection. In doing violence to herself, she had, so to speak, done violence to him, and he sought now some shield behind which he could withdraw and take care of his deep wound. 'Oh that I had wings like a dove! for then would I fly away, and be at rest.' In the coming months James may have read this psalm; for in it he probably found his deepest feelings of this terrible moment in his life; and in it he found the title of the novel that he would ultimately write about a death in Venice.

The evolution of his feelings are documented for us in the letters he wrote during the ensuing days, and throughout this year – 1894 – which he thought he would consecrate to the drama, but which was devoted much more to a spiritual altar of the dead. Writing on the day after his decision not to go to Rome, to his friend, Margaret Brooke, the Ranee of Sarawak, who was in Italy, he could not avoid pouring out his inner grief:

For the last two days it has seemed to me probable that I might see you very soon, for in consequence, I grieve to say, of some terribly sad personal news from Italy, I was all prepared up to last night to start this morning [he was writing on 28 January] for Rome. Circumstances, at the eleventh hour, have made it impossible – and the reprieve, *in* these circumstances, is only an extreme relief. A close and valued friend of mine – a friend of many years with whom I was extremely intimate and to whom I was greatly attached (Miss Fenimore Woolson, the American novelist, a singularly charming and distinguished woman), died last Wednesday, in Venice, with dreadful attendant circumstances. Ill with influenza, aggravated by desperate insomnia, she threw herself out of the upper window of her house and died an hour later! It is too horrible to me to write about it – and I mention it really only to tell you that for the present I *can't* write.

He had never quite expressed it in this way – 'with whom I was extremely intimate'. Fenimore had always been his 'admirable' friend, his 'distinguished friend'. But the Ranee had not known Miss

Woolson, and he could speak to her, perhaps, more freely. In his telegram to John Hay he asked that some flowers be laid in his name beside Fenimore's grave. 'The only image I can evoke that interposes at all,' he wrote to Hay, 'is that of the blest Roman cemetery that she positively *desired* – I mean in her extreme love of it and of her intensely consenting and more than reconciled rest under the Roman sky. *Requiescat.*'

2

On the day of the funeral James wrote to Francis Boott: 'I feel how, like myself, you must be sitting horror-stricken at the last tragic act of poor C. F. W. I can't *explain* it to you – it is with my present knowledge too dreadfully obscure – and I am tired with the writing and telegraphing to which I have had to give myself up in consequence.'

Seeking explanations, reasons, motivations, James suggested to Boott that the event demanded

the hypothesis of sudden *dementia* and to admit none other. Pitiful victim of chronic melancholy as she was (so that half one's friendship for her was always anxiety), nothing is more possible than that, in illness, this obsession should abruptly have deepened into suicidal mania. There was nothing whatever, that I know of, in her immediate circumstances, to explain it – save indeed the sadness of her lonely Venetian winter. *After* such a dire event, it is true, one sees symptoms, indications in the past; and some of these portents seem to me now not to be wanting. But it's all unspeakably wretched and obscure. She was not, she was never, wholly sane – I mean her liability to suffering was like the *doom* of mental disease. On the other hand she was the gentlest and kindest of women – and to me an admirable friend.

Fenimore was buried in a corner of the Protestant Cemetery in Rome, not far from the Roman wall and near the point where the pagan pyramid of Caius Cestius thrusts its sharp diagonal beside the Christian ground. 'We buried poor Constance W. last Wednesday, laying her down in her first and last resting place,' Hay wrote five days later to Henry Adams. 'A thoroughly good, and most unhappy woman, with a great talent bedevilled by disordered nerves. She did much good and no harm in her life, and had not as much happiness as a convict.'

She lies under the tall cypresses, not far from the graves of Shelley and Trelawny, and a short distance from the graves where Keats and his friend Severn are placed side by side. In death, as in life, Fenimore was companioned by great literary figures. A modern visitor among these clustered tombstones cannot but be struck by the fact that she also was buried – fate so arranged it – almost in the very spot where Henry James had tenderly laid to rest one of his most famous heroines, with whom Miss Woolson had identified herself and who, she felt, had been misunderstood and rejected by the Jamesian hero. Here Daisy Miller had been interred, after she died of the Roman fever, on an April morning long ago, 'in an angle of the wall of Imperial Rome, beneath the cypresses and the thick springflowers'. It was still winter when the earth covered Miss Woolson's coffin. John Hay caused the plot to be planted with perpetually blooming violets, and in due course a wide marble coping was placed round the flower-bed, and a Celtic cross of stone laid within it. On the coping there is simply the name Constance Fenimore Woolson, and the year of her death, 1894.

13

Casa Biondetti

'THERE is much that is tragically obscure in that horror of last week – and I feel as if I were living in the shadow of it,' James wrote to Edmund Gosse, who read the paragraph in *The Times* and questioned him about his dead friend. To Mrs Bronson he spoke of 'the strange obscurity of so much of the matter' and said that it had the 'impenetrability of madness'. He added:

Nothing could be more incongruous with the general patience, reserve and dainty dignity, as it were, of her life. Save her deafness, she had absolutely no definite or unusual thing (that I know of) to minister to her habitual depression; she was free, independent, successful – very successful indeed as a writer – and *liked*, peculiarly, by people who knew her.

James was unable to penetrate the obscurity; he could only offer himself consoling thoughts. He learned that Miss Woolson had been delirious, he was aware of the deep depression that often accompanies influenza; he reminded himself again of the circumstances of solitude and melancholy. Gradually certain comforting thoughts asserted themselves. If Miss Woolson's life had been a life of chronic melancholia and loneliness, then all that he had done had helped to provide a measure of happiness – had helped even to keep her alive. 'My own belief,' he wrote to William, 'is that she had been on the very verge of suicide years ago, and that it had only been stood off by the practical interposition of two or three friendships which operated (to their own sense) with a constant vague anxiety.' To Lily Norton he wrote: 'Isolation she sought and liked, but it was not the right thing for her and I can't help thinking that, given the condition she had long been in, the event might have been averted by an accidental difference of circumstance – as it was precipitated by the catastrophe of her illness.' Again and again, to his inquiring friends, he repeated the sentence that 'half one's friendship for her was always anxiety', and he thereby discerned in his relationship with Fenimore those elements that had made for disquiet and uneasiness in himself. There had been, from the first, when he had known her in Florence, the obstacle of her deafness. Communication with her had never been easy; and doubtless it had been at its best in their correspondence. Had they really understood one another? Had her act been a partial consequence of frustration – of frustrated love for James? The promise of an annual visit was thin support for an elderly devoted spinster living in a comparatively soundless world. We do not know whether he entertained such thoughts; nor can we say what measure of guilt he may have felt – if he felt any at all. What is clear is that in time he took comfort in the thought that Fenimore had been seriously ill, and that she had not been altogether responsible for her actions.

He expressed this to Mrs Bronson: 'It was an act, I am convinced, of definite, irresponsible, delirious insanity, determined by illness, fever, as to its form, but springing indirectly out [of] a general depression which, though not visible to people who saw her socially, casually, had essentially detached her from the wish to live.' This was also his answer to William, who wrote to him that on the one occasion he had met Fenimore he had found her carefree, happy, lively and without sign of melancholia. Henry answered that it could not be visible in a casual social situation.

There was another question, of a practical kind, which may have been a source of anxiety to the novelist. This was his correspondence with Fenimore. The author of *The Aspern Papers* was all too aware of the hazards of what Dr Johnson had called 'The Great Epistolick Art'. One of the first entries in his notebook, after his sister's death, had been a worried paragraph about 'the idea of the *responsibility* of destruction – the destruction of papers, letters, records, etc. connected with private and personal history'. This had led him to write a little tale (*Sir Dominick Ferrand*) about a young man who finds a secret drawer in a desk containing scandal-provoking letters of a famous statesman; the young man, in his impoverished state, is faced with the conflict of selling the letters or upholding privacy. In the end the letters are burned with 'infinite method'.

James could make 'the private life' triumph in his fiction; but was it possible to do so in life? He was all too aware how many trunks Fenimore possessed; he had seen her constitutional difficulty in extricating herself from the clutter of her days. He could imagine – he who was intensely private and secretive – what piles of paper, notebooks, possibly even diaries, there might be lying at this moment in the rooms of the temporarily sealed apartment in the Casa Semitecolo. Fenimore had spoken of a will, shortly before her death; none was found. She had even – he learned later – told Francis Boott that her last testament would contain a 'surprise'. When Boott told James this, he replied it was 'just one of those numerous strangenesses that illustrate (as one looks back) her latent insanity'. In the absence of a will, Clara Woolson Benedict in New York, Fenimore's sister, fell heir to all her possessions. And James, in his correspondence with Mrs Benedict, suggested that he would meet her when she came abroad, escort her to Venice and give her all the assistance she might need in taking charge of Fenimore's belongings. He would, in this fashion, perform a generous act, an act of piety; and his good offices would be of great help to the bereaved woman, particularly since she spoke no Italian. At the same time there would be the comforting practical certainty that he would be in Venice when the Casa was opened up, and at hand to cope with whatever privacies might require safeguarding among the dead woman's papers. His task was the opposite of that of his narrator in *The Aspern Papers*. To dispose of, rather than preserve, certain documents, may have been a part of his goal in undertaking what at best was an irksome and lugubrious task for a busy man of letters involved in the theatre at this moment and not directly involved in Mrs Benedict's affairs – save as a sympathetic and interested friend of her dead sister.

He went unwillingly. Without divulging why he was coming to

Venice, he asked Mrs Bronson to find him some rooms. He had reached the age, he explained, when he no longer could tolerate hotels with rows of international shoes lined up outside bedroom doors at night. He went on to suggest that if possible she obtain for him Miss Woolson's rooms in the Casa Biondetti – those she had occupied before moving into the Semitecolo. 'A combination of circumstances, some of which I would have wished other, but which I must accept, makes it absolutely necessary I should be in Venice from the first of April,' he explained. He remembered, he said, that Miss Woolson had found these rooms particularly comfortable; and that the woman in charge had cooked for her. This would be ideal for the work he had in hand. He made no mention of Miss Woolson's sister. Mrs Bronson sent him a cable very promptly to say that the apartment had been secured.

I

By the time he made his arrangements to go to Italy at the end of March, the novelist had become accustomed to the idea of Fenimore's death; and the letter he wrote to Mrs Benedict was balm for his own wounds as well as on those he imagined to be hers and her daughter's:

Almost by this you will have heard from me that I will meet you at Genoa – be there when you arrive. I am sure Rome will be a very soothing, softening impression to you – that after a little the horror of the weeks you have been living through will be lost in the simple, assenting, participating tenderness with which (in regard to her memory and deep exemption now from everything that is hard in life) you will find yourselves thinking of her – till at last you will feel almost at peace in your acceptance. Meanwhile only live, and think of living, from hour to hour, and day to day; it is perfect wisdom and it takes us through troubles that no other way can take us through. Have no plan whatever in advance about Venice. There is no need for any. The whole question will simplify itself, settle itself, facilitate itself, after you get to Italy.

He reached Genoa five days before Mrs Benedict, and was on the pier on 29 March 1894 when the *Kaiser Wilhelm II* docked. She was accompanied by her daughter Clare. James helped them through customs and took them to the Hôtel de Gênes, where he himself was staying. The Benedicts went first to Rome, to visit the grave. James went directly to Venice, to await their coming. 'I found this pleasant little apartment quite ready for me and appreciably full of the happy presence of your aunt,' he wrote from the Casa Biondetti to Clare Benedict in Rome. He urged her and Mrs Benedict to stop in Florence on their way to Venice, to meet Dr Baldwin whom Fenimore had known. Baldwin had been a devoted and faithful friend and 'it will be such a comfort and relief to him – a very great good indeed'.

It was probably while he was waiting for the Benedicts that James visited, by himself, the little street behind the Casa Semitecolo and looked at the window from which Fenimore had jumped. 'The sight of the *scene* of her horrible act is, for that matter, sufficient to establish utter madness at the time. A place more mad for *her* couldn't be imagined.' Writing to Francis Boott, he added, 'I don't know why I remind you of these things, which only deepen the darkness of the tragedy.'

The Benedicts arrived within a matter of days. Henry, Grace Carter, Fenimore's two gondoliers and the dog Tello met them. On the morning after their arrival the seals were removed and the silent rooms were entered – 'a heartbreaking day, followed by many weeks of a task beyond words hard,' Mrs Benedict wrote in her diary. To a friend she wrote that 'Henry James met us at Genoa, and never never left us until all her precious things were packed and boxed and sent to America'. Mrs Benedict distributed mementoes to Fenimore's friends. James recovered such of his letters as were found and was invited to take such books of Fenimore's as he wished. He took eleven volumes of her Turgenev in French, bound in half-morocco; ('You are now our Turgenev,' she had once written to Henry); her personal volume of *Rodman the Keeper*, containing the place and date of each sketch, inserted in her own hand. He took also a bound copy of Fenimore's most popular novel, *Anne*. Clare Benedict kept the books which Henry had given to her aunt, the 'silent witnesses' of their various meetings. He regained possession, however, of his *Essays in London*, asking for it perhaps for sentimental reasons, since there was a note written in it in Miss Woolson's hand, at the end of his essay on Mrs Kemble. In this note Miss Woolson recalled the evening when she had gone to see Salvini and there encountered James with Mrs Kemble; he had surrendered to her his seat beside the aged actress. Mrs Kemble had turned to Miss Woolson and said, in her deepest tragic tones, 'I am *sorry* Mr James has introduced you to me. I shall be obliged to tell you, *now*, that I shall not *speak* to you, or *look* at you, or be conscious of your existence even, during the entire evening.' The volume remained in James's library. Miss Woolson's name, which had been written in it in pencil, was erased, and James wrote his own name over the erasure. On the title-page 'C. F. Woolson from H.J.,' also written in pencil, had been erased but the H.J. remains legible. James also took as a memento a small painting by an artist named Meacci which years later he returned to a little memorial room Mrs Benedict established in Cooperstown for Miss Woolson.

2

As Henry James had suspected, the literary remains were voluminous. The impression one gets from the diary of Mrs Benedict is that the novelist had ample opportunity – and doubtless would have been encouraged – to look through Miss Woolson's various literary papers. There were the notes she had been taking on the lagoons and islands of Venice. There was a commonplace book filled with comments on her reading. There were notebooks containing her reflections on art, music and literature, most of them of a distressing banality. Occasionally, however, an interesting thought crept in, a passage of singular insight. If James read these pages he must have come on a passage such as:

Many women, good women, think scenes in certain novels and plays 'so untrue to nature!' These are the women who live always in illusion! They believe in all sorts of romances which have never had the least actual existence. They think in their secret hearts that all men are more or less in love with them; they go swimming through life in a mist of romantic illusion. Ibsen, for instance, is to them horrible. Though they may have Noras in their own family, and Heddas too.

Or a note such as:

'He is interested in indexes,' said H. with profound stupefaction.

There were jottings of remarks she had heard; comments in drawing-rooms; ideas for stories. Many of her notes seemed to have been inspired by Hawthorne's notebooks, and were set down in his form:

To imagine an American business man seeing 'the late' prefixed in a newspaper to the name of some one he had known, and suddenly trying to imagine *himself* 'the late'.

To imagine a haunting face for years. Then to meet the person in real life.

The themes that haunted her, stated at greater length, were themes of women misunderstood and scorned :

To imagine a person (woman) always misunderstood; considered shy, sullen, cold, etc. – simply because she has never had about her people who really like her. To show the change – the gradual outburst, bloom and glow, even beauty – that follows an atmosphere of admiration, regard, sympathy and love.

A love story ... It tells how she loved him. He did not think of her at all; in fact he never noticed her.

To imagine a woman obtaining all the romance and sentiment of her life in distant and wholly imaginary lovers. She has one at every corner!

Imagine a man endowed with an absolutely unswerving will; extremely intelligent, he *comprehends* passion, affection, unselfishness and self-sacrifice etc. perfectly, though he is himself cold and a pure egotist. He has a charming face, a charming voice, and he can, when he pleases, counterfeit all these feelings so exactly that he gets all the benefits that are to be obtained by them.

An American who has lived so long abroad that he is almost denationalized, and *conscious of it fully*; which makes him an original figure.

There was one note above all which James may have seen and which could have been the source for an entry in his own notebooks. Fenimore wrote :

To imagine a man spending his life looking for and waiting for his 'splendid moment.' 'Is this my moment?' 'Will this state of things bring it to me?' But the moment never comes. When he is old and infirm it comes to a neighbour who has never thought of it or cared for it. The comment of the first upon this.

James's note, written seven years later, ran :

A man haunted by the fear, more and more throughout life, that *something will happen to him*; he doesn't quite know what ... Yet 'It *will* come, it will still come,' he finds himself believing – and indeed saying to some one, some second-consciousness in the anecdote. 'It will come before death; I shan't die without it.' Finally I think it must be *he* who sees – not the second consciousness ...

This was the germ from which Henry James would write *The Beast in the Jungle*.

3

For five weeks the novelist, Mrs Benedict and her daughter lived with the ghost of Constance Fenimore Woolson. Early in May twenty-seven boxes containing the effects accumulated during her sister's literary life abroad were dispatched to America. James, she recorded in her diary, 'came every day to see and help us – we could not have gone through it without him'. Apparently, once he had satisfied himself about Miss Woolson's literary remains, he reverted to his usual working hours, spending his forenoons and early afternoons at the Casa Biondetti. He would arrive at tea-time at the Semitecolo, and the three would go out for a couple of hours in the gondola. On most evenings he dined with the Benedicts. He wrote to William James of

the great hole bored in my time and my nerves by the copious aid and comfort I couldn't help giving to poor Mrs Benedict – Miss Woolson's sister – who, staying there five weeks, made daily demands of me to help her in the winding-up of Miss W's so complicated affairs, all left, so far as Venice was concerned, at sixes and sevens. This proved a most devouring, an almost fatal job.

He told Francis Boott that all the knowledge Mrs Benedict collected of Miss Woolson's last weeks 'tended directly to confirm the conviction she had already formed that an unmistakable lapse from sanity had occurred sometime before her death – that some cerebral accident had been determined the previous summer'. This is questionable; certainly the notes on the lagoons and the diary-entries of Fenimore's last Christmas show no lapse from her usual ability to observe and to record.

The novelist's own role in aiding Mrs Benedict seems to have occupied his first fortnight in Venice. A notebook entry of 17 April 1894, brief and pointed, suggests the term of his principal funereal duties, but suggests also the inner outrage he had suffered.

Here I sit, at last, after many interruptions, distractions, and defeats, with some little prospect of getting a clear time to settle down to work again. The last six weeks, with my two or three of quite baffling indisposition before I left London, have been a period of terrific sacrifice to the ravenous Moloch of one's endless personal social relations – one's eternal exposures, accidents, disasters. *Basta.*

Exposures, accidents, disasters. The mounting strength of each of the three words suggests the force of his Venetian experience. There had been danger of exposure; there had been accident; there was the disastrous inroad on his working time : there was the greater disaster of his personal hurt. We may guess that when he made this note – that is two weeks after the work at the Casa Semitecolo began – James had settled all the practical questions that concerned him in Fenimore's death, and he could relax. The most difficult part was over. The mystery of her life and death remained. As for the rest – *basta*!

4

Early in May the Benedicts left for further travels in Europe. The Curtises were in India and Palazzo Barbaro was let. Few of James's friends were in Venice. He could settle down to work that had been delayed. He had promised Henry Harland a long tale for the *Yellow Book*. One of the reasons he had been attracted to this hard-cover quarterly, of which he did not altogether approve, was that he would be allowed to write his *nouvelles* without regard to a word-count. The first issue, earlier that year, had contained his tale of *The Death of the Lion*. That sardonic tale was written just after Fenimore's death, and it masked, in its moments of savage wit, all the anguish of the time. Its picture of an elderly, neglected man of letters, unread and unknown, who becomes a 'lion' because a newspaper finally takes notice of him, was one of the bitterest – and most amusing – of the 'tales of the literary life' which James now began to write. The 'lion' is taken up by a sympathetic young man who constitutes himself his protector and his 'manager'. But he cannot protect him from the draughts at the home of Mrs Weeks Wimbush, the 'lion'-fancier. She collects celebrities and at her home a precious manuscript belonging to the great man is lost, as it is passed from hand to hand – unread. The 'lion' dies, unaware of the fuss around him.

The tale which James now set down in Venice, and which ran to great length, was *The Coxon Fund*, built around his recent reading of a life of Coleridge by James Dykes Campbell. He was struck by the personality of the poet-critic, 'wonderful, admirable figure for pictorial treatment'. There emerged his portrait of the gifted Saltram, who had magic in his talk, and lived his life unconcerned by the Philistines around him. The story is perhaps the first in which

James's 'later manner' begins to emerge : and one has the impression that he struggled in the writing of it to express, in a bolder way than ever before, his belief in the supremacy of the artist whose vagaries and idiosyncrasies society must learn to tolerate. Some of the story's force is smothered in verbal extravagance; however, its ironic message is sufficiently clear. The artist must be given full freedom : he must be forgiven his sins against the social body. He must be allowed his transgressions – his illegitimate children, his sublime ignorance of daily routine or method, his sexual irregularities – but it must be recognized that if he is too well endowed, he might cease to struggle altogether. When finally an American fund is established for the gifted Saltram, he lapses into benign indifference. 'The very day he found himself able to publish, he wholly ceased to produce.' His wife says he has simply become 'like everyone else'. Saltram draws his income, 'as he had always drawn everything, with a grand abstracted gesture. Its magnificence, alas, as all the world now knows, quite quenched him.' If James was thus re-imagining an endowed Coleridge, he was also prophesying certain aspects of an endowed James Joyce. The more personal message of *The Coxon Fund* was avowed by James in his later prefaces to this and other stories about writers – that they had gathered their motive from 'some noted adventure, some felt embarrassment, some extreme predicament, of the artist enamoured of perfection, ridden by his idea or paying for his sincerity'. And he also said that they proceeded from 'the designer's own mind' and were fathered 'on his own intimate experience'. These were but ways of saying that the 'tales of the literary life' – including *The Figure in the Carpet* and *The Next Time*, written shortly afterwards – expressed James's own disappointment in the market-place as well as in the world of letters. He felt that his work was misread – when it was read – and more often discussed without having been read at all. James was at last beginning to say that he did not care; that he had followed rules and conventions too long, and that he would go his own way, publicly and privately and – *que diable!* – take from life what he could get from it. In the Casa Biondetti that gruesome summer, he began to find the light for his later years.

This did not mean that the old ingrained puritanism in him foundered at this moment. The obverse of *The Coxon Fund* was still an individual carrying his bundle of guilt on his shoulders. And in the Casa Biondetti he set down the idea for a tale he would write many years later : that of a young man with some unspecified burden, who seeks someone to listen to him, that he may be eased. The young man has 'a secret, a worry, a misery, a burden, an oppression'. In our time James would probably not have pondered such a story too long, and the young man would have ended up on the psychoanalytic couch. However, in Venice in 1894 James could spin this personal idea, suggestive of the burden he himself carried, and of the young man's round of visits in which no one wants to share his misery. As he planned the story, he finally would have someone else unload a burden on the already-burdened young man. 'He is healed by doing himself what he wanted to have done *for* him.' And 'the charm and interest of the thing must necessarily be in the picture – the little panorama of his vain contacts and silent appeals'. The tale, *A Round of Visits*, was not written until 1910, by which time it underwent many modifications. But the note for it in Venice, at the time of the writing of *The Coxon Fund*, is revelant to the worries of that time.

While he worked in the Casa Biondetti, the hot weather came and with it something strange he had never before experienced in his beloved Venice. Ships had begun to ply directly from New York and Boston to Genoa; and Henry James discovered that this summer the Grand Canal was transformed into Marlborough Street and Back Bay. Venice became, 'if I may be allowed the expression, the mere *vomitorium* of Boston' He had never seen such an Americanized Venice, all mixed up with the Germans and other European tourists in the Piazza. 'They are all "our" people – yours and mine,' he wrote to Morton Fullerton, 'and they dis-Italianize this dear patient old Italy till one asks oneself what is at last left of its sweet essence to come to, or for. The accent of Massuchusetts rings up and down the Grand Canal and the bark of Chicago disturbs the siesta.' Late in May he decided to make the pilgrimage he had promised himself. Even as, years before, he had read William's letter to his father over the newly-dug grave in Cambridge, so now he would stand beside this other grave, in Rome. He would pay his visit to Fenimore; he would keep his solemn promise to her – and to himself.

14

Pilgrimage

WHEN Henry James left Venice, crowded with his countrymen, he felt like 'Apollo fleeing the furies'. On his way to Rome he stopped in Florence and climbed the hill of Bellosguardo. Fenimore's Villa Brichieri seemed to stare down at him 'with unspeakably mournful eyes of windows'. He visited friends in the Castellani. The place was for him 'a cemetery of ghosts'. He went to the Allori Cemetery, outside the Roman Gate, and for the first time saw Lizzie Boott's bronze tomb. 'Strange, strange it seemed, still to see her only so – but so she will be seen for ages to come.'

Rome seemed empty by comparison with Venice, and it happened to be cool. He had not been there for some years; his recent visits to Italy had been confined to Venetia and Tuscany. The city spoke to him 'with its old most-loved voice as if a thousand vulgarities perpetrated during the last fifteen years had never been'. He went to the Barberini and called on William Wetmore Story. He found him 'the ghost of his old clownship'. He, who had talked so well of old, was now 'very silent and vague and gentle'. And James brooded on the great unsettled population of statues in his studio which he knew Story's children did not like. Soon they would be turned 'loose upon the world'. Well, he mused, Story, fortunate man, had had fifty years of Rome.

Count Primoli invited James to luncheon in his picturesque palace in the Via Tor di Nona near the Tiber, and here he found himself sitting next to the 'she-Zola' of Italy, Matilde Serao, 'a wonderful little burly Balzac in petticoats – full of Neapolitan life and sound and familiarity'. There were other strange Roman types, male and female, present. Madame Serao told James the astonishing news that Paul Bourget had just been elected to the Academy – had arrived comparatively young among France's 'immortals'.

When he stood before Miss Woolson's grave for the first time it had already received its marble coping. It was purple with Roman violets; veins of newly-planted ivy crept round its base. James had always been deeply moved by the Protestant Cemetery. He never spoke of it without alluding to the pyramid, the ancient wall, the cypresses. We have no record of the day on which he paid his visit, or of the silent hour of communion he spent alone with the dead. But there may be echoes of this and of a later visit in his description of John Marcher at the grave of May Bartram in *The Beast in the Jungle*. There he speaks of Marcher's standing

powerless to turn away and yet powerless to penetrate the darkness of death; fixing with his eyes her inscribed name and date, beating his forehead against the fact of the secret they kept, drawing his breath, while he waited, as if, in pity of him, some sense would rise from the stones. He kneeled on the stones, however, in vain; they kept what they concealed.

He described the grave to Boott as 'beautiful – in a beautiful spot – close to Shelley's. It was her intense desire to lie there.' Thirteen years later, on his last visit to Rome, he made the pilgrimage again, for he wrote to the Benedicts:

The most beautiful thing in Italy, almost, seemed to me in May and June last, the exquisite summery luxuriance and perfect tendance of that spot. I mean, of course, that very particular spot below the great grey wall, the cypresses and the time-silvered pyramid. It is tremendously, inexhaustibly touching – its effect never fails to overwhelm.

If he used *overwhelm* in 1907, we may believe that he was overwhelmed when he saw the grave in its violet-sprinkled newness in 1894. 'I echo your judgment of her life and fate – they are unmitigatedly tragic,' he wrote to Boott. 'But to have seen something of her unhappiness is to find in her extinction something like one's knowledge of the cessation of a horrible pain.' To Fenimore, as to his sister, there had come a 'divine cessation'.

15

The Desecrated Altars

THE remainder of James's stay in Italy that summer of 1894 was a scramble and a continual heartache. He spent a few days in Naples; he returned to Rome; he went to Florence and stayed with Dr Baldwin. Under his roof he contracted influenza. The doctor quickly pulled him through. He went to Bologna, where it was quiet, and he had a few peaceful days. He didn't want to go back to Venice. He wondered whether he would ever return. Finally, at the end of June, he journeyed there just long enough to pick up some luggage, and even then he withdrew to visit Mrs Bronson at Asolo, at the uncomfortable La Mura. There were tourists everywhere. To this had his great American-European legend come. He, who had been its veritable historian, was now the spectator of a great invasion. 'Europe' – from now on he began to put quotation marks around the word – had been the great adventure of his youth and of his generation. The continuing American discovery of it had been the substance of comedy, irony and tragedy in his fiction. And now it was ravished – it had become history; it was as commonplace as the buttons on one's coat, or the noisy numbered streets of New York. One Mrs Jack Gardner, bestriding Europe, could be a source of amusement; a thousand Mrs Jacks was a catastrophe. He was to write in his notebook a year later of 'the chaos or cataclysm toward which the whole thing is drifting', and to speak of

the deluge of people, the insane movement for movement, the ruin of thought, of life, the negation of work, of literature, the swelling, roaring crowds, the 'where are you going?', the age of Mrs Jack, the figure of Mrs Jack, the American, the nightmare – the individual consciousness – the mad, ghastly climax ... the Americans looming up – dim, vast, portentous – in their millions – like gathering waves – the barbarians of the Roman Empire.

From Bologna he wrote to Henrietta Reubell that he dreamed of 'some Alpine pasture – some high hillside, under the great chestnuts, where I can hear the plash of a torrent and the tinkle of cattle bells'. As he paused in Venice he wrote to William: 'I am demoralized and my spirit broken by the most disastrous three months' attempt I have *ever* made to come "abroad" for privacy and quiet. These three months have been simply hell.' Early in July he went to the Splügen: he found the little river that girdled the hotel at Chur not as copious or pellucid as he had thought; it was thin and brown, 'and the voice of the compatriot rings over it almost as loudly as over the Grand Canal. For the compatriot is here in her hundreds (excuse the gender) on her way to the Engadine and this first brush with the dreadful Swiss crowd takes the heart out of my disposition to linger by the way.' His great temple had been desecrated; his altars ravished. The long quiet of his personal 'Europe' was shattered. He had planned to stay away from London until August. He was back in De Vere Gardens on 12 July. He had left the Continent, almost, for life. He would cross the channel but three times during his remaining years, and at very long intervals. At this moment all he felt was a relief to regain England, to turn his back on the American rape of Europe.

Shortly after his homecoming Walter Pater died, and James, writing to Edmund Gosse, spoke of 'his exquisite literary fortune'. He had achieved 'the mask without the face'. James added almost exultantly that there wasn't an inch in the total area of 'pale embarrassed, exquisite Pater', not even 'a tiny point of vantage for the newspaper to flap his wings on'. There spoke the writer who that summer had suffered 'exposures, accidents, disasters', and who had only recently written to his brother expressing fear lest Alice's journal fall into the hands of relatives: 'I seem to see them showing it about Concord – and talking about it – with the fearful American newspaper lying in wait for every whisper, every echo.'

There were importunate Americans in London as well; Mrs Gardner was on the horizon, and James left to pay rural visits. He could rely on tranquillity in the countryside. He spent some days at Torquay with W. E. Norris, a minor novelist of the time whom he had come to know, and whom he liked. He had a night and a morning with Rudyard Kipling, who 'spouted to me many admirable poems – but all violent, as it were – and all about stea͞ ͞ers and lighthouses'. *The Jungle Book* was 'thrilling, but so bloo ͞'. In mid-August he went to St Ives, in Cornwall, to stay near the Leslie Stephens. He had long been a friend of the taciturn Stephen, and an admirer of the beautiful Julia, his wife. He put up at the Tregenna Castle Hotel; and every day he went for long walks with his former *Cornhill* editor, 'the silent Stephen, the almost speechless Leslie', paying occasional visits to Talland House, the Stephen summer home. The world knows that house today and its personages, not as James saw them, but through the eyes of Virginia Woolf, then the twelve-year-old Virginia Stephen, whose delicate beauty struck the novelist from the first. The time had come when James was encountering the living substance of future novels as when he met, before their time, characters of Marcel Proust. For a fortnight James moved in the future landscape of *To the Lighthouse* and among its people; and went striding over the moors with the future Mr Ramsay. Although he had known Stephen since 1869 they still met and walked in great intervals of silence. James found this kind of English 'dumbness' a relief after the chattering tourists of the Continent. And the vigorous walks on moor and seacoast gave him the physical exercise and relief he had hoped to get in Switzerland.

I

At the end of the summer, quite without design, but by circumstances not altogether coincidental, he found himself housed once more with the ghost of Fenimore. The Bourgets had come to England to spend a brief holiday while their new apartment was being prepared for them in Paris. They went to Oxford and put up at the Randolph. James joined them, curious to hear about their recent American tour. To be in Oxford was to be in the very spot – as it happened, the very street – where Fenimore had spent her last months in England and where, on many occasions, he had visited her. 'Disturbing as it was to enter the house', James nevertheless walked the few steps from his hotel to No. 15 Beaumont Street to call on Fenimore's former landlady, a cultivated woman who had been a schoolteacher and of whom Miss Woolson had been very fond. This lady, Mrs Phillips, 'would have done anything for her and I wish she might have been free to do more,' he wrote to Clare Benedict. 'I was much moved by the spectacle of her emotion.'

He did not spare himself this re-encounter with a recent past; he not only invited it, but ended by taking lodgings in the same house as he had done in Venice. His letters during most of September 1894 and several entries in his notebook are dated 15 Beaumont Street, Oxford. He saw much of the Bourgets. He and his confrère would spend the day at their work and meet in the late afternoon for long strolls through college gardens and cloisters in the waning light. Bourget, for all his success, was deeply depressed; his election to the Academy, which would have gratified most writers, seemed to him one burden the more; his biographer speaks of his poisoning 'the very real joy' he felt in re-visiting Oxford by conjuring up the memories of the Oxford dead – Mark Pattison and Walter Pater. The image comes to us of James and Bourget, both rather short and stout, walking solemnly through the ancient town and its historic colleges, haunted by private phantoms, yet turning them into brilliant talk. This was the background for the theme James entered in his notebook one day in Beaumont Street, after the Bourgets had left. He wanted to write a tale called *The Altar of the Dead*. The name, he felt, was happy; he hoped the 'story may be half as much so'. At its inception the idea, for the tale was simply a 'conceit' that would take the form of 'a man whose noble and beautiful religion is the worship of the Dead'. The story he wanted to write was that of an individual who cherishes for 'the silent, for the patient, the unreproaching dead' a tenderness which finally takes the form of some shrine – some great altar in which a candle is lit for each person who is gone. 'He is struck with the rudeness, the coldness, that surrounds their memory.' James emphasized that the altar was 'an altar in his mind, in his soul'. Later in working out the tale he gave it material form: his hero, Stransom, actually arranges to establish the altar in a church, and even finds the Bishop, with whom he works out the details, 'delightfully human' and 'almost amused'. This tale was completed very rapidly in De Vere Gardens.

What James did not sketch out was the drama – the conflict – with which he endowed it. It is an eerie tale, flimsy in its materials, yet written in great prose organ-tones, and evocative in its symbolism: for it embraces the universal relation between the living and the dead; and it contains within it also the force of Christ's sermon:

Therefore if thou bring thy gift to the altar, and there rememberest that thy brother hath aught against thee; Leave there thy gift before the altar, and go thy way; first be reconciled to thy brother, and then come and offer thy gift. [Matthew v. 23, 24].

Stransom, lighting candles for all his dead, cannot bring himself to light one for Acton Hague, the friend who had once wronged him. He has forgiven Hague, but he will not include him in his particular shrine. Presently Stransom discovers that a woman is also worshipping at his altar. By a series of circumstances he comes to know that for her the entire altar is but as a single candle, lit for the very man he has excluded. Acton Hague had wronged her also. She had forgiven and she worshipped his memory. In this fashion she takes symbolic possession of the altar; and Stransom, who had expected that the last missing candle would be lit for himself, finds her insisting that it be lit for Hague.

There is however another side to the tale. This is a struggle for power between a man and a woman, each participating in the same obsession, and each determined to have his way. Like Isabel and Osmond, and so many other of James's characters, the struggle here is between mirror-images. In effect the woman in this tale takes from the man his 'altar of the mind'; there is no room for truce between them. She will have it only on her terms. At the very outset, when they begin to speak to one another, they admit 'they did not care for each other'. Presently Stransom recognizes that 'she used his altar for her own purpose'. If she had given him a worshipper, 'he had given her a splendid temple'; and again 'she was really the priestess of his altar'. In these circumstances he loses all taste for his creation. He feels his candles have been extinguished by her; there has been 'a dire mutilation of their lives'. There is little left for him to do. One day he dies before his ravished altar. She is contrite at the last moment; but she may well be. For he has surrendered; the triumph is hers. In the tale James made her into a writer who publishes her works under a pseudonym. Neither her name nor her pseudonym is given.

What we may read in *The Altar of the Dead* is that there had been between Henry James and Fenimore a strange matching of personalities, and strange distortions in their mutual vision of one another. He had ruled out women from his life and, in his bachelor state, had no desire to become involved with them. In Fenimore he had found a disinterested devotion – as distant as was consonant with his own sense of freedom and sovereignty. Then apparently, in some way, Fenimore had made him feel that she made claims on him – claims he had not been prepared to meet. The 'it won't do' of *The Aspern Papers* suggested at the time what he may have experienced at the Villa Brichieri; and the final 'arrangement' that he would visit Fenimore once a year in Italy had been apparently an ultimate compromise. Yet in the end she had performed an act of horror. His altar was spattered with her blood. And the mystery of her grave was intolerable to someone like James, who sought total vision and total insight. Had she died a normal death James would have taken possession of her and been able to light a candle for her within the altar of his soul where candles were lit for his near ones of Quincy Street; for Minny, long ago; for Lizzie; for his great literary comrades; for Turgenev; for the young dead of his recent years. How light a candle for Fenimore, when he could not possess her? She had possessed herself : she had arbitrarily cut herself off from him. Fenimore had asked for too much : and her legacy was an eternal secret.

2

The old and long-buried equations of James's life had been acted out in Fenimore's death. In the struggle between man and woman, in many of his tales, one or the other had to die. It was impossible for two persons to survive a passion – and in this case had it been a passion? Certainly not on his side. But on hers apparently it had. These were the mysteries which now began to haunt James, and were to haunt him for years, until he would find a partial answer – a decade later – in the tale of *The Beast in the Jungle*. But other experiences would intervene to offer illumination for that tale. An entry in his notebook late in November of 1894 suggests the phantoms with which he was struggling, and his feelings about the conflict of will that had prevailed between him and Fenimore. He envisaged a story in which 'a man of letters, a poet, a novelist' discovers after years 'of very happy, unsuspecting, and more or less affectionate, intercourse with a "lady-writer"' that she has been anonymously 'slating' his books in certain periodicals to which she contributes. He pondered 'the situation of the two people after the thing comes to light'. The reviewer had had one attitude to the writer as a writer, and another to him as a 'friend, a human being'. From this fantasy, so close to the mysteries of his relationship with Fenimore, he went on to an analogous one – it was the last of this fatal year – 'a small drama, in the conception of the way certain persons closely connected are affected by an event occurring, an act performed' which results in 'the contrasted opposition of the two forms of pride', the pride that stiffens the heart, and the pride that suffers. Decidedly Fenimore's act had stirred up in Henry James a sense of personal betrayal, a desecration of his private life, his altar of the mind. He never wrote these tales, but they are variants of the situation he had imagined and worked out in the muted yet precise language of *The Altar of the Dead*.

For the moment all he had was the silence of the grave in Rome, and the malaise that something had happened in his life: a great barrier, thrown across its roadway. In the past he had always 'taken possession'. And in his tales of artists it was always someone else who makes the sacrifice for the great man. In *The Middle Years*, the admiring young doctor had given up his post; in *The Death of the Lion* the dazzled young journalist had thrown up his job; in *The Coxon Fund* the young woman had given up her dowry to subsidize the genius. And years before – twenty-five years before – he had felt, when his young cousin Minny Temple had died, that she had surrendered her life to give him the strength to live. He had rejoiced that she lived on as a 'steady unfaltering luminary in the mind'.

His taking 'possession' of the dead is fully expressed by Stransom in the tale of the altar. 'There were hours at which he almost caught himself wishing that certain of his friends would now die, that he might establish with them in this manner a connection more charming than, as it happened, it was possible to enjoy with them in life.' The Henry James who had had difficulty in establishing full and charming connections with people in life, could do so when they were dead and locked within the crystal walls of his imagination. Fenimore had evaded this. She had hurt him, made him live with an unanswered riddle. He could find no crystal walls, no settled place for her in his imagination.

16

The Terrible Law

MINNY TEMPLE had died at the end of Henry James's 27th year, when he stood on the threshold of his literary life. Constance Fenimore Woolson had destroyed herself when he was in his 51st year, and a famous man. And now, before the long-burning candle of Minny, and the unlit candle of Fenimore, James found himself dreaming of a novel in which a young woman, with all life before her, an heiress of the ages, is stricken and must die. In the year of Fenimore's death he returned to his memories of Minny. Early in November, shortly after writing *The Altar of the Dead*, he set down his first notes for the large fiction that would become, almost a decade later, *The Wings of the Dove*.

This novel has always been regarded as James's attempt to recapture the drama of Minny's untimely end. He named his heroine Milly Theale, thereby echoing Minny's name; and in his autobiographies he spoke or having sought 'to lay the ghost in the beauty and dignity of art'. However, when he set down his first notes for the novel the figure of Fenimore also stood beside him. We can glimpse her in his search for a place where he would assemble his characters. 'I seem to see Nice or Mentone – or Cairo – or Corfu –

designated as the scene of the action.' This is a curious ranging about the Mediterranean. James had never been in Cairo or Corfu; but Fenimore had. Her eastern tour with Mrs Benedict was chronicled in the magazines and now appeared posthumously as a book, *Mentone, Cairo, and Corfu*. In the end James chose neither Cairo nor Corfu, nor Mentone, where Fenimore long ago wrote her poem about love. Her death in Venice, that for the time had changed the aspect of his days, became the death in Venice of *The Wings of the Dove*.

In that novel there would be the same struggle as in *The Altar of the Dead*. It would be embodied in the unyielding spirit of Kate Croy who bends Merton Densher to her wishes, and to her scheme to have him give his love to the dying girl so that they may inherit her riches. It is a sinister and cruel plot. The novel belongs to the later time, to the same period as *The Beast in the Jungle*. And at its end the image of the dead girl dominates the living, and changes the course of their lives. In *The Wings of the Dove* James incorporated the two women whose deaths he had faced at the beginning and at the end of the middle span of his life – Minny, the dancing flame, who had yielded everything and asked for nothing and whom he possessed eternally; and Fenimore, the deep and quiet and strong-willed, who had given devotion 'and intensities of fidelity' but had yielded nothing and had disturbed the innermost altar of his being.

The struggle for the altar was ended. In his tale the hero died. In life James endured. What remained was a dull ache, an unresolved, unanswerable riddle. The altar of art still shone, high and pure, and if the candles had momentarily dimmed, time would restore their former light. Standing on the edge of winter late in 1894, James turned from his contemplation of the dead to the problems of his life. George Alexander shook him out of his Oxford reverie. The play that was to have further delayed *Guy Domville* had had a short run. Suddenly the actor-manager was asking for more cuts and announcing rehearsals. James threw himself into the revisions, feeling as if the stage were exacting flesh from him every time he altered a scene. He had written to his brother that he would wage his theatrical 'siege' for 'one year more'. The year was running to its term. Presently rehearsals began, and early in 1895 the costume play would be produced on the stage of one of London's best theatres, and by one of London's best companies. Perhaps the novelist would have his *revanche*, retrieve lost ground, find again a reasonable show of fame, perhaps even a modest show of fortune.

'Ah the terrible law of the artist,' he had written when he had begun his theatricals, 'the law of fructification, of fertilization, the law by which everything is grist to his mill – the law, in short, of the acceptance of all experience, of all suffering, of all life.' James had long ago bowed to that terrible law. He bowed now, knowing that the genius, residing somewhere within his gouty and ageing body, still had courage and force and will. 'To keep at it – to strive toward the perfect, the ripe, the only best; to go on, by one's own clear light, with patience, courage and continuity, to live with the high vision and effort, to justify one's self – and oh, so greatly! – all in time: this and this alone can be my lesson from *anything*!'

His words might be weak, but

the experience and the purpose are of welded gold and adamant. The consolation, the dignity, the joy of life are that discouragements and lapses, depressions and darknesses, come to one only as one stands *without* – I mean without the luminous paradise of art. As soon as I really re-enter it – cross the loved threshold – stand in the high chamber, and the gardens divine – the whole realm widens out again before me and around me – the air of life fills my lungs – the light of achievement flushes over all the place, and I believe, I see, I *do*.

Such was his flight, his invocation to his muse, to the powers by which he lived. The period of his mourning was over. The recently-installed electric lights of the St James's Theatre burned like some twinkling mundane altar, lit in the Mayfair market-place, where his newest work, on which he had spent so much energy and lavished so much affection, would find its public. He knew that this time he had created out of all the experience of his dramatic years and the accumulated resources of middle life. In his tale of *The Middle Years* he had talked of a better chance, a new style, a 'later manner'. Perhaps *Guy Domville* would be his better chance. At Christmas of 1894, when one of the most tragic years of his life approached its end, he waited for the rising of the curtain on his new play – and on his future.

Part Three

An Excess of Simplicity

17

The Scenic Idea

ON the clock-stroke of 50 – in 1893 – Henry James had had, it will be remembered, his first attack of gout. But he had hobbled bravely in a split boot to stand at the grave of his beloved Fanny Kemble, for whom he had lit one of his brightest tapers on his personal altar of the dead. Then, in quick succession, he had had three further attacks, one while he was staying in the Hotel Westminster in Paris. He had dragged about his room, cushioning the offending toe and reading proofs of three books to be published that spring. The years were catching up with him – but not with his fertility. In a burst of alliteration he told Edmund Gosse he was 'moody, misanthropic, melancholy, morbid, morose'. The malaise was however more than gout. He had set it down in his notebooks. 'Youth,' he wrote, 'the most beautiful word in the language.' Henry James had a growing sense of ebbing time, of shrinking opportunities.

Everything spoke for the flight of youth. The old motherly Queen was now – had long been – grandmotherly. Her once-young son, the Prince of Wales, had grown bald and heavy with the good things of life, awaiting his turn in the royal hierarchy. People grew old; institutions grew old; the very century had grown old. Everyone talked of *fin de siècle*. It was a malady of unrest in which the pulse quickened and the calendar grew large on the wall. The Victorian Age was coming to an end and Henry James had called his new volume *Terminations*. Three of the tales were about writers, dying or moribund, ignored by the work-a-day world. If we read personal overtones in the title, we can do the same for the volume that followed. This was called *Embarrassments*.

I

Moody, misanthropic, melancholy, morbid, morose – embarrassment seemed a mild enough word for such states of feeling. But James had been trying to become a playwright since 1890 and his life in the theatre had not gone well; there had been endless delays; and his financial resources dwindled. Moreover his days were filled with personal relations not of his choosing. He was paying a heavy price for quitting his tower of fiction. He had told himself there would always be a line of retreat to his many-windowed flat in Kensington, to the peace of his writing desk. Nothing could prevent him (he assured himself) from dipping his pen 'into the *other* ink – the sacred fluid' of the novel. At various intervals during the five years of his theatre-life he spoke of 'this quiet, this blessed and uninvaded workroom', where he was sole master. 'Among the delays, the disappointments, the *déboires* of the horrid theatric trade nothing is so soothing as to remember that literature sits patient at my door.'

Literature sat patiently at his door – and he kept it waiting. Something in the theatre held him. He might complain of 'the vulgarities and pains' of stage production, yet he continued to suffer them. Perhaps he felt there could be no turning back; a kind of pride of endeavour possessed him. The 'vulgarities' fascinated him too much. Dull, egocentric stage-folk could be brilliant before the footlights. Their charm could be turned on and off like gaslight. There was a great deal of reality – and dream – behind the proscenium. Women were ethereal creatures to put into fiction; but in the stage-wings they were flesh and blood, with grease-paint covering the flesh, and beads of sweat on top of the paint. And then the crudeness of the managers and the pettiness of the actors and their monstrous vanity. He had worshipped Coquelin's art at the Théâtre Français during memorable evenings in the late 1880s. Meeting him now in London James saw only a monster of conceit. If he spoke of his contempt for the stage and for the thespians, he was less willing to recognize that there was a kind of contempt of himself too for having truck with the perpetual self-exhibition around him. He was not being true to himself as the artist of the study. And he rationalized his persistence in a little autobiographical story called *Nona Vincent* in which a young playwright sees a play through its production while he is counselled by a wise married lady and struggles to fit an actress into her part.

The scenic idea was magnificent when once you had embraced it – the dramatic form had a purity which made some others look ingloriously rough. It had the high dignity of the exact sciences, it was mathematical and architectural ... It was bare, but it was erect, it was poor, but it was noble ... There was a fearful amount of concession in it, but what you kept had a rare intensity. You were perpetually throwing over the cargo to save the ship, but what a motion you gave her when you made her ride the waves – a motion as rhythmic as the dance of a goddess!

As always, his tales of this time, little fables out of his own inner world, tell us much more than his busy, anxious letters. There is one tale in particular, of 1892, which contains a clear translation of the facts of his case into fictional fantasy. It is called *Greville Fane*, and is numbered among the stories James called 'anecdotes'. A busy lady writer of popular novels decides that writers are made, not born. To prove this she announces she will rear her son to be a novelist. The consecrated child takes to cigarettes at ten 'on the highest literary grounds'. By the time he is a young man his 'rings and his breast-pins, his cross-barred jackets, his early *embonpoint*, his eyes that look like imitation jewels' indicate to the narrator that he is working hard at 'life' – and at living up to his mother's expectations. 'The great thing was to live, because that gave you material.' He is so busy living – at his mother's expense – that his books remain unwritten. He is always gathering material. His mother has a secret dream her son might have a liaison with a countess; he persuades her without difficulty that he has had one. He dips into cheap French novels and talks glibly about the craft of fiction, making a better show in this than his mother 'who never had time to read anything, and could only be vivid with her pen'. In the end she writes herself to death to support the obese product of her 'system'.

James was saying in effect that he could never educate himself into being a playwright. And in another tale, one of his finest and briefest, called *The Real Thing*, he seems also to say that the 'real thing' is only that which we imagine, and in art one is either an amateur or a professional. An amateur is never 'the real thing'. An upper-middle-class couple, husband and wife, having lost their money, decide that they can serve as models to a fashionable painter, since they are socially 'the real thing'. In his studio, in spite of their smart appearance, they remain inanimate objects; nothing can turn them into the human stuff of illustration. But the artist's Italian houseboy and cockney maidservant, with a mere hint of the right clothes, can posture to perfection. They seem more real than 'the real thing'. The real thing, James says in this story, remains simply the real thing; only the imagination transfigures.

2

In spite of these insights, he had got a rude shock when he first had offered the scenario for *Guy Domville*, written in 1893 amid twinges of the gout, to Edward Compton and his wife. The Comptons had asked for a romantic play for their provincial repertory. James proposed a three-act drama of a young man destined for the priesthood who has to abandon his vocation and return to the world because he is the last of his line. He owes it to his family name to marry and produce children. The scenario provided a touching love affair; and at the end James planned to have the novice reject the world – and the woman – for the monastery. The Comptons promptly expressed alarm that there would be no happy ending. James replied that renunciation of love was 'the only ending I have ever dreamed of giving the play', indeed, he said, 'it *is* the play'. Would it not be 'ugly and displeasing' to the audience to marry off someone who has one foot in a monastery? The Comptons argued it would please English audiences very much. James answered stiffly 'my subject is my subject to take or to leave'. The Comptons did not take it.

James had a second thought. 'Do I mean something that your audience can't understand? It is a complete surprise to me to suppose so, for I have been going on with a great sense of security.' He had been in the same predicament long ago with Howells when *The American* was serialized in the *Atlantic Monthly*. Howells had wanted the hero to marry the aristocratic lady and James had replied, with similar *hauteur*, 'They would have been an impossible couple. I should have felt as if I were throwing a rather vulgar sop to readers who don't really know the world.'

He repeated to the Comptons that 'to make a Catholic priest, or a youth who is next door to one, *marry*, really, when it comes to the point, *at all*, is to do to spectators a disagreeable and uncomfortable thing'. What the Comptons could not convey to James was that the artistic discomfort was his own: it would not be the audience's. He wrote:

I have a general strong impression of my constitutional inability to (even in spite of intensity and really abject effort) realize the sort of simplicity that the promiscuous British public finds its interest in. Even when I think I am dropping most diplomatically to the very rudiments and stooping, with a vengeance, to conquer, I am as much 'out of it' as ever, and far above their unimaginable heads.

He *was* out of it. He could not conceive of the coarse. Nor did he recognize that an audience was entitled to a happy ending in a romantic work – that this was the tradition of romance. He had neglected 'the romantic property of my subject' in the novel of *The American*, as he came to recognize many years later. In 1893, however, his confusion between the romantic play he was writing, and his sense of reality, was strong. It was difficult for him, as a bachelor, to bestow a bride on his hero. Moreover, *The Second Mrs Tanqueray* demonstrated to James that a certain kind of English audience would accept an unhappy ending. He had taken *Guy Domville* to George Alexander with the feelings that the actor-manager had a larger view that the provincial-touring Comptons.

In doing this James felt that he was adhering to the code of the artist. One had to give the audience 'what one wants oneself – it's the only way; *follow* them and they lead one by a straight grand highway to abysses of vulgarity'. He told William: 'One must go one's way and know what one's about and have a general plan and a private religion.' To drag after the public, he said, 'simply leads one in the gutter'. He would not make his fortune in the theatre, but he added 'I know what I shall do, and it won't be bad.'

3

By 1894 he admitted to himself that four of his comedies, which he had passed around the London theatres for two years, stood little chance of production. He accordingly published them as *Theatricals* in two volumes with rueful Addisonian prefaces, acknowledging that it was 'an humiliating confession of defeat' to have to print unproduced plays. This was the first time during his dramatic years that he spoke of 'defeat'. He printed the comedies handsomely, with wide margins, and the names of the characters above the speeches, in the French manner. The prefaces are filled with polite rage : the rage of 'the perverted man of letters freshly trying his hand at an art of which in opposition to his familiar art, every rule is an infraction, every luxury is a privation, and every privilege a forfeiture'. Like his hero in *Nona Vincent* he likened himself to a ship's captain, obliged to throw most of his cargo overboard. This was his way of saying that the cuts imposed upon him by the managers were so drastic that in the end there was 'no room in a play for the play itself'. The implication was that plays by literary men should be produced as

they are written: the literary man knew what he was doing. In this
James seems to have taken his cue from Balzac's misadventures in
the theatre. Balzac with his strong novelistic sense, had treated the
theatre with disdain. Accustomed to dictate to publishers, he had
refused, until too late, to compromise with managers. 'The sole
thought of the manager, the producer, the actor, is to turn the play
into something other than the one you wrote,' Balzac had said. His
words were now being echoed by Henry James.

William James read his brother's plays when they came out and
found them 'unsympathetic'. He urged him to work for 'emotionality
and breadth', and he offered a pointed criticism. He had noticed that
the comedies depended wholly on verbal play and on characters not
understanding what they said to one another, so that they were
constantly explaining themselves. To such criticisms James's answer
was – he put it into one of the prefaces – that the stage demanded
of him 'an anxious excess of simplicity'. The word *anxious* catches
our eye.

4

George Alexander had in reality accepted *Guy Domville* for reasons
that had nothing to do with its ending. It was a costume play which
allowed him to be romantic in the first act, disillusioned in the second
act, visionary in the third. A series of costumes would display his
fine legs – and in a series of noble attitudes. He liked breeches and
jackets with long sleeves fringed with lace. He would be able to
strike poses which filled his matinées with sighing ladies; any play
he produced was assured of a month's run. Most audiences at the St
James's wouldn't know who Henry James was; but they knew their
George Alexander of the handsome profile and the trim legs. The
play, however, had to wait its turn. Alexander sat down to a critical
reading of *Guy Domville* late in 1894. For James it was a 'hideous,
supreme ordeal'. Scenes were cut and speeches were abridged. Alexander had 'a theory of the play so beggarly in its meagreness and
crudity, that it is absolutely nauseating'. James swallowed his pride.
He told Elizabeth Robins that his play had been 'abbreviated and
simplified out of all *close* resemblance to my intention'.

And then quite irrelevantly Alexander came down with German
measles and the novelist fretted through another fortnight, during
which he read with admiration Ibsen's *Little Eyolf*. He saw in this

play fine opportunities for Miss Robins. 'Really uttered, *done*, in the gathered northern twilight, with the flag down and the lights coming out across the fjord, the scene might have a real solemnity of beauty.' Then Alexander was well again and at the beginning of December 1894 the novelist was summoned to the St James's for rehearsals.

18

The Northern Henry

HENRY JAMES had first heard of Henrik Ibsen – 'the northern Henry' as he later referred to him – from Edmund Gosse. 'You must tell me more,' he had written as far back as 1889. The essayist and critic, who had begun as a specialist in the literature of northern Europe, obliged his friend; and in 1890 we find James writing to him: 'How provincial all these poor Dear Norsefolk, including the Colossus himself. They all affect me like intensely domestic fowl plucking behind a hedge – the big bristling hedge of Germany.' By 1891 he had read excerpts from *Brand* and *Peer Gynt* in translation and in January of that year he attended his first performance of Ibsen's *A Doll's House* with Elizabeth Robins. In April 1891 James was still protesting. He found *Rosmersholm* dreary; *Ghosts* shocked him. 'Must I think these things works of skill?' he queried Gosse. They seemed to him of a 'grey mediocrity'. They were simply 'moral tales in dialogue – without the objectivity, the visibility of the drama'. He added: 'I can't think that a man who is at odds with his form is ever a first-rate man. But I may be grossly blind.' He would not admit how much at odds he was with theatrical 'form'.

A few days after this he had gone to see Elizabeth Robins in her own production of *Hedda Gabler*. The play had 'muddled and mystified' him when he read it; now he was fascinated. Ibsen was actable, and Hedda – in the hands of the young American actress – was indeed 'uncanny'. He had sat through three performances and then had promptly written an article 'On the Occasion of Hedda Gabler', which placed him on the side of the Ibsenites against the Victorians of the old school. He recognized that Ibsen had 'sounded in our literary life a singularly interesting hour'. He could not, however, overcome his sense of Ibsen's 'bare provinciality'. Indeed he always found uncomplimentary adjectives to season his praise of Ibsen. He spoke of the dramatist's 'charmless fascination', his 'aesthetic density'; he was not happy with his evocation of 'a spare strenuous democratic community'. He was 'ugly, common, hard, prosaic, bottomlessly bourgeois' – and yet 'of his art he's a master'. But he recognized two things. The first was that Ibsen would be the 'adored' dramatist of the acting profession; he made it possible for actors 'to do the deep and delicate thing'. The second – and this touched him personally – was Ibsen's extraordinary skill in projecting a situation, in choosing a crucial hour in the lives of a group, and yet within that hour making the audience aware of the entire psychological history and 'the whole tissue of relations' between his people. In this sense Ibsen's influence on the later novels of Henry James was profound : it was Ibsen's 'admirable talent for producing an intensity of interest by means incorruptibly quiet, by that almost demure preservation of the appearance of the usual, in which we see him juggle with difficulty and danger and which constitutes, as it were, his only coquetry.' The sentence that follows, in the article on *Hedda*, shows exactly where Ibsen the artist had touched the artist in Henry James : 'There are people who are indifferent to these mild prodigies; there are others for whom they will always remain the most charming privilege of art.'

James did not discern at first Ibsen's symbolic power. He had complained of 'the absence of style, both in the usual and larger sense of the word'. This might have made Ibsen 'vulgar', for he was 'massively common and "middle-class," but neither his spirit,' wrote James, 'nor his manner is small'. These remarks prompted William Archer, most dedicated of drama-critics and one of Ibsen's translators, to a rejoinder. In a long letter he praised James for having written 'one of the very few really sane and luminous things that have been said on the subject in English', but he assured him that, in the original, Ibsen was a master of style – if style, on the stage, meant giving to every word a vital function. The secret of Ibsen, Archer told James, was that he was 'the greatest *poet* who has as yet enslaved himself to the conditions of realistic, or perhaps I should rather say everyday, drama'. In this sense Ibsen had a 'gigantic imagination', for he could seize a few fragments of experience and endow them with the depth and complexity of life. 'Remember,' Archer told James, 'it is not as a realist, but rather as a symbolist, that I chiefly admire Ibsen.' James was to remember this, for in a complementary piece, *On the Occasion of* The Master Builder, two years later, he spoke of 'the mingled reality and symbolism of it all' that 'gives us an Ibsen within an Ibsen'.

2

The record of James's flirtation with Ibsen makes amusing reading in his correspondence with Miss Robins and Mrs Bell. *The Master Builder* arrived act by act in London. James, receiving the translation piecemeal, was driven 'from bewilderment to madness'. He looked for a leading role for Miss Robins, but saw only the Master-Builder. 'The fact remains that the quinquagenarian architect *must* be the heroine,' he teased. 'Miss Elizabeth must do *him*.' And then there were the usual reservations: 'It is all most strange, most curious, most vague, most horrid, most "middle-classy" in the peculiar ugly Ibsen sense.' When he saw Miss Robins's great triumph in the play – he had attended the rehearsals – he recognized the triumph of Ibsen as well and he wrote of 'the hard compulsion of his strangely inscrutable art'. In *Little Eyolf*, he saw 'the small Ibsen *spell*, the surrender of the imagination to his microcosm, his confined but completely-constituted world'. Finally, seeing *John Gabriel Borkman* he praised 'the sturdy old symbolist' and his 'admirable economy', but as before he contended the plays had 'no tone but their moral tone'. He complained of 'so dry a view of life, so indifferent a vision of the comedy of things'.

Unable to read Ibsen in the original, James never consecrated to him the full-length article he might have written. However, as late as 1908, in his preface to his novel *The Awkward Age*, we find him still holding to his fundamental view, although he pretends to put the words into the mouth of a devil's advocate against the theatre. His argument is that playwrights like Ibsen and Dumas are forced in the theatre to renounce the fine for the coarse. James was arguing his own difficulties. Ibsen was clear, he said, only on a thesis as 'simple and superficial' as that of *A Doll's House*, but was confused and obscure from the moment he tried to say something finer, as in *The Wild Duck*. Even *Hedda Gabler*, for all its appeal, was enfeebled by remarkable 'vagueness'. These criticisms voiced, the novelist nevertheless recognized – as imaginative artists will – all that had meaning for his own work in the plays of the northern Henry.

The deeper influence of Ibsen on James's fiction belonged to the future; a direct influence could be seen in two plays projected in 1893, the year of his piecemeal reading of *The Master Builder*. Coming on Ibsen at the very moment when he himself was turning playwright, James seems to have asked himself whether he should enrol himself under the Norwegian's experimental – and then avant-garde – banner or go his own way. Decidedly Ibsen, still a playwright for a small coterie in London, was hardly a model for a novelist who wished to find a large audience. Miss Robins obtained her hearings for Ibsen through subscription evenings, special performances, subsidized management. Nevetheless James had Ibsen in mind when he planned *Guy Domville*. He shaped the play for a handful of characters and chose a critical moment in the hero's history; and late that year he first sketched the scenario for what ultimately became *The Other House*. Here he planned a 'bourgeois' drama and 'provincial' characters in the manner of Ibsen – creating a tense and violent 'Bad Heroine' who seemed ideally suited for the special talents of the acress who had played Hedda in England. But *The Other House* did not become a play in the 1890s. And *Guy Domville* waited another year before production.

19

Saint Elizabeth

THE battle for Ibsen brought James close to Elizabeth Robins and their friend Florence Bell. We can glimpse these interesting ladies in James's theatrical tale of *Nona Vincent*, written immediately after his experiences with *The American* in 1891. Miss Elizabeth is embodied in the ambiguous, faltering actress with the two-toned name of Violet Grey – for she had her grey side as well as her violet. And Mrs Bell, who was a wise and worldly English cosmopolite, is the quiet Mrs Alsager – very sage and purposeful – who helps the young dramatist find a producer. Miss Robins had played Claire de Cintré in James's play – and had played her very badly. James had wished that Mrs Bell, or the American beauty – the friend of the Prince of Wales – Mrs Mahlon Sands, might show the tense and earnest Miss Robins what was wrong with her acting. Miss Robins had but recently come to England; she had had considerable professional experience, but she could not play a Jamesian renunciatory lady. 'I am unhappy about Miss Robins's hair – but I wish she could see you!' he had written to Mrs Sands. The ending of *Nona Vincent* hinges on Violet Grey's finally having a talk with Mrs Alsager and turning her role from failure into success.

A young and energetic actress in her late 20s, Miss Robins was a presence of charm and vitality: but she was strenuous and lacked the repose of the older ladies. James's response was his courtly manner. She was sufficiently 'distant' to make him comfortable in her presence.

I

In a later time, Miss Robins published the letters Henry James wrote her during the years of his dramatic obsession and their common espousal of Ibsen. She called the book *Theatre and Friendship*. In spite of her own gloss, and the atmosphere she created of a deep and cherished intimacy, the correspondence is impersonal. The letters are lively, good-natured, filled with persiflage and elaborate courtesies; many are simply the equivalent of modern telephonic communication – appointments, comments, shared public enthusiasms. What one discovers in the book is the skill with which Miss Robins used James's letters to her friend Florence Bell to support and enhance those written to herself. One-fourth of the volume belongs to Mrs Bell, and by far the warmest letters are addressed to her. The book is indeed a record of a triangular theatre-friendship. Miss Robins and Mrs Bell were devoted friends. They wrote to each other daily, since Mrs Bell was much out of London in her north-country home. James on his side wrote to both about each other – and about himself.

The friendship between Miss Robins and James, begun during the days of *The American*, was one of backstage camaraderie and common dedication. The novelist, in his playwriting phase, nourished a dream of writing a great part for her. A handsome hard-working woman, Miss Robins could be all fire and passion – and perversity – as Hedda or Hilda; but she could do little with other parts and other plays. She knew this and became an Ibsen specialist, although James repeatedly warned her that she was narrowing her career. Leonard Woolf, who knew her at a later time, characterized her as 'gentle, soft, frail – and *iron*'. In the 1890s she was far from frail, but there was plenty of iron. She gave an effect however of softness. 'In talking with her one continues to *batter* one's self against that quiet individuality of determination – not to say perversity of it – which takes for me, at least, all sense of effect and fruit from my words.' Thus James to Florence Bell. 'She sees her life in a certain way – and that's the end of it. But she will, all the same, I think, arrive.' Miss Robins did 'arrive'; but not in the usual theatre-sense.

2

Elizabeth Robins had a way of disarming those who talked with her – and she talked mainly to the great. She was all attention; she had beautiful, attentive, lustrous blue eyes; she created an effect of hearing and understanding everything. By means of a quiet intensity she had managed, with extraordinary skill within a week after landing in London, to involve a dozen leading stage figures, (among them Beerbohm Tree and Oscar Wilde), in her personal affairs. Only Bernard Shaw cut through her pose and for a long time Elizabeth Robins feared and detested him. He rode roughshod over her Joan of Arc manner – he dubbed her 'Saint Elizabeth'. He understood her way of making herself the centre of her environment. 'The beautiful puritan charm, the St Elizabeth sanctity, the pure-toned voice, the unstagey beauty of movement' – these were the qualities he found in her playing in *The Pillars of Society*. He had interviewed her when he was still a round-the-town journalist, and before they had ended their talk Miss Elizabeth 'swore she would shoot me if I said anything she didn't approve of'. The situation he caricatures in a letter to Miss Robins at the time of *The Master Builder* was typical of the actress's way of arousing response in men and then retreating:

You send me for a cab, and contemptuously reward me with a lift, during which, being so near you, I cannot help being in love with you in a poetic and not in the least ignoble way; but though I do not venture on the faintest expression of my impulse, you discover it by a sort of devilish divination, and instantly I am seized and flung out of the vehicle into the mud, with wheels flying over me this way and that and horses dancing and stumbling on my countenance.

Elizabeth Robins, with her large liquid eyes and her inner toughness regarded men as creatures to be manipulated. She could love women; men were to be conquered and 'used', and her secret love affair with the critic William Archer – a story yet to be told – was a kind of collaboration in the theatre as much as a passion, a case of mutual professional respect transmuted into affection. There is even a mention of a child somewhere in her legend; and a bundle of passionate love-letters from the later poet laureate John Masefield. But while she kept a voluminous archive, she covered her tracks carefully. 'This mania for secrecy will undo you,' Shaw wrote to her. She remained secretive all her life. 'What the world wants from her is not noble conduct but acting' he told a friend. Miss Robins preferred noble conduct. And Shaw discerned one thing more – that Elizabeth Robins was a great actress only when she was acting her own life. He recognized that the emotion, so powerfully infused into Ibsen, was 'really yourself and not your acting'. In this the dramatist put his finger on her greatest secret. In later years Henry James also came to understand this. He told a friend that she had been wise to leave the stage – to abandon the false position of being engaged 'without a scrap or shred of artistic feeling, in an occupation which was all art'.

3

In America Miss Robins had married an actor named George R. Parkes; her widow's weeds proclaimed the fact when she arrived in England. That part of her life, however, was one of the best kept secrets of all. Parkes had wooed Miss Elizabeth in the 1880s at the stage door when they were both players in the Boston Museum. He offered her much attention and gallantry; he was ready to be her flunkey – and in her lonely youth, seeking to win a place on the stage, she was appreciative and even affectionate in her cold ambitious way. Photographs of Parkes suggest an elegant if flaccid 'masher' of the time; and Miss Robins, who had resisted a number of wooers, finally – after much conflict and secrecy – married Parkes almost as if it were a business arrangement. They rushed from the ceremony to the different theatres in which they were playing. Nothing could interrupt their careers. Matrimony was to be a kind of companionship and indeed Miss Robins treated her husband as if he were a younger brother. Between them they earned a comfortable income; they lived at good hotels; but Miss Robins always got better parts and more notice. Moreover Mrs Parkes spent much of her day sewing her costumes, dressing her hair, studying her roles. Being a tremendous blue-stocking, she also studied German and French at night and read serious philosophical books. Her husband was baffled and frustrated. Miss Robins seems to have considered sex superfluous in her marriage. But it is clear that Parkes was also a man of little resource, more capable of tantrum than self-assertion. He tried consistently to domesticate Elizabeth. He urged her to give up the stage and become a home-keeping wife. He planted her for a long hot summer in a dreary house at Medford with his dull mother and dull sisters. Elizabeth Robins paced the verandah like a caged lioness – like Hedda Gabler. Thus within months after her marriage she had lived out *A Doll's House* and *Hedda* – several years before she heard the name of Henrik Ibsen. The ending of this domestic strife was indeed to be like one of Ibsen's stark tragedies.

Parkes had always kept a suit of stage armour in his hotel room, although he never explained why. One day the suit was missing – and so was Parkes. Only Miss Robins knew what he had done. For in the letter he wrote and mailed to his wife he did not spare her any details. He was ending everything. He could not continue a loveless marriage: and as a sadistic refinement he gave Elizabeth the exact time at which he would be drowning himself, weighed down by the armour, in the Charles River. When she received the letter it was past the fatal hour. For ten days the actress did not know whether she was a widow or the subject of a grim joke. She lived in the glare of newspaper headlines and a police search. The body was finally recovered in Boston harbour. Parkes had tied the armour to his feet to pull him down. Ultimately it had dropped away and the corpse floated to the surface.

The widow's weeds which Elizabeth wore when she arrived in London in 1888 were a symbol of her shock and sense of guilt. In later years she forgot her troubled life with Parkes. She wrote of him in private memoranda as if their love had endured and as if his ghost were at her side. Fortunately she was young and her sense of self was strong. During a later suffragette phase she even nourished a fantasy that George would have approved of her militancy. She destroyed some of his letters but carefully packaged and sealed others in her archive. Fifty years after the tragedy she could not bring herself to part with these sad relics which included a batch of clippings from the Boston newspapers about the suicide. She died in her 90th year in 1952 with the seals unbroken.

Miss Robins's *Hedda* had been 'uncanny' to James, because the stifled exasperated lady of Ibsen's play incorporated the desperate desolation of the verandah in Medford; and when Hilda Wangel knocked on the door and sounded the fate of the Master Builder, Miss Robins was playing the 'St Elizabeth' who expected men to serve her as her husband had done, by total abdication of the self. Her success in *The Master Builder* was also related to a more remote part of her experience. At 16 she had been taken by her metallurgist father to spend a summer in a mining camp at Summit in Colorado. The 'Little Annie' gold mine was a profound adventure of her adolescence (she was at a later phase to go to the Klondike during the gold rush to be there with her favourite brother Raymond Robins). It was as if Ibsen had known Miss Robins and her Colorado life when he provided his English Hilda Wangel with an alpenstock and made her talk of great heights and castles in the air.

Miss Robins was intelligent and intuitive. She knew exactly on what plane to pitch her friendship with Henry James. She gave him a feeling of mystery; but she aroused no anxieties. In her cultivated simplicity she made him feel at home when he called, served him a cup of cocoa, listened to him until late in the night, while he talked of his play-troubles – and offered him the quiet encouragement of her blue eyes.

They were often at the theatre together. They went to see Coquelin and Duse. James's letters to her are pitched on a plane of bemused euphoria: 'Saturday evening will suit me down to the ground – or as I ought in your case to say, up to the skies: and I shall be eager – and not later than *nine*.' Miss Robins reports to Mrs Bell:

Third instalment of the Ibsen play. I am more in a maze than ever. I had a cosy chat over the fire with H. J. yesterday. I told him bits and read him bits (intensely private of course) under seal of secrecy except so far as you're concerned. He comes Tuesday of next week to hear if the Ibsen heroine has appeared yet and what she's like. He'll faint when he hears!

James found *The Master Builder*, on reading it, 'most unpromising for Miss Elizabeth or for any woman'. He felt the play to be a man's play, the master-builder's. But Miss Robins had quietly studied Norwegian – she had travelled in Norway before coming to England, in the company of the widow of the violinist Ole Bull – and did not have to rely on the hurried translations of Archer and Gosse. James little dreamed, as he later recognized, with what magic and witchery Miss Robins would render Hilda Wangel: nor would be ever know that all of herself was in the part. She was perhaps unconsciously acknowledging this when, in a lecture on Ibsen three decades later, she remarked 'make no mistake, you must let Ibsen play you, rather than insist on your playing Ibsen'. Everyone agreed there was something demonic in the way in which Miss Robins played her Ibsen roles.

The Isabel Archer side of Miss Robins understandably appealed to Henry James even though she came closer to possessing the histrionic self-absorption and self-centredness of his actress Miriam Booth in *The Tragic Muse*. (James with a flourish inscribed that novel to her as 'from her friend and colleague' during the run of *The American*.) He befriended her as a compatriot and as a woman of temperament. What he never discovered was that Miss Robins had, behind her mask of the stage, the mind of a journalist. She thus had a Henrietta Stackpole side to her as well. From her earliest days she had regarded all her experience as potential 'copy'. In the end, when there were no more Ibsen parts for her to play, she abandoned the stage and under the name of C. E. Raimond wrote a series of sensational best-selling novels based on 'questions of the day' – euthanasia, votes for women, white slavery. Dressed in a Salvation Army costume she gathered material at first hand from the prostitutes in Piccadilly. She doubtless would have kept this side of her endeavours undisclosed had not Mrs Patrick Campbell come upon some of her bundles of proofs in her flat. Mrs Pat could never keep a secret and Miss Robins was forced to admit that she was C. E. Raimond. The *nom de plume* embodied much more than met the eye. The initials C. E. R. were those of her father; and Raymond was the youngest and best-loved of the three brothers she helped raise. She absorbed into her career and existence the males who had meant most to her. She clung to her mass of papers, her minute diaries recording dates and meetings. Had James known that Miss Robins dreamed of turning all that happened to her into copy, he probably would have kept a greater distance. What saved Miss Robins was her innate discretion – and her indirection. She began too late to write her memoirs; the first volume barely covers her pre-Ibsen experiences in England. Virginia Woolf gave her the happy title for the book – *Both Sides of the Curtain* – but the picture of both sides had been too abundantly preserved. Drowned in the clutter of her days, Miss Robins produced a confused memoir of her earliest English years and never wrote the one which would have counted: that of her Ibsen triumphs.

3

Mrs Alsager in the tale of *Nona Vincent* has a large comfortable house in London, 'simply a sort of distillation of herself'. She is married to an indulgent wealthy husband and she throws 'her liberty and leisure into the things of the soul – the most beautiful things she knew'. This lady listens to the dramatist's play, introduces him to a producer, helps him on his way to success; and, as we have seen, ultimately shows the leading lady how to do her part. The attributes of Mrs Alsager would fit a number of James's literary lady friends; but they fit best of all Florence Bell, wife of the colliery-owner and iron-master Hugh Bell. She had grown up in France and from childhood had often sat in a box at the Comédie Française. James and Mrs Bell had common Gallic ground. A lady of delicate perceptions, she was warm, attentive, generous; busy always with her three children and two stepchildren (one of whom was the indomitable Gertrude Bell, explorer of Arabian deserts), she divided her time between her Yorkshire home at Redcar and her big house at 95 Sloane Street. When she was in London, James found her house a welcome place to spend a late afternoon, and Mrs Bell was an eager listener. He had given her the rare prompt-book of his old dramatization of *Daisy Miller*, which normally he would not have shown to anyone; he allowed her to read the manuscript of *The American*. He called her 'Lady of the full programme and rich performance'. They had met in the mid-1880s and had the habit of going to theatres and discussing plays when Elizabeth Robins came into their lives. James accepted Mrs Bell's opinions of his plays, for she had a flair for comic dialogue and could write witty comedies. One of them had been performed at the Théâtre Français by Coquelin. Others were the delight of amateur companies in the provinces. On attending an evening bill of these chamber comedies James urged Mrs Bell to 'follow the inclination of your mind, which is full of drollery and humorous resource'. And he also offered advice: 'Avoid simplicity as you would poison and the "obvious" as you would the devil.'

Their interest in Miss Robins was almost that of watchful parents trying to cope with an opinionated daughter. They agreed about Miss Robins's 'unworldly careering'. Reporting from seeing Elizabeth in *A Doll's House*, James said: 'She ought to take more what she can get – to do whenever she can, *any*thing she can – be it Norwegian or not.' He added: 'Too little, alas, however, comes her way – and she is, after all, indifferent (or it seems to me.)'

A great opportunity did come her way in the spring of 1893. Mrs Patrick Campbell, slightly younger than Miss Robins and less known, was offered the part of Paula Tanqueray in Pinero's play which Alexander had in production. She was under contract elsewhere and had to turn it down. Alexander, impressed by Elizabeth's playing of *The Master Builder*, asked her to take the part and she agreed. It was 'the kind of thing that comes along once in an actress's lifetime, seldom oftener'. In the interval Mrs Pat was released from her contract. With a show of renunciation worthy of a Jamesian heroine, Elizabeth decided that Mrs Pat had more claim to the part than she did and surrendered it to her. It was a handsome and gallant – indeed a Saint Elizabeth – gesture; it would have been understandable in a great actress who had already had great parts. It was also something the majority of dedicated actresses would not do. Given the shuffles and changes of the stage nothing had occurred that demanded so much sacrifice on Miss Robins's part. Moreover Mrs Pat was young enough, and promising enough, to have other chances, as she did, when she created Eliza in Shaw's *Pygmalion*. Miss Robins seemed to have thought neither of the future nor of her own needs. She wrote to Mrs Pat that she was consoled at losing the part by the fact that it had come to her fellow-actress. This was not a loss but a surrender. Miss Robins had made of the incident one of her Ibsenite moments. She signed her strange letter of renunciation with these words: 'There is to my mind no woman in London so enviable at this moment, dear savage, as you.' Miss Robins's friend and literary executor Dr Octavia Wilberforce was to grant that this showed that Elizabeth was not 'one hundred per cent actress' – but after a further thought she added, 'Elizabeth wasn't hundred per cent anything.'

Henry James was in Paris at that moment and seems to have gained the impression that the loss of the part was simply a bit of bad luck. He felt Miss Robins had behaved 'admirably well'. But here again others understood more clearly. Mrs Pat, who was to be for ever grateful, though not always loyal, recognized that the bluestocking in Miss Robins was in conflict with the actress. 'The peculiar quality of Elizabeth Robins's dramatic gift,' she said, 'was the swiftness with which she succeeded in sending *thought* across the footlights; emotion took a second place, personality a third.'

20

Oscar

THE bulky figure of Oscar Wilde had crossed Henry James's path at infrequent intervals during the previous decade. They had met long before – in 1882 – in a drawing-room in Washington, during Oscar's circus-like tour of America. James had confided to friends at the time that he thought Wilde 'an unclean beast', he found him 'repulsive and fatuous'. There was however no ill-will or animosity between them. Oscar simply irritated James; and the novelist regarded with curiosity and a certain condescension the public antics and public wit of the younger man. Wilde on his side spoke with respect but with understandable reservations concerning the fastidious American. His own relaxed amateurism, his emphasis on talk and performance rather than on creation, caused him to feel that James treated art as 'a painful duty' rather than as one of the amusements of life. They had no common bonds of temperament; and they represented diametrically opposed attitudes towards life and the imagination. If Wilde insisted on putting his talent into his art and his genius into his life (as he later told André Gide), Henry James did exactly the opposite. James's drawing-room wit was merely the surplus of his genius – and he lived for his art. The American writer was eleven years older than Wilde; he worked hard and was highly productive. Wilde had a lazy facility that James found 'cheap' – the cheapness of the actor who knows how to provoke applause: he had written very little and the American deplored the public display which had made the young Wilde the subject of Gilbert and Sullivan and of George du Maurier in *Punch*. There has been speculation that Gabriel Nash, the talkative aesthete in *The Tragic Muse*, incorporated some of Wilde's qualities: if this was so, James had drawn a singularly generous portrait. Nash's cultivated ineffectuality might be that of Wilde; his wit is that of Henry James, and so is his sentience. Whether James read *The Picture of Dorian Gray* when it came out in 1891 we do not know. What we do know is that Wilde turned to the theatre at the same time as James; and from this moment on, they were – from James's point of view – rivals, or fellow-contenders in the same arena.

I

In 1892 Henry James attended the opening of *Lady Windermere's Fan*. 'Oscar's play,' he wrote to Mrs Bell, 'strikes me as a mixture that will run, though infantine to my sense, both in subject and in form. As a drama it is of a candid and primitive simplicity, with a perfectly reminiscential air about it.' It contained things one had always seen in plays, and from this point of view there was nothing to analyse or discuss.

But there is so much drollery – that is 'cheeky' paradoxical wit of dialogue, and the pit and gallery are so pleased at finding themselves clever enough to 'catch on' to four or five of the ingenious – too ingenious – *mots* in the dozen, that it makes them feel quite *'décadent'* and *raffiné* and they enjoy the sensation as a change from the stodgy.

They thought they were hearing the talk of the *grand monde* – 'poor old *grand monde*' – and they felt altogether 'privileged and modern'. There was a perpetual attempt at epigram, and many of these fell flat, 'but those that hit are very good indeed. This will make, I think, a success – possibly a really long run.' There was no characterization; all the personages talked 'equally strained Oscar' and the central situation 'one has seen from the cradle'. As for Oscar's curtain speech, it may have been impudent but it was 'simple inevitable mechanical Oscar' that is, said James, the usual trick 'of saying the unusual – complimenting himself and his play'. James thought it wrong of the newspapers, which had criticized Oscar's levity, to be taking his remarks and his attitude seriously. To be deadly serious about his lack of seriousness seemed to James simply stupid. 'Everything Oscar does is a deliberate trap for the literalist, and to see the literalist walk straight up to it, look straight at it and step straight into it, makes one freshly avert a discouraged gaze from this unspeakable animal.'

Two days later he wrote a further account of the opening for Henrietta Reubell in Paris; she was a friend of Oscar's and he frequented her salon in the Avenue Gabriel.

I was at the *première* on Saturday last and saw the unspeakable one make his speech to the audience, with a metallic blue carnation in his buttonhole and a cigarette in his fingers. The speech, which, alas, was stupid, was only to say that he judged the audience felt the play to be nearly as charming as he did. I expected something much more *imprévu*.

James quoted some of the Oscarisms he had liked. 'There is nothing like the devotion of a married woman – it's a thing no married man knows anything about.' 'Yes. London is all sad people and fogs. I don't know whether fogs produce the sad people, or the sad people produce the fogs!' 'There is nothing so unbecoming to a woman as a nonconformist conscience.' And 'to love a good woman is a Middle-Class education'. The epigrams however sounded familiar to James 'and the idea of the play, of which the treatment is beneath discussion, is one that has been knocking about for fifty years'.

'*Ce monsieur*,' James wrote, 'gives at last on one's nerves.' One suspects however it was not only Wilde who made James nervous. It was his recognition that Wilde had an infallible sense of his audience.

2

During James's gouty winter in Paris, word reached him that Wilde's second play, *A Woman of No Importance*, was about to be produced. When he heard of its subject he became worried; the play sounded singularly like his own unproduced comedy, *Tenants*, which dealt with a woman 'unimportant' in the same sense as Wilde's, and her illegitimate son. A letter was posted promptly from the Hotel Westminster to Miss Robins: 'One thing I do wish you would do – tell me three words about Oscar W's piece – when it is produced; and if in particular the *subject* seems to discount my poor three-year-older that Hare will neither produce nor part with.' Miss Robins was busy arranging an Ibsen season. She did not reply. James wrote again, sending a subscription to her season and cautioning her against the danger of figuring in public 'as an Ibsen-actress only'. Also he renewed his appeal – he would welcome, he said, 'a spark of ecstasy over Oscar W's tragedy. I am consumed with curiosity but I eat my heart out in silence.' Miss Robins continued silent, and James turned to Mrs Bell for 'any stray crust or two about Oscar's play ... *don't* neglect Oscar'. A few days later another letter to Mrs Bell: 'I read with wonderment Archer's strange rhapsody over him in the *World*. However, I sit in darkness.'

He was satisfied only after his return to London. He found Wilde's play 'an *enfantillage*', 'a piece of helpless puerility'. Yet his own *Tenants* could be similarly described. He too had assembled all the Victorian stage clichés: a retired army officer, his illegitimate son, his ward, the love of the army man's legitimate son for the girl, the confrontation of the legitimate and illegitimate sons – a goodly collection of stereotypes, which James had adapted from an old tale in the *Revue des Deux Mondes*. He had writen the play before seeing any of Wilde's comedies, but he was attempting a similar though more serious kind of comedy. James's comedies were full of unexpected situations and drolleries, and his wit was often superior to Wilde's; but he lacked Wilde's common touch, the sense of what would amuse. James was not only too subtle, but also too earnest; and when he tried to be less subtle, he became banal. Wilde's humour was inherent in his air of improvised fantasy out of which his social caricature sprang. James's humour was all on the surface; it was built into the speeches, not the action.

We have the spectacle of two gifted writers each attempting in his own way to put intellectual comedy on the stage. Wilde accomplished his by being off-hand and casual, as if he were shrugging his shoulders. James anxiously cared; indeed he cared to excess. His subtlety was a fine theatrical instrument; and it had to be used finely. He was blunting it under the misguided belief that he must discover common ground with audiences whose needs he could not experience. He had never had to face such problems in writing his tales.

Returning from Paris, James went to see Eleanora Duse with her 'exquisite delicacy and truth and naturalness'. He also had some evenings at the Comédie Française then visiting London with his friend Rhoda Broughton, seeing Sarah Bernhardt. Duse had neither the temperament – nor the vulgarity – of Sarah, 'but a pathos, a finish, an absence of the tricks of the trade that are strangely touching and fascinating. No beauty – no wigs, no clothes, scarcely any paint – but a delicate refinement and originality. The total is rare.' In a sense one might have said that Sarah resembled Wilde. The qualities of Duse were in himself.

He went also to see Miss Robins in an Ibsen series and praised her work, but felt he was being exposed to a heavy dose of northern gloom.

21

The Young Bard

HE had gone, late in 1891, to Dresden, hurriedly crossing the channel to stand in a dreary little suburban cemetery at the grave of his young compatriot Wolcott Balestier. Balestier had been an unabashed success-seeker, a literary publisher who had helped James with the financial details of the dramatized *American*. The young man had come abroad bringing his own exuberance and the praises of William Dean Howells; and in a few months had made friends with most of the established English writers, and with the new 'infant prodigy' – for so James called him – Rudyard Kipling. Balestier lived in his picturesque but insalubrious quarters beside Westminster Abbey. Somewhere he had taken a drink of contaminated water; and now he was dead, of a virulent typhoid, in a strange city, his dream of rivalling (in partnership with Heinemann) the great Baron Tauchnitz, abruptly ended. James had developed a deep affection for him, and had willingly accompanied Heinemann to Dresden to bring solace to the youth's mother and sisters.

Wolcott Balestier was the first of several young men who figured in Henry James's middle life as beloved acolytes: and the tale *The Middle Years* seems to reflect something of their relationship, broken so early by Balestier's death. In a later time James wrote annually to Wolcott's mother on the anniversary of Dresden, mourning the young man almost as if he had lost a son. 'Strange and sad it seems to me when you bring home to me that it's eight years since we laid Wolcott to rest in those unforgettable Dresden days!' he wrote to Mrs Balestier in the last year of the century. 'His photograph hangs here beside me as I write – and he looks down at me meeting my eyes, as if he knew I am speaking of him. My memory, my affection, thank heaven, holds him fast – for all the swift, awful sweep of the deep stream of time, swifter, more noiselessly lapsing with each year.' Only with 1914 did he accept the thought that his young friend, so long dead, was well out of the terrible world into which he himself had survived.

Both Henry James and Edmund Gosse wrote memorials to the young Balestier. Gosse's portrait suggests the characteristic English view of the young American as an attractive if pushing publisher bringing to the British Isles the promise of overseas royalties. James rebuked Gosse. He thought one portion of the sketch 'ungracious'. 'To the young,' he told him, 'the early dead, the baffled, the defeated, I don't think we can be tender enough.' In his own memoir, which served as preface to Balestier's posthumous *The Average Woman*, James paid him perhaps the highest tribute of all; 'He had the real cosmopolitan spirit, the easy imagination of differences and hindrances surmounted.' In this way, he placed him on a footing with himself.

The cemetery in Dresden had seemed an ugly alien place for a young American to lie. The rite was 'monstrous' to James for the poor 'yesterday-so-much-living-boy'. He listened to the service read by a chaplain 'with soft, yet not offensive sonority', and handed to one of Balestier's sisters a pot of English flowers which Mrs Gosse had given him; she let fall this bit of English fragrance and earth into the foreign grave that would house her brother. The ceremony was soon ended and James came way with Balestier's sister, Caroline. She had asked him to ride with her in one of the lugubrious black-and-silver funeral coaches with German footmen also in black and silver. She had whispered she wanted to talk with him.

Caroline Balestier was a trim young woman with tiny features and tiny hands and feet. She was admirable in her grief in 'the intense – and almost manly – nature of her emotion'. James described her as concentrated and passionate, filled with force and courage. She was a worthy sister to 'poor dear big-spirited, only-by-death quenchable Wolcott'. What Caroline had to say in especial to the novelist in the baroque coach we can only surmise. What we know is that a month later (on 18 January 1892), Henry James, playing his paternal role with becoming gravity, gave Caroline Balestier in marriage to the young poet and story-teller, the great success of London, Rudyard Kipling. It was a quiet, almost a secret wedding – the family in mourning, the mother and other sister confined to their beds with influenza. Only four persons were present beside the bride and groom. 'Oh the "ironies of fate," the ugly tricks, the hideous practical jokes of life,' Henry had written to a friend from Dresden. Here was another irony, this marriage of the poet of Empire, from India, to this daughter of the New World. It mainly illustrated for James 'the ubiquity of the American girl'. 'I today, at All Souls,

Langham Place, "gave away" Caroline Balestier to Rudyard Kipling – a queer office for *me* to perform – but it's done – and an odd little marriage,' James wrote to Morton Fullerton.

I

It would seem always to James an odd little marriage, but he was to count the Kiplings as friends from first to last and to follow the interval of their life in America, in Vermont, with fascination. The novelist and the young genius met in 1890. 'I liked Rudyard,' he told Rhoda Broughton, calling him 'the young Bard'. Later he called him 'the star of the hour', 'the infant monster', 'the little black demon'. 'That little black demon of a Kipling,' he wrote to Robert Louis Stevenson, 'will have perhaps leaped upon your silver strand by the time this reaches you – he publicly left England to embrace you, many weeks ago – carrying literary genius out of the country with him in his pocket'.

In the first flush of his admiration for Kipling, and before he had been a principal at his marriage, Henry James had praised his precocity by writing an introduction to the American edition of *Mine Own People*. He had done this as a favour to Balestier, who arranged for the preface, because he felt that so new a writer needed introducing in the United States. James's introduction was hedged with precautions : he spoke of this 'strangely clever youth who has stolen the formidable mask of maturity'; he characterized him as having 'an identity as marked as a window-frame'. Kipling was 'shockingly precocious'; he had delight in battle; he was cheeky about women, 'and indeed about men and about everything'. James noted his love of the private soldier and the primitive man; he felt it a bit of good news that 'in the smoking room too there may be artists'. He prophetically remarked that if invention should ever fail Kipling 'he would still have the lyric string and the patriotic chord, on which he plays admirably'. He observed that 'Mr Kipling's actual performance is like a tremendous walk before breakfast, making one welcome the idea of the meal, but consider with some alarm the hours still to be traversed'.

Disillusionment set in quickly. He had praised Kipling's 'extraordinarily observed' stories of barrack-room life; but he began to have doubts when he read *The Light That Failed* – 'there,' he wrote, 'the talent has sometimes failed', even if that talent was enormous.

Kipling's violence was deep-seated. He had outdone the brutal stories of Rider Haggard and triumphed; but James could not stomach the new violence. By 1893 Kipling was living in America near Brattleboro and writing James of the winter cold, the rude conditions, the delights of being driven 'over stone walls in an oxcart' and how he had met Henry Adams in New York, finding him 'painfully civilized' and wearing a tall silk hat, a thing he hadn't seen since he left England. James confided to a friend he believed the writer well-satisfied – 'he needs nothing of the civilized order'. And he went on, 'He charged himself with all he could take of India when he was very young, and gave it out with great effect; but I doubt if he has anything more of anything to give. All sorts of things – i.e. symptoms and indications – seem to me to point to that. But what he *did* – in two or three years – remains wonderful.'

This was James's verdict in July 1893, and a year later, when he read *The Jungle Book*, Henry James exclaimed '*how* it closes his door and sets his limit! The rise to "higher types" that one hoped for – I mean the care for life in a finer way – is the rise to the mongoose and the care for the wolf. The *violence* of it all, the almost exclusive preoccupation with fighting and killing is also singularly characteristic.' He repeated that he expected nothing from Kipling 'save some beast stories'.

2

For a while James had hoped Kipling might have in him the seeds of an English Balzac. Presently he came to recognize that there was in him 'almost nothing of the complicated soul or of the female form or of any question of *shades*'. The novelist and poet of civilization had looked carefully upon the poet of the jungle and the barrack-room and by the turn of the century he delivered his final judgement to Grace Norton.

My view of his prose future has much shrunken in the light of one's increasingly observing how little of life he can make use of. Almost nothing civilized save steam and patriotism – and the latter only in verse, where I *hate* it so, especially mixed up with God and goodness, that that half spoils my enjoyment of his great talent.

James had been alienated from Kipling

in proportion as he has come steadily from the less simple in subject to the more simple – from the Anglo-Indians to the natives, from the natives to the Tommies, from the Tommies to the quadrupeds, from the quadrupeds to the fish and from the fish to the engines and screws. But he is a prodigious little success and an unqualified little happiness and a dear little chap.

He also remarked 'and *such* an uninteresting mind'.

Kipling destroyed many of his letters. But a typed copy of one from James (30 October 1901), acknowledging *Kim*, suggests the verbal legerdemain the latter practised in his relationship with Kipling. He rejoiced, he wrote, 'in such a saturation, such a splendid dose of you'. He had read *Kim* 'with comment and challenge ... in other words I have some small reserves and anxieties – as to your frequent *how* of performances'. Yet he did not allow these things to matter: he had 'surrendered luxuriously to your genius ... I take you as you are. It might be that I wished you were quite different – though I don't.' Continuing this counterpoint of ironic qualification and praise, he adds

you are too sublime – you are too big and there is too much of you. I don't think you've cut out your subject, in *Kim*, with a sharp enough scissors, but with that one little nut cracked – so! – the beauty, the quantity, the prodigality, the Ganges-flood, leave me simply gaping as your procession passes. What a luxury to *possess* a big subject as you possess India!

He ended with the suggestion that Kipling 'chuck public affairs, which are an ignoble scene [by which he meant his patriotic verses at the time of the Boer War] and stick to your canvas and your paint box. There are as good colours in the tubes as ever were laid on, and *there* is the only truth. The rest is base humbug.'

22

The 'Wanton' of the Pacific

THE recipient of Henry James's confidences – his ambitions and misgivings in the theatre – was his old friend Robert Louis Stevenson. To far-away Samoa Henry James dispatched from time to time a record of his hopes and his doubts in the strange medium to which he had turned. While he boasted in London of the 'honourable' run of *The American*, he candidly told Stevenson in 1891 that it had been a 'public humiliation', and 'the papers slated it without mercy'. The word 'dishonour' crept into another letter. 'I am working with patient subterraneity at a trade which it is dishonour enough to practise, without talking about it: a trade supremely dangerous and heroically difficult – *that* credit at least belongs to it.'

But Stevenson, whom James loved with a tenderness of memory unique among his friends, had by this time become a wraith. James remembered how in 1885 he had first visited the Stevensons near Bournemouth, and how ill Louis had been at the time. He rejoiced in Louis's new-found vigour in the South Seas, yet he could no longer invest him with reality. Some of James's most touching letters were written during these years to the absent friend and they are virtuoso performances of a stylist aware that he is writing to a stylist. The refrain is constant. James felt as if he were addressing a company of ghosts – 'you are too far away, you are too absent – too invisible, inaudible, inconceivable'. He teased his friend; he had become 'a beautiful myth', a kind of 'unnatural uncomfortable *mort*'. The visual-minded James wanted always to see – and Stevenson's adventures in Polynesia seemed to belong to fairy tales. Again and again James pleaded for more description of 'people, things, objects, faces, bodies, costumes, features, gestures, manners' – what he called 'the personal painter-touch'. He had seen some snapshots; these only whetted his appetite. When John Hay sent him certain of Henry Adams's letters from the Pacific, including an account of his visit to Stevenson, James complained that Adams had not given him 'the *look* of things'.

James regularly sent Stevenson books and journals. When he came upon the Napoleonic volumes of Marbot, he dispatched them in haste. He sent him Bourget and Anatole France, and talked of Thomas Hardy, whose Tess he considered 'vile', and of the genius of Kipling. There is, in all his letters, a great embracing tenderness. He told him his friends brandished laurel over his absent head and he called him a 'buccaneering Pompadour of the Deep' and 'a wandering wanton of the Pacific', and when Stevenson misdated a letter by two years James twitted him as 'my dear time-deluded islander'. He saluted Stevenson's family as 'your playfellows – your fellow-phantoms. The wife-phantom knows my sentiment. The dim ghost of a mother has my heartiest regards.' He grieved over Louis's 'permanent secession'. He was too far away – he had become a legend – but a legend of 'opaline iridescence'.

I

From beyond the seas there appeared in London at the moment of Balestier's death the ghostly figure of Henry Adams and the distant ghost of James's Newport youth, John La Farge. They brought news of Tusitala – Louis's native name – and his rough-hewn quarters on the Samoan hilltop.

James had not seen Adams since before the suicide of his wife, in 1885. Now the melancholy historian was in the British capital again, remembering how he had come originally with his father, Charles Francis Adams, during the civil war. In his *Education*, Adams uses the word 'extinct' repeatedly as he describes his emotions of this time. Thinking of Polynesia, he found himself wishing, during a week he spent in a nursing home in Wigmore Street, that he might 'sleep forever in the tradewind under the southern stars, wandering over the dark purple ocean, with its purple sense of solitude and void'. Life, he wrote, 'had been cut in halves' for him. He brought his countenance of despair to Henry James in De Vere Gardens.

James tried to cheer him up. On one occasion Adams found him excited by Kipling's marriage which he had witnessed six days before; the two friends gossiped about the poet and his American bride. Adams began by seeing Kipling as a Bohemian, a wanderer 'of the second or third social order'; he felt he had 'behaved well about his young woman', had married in the face of family opposition. James gave him the impression that Caroline Kipling was 'without beauty or money or special intelligence'. He also told Adams how his friend Sargent had lost his temper when he had been scolded by a Cotswolds farmer for riding his horse over the farmer's spring wheat. Sargent had been enraged when the farmer suggested he was no gentleman. The painter returned to the farm-house, called out the farmer, and gave him a thrashing. Now he faced a jail term for assault.

All this, Adams reported to a friend in Washington,

much distresses Henry who has a sympathetic heart. As Sargent seems not to distress himself, I see no reason why James should do so. But poor James may well be a little off his nerves, for beside Balestier's death, the long, nervous illness of his sister is drawing slowly to its inevitable close, and James has the load of it to carry.

Adams had called at Alice James's house on Campden Hill and had sat for two hours with her companion and friend, Miss Loring. We gather from Alice's journal that among the subjects of their talk was the helplessness of English doctors when faced with American patients.

To Elizabeth Cameron, his Washington confidante, Adams wrote 'I feel even deader than I did in the South Seas, but here I feel that all the others are as dead as I'. It was in this letter that he called James 'a figure in the same old wall-paper'. James on his side wrote to his Scottish friend, Sir John Clark, and the laird of Tillypronie: 'I like [Adams] but suffer from his monotonous, disappointed pessimism.' Adams, he remarked, was 'a man of wealth and leisure, able to satisfy all his curiosities, while I am a penniless toiler – so what can *I* do for him? However, when the poor dear is in London, I don't fail to do what I can.'

Each thus seems to have believed he was comforting the other; in reality they made each other uncomfortable.

2

When Stevenson told James that he had been visited by Adams and La Farge, the novelist replied: 'Henry Adams is as conversible as an Adams is permitted by the scheme of nature to be; but what is wonderful to me is that they have both taken to the buccaneering life when already "on the return" – La Farge many times a *père de famille.*'

Stevenson had gone on horseback to visit the western wanderers, swimming his horse through a river to get to them. He had to borrow dry clothes from the American consul. He described the way in which he was clearing the land and creating his Vailima home in the hills above the sea; and how he and his wife had not yet managed to arrange their food-supplies. Adams and La Farge, returning the visit, sent food ahead, and after a long weary tramp arrived and spent several hours. At the end, the frail and sickly Stevenson seemed greatly refreshed, while Adams was completely exhausted. Stevenson's fragility, Adams observed, 'passes description, but his endurance passes his fragility'. The eye of Quincy and of Lafayette Square never understood the carefree ways of the Bohemian; and Mrs Stevenson in her dirty work-a-day *muumuu* had seemed to him to be a lady in a nightdress. Their mode of existence was 'far less human than that of the natives'; compared with the Stevenson shanty Adams considered the native houses palaces. He decided that Stevenson's ability to live in this 'squalor' was due to his education. 'His early associates were all second-rate; he never seems by any chance to have come in contact with first-rate people, either men, women, or artists.' This was spoken like an Adams; it was like his judgement of the second- or third-ratedness of Kipling. How he reconciled Stevenson's knowing the first-rate Henry James we do not know. Adams moreover felt uncomfortable in a belief that Stevenson, with his gregarious nature, had contempt 'for my Bostonianism'. Stevenson however had written to James 'we have had enlightened society; a great privilege – would it might endure'.

To Sir John Clark again, Henry James voiced his wonder 'how Adams and La Farge could, either of them, have failed to murder the other'. He had finally decided that 'each lives to prove the other's self-control'. La Farge, passing through London briefly on his way back to America, felt that James did not understand Adams: and probably there had been peace in Polynesia between the restless La Farge and the melancholy Adams only because La Farge was too busy absorbing the painter's visual world and the South Sea colours, and Adams, in his effort to get outside himself, tried very hard to keep pace with him. James wondered afresh at 'La Farge's combination of social and artistic endowments'. He characterized him to Stevenson as 'a strange and complicated product'. He was delighted however to find that neither his charm nor his talk, had changed; for a brief moment they were back in Newport. 'I was all young again,' La Farge wrote to Adams.

It was probably with a sense of relief that Henry James saw Adams off to America in February of 1892. The latter had hardly emerged from his cabin to take the sea air, 'when I fell into the arms of Rudyard Kipling and his new wife, and wife's sister, and wife's mother'. 'Henry James,' he wrote to a friend, 'is responsible for this last variation on my too commoplace existence.' Adams quickly changed his mind about Kipling; he wasn't second- or third-rate; he judged him one of the rare Englishmen he had met whom he did not experience as condescending to an American. 'Fate was kind on that voyage,' he remembered in the *Education*. 'Rudyard Kipling, on his wedding trip to America, thanks to the mediation of Henry James, dashed over the passenger his exuberant fountain of gaiety and wit – as though playing a garden hose on a thirsty and faded begonia.'

3

That had been almost two years before and now in the midst of the rehearsals of *Guy Domville*, on 17 December 1894, James read in the newspapers that Louis was dead. The news had travelled slowly from Vailima where Stevenson had been buried on his hilltop – Tusitala, the teller of tales – in his permanent sleep under the bright and starry sky. 'This ghastly extinction of the beloved R.L.S.,' James wrote to Gosse that evening, 'it makes me cold and sick – and with the absolute, almost alarmed sense, of the visible material quenching of an indispensable light.' James felt as if in the place Stevenson had occupied 'there had descended an avalanche of ice'. It was a relief for Louis – he had suffered enough, 'but for us the loss of charm, of suspense, of "fun" is unutterable'.

Into his mourning for the newest of his dead there was now introduced a curiously unexpected note. James found himself named one of Stevenson's executors. He had not been consulted; but the will did provide alternatives. James, who had been his father's executor, had no relish for the task. 'It would be a dreadful disaster to his heirs,' he said, asking to be excused.

The long letter which he wrote to Mrs Stevenson is one of his finest epistolary elegies. Louis had died 'in time not to be old – early enough to be so generously young and late enough to have drunk deep of the cup'. The note from the first was that of a requiem: 'What can I say to you that will not seem cruelly irrelevant and vain? We have been sitting in darkness for nearly a fortnight, but what is *our* darkness to the extinction of your magnificent light?' And the image of the light is taken up again a few sentences further – 'he lighted up a whole side of the globe, and was himself a whole province of one's imagination'. James saw Stevenson's death as having its glorious side – 'struck down that way, as by the gods, in a clear, glorious hour', for he had had the best of life, 'the thick of the fray, the loudest of the music, the freshest and finest of himself. It isn't as if there had been no full achievement and no supreme thing. It was all intense, all gallant, all exquisite from the first.'

From the eloquence of this tribute James returned to the rehearsals of his play. They seemed 'tawdry and heartless'. Stevenson's ghost 'waves its great dusky wings between me and all occupations', he told Edmund Gosse.

23

Preparations

HE had looked forward to the first rehearsal of *Guy Domville* when he would read the play aloud and expound it to the English actors in the French tradition. However, on the morning of the first reading (at the beginning of December 1894), he awoke with acute laryngitis, and he had the chagrin of sitting in the dark empty theatre while Alexander read the play for him. Then, day after day, for four weeks, he came in the wet and cold to the West End to participate in 'the poverty and patchiness of rehearsal'. It involved him in a great deal of anxiety; and also amusement. In his tale of *Nona Vincent* the young dramatist expects every actor 'to become instantly and gratefully conscious of a rare opportunity'. Things were different in Alexander's theatre; everything was done with a quiet efficiency; the manager was a masterly technician. He had assembled a highly professional cast, a group of polite, hard-working actors. Ellen Terry's gifted sister, Marion, had the lead opposite Alexander; the second male part was entrusted to Herbert Waring, who had recently played Solness with Miss Robins in *The Master Builder*. The other parts were in competent hands; one was played by the talented man of the stage H. V. Esmond, whom James judged to be the one 'true' actor in the piece. The villain, however, with the satanic name of Lord Devenish, was played by W. G. Elliott; he had begun as an amateur and the stamp of the amateur remained. He grimaced too much; he was 'stagey'. His memoirs suggest that James tried to tell him he should play his part in a more human way; for he quotes James as saying he should make the dissolute peer 'as much of a gentleman as is feasible – possible – to you'.

James told Miss Robins the rehearsals were 'very human and tranquil'. He alternated between approval of Alexander and doubt; the manager did have a distinct flair; yet he was all profile and posture, with an almost metallic suavity. As regards material things, he spared no expense. Doors could be banged without shaking the set. The hedges of the garden in the first act seemed real. The white parlour of the third act impressed by its sense of having been lived in (and was to do service in a number of Alexander's later productions). The costumes were meticulously faithful to the late eighteenth century. James was euphoric one day and in the depths of despair the next. He complained that rehearsals cut a gaping hole in his days; yet he never missed a rehearsal. Fatigue did overtake him – so that he could speak of his 'demoralizing and exhausting and incongruous ordeal'; and he was overtaken finally by nervousness, then panic.

'I am *too* preoccupied, too terrified, too fundamentally distracted, to be fit for human intercourse,' he told a hostess who invited him to dinner during the Yuletide of 1894. 'I would be a death's head at the feast.' On the last day of the year, with the first night but five days away, he wrote a long letter to Miss Reubell telling her he was about to sit through the dress rehearsals. This he found amusing, and promptly qualified it with 'as amusing as anything can be, for a man of taste and sensibility, in the odious process of practical drama-tic production. I may have been meant for the Drama – God knows! – but I certainly wasn't meant for the Theatre.'

James felt he had staked everything on this production. 'One can have a big danger, in the blessed theatre, even with a small thing,' he explained to his architect friend, Edward Warren. He told Miss Robins the production would be 'a very creditable performance, and a very finished production'; however he seemed to discern 'a bad theatrical *wind*' rising. A play at the Garrick had just failed and 'I have a superstitious sense that such influences are contagious.' He began to discuss with Edmund Gosse what to do on the first night. During *The American*, in the provinces, James had had the run of the backstage. Alexander wanted no nervous authors near the dressing-rooms. James first said he would go to an adjacent pub and Gosse promised to come between the acts to tell him how things were going. Thinking upon this, the novelist realized however he would need more distraction. Finally he decided he would go to see some other play.

With the actors James was tenderly affectionate. 'I don't want to worry you,' he wrote to the leading lady a few hours before the opening,

on the contrary; so this is only a mere word on the chance I didn't say it a couple of nights ago *distinctly* enough that your business of the end of Act I – your going and leaning your face against the pillar of the porch – couldn't possibly be improved. Please believe from me that it is per-fectly beautiful and *right* – like, indeed, your whole performance, which will do you great honour.

He closed his note : 'Rest quiet, this weary day, at least about *that*.'

24

The Three Critics

On the day of the opening – 5 January 1895, a Saturday – Henry James found his nervousness unbearable. He went for a long walk through London parks and streets. The weather was cold and dreary. In the late afternoon he returned to 34 De Vere Gardens in a state of panic. He now tried letter-writing to calm himself. To Madame Bourget: 'It is five o'clock in the afternoon and at 8.30 this evening *le sort en est jeté* – my poor little play will be thrown into the arena – like a little white Christian virgin to the lions and the tigers.' Madame Bourget had mentioned that a friend of hers, an American lady named Edith Wharton, sent good wishes and James replied, 'I cling to *you* ... with the agitated clutch of this instant, and please say to Mrs Wharton that I cling a little, if she will permit it, even to *her*.' He added, 'I offer Mrs Wharton all thanks for her sympathy.' In concluding he invoked prayer, *Domine in manus tuas*. A few minutes later he scribbled a hasty, almost illegible, note to his brother. Alluding to William's interest in spiritualism he counted on 'psychical intervention from you – this is really the time to show your stuff'. And then, 'This is the time when a man wants a religion.' Alexander had told him there had been a large advance sale of seats, 'but my hand shakes and I can only write that I am your plucky, but all the same lonely and terrified Henry'. He added after the signature the date and the hour. It was 5.45 p.m. James decided it would help speed the dragging clock to go and see Oscar Wilde's new play at the Haymarket.

I

Mr Bernard Shaw, the drama critic of the *Saturday Review*, who had attended the first night of Oscar's play that week, was preparing to review *Guy Domville*. He was new in his job: he had assumed his duties five days before. Shaw was 38 and comparatively unknown. He had been a music critic for some years but to the musical public he signed himself Corno di Bassetto. He had also recently produced a play, *Widower's Houses*; it had attracted little attention.

A second play, about prostitution, *Mrs Warren's Profession*, had been refused a licence by the Lord Chamberlain. Shaw was known, however, in socialist circles as an indefatigable pamphleteer and a speech-maker to working-men's clubs; and he was a familiar figure among the journalists. A lanky Irishman, he had red scraggly whiskers and bushy brows and the pallor one finds in red-haired persons. For some years he had sought every possible public platform to teach himself to be fluent and authoritative. He spoke now on a variety of subjects and with increasing ease : Marx and Wagner, wages, common sense, food – the joys of being a vegetarian, the barbarism of meat-eating – the importance of Henrik Ibsen. He had learned to face audiences and to amuse them by paradox and persiflage; he offered a mixture of wisdom and vulgarity. By trial and error he discovered himself most comfortable when he could build a wall of words between himself and the world. Paradoxes came to his lips as naturally as epigrams did to his compatriot Oscar.

He had arrived in London from Ireland in 1876 – that is, in the same year that Henry James had come from Paris to settle in Bolton Street. Shaw had been 20, James 33. Two years later the American had won renown at the moment the Irishman was writing a novel entitled *Immaturity*. James was a finished cosmopolite; Shaw was from the provinces, from John Bull's other island, a clumsy Dubliner with a shrewd sense of practical affairs and a love of music. During the 1880s, when James wrote a novel on a social theme, *The Princess Casamassima*, Shaw was helping found the Fabian Society and in the parks and on the Embankment had begun his socio-economic discourses. He read Karl Marx in the British Museum and studied Wagner. He was a bohemian and a philanderer; ladies pursued him; he wooed them with words. And yet, as with James, who was also interested in women but kept a proper distance, there was something eternally virginal and fresh in Shaw. His eyes sparkled; his wit flashed. His sexual investment was in his intellect, in the power of language. He lived for ideas, for common sense, for histrionic display. No man of his time seemed more involved with the world or had more opinions on anything and everything; and no man – as Leonard Woolf in particular has shown – was more removed and dissociated in his personal relations. Shaw liked the clash of minds and knew the vitality of ideas. He also liked to make logic out of life's inconsistencies. People were more difficult. His way of meeting them was to charm them by being charmed with himself.

Henry James on the other hand liked the contradictory ironies of life; he knew the meaning of ambivalence; he lived for art. Shaw railed at ugliness and poverty and wanted to change the world. James was troubled by the crudities of existence and hoped to exorcize them by devotion to beauty. He held with Balzac that the artist must take the world as it is; he held with Voltaire that he must cultivate his own little garden; his task was to make – not to *remake*. Shaw was an articulate revolutionary who performed his revolutions on paper; and he tried to make the world his classroom. Yet he knew the nature of art. 'You cannot be an artist until you have contracted yourself within the limits of your art,' he wrote to a friend shortly after the production of *Guy Domville*. At the same time James was writing 'Art should be as hard as nails'. Both the American and the Irishman were concentrated egotists – Shaw with an open and good-humoured though often garrulous public aggressivity; James behind a façade of discretion, civilization, secrecy. Shaw was journalist and preacher; James was a finder and maker.

What was happening, however, in the waning years of the century, was that James was attempting to woo the world in a manner closer to Shaw's nature than to his own. Both wanted to conquer the theatre. When someone in 1892 booed *Widower's Houses*, which Shaw had called 'an original and didactic realistic play', the dramatist subdued the audience with a three-minute speech and changed the boos into applause. In the theatre the two men were at this moment equal failures. The difference was that James had a reputation at stake, and Shaw had a reputation to make. The would-be playwright, Bernard Shaw, was a critic of other men's plays. On this first Saturday in January of 1895 the Irish critic donned his corduroy jacket, and made his way from Fitzroy Street in Bloomsbury to St James's through the cold and wet to see the American novelist's long-awaited play.

2

The critic of the *Pall Mall Gazette* was also new at his job. He was a thin, undernourished, wispy man, with short legs, long moustaches, and a squeaky voice, named H. G. Wells. He had been offered the post on the newspaper a few days before, and on 3 January had reviewed Wilde's play at the Haymarket. Child of a below stairs marriage, he knew that the upper classes always dressed for important occasions. One of his first questions, when his editor gave him tickets for *An Ideal Husband* and for *Guy Domville* was 'one wears evening dress?' The editor answered 'oh yes, tomorrow night especially', for the Oscar Wilde première drew all of London society. Wells described in his reminiscences how he rushed to a tailor and had a suit made in twenty-four hours, in time for him to be at the Haymarket opening in full regalia. He had actually only been to a theatre twice, and when he told his editor this, the reply had been 'Exactly what I want. You won't be in the gang. You'll make a break.' Apparently his first review, written late into the night, had satisfied the editor. Wells went to James's play, in his new dress suit, with greater assurance. He was to explain later that he never really cared much for the theatre. He had been trained as a scientist. Make-believe was not his sort of thing.

His childhood might have been written by Charles Dickens. His mother was a housemaid, his father a gardener who later became a shopkeeper. He had served an apprenticeship in a draper's shop; later he was a chemist's assistant. He was alert, brilliant, articulate. He had become an usher in a grammar school and in spite of bad health and poverty had obtained a scholarship. At the University of London he studied under T. H. Huxley and took his degree in 1888. He had embarked on a career in science; he discovered now he had a flair for journalism. Magazines accepted his pieces and paid him decently; and he had just written a novel called *The Time Machine* which promised to be successful. His job on the *Pall Mall Gazette* would be short-lived, and the only regular job (save for the early apprenticeship) he ever held. No one would have predicted on the night of *Guy Domville* that this immaculately dressed little man was to be the founder of modern 'science fiction' and perhaps the most brilliant of literary and political journalists of his time. He was also to have a long and as he called it 'a sincere and troubled friendship' with the author of *Guy Domville*, whom he considered 'a sensitive man lost in an immensely abundant brain'.

Like Shaw, Wells was interested in working-class movements. They were both atheists and socialists. Wells was to say later that Shaw did not have as sustained and constructive a mental training as he had, and this was true; however, the Irishman had been saturated with good conversation, good music and 'the appreciative treatment of life', something Wells lacked. Thus in the theatre that night 'the new men' of James's time were sitting in judgement on his play. Wells, felt, however, that he was the newest of the new: that science put him in the forefront, and that in their devotion to art, Shaw and James lagged behind. Wells put the difference between himself and Shaw as follows: 'To him, I guess, I have always appeared heavily and sometimes formidably facty and close-set; to me his judgements, arrived at by feeling and expression, have always had flimsiness.' Wells always accused Shaw of philandering with Fact.

In that formally dressed audience on this first night, however, it was Shaw who burst through fact: he broke the ranks of the boiled shirts and the black and white ties in the stalls with his modest brown jacket suit. It was Wells who, more rebellious and *gamin* than Shaw, had conformed to job and society by dressing the part assigned to him. The two men, future 'prophets' of their generation, met for the first time at the James play.

3

Still another 'new man' sat in the audience at the St James's that evening as critic of *Guy Domville*. He was wholly unknown – an assistant editor of a magazine named *Woman*, given to signing his articles Barbara (if he reviewed books) or Marjorie (when he wrote town talk) and Cécile (when he reviewed plays). His name was Enoch Arnold Bennett. Like Shaw and Wells he had come to London from the provinces, from the midlands, where he had been a potter's son; he had grown up to middle-class comfort and philistinism. If Shaw had sublime self-assurance and Wells was an uncertain aspirant in literature, and in considerable conflict about his place in society, Bennett was simple, shy, insecure, ambitious. He had a marked stammer. He wore a boiled shirt, and probably would not have dreamed of wearing anything else. He knew the solid materialistic world in which he had moved from decent poverty to the professional class of the town, for his father had succeeded in leaving the pottery and making himself into a lawyer. Enoch Arnold Bennett had worked first as a shorthand clerk in his father's office. A year after Wells came down from university, Bennett arrived in London determined to make himself into a man of the world.

In that brilliant series of cartoons in which Max Beerbohm caricatured London celebrities, none was more successful than his drawing of Bennett's Old Self saying to the Young Self: 'All gone according to plan, you see'; to which the Young Self replies: 'My plan, you know.' Bennett had published a tale in the *Yellow Book* after his arrival in London and borrowed £300 to buy himself a share in the magazine *Woman*, thereby becoming assistant editor. Later he was its editor. In this school of practical journalism he learned to be a commentator on London life. He was to become a famous novelist, and like Wells a giver of opinions to the average man through the medium of the press. But where Wells was brilliant and erratic, prophetic and often tried to be Olympian, Bennett spoke with a kind of plodding honesty, a supreme matter-of-factness. He was six months younger than Wells and the two were not to meet for some time. Wells was to remember that 'we were both hard workers, both pushing up by way of writing from lower middle-class surroundings, where we had little prospect of anything but a restricted salaried life, and we found we were pushing with quite surprising ease'. They were both liberal and sceptical, but Bennett, even more than Shaw or Wells, felt himself in James's camp. He had an ideal of art, a desire to be a storyteller; he saw the world brighter than it was. He wanted success and all the glitter of success; unlike Shaw and Wells he believed in the fairy-tale of achievement; and he was to live the tale to the full.

James, product of an American aristocracy of the mind, would have held it an irony that in this theatre, where his future as a playwright was to be decided, the plebeians were sitting in judgement on him: men whom he would get to know reasonably well – one of them intimately – and whom he in turn would criticize when they came to practise his own art. On this occasion (as we can now see) the Edwardian world-to-come was already present to review a play of the Victorian world. The names of Shaw, Wells and Bennett were to be linked constantly in the next three decades and would be – with certain others – among the supreme literary names of the new time.

At the Haymarket, Henry James fidgeted uneasily. Oscar Wilde's newest epigrams burst from the stage like well-timed firecrackers. 'Men can be analysed, women merely adored'; 'only dull people are brilliant at breakfast'; 'morality is simply the attitude we adopt towards people whom we personally dislike'. The play did not have a soothing effect. Perhaps no play could alleviate James's panic, his sense of disaster.

25

The Last Domville

THERE were in reality two audiences at the first night of *Guy Domville*. Literary and artistic London came to see an Alexander production of a James play : it seemed a happy combination; and then many of the members of that audience were friends of the novelist. The world of art was represented by such figures as Leighton, Burne-Jones, Watts, Du Maurier (doubly famous now as the author of *Trilby*), Sargent and members of the 'Broadway' group such as Millet and Parsons; letters were represented by Edmund Gosse, Mrs Humphry Ward, Mrs W. K. Clifford, W. E. Norris, members of the critical 'establishment', and other late Victorian luminaries; there were several well-known actresses in the audience, not least Miss Robins; there were representatives of the English aristocracy who had always admired James. These constituted the first audience which came prepared to applaud and to praise. The second audience had queued up in the winter damp and sat in the gallery seats. It had never heard of James; it had come to be entertained by Alexander. 'Alex' could be relied upon to put on a good show.

I

The theatre itself, where gaslight had just given way to electricity, was warm and cheerful; and by the time the little curtain-raiser had been acted, and the orchestra had fussed through an overture, the distinguished and well-dressed were in their places. The curtain rose on a set visually pleasing, the garden of a wealthy young widow, Mrs Peverel, near Richmond in 1780. The aim had been to suggest peaceful rural charm and there was a close-cut privet edge, with clustering rose-bushes and honeysuckle trailing around quaint lattice-windows. In this pleasant setting James developed with great simplicity and charm of dialogue the dilemma of young Guy, devout and dedicated on the eve of his departure for France, strong in his determination to become a Benedictine monk. He has been tutor to Mrs Peverel's son; he loves Mrs Peverel; his love for the Church however has not permitted him to recognize his deeper feelings. Mrs Peverel is devoted to him, and thinks of him as an earthly saint. She has accordingly resigned herself to losing him to the Mother Church. Guy is also fond of a neighbouring squire, Frank Humber, who pays courts to Mrs Peverel. Since Guy will not have the widow for himself, he is prepared – like Miles Standish or Cyrano de Bergerac – to plead his friend's cause.

All this James set forth with considerable charm; it won both audiences: the gallery, knowing Alexander as a romantic hero, lived in hope that he would throw over the church and marry Mrs Peverel – as the Comptons had warned James two years earlier. The more sophisticated members of the audience experienced, after seasons of tawdry and violent drama, the delicacy of James's dialogue. Guy Domville's conflict quickly became, however, much more than that of spiritual love versus the spiritual life. Into the quiet of this garden there enters Lord Devenish, the Mephistopheles of the drama. He brings the news that Guy's kisman has just fallen from a horse and been killed – 'he was mostly too drunk to ride'. Guy is the last of his line. He must renounce religion, take over the encumbered estates, make an advantageous marriage. The Domvilles must not be allowed to die out.

Mrs Peverel's hope revives and she urges Guy to take the worldly course. Lord Devenish also urges this as envoy of the newly-widowed Mrs Domville, now reduced to the dower-house but possessed of a marriageable daughter. Guy speaks in touching lines of his devotion,

Break with the past, and break with it this minute? – turn back from the threshold, take my hand from the plough? – The hour is too troubled, your news too strange, your summons too sudden?

The act was filled with such lines and Bernard Shaw's ear was sensitive to them. He was delighted with the play's literary spirit. Like the other critics however he was troubled by the rude shifts of feeling. Guy, who speaks of his vocation, who to his friends had 'such an air of the cold college – almost of the cold cloister', suddenly makes a grand exit shouting 'long, long live the Domvilles'. Just before doing this, still blind to love, he commends Mrs Peverel to his friend Humber. The last of the Domvilles is ready for London and the world.

The second act, at the villa of the dowager Mrs Domville, banished all the sympathetic characters of the first act. Only Guy and Lord

Devenish were retained. Guy has shed churchly black for the breeches, lace and wig of a man-about-town. He has learned very quickly to play cards and to drink; he is ready to marry his cousin, the dowager's daughter. Into this act James poured the clichés of the boulevard theatres of Paris: the cousin turns out to be the illegitimate daughter of Lord Devenish and Mrs Domville; she in turn is in love with a naval lieutenant. When Guy learns the truth, he aids in their elopement. In the midst of the act he indulges in a mock drinking scene – borrowed from Émile Augier's *L'Aventurière* – in which the naval lieutenant and Guy pour glass after glass of port into the flower pots while pretending to make each other drunk. H. G. Wells pointed out that the characters came and went in this house 'like rabbits in a warren'. At the end, having found nothing but deceit around him, Guy again reverses himself. He has strayed from his true vocation. He must, after all, go into the Church.

The third act, even though it brought back the sympathetic Mrs Peverel and her suitor, could not repair the damage. Lord Devenish rushes to Mrs Peverel; if he can't marry off Guy to his illegitimate daughter, he may still save him for worldly things, and his own devices, by marrying him to Mrs Peverel. Guy returns, and in another scene of great delicacy shows a glimmer of awareness of Mrs Peverel's love. But Lord Devenish has left his gloves in the room; and the sight of these freezes the novice into a sense of the world's treacheries. All hesitation is gone; he will say good-bye to everything.

GUY: I'm the *last*, my lord, of the Domvilles! [*Then, anticipating* DEVENISH'S *reply and speaking on his quick gesture of impatient despair*.] You've been so good as to take a zealous interest in my future – and in that of my family: for which I owe you, and now ask you to accept, all *thanks*. But I beg you, still more solemnly, to let that prodigious zeal rest, from this moment, for ever! I listened to your accents for a day – I followed you where you led me. I looked at life as you showed it, and then I turned away my face. That's why I stand here again; for [*with intensely controlled emotion*] there are other things – there are partings. [*Then very gently to* MRS PEVEREL.] Will my conveyance have come back?

MRS PEVEREL: [*Listening an instant, and as if subjugated by his returning sanctity*.] I think I hear it now.

GUY: Then I start this moment for Bristol. [*Sadly, kindly smiling*.] Father Murray has had patience. I go with him to France, to take up my work in the Church! if the Church will *take* again an erring son!

MRS PEVEREL: She'll take him.

LORD DEVENISH: And *you* give him?

MRS PEVEREL: To *her*!

LORD DEVENISH: [*with high sarcasm, to* GUY] I hope you do justice to this lady's exemplary sacrifice!

GUY: [*blank.*] Sacrifice?

LORD DEVENISH: That of a sentiment consideration for her forbids me to name.

FRANK: She loves you, Guy!

LORD DEVENISH: He doesn't deserve to know it. [*Then smiling, gallant to* MRS PEVEREL.] If it were *me*, Madame! [*From the threshold.*] Pity me!

MRS PEVEREL: It was a dream, but the dream is past!

GUY: [*Gathering himself slowly from a deep, stupefied commotion.*] The Church *takes* me! [*To* MRS PEVEREL.] Be kind to him. [*To* FRANK.] Be good to her. [*At the door.*] Be good to her.

FRANK: Mrs Peverel – I shall *hope*!

MRS PEVEREL: Wait!

2

This was the play on which James had placed all his hopes and it had much in it that was literary and fine. But while the novelist was sitting at the Haymarket Theatre squirming over Wilde's play and the audience's enjoyment of it, curious things, which had nothing to do with James's text, occurred on the stage of the St James's. In the first place there was the acting of Elliott as Lord Devenish; he played his devilishness with a villainy so obvious as to wither (Shaw said) 'all sense and music out of James's lines with a diction I forbear to describe'. Wells remarked that 'he might have come out of Hogarth, but he has certainly no business to come into this play'. This in itself would not have sufficed to alienate the audience, had not another distraction occurred in a curious and unexpected form. Mrs Edward Saker, in the role of the dowager Mrs Domville, appeared in what Shaw described as 'a Falstaffian make-up'. She wore not only an elaborate gown of the period, a voluminous skirt of black satin over a panier crinoline of huge dimensions, but an enormous hat, one of those extravagant creations to which ladies were addicted in the late eighteenth century. It was tall, made of velvet and shaped like a muff; it towered on her head under nodding plumes. Her entrance with this piece of extravagant headgear came at a moment when the audience's patience had been tried by the fuss of the second act. The gallery, in which there had been a great deal of coughing and shuffling of feet, now began to titter. Mrs Saker, struggling with her huge skirt, was unnerved. Graham Robertson, the designer, who had come with John Singer Sargent, later said that the dress was particularly good, but 'it wanted wearing; the huge hoop, and great black hat perched upon a little frilled undercap should have been carried by one filled with the pride of them and consciousness of their beauty'. Mrs Saker at this moment had neither pride nor awareness of anything but discomfort. She tried to be as self-effacing as possible : but her costume filled a large area of the stage and her plumes waved with every motion she made. Illusion was gone. Alexander, unaccustomed to signs of discontent in his audience, displayed his nervousness in his acting. 'Why does he open his mouth on one side like that?' Sargent whispered to Robertson. 'It makes his face all crooked.'

The drinking scene which followed the hat incident could provide – after this – none of the intended comedy. The actors were play-acting drunk, and Shaw was to recount many years afterwards, with unforgotten amazement, the surreptitious pouring of the drink into the flower-pots. Alexander played his scene, Shaw said, 'with the sobriety of desperation'. James had once said of the Augier play he was imitating that its charm resided in 'the delicacy with which the deepening tipsiness was indicated, its intellectual rather than physical manifestations, and in the midst of it, the fantastic conceit which made [the character] think that he was winding his fellow-drinker round his fingers'. There was no suggestion in the scene in *Guy Domville* of any kind of 'intellectual' drunkenness.

The third act, with its fine setting, did little to restore the damage. The unintended comedy had thoroughly demoralized the gallery; the doors with their genuine brass knobs, the solid shelves, the handsome grandfather clock – not to speak of Mrs Peverel all love, and Guy all renunciation – had lost all meaning. The last lines with their subtlety of phrasing and calculated repetitions irritated the audience. There would be no romantic ending. Moreover, the audience's sympathies were no longer with Guy or the actor who embodied him. The audience tended to agree with Lord Devenish that Guy didn't deserve to know of Mrs Peverel's love – he seemed so insensitive to it. His vocation for the church had been insufficiently strong when it was a question of the family name and a worldly marriage; and yet it became strong when confronted with a deep and devoted love such as Mrs Peverel's.

When Alexander delivered himself of what, in other circumstances, might have been a touching and deeply felt speech, 'I'm the *last*, my lord, of the Domvilles!' there floated out of the darkness a strident voice from somewhere in the gallery: 'It's a bloody good thing y'are.'

3

Henry James remained to the end of the Oscar Wilde play. He listened to the final epigrams, heard the audience break into prolonged applause and left the theatre with the applause ringing in his ears. It was late evening. He walked down the short street leading into St James's Square. Oscar's play had been helpless, crude, clumsy, feeble, vulgar – he later would throw all these adjectives at it. And yet – it was almost unbelievable – the audience had liked it. This suddenly made him stop midway round the Square. He feared to go on to hear about his own play. 'How,' he asked himself, '*can* my piece do anything with a public with whom *that* is a success?'

He entered the St James's Theatre by the stage door. On stage Alexander was backing away towards the exit, saying to Mrs Peverel with some awkwardness in slowly measured accents, 'Be kind to him', and to Humber 'be good to her'. As H. G. Wells heard it it sounded like 'be keynd, be keynd'. Alexander had a long face, but to Wells it seemed now, 'with audible defeat before him', the longest and most dismal face he had ever seen, and the slowly closing door reduced the actor to 'a strip, a line, of perpendicular gloom'.

Backstage in these nervous moments no one said anything to James about the evening's accidents. The curtain came down and the panic-stricken author faced the angry manager. Outside there was a great roar of applause. Alexander took the curtain calls. He received the ovation to which he was accustomed. Then James's friends in the orchestra began to call 'Author, author.' The press reports of the evening agreed that a manager who knew the temper of the audience would have left well enough alone. But Alexander was unnerved. Perhaps Wells was right when he speculated that 'a spasm of hate' for the writer who had given him such a play seized Alexander. Or Alexander may have hoped, by acceding to the call, to placate those troublesome voices that had jarred him so painfully at intervals during the play.

He brought James on, leading him by the hand. The novelist, having heard applause, came forward shyly, hesitantly; and at that moment the gallery exploded. Jeers, hisses, catcalls were followed by great waves of applause from that part of the audience which esteemed James and recognized the better qualities of the play. The two audiences declared war. The intellectual and artistic élite answered the howls of derision; the howls grew strong in defiance. This was an unusual kind of passion in an English theatre, where feelings were so seldom expressed. 'All the forces of civilization in the house,' Henry later wrote to his brother, 'waged a battle of the most gallant, prolonged and sustained applause with the hoots and jeers and catcalls of the roughs, whose roars (like those of a cage of beasts at some infernal zoo) were only exacerbated by the conflict.'

James faced this pandemonium; his dark beard accentuated the pallor of his face and his high bald dome. He showed, some of the witnesses said, a 'scornful coolness'; others described it as a display of 'quiet gallantry'. At this moment various of his friends – Sargent among them – experienced an intense desire to leap across the footlights, to lead James out of the zoo-cage in which he was for the moment trapped. Alexander shifted nervously from one position to the other and followed with quick paces as the novelist fled. Two members of the cast, years later, said they had never forgotten the expression on James's face as he came into the wings. To Franklyn Dyall, who was just beginning his career, James seemed 'green with dismay'.

The brawl in the audience continued. Philip Burne-Jones was seen to turn in his box and applaud in the direction of the gallery. The gesture renewed the noise. James had once argued that certain plays should be hissed, since 'the deceived spectator ought to hold in his hands some instrument of respectful but uncompromising disapproval'. This was hardly 'respectful'; moreover he had prescribed it for the play, not the author.

Alexander, feeling that the situation in the theatre was getting out of hand, reappeared in front of the curtain. He held up his arm. English courtesy and discipline reasserted itself. He said slowly and with emotion that in his short career as actor-manager he had met with many favours at the hands of his audiences and 'these discordant notes tonight have hurt me very much. I can only say that we have done our very best.' He added that if he and his company had failed 'we can only try to deserve your kindness' by doing better in the future.

A voice from the gallery said: 'T'aint your fault, guv'nor, it's a rotten play.'

The house lights came on. The well-dressed poured into the small lobby to wait for their carriages; the gallery emptied itself into the cold streets. H. G. Wells spoke to Shaw. They walked away from the theatre together. James escaped as soon as he could. He had his answer. He had said he would 'chuck' the theatre if *Guy Domville* did not succeed. The theatre had 'chucked' him.

BOOK TWO
THE TREACHEROUS YEARS
1895–1900

Never say you know the last word about any
human heart.

HENRY JAMES

Part One
The Black Abyss

26

Postscripts

WE know that Henry James walked home in the cold damp from St James's to Kensington after he left the theatre on the night of 5 January 1895. He later said that he felt weary, bruised, disgusted, sickened. 'I swore to myself an oath never again to have anything to do with a business which lets one into such traps, abysses and heart-break.' The audience – that is, the gallery – had behaved, he said, like a set of savages pouncing on a gold watch. James's choice of image was apt. To him *Guy Domville* had been like a tightly-built gleaming golden piece of machinery, an artefact of which he was extremely proud. The play had had every advantage of production. And yet it had failed. In that strange and necessary way in which we defend ourselves against demons and accidents James sought, in his anguish, blame outside his art, outside himself. One couldn't hand a gold watch to a set of savages and expect it to survive; one couldn't make a sow's ear out of a silk purse. And yet he had been trying 'heroic-ally', as he said, to convert the sow's ear into something fine, even exquisite. It was time to purge himself of such heroisms.

From all that he wrote later it was clear that he returned to De Vere Gardens in a deeper state of shock than he knew. He had made mental allowance for possible failure; that could happen to the best of dramatists. He had not allowed however for a display of violence against himself – he who had been an unobtrusive figure in the London literary world for so many years. He had been hooted by a brutal mob as if he were some old-time criminal, led through the streets for execution. He felt numb; too numb and indignant to experience the full pain of his hurt. He thought of his play as a bird winged by a huntsman, doomed to early death. These had been, he said, 'the most horrible hours of my life'.

I

Early next morning [Sir Edmund Gosse would write twenty-five years later] I called at 34 De Vere Gardens, hardly daring to press the bell for fear of the worst of news, so shattered with excitement had the playwright been on the previous evening. I was astonished to find him perfectly calm; he had slept well and was breakfasting with appetite. The theatrical bubble in which he had lived a tormented existence for five years was wholly and finally broken, and he returned, even in that earliest conversation, to the discussion of the work which he had so long and so sadly neglected, the art of direct prose narrative. I recall him saying to me, after the fiasco of *Guy Domville*, 'At all events, I have escaped for ever from the foul fiend Excision!' He vibrated [so Gosse remembered] with the sense of release, and he began to enjoy, physically and intellectually, a freedom which had hitherto been foreign to his nature.

Memory has a way of telescoping fact; and Sir Edmund's testimony must be retouched by documentary evidence. It is doubtful whether Gosse called alone early the next morning. He had been invited to lunch, with at least three other guests, W. E. Norris, the Victorian novelist, who had come to London from Devon to see James's play; Julian Sturgis whom James had known as a boy, and Philip Burne-Jones, son of the painter and himself a skilful sketcher. This was the young man who had shown such militancy the previous evening towards the ill-behaved gallery. James received his guests with melancholy politeness. He had planned the luncheon and he went through with it. 'You would have been proud of your friend,' he later told Margaret Brooke, Ranee of Sarawak. He was far from being 'perfectly calm', as Gosse would claim; he was in a state of nervous exhaustion. But he put on a bold face. He confessed a day or two later to Norris that he had become aware, sitting at the table, how great was his weariness after five weeks of intensive rehearsal and the rude climax of the previous evening. He told Norris he would never forget 'your kind, tender-embarrassed face when you came in to see me'. His fatigue, he explained, made him 'mingle but poorly in the fine, rich gossip of some of my guests'. This suggests that James was silent much of the time, and that Gosse and the younger men bridged the awkwardness with anecdote.

James felt much better the following day, after a good night's rest – sufficiently well to return to the theatre and sit in quiet anonymity in the gallery where the rumpus had occurred. The audience was well-behaved; the production went smoothly. Alexander had made some furthers cuts, to which James reluctantly consented. Nothing occurred to disturb the players. At the end there was warm applause for the cast. In this way James satisfied himself that the events of the first night were not altogether induced by what he had written. Alexander showed him an unsigned telegram received on the opening night, 'with hearty wishes for a complete failure', sent, he discovered, by two women from a nearby post office. The press carried reports that there had been an anti-Alexander 'cabal'; certain individuals, it was said, were avenging a slighted young actress. Various witnesses testified that the roughs had a leader and 'refreshed themselves copiously between the acts'. There had been apparently a variety of motives in the behaviour of the audience. But the central fact was that *Guy Domville* had been a failure.

2

James's play had a good reception from the establishment critics; he spoke with approval in particular of the notices of William Archer and Clement Scott. He made no mention however of Bernard Shaw's review, one of the most cordial given the play. Was it good sense, Shaw wrote, to accuse James 'of a want of grip of the realities of life because he gives us a hero who sacrificed his love to a strong and noble vocation for the Church?' And yet when some unmannerly playgoer, untouched by love or religion, howled at this, the intelligent spectators were asked to admit 'if you please, that Mr James is no dramatist, on the general ground that "the drama's laws the drama's patrons give." Pray, which of its patrons?' queried Shaw, 'the cultivated majority who, like myself and all the ablest of my colleagues, applauded Mr James on Saturday, or the handful of rowdies who brawled at him.' He added: 'It is the business of the dramatic critic to educate these dunces, not to echo them.' James's dramatic authorship was valid when the right people were in the theatre. 'Line after line comes with such a delicate turn and fall that I unhesitatingly challenge any of our popular dramatists to write a scene in verse with half the beauty of Mr James's prose.' He likened the music in James's lines to an evening of Mozart after Verdi. *Guy Domville* was a story and not a mere situation – a story of fine sentiment and delicate manners. Wilde, Pinero, Jones had treated Alexander as if he were a tailor's dummy. James treated him, Shaw said, as if he were an artist.

Wells's review was written in the tone of the scientist. It was question of a prognosis – and the prognosis was bad. The play had too many faults. The principal one was Alexander. 'In the first act Mr Alexander is a didactic puritan; in the second a fine generous

blade; in the third he is that impossible, noble, iron-grey Mr Alexander that we have seen before.' This sounded as if it were written by a
frequenter of the theatre rather than a novice. The play, said Wells,
was a fine conception, weakly developed; it was beautifully written
but too delicate for acting, 'and whether that is the fault of player
or playwright is a very pretty question'. Everything pointed to 'an
early deathbed'.

Arnold Bennett, disguised as 'Cécile', offered a conscientious and
platitudinous notice, tailored for his feminine readers. The future
author of *The Old Wives' Tale* found 'fitful beauty' in James's work
and certain 'exquisite scenes'. The first act was 'studded with gems
of dialogue', of 'too serene a beauty' to suit audiences accustomed
to the 'scintillating gauds' of Oscar Wilde and Henry Arthur Jones.
The melodrama of the later acts however was hardly in keeping with
the 'unrivalled work which Mr James has produced in fiction'.

In this fashion the 'new men' of the 1890s rallied to the side of
art – and indeed of courtesy. The older reviewers were staunchly
with James. A. B. Walkley brilliantly contrasted Wilde's new play
with *Guy Domville*. Wilde's, he wrote, would not move the English
drama forward an inch, nor would it add to his reputation. James's
play was 'a defeat out of which it is possible for many victories to
spring; in gathering the enemy's spears into his heart he has made
a gap through which his successors will be able to pour in triumph'.
James himself took no such heroic view of what he had done; but he
came to see that he had, in spite of his stooping to conquer, struck
a blow for literature and for a new drama. *Guy Domville* ran through
its allotted month, the minimum time required to exhaust the credit
of Alexander's loyal followers, and even a few days longer to include
some profitable matinées at Brighton. Then came a crowning bit of
irony. Faced with failure, Alexander rushed into rehearsal a play
by the very dramatist whose work was being compared with James's,
whom James himself had used as a measure and augury for his own
work. *The Importance of Being Earnest*, Wilde's comic masterpiece,
settled in promptly at the St James's for a promising run.

'There is nothing, fortunately, so dead as a dead play – unless it
be sometimes a living one,' Henry wrote to his brother. 'Oscar
Wilde's farce which followed *Guy Domville* is, I believe, a great
success – and with his two roaring successes running now at once
he must be raking in the profits.' *Guy Domville* had yielded James
£275 in royalties, token of the prosperity that would have awaited

him had he succeeded. On the closing night James said good-bye to the cast. 'It has been a great relief,' he wrote to Elizabeth Robins, 'to feel that one of the most detestable incidents of my life has closed.'

27

Embarrassments

JAMES went, five days after the *Guy Domville* opening, to pay a promised visit to the Archbishop of Canterbury, Edward White Benson, at the archiepiscopal residence, Addington, outside London. The Archbishop had at various times expressed admiration for James's work; on one occasion he had quoted from *Roderick Hudson* in a sermon. It must have been soothing to the injured playwright's self-esteem to be received in the ecclesiastical family circle with warmth and affection. In the great house James found two of the Archbishop's sons, Arthur Christopher, then a master at Eton, a prolific writer of verses and of Victorian 'familiar' essays, and E. F. Benson, later to be a popular writer of light novels. Both remembered James's talk and recorded it. He said he had been, during his play-writing, in a dim 'subaqueous' world – had been 'bewildered and hampered by the medium'. Now, he said, he felt he had got his head 'such as it was', above the surface; he had at last 'a new perspective and an unimpeded vision'. This picture of himself as a drowning man suggests the depth of his melancholy; and equally suggestive was James's fascination, as he sat and conversed with the Archbishop over a cup of tea, with a little anecdote which the ecclesiastic told him. They had been talking about ghost stories. Both agreed that the best had been told; that psychical research tended to wash ghosts clean of all mystery and horror. 'Recorded and attested ghosts,' James was to write, 'are as little expressive, as little dramatic, above all as little continuous and conscious and responsive, as is consistent with their taking the trouble – and an immense trouble they find it, we gather – to appear at all.' Having dismissed 'certified ghosts', and lamented 'a beautiful lost form' the Archbishop, in the waning light, spoke of an incident he had heard long ago, of a couple of small children in some out-of-the-way place to whom the spirits of certain 'bad' servants were believed to have appeared; they had seemed to beckon, invite, solicit across dangerous places, such as the deep ditch of a sunken fence, so that the children might destroy themselves. The Archbishop was vague – but the ghostliness, the mystery, the terror was in the anecdote; the terror of nightmare, the fright of innocence before the unknown. It was dim, eerie, the very 'shadow of a shadow'. And it touched a raw nerve at this moment in the life of the novelist.

He had talked of his struggle in a dim water-world, as if he were drowning; he had suddenly been hurt by violent and uncontrollable forces. Henry James could indeed muse on a tale of horrible threats to children, the baleful influence of the extra-human that lies in wait for man in the very midst of serenity. In James's infancy there had been the 'vastation' of his father, who in the quiet of the domestic dining-room had been suddenly seized with a terror of the soul, as if some horrible goblin squatted in the room beside him. For months after, the elder Henry's mind had been haunted by this vision. His experience had been personal, subjective, private; the son's recent ordeal was actual, physical, public. Yet the two episodes were related. Both represented the beasts that lie in wait for men within the depths of life, the element of mystery – the nameless terror of nightmare.

Returning to De Vere Gardens Henry James scribbled in his notebook: 'Note here the ghost-story told me at Addington (evening of Thursday the 10th) by the Archbishop ... the mere vague undetailed faint sketch of it.' Three years would elapse before he would be ready to write *The Turn of the Screw*.

I

He had pronounced the detestable incident closed; but he could not stop the pain as easily as he could lower the curtain on his play. The behaviour of the audience at the St James's had struck at the very heart of his self-esteem, his pride and sovereignty as artist. He spoke of the theatre as an abyss – an abyss 'of vulgarity and British platitude' – and also as 'a black abyss'. The theatre doubtless had been one kind of hell, and he was now out of it. He lived on however in his other, his private hell – wounded, sore, depressed. In one of his letters of this time he spoke of being plunged into 'the nethermost circle of the Inferno'.

This was James's journey through the wastes of the symbolic sea of ice, the 'heart of darkness' of which one of his admirers would write. His personal letters after *Guy Domville* were a cry of outrage and defiance. Later there came the nursing of private grief, the search for balm, the rationalization and self-consolation that might ease his spirit. To his brother he wrote:

I no sooner found myself in the presence of those yelling barbarians of the first night and learned what could be the savagery of their disappointment that one wasn't the *same* as everything else they had ever seen than the dream and delusion of my having made a successful appeal to the cosy, childlike, naïve, domestic British imagination (which was what I had calculated,) dropped from me in the twinkling of an eye. I saw they couldn't care one straw for a damned young last-century English Catholic, who lived in an old-time Catholic world and acted, with every one else in the play, from remote and romantic motives. The whole thing was for them remote, and all the intensity of one's ingenuity couldn't make it anything else.

He recognized that the attitude of the theatregoer towards a story in a play was different from his attitude towards a story in a book. And so, with many nuances, he found explanations. But the one to which he adhered above all, and which was the fundamental truth, was that his was too refined and subtle a talent to reach the 'common man'. The truth had been before him during all his 'dramatic years' and he could not say that the Comptons had not warned him. Yet it had required a rebuff of the most violent kind to bring it home, so deep had been his ambition and determination to achieve stage glory – and the royalties that went with success. 'Produce a play,' he wrote to William, 'and you will know, better than I can tell you, how such an ordeal – odious in its essence! – is made tolerable and palatable by great success; and how in many ways accordingly non-success may be tormenting and tragic, a bitterness of every hour, ramifying into every throb of one's consciousness.' When he looked at his curious experience through the light of his intellect he could see it with wry and sardonic humour, charged with irony and paradox; and he wrote this into a series of stories about writers who are applauded, although their works are unread, or who try to 'take the measure of the huge, flat foot of the public' but who succeed only in writing another distinguished failure. Commenting on the deluge of mail which descended on him, James said that twenty-five years of 'literary virtue and of remarkable prose never have brought me a five-and-twentieth of the letters that fifteen vulgar nights of the odious stage have caused to descend upon me'. To the end of his days James was to wonder at this anomaly between achievement and the image – particularly the newspaper image – of the artist: the audience-worship of the personality without the understanding of the *persona*. He was to see, a few months later, the massive Victorian funeral offered the votary of classicism in painting, Lord Leighton, and to muse on the elaborate mourning and the way in which Leighton's artistic relics were ignored; buried, the painter was quickly forgotten. James had once put Leighton into one of his stories (*The Private Life*) as an individual who was a superb performer in public and who ceased to exist the moment he had no audience. 'So much beauty and so little passion,' James mused. The public could recognize neither the presence of the one, nor the absence of the other.

2

He was in mourning for himself, for his dead self, who had floundered and struggled when the waters of disaster closed over his head. In his notebooks, he now returned to the idea for a story recorded a year earlier.

I was turning over the drama, the tragedy, the general situation of disappointed ambition – and more particularly that of the artist, th man of letters: I mean of the ambition, the pride, the passion, the idea of greatness, that has been smothered and defeated by circumstances, by the opposition of life, of fate, of character, of weakness, of folly, of misfortune; and the drama that resides in – that may be bound up with – such a situation. I thought of the tragic consciousness, the living death, the helpless pity, the deep humiliation.

And then – 'the idea of *death* both checked and caught me'. He began to toy anew with the story of this man, 'the spectator of his own tragedy'.

Pride, passion, pity, humiliation, 'the living death'. James's words help us to glimpse a few of the deeper feelings of the struggling artist, caught in mid-life, 'smothered and defeated by circumstances' – some of his own making. He went on to think of this man whose passional and sentient life is dead, as finding renewed life in some woman. James was pushing away from himself the most painful part of his experience, and in fantasy making a woman the repository of his anguish (as he would do in *The Beast in the Jungle*.) 'She *is his Dead Self,'* he wrote, underlining the words, *'he is alive in her and dead in himself.'* Having written out the note he finally abandoned the idea; he feared 'there isn't much in it : it would take a deuce of a deal of following up'. It would require more than this : the fortitude to deal with his own failure.

Outside his notebooks, his letters reflect his soreness of heart. 'My youth is gone,' he writes to his old friend, Sarah Wister. 'Life's nothing – unless heroic and sacrificial,' he tells the Archbishop's son, Arthur Benson. 'I pay the penalty of my magnificent imagination,' he also writes, and twice he speaks, in a letter and in a novel, of having 'the imagination of disaster'. He remarks that 'one outlives some of one's complications – if one doesn't live into too many others'. He is weary of London; he feels as if he were homeless. He had had this experience after the death of his parents, and the end of the family house in Cambridge. His comfortable De Vere Gardens flat no longer seemed to suffice. He talks of finding 'a much needed bath of silence and solitude' in some rented house in the English countryside. His preoccupation with houses and children fills his writings at this moment – children, unwanted, displaced, seeking an anchorage and love.

He spoke of himself as unwanted a fortnight after the collapse of his play in a letter to his old friend William Dean Howells who, with a certain prescience, had written before *Guy Domville*, to remind James that whatever the outcome of his theatrical ventures, he was still primarily a novelist, possessed of a public that waited to read everything he wrote. In some such words (for the letter does not appear to have been preserved) Howells touched James's artist-sense, and implied that the winds of the market-place could not alter the record of James's achievement nor his ability to create – nor the devotion of his old friends. In the midst of rehearsals James had read Howells's letter hastily. Now, taking it up to answer it, he found unexpected comfort in it.

You put your finger sympathetically on the place and spoke of what I wanted you to speak of. I *have* felt, for a long time past, that I have fallen upon evil days – every sign or symbol of one's being in the least *wanted*, anywhere or by any one, having so utterly failed. A new generation, that I know not, and mainly prize not, has taken universal possession. The sense of being utterly out of it weighed me down, and I asked myself what the future would be. All these melancholies were qualified indeed by one redeeming reflection – the sense of how little, for a good while past (for reasons very logical, but accidental and temporary) I had been producing. I did say to myself 'Produce again – produce; produce better than ever, and all will yet be well.'

'Every sign or symbol of one's being in the least *wanted*, anywhere or by anyone.' James spoke not only of recent history; one of his reasons for attempting plays had been the poor sale of his books, and his waning position in the magazines.

Until the other month Henry Harper, here, made a friendly overture to me on the part of his magazine, no sign, no symbol of any sort, has come to me from any periodical whatever – and many visible demonstrations of their having, on the contrary, no use for me. I can't go into details – and they would make you turn pale! I'm utterly out of it *here* – and *Scribner*, the *Century*, the *Cosmopolitan*, will have nothing to say to me – above all for fiction. The *Atlantic* and H[oughton] and M[ifflin] treat me like the dust beneath their feet; and the Macmillans, here, have cold-shouldered me out of all relation with them. All this I needn't say, is for your *segretissimo* ear.

Howells had at least assured him about his 'book-position'. James had never, in any event cared for the magazine world, he told his friend. 'I hate the hurried little subordinate part that one plays in the catchpenny picture-book – and the negation of all literature that the insolence of the picture-book imposes.'

This communion with his old-time editor had a tranquillizing effect. On the morning after writing the letter James roused himself and set down, with an air of finality, the following words in his notebook:

I take up my *own* old pen again – the pen of all my old unforgettable efforts and sacred struggles. To myself – today – I need say no more. Large and full and high the future still opens. It is now indeed that I may do the work of my life. And I will.

After this moment of resolution, he set down a row of crosses, as if to denote a contemplative pause. Then, 'I have only to *face* my problems.' Another row of crosses. Then, 'But all this is of the ineffable – too deep and pure for any utterance. Shrouded in sacred silence let it rest.'

28

The Young Heroes

DURING the first phase of his work in the theatre, in 1891 and 1892, Henry James had written two tales whose pages are filled with personal history. One was a story of an itinerant family on the Continent and the fate of their gifted son – Americans as footloose as his own family had been long ago. The other was a story of a rigid military family, whose tradition was to supply gallant soldiers for England's army. In the first story, *The Pupil*, the sensitive boy is ashamed of his down-at-heels parents who lead a hand-to-mouth existence and expect the world to provide for them. In the second, called *Owen Wingrave*, the young Owen, a few years older than the pupil, struggles with his family's militarism. He is determined to study the art of literature rather than the arts of war. Both heroes have in common their perception of the false values by which their families live; and both die as a consequence of their self-assertion. Women play a cruel role in their death. Morgan Moreen dies at a moment when his mother ceases to offer him the protection of her shoddy way of life. Owen dies proving to a hard and demanding fiancée that he is not a coward. The stories are markedly different: the life-myth they embody is the same.

I

James got his hint for *The Pupil* from his Florentine friend and doctor, William Wilberforce Baldwin, a gifted healer who had attended a generation of wayfaring Americans as they passed through Italy. Even Baldwin's envious rival, Dr Axel Munthe, who practised in Rome, admitted that Baldwin had 'the inestimable gift of inspiring confidence in his patients'. He had, said Munthe, 'a striking personality, a fine forehead, extraordinary penetrating and intelligent eyes, a remarkable facility for speaking, very winning manners'. Baldwin had ministered to James after his attack of jaundice in Venice in 1887. He had been Miss Woolson's doctor as well. He would have other distinguished patients, Mark Twain, and Howells, and in the new century Edith Wharton. James spoke of him as an 'American physician of genius' and as 'a charming and glowing little man'. Son of a New York State clergyman, he had earned his way as a school-teacher, studied medicine in Long Island Hospital, and after a brief period of practice in Connecticut had gone abroad to work with the great heart-specialists in Vienna. He had set up practice in Florence and became a civic leader; he helped purify the city's water and kept a cow to supply milk for his own children; his curiosity and alertness never left him. He knew the medicinal value of most spas on the Continent.

During Henry James's 1890 visit to Italy, Dr Baldwin had proposed to him that they tour small out-of-the-way Etruscan towns, using rail and carriage as available, and walking to less accessible spots. Baldwin knew these places well; he was in the habit of setting up clinics for the peasants in the Abruzzi during the summer. Accompanied by an obese Falstaffian friend and language-tutor of Baldwin's, named Taccini who was their guide, they visited Volterra, Montepulciano and Torrita, and certain villages in between. They stayed nights in peasant homes and James never used the common trough for his ablutions, insisting always on a morning bath even when he had to take it in the large deep tub in which the farm's bread was kneaded. The little trip proved however too hot and fatiguing to James, who had, of old, been a long-distance walker. He came way from this adventure, nevertheless, with one of his finest tales. 'Years ago, one summer day, in a very hot Italian railway-carriage, which stopped and dawdled everywhere, favouring conversation, a friend with whom I shared it, a doctor of medicine, who had come from a far country to settle in Florence, happened to speak to me of a wonderful American family.' In his preface James went on to describe this family to which, briefly, Baldwin had been doctor. It was an itinerant family; it jumped its hotel bills; its members were an 'odd, adventurous, extravagant band of high but rather unauthenticated pretensions'. They had a small boy, who was precocious, but who had a weak heart. The boy saw the prowling and precarious life of his parents and siblings, 'and measured and judged them'. Here, James wrote, was 'more than enough for a summer's day even in old Italy – here was a thumping windfall'.

2

This was indeed a windfall and James wrote *The Pupil* at the end of that summer of 1890 when he was back in London. He too had been a precocious boy on the Continent; his father, though not as much 'a man of the world' as the parent described by Baldwin, had dragged his family about from place to place; Henry and his brothers had been 'hotel children'; they had known the loneliness of strange places and been confided to tutors and governesses. He had memories of anxieties provoked by money shortages, for there had been a moment during the American depression of 1856–7 (when he was 14) which caused his parents to beat a hurried retreat from a luxurious apartment in Paris to an economical house at Boulogne-sur-mer. Out of this personal past and Dr Baldwin's anecdote, James wove his tale of a sensitive boy and his attachment to his tutor, the first of a series of the 1890s in which children suffer from parental neglect and indifference, and little boys die asserting their claim to live.

A poignant tale (we see the boy between the ages of 11 and 15), *The Pupil* was written with the technical virtuosity of these years. It was told through a double-vision : the boy's 'troubled vision' of his family 'as reflected in the vision', James explained, 'also troubled enough, of his devoted friend' the tutor. Like the James family, the Moreens are a country unto themselves, and 'ultramoreen' is a key word in their private vocabulary. Little Morgan knows from the first that his tutor, Pemberton, a graduate of Yale and sometime student at Oxford, will never be paid for his services; he attaches himself to him with the tenderness of a loved and neglected child who feels also guilty and ashamed at his family's improvidence and dishonesty. The tutor, on his side, becomes attached to his charge; he stays on, unpaid, in conflict between his personal needs and his feelings for Morgan – but not a little also because there is something irresponsible and shiftless in his own character; for we learn early that he spent all his resources, during a year on the Continent, in 'a single full wave of experience'. He too had a touch of the 'ultramoreen'.

There is humour and pathos in the way in which James describes the life of the vagabond Moreens, first at Nice, then in Paris; their dash to a wintry and harsh Venice, their return to a further shabby life at Nice. Their false standards and values, their façade of arrogance and helplessness – 'a houseful of Bohemians who wanted tremendously to be Philistines' – their belief in a providing world that doesn't provide, their petty luxuries and pretence to style – all this is shown as it affects the growing child. Quick of mind, Morgan is thoroughly aware of his mother's shameless use of Pemberton's love for him; if the tutor finds happiness in the family, she reminds him, he needs no other reward; she even borrows money from him. The ultimate parental decision to take advantage of the attachment and 'unload' Morgan on the tutor leads to a swift and complex ending. Pemberton had had a fantasy that the two might some day go off to lead a life together, away from the Moreen cares and improvisations. Morgan entered into this fantasy as if it were an 'escape' story in a boy's magazine. Suddenly he discovers the power of reality over the imagined fiction. Expecting to find Pemberton enthusiastic, he sees him wavering. In that 'morning twilight of childhood' which Henry James so clearly understood, in which there was 'nothing at a given moment you could say a clever child didn't know', Morgan learns the terrible truth – and his life becomes a void. Betrayed by his parents, frightened by the glimpse of vacillation in the beloved tutor, not old enough to tolerate disillusion, he feels himself suddenly alone. The panic is too much for his weak heart.

The tale, coming to James from the case-book of the gifted Baldwin, brilliantly re-imagined out of his own life, inaugurated the novelist's great decade of the short story. However, for all its remarkable qualities it suffered a misadventure at the start. The novelist had received a request for a series of tales from the new editor of the *Atlantic Monthly*, Horace Scudder, and he dispatched *The Pupil* promptly. Scudder had a sharp negative reaction, and for the first time in the history of his relation with the *Atlantic*, one of James's stories was rejected. Scudder may have been worried by the hint of unconscious homosexuality in the attachment between tutor and boy. Yet there is no evidence that in the early 1890s – before the trial of Oscar Wilde – there was any such awareness or alertness to deviation among readers or editors: friendship and affection between tutors and their charges was regarded as normal in the Victorian age. A more plausible theory is that the prosaic Scudder was worried that the *Atlantic*'s readers would resent a story about an American family which jumped its hotel bills and behaved with such deliberate mendacity. Americans were not supposed to do such things. James expressed his 'shock of a perfectly honest surprise' at being rejected. He felt the responsibility to the magazine's readers, when it was a question of 'an old and honourable reputation', should be left to the author himself. *Longman's Magazine* accepted the tale in England; it was reprinted thereafter many times, and remains one of James's most popular stories.

3

Owen Wingrave was written early in 1892, just after the death of Alice James. 'Owen' is a Scottish name; it means 'the young soldier'. The title of James's tale accordingly meant 'The Young Soldier Wins His Grave'. James later said he got his idea one day when he saw a young man in Kensington Gardens, reading a book, in one of the penny chairs; this had furnished him with the image of his young pacifist. James's notebooks supply another source. The idea occurred during a reading of the memoirs of Napoleon's General Marbot – a three-volume work popular in England throughout the 1890s. The flood-tide of Napoleonic memoir-writing was at its height; old diaries were being found; old memories were being searched. And James's notebook-entry begins with the words:

The idea of the *soldier* – produced a little by the fascinated perusal of Marbot's magnificent memoirs. The image, the type, the vision, the character, as a transmitted, hereditary, mystical, almost supernatural force, challenge, incentive, almost haunting, apparitional presence, in the life and consciousness of a descendant – a descendant of totally different temperament and range of qualities, yet subjected to a superstitious awe in relation to carrying out the tradition of absolutely *military* valour – personal bravery and honour.

James's idea was to create a hero who was a soldier in every fibre, but who had a horror of 'the blood, the carnage, the suffering'. He would make his hero perform a brave soldierly act even while defying militarism.

This detailed note, at first glance, seems unrelated to the death of James's sister; but the story he wrote during 1892 in its picture of the dead weight of 'family' and personal past as brought to bear upon the living, reached very far back into the novelist's experience; it stemmed from the time of late adolescence, from the days of the Civil War when public opinion had told him he must become a soldier while his own terror of violence and fratricidal murder, his own will to peace and to poetry, held him back. The three volumes of Marbot's memoirs which James read have survived in their expensive bindings; they disclose in their marked pages what James himself felt when he spoke of 'fascinated perusal'. Marbot was one of Napoleon's most articulate generals; he was the second son of a soldier, and James was always interested in second sons. Marbot had written his memoirs in obedience to the Emperor's wish that he 'continue to write in defence of the glory of the French armies'. Now almost a century after the Napoleonic era, Marbot's family had published the manuscript. The numerous page-numbers pencilled in James's hand at the back of each volume refer us to particular passages of violence and glory – the description of a cavalry charge, the courage of the unknown, the battles of Austerlitz and Aspern, the coincidences of combat: Marbot coming to consciousness after being wounded and finding himself naked in the snow, stripped of uniform and gear by those who gave him up for dead; Marbot's constant references to his mother; the Emperor saying to Marbot, 'Note that I do not give you an order; I merely express a wish'; Napoleon's 'magic personality' and its effect on the troops; the great cold at Vilna; the delight of the bed, after weeks in the open – one gets the impression in the sections marked by James that he read the memoirs with a deep identification and absorption but with confused feelings. He abhorred violence, he respected courage. He was impressed, as his notebook shows, with the sense of military tradition. The Marbots had all been soldiers, and the sons of soldiers. General Marbot fights only when it is a question of combat; the battles with brigands and looters, the summary executions, he leaves to others. He is single-minded; he serves only the Emperor – only *gloire*.

From the dates on the bindings and of publication, it is clear that James bought at this time a large number of volumes about the First Empire; some show signs of careful reading and contain marked passages. In his library the novelist had, in addition to Marbot, the memoirs of Marshal Macdonald, Masson's book about Napoleon and women and his volume of anecdotes about the Emperor's private life; the reminiscences of General Bigarré, the aide of King Joseph (James seems to have read with particular interest his account of his adventures among the blacks); Arthur Levy's *Napoléon Intime* of 1893; Barry O'Meara's earlier two-volume account of Napoleon on St Helena. James also owned Lanfrey's five-volume life of Napoleon as well as dozens of volumes of letters and biographies of figures in the Empire and after. Napoleon had cast a long shadow; and Henry James, who had seen the pageantry of the Second Empire and lived in a Paris in which the memories of Napoleon remained vivid, was clearly attracted to him more as a man of action and a symbol of glory than as a soldier. In all probability his feelings for Napoleon were derived also from his close reading of Balzac; for it was in the pages of Balzac during his youth that James had found a supreme example of imagination resolved into action, the will – and the egotism – of grandeur, pushed to a denial of the impossible. We find in James's memoir of Wolcott Balestier words about the young man's having 'Napoleonic propensities' – a 'complete incapacity to recognize difficulties, his immediate adoption of his own or, in other words of an original solution.' It charmed him in the young Balestier; it dazzled him in Balzac. And it dazzled him in the records of the Empire. But he had no illusions about Bonaparte, for in *Owen Wingrave* (where the young tutor has 'the stature of the great Napoleon') Owen believes him 'a monster for whom language has no adequate name'.

4

The tale of the young soldier is rooted in James's experience and vision of a whole era and linked also to the bloodshed – and glories – of the American Civil War. The actual story contains the usual James family constellation; it reminds us in particular of the way in which Henry was under pressure as a young man to leave art alone, urged by his father, his practical mother and his elder brother, to take a steady job and avoid the hazards of publication. He had wanted simply to be 'literary'; he had resisted the family pressure and achieved what it had regarded as impossible. He had refused to study science. He had thrown away his law books. He had quietly and determinedly locked himself in his room and written his tales and read novels while his brothers banged and shouted. So young Owen Wingrave goes into the park carrying the poems of Goethe when he should be reading the hard prose of Clausewitz.

Owen is a second son like Henry; the older brother has been locked away, a mental case; and upon the second son falls the burden of upholding the family name. The name has a single historical virtue: that of the soldier. Aunt Jane Wingrave represents 'the expansive property of the British name'. She is a veritable grenadier. 'If she was military it was because she sprang from a military house and because she wouldn't for the world have been anything but what the Wingraves had been.' James adds : 'She was almost vulgar about her ancestors.'

Owen's father died of an Afghan sabre-cut. Owen's grandfather, Sir Philip, survived to 80, 'a merciless old warrior'. At Paramore, seat of the Wingraves, there is a haunted room; here a miltary ancestor killed a son as rebellious as Owen. The drama of the tale fills one evening. To Paramore come Owen's 'crammer' Spencer Coyle, who is preparing him for military college; his best friend, also destined for the army and his intended, Kate, who never knew her father, for he was killed in a war. All assail young Wingrave. Sir Philip will cut him off without a penny. His friend and his coach believe in more subtle modes of coercion; to the sweetheart he is simply a 'coward'. She will not believe that he has already slept in the haunted room. Owen resists this terrible pressure. He would have war set down as a capital crime; he would hang cabinet ministers who declare it. The youth is handsome, original, talented; we see him largely through the eyes of his 'persecutors'. Owen has read his military lore – Caesar, Marlborough, Frederick; he talks of the miseries of war, the widows, 'bereavement and mourning and memory ... the echoes of battles and bad news'. His friend reports that 'he hates poor old Bonaparte worst of all'. The coach rejoins, 'Well, poor old Bonaparte *was* a brute. He was a frightful ruffian.' When Wingrave's friend questions whether he has 'the military temperament' of his ancestors, Owen's rejoinder is 'Damn the military temperament!'

We do not hear his quarrel with his sweetheart; but we know their voices were raised, and that he locks himself into the haunted room. There he is found in the eerie dawn, after strange noises have been heard during the night. Owen lies on the floor, dressed as he had last been seen. In the original version of the tale James wrote, 'He looked like a young soldier on the battlefield.' In the revision fifteen years later James changed this to 'He was all the young soldier on the gained field.' Thus he heightened the story's irony. The young pacifist has been a soldier in spite of himself : he has won a victory for his own beliefs. But the victory has in reality been won by tradition, by family. Owen could not escape his fate.

A vivid tale, it is one of the most 'deterministic' James ever wrote. He took small stock in it, for he had conceived of it as for the larger public – 'a little subject for the *Graphic* – so I mustn't make it "psychological" – they understand that no more than a donkey understands a violin'. Nevertheless he had embodied in *Owen Wingrave* the single theme which haunts his work throughout his middle years – that of the son, usually the second son, who must bear the responsibility for the family's traditions; he is coerced by his 'past'; he must struggle to find a free life for himself.

5

The two tales – those of the unhappy pupil and the young pacifist – were recollections of adolescence. They were of a piece with the experience of *Guy Domville*. It was as if James had to return constantly to a dream of second sons, forced to take up family burdens; Owen Wingrave was supposed to be a soldier when he wanted to be a poet; young Domville wanted his monastery, but was told to go into the world and have children; Nick Dormer (*The Tragic Muse*) wanted to be a painter; but his family expected him to follow his father's footsteps and be a politician. The young heroes are subjected not only to family pressure, but to a kind of inexorable weight of history. And resistance is punishable by defeat – or death. Nick Dormer lived, after defying his family, but his price would be the loneliness of art. Guy Domville renounced 'life' to take his vows in his monastery. The ivory tower, the religious cell – there one could live with the eternal, and avoid the passions and the demands of flesh and family. But for those who did not withdraw, the young, the self-asserting, the verdict in James was death; and women were at hand to preside at the execution. Life had, indeed, stepped in to prove to James the truth of his fictions. He, a second son, had asserted himself by writing plays in defiance of his long-established reticences. He had left his ivory tower. His punishment had been inevitable. The world he strenuously wooed had told him he was not wanted. He had suffered a kind of spiritual death like the young Owen, killed by irreversible forces, by the fates; or like Morgan Moreen for whom there seemed to be no escape, for whom 'family' was more than an historical weight. It was a pressing humiliation, an eternal shame.

On 15 January 1895 James wrote to a friend that the theatre was an abyss of 'vulgarity and platitude, and I suppose one ought to be glad of any accident which disengages one from it'. Three weeks later he was planning a new play. Did he still see some glimmer of hope? was there still a fantasy of recovery and conquest – and revenge? The impulse had a generous prompting. Ellen Terry, the reigning actress, had attended the first night to see her sister play the lead in *Guy Domville*. She had witnessed James's humiliation. A woman of quick sympathies and openness of feeling, she invited him to call on her. In his notebook of 6 February 1895 he records 'I went yesterday, by appointment, to see Ellen Terry'. Miss Terry asked him to write a one-act play; she was going to the United States with Sir Henry Irving; and she had a fancy to play an American woman. What better than a curtain-raiser from the pen of Henry James, for his compatriots? Ever practical, and pushing aside all vows, he re-read an old note, a sketch for a comedy he had wanted to write for Ada Rehan two years earlier. The idea of being played by Miss Terry – and in America! – was irresistible.

Strangest of all was the plot of the play he wanted to write – 'an American woman as the beneficent intervening agent in the drama of an English social, an English family, crisis.' He envisaged 'a wild ostensible radical of an eldest son' and 'a sympathetic and sensible younger brother'. The younger brother, as usual in James, would be called upon to assume responsibility for an old house. (Later James would eliminate the older brother altogether.) The second son would be the radical, and like Owen, like Guy, like Nick Dormer, he would be expected to sacrifice his feelings and ambitions for family. He must forget his radicalism, cross party lines, become a Tory – and all to retrieve an encumbered estate, a decaying old family house. This was James's newest fancy – almost as if he were rewriting *Guy Domville*. He was interested in the twist he would give to this personal myth. The young radiant American woman – this would be Miss Terry – would arrive at the house, convince the radical he must change politics, buy up the mortgages, maintain the family tradition. And she would be the fairy godmother. American democratic sentiment would support British conservatism: American dollars would bring about the triumph of Family. All would be saved – all but the hero's political integrity, a point James chose to overlook, as he had overlooked the Catholic vocation in Guy Domville's switch from the Church. This was his cheerful re-dreaming of the theme, his summoning of magical aids to pull him out of despair. Mrs Gracedew is one of James's charming American heroines. One imagines her in the form and figure of Miss Terry, offering the novelist, at this moment of crisis, the beneficent assurance that if the world did not value its play-writing son, she at least was prepared to do so. The play would be written that summer – and in the ensuing years would have a complex history.

29

Discoveries

BY the middle of February, little more than a month after *Guy Domville*, Henry James had begun to dissociate the disaster from himself – 'it is rapidly growing to seem to have belonged to the history of someone else'. This transference of the unbearable burden to mythical shoulders, made it possible for him to try to work again. 'I have my head, thank God, full of visions,' he wrote in his notebook. 'One has never too many – one has never enough. Ah just to let one's self go – at last.'

But he couldn't let himself go. Two forces contended within: his intellect and his buried emotions. His intellect was as powerful and as active as ever; indeed it now began to discover all kinds of solutions – artistic solutions. His emotions were blocked, defended, confused, full of past and recent hurt. At this moment, therefore, James begins to use the supremacy of his intellect. He concerns himself more intimately with 'method' than ever before. Rational form and mind are interposed against confusions of feeling. If he allowed himself to feel too much he would have to surrender to despair, face imperious questions about his identity, his goals, his life. His best, his 'safest' identity was the intellect of art; there he was in full command. In this way James arrived by stages at the idea of moving the architectonics of the theatre into his De Vere Gardens study. For the first time he began to write scenarios for his novels. He had hitherto written them only for his plays.

Below the surface of his intellectual inquiry – or strategy – the spiritual wound remained deep and raw. We arrive thus at a paradox involving the mystical forces of human survival. At this moment of defeat Henry James seized the skills of his 'technique' as if they were a life-belt, and indulged in a vigorous and mature inquiry into forms not hitherto questioned. Simultaneously we have an emotional retreat – that retreat of which man is capable in order to nurse and heal his spiritual as well as physical wounds. One part of James remained in his study, vigorously engaged in artistic inquiry while the other part took to its sick bed. The Catholic 'retreat' symbolizes this in religious experience; the biological process illustrates it in the physical world: and we know how the evolutionary process, confronted with obstacles, invents alterations and mutations. Or in James's own image, within the dim water-world of his inner being, fancy and dream took over in the service of his wounded ego – even while the active novelist continued, in the world, to use his artistic tools with greater skill than ever. In the materials of James's writing, and the forms he gave them, we can discern the life-in-death, health-in-sickness struggle. There was both progress and regression. His mind moved forward – his feelings turned backward to childhood. Instinctively reaching for insights into his dilemma, James recovered buried infantile memories. The technical progress is palpable; we can study the form of his work. The regression is available to us largely in the fabric of the novels and tales written between 1895 and 1900.

I

Howells had reminded James that he was in reality a novelist not a playwright; and the comfort James found in this was that he was made suddenly to recognize that his failure in the drama was not total. So, in the wake of his answer to his friend, and his first jottings in the notebook, we come upon James's linking of his play-experiments to the novel. The entry in his notebook of 14 February 1895 shows him becoming aware that if he had been a novelist turned playwright, he might think now of these roles as reversed; he could be a playwright turning back to the novel. On this day James begins by looking at his old notes for the story that will become *The Wings of the Dove*. He goes on to read a note that represents a first sketch for *The Golden Bowl*. At this time of despair his imagination is already committing itself to his largest works. The note for *The Golden Bowl* troubles him, for it contains too much of 'the adulterine element'. Harper's had asked for a light tale, and this wouldn't do. 'But may it not be simply a question of *handling* that? For God's sake let me try: I languish so to get at immediate creation. *Voyons*, *voyons*; may I not instantly sit down to a little close, clear, full scenario of it?' The word *scenario* is 'charged with memories and pains'. Yet it touches a new chord of association. And in that ruminative conversational fashion which is the great charm of his note-books, James suddenly has a series of illuminations.

Compensations and solutions seem to stand there with open arms for me – and something of the 'meaning' to come to me of past bitterness, of recent bitterness that otherwise has seemed a mere sickening, unflavoured draught.

And then :

Has a *part* of all this wasted passion and squandered time (of the last five years) been simply the precious lesson, taught me in that round-about and devious, that cruelly expensive, way *of the singular value for a narrative plan too* of the (I don't know *what* adequately to call it) divine principle of the Scenario?

If this was so, he was ready, he told himself, to bless the pangs and pains and miseries of his tragic experience.

If there has lurked in the central core of it this exquisite truth – I almost hold my breath with suspense as I try to formulate it; so *much* hangs radiantly there as depending on it – this exquisite truth that what I call the divine principle in question is a key that, working in the same *general* way fits the complicated chambers of *both* the dramatic and the narrative lock ... why my infinite little loss is converted into an almost infinite little gain.

This was 'a portentous little discovery, the discovery, probably, of a truth of real value even if I exaggerate, as I dare say I do, its *portée*, its magicality'.

2

What happened can be read in Henry James's writings from this point on. The image of the key and the lock was apt : and it applied to his life as well. He was closing a door behind him. He was open-ing a door on his future. He would never again write the kind of novel he had written during his earlier years, before he began play-writing. The stage had given him new technical skills; these he would now use in his fiction. A story could be told as if it were a play; characters could be developed as they develop on the stage; a novel could be given the skeletal structure of drama. The novel in England and America had been an easy, rambling, tell-the-story-as-you-go creation; novelists had meandered, sermonized, digressed and long enjoyed the fluidity of first-person story-telling; they had taken arbitrary courses ever since the days of Richardson and Fielding. Henry James now saw that he could launch an action and then let it evolve with the logic of a well-made play. Beginning with *The Spoils of Poynton*, written during the ensuing months, there emerged a new and complex Jamesian novel. His work required also a new and complex reader: one who had to be aware he was 'following', not simply reading, a story. In earlier years a brief notation had sufficed in James's working journals to record ideas for tales: now we observe him setting down detailed and seemingly mechanical scenarios, even for short stories. 'What then is it,' he asks himself as he works on *The Spoils of Poynton*, 'that the rest of my little second act, as I call it must do?' And he continues:

What I feel more and more that I must arrive at, with these things, is the adequate and regular practice of some such economy of clear summarization as will *give* me from point to point, each of my steps, stages, tints, shades, every main joint and hinge, in its place, of my subject – give me, in a word, my clear order and expressed sequence. I can then *take* from the table, successively, each fitted or fitting piece of my little mosaic.

James did not achieve at once a full-blown dramatic method for his fiction. He proceeded by trial and error, to the exasperation of his readers and the bewilderment of his critics. His art had been the art of lucid narrative. He possessed the closely observed life of the society of his time; he had forged for literature the American-European myth. From this point on, he entered the company of the great artists who, in their late years, find themselves in command of unsuspected energies and resources. So Michelangelo, long ago, could work with undiminished vigour into old age; and Shakespeare, who died much younger, could free himself to write *The Tempest*. Beethoven wrote his greatest quartets at the end, and Bach, after a lifetime of labour, planned *The Art of the Fugue*. Yeats at a later time would shed the earlier trappings of his poetry, and remake his art into the maturity of his life. Examples of such growth are rare in the annals of literary art. In the art of the novel, James moved to new and difficult experiments at the very time when other novelists of his age find their talent 'written out'. His quest for 'compensations and solutions', his desire to assuage and heal his injured spirit with the awareness of his unimpaired vitality, led him to seek newer modes of expression instead of staleness and withdrawal. 'Oh yes,' he was to recognize in a later note, 'the weary, woeful time has done something for me, has had in the depths of all its wasted piety and passion, an intense little lesson and direction.'

He experimented with systematic scenic alternation; with telling a story wholly in dialogue; with devices by which he left out certain scenes and supplied material through retrospective action. He tried to create 'informing' characters as aids to narrative; and he arrived at the ultimate integration in his work of 'picture' and 'scene'. Above all he grew watchful, as if he were a lens, over 'point of view'. He had begun long ago by thinking of storytelling as a form of painting; he now merged the idea of painting with drama. On the surface some of the later novels seem the very opposite of dramatic; the situation appears static, for James, in his great elaboration, slowed his action. And often we are placed in the minds of his super-subtle observers to the exclusion of much of the 'normal' detail of the conventional novel. It was a case of the novelist skilfully withholding information rather than giving it; that is, doling it out and asking the reader to keep track of it. In his earlier novels James had emulated the richness of Balzac by creating a large background and describing an entire environment. Now only relevant stage 'properties' are described. No chair is mentioned if a character is not to sit on it; a mirror is on the wall only because we see the heroine looking in it. There exists a frugal economy of pictorial substance in these novels; and all characters are used 'functionally'. With this, perhaps to compensate for economy of situation, closeness of scene and sparseness of stage 'properties', James furnished his novels with an extravagance of image and a largeness of metaphor, a general and ever-increasing embroidery of style, infusing poetry into his prose pages. In his late prefaces the recurring motif is 'dramatise, dramatise'. He was to be endlessly delighted with 'the charm of the scenic consistency', with 'the blest operation of my Dramatic principle, my law of successive Aspects', and with those 'scenic conditions which are as near an approach to the dramatic as the novel may permit itself'.

3

He had been unable to meet the conditions of the stage. Now he imported the stage into his novels. He had no need of managers, actors, scenery. He had abandoned all hope of box-office earnings;

but he had gained an artist's grasp of what narrative fiction might be if he had a plan, a design, a method. His protagonists were to be shown at crucial moments in their lives as in Ibsen, caught in the workings of their destinies. He could at last create the 'organic' novel of which he had long ago spoken, so that everything in his story was related to everything else, as the organs are in the human body. He gave to his fictions an intricate cellular structure. Each experiment justified itself and required a separate solution. He learned that he need be neither a 'realist' nor a 'naturalist'; the new symbolism, especially as Ibsen and Maeterlinck used it on the stage, gave him a freedom from material things and a liberty to imagine : if what he created was real to him it could be real to others, though not necessarily to some of the critical fraternity and those who wanted him to go on doing what he had done before. His final novels were a synthesis of all that he had learned about his art, and he wove into this the complex civilization of his mind, his vision of essences.

Almost fifteen years later, after these last novels were written, and he was still hoping to write others, he could speak of the sense 'divine and beautiful, of hooking on again to the sacred years of the old De Vere Gardens time, the years of the whole theatric dream and the "working out" sessions, all ineffable and uneffaceable, that went with that, and that still live again, somehow (indeed I *know* how!) in their ashes.' The years devoted to the writing of plays were to become, after a long period, 'the strange sacred time' – strange because of the suffering, the pain and mastery of technical resource in the teeth of failure; sacred, because there resided in this the mystery and passion of his imagination, which enabled him to triumph again and again over 'the sacred mystery of structure'. The word 'sacred' is constantly on his lips. In the end, Henry James's dramatic years, would be 'the sacred years'. But in another part of his being, in that part which masked a continuing despair, these might also have been called 'the treacherous years'; they had harboured within them false prospects, false hopes, cruel deceptions, private demons.

30

In Ireland

EARLY in March of 1895 – five weeks after the closing of his play – Henry James went to Ireland. He had little heart for visits, but he had promised his old friends, the Wolseleys, who were living in state in Dublin, that he would spend a few days with them. Lord Wolseley was Commander-in-Chief of the English forces, the army of 'occupation', as James remarked. And then the novelist had found in his *Guy Domville* mail a friendly note from the second Lord Houghton, the Lord Lieutenant of Ireland, inviting him to spend a week at the viceregal court. The first Lord Houghton, the viceroy's father, had been the 'world-wrinkled' Victorian, the 'bird of paradox', who had befriended James long ago. Now the son, emulating his father, made a timely gesture to the rejected playwright. James appears to have felt that it would be graceless to decline; and he welcomed the opportunity at the same time of keeping his promise to the Wolseleys. He crossed to Dublin on 9 March. The 'unwanted' dramatist was still very much *persona grata* in the high world. He was guest both of State and Army in the embattled land of his forefathers.

I

James had visited Ireland twice before. In 1883 he had stopped in Cork and Dublin after a transatlantic crossing. These cities were filled at that moment with soldiers and he had cut short his stay. Then, almost a decade later, after a bad influenza, he had recuperated at Kingstown, near Dublin. Ireland was best known to him in the continuing Home Rule struggle in parliament, in the recent drama of Parnell, which he and his sister had followed with deep feeling, and in fairy-tale memories out of his childhood. The senior Henry James had made much in old bedtime stories of his visit as a young man to the County Cavan village from which the first William James had emigrated to America. He had taken with him the family Negro servant in Albany, Billy Taylor; and he had arrived, as his son put it, 'a gilded youth' to create a sensation among the villagers.

There had been other elements in the story – whisky abundantly poured out by the local doctor and lawyer, and a girl named Barbara who ate gooseberries in a garden 'with a charm that was in itself of the nature of a brogue'. All these memories belonged to the lore of Henry James's childhood. With a strong sense of the 'Irishism' of his family, he now set foot on the ancestral soil, but with less exuberance than his father and with a sceptical eye.

The visit proved from the first 'explosive'. James intended nothing more violent by the word than the fact that it represented an extraordinary variation from his life of 'small decorous London observances'. As prelude he went first to stay with Lord Houghton's private secretary, Herbert Jekyll – 'the kind and clever Jekyll' – in his lodge in Phoenix Park. Then his brief taste of viceregal life at the Castle began. Here he had a feeling of shock – 'the sense of the lavish extravagance of the castle, with the beggary and squalor of Ireland at the very gates'. The novelist however seems to have made little allowance for Lord Houghton's goodwill and his difficulties in his office – 'the most thankless,' John Morley was to say, 'that any human being in any imaginable community could undertake'. The viceregal court was boycotted by the Irish aristocracy, the gentry and the landlords, since Houghton was the appointee of a Home Rule government and had been close to Gladstone during the writing of the first Home Rule bill. In his isolation, Houghton sought to enliven his court by inviting large parties from England. James grew ironic over the *bleu-ciel* coats lined in azure of the eight aides of the viceroy. He developed lumbago and found it a weariness to have to stand all evening 'on one's hind legs' during the four balls given by the viceroy in the six days of his stay. The young Lord Houghton was attractive, intelligent, artistic; a widower with three daughters, he was constantly under the hopeful gaze of dowagers with available sons. He had lately inherited great estates from his uncle the Lord Crewe (and was indeed to become himself the Marquess of Crewe). With his large resources, he passed his uncomfortable time in Ireland bestowing luxurious hospitality. James squirmed at this 'grandeur in a void'. He described the Castle as 'tarnished and ghost-haunted'; he considered Lord Houghton to be leading 'a strange and monstrous life of demoralization and frivolity'. It gave him 'a haunting discomfort', and made his visit 'a gorgeous bore'. To some friends he was even more candid: the visit had been 'an unmitigated hell', 'a weariness alike to flesh and spirit', 'a Purgatorio'. He was deeply moved by 'the tragic shabbiness of this sinister country'. It was too much for the grandson of the County Cavan William James. With great relief he bade farewell to the well-meaning viceroy, and drove to the Royal Hospital in another part of the city for his stay with the Wolseleys.

2

The transition from hollow viceregal splendour to the military alertness of the Wolseley establishment was a welcome relief. Lady Wolseley gave James the run of the Sèvres room in the mornings, and he described the inkpot on the desk as the largest he had ever used, overflowing 'like the Wolseley welcome and their winecups'. He seems to have made little use of the inkpot, for he found the fine clean-cut young military men 'charming and wholesome' in their soldierly deportment. He liked being in 'an intensely military little world of aides-de-camp, dragoons and hussars'. There were amiable colonels to take him on tours; and he visited the old red-coated cocked-hatted Irish pensioners of the English armies. He was full of admiration for the place, built by Charles II, and in particular the great rococo hall 'one of the finest great halls in the British islands', where Lady Wolseley staged a beautiful costume ball. She allowed James to come in evening dress and he proved the only black-coated figure present. The women – it had been Lady Wolseley's whim – dressed like ladies in the paintings of Sir Joshua, Gainsborough and Romney. The men were in uniform, or court dress, or 'the prettiest of all the fopperies of the English foppish class', evening hunt dress. James spent ten delightful days in these surroundings, watching the sentinel-mounting and a great deal of military ritual.

For a 'man of peace' (as he constantly reminded Wolseley) he was happier among soldiers than among courtiers. But then he had known the Wolseleys for many years, indeed since his first dinings-out in London when he had been made welcome at their great house in Portman Square. Lady Wolseley, who was English, seemed to James to have the best attributes of an American woman; the former Louisa Erskine was attractive in her younger years, dark-haired and dark-eyed, and from the first he became, as he said, 'quite thick' with her. The more than 100 letters written to her during four decades show how much he liked her and her expertise in old houses and old things; she had a connoisseur's eye for antiques and furnishings. The

Queen Anne bric-à-brac at the Wolseleys long ago had been abundant 'to a degree that quite flattens one out'.

As for her husband, he was one of Victoria's bravest and most renowned soldiers. James liked his eye of steel – the one that remained, for he had lost the other in the Crimea. He liked Wolseley's rosy dimples, his simplicity, his belief in 'glory'; he admired his record in all the colonial wars of the era. Badly wounded in the Crimea, Wolseley became a captain at 20; he had fought in the Burmese war, had been at Lucknow and in China; he had gone to the relief of Gordon in Khartoum. Stationed at Ottawa he had handled the Red River rebellion in Manitoba and had crossed into the United States to cast an expert British eye on the Civil War, slipping through the embattled north to the Confederacy to meet Stonewall Jackson ('a glorious fellow', said Wolseley) and to have a long talk with Robert E. Lee ('an English gentleman'.) He also admired Lincoln, and had praise for Grant. His exploits in the Ashanti campaign were legendary, and on his return to civilian life, he had been a great leader in the War Office for reform of the British Army. James found 'an extraordinary charm in his unquenched youth'. Wolseley on his side delighted in James's conversation.

A decade later, when Wolseley had been named Field-Marshal and Viscount, he wrote his *Story of a Soldier's Life*. James read these two stout volumes with the same fascination as the memoirs of General Marbot, and his pen again marked salient passages describing personal heroism and the glory of arms. The Field-Marshal, whom James judged 'a singularly and studiously delightful person' and a supreme example of the 'cultivated British soldier', believed in the glory of arms as in 'a national religion'. James marked the passage, 'a nation without glory is like a man without courage, a woman without virtue ... glory to a nation is what sunlight is to all human beings'. He also marked the passage in which Wolseley recalled his first cavalry charge : 'You are for the time being lifted up from and out of all petty thoughts of self and for the moment your whole existence, soul and body, seems to revel in a true sense of glory.' The novelist wrote the Field-Marshal a long and enthusiastic letter : 'It's a beautiful, rich, *natural* book – and happy the man whose life and genius have been such that he has only to *talk*, veraciously, and let memory and his blessed temperament float him on, in order to make one live so with great things and breathe so the air of the high places (of character and fortitude.)' James added that what, as a dabbler in the spectacle of life, I think I most envy you, is your infinite acquaintance, from the first, with superlative *men*, and your having been able so to gather them in, and make them pass before you, for you to handle and use them. They move through your book, all these forms of resolution and sacrifice, in a long vivid, mostly tragical procession.

It was the masculinity of heroism and glory rather than the masculinity of the barracks and the smoking-room, that James cherished. He had no stomach for the violence of Kipling, but he had a deep admiration for the probity of a soldier such as Wolseley. Thus he could write, at the end of his stay in Dublin – of that part of it passed at the Royal Hospital – that 'the military *milieu* and type were very amusing and suggestive to me'.

For the rest, he was completely clear about his stay at the Castle. 'I was not made for viceregal "courts," especially in countries distraught with social hatreds.'

31

A Squalid Tragedy

THE Oscar Wilde case burst upon London a few days after Henry James's return from Ireland with a kind of moral violence that fascinated and disturbed Henry James. From the first he characterized it as 'a very squalid tragedy, but still a tragedy'. The brilliant maker of epigrams, the wit of London society, the reigning playwright, had fallen from his high estate. He was convicted of homosexual offences and sent off to serve two years' hard labour. Oscar's two successful plays were immediately pulled from the boards. *The Importance of Being Earnest* was killed by the outcry of an outraged Victorian society, and George Alexander, for the second time in two months, found himself without a play. James's disaster in Alexander's theatre had been almost private by comparison.

Two days after Wilde was committed for trial, James wrote to Gosse that he found the affair 'hideously, atrociously dramatic and really interesting' but added that its interest was qualified by 'a sickening horribility'. It was, he wrote

the squalid gratuitousness of it all – of the mere exposure – that blurs the spectacle. But the *fall* – from nearly twenty years of a really unique kind of 'brilliant' conspicuity (wit, 'art,' conversation – 'one of our two or three dramatists, etc.') to that sordid prison cell and this gulf of obscenity over which the ghoulish public hangs and gloats – it is beyond any utterance of irony or any pang of compassion. He was never in the smallest of degree interesting to me – but this hideous human history has made him so – in a manner.

James sealed this letter. Then he had a further thought. He scrawled across the back of the envelope, in French, that it was both a pity – and a blessing – that John Addington Symonds was no longer alive. *Quel dommage – mais quel bonheur – que J.A.S. ne soit plus de ce monde,*

I

The allusion to John Addington Symonds would have been lost upon most Victorians had they read James's words. It had a particular meaning for Gosse. Both he and James had known for some years that Symonds had been a crusading homosexual, eager but unable to proclaim from the housetops the ecstasy he felt in love between men. He would have been the André Gide of his time and made the world his confessional – had the time been more propitious. Erratic, disturbed, tubercular, he had wandered in search of his health as D. H. Lawrence would do thirty years later. He might be described today as the D. H. Lawrence of homosexuality whom circumstance, and the climate of his time, prevented from writing a 'Lord Chatterley's Lover'. Wilde, in an impulsive and self-destructive way, brought his tragedy on himself by denying the truth and suing for libel when he was called a sodomite. Symonds, wavering between caution and the need to protect his wife and daughters, carried on a subterranean crusade on behalf of inversion, using the Greeks, and the example of the *Symposium*, to discuss the subject most intimate to him. He also circulated privately-printed pamphlets, and wrote passionate poems about what was spoken of in those years as 'the love that dare not speak its name'.

Gosse had been in Symonds's confidence since the mid-1870s. At the beginning Symonds made cautious epistolary overtures to him, saying he discerned in his writings a 'tender sympathy with the beauty of men as well as women'. Symonds's biographer says Gosse reacted with some 'alarm', and Symonds retreated with the explanation that his Greek poems were 'distinctly archaeological'. Some time would elapse before Symonds would make a complete avowal to him. Indeed it was not until fifteen years later, in 1890, that Symonds returned to the subject in a fully open manner and Gosse, now a man of the world and a power in literary London (and much less alarmed by such matters) wrote an 'understanding' reply which has been grossly misinterpreted as an admission by him of his own homosexuality. He was to write a similar 'understanding' reply to Gide a quarter of a century later, and the two letters, read side by side, testify essentially to Gosse's need to ingratiate himself with his fellow writers rather than cultivate the confessional mode. Gosse did say to Symonds in this letter that there was an 'obstinate twist' in his life, but the fuller text of the letter shows that he was alluding not to inversion but to his 'cowardice' in not taking a large-minded and generous view of Symonds's 'problem'.

James met Symonds at lunch early in 1877 with Andrew Lang. He reported to his brother that he found him 'a mild, cultured man, with the Oxford perfume, who invited me to visit him at Clifton'. James never accepted the invitation; and shortly thereafter Symonds went to live in Switzerland. So far as we know they only exchanged letters once. This was when James's essay on Venice appeared in the *Century* in 1882. The novelist sent a copy to Symonds

because it was a constructive way of expressing the good-will I felt for you in consequence of what you have written about the land of Italy – and of intimating to you, somewhat dumbly, that I am an attentive and sympathetic reader. I nourish for the said Italy an unspeakably tender passion, and your pages always seemed to say to me that you were one of a small number of people who love it as much as I do – in addition to your knowing it immeasurably better.

James added that 'it seemed to me that the victim of a common passion should sometimes exchange a look, and I sent you off the magazine at a venture'.

Symonds was concerned with a different level of 'common passion'; and James never knew how critical Symonds was of what he called 'the laborious beetle-flight of Henry James'. The English writer's proselytizing letters – his attempts to engage friends and strangers in a kind of continuing symposium on homo-eroticism – is now a matter of record. James was aware that Symonds corresponded with his old Newport friend, T. S. Perry. As is known, Symonds singled out Walt Whitman above all as a potential ally, and cross-examined him particularly on the subject of *Calamus*. The elderly poet grew increasingly impatient; he responded to the praise but not to the verbal embrace; and in his final rejoinder summarily informed Symonds that he had fathered six illegitimate children – as if to set at rest once and for all any question about his heterosexuality.

2

Early in their friendship Gosse told James the history of Symonds's unhappy marriage, without apparently divulging that Symonds had sought a wife in an attempt to escape from his homosexuality – if indeed Gosse at that time, in the early 1880s, himself knew all the details. James's notebook entry of 26 March 1884, a month after he had corresponded with Symonds, substantially foreshadows his tale of *The Author of Beltraffio* as he set it down shortly afterwards – 'the opposition between the narrow, cold, Calvinistic wife, a rigid moralist, and the husband impregnated – even to morbidness – with the spirit of Italy, the love of beauty, of art, the aesthetic view of life, and aggravated, made extravagant and perverse, by the sense of his wife's disapproval'. The delicately-told yet lurid little tale culminates in a violent Medea-like action: the mother prefers her child dead rather than have him survive to a pagan-spirited father. 'I am told, on all sides here,' Henry confessed to his brother William, 15 February 1885, 'that my "Author of Beltraffio" is a living and scandalous portrait of J. A. Symonds and his wife, whom I have never seen.' Gosse told James, in praising the tale, that he had shown great insight into the secret of Symonds's character, for the novelist promptly asked to be told what this secret was. 'Perhaps I *have* divined the innermost cause of J.A.S.'s discomfort – but I don't think I seize on page 571, exactly the allusion you refer to.' Page 571 of the serialization of the story (in the *English Illustrated Magazine*) has this significant passage about James's fictional author of *Beltraffio*: 'I saw that in his books he had only said half of his thought, and what he had kept back – from motives that I deplored when I learnt them later – was the richer part. It was his fortune to shock a great many people, but there was not a grain of bravado in his pages.' *

---

* It is interesting to read the same passage in the New York Edition as James revised it almost a quarter of a century later when he had for years possessed the full personal history of Symonds: 'It came to me thus that in his books he had uttered but half his thought, and that what he had kept back – from

This might not altogether fit Symonds, but it was certainly true that he would have liked to say publicly much that he spoke only in private.

In writing to Gosse about his glimpse into the 'innermost cause' of Symonds's 'discomfort' James said he was 'devoured with curiosity as to this revelation. Even a postcard (in covert words) would relieve the suspense of the perhaps-already-too-indiscreet H.J.' We know James ultimately was made a party to Gosse's intimate knowledge and even shown some of Symonds's papers.

His privately-printed pamphlet *A Problem in Modern Ethics* of 1891 prompted much private discussion; and when Gosse showed the booklet to James, the novelist thanked him for 'bringing me those marvellous outpourings'. He added:

J.A.S. is truly, I gather, a candid and consistent creature, and the exhibition is infinitely remarkable. It's, on the whole, I think, a queer place to plant the standard of duty, but he does it with extraordinary gallantry. If he has, or gathers, a band of the emulous, we may look for some capital sport. But I don't wonder that some of his friends and relations are haunted with a vague malaise. I think one ought to wish him more *humour* – it is really *the* saving salt. But the great reformers never have it – and he is the Gladstone of the affair.

James, perhaps to exemplify the humour of which he spoke, signed the letter 'yours – if I may safely so say so! – ever H.J.'

3

Symonds died in 1893, and when Gosse wrote to give James the news the novelist responded warmly in tribute to the 'poor much-living, much-doing, passionately out-giving man'. He had never had a clear vision of him, he said, but he felt the news as a pang; yet the end had perhaps come at the right time. Symonds had done his work and was spared living into feverish over-production and repetition. There had been an 'achieved maturity' – 'the full life stopped and rounded, as it were, by a kind of heroic maximum'. When Horatio Brown's biography of Symonds appeared early in 1895 James read the two volumes promptly. The memoir is discreet and measured; and James

---

motives I deplored when I made them out later - was the finer, and braver part. It was his fate to make a great many still more "prepared" people than me not inconsiderably wince; but there was no grain of bravado in his ripest things.'

marked a few passages in it – one relating to an early trance described by Symonds; another to the effects of chloroform upon him; and one passage in which Brown described how Symonds abandoned speculation, inquiry and analysis in a metaphysical sense and concentrated 'on man, on human life', so that he had discovered the sensuous and sentient existence of the artist.

Just before leaving for Ireland, James had been urged by his Venetian friend, Mrs Curtis to write an appreciation of Symonds. James replied he was too busy; moreover 'the job would be quite too difficult', indeed the difficulty was 'insurmountable'. There was, wrote James, an entire side of Symonds's life which was 'strangely morbid and hysterical and which toward the end of his life coloured all his work and utterance. To write of him without dealing with it, or at least looking at it, would be an affectation; and yet to deal with it either ironically or explicitly would be a Problem – a problem beyond me.' James thus injected Symonds's own term for homosexuality.

While the Oscar Wilde trial was in progress Gosse sent to James a large bundle of Symonds's letters. As on the occasion of his reading of *A Problem* the novelist referred to these as 'the fond outpourings of poor J.A.S.' His attitude towards Symonds suggests that James passed no moral judgement on his homosexuality or his passionate private crusade. What seems to have bothered James was Symonds's desire for public display in matters the novelist deemed wholly private. Both in his friendships, up to this time, and in his correspondence, James seemed to maintain the 'distance' he had always kept from questions of sex. A kind of cool formality intervened – and almost a touch of condescension towards his more 'involved' friends. The words 'fond outpourings' had in them a note of irony, tolerance, condescension. Symonds must have sensed this: for although he expressed pleasure at James's writings about Venice, he complained to Horatio Brown of James's 'real critical obtuseness', singling out his essays on Maupassant and Pierre Loti. The choice was significant; in both of these essays James criticized the eroticism of the writers and in his paper on Maupassant accused the French storyteller of dwelling too exclusively on the physical and the sensual, leaving out the reflective and meditative side of man.

4

This 'distance' from people and from passion enabled Henry James to be both cool and compassionate to Wilde as well. In the same letter in which he wrote to Gosse about Symonds's 'outpourings' James thought he saw a gleam of hope for 'the wretched Wilde' in 'the fearful exposure of his (of the prosecution's) little beasts of witnesses. What a nest of almost infant blackmailers!' On 26 April he wrote to his brother,

you ask of Oscar Wilde. His fall is hideously tragic – and the squalid violence of it gives him an interest (of misery) that he never had for me – in any degree – before. Strange to say I think he may have a 'future' – of a sort – by reaction – when he comes out of prison – if he survives the horrible sentence of hard labour that he will probably get. His trial begins today – however – and it is too soon to say. But there are debts in London, and a certain general shudder as to what, with regard to some other people, may possibly come to light.

To Paul Bourget he wrote, once the sentence had been pronounced, that he considered it 'cruel'. Solitary confinement, he said, rather than hard labour, would have been more humane. Later that year James was approached to sign a petition drawn up by the American poet, Stuart Merrill, and circulated on behalf of Wilde among French and English writers. The overture was made through Jonathan Sturges, who was then in a London nursing home. This was in November of 1895, when Wilde had been in prison eight months. To Merrill, Sturges wrote:

James says that the petition would not have the slightest effect on the *authorities* here who have the matter in charge and in whose nostrils the very name of Zola and even of Bourget is a stench and that the document would only exist as a manifesto of personal loyalty to Oscar by his friends, of which he was never one.

In a letter to Francis Vielé-Griffin, the Franco-American poet, Sturges reported that James was convinced that given the public attitude towards the case, Wilde would best be helped not by petitions or publicity but by quiet and authoritative pressure on the Home Office.

To what extent James himself intervened behind the scenes we do not know. But he did discuss the Wilde case with a Member of Parliament (probably R. B. Haldane) who, during the short-lived Rosebery Government, sat on the commission for penal reform and visited Wilde in jail. On 10 November 1895 James wrote to Alphonse Daudet that he had had news from this man that Wilde was '*dans un état d'abattement complet, physique et moral*'; that Wilde had lately been ill in the infirmary, and that some easing of conditions for him might occur. He said also his political friend had discerned in Wilde no will to resistance, no faculty for recuperation. If he had this faculty, James added, 'what masterpiece might he yet produce!'

32

The Two Romancers

IN June 1893, when he had been actively corresponding with Robert Louis Stevenson, Henry James had written of his recent trip to the Continent.

I saw Daudet who appears to be returning from the jaws of slow death – getting over creeping paralysis. Meredith I saw three months ago – with his charming *accueil*, his impenetrable shining scales, and the (to me) general mystery of his perversity. That perversity is flowering, I believe, into two soon-to-be-published serials.

When James coupled Alphonse Daudet and George Meredith in his little budget of news for the South Seas, he little dreamed that two years later he would be present at – would indeed be an agent in – a memorable meeting of the two romancers. Daudet was fixed for him irrevocably in Paris; Meredith in his cottage at Box Hill, near Dorking, in Surrey. Both were crippled by similar forms of paralysis. Daudet made no pretension to understanding England and the English. Meredith's main fault, to James was 'that he thinks he is French, which he isn't'. James was instrumental, however, in bringing together the Provençal Gaul and the English 'Gaul' – in a touching little comedy that played itself out that spring, in the very midst of the Oscar Wilde headlines.

I

Of the generation of French writers whose members he had met when he had first settled in Europe, Henry James had come closest to Alphonse Daudet. Maupassant had been a mere acquaintance, in the days of Flaubert's *cénacle*. Zola had fascinated, but also bored;

and he knew him only casually, had seen something of him in Paris and more recently in England. Edmond de Goncourt had received him at Auteuil, where they had gossiped politely. But between Daudet and James a deeper chord had been struck; part of this had gone back to their common attachment to Turgenev. A greater part resided in Daudet's meridional expansiveness and his vivid and pictorial style. 'He cannot put three words together, that I don't more or less adore them,' James wrote. On his side, the French novelist had a marked respect for James, not least for his command of the French tongue. '*S'il se tire de sa langue comme de la nôtre, c'est un rude lapin*,' he had written to the English journalist Theodore Child. 'What a dear little note from Alphonse,' was James's comment. 'My heart warms to him and I am most grateful to him for the rank he assigns to me in the animal kingdom.' His heart continued to warm towards the French writer, sufficiently for him to have translated in 1889 the last of the *Tartarin* series. Friendship – and the fat fee given him by Harper, £350 – induced him to go to Paris to do the work at high speed from Daudet's galley-proof.

Even before that time he had been a welcome visitor in the Rue de Bellechasse, in the Faubourg. He had been struck by the novelist's courage in face of his creeping paralysis, the fruit of indiscretions in his bohemian days. And he noted, half bewilderedly, but not without a touch of awe, that Daudet, in the naturalistic mode, studied his own symptoms intending to make capital of them in a novel he would have called (had he ever written it) *La Douleur*. In James's correspondence with Child, Daudet figures as 'the little thing', an affectionate reference to his smallness of stature and charm of manner (an allusion, also, to Daudet's autobiographical novel, *Le Petit Chose*). The French novelist had large dark liquid eyes and a vivid bearded countenance; it revealed his ill-health and suffering, but it was endlessly lively, endlessly alert. The last thing James expected, however, was that Daudet, with all his infirmities would want to travel. In the midst of the Oscar Wilde excitement, came a letter from Paris – 'the little thing' wanted to pay a spring visit to London, doubtless in emulation of Zola's recent trip. He planned to bring his wife, his sons, Léon and Lucien, his young daughter Edmée. There would also be Victor Hugo's grandson and his wife. Would James dig up some comfortable rooms for all seven of them? 'I will probably inflict a thousand annoyances on you,' Daudet had written – *je compte bien vous infliger mille ennuis* – and Henry remarked to his brother 'he will doubtless be as good as his word'. But if there was annoyance, there was also amusement. James arranged an intimate dinner in Daudet's honour at the Reform Club, took a suite of rooms for him at Brown's Hotel, sent off letters of advice and guidance, and arranged to bring Daudet to visit George Meredith at Dorking.

2

For Meredith, James had an affection much more profound and intimate than for Daudet. He had met him long ago (in 1878), and admired the man rather than the novelist. He liked his wit, his paradox, his brilliant intelligence, his faculty for piling fantasy upon fantasy to some ultimate absurdity, until it all collapsed amid his own hearty laughter. He would have liked to see more of him. But as it was, he went periodically to Dorking and spent long hours with his distinguished *confrère*. 'He is brilliantly intelligent and the wreck of a prodigious wit,' James wrote in 1888. 'He is much the wittiest Englishman, and the most famed for conversation, that I have ever known – for playing with intellectual fire.'

The 'intellectual fire' is suggested in James's notebooks, where he recorded two ideas furnished by his talk with Meredith. One evolved into the tale *The Great Condition* written in 1899, which tells of a man who becomes worried about the past of the woman he is to marry. The woman replies 'Give me six months. If you want to know it *then* – I promise I will tell you.' James turned this into a story in which the fiancé breaks off his engagement and another man wins the woman who, we gather, has no secret to tell. An earlier idea, of 1894, which much appealed to James, he was however unable to write; perhaps because there was too much sex in it. Note at first leisure the idea suggested to me by George Meredith's amusing picture – the other night – of the bewilderment of A.M. in the presence of the immense pretensions to "conquest" (to "having repeatedly overthrown Venus herself") of A.A.' A.M. was probably Admiral Maxse, who had fought in the Crimea, an intimate of Meredith's, and A.A. we may hazard a guess, was Alfred Austin, soon to be appointed poet laureate. James had the idea that the man who boasted about his conquests of Venus was in reality a fraud; and that the man who kept quiet and was bewildered by the boasting had himself had great successes in the bedroom. He toyed with the story in the days after Fenimore's death in Venice, but never wrote it. In

1892 we find James speaking of 'the great once-dazzling George Meredith, whom I like, and whom, today, one can't but be tender to in his physical eclipse – overtaken by slow (very gradual) paralysis.'

3

On 6 May 1895, Henry James met the Daudet party at Victoria Station and conducted them to Brown's. Daudet was insatiable; when he could not stagger into places on his own legs, he arranged to be carried in a bath chair. In this condition, he visited Westminster Abbey and was given tea in the Westminster Deanery. James remarked that the French novelist was surprised to find in the Abbey statues of actors – John Kemble, Mrs Siddons. 'In France,' he noted, 'the drama is primarily the Author ... the actors are kept more in their places.' Madame Daudet was counselled by James as to the proper hour to observe London society in Hyde Park. He enjoyed talking to the sons, although he strongly disliked the 27-years-old Léon Daudet, a gifted stylist and polemicist, also a notorious royalist and anti-Semite. James privately predicted that Léon would some day 'swing', a shrewd judgement. Léon Daudet died a less violent death but led a turbulent life. For the younger son, Lucien, then 17, James had much sympathy. Madame Daudet impressed him as worldly and amusing; she was 'rotund and romantic ... had very good clothes and golden bronze hair'; he enjoyed her comments on the way Englishwomen dressed – or rather failed to dress. There were times when James lost patience with his visitors, particularly with Alphonse's 'mania for being interviewed and all à propos of three weeks at Brown's hotel'. On one day of the British spring, which that year was rainless and mild, James took his French celebrities to Oxford; on another to Windsor. Daudet was tired and contented himself with looking at Windsor Castle from his carriage. They drove past A. C. Benson's picturesque cottage at Eton, where James left a card, and later apologized for not arranging a visit for his guests. 'Ah, si vous saviez comme ces petits coins d'Angleterre m'amusent,' said Daudet.

The dinner at the Reform Club was staged by Henry with his customary care and we gather with some trepidation, for he wrote to Gosse that his guest had 'a malady of the bladder, which makes him desire strange precautions – and I see – I foresee singular complications – for the flow of something more than either soul or champagne at dinner'. But the occasion seems to have gone well, and James mustered a dozen French-speaking notables in London (Daudet spoke little English) – among them John Morley, George du Maurier, Arthur Balfour, Lawrence Alma-Tadema, Sir Edward Burne-Jones, Admiral Maxse, the old dilettante Hamilton Aïdé, and Gosse. The latter in his recollections of Daudet seems to be referring to this occasion when he described how the French novelist struggled up a short flight of stairs and once seated at table 'a sort of youth reblossomed in him'. Daudet was silent at first, almost motionless, and then head, arms, chest 'would vibrate with electrical movements, the long white fingers would twitch in his beard, and then from the lips a tide of speech would spout – a flood of coloured words'. At dessert he began to talk of the melon-harvest at Nîmes. 'In a moment,' Gosse remembered, 'we saw before us the masses of golden-yellow and crimson and sea-green fruit in the little white market-place, with the incomparable light of a Provençal harvest bathing it all in crystal.'

Léon Daudet was to record that 'every day Henry James came to fetch us for a walk, a tea, a lunch, a dinner at the Club', and he described the American novelist as having 'a noble and complete nature, a spirit marvellously lucid'. James seemed to Léon Daudet like a doctor or a judge who 'inspired serenity and confidence'. There were days when James and his illustrious visitor simply sat at the window of Brown's and watched the life of the street below. 'What an air of pride these English soldiers have!' Daudet remarked looking at a military figure walking down the street. 'How well-set they are for marching on parade in their fine-figured strut.' James rejoined, 'My dear Daudet, they have to be thus, they have to take account of the young and pretty servant-girls looking at them from the windows.' The journalists often spoke of Daudet's emaciated and exquisite features as 'Christ-like' and James said, 'I felt as if I should go mad if I even once more, let alone twenty times more, heard Daudet personally compared (more especially facially compared, eyeglass and all) to Jesus Christ.' We get another view of these moments in James's letter to Lady Wolseley, after the Daudets were gone: 'They clung to me like a litter of pups to an experienced mamma. They were very amiable, very uninformed, very bewildered, very observant and perceptive, on the whole, and very overwhelming.'

4

The meeting of Daudet and Meredith occurred on 16 May, bringing together three novelists of widely different talents – the loquacious Daudet, with the sun of southern France in his talk, Meredith, the poet-novelist of England, and the transatlantic James, who stood aside as intermediary and left the foreground to the other two. Daudet and his son Léon made the trip by train from Charing Cross to Dorking, accompanied by James. With great effort Daudet climbed from the train and almost fell into the arms of the tall, white-bearded, white-haired Meredith. The dark-eyed meridional and blue-eyed Briton embraced. Henry described the scene to his brother William:

Strangely and grotesquely pathetic was the meeting between the French and the English romancer – *coram publico*, on the railway platform each staggering and stumbling, with the same uncontrollable paralysis into the arms of the other so that they almost rolled over together on the line beneath the wheels of the train.

Meredith leaned on the arm of Admiral Maxse; Daudet was supported by Léon. The little party slowly got into the carriage and drove to Flint Cottage where Meredith was giving dinner to his guests before they would take a later train back to London. Daudet spoke of the meeting – 'the ironic fraternity, two novelists dragging a wing, like two wounded seagulls, maimed birds of tempest, punished for having affronted the gods'.*

For other recollections of the occasion we must rely on Léon Daudet's embellished memoirs: but it seems clear that Meredith professed his love for Daudet and told him that he had set aside some bottles of Côtes-Roties '54 in the hope of such an occasion. 'His old Southern God is in that wine,' said Meredith to James, who also spoke of the occasion as an English version 'of a Provençal May Day'. Daudet was delighted to see on the table Mistral's *Mirèio* and *Calendau*. The English poet-novelist read aloud the *Poème du Rhône*; certain of the passages in the Provençal, Meredith could not decipher. 'I live here in the midst of Scythians, you understand, don't you, Daudet,' Meredith said. And later he remarked to his guest, 'How lively you are,' and as if to explain his appreciation of this liveliness he

* C'est une sensation de fraternelle ironie, ces deux romanciers qui trainent l'aile comme deux goelands blessés, estropiés, ces oiseaux de tempête, punis pour avoir voulu affronter les dieux.

added, 'You know I'm not really English; I'm a Gaul.' When the name of Wilde came up, Meredith said 'a mixture of Apollo and a monster'. To James, Daudet was 'very appealing and pathetic in his advanced and yet combated infirmity – wasted and worn, saturated with morphine and chloral'. '*Depuis dix ans,*' Daudet told him, '*je n'ai que le sommeil artificiel.*' A few days after the visit to Box Hill, Meredith came to London to dine with Daudet; and he returned again, in spite of his infirmities, to go to Victoria station to say good-bye to the visitors. The two invalids clasped hands through the window as the train began to move – and with their muscular infirmities disengaged them with difficulty.

Daudet was expansive to the last. Within a day of his return to Paris he wrote James that he had had great admiration for the subtleties of his talent and the profundity of his spirit; but that now after spending three weeks near to him 'during which I looked at you closely, I want to give you all my friendship and I demand all yours. Let's have not another word on the subject.'*

'That is charming,' Henry commented to William, 'and genuine, I think, and I am sincerely touched, but it is a rather formidable order to meet. However, he inspired great kindness.' He answered Daudet tactfully, 'I will best show you how touched I am by receiving your words in affectionate silence.' The Daudets had made James promise he would some day visit them at Champrosay. The promise was never kept; James did not go abroad for several years, and in 1897 Daudet died. He had been 'as warm as the south wall of a garden or as the flushed fruit that grows there', and of all finished artists he had been, said James, the most 'natural'. He was at the opposite pole from Flaubert in this respect. Flaubert, with 'a kind of grand, measured distance from his canvas – paced as if for a duel – seemed to attack his subject with a brush twenty feet long'. Daudet's charm lay in his agitation, and his nerves. 'His style is a matter of talking, gesticulating, imitating – of impressionism carried to the last point.' And James also said, 'The sun in his blood had never burnt out.'

---

* Je ne veux vous dire aujourd'hui qu'une chose: avant d'aller à Londres j'avais pour votre talent subtil la profondeur de votre esprit, une sympathie très-grande; maintenant, après ces trois semaines vécues en commun, pendant lesquelles je vous ai bien regardé, c'est toute mon amitié que je vous donne et toute la vôtre que je vous demande. Ainsi, plus un mot là-dessus!

33

The Figure in the Carpet

AFTER the Daudets left, Henry James had a violent attack of gout – his foot was 'like the Dome of St Paul's'. To Dr Baldwin he wrote of his 'fruitless six months, with gout, sore throats, a futile month's visit to Ireland, interruptions innumerable, and just lately, to finish, the whole Alphonse Daudet family'. He would not be going to Italy this year, he told Baldwin, and referring to a recent earthquake there he added, 'Our earthquake, here, has been social – human – sexual (if that be the word when it's all one sex). You probably followed in some degree the Oscar Wilde horrors.'

There had been also his personal earthquake. The passage of the six months since *Guy Domville* had not diminished his indecision nor his melancholy. He was face to face with a long summer and did not know where to turn. He had done very little work, had written only one tale published in the *Yellow Book* (*The Next Time*), and was having difficulty getting on with a novel. He had never felt so much at a loose ends. His decision to remain in England could have been foreseen; he had found too many American tourists in Italy and Switzerland during the previous spring and summer. And the death of Fenimore had blunted his desire to go abroad. He talked much of abandoning London for the English countryside but shrank from doing so. He would have to face solitude and work, and he had no appetite for either. Instead he involved himself with passing Americans. 'There is a compatriot for every day in the week,' he said. John La Farge appeared, after the failure of an exhibition of his South Sea watercolours in Paris. He revived old memories, but seemed 'Americanly innocent'. And he was thoughtless. He sent three French ladies to James, to be guided through London. 'What does he expect me to do with them?' James wailed to Henrietta Reubell. Then Mrs Jack Gardner came and for a few days he played out his usual comedy of pretending he was her most abject courtier; but her queenliness no longer amused him. He left her with one of his usual flourishes, after taking her to a couple of art-exhibitions. Life, he told her, was too 'complicated and conflicting'. With characteristic irony he added 'you are a great simplifier – I wish you would simplify *me*!' Nothing seemed simple now. London was 'a seething hell'.

I

He lingered until late July amid the visiting 'barbarians' and then suddenly bolted to Torquay in Devonshire where he had spent a few days the previous year. He obtained a fine suite in the Osborne Hotel on Hesketh Crescent, with a large sitting-room and a balcony. A six-foot chambermaid prepared his hot bath every morning. He took bicycle lessons and boasted of his black and yellow bruises. He paid calls on W. E. Norris, who lived in a large villa on a nearby hilltop, and had shown James much sympathy at the time of *Guy Domville*. He described him as 'the mildest, kindest, cleanest of novelists and of gentlemen – tremendously old-fashioned at 45', and 'the gentlest and sweetest of men, one quite loves him'. Norris apparently felt the same about James. They ran out of conversational subjects during the first quarter of an hour every time they met. This did not trouble Henry. Norris was 'accepting' – and he needed this now more than anything else.

'Peace wraps me round,' he wrote to Miss Reubell. He liked the view; the sea had a lovely Italian blueness. And the tranquillity – 'not a cat in the house!' So it seemed, at least for three weeks. During this time he completed his one-act play for Ellen Terry. Then, perhaps because life was too tranquil, perhaps because he still had stage-fever, he went back to London 'for two or three compulsory weeks'.

His main reason for returning, after fleeing, was a need to talk to Miss Terry; but she was on the verge of sailing for her American tour and gave him only a brief rendezvous in her box at the theatre. She had written that she liked *Summersoft*, as the one-actor was titled, and James replied 'you are indeed the Gentle Reader; you read with imagination ... I want to write you another (already!) one-act play – yearn after such'. The actress paid him £100 and told him she would not produce the one-acter in America – she was scheduled to play *Madame Sans-Gêne*. The theatre seemed as fickle as ever but she promised production on her return. 'It will seem a long year – but art *is* long, ah me!' James replied. 'At all events, if the Americans are not to have the Gem, do excruciate them with a suspicion of what they lose.' This was his final gesture to the theatre. Miss Terry would never produce *Summersoft*, and two years later he converted it into a short story.

If the actress was the principal reason for James's dash to London, there was also another which few of his friends knew. A diary-entry in the journals of Clara Benedict, Miss Woolson's sister, tells us that 'Mr James said he would come up from Torquay and be with us the week before we sailed'. He was as good as his word. After a twelve-month, he still seemed to feel some sense of duty or obligation, some need for common kindness, and piety to Fenimore. He took the Benedicts to dinner at the Indian exhibition to which all London was flocking. They dined also in Mayfair and he saw them off to America. How he felt about them we know from his saying to Dr Baldwin that the United States had 'swallowed them up – and will keep them I suppose – till it heaves them forth again'. To another friend of Fenimore's – Francis Boott – he characterized Mrs Benedict as 'very considerably mad', and spoke of her and Miss Woolson's niece as 'very futile and foolish, poor things'. Nevertheless, some attachment to Fenimore's memory caused him, and would cause him in future years, to a continued excess of generosity towards the Benedicts.

After they sailed, James was free to return to Torquay. Instead he remained entangled with visitors and London society. He saw the Kiplings, on the eve of their return to America. The poet was 'strangely ungrowing'. He spent a Sunday in the country with the Humphry Wards. He entertained Graham Balfour, who brought him news of Fanny Stevenson in San Francisco. He spent some time with Mrs Mason. Count Primoli, the Bonaparte dillettante, turned up from Rome with his usual stories about the Princess Mathilde, and in his company was the young Prince Karageorgevitch of Monte-negro. James described the prince as 'not a bit of a personality, an individual – only a well-directed little faintly-perfumed spray of fluid, of distilled amenity'. He entertained Barrett Wendell of Harvard and complained to William when the professor sent him his book on Shakespeare. 'Besides being critically very thin and even common,' he wrote, 'it is surely not written as the Professor of English of Harvard should write. It has made me unhappy.' He wrote Wendell 'with anguish, a mendacious letter of thanks'. Still complaining of being 'confined to the torrid town', he went off to spend a week-end with George du Maurier at Folkestone. *Trilby* was breaking records as a best-seller, and would be a roaring success as a play. The quiet and gentle du Maurier, a professional artist but an amateur writer, was having the very kind of success James needed. Yet he found du Maurier depressed 'in spite of the chink – what say I, the "chink" – the deafening roar – of sordid gold flowing in to him'. James wrote to Gosse: 'I came back feeling an even worse failure than usual.'

2

It was now early September. James made arrangements for installation of the electric light in his De Vere Gardens flat. As painters, paperhangers and electricians took over, he left once more for Torquay. His Devonshire retreat promised to be sociable. The Paul Bourgets, passing through London, had once again decided to join him for a month. There had been their sojourn in Siena in 1892; and then the previous year they had lived side by side in Oxford. They were much less demanding than the Daudets. The pair clung to James; he in turn clung to them and to Norris. 'Bourget's mind is, in the real solitude in which I live, beneath what has been so much social chatter, a flowering oasis in conversational sands.'

Writing to Francis Boott he described Norris's hilltop villa in terms of Italy. It had a lovely view and Norris lived with an only daughter

exactly as you used to do at Bellosguardo. Torquay was all dusty roads and villa walls ... Norris is a dear like you, and passionately fond of music, like you. His daughter too, is Lizzie's age: the age Lizzie was (23!) but there the resemblance ends. She doesn't care a straw for 'art' – or only for the art of foxhunting. She is a pure amazon – one of these frequent English types who is exclusively horsey and yet not a bit 'fast'.

Norris played golf every morning, during the hours James was writing. The English novelist wrote

at the inconceivable hour of three till five. Then he potters in his garden; then, at six, I, finishing my longish and solitary walk, drop in, or rather climb up, and have tea with him. At eight he dines *tête-à-tête* with his daughter, both infinitely dressed – and after dinner he plays the piano. So you see it's all much like you.

As for Norris's books, 'ah, his books – nothing would induce me to tell you what I think of them! Seriously, I don't think anything at all.' Norris once spoke of 'my rather absurd old-man's fad for hearing from all the people I care for at Christmas'. During James's late years, no matter where he was, a long Yule letter was invariably dispatched to Torquay.

3

James had promised Heinemann two novels during the coming year; and he was supposed to write three tales for the *Atlantic Monthly*. He felt a certain pressure not only to fulfil these agreements, but to begin earning money again. His vain theatrical experiments, he wrote William, had brought him 'to the verge of bankruptcy'. Once again he communed with himself in his notebooks, 'I am face to face with several little alternatives of work. I must thresh out my solutions, must settle down to my jobs.' Then, impatiently, he told himself, 'It's idiotic, by the way, to waste time in writing such a remark as that! As if I didn't feel in all such matters infinitely more than I can ever utter.' He had lost sight of

the necessary smallness, singleness of the subject. I've been too proud to take the very simple thing. I've almost always taken the thing requiring developments. Now, when I embark on developments I'm lost, for they are my temptation and my joy. I'm too afraid to be banal. I needn't be afraid, for my danger is small.

The danger was small, but he was caught now in the complexities of his troubled imagination as well as his desire for experiment. By telling his stories in short dramatic scenes, he required more words than had been necessary in his *laisser-aller* days. Even when he tried subjects that were small, the process of dramatizing them required a larger statement. His goal was 8,000 to 10,000 words; and now he nearly always ended with 18,000 or 20,000. He had begun a story for the *Atlantic* about a squabble between a mother and son over some antiques. At 25,000 it was not yet complete. He set it aside and began what seemed to him another small tale which he called *The Awkward Age*. When it reached 15,000 he wrote to the editor, 'I must try again for you on a tinier subject – though I thought this *was* tiny.' And he confessed that 'I can't do the very little thing any more, and the process – the endeavour – is most expensive – it is so long and complicated'. He attempted a new story inspired by having seen, while riding on top of a London bus, an attractive woman's face disfigured by a pair of abnormally large spectacles. It took him almost a month to write *Glasses*, and then he ruefully informed the *Atlantic* it had exceeded 15,000. Apologetically he asked the editor to print it in two instalments, 'The thing is so highly finished ... that is is a double pity it's so ill-starred. Of course, however, you may say

"Who in the world cares for high finish?"' The editor, Horace Scudder, liked the tale and ran it in a single issue. James was elated. 'Ask *anything* of me then – I won't refuse it!' Scudder offered to take the overblown story about the squabble over a houseful of antiques as a three or four instalment novel of about 35,000 words. James bargained for 5,000 words more; by the time he finished it, it had become a 75,000 word novel, published in seven instalments as *The Old Things*. In book form it would be *The Spoils of Poynton*.

What had happened to the author who could, with his turning hand, produce tale after tale, sometimes one or two a week? We may surmise that at this stage, given his mood and his despair, he resisted writing altogether. His notebooks contain over-elaborate scenarios, even for short things. In the old days he wasted no time for such preliminaries. He still possessed the art of brevity in spite of his new techniques; but the combination of psychological 'resistance' and his quest for original forms, proved too much for him. And then the substance of his tales – the four he would complete in 1895 – showed a state that he himself called 'embarrassment'. One feels that at this moment James wanted simply to be left alone; to have the consoling company of Norris; to ride his bicycle, and brood on his problems or dawdle on the Torquay Crescent. Instead he had to keep at his work, to refill his empty purse. A fantasy he set down in his notebook clearly suggests this. He begins by recalling that old Mrs Procter long ago described how pleasant it was simply to sit by her fire and read a book. He began to plan a tale about an 'old party' who finds delight in simple elderly pastimes – 'a quiet walk, a quiet read, the civil visit of a friend, or the luxury of some quite ordinary *relation*'. In his fantasy however the 'old party' is ousted from his fireside by his estranged wife who now turns up. 'I see it all, I feel for him.' The old party disappears, he 'vanishes away, leaving the wife in possession'. She takes over his quiet, his fireside, his book. 'I see *her* – having exterminated him – given up to the same stillness as *he* was. She is in his chair, by his lamp, at his table, she expresses just the same quiet little joy that he did.' The theme is very much like that of *The Altar of the Dead* written a year before, in which a woman takes over a man's private altar – and uses it to mourn the very individual he hated. The tale of the altar had reflected his feeling that Miss Woolson, by her suicide, had ravished his inner quiet. In killing herself, Miss Woolson had made him feel that in some strange way she had 'exterminated' him. He did not write this tale of the 'old party', but instead wrote another, about an author and an unfathomable secret.

4

James's re-exposure to the Benedicts in London and the reawakened Bellosguardo recollections at Torquay seem to have prompted a story reflecting his own secretive nature. Miss Woolson had, long before, written a story about a woman writer like herself, who takes her work to a successful literary man. Dissatisfied, he tries to edit it, only to discover that it contains 'an especial figure in a carpet', which unravels when he tampers with the copy. Whether James remembered that image, or found it elsewhere, he now planned a tale called *The Figure in the Carpet* and wrote it shortly after his return to town, under the new electric lights in De Vere Gardens.

It is one of James's artificial conceits about authorship. A young critic has reviewed the latest novel of Hugh Vereker and he hears Vereker call his review 'the usual twaddle'. Later Vereker discovers the identity of the critic, and is contrite; he explains to the young man that no one has understood his work nor discerned its secret – its 'figure in the carpet'. He speaks of this as his 'general intention'. Vereker says he has not tried to conceal anything; it is simply something everyone has overlooked. It resides in 'the order, the form, the texture' of his novels. Pressed further by the critic, the novelist says that what nobody had ever mentioned in his writings was 'the organ of life'. In the context of James's total work, it is not difficult to suggest what James was thinking of when he wrote this tale. We have his pronouncements, often reiterated, that it was art that *made* life. Consequently we may say that the 'organ of life' is art. 'Who in the world cares for high finish' – his words to the *Atlantic* editor – had expressed this. The order, the form, the texture of a work constituted the art with which it was written. And then in his writings James incorporated works of art and literary allusions as if they were 'life', as Adeline Tintner has shown in her many studies of James's 'iconography'. Vereker wryly observes to the young reviewer, 'It's quite with you rising young men that I feel most what a failure I am.'

The unnamed young critic tells all this to a fellow-critic, George Corvick, who begins a systematic search for the author's secret. He also tells his fiancée, Gwendolen Erme, who at 19 had written a three-decker novel James whimsically called *Deep Down*. Perhaps here James remembered Vernon Lee's novel and her caricature of him. Things have not gone well between Corvick and his girl friend, but now in their common pursuit of Vereker's 'exquisite scheme' they find true common ground. Art proves a more powerful force than life in the wooing. Corvick finally makes his discovery; he journeys halfway across the world to consult Vereker who confirms it. And Gwendolen marries him.

The marriage is short-lived. Corvick dies in an accident during his honeymoon. Later Vereker dies; and after him his wife. Only Corvick's widow now knows the secret and the curious little narrator asks her bluntly for it. She is just as blunt : 'I mean to keep it to myself,' and with this knowledge she writes a better novel, called *Overmastered*. When the narrator pursues her with his questions about the 'figure', she tells him 'It's my *life*.' Like the narrator in *The Aspern Papers*, the busy and curious little critic wonders whether he shouldn't try to marry her – the figure in the carpet seems traceable and describable 'only for husbands and wives – for lovers supremely united'. However, she marries a third-rate critic; and when, after a time, she dies, the narrator discovers that she never told this husband Vereker's secret. 'I was shut up in my obsession forever – my gaolers had gone off with the key.'

We have a convergence in this tale of the two themes that constituted James's 'embarrassment'. The first, the more obvious one, was his sense of being a misunderstood author; criticism was blind; it cared not one bit about the clever secrets of his art – his own figure in his Persian carpet. No one really understood what he wanted to do. The *Guy Domville* audience had behaved like a bunch of savages with a gold watch. The second theme was the burden of Miss Woolson. Had it been a secret of human relations, a defect in his own 'system' of friendship? He was left shut up in his obsession – for ever! How deeply this troubled him we may judge by the tale, *The Way it Came* (later renamed *The Friends of the Friends*), which immediately followed the story of Hugh Vereker. In the tradition of Defoe, it is a tale of a man who will never know whether he talked to a woman just before or after her death. His fiancée, who narrates the story, is also left in eternal doubt. Did her fiancé have a tryst with a living woman or with a ghost? As she kneels by the bedside of the dead woman, her thought is that 'Death had made her, had kept her beautiful; but I felt above all, that it had made her, had kept her, silent.' Again his image is that of a key – 'it had turned the key on something I was concerned to know'.

From this moment on – and for the next five years – his stories would be about little girls and young female adults who want to know – who try to probe the secrets of the world around them, but who do not possess enough facts for their inductions and deductions. In these tales James seems to have worked towards a single conclusion : the facts of life were crude and raw, and art coloured and gilded them. The human imagination brings life into existence. And the created life – the art and artefacts of the ages – became a part of human history. The greatest records of man are the records of his imagination.

5

James remained at Torquay for two months while his apartment was renovated. During the last days of his stay, Jonathan Sturges came to be with him. His crippled friend, usually cheerful, sardonic, a veritable 'little demon', was downcast and unhappy. James believed he had fallen in love with some woman in France; and for the first time had had to face the fact that in his helpless state he could not hope for love as other men. In this mood, one evening, Sturges began to tell James a little incident that had occurred months before in Paris. He had met Howells one day in Whistler's garden in the Rue du Bac. Howells had just arrived. Paris was beautiful. And he had to leave, recalled to America because his father was dying. In the garden-setting Howells said to young Sturges : 'Oh, you are young, you are young – be glad of it : be glad of it and *live*. Live all you can : it's a mistake not to. It doesn't much matter what you do – but live.' Howells had added 'I'm old. It's too late.' Listening to Sturges James could see and hear Howells – and he listened as if the message were for him. He felt old. His best years had fled. He was aware of his unlived life rising within – and yet it seemed 'too late'. The little anecdote touched the heart of James's melancholy. He could do no more, in his own black abyss, than put down Howells's words in his notebook. Five years later they would speak to him again : and then he would pay attention not to the words 'too late' but to the words 'live all you can'.

Part Two

The Turn of the Screw

34

A Quiet Hermitage

HENRY JAMES returned to London at the beginning of November 1895, having had two full months of the autumn at Torquay. He would have lingered in Devonshire but for the increasing illness of Jonathan Sturges. Rather than risk having a seriously sick friend on his hands, he got him to London. The doctors put Sturges straight into a hospital – 'where,' James wrote to Miss Reubell, 'he is (very successfully and comfortably) having his illness now.'

'I loved my Torquay to the end,' James told Miss Reubell. He found London lively and 'lots of people about'. A day or two after his return he helped to entertain Georg Brandes, the Danish critic who was on a visit to England, dining with him and Andrew Lang and afterwards taking him to the Saville Club and plying the abstemious celebrity with lemon squash. He found him of 'a very bright and large intercourse' and he told Gosse that Brandes 'did me good – great good; it is such a joy to encounter a fine free foreign mind. But it's a peril – it spoils one fearfully for some of one's other contacts.'

James rejoiced in the fresh paint, and the brightness of his new electric lamps. He wrote two tales and resumed work on his serial for the *Atlantic*. To Mrs Wister he said he cared more than ever for his work. With the 'necessary isolation the years bring with them (quantities of *acquaintances* – oh yes!)' his fiction was 'almost the only thing I do care for'. James spoke also in this letter of the death earlier that year of Leslie Stephen's wife (the mother of Virginia Woolf).

I had a great affection for her, and she was – where she was – such a perfectly precious force for good that one doesn't know what to make of the economy of things that could do nothing with her – as far as our measure of the matter goes – but suppress her. She was beautifully beautiful, and her beauty and her nature were all active *applied* things, making a great difference for the better for everybody. Merely not to see her any more is to have a pleasure the less in life.

Before the Yule season, James visited George Meredith who was about to bring out *The Amazing Marriage*; and he wrote to Daudet about du Maurier's *Trilby* which in its play form seemed destined to run for at least two or three years. 'See what it is to take the measure of the foot – as we say – of the gross Anglo-Saxon public. The rare Meredith is not that kind of shoemaker – nor,' added Henry, 'the poor James.'

I

On 18 December 1895, the London newspapers brought the novelist a horrible war scare. There had been for some years a boundary dispute between Venezuela and British Guiana. To a public unaware of the dawning American sense of hemispheric sanctity, the Latin country disputes seemed remote. Suddenly President Cleveland re-asserted the 70-year-old Monroe Doctrine. He denounced British 'aggression' against Venezuela and declared that the United States had a serious interest in the determination of the boundary. 'The American outbreak has darkened all my sky,' James wrote to Norris.

He had for so long taken for granted the continuing friendship of the English-speaking peoples – which his own career symbolized – that it came to him as a violent shock to discover how deep trans-atlantic animosities could run. He knew only too well that the English could be condescending and haughty to their American cousins; but it was new to him to see how nasty some of his fellow-countrymen could be to the English. Feelings between the two nations had been on the whole friendly since their differences during the Civil War. James had witnessed good diplomatic relations during Lowell's ministry, and an amicable tone of converse between London and Washington in subsequent years. Now Cleveland's belligerence, and a huge outcry against England in the American press, shook the foundations of his security. Cleveland, he remarked, had made the United States sound 'like one of the big European powers, particularly the Germany of Bismarck'.

His letters during the early weeks of 1896 show how profound was his anxiety. If there were a war he would have to make a choice, for his allegiance was double; his sympathies lay in London, in Europe, in the cosmopolite world. 'One must hope that sanity and civilization, in both countries, will prevail,' he wrote to his brother.

But the lurid light the American newspapers seem to project on the quantity of resident Anglophobia in the U.S. – the absolute war-hunger as against this country – is a thing to darken one's meditations. Whence, why does it, today, explode in such immense volume – in such apparent preponderance, and whither does it tend? It stupefies me – seems to me horribly inferior and vulgar – and I shall never go with it.

In an outburst of feeling he added: 'I had rather my bones were ground into British powder!'

James experienced in part the fatalism of the newspaper head-lines, the daily presentation of violent alternatives – as if all de-cisions had to be made on the instant. The British put on their coolest diplomatic manner; and as days passed, and belligerent words were succeeded by cautionary moves, James could write to the painter, John Everett Millais, 'The madness will evaporate.' To Howells he confessed that the war-scare had brought home to him the length of his absence from America. He had been away twelve years, and the American 'delirium' reached him 'as if it came from China or another planet'. To his despair, at the end of this terrible year of personal upheaval, was now added a sense of distance from his own country. 'Those were weeks of black darkness for me,' James told Howells.

2

In mid-winter of 1895–6, James was invited by the *Century* maga-zine to write a commemorative article on Dumas the Younger who had died recently. He did so promptly; it was a chance to talk 'theatre', and Dumas had been a dramatist remembered from his early years; he had heard his name when he was a small boy. He had not been allowed to see *La Dame aux Camélias* because it hadn't been suitable for his time of life. In his article he discussed the Anglo-Saxon tendency to be moral and the French tendency to *moralize*. Dumas had been a 'professional moralist', a student of the passions. One of Dumas's great contentions had been 'that seduced girls should under all circumstances be married – by somebody or other, failing the seducer. This is a contention,' James wrote, 'that, as we feel, barely concerns us, shut up as we are in the antecedent conviction that they should under no circumstances be seduced.' When James dispatched his manuscript, he received word from Robert Under-wood Johnson of the *Century* that it wouldn't do. The *Century* was a 'family magazine'. Relations between men and women, not least the seduction of young girls, could not be discussed in its pages. James promptly noted that this would make 'a lovely little ironic tale'. He wrote it during the following year – *John Delavoy* – and the editor in it tells a young critic emphatically he cannot write about the relations of the sexes. 'If you want to know what our public won't stand, there you have it.' The *Century* had wanted the article because Dumas was famous. He was famous because he had written certain things – 'which they won't for the world have intelligibly mentioned'. James may have taken ironic satisfaction when he sold the article to the New York *Herald* and the Boston *Herald*; it appeared in both under large headlines, as if indeed James had written a shocker – '[Dumas's] Reputation for Immorality due to Alien Judgment' and 'Life to him Appeared Wholly a Fierce Battle Between Man and Woman'.

3

James agreed that winter to do a serial for an unusual medium – for him – the *Illustrated London News*. His friend, Mrs W. K. Clifford had hinted to the editor Clement Shorter that James might be willing to strike a 'popular' note and he was very positive about this. 'I should be very glad to write you a story energetically designed to meet your requirements of a "love-story,"' he wrote, and he bargained for a higher price than was offered. They settled for £300. 'I shall endeavour to be thrilling,' he said. With the final chapters of *The Old Things* still to be written for the *Atlantic*, James decided to quit London early and get his books done in some quiet corner of England. He had nursed a dream of going that spring to Italy, but Torquay had demonstrated that England had eminently practical places of refuge. If he could find a house near London, he could be in and out of the city as necessary. Moreover, there had always been the question of his servants in De Vere Gardens, who took to drink during his absence. He began to lay plans in February 1896.

The house was found for him by an architect friend, Edward Warren, and punctually at the end of April James moved in. 'I recapture a cottage on a cliffside,' James would remember,

to which at the earliest approach of the summer-time ... I had betaken myself to finish a book in quiet and to begin another in fear. The cottage was, in its kind, perfection; mainly by reason of a small paved terrace which, curving forward from the cliff-edge like the prow of a ship, overhung a view as level, as pure, as full of rich change as the expanse of a sea; a small red-roofed town, of great antiquity, perched on its sea-rock, clustered within the picture off to the right; while above one's head rustled a dense summer shade, that of a trained and arching ash, rising from the middle of the terrace, brushing the parapet with a heavy fringe and covering the place like a vast umbrella.

It was called Point Hill, located at Playden in Susssex. The novelist got a three-months' occupancy, from May to August 1896. The town at which James looked was one of England's ancient Cinque Ports – Rye in Sussex, unique in Britain in the way in which its red-brick houses, many of them extremely old, huddled about the town's church, set on the highest point of the rock – a church part Norman, with a square tower. For all the world, in the fading light, amid a thick purple haze, it looked from Playden like a miniature Mont St Michel or one of James's beloved Italian hill-towns rising above the Umbrian valley.

When he explored Rye he found it to be filled with old-world charm. It had an ancient tower, built in the twelfth century as a watch-tower; on the London side the town had a Landgate, also a remnant of the middle ages. The waters had long withdrawn from the base of the rock and the marshes had been drained, so that Romney Marsh, once covered by the sea, now had hundreds of sheep peacefully grazing. The High Street was filled with old shops, small-paned and reminiscent of old novels; at night when they were lit by candle or smelly oil-lamp it seemed as if he were back in the eight-eenth century. Cobbled Mermaid Street, with its Elizabethan houses, went back much farther. During his rambles James was particularly struck by a stout red-bricked Georgian house, at a curve in the steep street leading to the church; next to it was a curious little hall that looked like a chapel or a banqueting hall. He was told that the house had for decades been in the hands of the Lambs, one of Rye's promin-ent families.

'It is delightfully quiet and quaint and simple and salubrious, and the bliss of the rural solitude and peace and beauty are a balm to my spirit,' James wrote to William after a month at Point Hill. 'This little corner of the land endears itself to me.' His servants took good care of him; the weather was exceptionally fine, and every evening in the thickening twilight he would dine at eight on his terrace, as if he were living in a Florentine villa. He had brought his other com-panions with him – his faithful fat old dog, Tosca, and his canary in its cage, a recent gift from the London beauty Mrs Mahlon Sands. When he was not walking the hilly streets, he took to the circling

sea-roads on his bicycle, going to nearby Winchelsea, where Ellen
Terry had her cottage, and to a host of little towns with soft quaint
names – Brookland, Old Romney, Ivychurch, Dymchurch, Lydd. As
the summer deepened, as the shepherds and their dogs passed him
in the grassy meadow, Henry James was reminded of his younger
years when he had galloped on horseback past Italian shepherds and
their flocks and felt the stir of ancient things in the Roman Campagna.

4

Long before the first of August when he was supposed to surrender
Point Hill to its returning owners, James decided he did not want
to leave. A systematic hunt yielded him a haven for the rest of the
summer. This was the town's Old Vicarage, as it was formally called,
situated in Rye itself, to which Jamed moved bird and dog and servants, and his masses of proof and manuscript. The 'musty,
bourgeois parsonage' gave him no view, and brought him down to
the cobbles of Rye itself; but he was able to work well within it. He
liked its 'very ancient and purple brick-walled garden, where the
pears grow yellow in the September sun and the peace of the Lord
– or at least of the parson – seems to abide'. He amusedly gave himself out as leading the 'prosy' life of a *curé de campagne*. 'Think of
me in a vicarage,' he wrote to the church-doctrined Mrs Humphry
Ward; and he clung to it until it was time to surrender it at the beginning of October.

  'I am nearing the end of a very quiet summer,' he wrote to Grace
Norton, 'I like the country, which is really rustic, and for the most
part remarkably pretty – I like, now, almost *any* country; and I like
even a little unsophisticated town, like this, perched picturesquely
on its pedestal of rock.' A little red-roofed and clustered old-world
town, James told Miss Norton, was 'in a manner a small and homely
family'. The image was apt. For the Henry James, who ever since
Guy Domville had felt 'homeless', whose mind wandered to the rent-
ing or even acquiring of an anchorage (and who indeed was writing
three works in succession involving houses) the parochial domesticity of this one of the guardian ports of England offered a kind of
solitude and friendliness which he could not find in London. James
said he recognized how intensely Rye must have been a 'family' 'in
the old days of its loneliness, when the French repeatedly harried

and took it'. In later decades it had been a great centre of smuggling. All this was but 'a quaintness the more, when on one side, away from the steep little street, where the sound of wheels is almost never, one's windows in the rear have a garden and a great country view'. Before leaving he mentioned, in chatting with the local ironmonger, that he·was interested in finding a year-round house in Rye. The ironmonger would remember.

35

Houses and Old Things

I

The Spoils of Poynton – a story of an old house and 'old things' – marked a turning-point in the fiction of Henry James, although the novelist, struggling with his work on his terrace overlooking Rye, seems hardly to have been aware of this. Re-reading The Spoils today one is struck by the dramatic quality of its slight but strong theme – the struggle between a mother and son for possession of a houseful of antiques; the scenic deployment of its four principal characters; the shrewd study of personal relations. The novel deals with a woman who values property above people, whose 'fine arrogance' and 'sense of style' involve the manipulation of persons weaker than herself. But the novel is also – within its technical virtuosity – an amused commentary on the collecting spirit, 'that most modern of our current passions, the fierce appetite for the upholsterer's and joiner's and brazier's work, the chairs and tables, the cabinets and presses, the material odds and ends, of the more labouring ages'. These are the grouped objects, 'all conscious of their eminence and price' which the dedicated owner of Poynton, on the death of her husband, seeks to prevent her son from inheriting – unless he can marry a wife capable of caring for them as she has done.

The 'old things' of this novel are moved about a great deal; and we are made to see that certain houses are right for them and others wrong. There is Poynton itself 'written in great syllables of colour and form', held in the embrace of England's composed landscape. There is the dower house of Ricks, a 'shallow box', symbol of Mrs Gareth's dispossession. Here the treasures are rearranged in a dubious compromise. Finally there is Waterbath, 'trumpery ornament and scrapbook art', which the embattled Mrs Gereth regards as enemy territory. She has made a successful work of art of Poynton. She has not succeeded in making her son into anything but a pleasant, weak young man. And the story involves her attempts to rectify her failure and his artlessness, to supply him with a woman capable of making up for his deficiencies, that is someone as discriminating and as skilled in manœuvre as herself.

2

The original idea for *The Spoils* had been jotted down in James's notebook two years earlier, during one of his London dinners, when the woman next to him had spoken of 'a small ugly matter' in which a widowed Scottish lady was suing her son over the rare furnishing he had inherited and which she refused to yield. The anecdote became long; and James didn't want its cluttered details. He closed his ears to the rest: he had his situation in the first few words. In the notebooks we can see that he began by wanting to be sorry for Mrs Gereth, the displaced and deposed mother, sent away from her grand house and her antiques by the English custom of relegating widows to a dower house. This very American view of the perpetual 'queenship' of the mother faded considerably as James got into his story. What emerged was Mrs Gereth's destructive rage and her determined effort to marry her son off to the helpless Fleda Vetch, whose name does not suggest the fineness James sought to give her character. She is a young artistic girl, and James regarded her as the moral force of the novel. Mrs Gereth is clever, but not intelligent; Fleda is intelligent, but not clever. And Mrs Gereth places her in the impossible position of having to pursue her light-hearted son, who is himself pursued by the ruthless philistine Mona Brigstock. James thus constructs a chain of personal pressures. Mrs Gereth exerts pressure on Fleda. Fleda in more subtle ways exerts moral pressure on Owen, while Mona presses him from her side. The young man's weakness is greater than his amiability and he has three women on his back. Mona will marry Owen only if he obtains Poynton. Fleda wants to marry Owen, but holds back out of moral scruples, indecision, and an inability to assert herself; perhaps also because she believes her love for him is worthy of more direct recognition. She will marry Owen only if she is sure he can disengage himself from Mona with honour. One develops sympathy for the artless Owen, who is valued largely in terms of a houseful of antiques. Only Fleda shows love for him; but he is passive; and she on her side is more passive still; she seems to value honour and protocol and priority as much as love. The intensity of her passion is expressed when she says, 'I don't know what girls may do, but if he doesn't know that there isn't an inch of me that isn't his –.' Thus Fleda to Owen's mother. This same intensity however does not lead to action. Moreover she feels too much 'advertised and offered'. We have been told that she was armed for 'the battles of life' by a season of study with an impressionist painter. Her impressionism, her vacillation, make for self-defeat; holding all the trump cards in her hands she throws them away. These are the emotional and 'interpersonal' dilemmas of James's little drama.

Critics have been puzzled by the character of Fleda Vetch and her ill-motivated renunciation of Owen. Her reasons are noble; yet they have no relation to the realities James incorporated into his story. His scenario shows James at odds both with his characters and his plot. He seems to have fixed his mind on the ultimate destruction of Poynton; in the end no one is to have anything – as he had been left with nothing when his own artistic work went up in smoke at the St James's. The novelist begins, in effect, with the idea for one kind of novel, that of the dispossessed mother, and ends with another. He removes Mrs Gereth from the centre of the stage and puts Fleda in her place. To read James's late preface and his description of his heroine is to recognize that he 'thought' one character but created another. The Fleda of his preface, the 'superior' girl with the 'demonic' mind and 'free spirit' is not in the book. In the book she is as confused and filled with tergiversation as James had been in the theatre. His traditional ending would have been the triumph of the philistines and the defeat of the noble-minded. But he substituted melodrama instead; perhaps because he had himself been forced to abandon the stage, in a bit of melodrama not of his own making.

His imagery went further back however than the recent disaster in the St James's. In describing Mrs Gareth's departure from Poynton and her loss of her antiques, *her* work of art, James wrote 'the amputation had been performed. Her leg had come off – she had now begun to stump along with the lovely wooden substitute; she would stump for life, and what her young friend was to come and admire was the beauty of her movement and the noise which she made about the house.' Thus James had recourse in this work to one of the most personal images out of his childhood. It suggests how vivid for all his lifetime was the memory of his father's amputation and 'the noise ... about the house' of his wooden leg. Amputation and fire: these symbols out of the past now forced themselves into the story he was telling. Poynton and its 'spoils' had to be destroyed as *Guy Domville* was destroyed: and Henry James felt himself amputated — as his father had been after a stable fire. James's five-year struggle to sacrifice art to the Moloch-materialism of the stage was retold in *The Spoils of Poynton* in the form of an irrational issue of a rational conflict, and in terms of irrational behaviour. In life everything had been irrational. And the violence of the *Guy Domville* audience had revived the violence of his childhood. Later stories would show just how much had been reawakened. It was as if the injuries of long ago had re-occurred within his adult consciousness, and he had to purge himself of them. He was doing this in the only way he knew — he relived them in his art.

3

If *The Spoils of Poynton* represented James's first attempt to use his scenic method and his play-writing techniques, *The Other House*, which he wrote immediately afterwards, was a direct adaptation into the novel-form of a play scenario. The play had been sketched for Edward Compton early in 1894. The actor had shown little interest, and James had put it aside.

The punctuality with which he dispatched his instalments from Point Hill, and later from the Old Vicarage, suggests that the scenario must have been in effect a first draft of the play. The work is almost entirely dialogue, save for settings and occasional brief narrative passages. James was to regard the lessons he learned from turning scenario material into fiction as a landmark in his work, for he exclaims in an entry in his notebook, as late as 1910, 'Oh blest *Other House*, which gives me thus at every step a precedent, a support, a divine little light to walk by.'

There are two houses in this novel: Eastmead and Bounds. They are separated by a garden and a near-by stream connects them; they are also connected by being the homes of the partners in the banking firm of Beever and Bream. Mrs Beever, who inherited her husband's share in the bank, lives at Eastmead and to her, Bounds is 'the other house'. Eastmead is 'a great, clean, square, solitude', and everything we discover about it reinforces our impression of its calm, its order, its uncluttered state. Mrs Beever's own life is equally ordered – 'like a room prepared for a dance; the furniture was all against the walls'. A strong, masculine woman, her only concession to maternity is her desire to marry off her son, when he graduates from Oxford, to a girl of her choice. Her choice is a 'slim, fair girl', whom James in his notes has designated as his 'Good Heroine'.

The 'Bad Heroine' is installed in 'the other house'. Unlike Eastmead, Bounds is the reverse of calm; it is in some ways the grander house, handsomely and expensively renovated by the younger partner in the bank, Anthony Bream. In the prelude to this odd story, Bream's wife has just given birth to a daughter. The mother is certain she will not survive childbirth. She has a morbid fear of stepmothers; her own had been too demanding. She accordingly exacts a promise from Tony Bream that if she dies, he will not remarry, so long as her child lives. At the end of the first 'act', she does indeed die, and the Ibsenite drama can now act itself out, between the two houses, the house of quiet and the house of passion, between the Good Heroine Jean Martle and the Bad Heroine Rose Armiger, who is as desperate and frustrated, as intense and as determined as Hedda Gabler.

Rose had been an old companion of Mrs Bream's. A difficult and exasperated woman, she had loved Tony without hope so long as her old friend lived; and she is now prevented from marrying him so long as the child, Effie, lives. Tony on his side is much more interested in the Good Heroine, Jean Martle, than his wife's friend. The little girl protects him, in a sense, against Rose and indeed against remarriage – as his wife had intended. The Good Heroine is a sort of child-woman, with a fine complexion and beautiful hair : she is Henry James's idealized female, a simpler Isabel or Mary Garland. Tony is attracted to her in the way in which James was attracted to women, to Miss Woolson, for instance – 'there was no one he had ever liked whom he could quite like so comfortably'. Tony asks himself what his appreciation of this girl might lead to, and he provides the answer – 'it would lead to exactly nothing – that had been settled all round in advance. This was a happy, lively provision that kept everything down, made sociality a cool, public out-of-door affair, without a secret or a mystery – confined it, as one might say, to the breezy, sunny forecourt of the temple of friendship.' Everything would be kept 'down', as at Eastmead; and the words *cool*, *public*, *out-of-doors* are eloquent. No sex, no passion, no secret, no mysteries – a comfortable Platonic relation.

As for the other girl, she is frightening. She belongs to the intensity and passion expressed by Tony's own dead wife who exacted the sacred promise. Tony looks into Rose Armiger's eyes. They seem at first deep and exquisite. Then he sees something else, a kind of 'measureless white ray of light steadily revolving' and he notes that she could sometimes turn this light away. Nevertheless it was 'always somewhere; and now it covered him with a great cold lustre that made everything for the moment look hard and ugly'. It *is* hard and ugly; for the frustrated passionate Rose drowns little Effie (the child is 4 when the crime is committed), and tries to fix the guilt on the Good Heroine. The hero is left undefended.

This is the melodrama James devised for the readers of the *Illustrated London News*. It is the only novel he ever wrote (he did not consider it part of his fictional canon, always recalling its 'inferior' origin in the theatre) in which violence occurs. James had toyed with having the Bad Heroine administer poison to the child; but he chooses death by drowning instead, and we are reminded how little more than a year before he had spoken of being himself 'subaqueous'. At the end Tony Bream must ponder 'to what tune he had been liked' – which was what James had had to ponder after Fenimore's violent end in Venice.

The Other House is an unpleasant novel : a piece of subtle mechanical play-tinkering with powerful stuff of the emotions which he does not seem to understand or to command : an outburst of primitive rage that seems irrational however much it is dramatically 'motivated'; and with a crime which defies the tradition of murderstories by going unpunished. It is an Ibsen play without Ibsen's morality – or his insight; we can find in it certain resemblances to *Rosmersholm*, which Miss Robins produced during the year *The Other House* was first planned. Perhaps James felt that his Bad Heroine's future would in itself be sufficient punishment. But the reader puts down the work feeling that for once James has been clever rather than intelligent; that some powerfully controlled areas of feeling within him have burst their bounds (symbolically the house in which the melodrama is enacted is called Bounds). Reading the cultivated dialogue, and watching the men struggle to shield Rose from punishment, we sense that for once in his career as artist

James has seriously faltered. Some instinct told him that he had; for he published the novel amid the pictorial sensationalism of a journal he disliked.

Thus the two novels which James wrote at the outset of this new period of creativity contain within them the violence that had come into his own life. The sudden burning of Poynton was the metaphor for the sudden destruction of his play; the passion of Rose Armiger and its destruction of the little girl meant the murder of innocence – as if some remote little being within James himself had been 'exterminated' by the audience during that crucial night a year and a half earlier, and left him open to the indifference of the world. *The Spoils of Poynton* becomes the portal through which we pass into the most curious series of novels James devised in his entire career as a writer : a terrible world of blighted houses and of blighted childhoods – of little girls – and a strange world of female adolescence. The works he now wrote suggest that in the midst of the sun and sea and summer of Rye, the long rides on his bicycle, the change from urban life to quiet English ruralism, James continued to live in his deepest self in a struggling nightmare world, a return to the sensitive hurts of his early life. The quest for inner peace continued.

36

Paradox of Success

ON 30 July 1896 Henry James broke his stay at Point Hill – he was on the verge of moving into the Vicarage – to attend the funeral of a friend in London, a great American beauty, Mrs Mahlon Sands, who had died quite suddenly at 41. Her maid had been helping her to dress in her great house in Portland Place; she left the room for two minutes and returned to find her mistress dead on the floor. Three days earlier Mrs Sands had written to Henry James, at the climax of the London Season : 'Are you not coming up at all? I am sick of the whole thing.' He came up for the service in St George's, Hanover Square, on an exquisite summer's day; and amid the flowers and elegant mourners – Harcourts, Rothschilds, Rowtons, Algernon West who had wanted to marry her – James could hear the irrelevant worldly bustle of Bond Street close at hand. Mrs Sands had conquered

London fifteen years earlier, almost as if she were one of his heroines. She had been a friend of the Prince of Wales, had known Gladstone, all the late Victorians, moving with ease through the great houses. James had been fond of her, driven, nervous, tense creature though she was, enmeshed and trapped in Society. There was 'nothing small or mean' about her and she had had 'a beauty that had once been of the greatest'. Sargent had painted her and James had written her instructions how to pose –

you can't collaborate or co-operate, except by sitting still and looking beautiful ... it's *his* affair, yours is only to be as difficult for him as possible; and the more difficult you are the more the artist will be condemned to worry over you, repainting, revolutionizing, till he, in a rage of ambition and admiration, arrives at the thing that satisfies him and that enshrines and perpetuates you. There are as good eyes on his palette as ever were caught, and yours on Sargent's canvas will still be the mystification of posterity, just as they often are that of yours most didactically Henry James.

Before beauty, the novelist could be humble and voluble. To Ethel Sands, the daughter, a painter and a distinct personality in Chelsea and Bloomsbury, James wrote a few days after the funeral :

She had no vocation for any *common* happiness, or common answers, small answers, to great questions, and she *had* a great aptitude to struggle and suffer. Better than I too you know her sweetness, her grace, her gifts – you had lived in her beautiful presence. Nothing small had any part in her – and she is an exquisite ineffaceable memory.

It was Mrs Sands who had sent him the golden canary that warbled away the days in Sussex that summer.

I

James experienced a different kind of sorrow that autumn, when he returned to London. His old and cherished friend, George du Maurier, died early in October. James had loved his cartoons in *Punch* long before he had met him; he had studied them as a boy stretched out on the rug before the fire in Fourteenth Street. And then in his first years in London du Maurier had become his friend. He had illustrated *Washington Square*, or as James put it, had consented to make drawings 'for a short novel that I had constructed in crude defiance of the illustrator'. James liked the mixture of French seriousness and English drollery in du Maurier; du Maurier liked James's American observation and his French wit. On Sundays James used to climb the hill to du Maurier's house in Hampstead; they walked on the Heath and in that suburb, amid 'red walls and jealous gates, the old benches in the right places'. There was one such bench which figures as frontispiece to James's volume of tales of the literary life in the New York Edition. Here they sat for hours talking about Flaubert and Paris and English life. James had always admired the comedy and craft of this supreme gentle satirist – du Maurier's ability to capture people's postures while they wait for dinner, while they are thinking what to say, pretending to listen to music, making speeches they don't mean. Du Maurier could reproduce to the life the gentleman who stares at his boots, the lady who gazes at the ceiling. And then no one had drawn lovelier women and children. Du Maurier seemed to see all the English as tall and handsome. The world for him had a wonderful simplicity; things were either ugly or they were beautiful.

Du Maurier was blind in one eye, but when they walked his other eye had an extraordinary optical reach. 'I always thought I valued the use of my eyes and that I noticed and observed,' James wrote, 'but the manner in which, when out with him, I mainly exercised my faculty was by remarking how constantly and how easily his own surpassed it.' James and the artist would go on long rambles in Bayswater 'with dusk enough for the lighted shop-fronts to lend a romantic charm to Westbourne Grove'. The novelist remembered du Maurier's alertness: he saw mystery, reality, drollery, irony, in everything.

And then du Maurier had 'a sociable habit of abounding in the sense of his own history and his own feelings, his memories, sympathies, contacts, observations, adventures'. There were summers when James had gone to the Yorkshire coast, to Whitby, to visit him and to be near Lowell who also stayed there. They used to walk by cold cliffs and beside a cold sea, or on the warm moors, or in Whitby's big brown fishing quarter. Du Maurier used to like the bleak breakwater, a long wide seawall with a twinkling lighthouse at the end; he expressed delight in the bronzed and battered faces of the fishermen and the long procession of their boats. The artist was a marvellous spinner of tales. One night he told James a fantastic story of a pair of lovers changed into albatrosses. They were shot and wounded; one resumed human shape and waited and watched in vain for the other. The germ of *Peter Ibbetson* seemed to be in this tale and du Maurier's idea of 'dreaming true'. And then there was the famous evening, of 25 March 1889:

Last evening before dinner I took a walk with G. du Maurier in the mild March twilight (there was a blessed sense of spring in the air), through the empty streets near Porchester Terrace, and he told me over an idea of his which he thought very good – and I do too – for a short story – he had already mentioned to me – a year or two ago, in a walk at Hampstead, but it had passed from my mind.

James then recorded the story. It dealt with a girl with a wonderful voice but no genius for music, who is mesmerized and made to sing by a little foreign Jew 'who has mesmeric power, infinite feeling, and no organ'. *Trilby* acquired existence first as a note in James's scribbler. James decided he could not write it, though du Maurier urged him to do so: 'the want of musical knowledge would hinder *me* somewhat in handling it'. He then urged du Maurier to tell it himself. Du Maurier tried but found himself dealing with a different theme. He wrote *Peter Ibbetson*, about a hero whose dreams become his only reality. Six years after their evening walk *Trilby* was published – with the results the world knows.

2

As James stood in the fine old Hampstead churchyard, amid the élite of England, beside the grave of the man he had seen so often during his London life, and whom he had dearly loved, *Trilby* was selling in the tens of thousands and people were flocking to see the play version on both sides of the sea. For James there was a striking – and mocking – psychological drama in the final events of his friend's life. Du Maurier had for years lived his private Hampstead life, with his wife and children and dog, his drawing-board and his notations of London comedy and London society. Then he had written *Trilby* as a piece of natural and intimate story-telling. James had expected that it would be liked; he had not thought it would take the public by storm. The amateur, writing his tale as it were on the edge of his drawing-board, had achieved what James with all his consummate art of story-telling could never do. He was not jealous of his friend, but he was amazed by the paradox of 'success'. Life was recreating so many of his stories of authorship. In the end *Trilby* seemed to have murdered her creator. The old witty intimate du Maurier disappeared; in his place there remained a melancholy successful man. He did not want to be a public figure; fame insisted on making him one late in middle age. 'I dearly loved George du Maurier,' James wrote to Paul Bourget. He had had, late in life, on the edge of his sixties, the success of a celebrity and of personal fortune, to which he attached no importance, and which seems not to have given him much pleasure. He has died in the midst of this of melancholy and indifference.' What did it mean, this showering of adulation on a man who loved privacy and quiet? The long article James dedicated to his friend takes up this question but finds no answer. Why was du Maurier so 'overtaken and overwhelmed?' Why had the public pounced on his gentle writings with such eagerness, such greed? He 'passed away, I think, with a sigh that was a practical relinquishment of the vain effort to probe the mystery of its [*Trilby*'s] success. The charm was one thing, and the success quite another, and the number of links missing between the two was greater than his tired spirit could cast about for.'

Du Maurier had let loose the elements, and 'they did violence to his nerves'.

The whole phenomenon grew and grew till it became, at any rate for this particular victim, a fountain of gloom and a portent of woe; it darkened all his sky with a hugeness of vulgarity. It became a mere immensity of sound, the senseless hum of a million of newspapers and the irresponsible chatter of ten millions of gossips. The pleasant sense of having done well was deprived of all sweetness, all privacy, all sanctity.

Du Maurier had wanted to simplify, but 'the clock of his new period kept striking a different hour from the clock of his old spirit'. One more door had closed on James's old 'London life', and its closing illustrated the ironies of 'success', the strangeness of 'reputation'. If one part of his memorial to du Maurier dealt with a deeply personal friendship, the other part was a kind of memorial for his own dream of theatrical fame, an attempt to tell himself that this fame would have been in reality worthless, perhaps fatal.

37

A Fierce Legibility

BETWEEN 1895 and 1898 the twentieth century began to knock loudly at Henry James's door. He had installed electric light in De Vere Gardens in 1895; in 1896 he had begun to use the bicycle whenever he was in the country; in 1897 he purchased a typewriter and engaged a part-time typist; in 1898 he went to one of the earliest movies, the 'cinematograph – or whatever they call it' to see pictures of the Fitzsimmons–Corbett prizefight. 'We quite revelled,' James told Mrs Wister. But it was the purchase of the typewriter that brought the greatest change into his life.

I

When the use of the typewriter had become general in the 1880s he began to send his manuscripts to a public stenographer. In earlier years he had simply dispatched his pages, written in his rapid hand, directly to editor and publisher; if he was writing a serial he worked from proofs. Early in 1896 he had become aware of increasing pain in his right wrist; he described it as rheumatic and it was probably the familiar writer's cramp, understandable enough in a man who for years had worked six to eight hours a day at his desk. His brother who had acquired stenographic help at Harvard, described the delights of dictating. Henry agreed he might come to this – for his correspondence. It did not at first occur to him that it might also serve for his fiction. During the autumn and winter of 1896–7, when he was working on *What Maisie Knew*, his wrist condition became chronic. He accordingly engaged a stenographer, William Mac-Alpine, a silent Scot from Aberdeen and Edinburgh, who worked regularly as shorthand reporter for medical societies, but had his mornings free to take James's dictation. The novelist began by letting him take letters in shorthand. The typewritten letters from the first announced themselves in elaborate apologies for 'this cold-blooded process', this 'fierce legibility' – 'the only epistolary tongue of my declining years'. By the end of the first month, he was dictating directly to the typewriter; it saved time and enabled him to do much more. 'I can address you only through an embroidered veil of sound,' he dictated to his Parisian friend, Morton Fullerton. 'The sound is that of the admirable and expensive machine that I have just purchased for the purpose of bridging our silences.' He added: 'The hand that works it, however, is not the lame *patte* which, after inflicting on you for years its aberrations, I have now definitely relegated to the shelf, or at least to the hospital.'

James discovered early that the repose enabled his wrist to do a certain amount of letter-writing in the old way, so that part of his correspondence was relegated to the evenings, and remained private; he did not like to share it with his Scot. A certain number of letters continued to be typewritten; but the machine in the end was reserved for his art. He became so accustomed to its sound, that he was unable to dictate one day when it broke down and an alien typewriter temporarily replaced it. Very early, Morton Fullerton raised the question: what would the typewriter do to James's style? 'I can be trusted, artless youth,' James answered, 'not to be simplified by any shortcut or falsified by any facility.' He ended this letter with, 'am I not meanwhile only more discernibly yours, Henry James?' To Mrs Curtis of Venice, who put a similar question, he said that dictation did not hamper him in the least, 'in letters quite the reverse, and in commerce with the Muse so little that I foresee the day when it will be pure luxury'. There was no question that he was more 'discernible', and some of his friends claimed they could put their finger on the exact chapter in *Maisie* where manual effort ceased and dictation began. Henry James writing, and Henry James dictating, were different persons. His sentences became, in time, elaborate – one might indeed say baroque – filled with qualifications and parentheses; he seemed often, in a letter, to begin a sentence without knowing what its end would be, and he allowed it to meander into surprising twists and turns. After several years of consistent dictating, the 'later manner' of Henry James emerged. Some part of it would have been there without benefit of the Remington. Certain indirections and qualifications had always existed. But the spoken voice was to be heard henceforth in James's prose, not only in the rhythm and ultimate perfection of his verbal music, but in his use of colloquialisms, and in a more extravagant play of fancy, a greater indulgence in expanding metaphors, and great proliferating similes. James was Proustian before Proust; and doubtless having a companion always in his work-room brought into his creative work elements of the

'interpersonal'. It would be a long time before James would obliter-
ate from his vision the presence of the typist. The actor in him could
not resist exhibitory flourishes.

The typewriter was, in those days, a large and not easily trans-
ported object. It never occurred to James – and doubtless he would
have been very clumsy at it – to learn to typewrite, as writers would
learn to do in the new century. Acquisition of his machine meant
not only that he lost his mobility, but that he was dependent upon
help to get his daily work done. For more than thirty years he had
been able to take his writing-portfolio wherever he went. He could
not travel with his machine; and it would have meant employing
the typist full-time. And he would have to lodge and feed him as he
journeyed. He explained this in detail to a friend in June 1897:

The voice of Venice, all this time, has called very loud. But it has been
drowned a good deal in the click of the typewriter to which I dictate
and which, some months ago, crept into my existence through the crevice
of a lame hand and now occupies in it a place too big to be left vacant
for long periods of hotel and railway life.

2

He passed one of his 'quietest, sanest, simplest' winters in London.
He went regularly to visit Jonathan Sturges in his nursing home; it
was almost as if he were back in the time when he regularly visited
his ailing sister. He declined invitations, worked at his dictation,
occasionally went to the theatre. For a few evenings he helped Miss
Robins put into English Echegaray's *Mariana* from a literal Spanish
translation, for one of her productions. He applauded the actress in
Little Eyolf, and Ibsen's mastery of form in *John Gabriel Borkman*.
While writing *Maisie*, he also wrote a monthly letter for *Harper's
Weekly*. He was well paid, but in most of the letters he sounds as
bored as his readers must have been. When *Harper's* dropped him
after ten such letters he was as always indignant. It was his *Tribune*
experience all over again. He had been dismissed 'as you scarce
would an incompetent housemaid. And yet I tried to be so Base!' As
in the theatre, and in other attempts at such correspondence, he
began with contempt for the task; and a part of his haughty anger
was anger at himself for stooping to literary drudgery. The best of
these letters were reprinted years later in *Notes on Novelists*.

With the spring London readied itself for Queen Victoria's diamond jubilee. James was impatient with the scaffold-carpentry, the defacing of the capital, the bidding for seats; this was a drab commercializing of national sentiment. He looked for another house in the country, but found none to his liking. So he remained in town, promising himself he would leave just before the 'Victorian Saturnalia'. He described the preparations as 'a great incommodity' – 'the gross defacement of London, the uproarious traffic in seats, the miles of unsightly scaffolding between the West End and the City, the screaming advertisements, the sordid struggle'. This was, he said, 'the great clumsy, ugly fate of everything today that's done at all. The machinery of insistence and reverberation – the newspaper deluge and uproar – deflowers and destroys and maddens.'

He told William he 'saw not the tip of the tail of any part of the show'. The young George Vanderbilt offered him a place on his large balcony overlooking Pall Mall. James declined, and left for Bournemouth. His typist was free and he took him along to the seaside, leaving the 'Babylonian barricades' to the hordes. 'For all the world like a cabinet minister' he engaged rooms at the chateau-like Royal Bath Hotel for himself and his typist and in a Bournemouth utterly deserted spent the show-day by a hot blue sea. The place was prosaic but salubrious; and it was filled with two ghostly presences, his sister Alice and Robert Louis Stevenson.

James spent most of July 1897 in Bournemouth, enjoying the emptiness of the place. He bicycled; he purchased a bicycle for MacAlpine, thus providing company for his rides. The Bourgets visited him, as had become their custom, but stayed only four days. Bourget went to Oxford to lecture on Flaubert and James journeyed through encumbered London to attend. Oxford still treated fiction as the Puritans had treated plays; but James could not resist the singular honour done to his craft and his two friends – the dead Flaubert and the living Bourget. He was, however, not sure the 'moderns' should be studied in universities. Their job was 'the established old'. It might lead, he said, to 'unexpected raptures' and failures in critical perspective.

The rest of the month was spent in daily dictation and seaside relaxation. MacAlpine was an excellent typist but a dull companion. James did have to return to London at the end of July, summoned unexpectedly to jury duty; he had learned aliens were not exempt from civic obligation after a ten years' residence in England. The case, apparently a banal divorce hearing, lasted only two days at the Court of Queen's Bench, and all we know of the experience is recorded in Henry's remark to William, 'Doing British Juryman threw lights – and glooms!' – which would suggest that the novelist was not bored. He had described a divorce in the opening instalment of *What Maisie Knew* – but by the time he went to the court he was at work on the final pages of the novel.

3

What Maisie Knew was a short novel, serialized in *The Chap-Book*, a semi-monthly published in Chicago between January and August of 1897 and in England in the *New Review*, where it ran from February to September. A work of intellectual wit, it reflects James's awareness of how a child's world is a piecemeal world, containing quantities of literal observation but lacking clues to wider connections. Many serious things are said in the presence of Maisie, and many bawdy things; but she, like a kitten, keeps her eye on the piece of string, or the direction in which a hand is moving. She ingeniously parrots adult phrases; they seem the right thing to say; but she doesn't know the meaning of what she is saying. Handed over, in a custody suit, to periodic visits with each of her parents, she becomes the carrier from one to the other of hatred and rage. Presently she is moving in the world of their adulteries and those of her surrogate parents.

James could now deal more directly with sex and his short novel is a brilliant comedy. Maisie moves through an amoral world with her innocence intact; we never know how much it has been damaged. When the handsome Sir Claude, the 'masher' of the novel, evades her and the governess, Mrs Wix, once too often, she chooses to live with the shoddy governess and her 'moral sense' rather than with unstable multiple parents. The decision accords with a child's instinct for safety. No digest of the story can suggest the skill and subtlety with which James keeps the reader constantly within the eye-vision of the little girl; nor his humour and wit. It is choreographic fiction : men and women come together and separate, and the little girl dances alone on the stage among them. The story is written scenically, like the *Spoils*, and shows in its form and tightness that James was not as yet yielding to the prolixity of dictation.

Like the works of this period it illustrates to an extraordinary degree the way in which the adult mind and professional skill can create a work in the face of inner bewilderment. Maisie's bewilderment and isolation is James's – it is the bewilderment he had felt since the collapse of his world in *Guy Domville*: but the world's cruelty and hostility are recreated into a comic vision of benign childish curiosity. Nevertheless, if one looks away from the smooth surface and the intellectual power of the story, one perceives a world of horror: a down-at-heels middle-class world that treats its children cruelly, and lives in a state of perpetual sexual confusion. In the depths of this novel – which on the surface is very much like a bedroom farce – we can discern James's own confusion before the collapsing Victorian moral façade. The worldly bachelor of Kensington and Mayfair, in this work, still possessed a fund of innocence and wonder and bewilderment disguised for the moment in the garments of ironic comedy. Maisie's 'small demonic foresight' as James was to describe it, harboured his own; and the word 'demonic' was apt, for what James was telling in the comic guise was a story of 'the death of childhood' – the phrase is in the preface he wrote to the book a decade later. 'Small children,' he wrote, 'have many more perceptions than they have terms to translate them; their vision is at any moment much richer, their apprehension even constantly stronger, than their prompt, their at all producible vocabulary.' There was 'the rich little spectacle of objects embalmed in her wonder' and 'she wonders to the end, to the death – the death of her childhood'. It is Maisie's sense of wonder that makes the sordid elements of her life appear phantasmagoric, like a child's fairy tale, or the images projected by a magic lantern. The reader sees both the wonder and the nightmare.

38

A Question of Speech

ON 3 July 1897, at Bournemouth, while reading the letters of the Suffolk genius, Edward FitzGerald, whose rendering of *Omar Khayyam* had brought an emanation of – a breath of – hedonism into Victorian England, James came on the name of Saxmundham which had for him a certain 'strangeness and handsomeness'. That same afternoon, during a long beach-walk, he encountered a rugged boatman from Suffolk – from Saxmundham – whose brother, Fitz-

Gerald's boatman, figured in the letters James had just read. On returning from the walk, he found a letter from Saxmundham, from an American cousin, sister of the long dead Minnie Temple, who was staying in the FitzGerald country, at Dunwich on the Suffolk coast with her three daughters. She urged James to join her. The coincidence of a thrice-encountered mouth-filling topographical name and his feeling that he should get to know his American cousins better, combined to make James promptly agree. Moreover, he was at a loose end. He had not known what to do with the rest of his summer. Thinking perhaps of *Omar Khayyam* he wrote to his cousin Ellen Hunter (who had been Ellen James Temple in his Newport days), that she had described 'a little Paradise'. He beseeched her 'to keep a divan for me there'. He would come for most of August. He hoped a room could be found also for his typist.

I

Elly Temple had married one of the New York Emmets. A sister had married his brother. There was a proliferation thus of Temple Emmets to whom James would apply a generic term, 'the Emmetry'. The novelist had seen the widowed Elly (now remarried to an Englishman) the previous winter, at Harrow, but had not yet met her two elder daughters who were studying in Paris. The three Emmet daughters were described by one of James's nephews as being 'of devastating charm and attractiveness'. The eldest was Rosina, then 24, who had sent her uncle some of her writings and had been warned by him against introducing too much low life and slang into fiction. 'There is, after all, another psychology than that of the brutes and another vocabulary than that of the slangermongers.' Her sister, Ellen Gertude, called 'Bay', 22, had been studying art in Paris. The youngest, just turned 20, was Edith Leslie. The three were lively, buoyant, curious; they had had little systematic education; it had been interrupted by their displacement from America to Europe. 'They just knew everything by instinct,' the nephew used to say; but their instincts were on the whole good.

Ellen and her three daughters, and another Emmet cousin named Jane, seem to have awaited the coming of the novelist as if he were a royal personage. The bedroom and sitting-room were found in one of the local houses, although Ellen could not guarantee the softness of the Omaresque 'divan'. Cousin Ellen had a more serious problem:

there was neither butcher, baker nor grocer in Dunwich, a decayed little seaport where there had been centuries of erosion by the sea. However she organized the food services 'Bonapartistically', James was later to say. Delayed by jury duty at the end of July, he sent MacAlpine ahead. We get some feeling of the excitement the awe-inspiring writer-cousin created in a letter by the visiting Jane:

Henry James is expected to arrive *sans faute* tonight. I don't believe there is such a person. I think it is always exciting to see a person you have heard of all your life, especially if you have been so delighted and amused as I have always been by his books. H. James's horrible young meek Scotch typewriter came down a day or two ago.

2

From Jane Emmet (later Mrs. Wilfrid Von Glehn) in Dunwich, Saxmundham, Suffolk, to her sister Lydia Emmet, 6 August 1897:

Well, at last Henry James arrived, and he is the nicest thing, but what a mental epicure. He is awfully sweet and affectionate and non-terrifying, and tragic-eyed. He hangs poised for the right word while the wheels of life go round. This afternoon Rosina, H.J. and I went for a walk and got caught in the rain and had to wade through ponds of muddy water to Henry James's unfeigned horror. I don't think he has been through a mud puddle for years. He rides a bicycle which is his only attempt at sport. Poor thing, he must miss so much, being so horrified by accent. He can't get past it. He must miss so much real refinement and cleverness and niceness. We do nothing but thank our stars that we are not Henry James. I am afraid our voices and sentences hurt his ear-drums. He and his typewriter spend their mornings together and the simple villagers of Dunwich may hear subtleties being dictated from ten to one.

From Henry James in Dunwich, Saxmundham, Suffolk, 1 September 1897, to William James in Cambridge, Mass:

The resources of Dunwich are not infinite, and I should, without the cousins, have made a briefer dip of it. It was of course for them I came and for them I am staying on a little. The girls accept with the extreme sweetness and tact that, I think, they show in all relations to the situation their mother has made for them, a rather extended stretch of a place offering a good deal less luxuriance of charm than many another they might, with more chance to look about, have found for their English summer. Meanwhile this little corner, where all is in the minor, the minimum key, is not without sweetness and character. I have done. with great pleasure and profit, a good deal of the bicycle; for which this region offers every inducement that can be offered without roads. We are miles from a good one – which is partly indeed why we are quaint and curious ... But I stray, even now, from the Cousins – as to whom you will be glad to hear more of whatever there may be to say. This last is summed up in a nutshell: they would be thoroughly 'sympathetic' if they only had a language to be it in! Their speech, absolutely unaffected as yet, so far as I can see, by a year of Europe – thanks to the antecedent cycle of Cathay – remains really their only fault. But it is a grave one. I attack it, however, boldly, and as much as I can. It will be hopeless, I fear, ever – or at least for a long time – to interfuse Bay and Leslie with a few consonants, or to make any of them sound the letter 'i' in any of the connections in which it occurs and especially in the word 'him' and 'it' where they replace it inveterately by 'o', 'u' and even 'a'! However, they *want* to improve, and are full of life and humour and sentiment and intelligence.

Small wonder that among the enduring memories of the Cousins were those of his efforts to improve their speech. In later years Rosina would tell how on one of their walks Henry James, with much affection, and yet a kind of merciless regularity, kept her attention fixed on the sound of her own voice. Hoping to engage him in conversation, she had commented on how charming she found the jewel in his tie-pin.

'Jew-*el*, not *jool*,' her Distinguished Cousin rejoined, ignoring the compliment.

'I'm afraid American girls don't speak their vowels distinctly,' Rosina ventured.

'Vow-*el*, not *vowl*, Rosina.'

Tears came. 'Oh Cousin Henry, you are so cruel.'

'Cru-*el*, not *crool*, Rosina.'

And the youngest cousin Leslie remembered that when she said, 'I must go upstairs and fix my hair,' Cousin Henry looked at her fixedly, and then, solemnly:

'To fix your hair, my dear Leslie, to *fix* it to what – and *with* what?'

In later years, the language of the American young, and the ways in which they spoke was to become an obsession with Henry James. Language was sacred; speech was sacred. Invited to speak at the Commencement at Bryn Mawr, during his 1904-5 visit to the United States, Henry James found occasion for his fullest statement to his young and captive audience. He titled it *The Question of Our Speech* and with good humour appealed seriously for a 'tone-standard'. He reminded his hearers that 'the human side of vocal sound' was being corrupted by slovenly speech and kept 'as little distinct as possible from the grunting, the squealing, the barking or the roaring of animals'. He deplored the failure in the 'emission of the consonant', so that speech became 'a mere helpless slobber of disconnected vowel noises – the weakest and cheapest attempt at human expression that we shall easily encounter, I imagine, in any community pretending to the general instructed state. Observe, too, that the vowel sounds in themselves, at this rate, quite fail of any purity.' His illustration was the way in which 'Yes', became 'Yeh-eh', and when the need for a final consonant showed, it became the still more questionable 'Yeh-ep.' He had many more examples, all testifying to his conscious ear, and to his belief that language – one's own – was to be learned and cultivated and cherished and not allowed to degenerate.

3

That he enjoyed himself enormously at Dunwich, in spite of the absence of luxuries and the bad roads, is clear from the lengthy article he wrote for *Harper's Weekly*, one of his last fugitive travel-pieces – he had written so many in other years. There was enough to fascinate in Suffolk – the wide pebbly beaches, the towns that had disappeared in the great wash of the sea during the centuries, the boatmen and coastguard men with whom he talked on every occasion, garnering their tales as FitzGerald had done. He remembered that he was in the country of David Copperfield; and that nearby Aldeburgh was the birthplace of the poet Crabbe. He delighted in names such as Great Yarmouth, Blundeston and of course Saxmundham, and in the appeal of 'desolate exquisite Dunwich'. He surveyed with his professional eye the ruins of the great church and its tall tower, and the crumbled ivy wall of the Priory, where Fitz-Gerald had admired the pale Dunwich rose that grew on its walls; the low heathery bareness of the countryside, the rare purple and gold that ran to the edge of the sea. There was enough left by the predatory sea to feed the fancy, 'what is left is just the stony beach and the big gales, and the cluster of fishermen's huts and the small, wide short street of decent, homely, shoppy houses'.

There were afternoons when he would go on long bicycle runs to a main artery six miles inland; he remembered stopping at such sleepy towns as Westleton to refresh himself at an old red inn with lemonade and a 'dash' – only of beer – but the refreshment was 'immense'. He wore his old baggy trousers and his rough-textured Norfolk jackets, jaunty bow-ties and golf cap. Snapshots taken by the cousins show that by this time he had trimmed his beard to a spade-like shape. There is one picture of James standing with a large grin beside a lifeguard on the stony beach; and another of him leaning on a cane as if he were Neptune. Best of all he liked his talks with the seafaring folk. 'I had often dreamed that the ideal refuge for a man of letters was a cottage so placed on the coast as to be circled, as it were, by the protecting arm of the Admiralty.' As if it were a private thought he added, 'may the last darkness close before I cease to care for sea-folk'.

As he left in September, he wrote a long letter to his brother and in it he spoke of his sense of being a nomad. 'I should like to put in a couple or more months in the country – but am tired of oscillating between bad lodgings and expensive hotels.' He had had a 'casual' summer; later he called it 'my rather incoherent summer ... of a rather patched-together, hand-to-mouth, unhoused and accidental sort'. This would continue to be his lot, he said, 'until I can put my hand on the lowly refuge of my own, for which, from year to year, I thirst'. And he added, 'On the day I do get it – for the day must come – I shall feel my fortune is made'. The day was only a fortnight away.

39

Lamb House

DURING the winter of 1895–6 Henry James had seen in the Cowley Street home of Edward Warren, the architect, a pleasant little water-colour of the front of a house in Rye, with Roman-arched bow-windows rising above the street in solid brick, a peaked roof, an old-fashioned lantern set in the wall and ivy climbing up one side. Warren told him it was the detached 'garden-room' of a house known as Lamb House he had lately sketched. The following summer, when James lived at Point Hill and later in the Old Rectory, he saw the house often and became fond of it. During this period it will be recalled he had casually mentioned to the local ironmonger, a man named Milson, that he was house-hunting.

Now, a few days after his return from Dunwich, he went on a long day's bicycle ride with Warren. They had a talk about houses. Lamb House was mentioned. Two days later came a brief note from the ironmonger. He wished James to know that Lamb House had fallen vacant and was available on a long lease. 'Telepathy does indeed mark the case for its own,' James wrote to Warren. Confronted with a possibility that might affect his entire way of life, James strangely felt the news to be 'a little like a blow in the stomach'.

Dream houses were delightful; the reality made him anxious. James rushed off to Rye, and Warren promised to give the house professional inspection.

I

Lamb House stands at the top of steep and cobbled West Street which climbs the hilltop out of the High Street. It is located at the turn, where West Street curves towards St Mary's Church. The house looks towards the ancient church, while the detached garden-room, which Warren had sketched, looked down the hilly street up which James had come. The garden-room was called the 'banqueting room'; doubtless the Lamb family (its members had been mayors of Rye for over a century) had used it for civic purposes. Rye itself had long ago received a visit from the great Elizabeth, and Lamb House had provided shelter for the first George whose tempest-tossed ship, homeward bound from Hanover, put in at one of the Cinque ports. Thus the house had a 'King's Room' in which later, George II and his son, the Duke of Cumberland, also slept during visits to the town. The house was of red brick that had turned russet; the garden-room at a right angle to it, built somewhat later, was of brick that had faded to a tawny colour.

James probably entered Lamb House for the first time by its high-canopied Georgian doorway; the knocker had to be turned sharply to the right to unlatch the door. Inside, the precautions of more violent times were visible: bolts, latches, chains: the door could be fastened in nine different ways. A well-proportioned and handsome balustraded staircase of oak faced the entrance. To the right was a small panelled room, a kind of waiting-room, that might serve as a small *cabinet de travail*. On the left was an oak-panelled parlour, or so James was assured, for the panelling had been covered by modern wallpaper. A door opened from the parlour into a comfortable stretch of garden – a little less than an acre. Next to this room was a squarish dining-room, with another French door giving on the garden, very much as James would describe it in *The Turn of the Screw*. Opposite, under the stair, the novelist passed into a high and spacious kitchen. The upstairs was laid out similarly; the King's Room, wainscoted from floor to ceiling, but also papered, with a bench window, looked towards the church; across the hallway on the right was a small square panelled room looking towards Winchealsea and on the Lamb House garden. There were two more bedrooms, also a dressing-room, with a handsome pedimented cupboard leading to the bathroom. On the floor above were four attic rooms that could be servants' quarters.

James passed through the ground-floor parlour into the garden; to the left was a short flight of curved stone steps, with a graceful iron hand-rail leading into the garden-room. This was spacious and would make an ideal study and work-room; its bow window commanded the downward sloping street and a fine expanse of the changeable Sussex sky. The house was not, as family houses go, large; all the rooms except the garden-house, were small; but with four bedrooms on the second floor and four in the attic, Lamb House was more than sufficient for a sedentary writing bachelor. One of the upstairs bedrooms – it would be known as the Green Room – would serve as a second study.

The garden was charming. There was a big mulberry tree offering generous shade; there was a kitchen garden at the upper end and a row of greenhouses. There were peaches – a memory of Albany – and an old bignonia which had climbed the south-west corner nearly to the roof. There was also an annexe to the property, a studio, with a pillared entrance in adjacent Watchbell Lane which James would be able to use or to let. Behind Lamb House proper was a cobbled court and a delivery-entrance to the street.

The house was in good condition, and Warren's verdict was favourable, even enthusiastic. The paper could be peeled from the fine old panels; some improvements in the sanitary arrangements were needed; the place required redecorating. The renovation could be done during the coming winter; the house would be ready for the spring. Alfred Parsons, the landscape painter who had done the sets for *Domville*, inspected the garden for James and pronounced in an equally favourable manner. The back windows of houses facing the church threatened the privacy of the garden but could be screened by planting Lombardy poplars at that end. High trellises on the walk would do the rest.

Before the end of September 1897 James had signed a twenty-one-years' lease. He got the house for £70 a year. The large parchment, setting forth the usual commitments of lessor and lessee, bound James, among other things, to horticultural pastimes, or at least the employment of an efficient gardener. The novelist undertook to keep the garden, the hothouse and greenhouses 'well and properly stocked, cropped and manured'. He promised to 'improve, prune and preserve all the flowers, shrubs and fruit trees, plant vines and other trees'. He convenanted to replace such plants or trees as decayed or died, by others 'as good or of the better sort'. He agreed to repaint the woodwork with three coats of 'good oil colour' at the end of the seventh and fourteenth years of his lease; and at the end of these years he had the option to surrender the lease if he wished. To A. C. Benson he wrote that his house was 'really good enough to be a kind of little becoming, high door'd, brass knockered *façade* to one's life'. This indeed was what Lamb House became.

2

In the midst of his joy at his acquisition Henry James had a sense of great complications. There was the problem of what to do with De Vere Gardens during his long absences; there was the need to find a gardener and to deploy his servants, the bibulous Smiths. Looking ahead to the time when he might spend a greater part of his year in the country and would therefore get rid of his flat, he put himself down at the Reform Club for one of the bedrooms looking out on Carlton Gardens. These were let by the year, and it would be some time before a chamber would be vacant. He would thus be assured of a *pied-à-terre* in the city.

Then there was the question of furnishings. He could hardly despoil De Vere Gardens if he wanted to sublet, though he would want to move some of his books. Lamb House fairly obviously would need 'old things', preferably eighteenth-century, certainly not of the costly 'Poynton' kind; nor could he afford the rarities Mrs

Jack captured on her European forays. Some good mahogany and brass, some Chippendale and Sheraton, a little faded tapestry, he gaily said in one letter, 'a handful of feeble relics', would do. He began his search immediately, for he wrote Warren from Northumberland, 'I have bought two maps, five prints and a chest of drawers.' He was to have long winter rambles that year visiting in London curiosity shops, as in the days, a decade earlier, when he had furnished De Vere Gardens. Mrs Warren announced she would take care of his curtains.

To accomplish all this, however, he would need extra funds. In other years James had skilfully mobilized his resources to pay for his trips to the Continent. Now with the same alertness he committed himself to a monthly 'American Letter' for a new journal, *Literature*, published by *The Times* (it would be a precursor of the *Literary Supplement*.) This would yield him £40 a month. Then the family of W. W. Story renewed a plea made earlier that James write the sculptor's life. James had delayed his reply, suggesting he would study the family papers when next in Rome. But now, when the Waldo Storys sent him a sampling of the material, James wrote to William Blackwood, in Edinburgh, who had published Story's amateur verses, plays and essays. He explained that his time was 'too valuable, much, for me to write Mr Story's life, even on the restricted scale on which alone I should be willing to proceed, as a mere friendly and unremunerated task'. He found it embarrassing to discuss 'business' with the Storys. 'It would be possible for me to do the book only for a definite *fee* on its completion – which should exhaust my interest in it.' He recognized that there must not be undue delay; but he would have to determine the deadline. Blackwood was sufficiently interested. He paid James £250 in advance, and agreed to pay £100 after 7,000 copies were sold and a like sum for every 2,000 copies sold thereafter.

Within a month of the lease-signing, James had thus provided himself with a financial 'cushion'. Now he had a further bit of luck. Howells suddenly turned up in Europe. They had not seen each other in many years. They had a long *déjeuner* in De Vere Gardens on a morning of thick fog, and talked for six hours. Howells had come (as James was to tell him later) at a 'psychological' moment. James had been too long away from America; he no longer knew how to place his work there, nor what prices to ask. James later wrote of the 'miraculous' effect of 'your admirable counsel and comfort'. He had come to feel, in the market-place, he said, 'like an old maid against the wall and on her lonely bench'.

Howells acted promptly on his return to America, with the result that *Harper's Weekly* expressed an interest in a serial and James asked a steep price, $3,000. He promised them the tale that had begun to shape itself as a novel, *The Awkward Age*. Even before this, James had contracted to do a short serial for *Collier's* to be delivered by the new year. This he would have to write at once, since it would carry an illustrative headpiece by his old friend La Farge, and another illustrator would do a series of scenes from the story. James's efforts to give himself financial leeway for his installation in Lamb House were more than successful: his earnings for the next year would be much larger 'than for any year of my existence'.

He could now talk with greater sureness of his house to his own family; but it wasn't until Howells had come and gone, and more than two months had elapsed, that he described his good fortune to Mrs William James. He told how he had two years before made 'sheeps' eyes' at the place 'the more so that it is called Lamb House'; he was writing at the beginning of December 1897, and he could report that on the southern exposure of the russet garden wall pears and apricots, plums and figs were still flourishing. The letter is cheerful and filled with a sense of possession. It also contained a significant piece of literary intelligence. 'I *have*, at last, finished my little book – that is *a* little book.' This was the story for *Collier's*. It was called *The Turn of the Screw*.

40

The Little Boys

HENRY JAMES'S decision to take Lamb House on a long lease sounded eminently sensible – and practical – as he described it to his sister-in-law. He was forsaking London. He was providing for his old age. He had chosen the kind of house that suited the taste and sensitivities of an artist. It was a reversal of all that he had done in the past. He had been from the first a foot-loose American in Europe; his expatriation had been in part a revolt against embeddedness. The lodging house, the foreign *pension*, the hotel, had been his way of life for the greater part of a quarter of a century – or at least until he had committed himself to De Vere Gardens in 1886. But even possession of a London flat had not altered his practice of spending many months on the Continent – Paris, Venice, Florence. Moreover he had always travelled 'light'. His most important baggage had been his writing portfolio. All this, to be sure, had had to be revised, ever since the typewriter had begun to limit his freedom. And then he was also accustomed to the sounds of cities and towns as he worked, the feeling that he moved in a dense human medium, always available to him whether urban or seaside. He depended on his clubs in London, and friendly houses both at home and abroad, a mode of existence that combined great industry with civilized amenities. Even his later dream of a 'great good place' envisaged an escape from worldly pressures into a brotherhood, all discretion and quiet, the house of an Order, celibate and fraternal at the same time.

But his deeper feelings seem to have been that in Lamb House he would be an anchorite, a lonely dweller, a 'prisoner' beyond the suburbs. His immediate emotional response to his contemplated change was a tale of nightmare terror. He had set down the idea for *The Turn of the Screw* in his notebooks two years earlier, when he had described himself as 'drowning' after the *débâcle* of *Guy Domville*. He had been writing tales about children victimized by an adult world – murdered Effie, tormented Maisie – and he had written stories in which houses occupied the centre of the scene – Poynton, Covering End, Eastmead, Bounds. Preparing now to settle in Rye, in Sussex, he called his fictional house Bly, and placed it in Essex; and to this house he dispatched a young governess, who would narrate eerie events, involving a boy and girl, that would give an extra 'turn' to the screw – by which, in old torture-chambers, pain was made excruciating. To be confronted by the possibility of Lamb House had felt 'a little like a blow in the stomach'. The remark indeed turns up early in the tale. When Mrs Grose is told by the governess that she has seen the ghost of Miss Jessel, she takes it 'as she might have taken a blow in the stomach'. There are similar strange remarks in James's letters at the moment he signs the lease. 'All my inclination is to take it – I feel in fact *doomed* to do so.' This was a curious way of describing fate or destiny, when the fate had made his wish come true. It sounded rather as if some extraneous coercion were occurring, some ominous oracle had intervened. The word 'coerce' is used also in a letter to the Emmetry; he felt 'coerced by some supernatural power that relieves me of all the botheration of a decision or an alternative. I feel quite absolutely foredoomed to take a lease.' What followed seemed to be a period on the rack.

James is clearly invoking an idea of magic. It had seemed un-canny. He had looked at the house, liked it – and suddenly he had been told he could have it. This was like rubbing a lamp in some old tale of the *Arabian Nights*. It was also a way of absolving himself of all responsibility. The fates had decided; it was a 'turn of the screw'; he was 'doomed'. From this kind of magical fantasy to a tale of the supernatural might seem a logical step in a writer of imagina-tion; but that the tale should be one of the greatest horror stories of its kind – as posterity would judge it – suggests that James was in some kind of abject terror himself, over a decision he believed not to have been his own. Something far deeper within him had been touched than the mere thought that he was leaving bright London and 'the world' for a rustic and rural life of solitude. *The Turn of the Screw* is a tale of a governess frightened by her own imaginings. And we must look at it closely, to see what were the hidden imagin-ings of its author.

I

'The imagination,' Henry James was to say to Bernard Shaw, 'leads a life of its own.' Between September and December 1897, James rapidly dictated the strange history of an untried young woman, fresh from a Hampshire vicarage, who is sent by her employer to a remote house to care for his nephew and niece, aged 10 and 8. The employer is a handsome man who lives in Harley Street, and the governess's girlish 'crush' on him prevents her from recognizing how callous he is towards the orphaned children. In effect, he washes his hands of them; he makes her the head, in spite of her inexperience, of the small household at Bly, and instructs her not to trouble him, not even to write him letters. The governess, flushed and anxious with her new-found authority, arrives at Bly in a state both of euphoria and anxiety. She finds her little charges precocious and charming. She is seconded in her responsibilities by Mrs Grose, the housekeeper, a good-natured, efficient woman, who acts as a kind of semi-articulate chorus in the story.

The governess's tale begins in June, during the long English twi-light, when the rooks circle above the crenellated towers of Bly and the evening's hush is on the land; it ends in bleak November, when the trees in the churchyard are bare and Bly has been blighted. In these few months the narrator – the governess – with eyes 'unsealed', encounters the apparitions of Miss Jessel, the governess who preceded her, and Peter Quint, the master's valet, both of whom had died some time before. She puts on a bold show of courage, always thinking that her heroism will win the approval of her handsome employer, who is constantly in her thoughts. But her courage is a mask for a deep hysteria, which is unveiled for us in two crucial scenes: that in which she confronts the little girl on the far side of the pond, and the final one in which she confronts the boy. Exalted and arrayed against the works of the devil, she believes the ghosts have come for the children; a true daughter of the manse, she is determined to exorcize the evil that she feels and sees around her. Bly, however, is filled not so much with the evil of the ghosts, as the terror of the governess, her wild suppositions and self-consoling explanations. There are the escapades of the children, which seem harmless, but which she describes as sinister; and there is the shock of the 'recognition' scene, when the governess tells Mrs Grose of the man on the tower and leads her, by elaborate cross-examination, to pronounce the name of Peter Quint and to use the words (Joseph Conrad would echo them in another tale of evil, *Heart of Darkness*, in the following year), 'Mr Quint is dead.' The controversial 'recognition' scene is filled with ambiguities, and it tends to draw the reader's attention away from the essential data, which is not the identification of the ghosts, but the history of the governess and her relations with the children and the housekeeper. As the summer advances, and the children grow restless under the constantly protective eyes of the governess, she sees confirmation of her suspicions. She expects them, in her own immature understanding of how children behave, to confide everything to her. And when little Miles, in the country churchyard, reminds her that he is a boy and doesn't want to be cooped up with females she regards this as an act of rebellion. There is a parallel scene with Flora in which the governess accuses the little girl of communicating with the apparition of Miss Jessel. Defied by Flora, who has all the aplomb of Maisie, the governess has a moment of amnesia, and finds herself stretched out and sobbing on the damp ground. We are in a kind of Brontë world in which calm and hysteria mingle – and we are in the Brontë period, for James carefully places the decade of the tale (which we can determine with the aid of simple arithmetic) in the 1840s. It happens to be also the decade of James's own childhood.

As the tale unfolds, it gives us a picture of the constantly-haunted state of the governess. Her 'turn of the screw' of pain resides in her belief that evil has come into the lives of the innocent. There is, however, a further 'turn' for the reader; consciously or unconsciously we begin to sense that it is the governess herself who haunts the children. For by all the testimony of the story, she alone sees the ghosts: neither the children nor Mrs Grose ever see them – their eyes, as she puts it, are 'sealed'. Peter Quint and Miss Jessel are private phantoms. James was very clear about this, both in the story and in his remarks in the preface he wrote ten years later. The ghosts are not ghosts at all, 'as we now know the ghost, but goblins, elves, imps, demons, as loosely constructed as those of the old trials for witchcraft'. When we remember the testimony of the bewitched children of Salem, saying with the discernment of childhood what their approving elders wanted to hear, we have a fundamental clue to *The Turn of the Screw*. In the charged testimony of the governess, with her phantoms, her 'certitude', her suppositions which she turns into 'fact', her facts which are mere suppositions, we recognize the materials of the witch-burners and executioners of old. Her narrative, told with such a consummate weaving of paranoid fancy and circumstantial reality, is indeed capable of making readers pronounce the innocents guilty.

Here lies the deepest horror of James's story: an attentive reader becomes aware of the ways in which Flora, Miles and Mrs Grose seek constantly to accommodate themselves to the governess's strange behaviour. The children are direct and guileless; the governess is indirect and filled with guile. She is always putting words into Mrs Grose's mouth; she asks the children questions they cannot understand or answer. Small wonder that little Flora, whose beautiful 8-year-old innocence has been carefully described for us, responds to the governess's hysteria at the pond with all the force of her childhood – 'I don't know what you mean. I see nobody. I see nothing. I never *have*. I think you're cruel. I don't like you!' The governess gets as firm a dressing-down as if she and the child had changed roles. To Mrs Grose the little girl turns and says, 'Take me away, take me away – oh, take me away from *her*.' Her instincts are right. In the last scene, which Oscar Wilde likened to an Elizabethan tragedy, Miles never sees Quint. The boy is described as if he were a dumb trapped little animal seeking a way of escape from the smothering presence not of the ghost but of the intense and pressing governess. 'No more, no more, no more,' she shrieks, thinking she has banished the phantom. When Miles, after guessing wrongly, dredges up the name she wants him to pronounce, that of Peter Quint, he is able in his frightened state to add the words 'you devil!' A careless reader might think that he is addressing the apparition. However throughout this scene, Miles has his back to the window where the governess sees the ghost ominously hovering. It is indeed the governess who has become the devil; and the subtlest twist of the story is that the demon she seeks to exorcize is within herself. She rids herself of her private ghost; and in the process little Miles's heart is 'dispossessed'. She is left 'alone with the quiet day', the dead boy in her arms – as in the old medieval tales of possession. The evil spirit has been driven out : but innocence has died.

2

James had never written at a greater pitch of intensity. In his series of brief scenes he wove a hell-fire tale and gave it a horrible tension, made it vague, ambiguous, filled with overtones of mystical and supernatural terror. What arrests our attention when we re-examine the story is his choice of a young boy as protagonist at a season of James's life when all his stories dealt with little girls, in various stages of their growth. Little Miles is the sole masculine figure in the series of Effies, Maisies, Aggies, Nandas, including the young unnamed governess herself and the unnamed girl 'in the cage'. Miles's fate resembles that of earlier little boys – the murdered Dolcino of *The Author of* Beltraffio, killed by a Medea-mother who, like the governess, would save him from external evil; or Morgan Moreen, whose young heart gives way at the very moment when his hope of freedom seems frustrated; or the young adult, Owen Wingrave, who in the old haunted mansion of Paramore proves his bravery by facing the family incubus – and dying. In James's world little boys died. It was safer to be a little girl. They usually endured.

In this light, the earlier confrontation scene between the governess and Miles in the country churchyard, in which they deal not with supernatural events, but with Miles's normal wish to go back to school, illuminates a large area of Jamesian experience. The scene is striking in its sharpness and 'objectivity'. They walk to church on a crisp autumn morning; and the governess describes Miles in terms of his masculinity – 'turned out for Sunday by his uncle's tailor, who had had a free hand and a notion of pretty waistcoats'. She notes the boy's 'grand little air', his 'whole title to independence' and 'the rights of his sex and situation'. At the same time she admits to herself that she has been over-possessive – 'I had all but pinned the boy to my shawl ... I was like a gaoler with an eye to possible surprises and escapes.' Thinking this, she remarks that if the boy struck for freedom she would find herself with nothing to say.

There was, as a matter of fact, a great deal she could say. Miles has been expelled from school with no explanation from the head-master. Instead of asking the boy, she has silently waited for his confession. This makes the conversation in the churchyard – in the little city of the dead under the leafless trees of autumn – a mixture of the governess's deception and the boy's candour. What Miles asks is, 'When in the world, please, am I going back to school?' His complaint is that he spends all his time with a lady – the governess; or his sister Flora whom he considers a baby. 'I want my own sort,' says little Miles. 'I want to see more life.' Also, 'I'm a fellow, don't you see?'

Two things emerge from this: Miles's strong sense of his role as a boy and his feeling of confinement in a house wholly in the company of females. In the days when Peter Quint was alive the boy had had a male companion; but now he demands the company of his peers. Later, when the governess finally asks him about his expulsion his answer is direct: 'I said things.' He had said them to boys he liked; and the boys had said them to others, and what he had said had finally reached the ears of the masters. James supplies no clue as to what he said, and by his policy of letting the reader's imagination fill such blanks, we can choose between blasphemy and obscenity. The tale keeps the misdemeanour in the realm of speech, not sex. Miles probably used words he had heard from Peter Quint. It little matters. The essential point is Miles's wish to be a boy among boys – and the fact that his expression of such a wish is deemed evil by the governess.

3

We are reminded as we think of the trapped and dead little boys and young adults in James's fictional world – the boy Miles, the adolescent Morgan, the young Owen – of events in James's own life, during the long-ago period of his rivalry with his strong and active elder brother. William was masculine and active, and punished often for his excess of activity; and Henry his junior, as spectator and outsider, repulsed by his elder brother, discovered that it was dangerous to be like him; he was safest when he identified himself with his younger sister, and stayed at home with his mother and the vigorous Aunt Kate. 'I play with boys who curse and swear,' William James had said when Henry was about as old as little Miles. It was William's way of telling Henry that he wasn't good enough for the company of older boys. The novelist, remembering this in his old age, looked sadly on his boyish self and agreed he 'simply wasn't qualified'. William could 'say things' *he* apparently had not yet learned. He smarted at being 'mere junior', and the picture we have of him at a later stage at Newport (in the memories of T. S. Perry) is that of a lonely adolescent, sitting on a window seat reading, 'while the rest of us were chattering'. This 'certain air of remoteness' was the first thing that struck Perry when they met. Another young man, a friend of William's, had a further memory. Steele MacKaye long after (when he was famous as a stage designer and actor) described how the older boys had called Henry 'sissy' at the time when he was beginning to write. James felt divorced from masculine activity when he recalled his life in New York, during his 32nd year. He had felt shut out – because he was a writer – from the great male business world of 'downtown'. Like his father before him, Henry was 'uptown' and 'at the very moderate altitude of Twenty-Fifth Street' he felt himself 'day by day alone . . . with the music-teachers and French pastry-cooks, the ladies and children'. Like Miles, he was not with his own 'sort'. He was in a feminine world.

We have then evidence, at different stages of Henry James's life – from childhood to maturity – of the masculine-feminine problem exemplified repeatedly in his fiction. There was, in the novelist, a compelling drive to masculinity which Miles expressed; but it had been driven underground. To be male was to risk (in the remote fantasy of childhood) such things as his father's amputation; females seemed the most serious threat to his sense of himself, as a boy, and later – by the disguises of the imagination, by thinking himself a little girl and by being quiet and observant – he could escape 'amputations' and punishments. The stratagem succeeded. His mother had called him 'angel'. He could wear the mask of an observant curious young female. The disguise of femininity was necessary mainly when he was confined to 'Family', and had to contend with his elder brother; in that relationship he always saw William as strong and active and himself as inhibited and passive. This is true in the many tales in which the old rivalry is re-imagined, and in which William is present, but usually reduced to a shoddy adventurer, an impostor, or a weakling. In the stories in which older brothers are banished, the second son can be his masculine self; but this makes him feel guilty and it can have fatal consequences. Owen's older brother we remember was locked away in an asylum, and the full responsibility of the Wingrave name fell on the second son. In *The Pupil* the older brother is an effete young man; it is little Morgan who is the focus of family attention – and neglect. There remained in James (as we can see in *The Turn of the Screw*) a young assertive male who wanted a life of action and of courage, who wanted to curse and swear with his fellows and possess the heroism of the Napoleonic Marbots or the seasoned Wolseley. Inhibitions, reinforced by later experiences, had been his defence.

Such personal history enables us to understand the lack of conviction that lay behind *Guy Domville*. His self-assertion in the theatre had been half-hearted out of a fear to commit his art totally to 'the world'. He had tried; and, because he had been half-hearted, he had lessened his chance of success. Failure confirmed him in his constituted mode of being. The very subject of the play expressed this: the young priest had been called upon to be a man, go into the world, have progeny. James, in effect, had concluded that Guy was incapable of this. The world was too bad, too dangerous. He would be safer in his monastery.

In this light it is possible to surmise what the 'blow in the stomach' was, when Lamb House fell easily, almost magically, into his hands and fulfilled a profound wish. The house symbolized the world of his childhood, the danger of self-assertion; he had been least free, when he had had to resort to disguise and subterfuge in order to possess himself and his identity. In the house of Family he had had to defend himself to escape William, and also to avoid the restrictions he saw placed upon William's excess of activity. To change from London to Rye, to take a house, represented (for one part of Henry James) an act of assertion not unlike Owen's act in sleeping in the old haunted family room at Paramore. In *The Turn of the Screw* James was saying, on the remote levels of his buried life, that Lamb House was a severe threat to his inner peace. It was haunted. It contained all the ghosts of his boyhood – pushing, demanding governesses, Aunt Kate, his mother in her moods of severity. He could not be 'a fellow, don't you see?' in such an environment. In the house of Family, Henry had always thought of himself as a claimant, as his early tales had shown. To establish his claim, to take possession, carried with it the certitude of punishment – the demanding ghosts would exact their price, and little Miles's, or Owen's, or Morgan's sacrifice had shown in the irrational feelings of childhood what the price for such assertions could be.

These, we may see, were the ancient emotions that arose within the adult Henry James in a kind of conscious nightmare called *The Turn of the Screw* – within an atmosphere of the uncanny and the supernatural. We can understand why he felt 'doomed' in the inexorable way in which oracles doom men to prescribed experience. The children and the governess are the voices of James's past, early terrors re-expressed through his imagination and through art – the eternal power of fantasy and thought that can turn the calm quiet of day into a place of evil and horror. All this had been 'triggered' by *Guy Domville* and the attendant night of terror.

4

The Turn of the Screw was promptly serialized in *Collier's*, from January to April 1898. Later that year it appeared in a volume to which James gave the title *The Two Magics*, its companion piece being *Covering End*, a story version of the Ellen Terry play – two tales of houses, and the title embodied the element of 'magic' relating to them – black magic and white, the baleful and the benign. Not since *Daisy Miller* had James written a tale that had so caught the public fancy. As inquiries from mystified and fascinated readers poured in, James was careful not to give away his secret. Like all artists, he did not like to 'explain' his art, and he was determined not to spoil the mystification he had created. He was to tease both readers and critics in his later preface by saying the story was 'a trap for the unwary', and he quite regularly reminded questioners that he regarded the tale as a piece of hack-work. Doubtless it was, in the sense that he wrote it in a hurry and for money; but James himself knew that what sometimes begins as hack-work can end as a masterpiece.

When one psychologist, interested in the unconscious, queried James about his intentions he replied that he blushed 'to see real substance' read into his 'wanton little tale', and added 'ah, the exposure indeed, the helpless plasticity of childhood that isn't dear or sacred to *somebody*'. To his brother's friend, F. W. H. Myers, the psychical researcher, James described the tale as a 'very mechanical matter', but he did add that he had wanted to create the impression of 'the communication to the children of the most infernal imaginable evil and danger – the condition on their part, of being as *exposed* as we can humanly conceive children to be' – exposed, we judge, to the too-vivid imagination of one of their elders. To H. G. Wells, who asked him a story-teller's question – why he had not described the governess in greater detail – he gave a fellow-craftsman's answer. He had sought 'singleness of effect' and so had confined himself to letting the governess strike her own 'little note of neatness, firmness and courage'. He was to elaborate on this in his preface, writing 'we have surely as much of her own nature as we can swallow in watching it reflect her anxieties and inductions'.

There exists evidence that James said in private exactly what he said in public about *The Turn of the Screw*, and the elaborate divagations of some of the critics of this much-discussed tale have never sufficiently taken this evidence into account. The private comment was made in his physician's consulting room; and it is known only because the doctor recorded the conversation in a learned study on *Angina Pectoris*, without discerning the uniqueness of *The Turn of the Screw*. It figures as 'Case 97' in a series of cases described by Sir James Mackenzie, a great Edwardian heart-specialist, who dealt with emotional factors in heart ailments.

I was once consulted by a distinguished novelist. Just before he came to see me I had read one of his short stories, in which an account was given of an extraordinary occurrence that happened to two children. Several scenes were recounted in which these children seemed to hold converse with invisible people, after which they were greatly upset. After one occasion one of them turned and fled, screaming with terror, and died in the arms of the narrator of the story.

'You did not explain the nature of the mysterious interviews,' Mackenzie said to his distinguished novelist. The latter then explained to Mackenzie the principles on which to create a mystery. "So long as the events are veiled the imagination will run riot and depict all sorts of horrors, but as soon as the veil is lifted, all mystery disappears and with it the sense of terror.'

This idea is expressed in James's theory of the ghostly tale. He liked 'the strange and the sinister embroidered on the very type of the normal and the easy'. In a word, terror exists for us anywhere, and at any moment that we imagine it. That is why James preferred daylight ghosts. And the secret of his story, as he finally revealed it in his late preface, was that he allowed his readers to imagine for themselves horrors never named. For an author to produce the corpse or rattle the chains, was to limit the potential of nightmare. 'Explained' ghosts and attested, certified psychical phenomena did not interest him. He sought to 'make the reader's general vision of evil intense enough ... make him *think* the evil, make him think it for himself'. By doing this the author was released from weak 'specifications'.

James wrote *The Turn of the Screw* accordingly on a theory of unexplained extra-human terror, that terror within himself that could not tell him why he had felt a sinking of the heart, at the simple daylight act of providing himself with an anchorage for the rest of his days.

Part Three
The Great Good Place

41

Two Diaries

I

Excerpts from a diary kept by Henry James, aged 19, son of William James and nephew of the novelist, during a summer's journey abroad:

Lamb House, Rye, Friday July 14, 1898 – I came down here a week ago last Wednesday and was met at the station by Uncle H. who brought me up the hill to the house, showed me over part of it, holding me by the arm and keeping up a perpetual vocal search for words even when he wasn't saying anything. He left me in my oak panelled room to dress, with the injunction that I must 'come down' bursting with news. In the evening he walked me about the town, to the old tower with its little terrace, to the 'land-gate', down round the back past the bit of shipping. It is all extremely pretty, pleasant, charming, or picturesque, but owing to my self-consciousness and slowness to expression I was much bothered by the duty of seeming properly appreciative.

I doubt myself how much H. cares for me. He takes no interest at all in my plans projects or ambitions and at any rate does not wish to show any curiosity about my tastes or peculiarities. And as his only way of condemning seems to be by faint praise, I don't feel much reassured by his commendations. But on the other hand he is always most kind and seems most anxious that I be properly amused, and I am beginning to think that he is naturally, socially rather duller and less genial than I thought. When a man named Orred came here to lunch a couple of days ago he was just as conversationally short-winded and nervous as with me. He knows it all so that I can't tell him anything (about my impressions of England etc.).

[Harrow] July 26, 1898 – Got a note from Uncle H. a couple of days ago saying he missed me. He told me he cherished me when I left. These things encouraging ...

Aboard the cattleboat *Armenian*, one day out of Boston Harbour, September 27th 1898 –

This diary has not been kept with the greatest regularity after all, but I shall jot down a word or two of what followed during the summer. The week and a half that followed were the best of those that I spent at Rye. Poor Rosina was pitifully personal and limited in her point of view and also over-prone to talk self and her own friends ... This, especially when addressed to strangers, appalled Uncle Henry. Yet he never made a sign and treated even her most Rosinaish outpourings and questionings with perfect respect. It was, however, but what was to have been expected of him. It [had] the effect of waking him conversationally, and when Edmund Gosse, a very perceptive, but genial and at times almost playful personage, came down he [H.J.] came out of himself completely, was at times quite frolicsome and even descended to a pun.

One evening they got to talking about Meredith and about his origin. Gosse knew a lady who had been a friend of Meredith's when he was a very young man ... He had married first at the age of 18. Later his wife ran away from him and Meredith subsequently disappeared. Where he had been was not known, but Gosse said that he supposed he had been in Germany during the two years. Uncle Henry said he thought he had never been in Germany, that he had once been a war correspondent in Austria (if I remember rightly) and that 'of that experience he had made the very utmost' ... Uncle Henry said that he lived out of the world in a rather shabby little house with a beautiful garden. He had wonderful wine of which he drank very little ...

From the diary of Mrs J. T. Fields, of 148 Charles Street, Boston:

Monday, September 13, 1898 – We [Mrs Fields and Sarah Orne Jewett] left London about 11 o'clock for Rye, to pass the day with Mr Henry James. He was waiting for us at the station with a carriage, and in five minutes we found ourselves at the top of a silent little winding street, at a green door with a brass knocker, wearing the air of impenetrable respectability which is so well known in England. Another instant and an old servant, Smith, opened the door and helped us from the carriage. It was a pretty interior – large enough for elegance, and simple enough to suit the severe taste of a scholar and private gentleman. Mr James was intent on the largest hospitality. We were asked upstairs over a staircase with a pretty balustrade and plain green drugget on the steps; everything was of the severest plainness, but in the best taste, 'not at all austere', as he himself wrote us. We soon went down again after leaving our hats, to find a young gentleman, Mr MacAlpine, who is Mr James's secretary, with him, awaiting us. This young man is just the person to help Mr James. He has a bump of reverence and appreciates his position and opportunity. We enjoyed our talk together sincerely at luncheon and afterward strolled into the garden. The dominating note was dear Mr James's pleasure in having a home of his own to which he might ask us. From the garden, of course, we could see the pretty old house still more satisfactorily. An old brick wall concealed by vines and laurels surrounds the whole irregular domain; a door from the garden leads into a paved courtyard which seemed to give Mr James peculiar satisfaction; returning to the garden, and on the other side, at an angle with the house, is a building which he laughingly called the temple of the Muse. This is his own place *par excellence*. A good writing-table and one for his secretary, a typewriter, books, and a sketch by du Maurier, with a few other pictures (rather mementoes than works of art), excellent windows with clear light, such is the temple! Evidently an admirable spot for his work.

42

A Russet Arcadia

HENRY JAMES slept for the first time in Lamb House towards the end of June 1898, probably on the 28th. The furniture acquired during the winter months was moved on 9 June; his servants followed – the liquor-loving Smiths, who showed some uneasiness and took to the bottle in anticipation of exile from London. James's uneasiness, at the time of the signing of the lease, had long been banished. *The Turn of the Screw* had taken care of the ghosts. Presently carpets were laid and curtains hung. James supervised every detail; he remained in flurried consultation with his architect; he acted with a sense of well-being and happy accomplishment. He engaged a local gardener, George Gammon. He brought with him his amanuensis, MacAlpine, complaining however that his work was uneven. He described it as a mixture of 'capacity and failure', which he found surprising in a Scot. Scots, he explained to his nephew, usually made the most of their capacities, even if these were limited. 'He is excellent for my work,' he explained, 'but with the fault that there's too much – *much* too much – of him for it.' However, he kept him that summer and into the autumn for the writing of *The Awkward Age*. Later MacAlpine worked only occasionally for the novelist and boarded out in Rye, so that James did not have to cope with his presence in Lamb House during non-working hours.

In the midst of James's installation, and because there was chaos both in De Vere Gardens and in Lamb House, he paid country visits and just before he finally quitted town he went to Brighton and thence to Rottingdean to the funeral of his old friend Sir Edward Burne-Jones. He stood in the grey-towered churchyard, which was smothered in spring flowers, and watched the committal of the ashes, in sight of a glistening sea. He had known the painter since his earliest days in London and he wrote another elegiac tribute, this time to Charles Eliot Norton, who had originally introduced him to Burne-Jones. 'There was no false note in him. He knew his direction and held it hard – wrought with passion and went as straight as he could.'

I

Rye proved a constant delight, a 'russet Arcadia'. He liked the brown tints in the town and the glimpse of the Channel; the quiet at night seemed almost audible; he could hear with great comfort in every room the friendly tick of the clock in his hallway. His new life had begun with the visit of his nephew, and namesake, the eldest son of William, who came to England to spend a few weeks. 'I have but just scrambled in here by the skin of my teeth,' he wrote to the young Harry James who was arriving on a cattle-boat at Liverpool, 'and am all ready – nay yearningly impatient for you. (I have slept here two nights – tonight the third, and shall feel an old inhabitant.) Your room awaits you – right royally – and the garden grins in anticipation'. His first visitor to his new domain was, appropriately enough, 'family' and the 'right royally' indicated he was installing his nephew in the 'King's Room'.

At the time of his visit to his uncle, James's nephew Harry was a solemn, rather conceited youth, as his diary-notes show, articulate, thoughtful, but a little too much absorbed in himself to note what was going on around him. Henry James found himself drawn to him and pronounced him extraordinarily nice 'only too silent and inward for absolutely easy intercourse'. If Harry wasn't sure, during his stay, whether his uncle liked him, he soon had abundant evidence in warm, affectionate letters filled with travel-advice and urging an early return to Lamb House, where the uncle expected a visit from the charming if 'incurably crude' Rosina – she of the missing vowels.

So began a famous tenancy that would link Henry James to this corner of Sussex. The novelist's first two months in Lamb House were a cavalcade of visitors. In letter after letter James reported 'the bump of luggage has been too frequent on my stair'. This also meant anxious conferences with his cook. It was one thing to entertain at luncheon or dinner in De Vere Gardens; it was another to have friends and relatives descend at the little Rye station to spend twenty-four hours or more. James invariably met the train, escorted by his servant, who brought a little hand-cart or wheelbarrow for the luggage. If guests were elderly, he sometimes had a carriage; more often he would saunter with them up the cobbled hill, pointing out the delights of his rural existence. In fast succession that first summer came his old friends, the future Justice Holmes, Mrs Fields and Miss Jewett, the Bourgets, the Curtises, the Edward Warrens, the Gosses, Howard Sturgis – 'a good many irrepressible sojourners' – and Henry James complained that he did not achieve at first 'all the concentration I settled myself in this supposedly sequestered spot in search of'.

However he himself issued the invitations. In spite of his joy in the place he felt abruptly cut off from London. He could not shed so easily the habits of twenty years; he felt 'out of things'. He wanted to know what was going on in Mayfair. He was reduced now to communication with London friends by letter and telegram; indeed, the telegram began to play a new role in his life. The medium itself provided a delightful challenge. 'Are you utterly absent or can you dine with me Friday at seven to go afterwards with three others to the theatre,' was a typical message dispatched that summer when he planned a foray into town. This sense of isolation from his clubs and the murmurs of London society contributed probably to his tale – the first written in Lamb House – of a young girl confined to her cage in a branch post office at the back of a Mayfair grocery store, seeking to deduce from the telegrams she handled the goings-on of society. As with the story *The Great Good Place*, which he wrote just before he moved, James created *In the Cage* out of immediate emotion. And however much he might complain, as guests descended from the Ashford local, and the luggage bumped on his eighteenth-century stairs, he actually felt himself protected by visitors against the solitude of country life with which he would now have to make his terms.

Bit by bit, however, the sense of the place asserted itself. The morning click of the typewriter in the Garden Room became known to Rye – and the distant sound of a grave and measured voice weaving sentences. By midsummer Henry James was offered (and declined) the vice-presidency of the local cricket club. Later he would join the Golf Club, not to play golf, but to partake of tea in the clubhouse. He had indeed found a great good place; and late that year he could proclaim to Francis Boott, his Florentine friend, now living in Cambridge, Massachusetts, 'Lamb House is my Bellosguardo.' He had never dreamed, in the old Italian days, when he envied Boott and his daughter Lizzie their tranquil existence in the Villa Castellani, that he too would have something resembling a villa, in – of all places – a rural and decayed out-of-the-way corner of England.

2

He had planned his move from London with the greatest care. Workmen had peeled off the paper and disclosed the handsome panelling in certain rooms; fresh paint had been applied; tile fireplaces had been repaired. 'Getting into' Lamb House, the novelist wrote to his brother, 'is the biggest job of the sort I have ever tackled and the end is not yet.' He had bought, aided by Lady Wolseley, discreet pieces of Georgian mahogany, 'a handful of feeble relics,' he said – and some of his books were moved from De Vere Gardens. He hoped he would ultimately be able to let his flat for part of each year.

His possessions were not as 'humble' as he suggested; they showed discrimination and taste. If he had not assembled a Poynton, he had nevertheless taken care of creature comfort, with modest elegance. The Green Room would lodge many of his books; and presently certain pictures were hung – a Burne-Jones, an inscribed photograph from Daudet, a small portrait of Flaubert, some illustrations from an edition of *Daisy Miller*, a Whistler etching. Elsewhere he would place family portraits, and prominently, a picture of Constance Fenimore Woolson. The garden-room was also furnished for work, and James installed here many of the inscribed volumes received from author-friends, as well as works of reference. There were books in the entrance hall, in massive bookcases. James's library was not that of a systematic book-buyer; he did much of his reading at his clubs. His Lamb House shelves contained volumes from his early years, sets of major English and French writers, a good deal of history and memoirs – he read eagerly anything that related to manners, customs, rituals in older societies – a goodly amount of Napoleonic material and certain books, pencil-marked and scrawled over in his large hand, which he had reviewed in the days of his literary journalism. It would be some time however before his library would be weeded out and fully transferred from De Vere Gardens, where he had at this moment more than Lamb House could accommodate.

At first James's staff consisted of MacAlpine, the Smiths, husband-

and-wife from De Vere Gardens and his newly-acquired part-time gardener. Later there would be a housemaid; and early in his life at Rye he took in an 'apprentice', a diminutive local lad named Burgess Noakes. Burgess was a mere 14 and still lived at home when he became James's house-boy. His master treated him as he would a son; corrected his English, taught him manners, made him conform to personal ritual. Ultimately he was James's valet. Burgess learned, in the new century, to shave the novelist and minister to his personal wants; looked after his clothes, did his errands. He remained small, wiry, athletic, with a love for football and boxing. 'My gnome Burgess,' James used to say of this sturdy bantamweight – he ultimately won the Sussex championship – and there was always pride and loyalty in this relationship. He survived, like James's fictional butler 'Brooksmith', a cultivated emanation of his master, a relic of the civilized Edwardian life of Lamb House.

3

The visit of Mrs Fields, bringing with her the delicate and gifted Miss Jewett, was an echo from an early time, a revival of memories of youth. Mrs Fields had been a beautiful Bostonian in James's apprentice years; her husband had published him in the *Atlantic*, and she had welcomed him as a precocious young man of letters to her salon in Charles Street. James remembered her as a singularly graceful young wife, with a beautiful head and hair and smile and voice and as a singularly winning hostess, who had enabled him to meet Mrs Stowe, and to hear Julia Ward Howe recite the 'Battle Hymn' with her finale of a great clap of hands as she rose to deliver the last line, 'Be swift my soul to welcome him, be jubilant my feet.' To receive a note from Mrs Fields, from London, after all these years, was to receive a flood of revived Charles Street memories; and James invited her and her companion to Lamb House to spend the night. The ladies preferred to come to luncheon and return by a late afternoon train.

Mrs Fields on her side had other memories of Henry. What she had experienced – she had recorded it long ago in her journal – was the freshness of James's youthful tales which her husband brought home, in their large sprawling handwriting. One such occasion is recorded, how the couple, on a beautiful summer's day went to a nook in the pasture 'where we could hear the sea and catch a distant gleam of its blue face', and lying in the cool grass she read Henry James Jr's tale called *Compagnons de Voyage* (later published in the *Atlantic* with the English title *Travelling Companions*). 'I do not know,' she had written, 'why success in work should affect us so powerfully, but I could have wept as I finished reading, not from the sweet low pathos of the tale, which was not tearful, but from the knowledge of the writer's success.'

They met now, in middle age, with this long backward reach to the Civil War. Boston – Charles Street – had come to ancient Rye. As James put it a few days later, writing to Mrs Humphry Ward, 'Mrs Fields took me back to my far-away youth and *hers* – when she was so pretty and I was so aspiring.' She wore, for her visit, a black lace mantilla, allowing it to descend from the head, as George Eliot had done; it gave Mrs Fields, with the traces of her earlier beauty, 'a general fine benignity'. In Miss Jewett, whose tales James had admired, and whom he now met for the first time, he found 'a sort of elegance of humility or fine flame of modesty'. Her work was minor; it combined the sober and the tender note. By the evidence of Mrs Fields's diary of that day at Rye, Henry James cross-examined Miss Jewett closely, and in its pages we seem to hear the talk in the parlour of Lamb House after the lunch.

'It is foolish to ask, I know,' said James to Miss Jewett, 'but were you in just such a place as you describe in the *Pointed Firs?*' 'No,' replied Miss Jewett, 'not precisely; the book was chiefly written before I visited the locality itself.'

'And such an island?' James persisted.

'Not exactly,' she said again.

'Ah! I thought so,' the novelist said. And then perhaps sensing the aggressiveness of his questions, he told Miss Jewett that her famous sketches were done with 'elegance and exactness', they were 'absolutely true – not a word overdone'.

James had ordered a carriage, and he took his two visitors to Winchelsea where he showed them the ancient village and Ellen Terry's cottage. After that they took their respective trains, the ladies back to London, the novelist back to Rye.

4

Aside from his hospitality, much of the novelist's time was given over to exploring the region; there were long leisurely spins on his bicycle and a slow and deliberate 'living into' the new-found Arcadia. He would go to Winchelsea, the decayed sister-port and study the view of Rye in the distance – the crowned hill, of which he now had such complete possession. Was there a touch of Mont St Michel in the aspect of the Sussex town – the little churched hilltop, rising from the lonely marshes, the open gates, the walls, the towers? James made such a comparison, but his thoughts ran rather on the Robert Louis Stevenson aspect of the place – the contraband running from the Continent and the yards where once the King's ships had been built out of solid Sussex oak, until iron began to be used. The shipyard had declined, as had the town itself, from its ancient commerce. But there were always three or four fishing-boats on the ways and some ship in the shrunken harbour. James liked to go to pubs and talk to the sailors; to wander on his bicycle to every nook and cranny. He re-read Thackeray's unfinished *Denis Duval* which was set in this region, and daydreamed of Thackeray, ensconced in his own garden-room, writing this novel. In an article on Rye and Winchelsea, written a couple of years later, when James had thoroughly made himself a part of the place, he indulged in this Thackerayan fancy. He spoke of

the open, sunny terrace of a dear little old garden – a garden brown-walled, red-walled, rose-covered on its other sides, divided by the width of a quiet street of grass-grown cobbles from the house of its master, and possessed of a little old glass-fronted, panelled pavilion which I hold to be the special spot in the world where Thackeray might most fitly have figured out his story. There is not much room in the pavilion, but there is room for the hard-pressed table and the tilted chair – there is room for a novelist and his friends. The panels have a queer paint and a venerable slant; the small chimney-place is at your back; the south window is perfect, the privacy bright and open.

He was reminded he said of some 'far-away foolish fiction, absorbed in extreme youth', which made this place 'an echo of an old premonition'. 'I seem to myself to have lain on the grass somewhere, as a boy, poring over an English novel of the period, presumably quite bad, – for they were pretty bad then too, – and losing myself

in the idea of just such another scene as this.' Fiction had a way – in
the existence of Henry James – of becoming life. But the fiction, he
observed, 'couldn't have been so good as this'.

43

A Summer Embassy

HENRY JAMES'S installation in Lamb House was accompanied by
the alarums of the Spanish-American war. The *Maine* blew up in
Havana harbour in February 1898; and the press headlines, the dispatches from the United States, and finally the outbreak of hostilities in April, were a heavy burden to the novelist for whom any
conflict evoked memories of the Civil War, 'buried under all the
accumulated other emotions and years'. To his brother he wrote, 'I
see nothing but the madness, the passions, the hideous clumsiness of
rage.' He blamed the newspapers 'for the horrible way in which they
envenomize all dangers and reverberate all lies'. It was true that the
Hearst newspapers had been responsible for much of the war
hysteria in America.

James's letters however showed less anxiety than in the Venezuela dispute two years earlier. On that occasion his double-allegi-
ance was in conflict. The new hostilities, largely naval, touched his
ingrained pacifism; and from the outset he feared that America's
seaward cities might come under Spanish shells. Spain had been
for a long time, Henry remarked, 'a picturesque and harmless member of the European family', and England could be counted upon
to stay out of the fight. James said he was averting his eyes from
the press – 'one must save one's life if one can'. He was 'mainly glad
Harvard College isn't – nor Irving street – the thing nearest Boston
Bay'.

On the day after the United States issued its call for volunteers,
James wrote to his old friend Frances Morse in Boston that he felt
'in a vile unrest ... wretchedly nervous and overdarkened'. Once
again he was distant from his country; 'and besides, it's too late –
and one must swallow one's discriminations'. Less of a public figure
than his brother or Howells, he watched the war without declaring
himself; but then he always avoided talking to reporters. He received
at this moment, however, a letter from Howells pronouncing the

war 'the most stupid and causeless that was ever imagined by a kindly and sensible nation'. Howells added, referring to the drama of Dreyfus in France, 'If there could be anything worse than the Zola trial, it would be our behaviour to Spain.'

I

James was to be extremely well-briefed during this war that, in a matter of weeks, turned the United States into a world power – in the sense that its frontiers were suddenly thrust beyond the seas. The defeat of the Spanish navy at Manila, the blockade and destruction of the Spanish ships, the surrender of the Philippines, the ultimate cession of Puerto Rico, the freeing of Cuba, the annexation of Hawaii – all this James learned not only through the newspapers but from his friends at the American Embassy in London – the ambassador himself, John Hay and the first secretary Henry White. He had known both for many years.

In the autumn of 1897 the ambassador had invited James to join him and Henry Adams in a trip up the Nile. James, whose journeyings had always been confined to the European continent, was sorely tempted. But Lamb House beckoned; and he was guarding his finances. 'I can't go – I *can`t*.' James wrote to Hay; it was 'perversely *impossible*'. Hay was soon recalled to London from Egypt because of the impending war. And shortly after James had installed himself in Lamb House, he learned that the Hays, Henry Adams, Senator Don Cameron and his wife Elizabeth – the woman to whom Adams had been most closely attached in recent years – had taken the large Elizabethan manor house of Surrenden Dering, in Kent, a dozen miles from Ashford, the change-point for Rye. Thus a group of Americans – for the house was filled with Adams nieces and Hay children and transient relatives and friends – were within easy distance of Lamb House. Surrenden Dering, set in its large park, and described ironically by Adams as 'about the size of Versailles' became the 'summer embassy'. James could find, at any time, authoritative reports and the diplomatic background for the American history being written overseas. 'I have had,' he wrote, 'Henry Adams spending the summer not very far off – in the wonderful old country house of Surrenden Dering, which he has been occupying in the delightful way made possible by the possession of Shekels, in conjunction with the Don Camerons.' James could not visit frequently;

his own house was filled; but he did go for a short stay a couple of times.

He found the summer establishment interesting in many ways, for, as Adams's biographer remarks, 'behind the feudal scale of hospitality' there went on the work of diplomacy 'as the secretaries hurried back and forth to London'. Perhaps even more than the echoes of Washington within the greenery of Kent, James watched the human relations in this large house on the vast estate. He had been fascinated for some time by the way in which Adams was a part of Elizabeth Cameron's large entourage. 'Everyone is doing – to my vision – all over the place – such extraordinary things that one's faculty of wonder and envy begins at last rather to cease to vibrate,' he wrote to a friend in Boston. There were signs that his faculty of wonder, and his novelist's curiosity, were vibrating as strongly as those of his narrator in *The Sacred Fount*, whom he would place two years later on as peopled an estate as Surrenden Dering. Concerning Adams and Mrs Cameron he remarked that he 'envied him as much as was permitted by my feeling that the affair was only what I should *once* have found maddeningly romantic'. He had met Mrs Cameron on other occasions; she was, he found, 'hard' – considering her 'prettiness, grace and cleverness'. The word 'clever' in James's lexicon was not always a compliment. Mrs Cameron was indeed a skilful managerial woman – a Mrs Touchett or a Mrs Gereth. Adams's niece, Abigail, has testified that at the manor house that summer Mrs Cameron 'was not only the hostess for this big and complicated caravanserai, but she ran it as well, and I doubt if many details escaped her eagle eye'. She was 'the most socially competent person that I have ever met', the niece, writing in her old age, remembered – a woman who could 'tackle any situation and appear to enjoy it'. In his notebooks James wrote that he was 'somehow haunted with the *American* family, represented to me by Mrs Cameron', but set this aside as demanding 'a large, comprehensive picture'. He did not elaborate. The allusion would seem to have been to Mrs Cameron's ability to be a Senator's wife, keep tight control of his busy home and his social life in Washington, and at the same time be available as a social resource and comfort to the widowed Adams. James was to say, in a letter to Henrietta Reubell, two or three years later, in the vein of *The Sacred Fount*, that Mrs Cameron had 'sucked the lifeblood of poor Henry Adams and made him more "snappish" than nature intended'. He added that 'it's one of the longest and oddest American *liaisons* I've ever known. Women have been hanged for less – and yet men have been too, I judge, rewarded with more.'

2

It was at Surrenden Dering that John Hay that August received the cable from President McKinley summoning him to Washington to be Secretary of State. James had known the diplomat and writer for many years. It was John Hay's good offices which had obtained for Henry the Paris correspondence of the *Tribune* in 1875. And they had come to know each other well during a certain period in the 1880s when Hay and Clarence King, the geologist, were in Paris at the Grand Hotel. Henry found them there – the boon companions of Henry Adams – and had fallen into breakfasting with them and roaming the boulevards. Clarence King was a well-known 'charmer', a conversationalist of great spontaneity, and he quite eclipsed in interest the meticulous and politic Hay. Hay had in him something of the distance of a politician and statesman; and Henry had his kind of 'distance' as well. Thus their relations were framed within a double-distance; these were on the whole pleasant and warm, yet remained always formal. 'He cares nothing for me,' Hay remarked of Henry James. 'I have always known it, and it came out again, plainly, in Paris. But I care a great deal for him.' Hay continued throughout his lifetime to testify to this. Henry on his side remained a loyal and distantly admiring friend, although he had developed considerable tenderness for the statesman at the moment of Miss Woolson's death. Hay, in Rome at the time, had performed all the offices of friendship for James at her funeral. Otherwise, a kind of top-hatted ceremoniousness prevailed between them. How highly Henry thought of Hay may be attested, however, by the fact that he had journeyed to Southampton to greet him on his arrival as American Ambassador to England. Hay's writing activities were, from James's high professional point of view, simply gentlemanly ventures into literature. He read Hay's novel *The Breadwinners* and identified the author in spite of its anonymity. It had, he told his sister, much 'crude force' and imitated the best in American fiction – the best being, he wryly remarked to her, 'Howells and me.' He also read Hay and Nicolay's life of Lincoln, 'a wonderful gallery of pictures of the vast democratic American life', and called it an 'epic' biography. For Hay, the pillar of Republicanism, the one-time secretary of Lincoln, the ambassador and Secretary of State, James had all the respect of an individual outside politics who admires probity and distinction in public life. 'I shall never, never, my dear Hay,' he wrote to him once, 'forget that you are the person in the world who has said to me the three or four things about my lucubrations that have most uplifted me – and them.'

He came to Surrenden one September day to salute his honoured friend before his departure for Washington. He was to remember 'with the vision not denied me, thank God, of the drama of life' the way in which Hay 'paused before the plunge, on the great high Surrenden terrace'; and he had wondered often if Hay remembered that moment – the soft September day, the baronial quiet of the place, the general air of enchantment – as well as the 'lovely women and distinguished men just respectfully hanging on to your coat-tails'.

3

Hay, King and Adams were a kind of private Washington triumvirate, and their friendship – watched from a distance by James – would be memorialized by Adams himself in later years. Hay was the party office-holder and man of political action that the ironical and worldly-wise Adams could not allow himself to be: Clarence King, a man of the out-of-doors, who could accept the irrational and primitive forces within himself, represented that part of Adams which was most submerged in his New England rigidity. These two men – Hay and King – had become more than Adams's close companions. In the Conradian sense, it might be said, they had been his 'secret sharers'. They helped complete a life that Adams felt to be incomplete; for Hay and King, each in his own way, acted out what Adams sometimes scarcely allowed himself to feel. The son of Quincy, the habitué of Washington, who felt himself swaddled in his puritan heritage – and damned by it – could experience vicariously King's love for 'archaic races', (this was Adams's way of putting it) that is, his sympathy with the Negro and the Indian, and his corresponding dislike of their enemies.

Hay was simply 'the good Hay', in James's letters; but Clarence King he watched with the eyes of a storyteller and a lover of character. He found him 'charming, but a queer, incomplete, unsatisfactory creature'. One day King would be 'buying old silk tapestries or the petticoats of Madame de Pompadour to cover New York chairs', or 'selling silver mines to the Banque de Paris, or philandering with Ferdinand de Rothschild, who appears to be unable to live without him'. Then suddenly he would ignore Rothschild and dine 'with publicans, barmaids and other sinners'. James saw these paradoxes from his Olympus. 'The most delightful man in the world, Clarence King!' he said, yet he was also 'slippery and elusive, and as unmanageable as he is delightful'.

King on his side reads James with a closeness that the novelist would have appreciated and wrote to Hay:

How clever Harry James's London is, but how Jacobean. Whenever he describes the periphery, as anywhere over one cab-fare from his dear Piccadilly, there is a nervous, almost nostalgic, cutting and running for the better quarters of the town. Even when talking of Blackwall or Hampstead, you feel that he looks a little askance, that he wants to go home; and you positively know that before going into these gruesome and out-of-the-way parts of the town, he gathers up a few unmistakeably good invitations and buttons them in his inner pocket, so that there should be no mistaking the social position of his corpse if violence befell him.

King had apparently been reading *The Princess Casamassima*, and perhaps remembering some of his visits with James to the more unsavoury sections of London. He expressed admiration however for James's ability to create 'such airy webs' and drape them over the objective facts of life, 'so that the dew shall sparkle on them and the amusing little insects glitter and tangle in them, like the fabrics of the spiders. It is a charming gift. I wish I had a little of it. I'd give worlds to be able to spin one inch.'

'He was in his way a fascinator,' Henry said of King at the time of the latter's nervous breakdown, some years before his death. 'It's miserable to think one may never again see him as he delightfully was. In truth I never thought there was no madness at all in his sanity – and feel indeed as if there may be some sanity in his madness.'

4

Surrenden Dering was a minor incident in the crowded life of Henry James that summer, although it evoked old memories and kept him in touch with America and Americans. The war had been 'a deep embarrassment of thought – of imagination. I have hated, I have almost loathed it.' For some friends there was no qualification. 'I detest the war,' he said. When it was over, and America's frontiers were extended to the south-east, and westward, far into the Pacific, James shrank from the thought of 'remote colonies run by bosses'. At the same time – perhaps as a consequence of the rationalizations of diplomacy heard at Surrenden Dering – James began to take a more benign view of the matter. The extension of American power was perhaps a New World version of Britain's *imperium*; the British he felt had been good colonizers, and the cause of civilization had, on the whole, been advanced. This was the way in which he spoke, at any rate, to his British friends, combining a gracious attitude towards his host-country with the wish to put his own nation in the best light possible. He wanted, however, he said, 'to curl up more closely in this little old-world corner, where I can successfully beg such questions. They become a spectacle merely.' His probing intelligence nevertheless tugged them continually; and much as he hated the newspapers he read them with critical curiosity.

He put the matter in another way to his nephew Harry some months later, when he had had time to absorb the shocks of the war and the ramifications of the peace. 'To live in England,' he explained, 'is, inevitably, to feel the "Imperial" question, in a different way and take it at a different angle from what one might, with the same mind even, do in America. Expansion,' he said, 'has so made the English what they are – for good or for ill, but on the whole for good – that one doesn't quite feel one's way to say for one's country "No – I'll have *none* of it!" It has educated the English. Will it only demoralize *us*?'

Then he had another thought. 'I suppose the answer to that is that we can get at home a bigger education than they – in short as big a one as we require.' After offering these suggestive thoughts, he told his nephew he thanked God he had 'no *opinions* – not even on the Dreyfus case'. He was he said more and more aware of things 'as a more or less mad panorama, phantasmagoria and dime museum'. The truth was he did have opinions – not least on the Dreyfus case.

44

Brother Jonathan

IN London, that spring, before he had moved to Lamb House, Henry James reached a moment of intense weariness. The war was a burden to him; every morning there was the same little mountain of newspapers, the casual bundles of proof, journals, books from publishers, from friends, from booksellers, the tide of the world's words sweeping into De Vere Gardens and overwhelming him. What could any creature want of so much print? He was to ask the question, and to speak disconsolately of 'the irrelevant, destructive, brutalizing' side of life, in a fantasy called *The Great Good Place*. The tale was a prevision of Lamb House. *The Turn of the Screw* had recorded old lingering fears of childhood when the occupancy of Lamb House was in prospect; but once these fears had been expressed, once the terror had been siphoned off, James could dream peacefully, and pleasantly – and the 'place' he imagined was more than a private retreat. In his story (which waited two years for publication), the good and great place is a curious mixture of monastery, hotel, club, country house, an ideal cushioned silent refuge, 'some great abode, of an Order, some mild Monte Cassino, some Grand Chartreuse' accessible to the Protestant as a 'retreat', yet not a retreat of the religious sort: a place of material simplification.

The interest of the story, on its biographical side, is not only in its obvious wish for surcease from worldly pressure, but his desire for an exclusive man's world, a monastic Order, a sheltering Brotherhood. The tale has in it distinct homo-erotic overtones. The admiring acolyte who comes to the great writer, George Dane, sits beside him, puts a hand on his knee, and gives him at once a 'feeling of delicious ease'. At the mysterious 'place' the 'dream-sweetness' experienced by the harried writer resides in the absence of all demands upon him and in the discreet quiet – a place of 'slow receding footsteps' where 'slow sweet bells' are heard in the distance and the Brothers compose 'a landscape of quiet figures'. Above all there is the blessing of anonymity. Dane can exist 'without the complication of an identity'. He is freed from being a *persona* in the world; the inner life can wake up again. He can re-possess his soul.

This was a very old fantasy of Henry James's. In *Roderick Hudson* of 1875 he had depicted a similar place, near Fiesole, where Rowland Mallet finds peace within a cool cloister, and lays his hand on the arm of a Brother to whom he speaks of the temptations of the Devil. James had always been fascinated by the moment in Hawthorne's *Marble Faun* when Hilda, the little American dove-girl in Rome, filled with the horror of a crime she has accidentally witnessed, goes to confession – though a Protestant – to ease herself of her burden. In a monastery the world's burdens drop away; this had been the theme of the ill-fated *Guy Domville*; and we may capture some touch of James's 'associational magic' in noting that the names George Dane and Guy Domville have the same initials. The craving for a great good place and the touch of a Brother's hand had existed for years. There is, however, one other element in this dream-fantasy. It resides in George Dane's identifying himself with the young man who has come to his flat and who, while he sleeps, gets rid of the newspapers and proofs, and answers the letters and telegrams. The great good place is also the place of youth. James's fantasy expresses the wish to be young again, to be the younger Brother that he had once been. He had long ago embodied this fancy in his little tale of Browning, about *The Private Life*, in which the poet of the drawing-room carries his worldly burdens while his liberated other-self, in the quiet of the study, writes immortal verse.

The language of the passage in *Roderick Hudson* describing Rowland's visit to the monastery, written twenty-five years before, is close to that of the *The Great Good Place*. The feelings are exactly the same. In James's secular religion of beauty 'the great good place' is also 'the great want met' – and the want is not so much 'the putting off of one's self' as in a religious retreat; it is 'the getting it back – if one has a self worth sixpence'.

I

He was getting it back at Lamb House. The autumn that year was dry and warm and Rye seemed even more beautiful – more *nuancé* – as he said – than in the summer. He awoke on clear days 'no longer with the London blackness and foulness, the curtain of fog and smoke that one has each morning muscularly to lift and fasten back; but with the pleasant sunny garden outlook, the grass all haunted with starlings and chaffinches'. The war, now that it was over, seemed merely to have flashed by; whatever dreadful marks it had left were beyond his reach; he felt, more than ever, that he could stay close to his little plot of land and cultivate his little garden. He watched his gardener plant bulbs and seedlings – hyacinths, tulips, crocuses – for the winter's shelter, with the promise they held for the spring. He relished the mellow fruit of autumn from his south wall. The novelist decided to linger in Rye until Christmas. De Vere Gardens – London – could wait. Presently great gales blew and his garden shook off 'in each gust, some article of clothing'. To Francis Boott he wrote,

I like this place – I like my little old house and little old garden. It blows, today, it blew all last night – great guns; and I hear them magnificently boom in my old chimneys. But my little house stands firm and gives me most refreshing assurance of the thickness of its walls and the depth of its foundations. After so many years of London flats and other fearsome fragilities, I feel quite housed in a feudal fortress.

The summer's end had brought an end to the rush of visitors; the bump of the luggage had ceased. He had finished writing *In the Cage* shortly after settling in Rye and now, undisturbed, he worked steadily at the Harper serial, *The Awkward Age*. Jonathan Sturges came to stay with him for a few days in the middle of October and remained for two months. He was not as the other visitors; he made no inroads on James's working hours; in his crippled state he was accustomed to quiet and he was excellent company at other hours of the day. 'Brother Jonathan,' James had called him when he had met him eight years before; this was an evocation not so much of the old Roundhead or Puritan name (Sturges was not from New England but from New York); the allusion was rather to the early image – particularly the stage image – of the stock American, the predecessor of the traditional 'Uncle Sam'. 'Little Brother Jonathan has his share of the national genius,' James had written to Edmund Gosse, and this quality, plus his bright eyes, his mordant wit, his fund of gossip, made him always a delightful companion. Since his visit to James at Torquay, three years before, Sturges had been through a long illness. He was well now, that is, as well as he would ever be. He evoked in James, as always, the tender feelings the novelist had shown to his invalid sister; moreover, like Alice James, Jonathan Sturges had a sharp tongue, which was why James called him 'the little demon'. 'Do you remember young Jonathan Sturges?' he asked Henrietta Reubell.

He is full of talk and intelligence, and of the absence of prejudice, and is saturated with London, and with all sorts of contrasted elements of it, to which he has given himself up. Handicapped, crippled, invalidical, he has yet made his way there in a wondrous fashion, and knows nine thousand people, of most of whom *I've* never heard. So he's amusing, and to him (as I'm very fond of him), I make sacrifices. But they *are* sacrifices.

They were, insofar as James gave up total solitude, which he liked less than he was ready to admit. He got in exchange this 'mine of conversation and a little blaze of intelligence'. Having forsaken London, he had a small incarnation of London beside him. There was something more, however, than the amusing asperities and touching physical helplessness of the younger man (Sturges was 34). He was literary, he was sentient; he observed; he was a civilized presence. Among the papers of James's journalist friend in Paris, Morton Fullerton, there is preserved a fragment of a letter written by Sturges on Lamb House stationery. It suggests a little the qualities in the younger man which made him sympathetic to James. Sturges wrote to Fullerton,

I wish I could give you a picture of this little, red, pointed, almost medieval town with its sea-wall and its Norman relic of Ypres Castle which they call here 'Wipers' – perched on a hill in the midst of the grey-green, sand-coloured waste of Romney Marsh, an Anglo-Saxon Mont St Michel, long deserted by the sea yet with the colour and scent of the sea in its quiet brown streets, a brown of the tone of fishermen's sails and nets. The blue-jerseyed retired fishermen themselves are to be found at any hour, on the deserted bastion of Ypres Castle happily armed against the French invasion a hundred years ago. They address one another with a classical 'What Ho!' which seems almost too beautiful to be true, and through brass telescopes they study the sails upon the distant Channel. In south-westerly gales one hears the roar and sees the long white raselier* of the surf. The sheep huddle together upon the marsh and the fishing boats huddle with bare poles in The Robber in Rye 'Harbour', a hamlet like a Dutch picture against the wild grey sky – three miles away. The old house itself is early Georgian, an impression of red brick and white marble, oak-panelled rooms and brass knockers. There is a 'garden-house' in the garden and a quantity of beautiful old pink wall. And H.J. . . .

---

* Apparently a word coined by Sturges to suggest the 'shave-and-lather' effect of the surf. There is no such word in the French dictionaries.

At this point the fragment ends and we are deprived of Sturges's picture of Henry James in his rural setting. There is abundant reference to Sturges, however, in James's correspondence, for he admired the crippled young man's stoicism – 'he is only a little body-blighted intelligence – a little frustrate universal curiosity – and a little pathetic Jack-the-Giant-Killer's soul'. In *The Great Good Place* James had dreamed of being cared for in a company of Brothers. In Lamb House he cared for Brother Jonathan; and it was as if he were being cared for himself. For he had reached that time of life when he was turning to younger men to capture an image of his own youth.

2

If we are deprived of Jonathan Sturges's glimpse of Henry James at middle age in his rural retreat, we have another picture, set down a year later by an assiduous diarist, a schoolmasterly man who lived with his pen in his hand in a constant state of self-communion. This was Arthur Christopher Benson, the second son of the Archbishop of Canterbury. He memorialized James on various occasions; and this has suggested a closer friendship than actually existed. The younger man sent his early verses to James, and the novelist replied in large pleasing phrases that nevertheless showed he found them wanting; they lacked form, they were false poems, however much they seemed to render feeling. Benson was born in a school, his father was a schoolmaster and later an Archbishop, and his own career was divided between Eton and Cambridge. He was a writer of familiar essays; they came out in such quantity and sold so well, that someone said of him (and of his brothers) that the Bensons wrote as easily as they breathed – adding however that it was uncomfortable to have them breathing down one's neck all the time. A. C. Benson was a melancholy man and, like certain Victorians, a great mountaineer; he was much given to his books and his thoughts. In later years he had long fits of depression. James responded to his melancholy; he had a certain affection for him, but one gets the feeling of a cool and courteous distance between them; the novelist is mild, and friendly-yet-aloof. There was something dry and commonplace in Benson to which James could not respond; and yet there seemed also to have been a feeling of pity for him and his circumscribed academic-churchly world.

A. C. Benson came to spend a night in Lamb House at the beginning of the new century, after receiving a warm invitation – 'I want immensely to hear the history of your triumphant Book and to assure you of my participation in your labour, your rest and your success. The way you heirs of all the ages knock off these things! But I want the inside view – I want indeed, from you, many things.' The visit occurred on 17 January 1900 and Benson felt impelled to 'dip my pen in rainbow hues – or rather let me be exact, finished, delicate, to describe the charm of this place'. There followed in his diary a brief picture of Rye and of Lamb House; and then the picture of its master. James had met him at the station, as was his custom, but 'looking somewhat cold, tired and old'. He was as always affectionate in his greeting; he patted the younger man on the shoulder, and was 'really welcoming, with abundance of *petits soins*'. They dined simply at 7.30 with many apologies from the host about the fare. 'He was full of talk, though he looked weary, often passing his hand over his eyes; but he refined and defined, was intricate, magniloquent, rhetorical, humorous, not so much like a talker, but like a writer repeating his technical processes aloud – like a savant working out a problem.' They gossiped; and James talked also 'with hatred of business and the monetary side of art. He evidently thinks that art is nearly dead among English writers – no criticism, no instinct for what is good.'

Benson's diary records some of James's talk. They got on to the subject of Mrs Oliphant:

I had not read a *line* that the poor woman had written for *years* – not for years; and when she died, Henley – do you know him, the rude, boisterous, windy, headstrong Henley? – Henley, as I say, said to me 'Have you read *Kirsteen*?' I replied that as a matter of fact, no – h'm – I had not read it. Henley said, 'That you should have any pretensions to interest in literature and should dare to say that you have not read *Kirsteen*!' I took my bludgeoning patiently and humbly, my dear Arthur – went back and read it, and was at once confirmed, after twenty pages, in my belief – I laboured through the book – that the poor soul had a simply *feminine* conception of literature: such slipshod, imperfect, halting, faltering, peeping, down-at-heel work – buffeting along like a ragged creature in a high wind, and just struggling to the goal, and falling in a quivering mass of faintness and fatuity. Yes, no doubt she was a gallant woman – though with no species of wisdom – but an artist, an artist – !'

'Henry James works hard,' Benson wrote after his visit.

He establishes me in a little high-walled white parlour, very comfortable, but is full of fear that I am unhappy. He comes in, pokes the fire,

presses a cigarette on me, puts his hand on my shoulder, looks inquiringly
at me, and hurries away. His eyes are *piercing*. To see him, when I came
down to breakfast this morning, in a kind of Holbein square cap of
velvet and black velvet coat, scattering bread on the frozen lawn to the
birds was delightful ... We lunched together with his secretary, a young
Scot. H.J. ate little, rolled his eyes, waited on us, walked about, talked –
finally hurried me off for a stroll before my train. All his instincts are of
a kind that makes me feel vulgar – his consideration, his hospitality, care
of arrangements, thoughtfulness ... He seemed to know everyone to
speak to – an elderly clergyman in a pony-carriage, a young man riding.
Three nice-looking girls met us, two of fourteen and fifteen, and a little
maid of seven or eight, who threw herself upon H.J. with cooing noises
of delight and kissed him repeatedly and effusively, the dogs also bound-
ing up to him. He introduced me with great gravity ... We got to the
station; he said an affectionate farewell, pressing me to come again; I
went away refreshed, stimulated, sobered, and journeyed under a dark
and stormy sky to the dreary and loathsome town of Hastings.

3

The story called *In the Cage* which James published as a volume-
size tale in the autumn of 1898 is of a piece with his immediate feeling of being cut off from London. The profound change in his mode
of existence, his sense at times of being confined and 'out of things',
seems to have contributed at this moment to his imagining a young
girl confined daily to a little cage in a branch post office at the back
of a Mayfair grocery store handling the brief and cryptic telegrams
of the outer world, counting the words and reckoning the fees. She
is curious and sufficiently alert to take in the meanings of the messages; they tell her of certain scandalous goings-on in society. James
gives the girl no name. Like the governess in *The Turn of the Screw*
she is identified by her thoughts and her conversations with a lady
of some social pretension who works in the rich houses as an arranger of flowers. We know the girl only as a troubled observer,
using her inductive and deductive capacities to satisfy an insatiable
curiosity about her environment. The cage-girl and the governess
both feel shut out – or shut in – as James now felt shut out from the
great world in Rye, or as he had pictured Hyacinth Robinson long
before in *The Princess Casamassima*, wondering what went on behind the impressive closed doors of noble mansions in London. The
cage-girl's notions of the world are derived in part from romantic

novels; the telegrams handed in through the high aperture of her cage become a part of the fictional furnishings of her mind. Where the governess remains locked in her own imaginings and lives with phantoms which she tries to explain to the readers of her tale, the cage-girl constantly returns to reality – to her fellow-employees in the grocery shop, to her young man, Mr Mudge, and to Mr Buckton the manager, in a setting of hams and cheeses, dried fish and paraffin. She is always aware of her poverty, her station in life, and the contrast between this and the world's splendours about which she is so touchingly curious and with which she feels she must make her peace. The moment of tension is reached in the story when she rescues from some undefined imbroglio a dashing Captain Everard, by remembering a telegram he has sent. Her dream of romance is quickly ended however and she discovers the world's indifference when 'without a look, without a word of thanks, without time for anything or anybody' Everard strides out of the grocery shop, as if young telegraph girls were expected always to bail out embroiled young gentlemen. Reality has quickly reasserted itself. Society may be blind to people of her station – but she sees, and without the distortions that complicated the life of the governess.

By many delicate and subtle touches, In the Cage keeps us within the girl's limited range of vision (as well as the vision of her creator) and we are enabled to accompany her in her practice, in a modest and simplified form, of the deductive methods celebrated in Sherlock Holmes. She is a detective of her own confined soul; she must make the best of her world. In the Cage shows James going about the business of seeing what he can do with his own alienation from Mayfair. That he should assume the disguise of an adolescent girl is of a piece with his creation of his stories of little girls; they had served their purpose in the earlier stages of his progress from his hurt and bewilderment through the madnesses and terrors of his soul. Now in the stages of his recovery, he had reached the moment when he needed no longer to take refuge within the bright-eyed world of Maisie; he could substitute the cogitations of a young adult. But like the girl he feels abandoned – almost as if London had left him rather than he London – and like Captain Everard without so much as a 'thank you'. If he no longer had his London, he at any rate had his little plot of ground in Rye, as the telegraphist, once she leaves her cage, will have her modest home with Mr Mudge and be the humble wife of a tradesman. James had had, after all, his 'position in society', had it for a quarter of a century; indeed he still had it. But society had turned out to be full of pitfalls and deceptions. If *In the Cage* shows us an adolescent yearning for knowledge of this society, *The Awkward Age*, which James now wrote, showed an adolescent caught up in its treacheries. In a certain sense this novel seems to have been James's way of telling himself that he was well out of London and its corrupt society : for *The Awkward Age* was to be his strongest indictment of England's upper middle class, its arrogant sense of privilege, and its erosion of human values. With the writing of this novel, the most complex of his fictional experiments following *Guy Domville*, James was on the verge of becoming his own self again. He seemed ready to shed the protective disguises of girlhood he had assumed and to take his own shape in his fiction – that of the elderly and fastidious observer of his world, the grave figure observed by young Sturges and the melancholy Arthur Benson.

45

The Awkward Age

THE TURN OF THE SCREW had had its initial impulse in Henry James's anxieties over his impending retirement to the country; *In the Cage* reflected his sense of actual divorce from London – from that 'London life' which he had lived with such vigour and delight for a quarter of a century. *The Awkward Age*, which he now wrote, between September and December 1898, was a serious inquiry into the society he had abandoned. The work suggests that James, in this crisis of his middle age, was writing not only about the 'awkward age' of the female young, but about the awkwardness of ageing. His elderly character is named as if he were invoking the rejected metropolis – Mr Longdon. He gave him his own age, 55, the age at which he was writing the novel. Mr Longdon has lived for a very long time in the country, in Suffolk. His house is square and red-roofed and be-gardened and russet-walled, like Lamb House in Sussex; indeed the frontispiece to the novel, in the New York Edition, offers us a picture of the entrance to Lamb House. It is captioned 'Mr Longdon's'. At the beginning of *The Awkward Age*, Mr Longdon accompanies a younger man, Gustavus Vanderbank, to his rooms during a night of downpour. There they discuss at great length the drawing-room they have just quitted. It is like the rising of a curtain on a play. Mr Long-don seems to be the novelist's idealized self. James still wore his beard; his counterpart is clean-shaven. James was stocky and thick. Longdon is slight and delicate. James was bald; Longdon is silver-haired. But if he thus seems to be the image of what James would have liked to see in the mirror, he talks brilliantly, as James talked, of London and its *moeurs*; and he reminds his 34-year-old companion that he is an 'old boy, who remembers the mothers'.

I

Mr Longdon's descent upon London is like that of an ancient travel-ler visiting a remote civilization. He compares himself indeed to 'a stranger at an Eastern court, comically helpless without his inter-preter'. He cross-examines Vanderbank closely about the life of the Brookenhams in their expensive Buckingham Crescent flat. Their drawing-room is extremely articulate, but Mr Longdon has been 'rather frightened'. Vanderbank, a heavy fashion-plate, senses this. 'We're cold and sarcastic and cynical,' he says 'without the soft human spot.' The novel becomes the story of the elderly man's attempt to discover a 'human spot' for the young Nanda (Fernanda) Brookenham, a charming adolescent who mingles knowingly with her elders and hears outrageous things in her mother's entourage.

Decidedly Henry James was writing as if he felt 'out of it' – of the London scene. And 'what's London life?' Vanderbank asks point-blank. He provides the answer: 'It's tit for tat!' Everything has its price. 'Ah, but what becomes of friendship?' Mr Longdon inquires 'earnestly and pleadingly' – we might say almost ruefully. There is a poignant suggestion of isolation and loneliness in the question. It was as if, after his long inner struggle with the demons of 'success' and neglect, of feeling himself 'unwanted' and cast aside, James had to start all over again. Having once conquered London, and learned it intimately, he must now re-explore it from a new distance. He sees now a society hard-rimmed and cruel, an aristocracy in *déchéance*, savage in its civilization – 'through its own want of imagination, of nobleness, of delicacy, of the exquisite'. He was aware that 'every-thing is allowed to a closed caste persuaded of its superiority'; but there has been 'a great modern collapse of all the forms'; and with-out form society – life – was void and chaos. And then, had he really learned to know 'society'? – the British aristocracy? Had he really grasped from his novelist-cage what went on in the gilded salons? Behind the façade of bright and brittle talk he could now discern intricate human relations, meetings, partings. One couldn't be quite certain who was sleeping with whom. In the old days one didn't ask such questions. Mr Longdon's curiosity about what Nanda 'knows', is but an enlargement of the inquiry into what Maisie 'knew'. It is but one more stage in the curiosity of the governess, the cage-girl – or Henry James's own bewilderment and bachelor-innocence – that ingrained Adamic bliss bestowed on him by his unworldly father. He knew well that somewhere, in some extra-human zone of being, there was evil. He had never been as innocent as Emerson in that respect. But he had lived in a kind of luminous, sexless and unphysical world – at least until his descent into the theatre. That had been the beginning of change. He had become aware by degrees that women in life as well as in fiction were not immaculate; they were organisms, possessors of temperament and passion who like Miss Robins could serve him cocoa in her rooms amid a smell of powder and perfume and greasepaint, and talk about the men who fell in love with her. He had watched this calculating actress, in the world of fakery and illusion – so intelligent about the stage and about Ibsen, so interesting a sexual object – use poise and appearance to impress and advance herself, in her struggle for exist-ence and fame. James's world of Daisies and Pandoras and Isabels had indeed vanished. In the wings of the theatre, in the dowdy dressing-rooms, in the costly defeat he had suffered, a process of re-education had been going on. The young Henry James, for whom life had been codes and manners and observances had encountered the fleshly in place of the verbal and the ethereal. He had witnessed the pettiness and egotism of struggle for place and for power. He who had learned to trust the truths of his fancy had by a long and painful process been learning certain truths of fact. Mr Longdon, or the unnamed narrator of *The Sacred Fount*, or the curious New Eng-land 'ambassador' Lambert Strether, would re-embody a new, still slightly bewildered, novelist who had once chided Maupassant for looking too much at the monkeys in the monkey-cage. Perhaps Henry James had looked too much at the reflective side of man – and looked too far away from the monkeys? Edmund Wilson long ago remarked – was indeed the first critic to perceive – that in James's novels of 'the death of childhood', and in his final large fictions, there was a kind of 'subsidence' into himself. Now sex does appear – it becomes a kind of obsession – in a queer, left-handed puritanical way, as of a man who has never allowed himself to think about sexual intercourse save as something to be read in lemon-coloured French novels. 'There are plenty of love affairs now and plenty of irregular relationships,' wrote Mr Wilson, 'but there are always thick screens between them and us; illicit appetites, maleficent passions, now provide the chief interest, but they are invariably seen from a distance.' The 'distance' in the works of 1895–1900 is created in part by the limited vision of the little girls or the limited experience of the adolescents. There is another kind of distance in those works – the confusion of feeling in the author himself. He had dramatized, always, the loss of American innocence in its encounter with a corrupt and decadent Europe. Now, by the process of living, feeling, suffering, he seemed on the verge of losing his own safeguarded – almost unbelievable – innocence. In his citadel of art he had remained one of the pure of mind.

2

We are à l'ombre des jeunes filles en fleur in Henry James's The Awkward Age, although the novelist is hardly telling us the same story as Proust. The jeunes filles of James's story are English and Italian; they are products of two distinct methods in education. The English girl has been treated, as we now say, 'permissively'. She has put up her hair and come down into the drawing-room and been exposed to her mother's 'fast' set. The Anglo-Italian girl has been brought up by a determined English Duchess, her aunt, in the continental manner: she has been treated like 'a little ivory princess', hand-fed 'the small sweet biscuit of unobjectionable knowledge', in anticipation of an early marriage. This is the engaging subject – it seems almost 'quaint' in our time – of The Awkward Age. The era of 'emphasized virginity' is no more; but what makes James's treatment of the subject highly contemporaneous is his grasp of the dilemmas of adolescence. Published in 1899, The Awkward Age would qualify as an outmoded Victorian novel were it not for James's vision of the essence of his dual subject – and the formidable technique he used to give it a frame.

The 'frame' puzzled the early readers of the novel. In the manner of 'Gyp', the French countess who wrote dialogue-novels in the 1880s and 1890s James constructed his novel almost entirely out of drawing-room 'talk', and set scenes. His dialogue-book possesses thus the immediacy of a stage play. The reader tells himself that he reads the novel as he reads a play; he enjoys none of the usual privileges of fiction : little is told about the characters, save as they tell it themselves. The reader is asked to supply voices, inflections, gestures, the very things which actors give to a script. *The Awkward Age* must be read with the inner ear to grasp its tone and idiom. This done, the characters come to life, move about in their scenes, endow the novel with its enveloping emotion. *The Awkward Age* is no more artificial than Oscar Wilde's comedies, and it is considerably more humane. But it would be more accurate to compare it with Molière – the high wit and the self-characterizations remind us of the French dramatist; also the personages and the materials are in his tradition – two young marriageable girls, two duennas, two eligible but difficult young men, and a strange assortment of society characters who circle about the protagonists. The story is dramatized, as James put it, in a series of 'presented episodes'. Each episode is a piece of the building – and it is we who build as we read. In this way James demonstrated, after his own miserable failure in the theatre, that a fine dramatic comedy could be placed within the novel-form.

The technical mastery displayed in this work seemed at first to thwart the movement of the story. James must have felt this, for he gave to his Mr Longdon a special function. He is the invented observer, initially intended as a puppet-string character, but also a chorus. He asks the right questions; he insists on the right answers; he bridges gaps created for the reader by James's strict dialogue-method. He has however much more than a mere 'structural' function. He comes alive as one of the 'poor, sensitive gentlemen', for whom James had a predilection in his late works. Mr Longdon and Nanda reveal two kinds of innocence, those of age and of youth; and both are engaged in voyages of discovery. Mr Longdon re-discovers the London from which he has been long absent; he knew it in its Victorian prime, when Nanda's grandmother was alive, when society was fearfully respectable on the surface and all its corruptions were carefully concealed. Now the corruptions are in the open, embodied in fact in a civilized 'system' of wit and urbanity which is the mainstay of Mrs Brookenham's salon. Nanda's voyage of discovery is more painful. She has had to learn too early to struggle with alien 'instincts and forebodings'. And James recognizes that however much we may 'free' the young, the buds within the budding grove must still be given time to burst into leaf. *The Awkward Age* is the story of Nanda's growing up. James may seem, at first, to approve of the continental way of rearing young girls; yet he returns at the end to the truths of the Garden of Eden. Knowledge need not be dangerous, he seems to say to us, if men and women learn to face it with eyes unsealed, in full awareness of what is real and what is factitious in the world around them.

3

Once we are able to cope with its obsessive dialogue and its humorous gravity, we discover in *The Awkward Age* a kind of 'theory of education' for the female young. James had indeed been offering such theories or opinions in his works since Daisy Miller or the American *jeune fille* Pansy of *The Portrait of a Lady*. If he protested against the permissiveness in America's upbringing of its young, he also admired their spirit, their candour, their innocence. But what he now seems to be saying more clearly than before, though not without his old ambivalence, is that a corrupt society corrupts its young: that sentience and 'awareness', carefully cultivated, constitute a greater safeguard than ignorance. Mrs Brook's salon contains within it a queer assortment of characters: the complacent, the newly-rich, the divorced – idle women, scheming mothers, questionable 'affairs'. Like Molière, James is the wise and objective moralist, without falling for a moment into didacticism. Lord Petherton lives off Mitchett, the son of a boot-maker to royalty with a weak social position and vast wealth. Mitchy is one of James's characteristic weaklings. We have met him as Ralph Touchett, we will meet him in other forms in the later novels. Vanderbank, the hesitating, irresolute and handsome 'heavy' of the novel hesitates before Nanda as Winterbourne did before Daisy, two decades before; but he is at home with older women, with Nanda's mother, for instance. Mrs Brookenham, born of the aristocracy, is married to a nonentity who owes his small government job to his wife's good connections. Their son has an off-hand way of 'borrowing' five-pound notes from anyone, or helping himself to money if it should be left in a desk-drawer. Lady Fanny is on the verge of quitting her husband; Mr Cashmore wants Mrs Brook to 'square' him with his wife so he can philander; and Mrs Brook herself, in the end, is in competition with her daughter for Vanderbank, whom Mr Longdon, in desperation, tries to 'buy' for Nanda, by offering a handsome marriage settlement. Vanderbank isn't sure – above all whether Nanda, just becoming a young adult, still possesses the virginity of heart to go with that of her body.

Mrs Brook is the great creation of the novel: disillusioned, ambiguous, arbitrary, she is beset by all the troubles of her world, her vapid, ineffectual husband, her daughter who loves her lover, her light-fingered son; even her cherished salon is foundering in the crisis between mother and daughter. In the midst of her tottering empire Mrs Brook holds her head high, looks out at us with her 'lovely silly eyes' and speaks with an absurd wit that is often deadly serious, and with a wry twist in her logic that steers her through her perilous situations. Mrs Brook must place her daughter in life; and Nanda's exposure to the corrupt morals of the salon makes her unplaceable. Her virginity has been 'de-emphasized'. She will have difficulty finding a husband. Moreover she loves Vanderbank. In the end Nanda leaves her mother's precious salon; and what remains with us when we try to visualize this civilized, corrupt world is the sadness of the young, the awkwardness of the ageing.

We experience above all the touching predicament of Nanda, who between 18 and 21 has been asked to be solemn beyond her years. She has had to acquire the wisdom of Eve in an Edenless Victorian world that seems bent on depriving her of all that she has learned to value – truth of feeling, truth of statement, truth to life. She is indeed pure in heart but her exposure to her mother's world makes her tough in mind. Very much like the less fortunate Maisie, she moves us by the candour of her innocence. And when her bold front dissolves in tears – as it must – we can experience her ultimate pain that life is not always as arrangeable as her room, or its furniture. Life itself indeed *is* the arranger. Like all of James's late heroes and heroines, Nanda has to arrive at self-awareness through a vision of the cold determining world with which she must make her peace. In the process of muddling through, she recognizes that her most important discovery has been herself. She will not therefore judge little Aggie harshly, when that continentalized virgin runs wild the moment she is 'safely' married. 'Aggie's only trying to find out what sort of person she is,' Nanda carefully explains to the attentive Mr Longdon. 'How can she ever have known? It was carefully, elaborately hidden from her – kept so obscure that she could make out nothing. She isn't now like *me*.' Nanda *knows*. And she learns that one pays a price for knowledge. If she cannot have the younger man, Vanderbank, she will accept the protection of the elderly Mr Longdon. We recognize that the relationship will be chaste; she will be a treasured virgin, a priestess at a bachelor's altar. He will minister to her mind and endow her with eternal richnesses of the heart rather than the ephemeral exaltations and torments of passion.

The ageing moralist of 1898 ended his late novel almost as he had ended his first, *Watch and Ward*, twenty-five years before. In that fiction a female adolescent is reared by her guardian in the hope that he will ultimately be able to marry her. For the middle-aged Henry James such a consummation was not necessary. And it seems in *The Awkward Age* that in removing Nanda from her mother's drawing-room Mr Longdon achieved what Henry James had done all his life – harbour within his house, the house of the novelist's inner world, the spirit of a young adult female, worldly-wise and curious, possessing a treasure of unassailable virginity and innocence and able to yield to the masculine active world-searching side of James an ever-fresh and exquisite vision of feminine youth and innocence. For this was the androgynous nature of the creator and the drama of his novels: innocence and worldliness, the paradisial America and the cruel and corrupt Europe – or in other variations, youthful ignorant America and wise and civilized Europe.

The Awkward Age records a great disenchantment. James tells himself that he is well out of London, well out of its lies and camouflage. A letter written at this moment to Paul Bourget expresses his deepest feelings about the endowed classes. He had, he says, 'an inalienable mistrust of the great ones of the earth and a thorough disbelief in any security with people who have no imagination. They are the objects, not the subjects, of imagination and it is not in their compass to *conceive* of anything whatever. They can only live their hard functional lives.'

A compromise with functional living was however possible. If the creator has to maintain himself within an unimaginative world he can do so by cherishing certain illusions. In such a world, it is better to use harmless deception so long as one knows what the deception is: so long as one doesn't pretend that the lies are the truth. James was beginning to say that civilization and society, forms and manners which ennoble man and make rich his life, would founder without illusions, or artistic lies, the old 'suspension of disbelief'. In a word, society must have faith in its illusions and yet paradoxically remember they are illusions. It must have its mythology, like the Greeks; and live by its myths. This would be the philosophy of his last and greatest works.

46

The Little Girls

THE AWKWARD AGE was Henry James's last novel in the series dealing with female children, juveniles and adolescents, written between 1895 and 1900. He had, in earlier years, written about young adults – Catherine in *Washington Square*, or Daisy Miller, or Isabel Archer – American girls with an excessive sense of their own worth and a distinct will to freedom. But he had never, save for his early novel *Watch and Ward*, and the single scene of little Hyacinth's visit to his mother in *The Princess Casamassima*, concerned himself with childhood. In the years after his play-writing – the years of his life within the black abyss – he not only lived in a world of childhood wonder and terror, but wrote his stories in a remarkable sequence. His precocious little females grow a little older in each story, as if they were a single child whose life experience is being traced from the cradle to coming-of-age. *Watch and Ward* of 1872 had been a limited story of an 'education'; and in it he had traced Nora Lambert's growth from 12 to 20. He had written that novel during months of depression, when his future looked bleak, and his longing for Europe was acute. Was it mere coincidence, this return to childhood, during the years of public failure and depression or was there some inner need to relive forgotten experience, some compulsion to re-visit, step by step, the hidden stages of his own growth and development, within his safety-disguise of a little girl? – as if indeed these books were the single book of little Harry James of Washington Square and 14th Street, of Paris, Geneva, Boulogne and Newport?

Taking them in their sequence as he wrote them, we begin in the cradle with Effie, who is murdered at 4 (*The Other House*, 1896); she is resurrected at 5 (*What Maisie Knew*, 1897) and we leave her at 7 or 8, or perhaps a bit older. Flora is 8 (*The Turn of the Screw*, 1898) and the sole boy in the series, Miles, is 10: we are in the period of the child from 8 to 10. Then we arrive at adolescence: the adolescence of an unnamed girl in a branch post office (*In the Cage*, 1898). Little Aggie, in the next novel is 16, and Nanda Brookenham, 18 when the story begins (*The Awkward Age*, 1899). With the writing of this novel, James completes the series. He wrote also a goodly number of tales during this time, but the childhood sequence is embodied in the longer works. After the story of Nora in *Watch and Ward* which James had published in 1871, the novelist had gone to Italy. Now after recording the education of Nanda (and we pause over the associative recall of the names, Nora and Nanda, although they are separated by thirty years) James also goes to Italy. The repetition of old experience in new contexts is striking.

I

It is sufficiently clear from James's notes and prefaces that he wrote these novels one by one, not as a series; that he did not deliberately set out to create a sequence. And yet the sequence is there – and the astonishing fact that in his imagination he moved from infancy to childhood, from childhood to adolescence and then to young adulthood. Taken as a whole, the series shows the curiosity of these children, their challenges, their questionings, in terms of the bewilderment, wonder, imagination, phantasmagoria of their years – and their drive to attain omniscience in a world of negligent and terrifying adults. If we remind ourselves of the personal origin of these tales, we can discern within the total record a series of parables, an extensive personal allegory of the growing up of Henry James. Beyond the conscious intellectual exploration of states of childhood, Henry James was intuitively questioning his unconscious experience, reliving the long ago 'education' of his emotions. The murder of little Effie in *The Other House*, which inaugurates the series can be read as the age at which the little Henry, within the mature artist, felt himself annihilated by the brutality of the audience at *Guy Domville*. It will be recalled that James originally planned to have the child poisoned; but his selective imagination chose the form of death he himself had described at the Archbishop's when he had spoken of having been under water – 'subaqueous' – at the time of his *débâcle*. *Maisie* is a careful presentation of the Henry James of the late autobiography *A Small Boy and Others*: she possesses his curiosity, she is engaged in a systematic study of her elders, she searches determinedly for her identity amid her absent and estranged parents and governesses. Nanda describes this phase later in *The Awkward Age* – 'there was never a time when I didn't know *something* or other and that I became more and more aware, as I grew older, of a hundred little chinks of daylight'. Maisie is not 'real', her precocity partakes of James's boyish precocity. James endowed her with his own resistance to 'the assaults of experience' by having 'simply to wonder', and so preserve the integrity of her years. He gives her his own 'undestroyed freshness'. Her 'vivacity of intelligence' and her 'small vibrations' are those of a storyteller in the making. She might have been 'rather coarsened, blurred, sterilized, by ignorance and pain'. Art saves her and protects her innocence, as it had saved Henry; art and the ability he acquired to 'convert, convert, convert'; raw experience was always convertible into the stuff of poetry. Maisie is able to give us a vision of her shoddy mother which becomes 'concrete, immense, awful'. For the little girl follows, as her creator tells us, 'some stray fragrance of an ideal'. In his late preface he describes the 'exquisite interest' he found in his study of this little girl, for in reality she is a study of himself; unwittingly he has treated her as a kind of psychological 'case history'. *A Small Boy* gives us abundant data about Henry's governesses – those he had during his boyhood, that is when he was a little older than Maisie, and into his teens, particularly the memorable Augustine Danse, the most Parisian, 'the most brilliant and most genial of irregular characters', who was sent away – 'a cloud of revelations succeeding her withdrawal'. Shades of the shade of Miss Jessel! She had been 'all-knowing and all-imposing', and she had had a 'flexible *taille*' and 'salient smiling eyes'. James's boyhood memories endow her with strong sexual attributes. Her views had had 'a range that she not only permitted us to guess but agreeably invited us to follow almost to their furthest limits'. Little Maisie among her variegated parents is but another version of the slightly older Henry among various governesses.

After Maisie we arrive at the latency period, represented by little Miles, his boy in the series. We may speculate that Henry James, having sought the disguise of a little girl, remained fundamentally a little boy, strongly masculine, save when this masculinity was confronted by his older brother, or the pushing hands of governesses. The consequence of Miles's self-assertion was death; after that James reverted in his stories to the disguise of female adolescence. The anecdote he tells in his autobiography of his hiding under the table to listen to a reading of Dickens, his stories of himself as an observant little outsider, seem to parallel the adolescent girl who, from her cage, tissues together the society around her. Then, in Nanda and little Aggie of *The Awkward Age*, we may see a projection of the Henry of late adolescence – that part of him which was continentalized and ranged freely in the forbidden fruit of French novels, and the other side of him, the serious young literary novice who had to make what he could out of the New England environment to which he was brought – the life of Newport – when he was Nanda's age. We remember how Nanda at the end is surrounded by manyvolumed 'sets' of authors. Some such history of the psychical 'growing-up' of Henry James is traced in the depths of these stories. There has been a re-visiting of earliest childhood following the recoil from the horror of public rejection and the destruction of selfesteem. And as man uses his cells to rebuild a wound and create scartissue, we have in this sequence of stories a curious, logical, chronologically accurate remounting of the steps of early experiences of feeling. This was more than an intricate rewriting of the biography of James's psyche. In resuming the disguise of a female child, the protective disguise of his early years, James performed imaginative self-therapy. The record of these stories can be seen as the unconscious re-visiting of perceptions and feelings, in the service of his adult hurts. As his old feelings and imaginings had defended him long ago against the brutal world, they now served as aid against the new brutalities. He underwent a kind of 'self-analysis', strangely enough in the very years in which Sigmund Freud was undergoing his selfanalysis and writing his book on dreams. There is a striking historical parallel – the return of both men to the stuff of childhood; in the case of Freud it was partly voluntary and with full use of his ratiocinative powers and the data supplied by his patients. In the case of James it was an involuntary, intuitive, unerringly accurate historical search, conducted subliminally. In neither case was there a complete cure; but in the history of both Freud and James the process restored, after a period of crisis, their functional power – more important, their creative power. Each could move forward into new depths of adult experience.

2

Henry James was not wholly unaware of the process of 'unconscious cerebration' as he had called it as early as the writing of *The Figure in the Carpet* in 1895. He asked himself certain pertinent questions a dozen years later when he was writing his prefaces. But he did not press for answers, as Freud, working to other ends, might have done. His first question to himself was why had he shown such a predilection in these stories for little girls? His rational answer was that they were more sensitive recorders of their environment – more sensitive than 'rude' little boys. This answer satisfied him for a while. Suddenly a second question came up – and for a moment he looked at it. Then he simply set it aside. 'Rude' little boys, perhaps, he had said – but wasn't Morgan, for instance, every bit as sensitive as his girl-characters? And wasn't it curious that if the little girls were more sensitive than his boys, they certainly were tougher? As he put it, 'they bear up, oddly enough ... beyond their brothers'. He made this observation, but the answer would have led him too far into the spiritual transvestiture that he had practised. Besides, it is extremely difficult to read the riddle of the self. The masculine adult side of James could not explore the threats to his young masculinity – save as he had explored them in his inner dream-work, in his art – in the violence of the governess towards little Miles.

The little girls had thus emerged out of a personal healing process during the years 1895–1900. And this process had in itself, in its stages, served a fascinating function. The period of nightmare had been short-circuited by the writing out of the nightmare; the period of bewilderment over his buffeting by the theatrical world and its audience had been discharged in his study of the bewilderment of female adolescence. Each tale had eased some of his emotional suffering, so that from story to story he had dispossessed himself of certain intensities of pain. He had undergone a continuing moral rebirth and regrowth, as if his body were shedding dead skin. This mobilization of inner resources occurred while the novelist's outward self moved in the world in full command of its intellectual power. The mature Henry leased houses, visited friends, dined in clubs, wrote and discussed his art, grew in authority and dedication to his craft; struggled moreover against failure and commanded the attention of editors and publishers. Below or beyond the adult self, the hurt self was finding its healing substance. The subject, the essence, of these works was that of the growth and development of the human, the artistic, imagination. What else are these children doing if not trying to balance magic lantern phantasmagoria against reality? By the way of art, and within the form of his technical experiments, Henry James re-encountered his buried life, in the manner in which he had known it – as a struggling little girl, as a beleaguered little boy, as a troubled female adolescent. A striking instance of this kind of self-exploration of the personal myth is to be found in *Orlando* by Virginia Woolf, in which she retraces the history of her emotional education, seeing herself first as a boy in the Elizabethan era, and later becoming a young woman in the eighteenth century and a suffragette and matron in the time of Victoria. There was some such allegory of the self in Henry James's work of the late 1890s. Whether we call this a 'crisis of identity' or a 'middle-age crisis', the particular sequence of stories he created reveals the benign workings of the imagination – in this instance in chronological fashion – that moved from direct confrontation of disaster through the death of the spirit and to its re-emergence and growth in the familiar shapes of the past.

James had spoken four years earlier of his quest for 'compensations and solutions'. The language of his notebooks during these and later years, in his eloquent and mystical prayers to his Muse and his Genius, reflects his strong feeling that his art was the very source of his life. He speaks of his 'workings-out' of his stories as 'the dear old blessed healing, consoling way'. In the act of constructing a plot he writes, 'My troubled mind overflows with the whole deep sense of it all – overflows with reflection and perception.' By this awareness – perceiving. reflecting – he could discover he told himself 'all passions, all combinations'. 'Oh, sacred beneficence of *doing*!' he suddenly exclaims. And again, 'Oh, celestial, soothing, sanctifying process!'

Healing, consoling, soothing, sanctifying! Art was for James an anodyne, a balm, a religion, a sacred fount. In the service of art he renewed himself. As Proust was examining memory and association at the very moment when Freud was asking his patients to 'associate' and remember – remember their childhood – so Henry James, also at this moment, went in search of his, consciously for the purpose of creation, unconsciously in answer to the imperatives of his imagination, the demands of his spirit. Some geniuses at such crises turn to the anaesthesia of drugs, the artificial dream-worlds of opium or the modern acids of hallucination; others seek the consolations of alcohol, the numbing exhilaration of the bottle. James wanted no anaesthetic. His need was to stay awake, to perceive, to reflect; his art, and what he came to call in the end the 'religion of doing', steadied him and sustained him.

3

His long-deferred trip to Italy, including his promised visit to the Bourgets in France, suddenly became possible early in 1899 with the letting of De Vere Gardens on a six-months' lease. To make arrangements for this he had to go to London after his prolonged residence in Rye, and he had the sensation of his Mr Longdon, that of returning to the city as from another country. He felt himself an outsider; and he fled back to Lamb House. He had not yet acquired his room at the Reform, and his one-room lodging at the Grosvenor Club made him feel 'so on the streets'.

James had to read large bundles of proof of *The Awkward Age* before leaving. January and February were mild, however, save for winter gales; and he was alone in Lamb House for the first time. Sturges was laid up in London with the flu. MacAlpine had left on completion of the novel with the understanding that he would be available later as necessary and on a boarding-out arrangement. James settled down beside great fires in his hearths; he spoke with pleasure of the 'indoor winter cosiness'. Solitude meant a return to self-communion. 'This is a grey, gusty, lonely Sunday at Rye, the tail of a great, of an almost, in fact, *perpetual* winter gale,' he wrote in his notebooks.

The wind booms in the old chimneys, wails and shrieks about the old walls. I sit, however, in the little warm white study – and many things come back to me. I've been in London for three weeks – came back here on the [January] 20th; and I feel the old reviving ache of desire to get back to work. Yes, I yearn for that – the divine unrest again touches me.

The 'divine unrest' was in evidence – after his long troubled months; he wanted to write, to travel, to be in strange cities as of old. He even began to think charitably of the theatre. It was only a momentary thought. Alexander asked him to turn the tale of *Covering End* into a one-acter, it seemed so like a play. He was right; it had been the Ellen Terry play. James said he might do 'a fresh one-act thing', and in his notebook he mused on the way the very thought of the drama 'with the divine little difficult, artistic, ingenious, architectural FORM' could still make the 'old pulses throb and old tears rise again. The blended anguish and amusement again touch me with their breath.' However, he was in no mood for dramatic trifles. Rather than one-act plays he wanted to write 'big' novels – 'How, through all hesitations and conflicts and worries, *the* thing, the desire to get back only to the big (scenic, constructive, "architectural" effects) seizes me and carries me off my feet.' For the first time in many months he prayed to his muse, as of old –

Ah, once more, to let myself go! The very thought of it soothes and sustains, lays a divine hand on my nerves, and lights, so beneficiently, my uncertainties and obscurities. *Begin* it – and it will grow. Put in now some strong short novel, and come back from the continent, with it all figured out. I must have a long *tête à tête* with myself, a long ciphering bout, on it, before I really start. *Basta*.

His notebooks record, however, no *tête à têtes* on the subject of his contemplated novels – rather a series of jottings for tales, an idea for one given him by George Meredith during a visit early in February to Dorking; a return to other ideas noted during the past twelve-month. He could not think of big novels on the eve of his journey. He read his galleys; suffered a longish bout of influenza; made arrangements to have Jonathan Sturges live in Lamb House while he was away – it would give the servants something to do – packed his bags and late in February sat up till the early hours clearing his desk before his departure. 'I go to Italy after more than five years' interlude,' he wrote to a friend. At this moment he became aware that his room was filled with a smoky haze; and then he saw smoke squeezing through the planks of his floor, and around the edges of his rugs. He ran down the stairs to the dining-room below to see what was burning, but everything was normal. He then roused his servants. Smith hacked, sawed and pried up a couple of planks nearest the fireplace. Thick smoke poured out: a charred beam was smouldering under the hearthstone. It was a matter of minutes to douse it with water, and for safety's sake pack it with soaked sponges. The Smiths returned to bed, and James resumed his letter. He thanked his friend for being an agent in his discovering the fire: it would have been serious had he been asleep in bed. And he signed himself with a 'Good-night – it's 2.45 and all's well. I *must* turn in.'

All was not well. There was flame now beneath his floor. He shouted anew for the servants. Firemen and police were summoned. To reach the burning beam they had to pickaxe their way through the wall and ceiling of the dining-room below, for the underside had ignited and the flames were burning downwards. His parlour was smoked up a bit; but on the whole he felt he got off lightly for the firemen were 'cool as well as prompt'; moreover, they used water sparingly. His epistolary passion in the small hours of the morning had saved his house, perhaps his life. After a sleepless night, James despatched a long telegram to his architect which ended 'now helpless in face of reconstructions of injured portions and will bless you mightily if you come departure of course put off Henry James'.

Part Four

The Sacred Fount

47

L'affaire

IN the *New York Times* of 7 January 1895, prominently displayed, with large headline, is the account of the public humiliation of a Jewish officer on the parade-ground of the École Militaire in Paris. Found guilty of selling military secrets to Germany, the officer had been marched two days earlier before 5,000 soldiers for the removal of the symbols of rank and honour: his epaulettes were torn from his uniform, his sword was broken – while beyond the stiff ranks a mob hissed and jeered. Below this bit of ancient history in the press, the disgrace of Captain Alfred Dreyfus, one may read a small headline. It describes the jeering of Henry James in London on the first night of *Guy Domville*. The two different episodes reported on the same day, related only in time and emotional content: they speak of humiliation, outrage, hurt – and a howling mob. The military humiliation in France was sinister, tragic, world-shaking; the literary humiliation was minor, limited, private.

I

Henry James's response to the Dreyfus 'affair', in the ensuing years, may have had in it, in part, an unconscious element of recognition. He had from the first been fascinated by the sinister drama. More than four years had elapsed since the officer's incarceration on charges of high treason. Early in 1898 Zola, out of his profound sense of justice and his deep social convictions – but also with a strange and compelling megalomania – had published his letter to the President of the French Republic, known in history as *J'Accuse*. 'Truth is on the march and nothing will halt it.' In February 1898 he had been put on trial for libel. James had felt as if he were 'every a.m. in Paris by the side of the big brave Zola, whom I find really a hero'. He thought *J'Accuse* 'one of the most courageous things ever done and an immense honour to our too-puling corporation! But his [Zola's] compatriots – !' he added, as with a Gallic shrug, in writing to his cosmopolitan friend Henry Brewster. On the day that Zola was found guilty, James 'worked off' some of his emotions by writing a letter of support and encouragement to his old friend of the Flaubert *cénacle*. The letter does not seem to have survived among Zola's papers and one wonders whether it reached him at so difficult an hour; for Zola fled to England, to a retreat in Surrey, on the advice of his lawyers and friends. James believed Zola's life to be in danger.

He will appeal, and there will be delays and things will happen – elections and revulsions and convulsions and other things – but it was, I think – I fully believe – his sentence,* on Wesdnesday, saved his life. If he had got life or acquittal, or attenuation, he would have been *torn limb from limb* by the howling mob in the street. That's why I wrote to him.

Whether the two novelists met during Zola's exile is doubtful. James was too busy settling into his house in Sussex, and Zola was isolated in Surrey and unhappy to be out of France at this crucial a moment. 'I sit in the garden and read *l'Affaire Dreyfus*,' James wrote to Mrs Humphry Ward in September 1898. 'What a bottomless and sinister *affaire* and in what a strange mill it is grinding. The poor French.' He took the same attitude of sympathy with France in a letter to Bourget, who had written him in great detail and with much hatred of the Jews. James told Bourget his letter dealt

almost solely with these unfortunate things in France, about which you speak so sombrely and about which I can't offer you any word in the world that might be comforting. I don't understand, I am too distant both from the experience of them and the way in which you feel them. Nothing here corresponds to them – neither the good relations which we maintain with the Jews, and, in sum, with one another, nor the supreme importance we attach to civil justice, nor the 'short work' which we would make of the military if they attempted to substitute their justice for it. I can well sympathize however – to the point of tears – with your stricken country. Let us hope it will emerge by the door open to it (or the door that will be open to it) of revision [of the case]. I must confess that if France refuses to do this, I will find her less subject for sympathy – a less interesting sufferer. But France will not refuse.

---

* James means the verdict of guilty of 'Defaming the French Army'. Zola fled and sentence was never pronounced.

2

The Dreyfus affair was much in his mind, as he journeyed to Paris on 8 March 1899, and later to the Riviera, at the end of the month to visit the Paul Bourgets. He knew that his French friends believed in Dreyfus's guilt; and he was aware of Bourget's pronounced anti-semitism. James was stoutly convinced of Dreyfus's innocence, and he had no hatred for any peoples. He might satirize national manners or national idiosyncrasies, or use national stereotypes, but there was no touch of bigotry in his make-up. At the moment of his journey all France was split by *l'affaire*; and as a consequence of Zola's action and the clamour of the 'League for the Rights of Man', a court-martial was scheduled to review the case.

James had committed himself long ago to visit the Bourgets on the Riviera. He had always enjoyed Bourget's *art de dire*. He also recognized in the French novelist a certain discipleship, much as he disliked his novels. Now history was throwing up a barrier to their intercourse – history and Bourget's Catholic and conservative view of the world. 'The odious affair is rather in the air between me and that [Riviera] retreat,' he told Mrs Gardner. 'I don't feel about it as I gather our friends there do.' He added, 'one must duck one's head and pass quickly'.

He ducked his head at first by lingering in Paris. He explained his delay by saying that he was proceeding by slow stages and he remained at the Hôtel Meurice, reading page-proofs of his novel and receiving regular dispatches from Edward Warren about the repairs in Lamb House. The fireplace in the dining-room would be remodelled; the hazards would be eliminated. James's insurance would cover the costs. 'Reparation, amended and scientific reconstruction is already under way,' he reported to the Curtises in Venice. He was light-hearted and happy to be travelling again. Five years had elapsed since his last journey : and now he brought to old familiar scenes the eyes of middle age, eyes that saw things not only in their immediacy but in merging memories – old crossings, old associations, old emotions going back to his boyhood during the Second Empire. The early spring sun in the French capital was comforting; and he found in Paris his young cousins, Rosina and Leslie Emmet. Ever avuncular, he gave the young women the benefit of his Parisianism. 'I break-fasted, dined, theatr'd, museumed, walked and talked them,' he told William – without counting constant teas and little cakes of which he was a large consumer. He had lunch also one day with the young French novelist, Marcel Prévost; and he paid his usual homage to the salon of Henrietta Reubell, and the apartment of Morton Fullerton. 'This extraordinary Paris,' he wrote to Edward Warren,

with its new – I mean more and more multiplied – manifestations of luxurious and extravagant extension, grandeur and general chronic *expositionism* ... it strikes me as a monstrous massive flower of national decadence, the biggest temple ever built to material joys and the lust of the eyes, and drawing to it thereby all the forces of the nation as to a substitute for others – I mean other than Parisian – achievement. It is a strange great phenomenon – with a deal of beauty still in its great expansive symmetries and perspectives – and *such* a beauty of light.

The beauty would prevail over the poisonous items in the newspapers. During this visit he received a large impression of the capital that lingered in his memory; it would emerge in the novel he would begin to write within the year about an American returning to France in middle age.

3

After hanging back in Paris for a fortnight, James went to the Riviera in one straight jump; he spent a night at Marseilles and reached the Bourget villa, Le Plantier, at Costebelle near Hyères the next day. He enjoyed the warmth of late March, the flowers, the views, the terraces. Bourget, after endless travels around the world, had finally settled, for the winters at least, on a twenty-five-acre estate in one of the most beautiful spots on the Riviera. Everything spoke for the French writer's literary prosperity. There was the large house, and the guest-pavilion in which James was placed with another visitor, the Vicomte E. Melchior de Vogüé, a minor novelist and one of the early interpreters of the Russian writers in France. The estate was on a terraced mountain-slope; the walled park of pine and cedar afforded views both inland and to the sea. 'It's classic – Claude – Virgil,' James wrote to his brother. Before these splendours 'poor dear little Lamb House veils its face with humility and misery'. The 'misery' resided not so much in the difference in scale and landscape between Rye and Costebelle, as James's sense of his own modest income from his writings compared with that of the *mondain* and best-selling Bourget. For, almost in the same breath, he avowed that he was homesick for Lamb House – 'never again will

I leave it'. That James was not altogether at his ease with the Bourgets is clear enough from his letters; it is suggested also by his managing very promptly to set fire to the curtains in the guest-house. Nothing was damaged but the curtains. Still, the carelessness was not in character, especially after his own brief ordeal of fire in Lamb House.

James had always liked Bourget, in spite of his snobberies, his social platitudes, his aristocratic pretensions. For a Frenchman Bourget was uncommonly cosmopolitan; he had an interest in moral questions and psychology. James was prepared to stomach his rigidity, his dogmatism, even sometimes his conservatism and his fixed ideas, in order to enjoy the play of his mind and its lucidity. Bourget 'notes with extraordinary closeness the action of life on the soul,' James had written in an essay of 1888 but he added 'especially the corrosive and destructive action'. There was something corrosive in Bourget; and his being such a monument to success only sharpened James's ironic view of him. As James put it in 1900 to their common friend, Urbain Mengin (who had parted company with Bourget on the Dreyfus case) Bourget was primarily interested in the grand life, the life of luxury, the *spectacles de la grande richesse, de l'éternelle "élégance"* ', and this meant that he wished to perpetuate systems *'qui font fleurir ce genre de beauté'*. He added in English (for his correspondence with Mengin jumped from one language to the other)

the manner in which his imagination, his admirable intelligence and his generous and sensitive soul have been led captive by a certain abnormal vision of 'high life' remains for me one of the oddest and most indescribable facts with which literary, with which moral criticism, just now, has to deal. He's a moralist so strangely conditioned!

Bourget on his side recognized James's 'love for a complex experience of life', and publicly praised his technical virtuosity. 'No one,' he said, 'has rendered, as this master has, the exact nuance of remarks exchanged by New Yorkers or Bostonians in a corner of a drawing-room or around a dinner-table.' He greatly admired and imitated James's tales of the artist life. Out of his own airless view of the world, however, he saw James as 'subtle rather than colourful, delicate rather than powerful, inquiring rather than deeply moved'. James would indeed have said as much – and more – of Bourget.

In the guest-pavilion it amused the American novelist to observe the seriousness and assiduity of Melchior de Vogüé, whom he described as a *gentilhomme* turned journalist-novelist – in other words an amateur. Daily the Vicomte locked himself up to do his stint: he was running a serial in the *Revue des Deux Mondes*. James found in him 'a fine gentlemanly tension', but his mind was 'too conscious and too cultivated'. To William he spoke of 'the indigestible Midi of Bourget and the Vicomte Melchior de Vogüé'. The tense and gentlemanly fellow-guest observed all the amenities; his novel *Le Maître de la Mer* was found tucked away among a mass of French books in Lamb House years later, inscribed '*A mon éminent confrère, Henry James en souvenir des bons jours passés près de lui au Plantier de Costebelle.*'

4

The week at Le Plantier passed quickly enough. 'I treat the *Affaire*,' Henry wrote to William, 'as none of my business (as it isn't,) but *its* power to make one homesick in France and the French air is not small. It is a country *en décadence*.' There were sundry sociabilities, of which we have no record save that on one occasion Lady Randolph Churchill, who was editing an elaborate hard-bound journal called *The Anglo-Saxon Review*, paying a call on the Bourgets, made James promise to do a story for her. Since he was to be decently paid for it, James was to spend a goodly part of his subsequent visit to Venice, in the Palazzo Barbaro, keeping his promise. We judge that there were walks and talks – wide-ranging talks about current literature and the literary situation in France, for shortly afterwards James wrote a brief and sketchy essay summing up the century. He called it 'The Present Literary Situation in France'. Published in the *North American Review* six months after his visit to the Bourgets it contained James's one public allusion to the Dreyfus case. In discussing Jules Lemaître as critic, he regretted that when Lemaître finally developed a conviction, it had turned out to be one of the 'ugliest' – 'his voice was loud, throughout the "Affair" in the anti-revisionist and anti-Semitic interest'. Bourget and Vogüé were mentioned only in passing in the article, in which James did not conceal his feelings that men of the second rank now held sway in the Republic. He praised Bourget for having learned his trade in 'the school of reflection not hitherto supposed to be that of the novel'. His subject was always 'an idea' and he was capable of regarding an idea 'as a positive source of excitement'. But he also said of his friend that the outer world to him was 'a large glass case equipped with wheels, stoves and other conveniences, in which he moves over his field very much as a great American railway director moves over his favourite line in his "luxuriously-appointed" private car'. As for the Vicomte, James quietly brushed him off as 'the best instance of how the most characteristic French aptitude may assert itself even in dull days'. As usual James confined himself to prose. His end-of-century view was more retrospective than contemporaneous. 'The great historians are dead – the last of them went with Rénan; the great critics are dead – the last of them went with Taine; the great dramatists are dead – the last of them went with Dumas; and of the novelists of the striking group originally fathered by the Second Empire, Émile Zola is the only one still happily erect.'

One episode was to linger in Bourget's memory long after James's visit. It occurred on an evening when they sat by the fire and Bourget complained of the difficulty he had – and he spoke English fluently – in understanding certain verses of Kipling's. He mentioned in particular *McAndrew's Hymn*. Henry James took the book from his hand. He moved over in front of the fire. The Hymn contained terminology that might have given an English reader pause – 'thrust-block', 'coupler flange', 'cross-head jibs'. According to Bourget, James spontaneously began to read the poem in idiomatic French : a feat of translation which he admired and described years later to Mrs Humphry Ward.

5

'I've been here a week and depart tomorrow or next day. It has been rather a tension,' James wrote early in April from Le Plantier to his brother. A day or two later he journeyed to St Raphael and by easy stages proceeded to Genoa. If Hyères had induced tension, he now felt relief, for he wrote a lively and affectionate letter to Minnie Bourget. 'I am full,' he told her, 'of grateful memories and blessed pictures. The beauty and harmony and nobleness of your eternal medium – that nothing can injure, diminish or disturb – has added a great stretch to my experience.' And he all but wrote a short story, in his 'international' mode, as he described to Madame Bourget the curiosity of some British females at the *table d'hôte* at St Raphael.

One of them, by the way, (who had the longest chin in Europe and bi-cycled over that afternoon from Costebelle!) has a villa near Le Plantier and succeeded in worrying out of me the shy confession of where – at Costebelle – I had been staying.

'And where did you come from?'

'Well – from Hyères.'

'Ah, you've been at Hyères? What part of Hyères?'

'Well – properly, rather, the part near Costebelle.'

'*Near* Costebelle – do you mean *at* Costebelle?'

'Well, yes – it *was*, I suppose at Costebelle.'

'And at what hotel?'

'I was not at a hotel.'

'Then where were you?'

'I was staying at a villa.'

'Ah! – where was the villa?'

'Well – up rather high; out of the way, thank heaven!'

A silence.

'Not at La Luguette then?'

'No.'

'And not Le Bocage either.'

'No.'

Another silence.

'But with some English friends at all events?'

'No.'

'Then with some French.'

'Well, yes – more or less French!'

'Ah, the Léotauds?'

'No.'

'Oh, I see – higher up?'

'Yes – *much* higher up.'

'Ah, the P. Bourgets?' (*breathlessly*)

'Well, yes, with M. and Mme Bourget.'

Sensation – quick conversation of lady with other lady on her right and prostration of both so great that I was really left in peace (on that side) for the rest of the dinner. Your name is a talisman.

The clatter and chatter of Genoa came up into his hotel room as he wrote his letter to Minnie Bourget. He felt a great joy in the sunny warmth of the Italian air and the shuffle below of Italian feet. He was recovering again 'the little old throbs and thrills' of his old Italian journeys.

48

The Brooding Tourist

HE had fallen in love with Italy thirty years before, never again – as he put it – to fall out. In the eyes of his young manhood, Italy had been 'a dishevelled nymph'. Now, in his own middle age, the nymph seemed to have grown stout and orderly and become a votary of 'progress'. Later in Naples he would look with suspicion at big advertisements and 'restorations' designed to please touring Americans and the perpetual horde of Germans from over the Alps. In Rome there were irrecoverable changes. He had known the last days of Papal Rome when Pio Nono was still carried through the streets, and the middle ages and the renaissance were piled high on antiquity. The Risorgimento had secularized the city and straightened out too many corners. His 'little personal Florence' remained in spite of everything. He could still manage with it, but the 'very modern Rome' could not come up to his old sensations and memories – the years of his horseback rides in the Campagna and his visits to the great palaces where expatriate Americans like William Wetmore Story, whose life he was now supposed to write, lived in high style and undemocratic grandeur. He had now known Italy during three decades. In spite of the pleasure of recovered sights and sounds (as in Venice, where the splash of the water, the dustless air, the sun on marble and stone delighted him) he felt a certain oppression. He was aware of 'the tone of time', he hated the desecrations and erasures. Yet there were new sensations and new pictures as well. He was not one to allow nostalgia to efface immediate reality. Still, there was a change in his manner of looking. He had called himself of old 'the sentimental traveller'; in England he had been 'the observant stranger'. Now in Italy he was 'the brooding tourist'.

I

He did not linger long in Genoa. A couple of days – visits to friends on the Ligurian coast – and he was off to Venice where he had promised to stay with the Daniel Curtises at the Palazzo Barbaro on the Grand Canal. He had spent painful weeks in the water-city in 1894 after Miss Woolson's death; but he confronted these memories and allowed older ones to re-assert themselves. In a bravura passage in the travel-sketch he wrote but did not immediately publish, he described the 'dignity of arrival' by water at the Barbaro. With a touch of swagger, he adjured his readers,

Hold to it that to float and slacken and gently bump, to creep out of the low, dark *felze* and make the few guided movements and find the strong crooked and offered arm, and then, beneath lighted palace-windows, pass up the few damp steps on the precautionary carpet – hold to it that these things constitute a preparation of which the only defect is that it may sometimes perhaps really prepare too much. It's so stately that what can come after? – it's so good in itself that what, upstairs, as we comparative vulgarians say, can be better.

Still the *piano nobile* of the Curtises had its grandeur. The Barbaro was a high historic house, with 'such a quantity of recorded past twinkling in the multitudinous candles that one grasped at the idea of something waning and displaced, and might even fondly and secretly nurse the conceit that what one was having was just the very last'. There was no future for such manners and customs and the comprehensive urbanity of his host and hostess; but he would not bother with the future; it was better to stay with the picture into which Venice resolved itself. During this visit the Palazzo Barbaro placed itself more vividly than ever in James's imagination, superimposed itself on memories of earlier years. There is still a legend that he wrote *The Wings of the Dove* while he stayed there. He actually wrote this novel entirely in Lamb House, three years later; but he did work at the Barbaro on this occasion, to fulfil his promise to Lady Randolph Churchill. He wrote for her *Anglo-Saxon Review The Great Condition*, a variant on his old stories about women with a 'past'.

If he gave this task as his primary excuse for delay in going to Rome, there were other reasons as well. One was the presence of a charming older woman, a fellow-guest, Miss Jessie Allen. To read the opening pages of *The Beast in the Jungle* is to get a sense of the kind of Italianate comradeship that developed gradually between the two. Miss Allen was of a distinguished family and knew the great noble houses of the Scottish border; there was a legend that she had been raised to be a lady-in-waiting at the court, but did not possess the requisite lineage. At any rate she was a grand lady, full of good talk and lively gossip; and a delightful companion in the alleyways and tiny curiosity-shops of Venice. They wandered in the twists and turns of the passages, dipped into cool chapels when the heat became insufferable, evaded the parent-like vigilance of the Curtis servant Angelo, went on long gondola rides. Shortly after leaving Venice, James reported to Ariana Curtis that Miss Allen wrote thirty-page letters, 'very agreeable ones, reflecting the life of unbridled luxury and perpetual country house'. Also that 'she is very faithful — and seems to lead a labyrinthine life'. His own letters to her would be long and humorous and filled with verbal gallantries: more than two hundred survive. Miss Allen, in her flat at 74 Eaton Terrace, for the next fifteen years would pour tea for Henry James whenever he was in London.

We gain a picture of his stay with the Curtises, between the lines of *Two Old Houses and Three Old Women*, memories of Venetian glimpses and visits which he printed, ten years later, in *Italian Hours*. In it he describes an occasion when the Curtises were host to German royalty, to the Empress Frederick.

Such old, old women with such old, old jewels; such ugly, ugly ones with such handsome, becoming names; such battered, fatigued gentlemen with such inscrutable decorations; such an absence of youth, for the most part, in either sex — of the pink and white, the 'bud' of new worlds; such a general personal air, in fine, of being the worse for a good deal of wear in various old ones.

It was a picture to see the little Empress in the *piano nobile*, a throwback to 1830.

You profit to the full at such times by all the old voices, echoes, images — by that element of the history of Venice which represents all Europe as having at one time and another revelled or rested, asked for pleasure or for patience there; which gives you the place supremely as the refuge of endless strange secrets, broken fortunes and wounded hearts.

He carried away another picture as well. There was a meeting with three Venetian sisters, the old women of the title of his article, and the touch of his revived interest in George Sand and her Venetian adventures with Musset and Doctor Pagello: for the old ladies pointed to the house in which George Sand had lived after her first stage of romance with Musset at the Danieli. Publication of a large biography of Sand in the ensuing months would enable James to write anew of this novelist who had charmed him in his youth, even if this publication was 'a tub of soiled linen which the muse of his-

tory, rolling her sleeves well up, has not even yet quite ceased energetically and publicly to wash'. And then the three sisters – he did
not name them – took James (and probably Miss Allen) to see their
own house, the seat of an ancient Venetian family in decline. The
visit prompted in James a peroration that was a recall of the old
palazzo in the Rio Marin in which his own Juliana of *The Aspern
Papers* had lived with her memories of lost moments.

The charming lonely girls, carrying so simply their great name and
fallen fortunes, the despoiled *decaduta* house, the unfailing Italian grace,
the space so out of scale with actual needs, the absence of books, the
presence of ennui, the sense of the length of the hours and the shortness
of everything else – all this was a matter not only for a second chapter
and a third, but for a whole volume, a *dénoûment* and a sequel.

2

To visit Venice was to pay homage to his oldest friend in that city
– Mrs Arthur Bronson. They had met long ago at sea when she had
played cards in the salon with Anthony Trollope. In later years, in
the Casa Alvisi, she had received Henry James and Robert Browning,
and provided cigarettes and good talk and a splendid balcony on the
Grand Canal. He had celebrated the Casa Alvisi in a notable essay
on the Grand Canal in the early 1890s as 'the very friendliest house
in all the wide world, and it has, as it deserves to have, the most
beautiful position. It is a real *porto di mare*, as the gondoliers say –
a port within a port; it sees everything that comes and goes, and
takes it all in with practised eyes'. In the essay James also alluded to
the fact that Mrs Bronson had restored the nearby Madonnetta and
lit the red spark of a lamp within the shrine of painted and gilded
wood, for the worship of the *gondolieri*.

He found her now at La Mura, at nearby Asolo, a sadly aged and
limited figure – she who had once ruled over the Canal. It did not
minister to James's sense of the past to arrive with the flabby and
unhappy son of poets – Pen Browning; and in the little house, which
he had always found uncomfortable, he got a painful picture of the
waning of a life once filled with ease, power and relaxed and open-
handed generosity. 'That eternal glass cage,' he was to write to Mrs
Curtis, 'and that little swarm of beneficiaries.' Mrs Bronson had become 'the strangest mixture of folly of purchase and of discomfort
about necessaries'. There wasn't an easy chair in La Mura for her

to be ill in, or for him to sit comfortably. They had an immense quantity of talk after the years of his absence. But Mrs Bronson was helpless and demoralized, 'a great deal of rheumatism, an enormous appetite, not a scrap of possible action', with two nurses, a flock of servants and queues of shopkeepers trying to sell her antiques. Asolo still had its old charm; the plain stretched away like a purple sea from the lower cliffs of the hills and the white campanili of the villages. Here the fumbling red-velvet carriage of provincial and rural Italy had served Mrs Bronson instead of her gondola; they had long before made trips to Bassano, to Treviso, to high-walled Castelfranco. Mrs Bronson remained alert and fresh 'for pleasant surprises and proved sincerities'; these no longer included excursions and explorations. She was 'of this world that she so much loved', but she would not be for long. This was to be James's last vision of her.

3

He was overdue in Rome, where the Waldo Storys awaited him in the old many-roomed apartment of William Wetmore Story at the Barberini. But James had no desire to stay with them; he preferred to be near the Spanish Steps and he put up at the Hôtel de l'Europe, where he had a sitting-room that looked on the Piazza Mignenelli. To Bourget he wrote, 'Rome is always Rome — at this moment generally empty and quiet but more and more "modern" as I grow more and more antique.' To Howard Sturgis he described it as 'a warmish, quietish, emptyish, pleasantish (but not maddeningly so,) altered and cockneyfied and scraped and all but annihilated Rome'. There were social traps on all sides. He half-heartedly examined the large Story archive — 'this preposterous Story job' — letters from the Brownings, his old friend Lowell, Charles Sumner, the accolades of the world bestowed upon this amateur sculptor of strained awkward statues. It was clear to James that he could write Story's life with ease; but not perhaps with much pleasure. 'There will be all the Rome I can put into so small a compass, and as little Story as I can keep out,' he said to Grace Norton. Story's 'vast marble shop' he described as 'a huge system and worshop of marmoreal Bedizenment of Billionaires'.

For the rest, he paid calls as always and continued to tour — and to brood. He went to Castel Gandolfo to visit the Humphry Wards and promised to return for a stay; he took two English ladies, Angelina Milman and a friend, to Hadrian's Villa and the Villa d'Este; and he called with pleasure and some regularity at the studio of John Elliott and his wife, the former Maude Howe whom he had known for many years, daughter of Julia Ward Howe. He liked Elliott's work and he liked their charming place near St Peter's – a flowered terrace on the roof of the Palazzo Accoramboni. Elliott was working on the ceiling for the Boston Public Library; and with great ingenuity he had turned the vast apartment into a comfortable home. James admired the view – they looked down into the square of St Peter's and also on the Castle of St Angelo and beyond to the Pincio and the Villa Borghese, the Campagna and the Alban and Sabine hills. Maud Elliott was a niece of Mrs Luther Terry who still lived at the Odescalchi palace where James had often visited in the 1870s; and he met again, after long years, the indomitable Louise Von Rabë, whom he had once found so formidable (when she was Annie Crawford) and who was now elderly and widowed. Maud Elliott gave a dinner for her on the terrace under the pergola and James was toasted in Orvieto and said with great solemnity – as a brooding tourist might – 'this is the time when one lights the candle, goes through the house and takes stock'. Such was indeed the nature of this – the all but last of his Italian journeys.

One day Maud Elliott told James of Julia Ward Howe's visit to Rome the previous winter when her beauty of old age – she was 78 – had been remarked upon everywhere, so that she was referred to as a living Holbein, and all the artists had raved about her. Out of this grew one of James's subtle late stories, *The Beldonald Holbein*.

On another day at the Elliotts' Henry James was introduced to a young and vigorous American sculptor from Boston, of Norwegian birth. His name was Hendrik Andersen – it sounded very like the name James had given to the sculptor he had created long ago, Roderick Hudson. Andersen was of 'magnificent stature,' Henry wrote. He was much taken by his sincerity, his seriousness – and his handsome blond countenance. The sculptor responded to James's interest. He invited him to his studio in the Via Margutta. The place, the Roman art atmosphere, the young aspiring handsome American – it was as if James were back in the 1870s, in the days when he went riding on the Campagna and smoked cigarettes with the assorted American artists and talked art in this very street. James listened to Andersen and to his grand dreams. He wanted, like

Roderick Hudson, to do large statues, big conceptions. The novelist took him to lunch. They talked until it was time to have dinner. They continued to talk. In Hendrik's studio, James took a fancy to a small terracotta bust Andersen had done of the young Conte Alberto Bevilacqua. He praised it highly, and praised the sculptor's promise. But what he was praising was the charm of youth and what he was enjoying above all was a reliving of the past. To encourage the sculptor, James took the unusual step of purchasing the bust of Conte Alberto. The price was $250, the sum he usually got for a short story. Andersen said he would pack it carefully and ship it to Lamb House. He promised too that he would come to England to visit James.

49

Three Villas

MRS HUMPHRY WARD in a Roman villa, writing one of her novels – with an Italian background! The thought fascinated Henry James. He was due in Florence to talk to William Wetmore Story's daughter – the Countess Peruzzi – who had married a descendant of the Medici; but he could not resist the invitation from the 'irrepressible' Mrs Ward to return to the Villa Barberini. He had liked its high position at Castel Gandolfo, the great slope of the Campagna seaward, the ruins of one of Domitian's villas far below, the view of the Alban lake and Monte Cavo. At the end of May when he began to find the heat of Rome uncomfortable he arrived for a stay of a couple of nights. He remained a week. 'This place is a wondrous ravishment,' he wrote to Mrs Curtis. 'The villa itself bleak and bare, but the circumstances, garden, views, walks, drives, ramifications of every kind, the fullest splendour of the picturesque. It rains and almost freezes (yesterday it quite hugely *hailed*!) but pedestrianism triumphs – and the blood of Dr Arnold.'

Mrs Humphry Ward – Mary Augusta Arnold – was grand-daughter of the great Arnold of Rugby and niece of Matthew Arnold, whom James had long ago met in Story's apartment in the Barberini Palace. Now he was visiting the niece in the villa of the same noble house where the Barberini bee-emblem was much in evidence. It was a seventeenth-century villa, massive but carelessly built. 'We perch over the blue Alban lake by one set of windows – vast campagna by other sets,' James wrote. 'Mrs Ward reads and writes hard.' Something about her – perhaps her Arnold blood, certainly her high seriousness, her tremendous moral tone, her appeal to James's artistic wisdom – found him always ready to be kind to her. He had criticized her first novel – it dealt with an actress – and told her how he would have written it. From that time on he assiduously rewrote – in his letters – all her novels. She took his criticism in good spirit, she knew it was well-intentioned; she seemed however unaware of some of its ironies. 'One fears a little sometimes,' James had written her of *Robert Elsmere*, 'that he [Elsmere] may suffer a sunstroke, damaging if not fatal, from the high oblique light of your admiration for him.' Perhaps James experienced a little the same oblique light. 'She asks my leave,' he told Grace Norton, 'to print and publish two letters of gratulation that I appear to have written her on the issue of *Robert Elsmere* ... after the manner of testimonials in the advertisement of a patent medicine.' He gave rueful assent; but admitted to himself that there was a streak of opacity in the otherwise intelligent and erudite lady.

Mrs Ward had had enormous success with *Robert Elsmere*, the kind of success James envied. But then Mrs Ward's subject was Christianity, and her 'dissent' had even caught the eye of Mr Gladstone. She had called upon the clergy to occupy itself with good works as well as with sin. Mr Gladstone reviewed her novel under the portentous title, '*Robert Elsmere* and the Battle of Belief'. They had met, the Prime Minister and the formidable blue-stocking, and Mr Gladstone had suggested Mrs Ward was being 'visionary'. Mrs Ward replied courteously but firmly that for Mr Gladstone 'the great fact of the world and in the history of man is sin', while for her the great fact was 'progress'. James had satirized her kind of literary aspirations in *The Next Time*, in the person of Mrs Highmore, the woman who wished she could have an artistic rather than popular success. He, on his side, would have liked to win her kind of readers, but he knew he could not write her kind of novel. Yet patiently, consistently, he lectured her on the art of fiction – *his* art – in all the years of their friendship. 'She is incorrigibly wise and good, and has a moral nature as Patti has a voice,' James wrote to Edmund Gosse, 'but somehow I don't, especially when talking art and letters, *communicate* with her worth a damn. All the same she's a dear.'

Perhaps because she was a 'dear', Henry James had composed a
brief tribute to her during the 1890s at the request of the *English
Illustrated Magazine*. In sending it to the editor he wrote, 'Alas, alas,
I have found her deadly difficult to do and cursed the rash hour I
undertook her.' And when a correspondent asked him why he had
written the piece, he replied that it wasn't 'written', it was simply a
gesture, an act of loyalty to an old friend. The essay pays tribute to
the ascendancy of women in the field of fiction. And it praises Mrs
Ward's intellect, her 'fine, moral ripeness, a genial much-seeing
wisdom'. Of the art of fiction, which he usually invoked in discussing
novelists, there is not a word.

I

Mrs Ward went about her novel-writing with great thoroughness.
When she decided to write a novel about Italy on the Elsmere formula – one in which she would show 'progress' as prevailing over
Papal inertia – she felt a need to live herself into an actual background. In March, while Henry James was making his slow journey
along the Riviera and basking in the sun at Hyères, she had arrived
at the Villa Barberini. There was snow on the campagna and a wind
was moaning in the Alban hills. The villa was rudely furnished and
without heat; the kitchen was fifty-two steps below the dining-room;
the Neapolitan cook was formidable. Her husband, Humphry Ward,
who was an editorial writer and art critic for *The Times* of London,
predicted she would end up in a heated hotel in Rome. Even he did
not reckon with the blood of Dr Arnold. Stoves were brought in
and made to burn; books were unpacked; the meagre furnishings
were pushed about into comfortable positions, and Mrs Ward's
daughters and the staff of servants were mobilized against the elements.

Mrs Ward looked at James during this visit with new eyes. In
England she had known the social James. Now she discovered the
Italianate James – with his thorough knowledge of antiquity and
the artistic resources of the Roman countryside; and when, in London, or at Stocks, had she heard him speak Italian? She watched him
in fluent conversation with a brown-frocked barefooted monk, from
the monastery of Palazzuola, and what fascinated her was that this
supersensitive cosmopolite of the English drawing-rooms was drawing out the peasant on this Italian hillside, questioning him, looking

into his face with searching eyes, and 'getting at something real and vital in the ruder simpler mind'. What struck Mrs Ward – and she seemed surprised – was that James too could be erudite; this apparently had never occurred to her. She remarked that he wore his learning lightly, 'like a flower'; and in saying this she was probably remembering the compliment he had paid her in his letter on *Robert Elsmere*, 'What a lot you know ... your head carries it like a garland of flowers.' Mrs Ward found that James conveyed his knowledge of things Roman and Italian by indirect hints, a grave way of being politely certain that his listeners themselves knew all that he knew; then he walked 'round and round the subject, turning it inside out, playing with it, making mock of it, and catching it again with a sudden grip, or a momentary flash of eloquence'. The impressions of a man of genius, Mrs Ward observed, were many, the number of words few. James made the fullest use of the resources of speech.

I can see still Mr James's figure strolling along the terrace which roofed the cryptoporticus of the Roman villa, – the short coat, the summer hat, the smooth-shaven finely cut face, now alive with talk and laughter, now shrewdly, one might say coldly, observant – the face of a satirist – but so human! – so alive to all that underworld of destiny through which move the weaknesses of men and women.

The picture in Mrs Ward's memoirs is vivid, intimate: but Mrs Ward was reading her memories of the future into the past. At the time of his visit to the Villa Barberini James still wore the beard he had grown long ago, during the Civil War. It was now sharply trimmed, but remained a striking part of his public 'image'. The smooth-shaven finely cut face was yet to come.

One afternoon James, his hostess and her daughters, went on an excursion to the blue lake of Nemi visible on their horizon. They passed on their way over the great viaduct at Aricia, where Diana had been barbarously worshipped. Diana's priest was always a run-away slave who obtained office by killing his predecessor. In the late soft hours of the afternoon the landscape was bathed in golden light. Everywhere there were ruins and fragments, ghosts of the past – as Mrs Ward would put it, 'engulfed and engarlanded by the active present'. They crossed the Appian Way and the high ridge above the deep-sunk lake; the crossing is described in her novel *Eleanor*. The excursionists perceived the niched wall and the platform of the temple; they speculated that the historic spring – Egeria's spring – must be in an embrasure in the high wall – Egeria who had instructed Numa Pompilius, the second king of Rome, in modes of worship and who had honoured him with her love. The spring had been a sacred fount – and James's next novel would bear this title. He would allude briefly to Egeria in one of its passages.

During this excursion James's attention wandered elsewhere than to Diana or Egeria. Both in novel and the Ward memoirs there is allusion to a dark-eyed youth, encountered among the strawberry-beds in the vicinity of the temple of Diana Nemorensis then being excavated. The boy was full of talk of fragments and artefacts lying in the furrows of the freshly ploughed field. James walked beside him, unable to take his eyes from his face. He asked him his name and listened, and repeated it, the noble Greek name of Aristodemo. He was 'straight and lithe and handsome as a young Bacchus,' said Mrs Ward. Henry James paused, his eyes on the youth; he surveyed the sunset scene. He murmured the name: his voice, said Mrs Ward, caressed it – Aristodemo – a kind of caress of the boy himself. The youth, aware that he had the centre of the stage, was voluble about the diggings and the artefacts. He described to James a marble head he had found – yes, he! – complete, even the nose preserved. The sun sank, the enchantment lingered. 'For me,' James wrote to his hostess later, 'the Nemi lake, and the walk down and up (the latter perhaps most,) and the strawberries and Aristodemo were the cream' – and he added, as for emphasis, 'I am clear about that.'

2

Mrs Ward's excuse for sending James proofs of *Eleanor* some months later was that she had introduced an American girl into her story, a very churchy young Puritan, named Lucy Foster, stiff and awkward, badly dressed – *gauche* in every way. Eleanor is in love with her cousin; and she becomes Lucy's Egeria as well; she gets her to dress her hair, induces her to put on more stylish clothes, brings out her latent beauty, and the man in due course falls in love with her. Lucy and this man however are proponents of differing philosophies. Lucy is anti-Catholic and all for a democratic Italy. He defends the past, the Pope, the Jesuits. The novel was a successful serial in *Harper's* and in the United States at one time was selling 1,000 copies a day – more copies in one day than an entire edition of some of

James's works. In fact Harper had confined the printing of *The Awkward Age*, recently published, to exactly 1,000 copies.

James's letters to Mrs Ward about *Eleanor*, whose impending success he could foresee, are solid little essays on the art of the novel as he practised it. He thought Lucy Foster not sufficiently American. Her religious stiffness seemed to him untypical. The American reader would say 'Why this isn't us – it's English dissent,' 'keep in mind how very different a thing *that* is (socially, aesthetically, etc.) from the American free (and easy) multitudinous churches, that, practically in any community, are like so many (almost) clubs or Philharmonics or amateur theatrical companies'. Nor did he think an obscure American girl would be shocked by Rome, the Pope, St Peter's, kneeling, or anything of that sort.

She would probably be either a Unitarian or 'Orthodox', (which is, I believe, 'Congregational', though in New England always called 'Orthodox',) and in either case as Emersonized, Hawthornized, J. A. Symondsized, and as 'frantic' to *feel* the Papacy etc. as one could well represent her. In that case I should say 'The bad clothes etc. oh yes; as much as you like. The beauty etc. *scarcely*. The offishness to "Rome", – as a spectator etc. – almost not at all' ... Had I looked over your shoulder I should have said: '*Specify*, localize, a little more – give her a *definite* Massachusetts, or Maine, or whatever, habitation – imagine a country-college-town – invent, if need be, a name, and stick to that.'

He did not stop at this. He told Mrs Ward he felt she was throwing her story too obviously at the reader; no suspense, no 'crooked corridor', no attempt to keep him guessing for a while. Since Eleanor the Egeria was the focus, she should keep her at the 'centre', make her consciousness 'full, rich, universally prehensile and *stick* to it – don't shift – and don't shift *arbitrarily* – how, otherwise, do you get your unity of subject or keep up your reader's sense of it?' He concluded his letter with: 'Do let me have more of *Eleanor* – to rewrite!'

Mrs Ward seems to have replied that the question of a 'centre of consciousness' represented an 'old difference' between them. Moreover, she chided James for criticizing her novel before he had read it entire. This elicited from the novelist a 2,000-word answer. He did not think there was an 'old difference' between them; to say so made it sound as if he had a fixed idea about how a novel should be written. He admitted he was 'a wretched person to *read* a novel – I begin so quickly and concomitantly, *for myself*, to write it rather – even before I know clearly what it's about'. Nevertheless there were certain things he could say, and one was that the artist must know what he is doing and how he is doing it. The story must get its unity not from the personality of the author – as apparently Mrs Ward had argued – but from the nature of the subject.

The promiscuous shiftings of standpoint and centre of Tolstoy and Balzac for instance (which come, to my eye, from their being not so much big dramatists as big *painters* – as Loti is a painter,) are the inevitable result of the *quantity of presenting* their genius launches them in. With the complexity they pile up they *can* get no clearness without trying again and again for new centres. And they don't *always* get it.

What James was defending so ardently was not only his kind of novel – which Mrs Ward could never write – but the method of limited 'point of view'; he anticipated the criticism that this might restrict the freedom of his storytelling. When *Eleanor* was published a year later he offered Mrs Ward extravagant praise, calling it 'a large and noble performance', although confessing that in reading the work he had 'recomposed and reconstructed Eleanor from head to foot'. After the *éloge*, he damned the book as having an essential weakness – Lucy wasn't a genuine antithesis to Eleanor, she had 'no logical force'; moreover, 'irony should at its hour have presided' in the novel. Mrs Ward however saw only the praise in the letter and she printed it almost entire in her memoirs.

There was one page in *Eleanor* which James read with a certain humour and irony of his own. Mrs Ward had included a brief scene, irrelevant to the story proper, in which she introduced a man of letters, a poet, who visits Eleanor's villa. He was named Mr Bellasis, and he figures only as a 'walk-on' character. She made him stuffy, arrogant, self-important. 'So you have read my book?' is his first question and then he wants to know whether Eleanor has *re*-read it, 'my friends tell me in Rome that the book cannot really be appreciated except at a second or third reading'. The physical Bellasis does not resemble James; but something in the way Mrs Ward made him talk sounds familiar. Mr Bellasis has no use for critics, and he talks of style: 'Why the style is done with a magnifying glass! – There's not a phrase – not a word that I don't stand by,' he says. When Mrs Ward sent James her first instalment he answered: 'I've read every word, and many two or three times, as Mr Bellasis would

say – and is Mr Bellasis, by the way, naturally – as it were –
H.J.???!!!'

We do not know whether Mrs Ward answered his question.

3

A few days after his visit to the Villa Barberini, Henry James was
standing on the deck of the little steamer that took pilgrims – and
brooding tourists – from Sorrento to Capri. Far aloft, on the great
rock, was pitched 'the amazing creation of the friend' who was offering him hospitality – the San Michele of Dr Axel Munthe. His visit
to Munthe was to be an affair of twenty-four hours, a side-trip from
another he was paying in Naples. He had met the famous society
doctor on the train to Rome, almost a month before, and had received
several pressing invitations to come to him at Capri, to the villa
reared by Munthe among blocks of ancient marble on the site of the
ancient Villa of Tiberius. At the same time no less pressing invitations
had come to James from Sorrento, from the popular Italianate-
American novelist F. Marion Crawford – son of the sculptor Thomas
Crawford and nephew of Julia Ward Howe – to visit his elaborate
villa at Sant-Agnello di Sorrento where relatives of the American
Wards and Howes gathered for familiar and happy festivities. James
had scarcely known Marion Crawford when he used to visit Marion's
mother and stepfather, the Luther Terrys, in the Palazzo Odescalchi
in his far-away Rome of the 1870s. Now, in the fullness of time, the
occupant of modest Lamb House was finding the later generation
in villas that spoke for great affluence; in the case of F. Marion Crawford a best-selling prosperity not unlike Mrs Ward's. To his intimates
James wrote that Crawford was 'a prodigy of talent – and of wealth!
It is humiliating.'

The Italianate Americans, in their cushioned ease, had always been
devotees of amateur theatricals and musical evenings, and during
James's stay at the Villa Crawford his host would invite to his great
terrace after dinner the usual local quartet – violins, guitar, flute, the
musical barber, the musical tailor, sadler, joiner – the humblest sons
of the people and exponents of Neapolitan song. The novelist had
planned a brief visit. However, Crawford announced a grand *festa*
to celebrate his wife's birthday, and James promised to return after
his excursion to Munthe's. The Munthe week-end had been a continuous divertissement. There was first the fantastic villa itself with

its loggias and its statued pergolas hanging dizzily over splendid views. The white arcades and the cool chambers offered at every step some old fragment of the past, a rounded porphyry pillar supporting a bust, a shaft of pale alabaster upholding a trellis, some mutilated marble image, some bronze that had roughly resisted the ages.

'Our host,' James wrote, 'had the secret; but he could only express it in grand practical ways.' James however also had a feeling of discomfort; the villa of black Tiberius had overhung the immensity of Capri and this evoked 'the cruel, the fatal historic sense ... to make so much distinction, how much history had been needed!' The air still throbbed for James 'and ached with it'. Munthe attributed to James the statement that San Michele was 'the most beautiful place in the world'. But the private record, a letter to Venetian friends, gives us James's direct impression – 'a creation of the most fantastic beauty, poetry, and inutility that I have ever seen clustered together'. Munthe also had, James remarked, an 'unnatural simplicity'. The novelist seems to have enjoyed however the local feast-day of St Anthony. Munthe held open house that afternoon. Huge straw-bellied flasks of purple wine were tilted for all the thirsty – and the general thirst was great. When the wine-drinkers were gone the musicians came, as at the Villa Crawford, and the dancers of the tarantella.

It was all purple wine, all art and song, and nobody a grain the worse. It was fireworks and conversation – the former, in the piazzetta, were to come later; it was civilization and amenity. I took in the greater picture, but I lost nothing else; and I talked with the contadini about antique sculpture. No, nobody was a grain the worse; and I had plenty to think of ... It was antiquity in solution, with every brown mild figure, every note of the old speech, every tilt of the great flask, every shadow cast by every classic fragment.

After Munthe and Capri, the novelist had a few more days with the Crawfords, days of a continually festive kind. But the summer heat was over the land. James did not linger. He paid his visit to the Countess Peruzzi in the mountain coolness of Vallombrosa. While in Florence, James's hotel-room was rattled and shaken early one morning by an earth-shock. 'Praise be to earthquakes of small calibre,' he remarked; a little more would not have been at all amusing. Early in June he was in Paris: crossing the channel he went straight to Folkestone and to Rye. He had been away nearly four months. Lamb House, with its refurbished fireplaces and reduced fire-hazards, seemed to him a haven of coolness and greenness. 'Oh, it is a joy to be once more in this refreshed and renovated refuge!' he wrote to Edward Warren. He had had enough of villas built or rented with the proceeds of best-selling novels. Almost a decade would elapse before he would go again to the Continent.

50

A Young Sculptor

A FORTNIGHT after Henry James's return from Italy there arrived at Lamb House, carefully packed, the small terracotta bust of the young Conte Alberto Bevilacqua which James had purchased from Hendrik Andersen in the Via Margutta. The novelist set it in the niche of the newly-re-modelled chimney-piece in his dining-room where it would face him during lonely repasts for years – the neat amateurish head and shoulders of boyish adolescence, somehow weighted and lifeless, for Andersen did not care for such small and trivial things as busts: and his touch was heavy. His dream was of great equestrian statues gleaming in the sun; he wanted to work in the soaring and the colossal; his vision was of huge American cities displaying form-filled fountains – sculpted by Hendrik Christian Andersen. But he was young and obscure; and it was a new experience for him to receive a letter from a famous novelist in far-off Rye in England, which told him, 'I've struck up a tremendous intimacy with dear little Conte Alberto, and we literally can't live without each other.' James added: 'He is the first object my eyes greet in the morning and the last at night.' Equally exciting for Andersen were the famous writer's words that Bevilacqua was 'so living, so human, so sympathetic and sociable and curious'. It would be a life attachment, he said – 'Brave little Bevilacqua, and braver still big Maestro Andersen.'

The bravos rang loudly in the ears of the hopeful artist. He had been working in comparative obscurity, making such friends as he could among Roman-Americans and dreaming his dreams, as James's Roderick Hudson had done a quarter of a century before. To have James tell him that his little Bevilacqua would be a 'life attachment' seemed an augury of friendship, intimacy, patronage, And when the novelist wrote that the bust would 'make many friends here', Andersen immediately assumed this to mean James had written an article about him and his work. The novelist was quick to correct this impression. 'I'm afraid I said something (accidentally) that misguided you to suppose I have written in a journal ... I haven't.' He had simply meant that the bust would be visible in its niche to his many friends who came to Lamb House.

Andersen had planned to leave for New York that summer. In the light of James's praise, and his invitation, it seemed to him practical to go to America by way of Rye. James was delighted. He had hardly expected so prompt a response and at a moment when he was downcast and weary. His trip to Italy had made him feel old; and in Rye he was lonely. To have a splendid eager youth come rushing to his side at this moment made James feel that someone still cared, that he was not cut off from the world. Andersen was hardly the 'nervous nineteenth-century Apollo' the novelist had made of Roderick Hudson; he was strong and handsome, and full of energy. To be sure, he talked a little like Roderick – he wanted to do statues of Love, Equality, Peace, great abstractions as Roderick had proclaimed his plans for Adams and Cains and Beauty, Wisdom, Power, Genius. Sensing that Andersen had dreams of grandeur, James warned him that Lamb House was hardly a *palazzo* or even a villa. 'I feel you to be formidable, fresh from your St Peterses, Vaticans and Trattorie Fiorentine – formidable to my small red British cottage and small plain British *cuisine* – but you will be very welcome.'

I

The relationship between the two had its complexities from the first. James looked at Andersen with an inward vision of his own youth, his distant Roman days. On his side, Andersen saw a kind, indeed a benignant, fatherly figure, who might aid him in the hard climb to fame and fortune. He made himself agreeable, with a show of modesty on the one hand and of ambition on the other. It is doubtful whether James saw, at the beginning of their friendship, much beyond the chiselled countenance, the flaxen hair, the big frame, the vitality of the young sculptor. That Andersen lacked the intellectual and moral force – or the will to discipline – James demanded of himself in art was hardly perceptible at first, and it is doubtful whether

James cared. Nor was Andersen's grandiosity – which James sensed – likely to have troubled him. Youth was entitled to its dreams; the grander the better, so long as they were anchored in realities, as his own had been. James's feeling of tenderness and affection for Hendrik Andersen, and the appeal of the young man's physical qualities, sufficed. Andersen, on his side, knew he was admired, and responded warmly; but it is doubtful whether he had the depth to discern just how deeply he touched James. The ageing novelist felt attached to him from the first. Andersen seems to have thought mainly of how 'useful' James could be to him.

Coincidence indeed added a few charming touches. Henry and Hendrik – they bore the same name. The Hendrik evoked in James also the old name of that river which had nourished his young senses between Albany and New York; he had bestowed the name of Hudson on his first hero. And then his birthday and the sculptor's fell in the same month. They were second sons. They had talented brothers. Hendrik's elder brother, Andreas, was a skilful painter. From the first, James treated Andersen as if he were his *alter ego*. He tended to endow him with his own feelings about art – which may explain his later chagrin at discovering Hendrik possessed no such feelings. Hendrik in the presence of the novelist possessed a longer past than he knew. The old Henry and the young – it was as if Andersen had been fashioned out of James's old memories and old passions. A warm nostalgia filled their hours together during the sculptor's first visit to Lamb House. James seemed unaware of his own illusions. And it is doubtful whether he fully realized that the youth's presence had filled him with that precious essence that men have called from time immemorial – love. He bestowed on Andersen his own taste, his own high standards, his own feeling for beauty. He looked into the mirror and saw smiling and healthy youth instead of his obese and ageing self. The image charmed – one might say it enchanted.

2

We have no record of their talk, but it is possible to imagine its course in the light of the epistolary record and James's retrospective allusions. It was casual, easy, spontaneous. James was always to be happiest when his objects of affection were not too intellectual, not burdened with literary trappings. That was why he felt comfortable with the sailors and the lifeguards. Andersen met this qualification splendidly; he was singularly unlettered (James would later chide him for his spelling) and singularly self-centred. They talked of art, work, career, success, how to confront and woo the world; they discussed the old subjects of James's professional life, they spoke of intimate things, family, friends, affections. So Roderick and Rowland had talked long ago. The novelist could offer the wisdom of his decades and Hendrik listened with tender deference. They cycled to Winchelsea and back. They sat under the big mulberry tree in the Lamb House garden at the summer's richest hour. The splendid bignonia threw its red flowers up and down the south wall and the big purple clematis flushed as if in competition and envy. Andersen was all sincerity and respect – and Henry James was full of warm feelings. He was unexpectedly happy. One judges that Andersen's deference contained no awe; he was not one to be shy. Forgotten for the moment by James was the pride of reputation, the envy of the best-sellers, the weight of the world. He lived for a small, a cherished idyll, of happy summer months. And with his curiosity and questioning, he learned more intimately the simple facts of his new-found friend's life. Hendrik Christian Andersen was a remote relative of the teller of fairy tales – 'little Hans', James would call him, as if to give him the stamp of literature, but adding promptly the 'little' was uttered 'without prejudice to your magnificent stature'. The sculptor had been born in Bergen, Norway, and brought to America as a child by his immigrant parents. The family had lived in genteel poverty at Newport, where however the Howes and La Farges, and other old families, had taken an interest in the talented Andersen children. There were three sons, all artistic. The eldest was a skilful painter; the youngest a musician; and there was a young sister. The father was an alcoholic; ultimately he would be shipped back to Norway to drink away the years. The mother was long-suffering and devoted. The boys had little schooling; they had to go to work early. With some help from well-wishers, Hendrik had gone to art school in Boston; then he had lived in the Latin Quarter in Paris and attended the École des Beaux Arts. He showed much skill in drawing and a painting of his concierge's daughter attracted attention; he tended to stylize his subjects in imitation of the sixteenth-century Clouet, court-painter to François I. His emphasis was on clarity and draughtsmanship. After a while, he decided that he did not want to follow the footsteps of his elder brother, the painter Andreas. He took up sculpture and went to the Holy City where the secrets of Michelangelo were still remembered, and where he presently joined the art-life in and around the Piazza del Popolo. At the dawn of the new century all was still hope and hard work – a familiar story of zeal, dedication and the dream of Arcadia. A great tenderness seems to have welled up in Henry James as he listened. He had liked Hendrik from the first; and when the three-day visit was over he became aware in a strangely troubled way that he had deeper feelings for him than he had ever had perhaps for anyone outside his own family. To the Elliotts in Rome, in whose apartment he had met Andersen, he wrote, 'That most lovable youth, as he strikes me, Hans Christian Andersen, turned up in due course nearly a fortnight ago – came down, that is, spent two days and was as nice as could be; then whirled himself off into space after making me grow quite fond enough of him to miss him.'

We cannot doubt this – nor that Henry himself had been much comforted and braced. 'I would with joy have put him up for ever so much longer,' the novelist added, but Andersen had gone on to New York to try his fortune there. James told the Elliotts he had 'distinct confidence' in his future. It took courage, said Henry, to be a sculptor. Andersen 'doesn't, somehow, make one positively alarmed for him. But I shall watch over him there – as I hope to hear from him – with a great deal of anxiety, all the same, as well as sympathy.'

In the letters he began to write now to the young sculptor he hovered a great deal over him; he had advice and encouragement for him and an abundance of love. The letters show also an ache of absence unusual for James.

I was absurdly sorry to lose you when, that afternoon of last month, we walked sadly to the innocent and kindly little station together and our common fate growled out of the harsh false note of whirling you untimely away. Since then I have *missed* you out of all proportion to the three meagre little days (for it seems strange they were only *that*) that we had together. I have never (and I've done it three or four times) passed the little corner where we came up Udimore hill (from Winchelsea,) in the eventide on our bicycles, without thinking ever so tenderly of our charming spin homeward in the twilight and feeling again the strange perversity it made of that sort of thing being so soon *over*. Never mind – we *shall* have more, lots more, of that sort of thing!

He hoped he could put him into his Watchbell Street studio 'and we shall be good for each other; and the studio good for both of us'.

And James added, 'I feel in you a *confidence*, dear boy – which to show is a joy to me."

A few weeks later:

It *was*, last August – our meeting – all too brief, too fleeting and too sad. You merely brushed me with your elbow and turned me your back. I walked up from the station, that soft summer morning of your departure, much more lonely than I should have thought three days of companionship could, in their extinction, have made me.

James felt 'confidence', in Andersen, but he was to discover, as the months passed that the 'lovable youth' would have to be loved at a distance. They were to have in all only half a dozen meetings and at long-spaced intervals. Andersen was too busy with his career, his ambitions, his excess of confidence. He came again to Lamb House two years later, after abandoning New York, and only after much pleading on James's part; and finally some months afterwards. They met in America in 1905; they met in Rome in 1907. Each meeting brought a renewal of affection, renewed and often intense outpourings from James, who wrote to Andersen with a freedom not to be found in any of his other letters. The greater part of this attachment seems to have been expressed in words, in an ache of loneliness, in touches of jealousy, in a kind of brooding hurt that the young maestro was not properly pursuing his genius under the old Master's direction. In his old age, James would pour out ironies and protests at Andersen, as he denounced his pretensions and his larger-than-life statues. The ironies however would be lost on the rigid and unimaginative sculptor.

3

Two significant elements set apart James's letters to Hendrik Andersen – the saddest and strangest perhaps in his entire *epistolarium* – from all his correspondence up to this time. The first is the quantity of physical, tactile language: James repeatedly offers his *abbraccio* – puts out his arms to embrace the younger man, pats him tenderly on the back – in words. While these speak for a certain physical intimacy in their meetings, they can be seen also as forms of endearment in one who was overtly affectionate in public. There is abundant testimony that James in his late years embraced friends at his club or at a railway station in the Latin fashion, with much patting on the back. All this embracing and laying on of hands and tender benedictions in James's letters to Andersen may signify nothing more than a well-known demonstrative Jamesian hug. Nevertheless there is a quality of passion and possession in the reiterated 'I hold you close,' 'I feel, my dear boy, my arms around you,' or 'I meanwhile pat you affectionately on the back, across the Alps and Apennines, I draw you close, I hold you long.' James is at his most mothering – but also most intense – in letters written to Andersen in 1902 on the death of the sculptor's elder brother, when he enjoins him, as from Olympus to 'lean on me as on a brother and a lover'.

The sense that I can't *help* you, see you, talk to you, touch you, hold you close and long, or do anything to make you rest on me, and feel my participation – this torments me, dearest boy, makes me ache for you, and for myself; makes me gnash my teeth and groan at the bitterness of things ... I wish I could go to Rome and put my hands on you (oh, how lovingly I should lay them!) but that, alas, is odiously impossible ... I am in town for a few weeks but I return to Rye April 1st, and sooner or later to *have* you there and do for you, to put my arms round you and *make* you lean on me as on a brother and a lover, and keep you on and on, slowly comforted or at least relieved of the first bitterness of pain – this I try to imagine as thinkable, attainable, not wholly out of the question. There I am, at any rate, and there is my house and my garden and my table and my studio – such as it is! – and your room, and your welcome, and your place everywhere – and I press them upon you, oh so earnestly, dearest boy, if isolation and grief and the worries you are overdone with become intolerable to you ... I will *nurse* you through your dark passage ... I embrace you with almost a passion of pity.

The second element in the correspondence is James's unusual and reiterated cry for the absent one. The pain of separation is strong. Two years after the first visit James is writing, 'I miss you – keep on doing so – out of all proportion to the too few hours you were here – and even go so far as to ask myself whether visits so damnably short haven't more in them to groan, than to thank, for.' In 1903: 'Don't "chuck" me this year, dearest boy, if you can possibly help it.' In 1904 he signs himself 'your poor helpless far-off but all devoted H.J. who seems condemned almost and never to be near you, yet who, if he were, would lay upon you a pair of hands soothing, sustaining, positively *healing*, in the quality of their pressure'. In 1905: 'We must hold on in one way or another till we meet. It is miserable how little, as the months and years go on, we *do*.' In 1906: 'the

months are added to the months and we only don't meet'. In 1911,
when James is 68 and Hendrik 39, there is a final clinging to a hopeless wish, the tired words of an old man :

It's a sad business, this passage of all the months and years without our
meeting again save in this poor way [that is by correspondence] I wish
to heaven we could relieve it a little by finding ourselves again fondly
face to face. I want to see you – and I so hold out my arms to you.
Somehow it may still come – but it seems far off. Well, may life still be
workable for you, with the mighty aid of art. *Ci vuol anchea* little intimate affection too, *pure* (as they say) *che diavolo*! Therefore let us
manage it somehow.

And in 1913, when James is 70, he still speaks with a kind of faint
and forlorn hope that perhaps they 'will meet (and still embracingly)
over the abyss of our difference in years and conditions'.

The embraces were postponed; the abyss remained; it had been
temporarily bridged at the first, and James's search – *che diavolo* –
for affection, had long been turned elsewhere. But there lingered
this particular love, which flickered up whenever he heard from
Andersen, even when it was smothered by the sculptor's failures in
perception, his indifferences, or his insensitive belief that he could
induce James to be among the sponsors of his plan to build a city
de chic. The question that may be asked is whether the use of the
term 'lover' and the verbal passion of the letters, was 'acted out'. The
question, if relevant, cannot be answered. We simply do not know.
Most Victorians kept the doors of their bedrooms shut : certainly
Henry James did. Some might judge the question irrelevant in the
life of a writer who had defended himself for so many years against
sex, and had exalted the intellectual and emotional rather than the
physical in human relations. It is perhaps too easy to assume in our
time that the 'physical' would have to be a consequence of so much
epistolary passion. It well might be : but it would be presuming too
much to insist on its inevitability, particularly in the absence of
Andersen's letters to James. We must remind ourselves also, in
weighing this delicate and ambiguous evidence, that James had
hitherto tended to look at the world as through plate glass. Andersen seems to have helped James emerge from behind that protective
wall. If we let our fancy run, we might think of him as opening
James up to sensory feeling to a greater degree than had been the
case earlier; perhaps the touch of those strong fingers of the sculptor's hand may have given James a sense of physical closeness and

warmth which he had never allowed himself to feel in earlier years; and it is this which we read in his letters. Certainly a great fund of affection was there, and it was openly expressed. Allowance must be made for James's long puritan years, the confirmed habits of denial, the bachelor existence, in which erotic feeling had been channelled into hours of strenuous work and the wooing of *mon bon*, the available and compliant muse of the writing table. One also must remember that James had a fear of loss of masculinity. His highest praise of a writer – as with Turgenev – had been to stress the 'masculine' in his work. He had rigorously, in the inhibited Victorian fashion, transferred the seat of affection to his intellect; he had argued in his discussion of Maupassant that it was not the physical side of man, but his reflective side, that is most characteristic. James was constitutionally incapable of belonging to the underworld of sex into which Oscar Wilde had drifted. These elements must be weighed in any consideration of James's intimate life. Somerset Maugham used to enjoy telling his friends of an alleged attempt by Hugh Walpole to violate the Master, and of James's passionate recoil – 'I can't, I can't!' Since Maugham's feud with Walpole was notorious, we must regard the anecdote with suspicion; yet it may testify to an understandable reticence and even fear and anxiety in James. We may speculate endlessly on this theme, without discovering the answers. One thing is clear. The 'heavy' Andersen, whose brightness would fade so quickly, inspired feelings in Henry James akin to love – to a love such as Fenimore had had for him long before she ended her life in Venice. She had written of her loneliness and complained of the years that passed between their meetings as James now wrote to Andersen. She had known what it was to have the object of her love fail her, fail to recognize the depth of her feeling. This James would in due course discover.

For the rest, it is perhaps useful to invoke the inspired comment of Geoffrey Scott, in his *Portrait of Zélide*. Discussing the passion that developed between Madame de Charrière and Benjamin Constant, Scott observes that psychologically 'the character of their relation was abundantly clear; – technically the inquiry would be inconclusive'.

51

The Third Person

HENRY JAMES had returned from Italy vaguely depressed. He had fed much more on 'established memories' than on new impressions. There had been too many changes; there were too many intruding ghosts. 'All was charming, but all was haunted,' he wrote to Francis Boott. He set aside for the moment the proposed biography of Story. And if he had found the life of his fellow-writers in their fine villas – Bourget, Mrs Ward, Crawford – amusing, it nevertheless made him aware of the difference between their 'success' – and his. Then, just before leaving Rome, he received word that his brother William was coming abroad for his health. William had always seemed to Henry the embodiment of restless energy, a mind and body constantly questioning and active: now he was on his way to take the cure at Bad Nauheim, like so many elderly invalids. Seven years had passed since their last meeting.

Thinking that William, and his wife Alice, would go first to England, he offered them his London flat, at the moment tenantless. But the two sailed directly for Germany. Henry soon learned the essential facts. Dr Baldwin of Florence happened to be at Nauheim, also taking a cure. He examined William and reported to the novelist that his brother had developed a serious heart condition – a valvular lesion. Henry wrote to the doctor that what he learned made him 'rather sick and sore and sad; so narrow a squeak does he seem to have had'. Physiological details always terrified him and he would try to believe, he said, 'in the reality of the rescue'. To William he wrote that he was deeply moved by Baldwin's 'inscrutable physiological definiteness'; and he added, 'oh, how I want you convalescent and domesticated here!' Henry too began to worry about his heart. 'I am coddling my organ at such a rate that I no longer bicycle up anything less level than a billiard table,' he wrote to Dr Baldwin. Fortunately he had a billiard table of some twenty miles in the area of Rye.

I

A few days after his return from Italy, James learned that his land-lord had died and that Lamb House was for sale. The price was £2,000. This was substantial for the time, yet reasonable given the excellent condition of the house and the increasing value of real estate in Rye. James had lived himself sufficiently into the house to know that he wanted it. However he had very little ready money, and not much practical knowledge about financing such a purchase. He wrote promptly to his brother, who had for a long time handled his finances in America, and gave him the arguments for and against his making what would be the largest expenditure of his lifetime. He began in so portentous a tone that he had a second thought, and re-assured William with a 'don't be alarmed' and 'I don't mean that I've received a proposal of marriage.' He seemed once again to be the younger brother asking for guidance – even while announcing he had made up his mind. He was certain he could obtain a loan from his banker. Rye was becoming increasingly popular; the new golf-course was attracting visitors, and so on. His letter ran to many pages. He told William he had wept 'tears of joy at the thought of acquiring this blessed little house so promptly and so cheaply'. William, in the midst of debilitating baths and general fatigue, took Henry at his word. He had not yet seen the house; but Dr Baldwin had. Baldwin was physician to royalty. His conception of houses was on a palatial scale, and he had spent only one night in Lamb House. It had struck him as a kind of rural *pied-à-terre* for the London-identified novelist. He therefore judged $10,000 to be 'a very extravagant price'. Wil-liam passed the word along to Henry.

The effect of this on the younger brother was registered in a long letter of anger and frustration. William had sent 'a colder blast than I could apprehend'. Forgetting that he had asked for his brother's opinion, Henry exclaimed, 'I do, strange as it may appear to you, in this matter, know more or less what I'm about ... I am not yet wholly senile.' Brushing aside the question of cost, he told William his fondness for Lamb House was reason enough for acquiring it. As for Baldwin's opinion, the doctor had 'scarcely appeared to me to appreciate the place at all'. He wasn't qualified to judge. 'PLEASE, drop the subject altogether – with Baldwin. I hate it's being talked of with anyone but Alice.' Henry said he had taken counsel every step of the way with Edward Warren. The architect considered the house not only worth the price, but also an excellent investment. Moreover, Henry had learned that he needed only $4,000 – £800 – since the rest represented a mortgage he could take over at four per cent. He wouldn't have to borrow any money.

The obsessed pleading of the reply and the self-justification revealed anew how vulnerable Henry was to anything critical William might say. A word of disapproval and the novelist was taken back to the days when William repulsed him in their boyhood games. 'You after all, have bought and built, etc.,' he wrote, 'and I have never wanted faith! I *may*, of course, have made a mistake – anyone, everyone, always may.' But he added he would have been utterly depressed and shown no faith in himself 'or any courage for *any* act' if he had not taken advantage of this opportunity. His sense of inferiority and his anxieties were also transferred to more recent history; and there was a note of pathos as he wrote:

My whole being cries out loud for something that I can call my own – and when I look round me at the splendour of so many of the 'literary' fry, my confrères (M. Crawford's, P. Bourget's, Humphry Ward's, Hodgson Burnett's, W. D. Howellses etc.) and I feel that I may strike the world as still, at 56, with my long labour and my genius, reckless, presumptuous and unwarranted in curling up (for more assured peaceful production) in a poor little $10,000 shelter – once for all and for all time – *then* I do feel the bitterness of humiliation, the iron enters into my soul, and (I blush to confess it,) I *weep*! But enough, enough, enough!

2

Enough, enough, enough! His sense of outrage abated. William's Alice offered a loan from her personal funds. Henry gracefully declined; he no longer needed it. He apologized to William. He had felt, he said, 'the impulse to *fraternize* – put it that way – with you, over the pleasure of my purchase, and to see you glow with pride in *my* pride of possession'. This was the heart of the matter. For Henry, in spite of his childhood sense of rivalry had always wanted his brother's approval. A jumble of emotion out of the far-away world of the 'mere junior' had been re-awakened. The boy Henry would have done anything for a loving glance from William, a pat on the back. Now he shifted his old sense of second-class status to his relationship with his affluent confrères. *They* had elaborate villas. He was entitled at least to a small hermitage. William had once again – this time in the most innocent way imaginable – hit an exposed nerve.

3

William James, his wife and young daughter, arrived at Lamb House early in October of 1899. The brothers had not met since William's sabbatical year in 1892. In the intervening years the two had passed into late middle age. Henry had had his crisis; William's fame as philosopher had continued to grow. A snapshot of the brothers taken a few months after this time clearly shows their established relationship – William stands upright, his arm round Henry's shoulders; at the same time he pulls himself a little away from him. Henry's head is sharply and stiffly inclined towards him, as if he wished to lay his head on his shoulder. The picture has the intimacy of a couple posing for a camera, with Henry held firmly but at arm's length by his brother.

William felt tolerably well after his Nauheim cure. He responded with his old painter's sense to the greenish-yellow autumn light in which Rye was bathed. He found the town, with its miniature brick walls, houses, nooks, coves and gardens alternately suggestive of English, Dutch and Japanese effects. Lamb House itself seemed to him like a toy compared with his own large New England house in Cambridge; he wondered 'how *families* ever could have been reared in most of the houses,' they were so small. He characterized his brother's house as a 'most exquisite collection of quaint little stage properties', and his brother as still interested above all 'in the operations of his fancy'. He found Henry's face calm, his spirit 'equable'. In general he had his old view of his younger brother – that he was a 'powerless-feeling' temperamental fellow. 'Harry is extemely easy and genial, but his whole way of taking life has so little in common with mine,' he had written to his wife. He recognized that life in this out-of-the-way town must be lonely, yet he felt the novelist was in equilibrium with his loneliness. This was his fixed picture of Henry : and every time he saw him abroad, after an interval, some such vision of him was recorded. 'Harry is a queer boy,' he had written to his wife some years before,

so good and yet so limited, as if he had taken an oath not to let himself out to more than half his humanhood in order to keep the other half

from suffering, and had capped it with a determination not to give anyone else credit for the half he resolved not to use himself. Really, it is
not an oath or a resolve, but helplessness.

As usual, Harry was 'helpless' only in William's presence. He was
reticent, closed-in, on his guard, full of awe and respect, making no
allowance for his own reputation and achievement. They related
to one another intellectually as adults. Emotionally they were still
back in 14th Street, in the 1850s.

In these circumstances it can be understood how much anxiety
Henry, through the admiring eyes and affections of long ago, felt
over William's illness. At first William took everything in his old
stride, save that he tired easily after his walks. He sat in the garden,
he read, he worked at the Gifford lectures he hoped to give at Edinburgh on the varieties of religious experience. But within a fortnight
he began to complain of being unwell again, and quite suddenly one
day he had a return of the terrible chest-pains he had experienced
in America. Alarmed, Henry and Alice took him at once to London
and installed him in De Vere Gardens, with its spacious rooms and
big sky windows. They called in the eminent heart specialist Bezly
Thorne, a younger Harley Street man well-versed in the latest
theories concerning heart ailments. He ordered the unwilling William to bed, put him on a strict no-starch diet. This time the philosopher obeyed. As Henry put it, he at last 'consented to be really ill'.
And watching him, the novelist became aware that he was 'a graver
and more precarious case than I had dreamed of'.

After three weeks of this regimen the patient improved. Thorne
then dispatched him – it was December by now – to Malvern for
hydropathic treatment. Here the bitter cold of the season and the
rigours of the baths quickly made William ill again, and after about
ten days he rushed back with Alice to London. Henry however in
the interval had let his flat for the coming year. He met the two on
their arrival from Malvern, put them in a hotel, and the next day
brought them back to Rye.

In the waning days of the year, in wintry Rye, where the storms
raged and the wind roared, the brothers and the sister-in-law awaited
the coming of 1900. Its advent had been announced that autumn by
the guns in South Africa – the trumpets, as they would prove, of the
new era. The brothers had been together as young men in the other
war, the war between the States – and Henry wrote early in the new
year of remembering 'the general sense, the suspense and anxiety,

stricken bereavement, woe and uncertainty of that – and more still of the special sense of young men, sons and brothers, of one's friends, many magnificent, *égorgés* in their flower. Such grey battalions of ghosts!'

Once again William showed improvement. Henry built great fires in his reconditioned fireplaces; and writing to Rosina Emmet he could report just before Christmas that 'the quiet, the private conditions, the sunny outlook (for we *have* sun,) the garden, the birds, the rest, the comfort, the sense of protection from *me*! –' the novelist caught his slip, and corrected it without erasing it – 'by which I mean *by* me; all these things make so much for his gradual improvement'. He later spoke of how he had been 'worried, depressed, tormented in a high degree'. 'My spirits were in my boots about him and my time all went in trying to create for him here an atmosphere of optimism and an illusion of ease.' In these moments William's wife Alice became for him a counterpart of his own mother. He was seeing her for the first time at close quarters; they had hardly known each other in earlier years, and he grew greatly attached to her – 'I bless the high heaven hourly for her.' He spoke of the renewed sight she gave him 'of what a woman can do for a man. Her devotion, her courage, her cheer, her ability and indefatigability, her ingenuity and resource in his service, are pure magnificence. She is *always* in the breach.'

Peggy spent Christmas at Lamb House with her parents and uncle. As William grew stronger it was decided that he would go to the Riviera, to escape the hardest part of the English winter. A wealthy French savant, admirer of the philosopher, had made available to him his fine little chateau at Costebelle, not far from the Bourgets. In mid-January Henry escorted his brother and sister-in-law to Dover and saw them aboard the channel steamer.

4

In Henry James's early stories, at the time of the Civil War, it is fairly easy to see the presiding emotions. In the tales which now tumbled from his desk one finds a complex network of old themes, re-awakened by the anger he felt at William's seeming hostility to his acquisition of a home – anger which he could not discharge more directly, since his brother was seriously ill. The new stories contain a fund of the feline, and strange notes of cruelty. They are brilliant but unpleasant, and the old theme of revenge is stated in new and shrill terms. In James's earlier writings, revenge was often renounced – a guilty backing away from violence was required. The narrator still shrinks from such passions, but this only dramatizes Mrs Grantham's ferocity in *The Two Faces*. She is a woman scorned. Insult moreover is added to the injury when his lordship, after jilting her, turns round and asks her to help introduce his inexperienced child-bride into society. Mrs Grantham complies – the bride is 'overloaded like a monkey in a show'. She herself provides the proper contrast by attiring herself with *éclat*. We are left with the narrator's horrified vision of two faces: – May Grantham's, savagely triumphant, and the 'feverish, frightened' countenance of her young victim. In *The Beldonald Holbein*, the tale derived from Julia Ward Howe's triumph of elderly beauty in Rome, we also look at two faces: that of the beautiful and proud Lady Beldonald, who uses her plain companion to enhance her own beauty; and the companion, whose plain face triumphs. She is seen as a perfect Holbein. In *The Special Type* there is a sacrificial lady who helps the male egotist marry the woman he wants, but takes her own quiet revenge. The theme will be used in *The Tone of Time*, in which a woman painter is asked by a lady to supply her with the 'portrait' of an imaginary husband. Instead of imagining a face, the lady painter puts on canvas the countenance of the man who long ago jilted her, only to discover that this man figured in the life of the very woman for whom she is painting the 'portrait'. A terrible jealousy seizes her; she will not surrender the picture at any price; hating the man, she loves him enough to want to keep his remembered likeness for herself; and she is jealous enough to refuse his image to the other woman. If we recall that in these stories Henry is casting himself as the jealous woman, we recover elements of the little ballets of his old novel *Confidence*, written when William married Alice. These had incorporated his jealousy of his sister-in-law. They are like a series of *pas-de-trois*, in which the sex of the dancers is really irrelevant: what matters are the emotions they incarnate – old love, old jealousy, old anger – of the little Henry who yearned with all the intensity of his being for acceptance by his brother. In a more benign and pathetic mood, the legend of childhood took still another form that autumn in a tale Henry wrote just before William's arrival from Germany – before he began to feel the old envy again. He called it *Broken Wings*. In it a writer-lady and a painter-man avoid one another at a country house. They had been in love years before; yet each believed the other to be too successful for them to have a life together. Then they both discover they have had their fame without the financial reward that goes with it. Life together is now possible; their wings 'broken', they can face the future and recognize their old love. It is a wishful parable in which Henry equates his own recent failures with William's broken health. He seems to be saying in the story that perhaps now, at long last, he and William, their wings broken, are on the same footing – in the same boat.

These three-cornered ballets and tugs-of-war of the inner life of the novelist represent in essence the feelings of a brother scorned who equates himself with scorned women. Nothing had changed in his inner world; what had changed was his adult power of fantasy; his tales are richer and more jewel-encrusted; but they show him still trying to resolve old problems, even as in the themes of murdered little boys and surviving little girls. There could be also morbid variants, such as *Maud-Evelyn*, in which the stiff young man gives up the living woman he is courting to love a young woman whom he has never known – and who is dead. It is a tale of a kind of *folie à trois*, in which the girl's parents pretend their daughter lives. The young man falls in with their pretence; he even pretends that he marries her. He goes further still – pretends that she has died as his wife. He moves in fantasy from courtship of a ghost to becoming a ghostly widower. This venture into morbidity – to a feeling of the deadness of his past – however, had its counterpart in a different tale – a good-humoured story to which James gave the significant tale of *The Third Person*. One of his slightest ghost stories, it is eloquently biographical. It was written while William and Alice were with him that cold December of 1899. Its principal characters are two elderly ladies who live in the ancient town of Marr 'a little old huddled, red-roofed, historic south-coast town' high and dry on its hilltop from which the sea had long before receded. The cousins have inherited a fine old brick house in which 200 years of the 'little melancholy, middling, disinherited' town have 'squared themselves in the brown, panelled parlour, creaked patiently on the wide staircase and bloomed herbaciously in the red-walled garden'. We are in Rye, we are in Lamb House. Presently the two spinsters became aware of the presence of a man, who carries his head always distinctly to one side. He appears and vanishes – he haunts one and then the other. With the aid of the local clergyman, who knows the history of the place, the third person is established as an ancestor who had lived in the old house and who had been hanged for smuggling – that is why his head is so mournfully tilted. For a while the cousins enjoy having a man about the house – even if he is a ghost. But they have also tense little jealous moments. In the end they decide the troubled spirit must be returned to its rest. Each has her own theory, and the tale peters out in a joke – a smuggled Tauchnitz effectively allows the ghost's brooding spirit to depart.

This was perhaps the most direct statement of the recurrent themes in Henry James's creative consciousness that winter. William, laid low by his heart attack, was as shorn of his power as the hanged smuggler; the two women competing for him might be Henry and Alice; or they belonged to the perpetual triangles of the Jamesian childhood and youth, with himself or William cast as 'third person' – depending on the situation. It had been an eternal ballet, a shuffling of the same figures into familiar combinations involving not only the parents but that other third person in the family, the devoted Aunt Kate. Ghosts might be laid in tales: but they had a way of returning in life. They still could be recalled at a given signal, by anything that touched an ancient hurt.

52

The Visitable Past

ONE day that autumn Henry James took the Brighton train from London and went to Rottingdean to have lunch with the Kiplings. They were back from America and 'the great little Rudyard', inspired by the Boer War, had been spouting patriotic verses and publishing them in the press. On the day of James's visit, he had written a new poem. He seemed to thrive on violence and declamation and measureless chauvinism. James couldn't swallow these 'loud brazen patriotic' mouthings. It was like exploiting the name of one's mother or one's wife. Two or three times a century – perhaps. But every month!

He took the return train in the thickening dusk. F. N. Doubleday, Kipling's American publisher and friend, had talked to James about his doing another volume of ghost stories, like *The Turn of the Screw*. Thinking of this, he seemed to see, as the train sped him back to London, 'the picture of three or four "scared" and slightly modern

American figures', against European backgrounds. His travellers were 'hurried by their fate – from one of these places to the other, in search of, in flight from, something or other'. It would be, he noted, a 'quasi-grotesque Europeo-American situation'.

In search of, in flight from, something or other. He did not apply this to himself when he recorded it some days later in his notebooks; yet the statement contained James's essential life experience in eerie form. He had been the archetypal American in flight from home; he had gone in search of 'something or other' in the great House of Europe, with its centuries of bloodshed and *bric-à-brac*. And now his brother William had made him aware again – had brought into his immediate experience the things from which he had taken early flight – the whole life of Quincy Street, Boston, New York, the glaring daylight of a world that confined him to the invisible barriers of his childhood and youth.

The uncanny moment passed. The train sped him into the city. And James did not then write the story : all he could do was record the emotion and the terror. Instead, he set down a scenario for a tale of a young American who walks into a house he has just inherited in London – to find himself in the past. Part of his Brighton-to-London fantasy was incorporated into this scenario. The idea of something inescapable – of the past carrying its future; of the future – that is the present – going back to its past. Some such brooding nightmare sense of history involving Europe and America was woven into his plan – perhaps the thought of his own old and recent travels, when in Venice, Rome, Naples he had found the present invaded at every turn by his personal past. He had a title for his story almost from the first : he would call it *The Sense of the Past.*

I

James wrote the opening chapters in the early days of 1900, a time when men are inclined to be unusually conscious of the clock and the calendar. The idea, fascinating in its possibilities, proved extremely difficult. He could get his young man back into the old house and back into the past of 1820 : that was easy enough. But how arrange for his escape to the twentieth century? The choice of 1820 was carefully made. James did not want to venture into a century he did not know. It would have meant 'research', and factitious 'historical' writing. The year 1820 was his 'visitable past'. It was the period of his father's boyhood, the remembered family background. The visitor from the New World, trapped in an old house, in the Old World, the man from the present moving from city to city in a haunted past, enjoying yet fearing it – this had been a part of his experience, and it was a part of his theme. Wonderful as James's evocation and sense of old things were, he had always been able to enjoy the past from the perspective of a delightful, comfortable present. The past had the charm of remembered lamplight and candlelight, in the new era of electric light. There was much of the past in his memories of his grandmother, in Albany, in her old-time clothes, reading books with the candle set between her eyes and the printed page. This was distinctly a 'visitable' past, the kind to which Fanny Kemble used to transport him during long winter evenings by her fireside; or some of the crusty ancients, who like her could take James back to the eighteenth century, within the panelled walls of old London clubs and drawing-rooms, which belonged to still other centuries.

In invoking a 'visitable past', James in reality suggested his ambivalence towards old things, towards Europe itself. His horseback rides long ago in the Campagna had given him an uncanny – and uncomfortable – feeling of the insolence of power, the primordial cruelty and brutality of man. He liked the sense of the backward centuries, but he shuddered at their violence. The unreachable past partook of nightmare; it held within it man's accumulated evil, the terror of the ages. His early stories had fabled this – the Emperor's topaz that carried its old evil; it had had to be re-committed to the past – thrown into the Tiber. Or his tale of the Valerii, the excavated Juno which must be reinterred if the present is to be saved. The past could choke the present. The visitable past was palpable; it ministered to a faint antiquarian interest. Out of such ambivalent feelings, James wrote his fragment of *The Sense of the Past*, seeking to recapture a *Turn of the Screw* horror in it by having his twentieth-century man blunder cheerfully into history – and into the terrible discovery that he is its prisoner. Trapped by history! To be unable to escape into kindly, sheltering, secure and easy immediacy – that could be the ultimate nightmare!

In the opening pages of this story there is one of James's delicate passages in celebration of the past – the past washed of its centuries of misery, its dirt, its bad smells – the 'clean' past of the historian :

He wanted the hour of the day at which this and that had happened, and the temperature and the weather and the sound, and yet more the stillness, from the street, and the exact look-out, with the corresponding look-in, through the window and the slant on the walls of the light of afternoons that had been. He wanted the unimaginable accidents, the little notes of truth for which the common lens of history, however the scowling muse might bury her nose, was not sufficiently fine. He wanted evidence of a sort for which there had never been documents enough, or for which documents mainly, however multiplied, would never *be* enough. That was indeed in any case the artist's method to try for an ell in order to get an inch.

It was of course the artist's method, and more particularly the novelist's. The young historian in *The Sense of the Past*, pausing in the doorway of the house that will admit him to the world of 1820, has the thought that 'it was for the old ghosts to take him for one of themselves'. One hardly wants to believe oneself a ghost. This was interesting as a thought – but also frightening. It may account for Henry James's failure to finish this book.

2

The story James planned was composed essentially of his personal myth. His young historian, Ralph Pendrel, is an American who has never been abroad; he possesses a sense both of art and of history. He wants to marry a young New York matron with the picturesque name of Aurora Coyne, a name which expresses both the Homeric rosy-fingered morning of America and its monetary materialism. She will have Pendrel if he will promise to keep his national virginity – stay away from Europe. Going to Europe has become commonplace, an adventure of the mob. Pendrel's uniqueness was that he had always been a part of the new America, and Aurora feels that he must shape his future within the land of the future: tissue it out of American materials without the adulteration of Europe, the past of other lands. Pendrel's dilemma, in the artificial comedy of the opening chapter, is that he not only wants to go to Europe, but has a particular incentive to do so. Like his author, he has just acquired – indeed inherited – an old house, the house of the English Pendrels, located in Mansfield Square in London. The last of the English line had read Ralph Pendrel's brilliant *Essay in Aid of the Reading of History* and had rewarded his kinsman for his piety towards the past. In bestowing the house he has, so to speak, made Pendrel custodian of the family past. Far from being an American claimant, like James's early hero in *A Passionate Pilgrim*, Pendrel may make his pilgrimage with a feeling of full possession. At the end of the first part of the novel, written in January 1900, Aurora and Ralph reach a vague accord. She knows she cannot persuade him to stay in the United States. But she may agree to marry him if, after his adventure, he returns to America – and then promises to remain.

The ensuing two or three chapters, all James wrote at the time, take Pendrel to London. His visit to the house in Mansfield Square reminds us of James's own close stock-taking in Lamb House; and in his nightly wanderings he studies an old family portrait of a young man painted in unusual pose. His back is turned, looking, one gathers, to the past rather than the future. In these pages we feel James's masterly touch in the ghostly genre : the sense of the eerie grows for Pendrel, he expects to encounter some sign, some portent, some apparition. Lighting his candle late one night he does – it is the finest and spookiest moment of this section – and perceives himself holding his candle aloft in one of the mirrors to light his way. But he now has his shock : it is not a reflection in a mirror. It is himself, descended from the picture, his *alter ego* out of the past, who wants to visit the present. It is Pendrel who must now turn his back, take the pose in the picture : and the man in the picture will replace him.

Leaving the house, Pendrel has the certitude that on his return he will change places with his ghostly double, his dead ancestor. Before embarking on this adventure, before his possible disappearance into history, he has a long talk with the American Ambassador to London whom James set down in the image of James Russell Lowell. Pendrel in the dawn of the twentieth century tries to explain to the Ambassador that he is about to go back to the nineteenth – to 1820. The ambassador listens, comments, and thinks him harmlessly mad. 'I *am* the Future. The Future, that is, for *him*; which means the Present, don't you see – ?' Henry James's *Time Machine* story (he had recently read Wells's book) or his fantasy of the Connecticut Yankee in the Court of King Arthur did not get far beyond this point. The Ambassador takes Pendrel to the entrance of the house in Mansfield Square : from the pavement he watches the young man take hold of the knocker, hears the rat-tat-tat, and sees his supreme pause 'before the closing of the door again placed him on the right side and the whole world as he had known it on the wrong'.

In January 1900 James abandoned his story at this exciting moment. Later that summer he picked it up again, but could not go on with it. He was much too interested in another novel, dealing with other 'ambassadors'. He would not turn to this manuscript until 1914 made him want to escape from a terrible present into a remote past. At that point several further chapters were written, and part of a scenario, which suggests how difficult James found his theme. He was not comfortable with his handling of an imprisoning past: the history of the Pendrels, which in the later chapters becomes an almost commonplace tale of the kind James had written during the Civil War; one catches a glimpse of the Civil War young men James had created; even Pendrel seems to be one of them; and of his long dead cousin Minny Temple; and the formidable James family mother, and a sister, whose unpleasant brother is still another incarnation of the William of long ago. The atmosphere of James's old tales, the vivid past of the novelist, rather than of the remoter 1820, is to be felt in these late pages. That James should come to this at the outbreak of a new war suggests indeed that in this respect also we deal with a reliving of crucial moments at the time of the story's genesis: the Boer War, William's presence, the purchase of an historic house – the uneasy feeling that in acquiring it he was re-enacting the adventure of his long-ago 'passionate pilgrim' – and above all his malaise at the thought he was trapped in the past, *his* past. These were the thickly overlaid memories and emotions which prompted this novel. It was a story too large for him to write, a plot that would remain unresolved. By 1914 it would be too late. *The Sense of the Past* remains a fragment of what might have been an extraordinary ghost-novel, James's ultimate discovery – had that been possible – how to complete his journey into himself.*

3

There was still another meeting of recent and old experience in *The Sense of the Past*. In Ralph Pendrel, contemplating himself as a figure seemingly reflected in a mirror, but in reality confronting an *alter ego*, a 'double' out of history, we may see the visage of the three-day visitor of the past summer, Hendrik Andersen. The ghostly fantasy gives us a glimpse into the power of the imagination to re-weave and

* In another form the fragment caught the public imagination, twelve years after James's death, when it was dramatized as the play *Berkeley Square*.

combine old and new, in the symbolic language of the mind. The vision of Ralph in Mansfield Square was the vision Henry James had had of his younger self during the fleeting hours spent with the young sculptor. He had felt his own past stirring in this youthful presence: he had *seen* his *alter ego*, had been involved in a double-play of identity: the man out of the picture, standing facing him in the old room, holding his candle aloft, 'the young man brown-haired, pale, erect, with the high-collared dark blue coat, the young man revealed, responsible, conscious, quite shining out of the dark-ness'. He had wanted to see his face in the portrait, but it had been looking the other way. Then he saw it – 'the face – miracle of miracles, yes – confounded him as his own'.

To return to the past was to meet oneself. The present Henry James, writing these pages in the century's dawn, heavy with middle age, was living in the future of the young Henry James who had written about a young sculptor in Rome, or as he puts it to the re-summoned Lowell, on behalf of his character: 'I *am* the Future, the Future, that is, for *him*.' This was hardly a myth of Narcissus. It was the attempt of an ageing man to accept the hard fact of his ageing, and to tell himself that he could be both old and young at the same time. He could possess his past; he need not be swallowed up by it. *The Sense of the Past* was Henry James's way of bringing together all the fancies that his charged imagination had been dredging up, inventing, modifying, in the attempt to recover the integrity of his Self – that identity diminished in boyhood by the dramas of rivalry and made sovereign by escape into Europe – an historical past, in which Henry James had always intensely lived the life of the present. Small wonder that he would use the phrase 'the visitable past', in talking of his tale of Venice, *The Aspern Papers*; and Venice itself had been, in his imaginative life, the symbol of a dead past and a living present, both death-in-life and life-in-death, as he had shown in his story of the haunted Juliana and the publishing scoundrel, a dozen years before.

Encased in pages of James's unfinished novel we find the essential elements of what he himself had called 'the Americano-European legend' – *his* legend, and the legend of the world he had peopled. For him there had been the great drama – the voyage out of the men of England to the New World. In the fullness of time there had come the voyage back. His father had made it long ago when he revisited County Cavan in Ireland. He himself had made it in the memorable voyage of 1869, which he had retold in *A Passionate Pilgrim*. And then there had been the great adventure of his life : his embrace of Europe – of a past that had set him free. It set him free – but not without exacting its touch of nightmare, the nightmare of doubt that things might have been otherwise, had he stayed at home, or the feeling at moments that he might be immersed, shut in, lost, damned, beyond all rescue in the maelstrom of history. He would borrow from *The Sense of the Past* seven years later, for his tale of *The Jolly Corner*, to try to see himself in the American past *as he might have been* had he stayed at home. For the moment the vision of Hendrik 'shining out of the darkness', remained with him – Hendrik who now had taken a studio in New York and was attempting to make his way in America, the land of the future, while James watched from the land of the past.

53

A Rage of Wonderment

THE remarkable thing about Henry James's life during that crowded autumn of 1899 and well into the new year was that he worked – in spite of distractions, anxieties, interruptions – as if constantly pursued by the furies. If ever there was an 'economic motif' in his writing, it existed during these weeks. He wanted to pay for Lamb House and he turned out tale after tale, a series of articles, and then scenarios for two novels which his agent circulated among the publishers. He had acquired an agent after long hesitation. Howells had urged this step on him long before; a brief period with the old firm of A. P. Watt had been helpful; and James recognized that his wares needed special handling. To this end he enrolled himself in the literary 'stable' of James B. Pinker, a man who in a very short time made himself indispensable to James, as he did to all his authors. He was an experienced former magazine-editor, unobtrusive, thoughtful, respected in the literary world. His clients would be the most distinguished in the annals of literary salesmanship: James, Conrad, Wells, Kipling, Bennett, a veritable roll-call of late-Victorians and Edwardians. Wise, shrewd, tactful, friendly, he reviewed James's confused copyrights, a heavy accumulation of literary properties representing thirty-five years of continuous toil; he found new publishers; he reopened old relations. James spoke of 'the germs of a new career' as Pinker began to place his work. From this time on James's correspondence with his agent offers us a clear picture of his work and his earnings. The record of the winter of 1899–1900 is striking. For a while James produces a story a week – and most are sold at Pinker's standard price of £50 per story, a large sum for the time. *Paste* is sent by James late in the summer : two articles follow and are sold at £75 each. The records show the following : 8 September, *The Beldonald Holbein*; 17 September *Broken Wings*; 24 September, *The Special Type*; 3 October 'another short tale', not named; 11 October, *The Faces*, (later called *The Two Faces*). In December *Miss Gunton of Poughkeepsie* and *The Third Person*. James writes an article on *The Future of the Novel* for a many-volumed 'universal anthology', a travel-piece *The Saint's Afternoon*, recalling his wine-bibbing day at Munthe's. The scenario for *The Sense of the Past* is dispatched and an early scenario of *The Ambassadors* which will be rewritten late in 1900 into the long 'preliminary statement' which has survived. In the thick of winter three more tales are produced, *The Tone of Time*, *Flickerbridge* and *The Story in It*. William Heinemann, who considered himself a friend of James's and had published all his work from *The Spoils of Poynton* to *The Awkward Age*, balked at dealing with an agent. Pinker promptly established new relations for the novelist with Methuen and Constable. The tales of that autumn and winter were rapidly assembled into the volume *The Soft Side* for which Pinker obtained a £100 advance.

In the spring James began another short story, planned at 8,000 to 10,000 words. This one, however, ran away from him. By June it had become a short novel, *The Sacred Fount*, which Pinker sold to Methuen in England and Scribner in America, a publisher who had long wanted to have James. Thus began a relationship in New York for the novelist which would endure beyond his lifetime. The money for the initial payment on Lamb House had been speedily earned. Self-confidence was restored; and James had margin in his bank. The furious pace of production moreover would not stop. Three large novels lay ahead, as well as several major essays and the promised biography of Story.

I

The novel which had begun as an anecdote and had grown from 19,000 words to 70,000 was dispatched to Pinker at the beginning of the summer of 1900. 'A fine flight into the high fantastic,' James called it, describing it to Howells; and to Pinker he wrote, 'It is fanciful, fantastic – but very close and sustained, and calculated to minister to curiosity.' The novel has ministered to curiosity ever since. When it came out, Henry Adams told Mrs Cameron that 'Harry James has upset me' and that John Hay had found the novel 'close on extravagance'. Adams went on to say,

I recognized at once that Harry and I had the same disease, the obsession of the *idée fixe*. Harry illustrates it by the trivial figure of an English country-house party, which could only drive one mad by boring into it, but if he had chosen another background, his treatment of it would have been wonderfully keen. All the same it is insanity, and I think Harry must soon take a vacation, with most of the rest of us, in a cheery asylum.

In a later generation Edmund Wilson would find the book 'mystifying, even maddening'. Perhaps Adams discovered in *The Sacred Fount* echoes of Surrenden Dering; for the Newmarch of the novel is that kind of lavish establishment; and in the novel James continued to show an antipathy towards the English country-house and large week-end parties, that contrasted with the relish he had taken in them fifteen or twenty years before. He had expressed this sharply in the tale of *Broken Wings*, in which his artists speak of the quantity of imagination they must furnish the rich – as the latter 'have none themselves'.

The Sacred Fount is of a piece with the work of this period – it is the last of the experimental series from *The Spoils of Poynton* through the tales of the little girls and the record of their 'range of wonderment'. James's later preface uses the word 'range', although one wonders whether he might not have written the word 'rage'. These novels as we saw were studies in the 'phantasmagoric', in the ways in which the mind and the emotions, coping with realities, tend to invest them with beauty, terror, mystery.

The Sacred Fount is the only novel James wrote in which he used a first-person narrator as in his tale of the governess in *The Turn of the Screw*. James did not believe in first-person use in long stories, where he felt it tended to make for a 'fluidity of self-revelation'; but in this novel, the mystified 'I' is essential to his scheme. The unnamed narrator is turned loose among the weekenders at Newmarch. We are confined to his observations and theories. We accompany the 'I' as he goes to Newmarch on the train; and here, meeting some of the other guests, he is struck by the fact that Mrs Brissenden, who had married a man much younger than herself, has grown remarkably young. Later he will see that her husband, 'poor Briss', has grown appreciably older. Out of this he evolves his generalization : people are capable, vampire-like, of draining one another : Mrs Briss is acquiring her youth at the expense of her husband. Then, discovering another guest, Gilbert Long, 'a fine piece of human furniture', a man hitherto possessed of a banal mind, he now discerns that he has become alert, intelligent and witty. The logical narrator decides that someone is being drained by Long of wit and intelligence. The narrator's week-end quest is to discover this particular 'sacred fount', the one that has ministered to Long. His candour and his inquisitiveness are resisted by his companions; we are never sure whether they treat his inductions with genuine interest or are merely humouring him as an incorrigible bore. He is far from boring as a narrator. He may be vain, self-preoccupied, obsessed, but he also has the artist's touch, the wider imagination – and he imagines a great deal. He judges those around him as if they were objects in an inquiry. For one of the week-end guests he does have, however, a marked sympathy. She is his 'suspect'; once-beautiful and intelligent, she now seems drained of life. Her name is May Server. The narrator sees her fluttering restlessly and unhappily 'like a bird with a broken wing'.

In a word, *The Sacred Fount* is a kind of adult *What Maisie Knew* and the narrator who wants to know everything discovers invariably that inquiry, especially into the lives of humans, has well-defined limits. He assures himself that he is not using the methods of 'the detective and the keyhole'. The ugly thought crosses his mind that he is perhaps 'nosing about for a relation that a lady has her reasons for keeping secret', but he is reassured by the perceptive artist, Ford Obert R.A., one of his fellow-guests. An inquiry, Obert explains, is honourable so long as the investigator sticks to 'psychologic evidence'. He observes that 'resting on psychologic signs alone, it's a high application of the intelligence'. James, in this way, justifies what had always been his greatest art – that of seeing *into* human behaviour. Of all writers, he was the novelist perhaps most in tune with what people really said behind the masks they put on. The aggressive emotion that masquerades as a cutting witticism; the euphoria that disguises depression; the endearment that compensates for animus; the pleasant remark that is accompanied by a hostile gesture; the sudden slip of the tongue that reveals the opposite of what is intended – James had learned long ago to read the truths of such data. But within *The Sacred Fount* there seems to be an uneasy questioning: 'Have I been right? How can I be sure?' A little voice whispers that omniscient novelists can be wrong as well as right. 'People have such a notion of what you embroider on things,' Mrs Briss tells the narrator. Her assaults on his self-confidence are particularly violent: 'You see too much ... You talk too much ... You're abused by a fine fancy ... You build up houses of cards ... You overestimate the penetration of others.' These are some of the charges she brings during her long final talk late at night with the speculating mental detective. Her parting shot is, 'I think you're crazy.' Mrs Briss may be trying to cover up an involvement of her own; for the reader often suspects she is having an affair with Long, the 'heavy' who is believed by the narrator to have drained Mrs Server's wit. Certainly her remaining with the narrator into late evening and her intense need to set him right suggests that, in spite of her coolness, she is in some way disturbed by his 'investigations'. The effect of the final dialogue is to echo how reality can come barging in and destroy the fine fruits of theory. 'You're costing me a perfect palace of thought,' the narrator pleads with Mrs Briss. He feels indeed that his palace has become a house of cards. He fights for 'my frail, but, as I maintain, quite sublime structure'. But he is left shattered on the battlefield. 'I *should* certainly never again, on the spot, quite hang together, even though it wasn't really that I hadn't three times her method. What I too fatally lacked was her tone.' With these words the novel ends.

2

In *The Sacred Fount* James wrote the last of his series of tales of curiosity and wonder, his inquiry into the extent to which man lives not by bare realities but by the embroidery of these realities within his mind. There had been Maisie's little world, 'phantasmagoric' with 'strange shadows dancing on a sheet', and the world of the governess, frightened by her own thoughts. The world of the imagination, James seems to tell us, arrives at its own truths, and its own beauties; but it can hold within it the terror of the unreal, the delicate uneasy balance between thought and fact, man's eternal struggle between what is and what might be. 'Light or darkness,' says the narrator in *The Sacred Fount*, 'my imagination rides me.' In this novel the question of 'reality' is resolved into a little scene in front of a glass-covered pastel of a young man without eyebrows, like those of a circus clown, and a pale and livid face. He holds an object, some work of art, that appears on closer examination to be 'the representation of a human face, modelled and coloured, in wax, in enamelled metal, in some semblance not human. The object thus appears a complete mask, such as might have been fantastically fitted and worn.' The narrator remarks that this is the picture 'of all pictures, that most needs an interpreter'.

The interpretation is not offered: or rather, James leaves us with two interpretations which cancel each other out, thus inviting the reader to put his own imagination to work. One of the spectators calls the picture 'the mask of death'. The narrator however argues that the face in the pastel is more dead than the mask. He would call it 'the mask of life'. Thus, what is seen as life by one, is seen as death by the other: and May Server adds a further touch – perhaps out of her own depleted life – by discerning a grimace on the mask. The mask of life, if it is that, has indeed had a grimace for Mrs Server: and in the cliché of opera, the clown's mask of laughter always conceals a breaking heart. But the mask is art – the face is life. And the art which is a grimace and a mask, can express – in James's view – more life than life itself. We are reminded in this little 'set' scene, of James's tale of *The Real Thing* and the hidden meaning of *The Figure in the Carpet* – the 'real thing' was simply itself, photographic. Art transfigures.

The symbolic scene contains within it the essence of *The Sacred Fount*. The older woman has assumed the mask of youth, while her husband has taken on the mask of age. But the symbol-pastel suggests something else as well. It reminds us that the obsessed narrator is trying, in his compulsive way, to arrive at the meaning and unity of his abundant impressions. If the same picture can yield opposite meanings, how real – or how phantasmagoric? – are his own 'discoveries?' How much does he really see? – how much does he read into what he thinks he has seen? The narrator wonders whether he is indulging too freely in this 'idle habit of reading into mere human things an interest so much deeper than mere human things were in general prepared to supply?' He enunciates in effect the law of the artist – the burden of the charged and creative imagination, which (James implies) continues to function in the creative being as regularly as 'the organ of life', the beating of the human heart.

The pastel scene in the gallery of Newmarch may perhaps hold within it also a personal memory of James's – a remembrance of the afternoon long ago, in the time of his first fame, when he had spent an afternoon with Flaubert, and listened to the French novelist read Théophile Gautier aloud. Flaubert had been supreme among his peers in translating the ugliness of existence into the beauty of words; and he had bellowed the sonnet at James – about pastels of beauties, lying in antique shops or among the stalls on the quays, with specks of mud on the glass, the melancholy beauty spots of time on the faded and the dead.

> Le vent d'hiver, en vous touchant la joue,
> A fait mourir vos oeillets et vos lis ...

The poet had described the sad smile on the pastel faces at the memory of vanished gallantries, vanished lovers, vanished life. It is significant that in the Newmarch scene it is the fading beauty, May Server, who sees the grimace on the mask. And she is described as having a grimace on her own countenance as well.

3

The themes of this perhaps under-valued novel begin to disengage themselves: the ageing process, the invulnerability of art, indeed the 'madness of art', which insists on seeing more than the immediate 'real', and the vulnerability of love. In trying to decipher the 'story' of *The Sacred Fount* – the equations of who is 'draining' whom – critics have failed to see that the most touching and most beautiful theme within this novel resides in the person of the unhappy May Server. Her children have died; love has died; she flits pathetically from man to man, 'the absolute wreck of her storm', yet remains a person to whom 'the pale ghost of a special sensibility still clung, waving from the mast, with a bravery that went to the heart, the last tatter of its flag'. One almost seems to recognize her as the parable-figure for the other side of her creator, not the intellectual-imaginative side, but that side of James whose children – his fiction, his tales, his plays – seemed to die when launched in the world and who still tried to face society as the 'personality' he had been. May Server's broken wing is the broken wing of the writer in his recent pathetic tale about himself and his brother. More important, she becomes the haunting figure of James's awareness of his loneliness, the passing of youth, the passing of success. He had had his good years; he had had his fame – and now it all seemed like a house of cards. And he was vulnerable – as vulnerable as the lovely fragile May Server, who needs love, who craves affection, and seeks someone, in her loneliness as she flits like a ghost about the grounds at Newmarch – strange, beautiful, alienated from the impersonal and the gross, the social falsity, the lies and conventions of 'society'. Love depletes – James seems to say – not simple physical love, which offers momentary solace to the senses, but the love that is 'the great relation' – the states of feeling and being which humans engender in one another. The passages devoted to May Server in *The Sacred Fount* are suffused with poetry and pathos, and lead us to the narrator's – to James's – vision of the ravage of love: 'I saw as I had never seen before what consuming passion can make of the marked mortal on whom, with fixed beak and claws, it has settled as on a prey. She reminded me of a sponge wrung dry and with fine pores agape. Voided and scraped of everything, her shell was merely crushable.'

At last James, the egotist and 'man of the world', a great intellectual and artistic phenomenon, was allowing himself to feel not only the beauty of art, into which ugly life constantly intruded, but recognize that his exquisite 'palace of thought' was not enough. One had not 'lived' if one had not loved; one had to know the ache of love, the pain of absence, the need for communion with the beloved – one had to *feel* love, not as he had felt it in all the novels he had written – novels about egotists seeking power, seeking the world, seeking the high places of art and life, as Roderick, Isabel, Newman had sought them; or the helpless, crushed by the absence of power and recognition, like young Hyacinth.

Henry James's work had never dealt with love, save as a force destructive of – or in competition with – power and aesthetic beauty. Now, at the very last of the century, when in his loneliness in Lamb House he reached out to his younger friends, and mourned the absence of the bright young sculptor, and saw in the mirror the grey streaks in his once glossy brown-black beard, he knew the deepest ache, felt it with all the strength of his genius. This was the new awareness, the new insight. He was vulnerable: he too could love. Yet he still had the armour of his egotism. For the narrator of *The Sacred Fount*, who so busily tries to ferret out the secrets of his various couples, is still more interested in himself and his great strength of mind, his problem-solving power, than in the persons who furnish him with his facts. Only May Server touches him, with the poetry of her loss and her struggle to survive:

She went through the form of expression, but what told me everything was the way the form of expression broke down. Her lovely grimace, the light of the previous hours, was as blurred as a bit of brushwork in water-colour spoiled by the upsetting of the artist's glass. She fixed me with it as she had fixed during the day forty persons, but it fluttered like a bird with a broken wing. She looked about and above, down each of our dusky avenues and up at our gilded tree-tops and our painted sky, where, at the moment, the passage of a flight of rooks made a clamour. She appeared to wish to produce some explanation of her solitude, but I was quickly enough sure that she would never find a presentable one.

It is at this moment, that the narrator sees how 'crushable' May Server is; what survived out of the wreck and ruin of her storm was her still striving consciousness – 'with a force that made it struggle and dissemble. This consciousness was all her secret.'

In this trivial, yet often beautiful tale, Henry James embodied the last stage of his 'self-therapy', his long struggle to bring into balance his world of art with the human values of the world, the beauty of his vision with the tawdriness and ugliness of reality. He could now write his last books. The way was clear. He could stop looking at the past, and its entrapments; he could ask himself what uses the past may have for the present. The question that formed itself on his lips now, that brought with it perhaps the deepest ache, that he whispered to himself – or wrote into his notebook – was 'too late'. Was it 'too late? Too late? too late?' Out of this old remark of Howells to Sturges would grow – in the cleared vision of his sensibility, in his renewed power as artist – the history of the middle-aged American returning to Paris, starting over again the same voyage Henry James had made a quarter of a century before. He had settled then in the French capital, and written a novel about an American in Paris – a romantic tale of an American's quest for the refinement and beauty and nobility of the Old World. Christopher Newman was about to become Lambert Strether.

54

The Great Relation

Too late? Too late? Turning the pages of one of Turgenev's novels at this time, in the English translation – he had read it long before in French – James drew a pencil line beside the words, 'Youth, youth, little dost thou care for anything!' The title of the novel was *First Love*. He was discovering the insolence of youth; he knew himself young in thought and even in strength, and yet it was an anguish to contemplate the ravage of time. 'I like growing old: 56!,' he had written to Henrietta Reubell '– but I don't like growing *older*. I quite love my present age and the compensations, simplifications, freedom, independences, memories, advantages of it. But I don't keep it long enough – it passes too quickly.' He asserted his power every day as he dictated to MacAlpine, who remained his part-time typist, and expressed his irritation as the elements turned the roads to mud, immobilized his bicycle, and made walking impossible. Rye seemed at such times like a prison; its winter months were long, its tempests noisy.

Shortly after Hendrik's visit, Henry James had begun to reach out to younger friends. He now felt a new and strong affection for them. To Morton Fullerton in Paris, to Howard Sturgis (not to be confused with Jonathan Sturges) whom he had known as a boy, to A. C. Benson – indeed to any charming and civilized young man who came to him with introductions from friends – young men like the studious and amiable Gaillard Lapsley, sent by Mrs Gardner from America – James offered the hospitality of his home, the rural distractions of Rye, an anxious avuncular affection. James had known Morton Fullerton for a decade. They had spent many pleasant hours together in Paris, whenever James was there. In the novelist's letters he had been 'my dear Fullerton' from the beginning. Now he is addressed as 'dearest boy', and the letters are warm – and importunate. Had Fullerton been working too hard? He surely needed a rest what with the Dreyfus case and the vagaries of French politics – of course at Lamb

House! 'You shall be surrounded here with every circumstance of tranquillity and comfort, of rest and consecration. You talk of the *real thing*. But that is the real thing. *I* am the real thing.' Fullerton was ready to concede this : but he was embedded in Paris; he rarely crossed the Channel. Elegant, in his morning coats and striped trousers, looking more like a diplomat from the Quai d'Orsay than a journalist, with his fine big moustaches and melancholy eye, he was *un homme de coeur*, a genial poetry-quoting sentimentalist – from New England – every inch the gentleman-journalist. He had lived himself into a Gallic way of life. He would become so French in the end that he would shift from *The Times* to *Le Figaro*, and write articles in French on American politics and American life. He sent James the latest books. He responded to his affectionate letters. But he seldom left Paris. A few years later Edith Wharton would be charmed by him, and for a time they were lovers. On James's shelves there remained an old seventeenth-century volume Fullerton had found on the quays – he was a versatile bibliophile – and inscribed elegantly in French to James. It was a book of dialogues between two French *élégants*, Aristide and Eugène, who discourse on life, on nobility, on art, on emblems. We may see the gift as emblem of the civilized communion between novelist and journalist. Fullerton's inscription consisted of a passage saying how busy he was in Paris, how much he longed for 'a quarter of an hour' to call his own. Such were the delicacies of this friendship.

To Fullerton, late in 1900, James wrote one of his grandiose letters, a confessional document couched in the majesty of the late style. James was reading proofs of *The Sacred Fount* at the time; and Fullerton once again had told him that he was prevented from visiting Lamb House. He also asked James one of his thoughtful questions – what had been the 'port' from which the novelist believed he had taken sail – what had been, as the French might put it, the *point de départ* of his life? James rose to the question with all the organ-tones of his prose. First there was regret that Fullerton could not visit him and he put this in a sweep of Olympian resignation :

I *am* face to face with it, as one is face to face, at my age, with every successive lost opportunity (wait till you've reached it!) and with the steady swift movement of the ebb of the great tide – the great tide of which one will never see the turn. The grey years gather; the arid spaces lengthen, damn them! – or at any rate don't shorten; what doesn't come doesn't, and what does does.

So Lambert Strether would soon meditate aloud to young Bilham, in Gloriani's garden, in *The Ambassadors*. In his letter James told Fullerton he discerned some 'obscurity of trouble' in his tone and he wondered whether he mightn't be of help. 'Hold me then *you* with any squeeze; grip me with any grip; press me with any pressure; trust me with any trust.' As for the question about his 'port of departure', this might require 'a large synthesis'. Yet James felt he could, 'in a manner answer' –

The port from which I set out was, I think, that of *the essential loneliness of my life* – and it seems to be the port also, in sooth, to which my course again finally directs itself! This loneliness (since I mention it) – what is it still but the deepest thing about one? Deeper, about *me*, at any rate, than anything else; deeper than my 'genius', deeper than my 'discipline', deeper than my pride, deeper, above all, than the deep counterminings of art.

I

Within this awareness of 'the essential loneliness of my life', the loneliness of being which was both his art and his alienation as artist, James now moved towards a greater and deeper understanding of the essences of human experience : that life was to be viewed not as some puzzle, as the narrator of *The Sacred Fount* viewed it, but as a question of human relations. He spoke of 'the great relation' between man and woman, 'the constant world renewal', as he elegantly phrased the physical and moral relation – in a word, love, in its deepest meaning which he had not yet probed in his novels after all these years. In such fantasies as *The Sacred Fount* we see James still in bewilderment before the exigencies, depredations and vulnerabilities of love; but in his essays of this time there is a clairvoyance and vision new in his writings. His mind could grasp what his feelings were still probing. It is strange, perhaps, that at this moment James should write two essays on Italian writers. He had never done so; he would never do so again. He seized upon them, we may imagine, because they offered him the special critical 'case' and the opportunity to express what lay closest to his thought. This was that life was not a matter of who slept with whom, or of tearing passions to tatters, but of understanding and feeling – as he put it in his essay on Matilde Serao, the Neapolitan novelist. One could not get to know people simply by their 'convulsions and spasms'. It was not 'the passion of hero and heroine that gives, that can ever give, the heroine and the hero interest, but it is they themselves, with the ground they stand on and the objects enclosing them, who give interest to their passion'.

Love, at Naples and in Rome, as Madame Serao exhibits it, is simply unaccompanied with any interplay of our usual conditions – with affection, with duration, with circumstances or consequence, with friends, enemies, husbands, wives, children, parents, interest, occupations, the manifestation of tastes. Who are these people, we presently ask ourselves, who love indeed with fury – though for the most part with astonishing brevity – but who are so without any suggested situation in life that they can only strike us as loving for nothing and in the void, to no gain of experience and no effect of a felt medium or a breathed air.

If the novelist begins to treat physical sex in a close and intimate way, James argued, a strange thing occurs. On the eve of the sexually-liberated century he set down these prophetic words:

The very first reflection suggested by Serao's novels of 'passion' is that they perfectly meet our speculation as to what might with a little time become of our own fiction were our particular conventions suspended. We see so what, on its actual lines, does, what *has* become of it, and are so sated with the vision ... the effect then, we discover, of the undertaking to give *passione* its whole place is that by the operation of a singular law no place speedily appears to be left for anything else; and the effect of that in turn is greatly to modify, first, the truth of things, and second, with small delay, what may be left of their beauty.

In an essay on D'Annunzio, written in the autumn of 1903, this question was pursued to its ultimate end; for in that essay, based on James's close readings of a series of D'Annunzio's novels in the original (they remained in his library, heavily marked), he analysed the dangers of an art which blows aesthetic gold-dust over life's uglinesses, and masks with serious beauty the empty passions of persons possessed of nothing but their senses. Love in D'Annunzio is fragmented; it has no relation to human values. It is a simple physical act; the total beauty of his novels 'somehow extraordinarily fails to march with their beauty of parts'. In this James was giving new meaning to old ideas expressed in his essay *The Art of Fiction*, that a novel could not be better than the quality of the novelist's mind. Faced with the erotic, and choosing two Italian novelists of the time who offered him illustration not available in the English-speaking world, James now speaks of the wholeness and totality of love that will find expression ultimately in his symbolism of *The Golden Bowl*. He does not espouse the aesthetic view, which would seek beauty in order to look away from ugliness. His requirement is for both ugliness and beauty, the lies and deceptions as well as the truths of life; for only by knowing the lies is it possible to know the truth. 'The vulgarity into which he [D'Annunzio] so incongruously drops,' James wrote, 'is, I will not say the space he allots to love-affairs, but the weakness of his sense of "values" in depicting them.'

At the end of the essay he uses a striking image to characterize the emptiness of novels that isolate the physical from the act of living:

Shut out from the rest of life, shut out from all fruition and assimilation, it has no more dignity than – to use a homely image – the boots and shoes that we see, in the corridors of promiscuous hotels, standing, often in double pairs, at the doors of rooms. Detached and unassociated these clusters of objects present, however obtruded, no importance. What the participants do with their agitation, in short, or even what it does with them, *that* is the stuff of poetry, and it is never really interesting save when something finely contributive in themselves makes it so.

This passage would lead Max Beerbohm to draw one of his cele-brated cartoons of Henry James. He would portray the bewildered novelist, heavy-jowled, kneeling in a hotel corridor, before two pairs of shoes, a man's and a woman's, placed beside the shut door. The witty cartoon was of course a joke; but for the wider public it too literally portrayed a state of bewilderment that did not in reality exist. It belonged to the mental detective narrator of *The Sacred Fount*, not to the Henry James of the new century. In this simpli-fication of wit, Beerbohm expressed the opposite of what James was now saying. The mature statement resides in the plea that the novel use the fullness of life, and attempt new divinations and discoveries. D'Annunzio illustrated for James how much a novelist could over-look: he had seen 'neither duration, nor propagation, nor common kindness, nor common consistency, with other relations, common congruity with the rest of life'. Great territories were open to the 'future of the novel' – certainly to the novel in the English-speaking world. The English novel had done very well, wrote James, in dealing with the pirate and the pistol, the police, the wild and tame beast – but it had not yet studied 'whole categories of manners, whole cor-puscular classes and provinces, museums of character and condition'. Instead it had taken for granted that 'safety lies in all the loose and thin material that keeps reappearing in forms at once ready-made and sadly the worse for wear'. With these views James expressed his faith in the beauty and elasticity of the fictional form. For novels fulfilled one of man's deepest needs. 'Till the world is an unpeopled void,' he said, taking Stendhal's image, 'there will be an image in the mirror.' Everything would depend on the novelist's art. 'So long as there is a subject to be treated, so long will it depend wholly on treatment to rekindle the fire.'

Recording these views in his essays, James gave intellectual utterance to feelings adumbrated in his stories – and in this meeting of sentience and idea, his intellectual power and his new openness to feeling, he showed his readiness for a *vita nuova*. The masterpieces he would write were already sketched in his notebooks.

2

In his 'deep well of unconscious cerebration' Henry James had moved slowly from sickness to health. He had taken backward steps into the black abyss in order to discover his power of self-recreation, and now he had emerged again a whole man in spite of assaults and misfortunes. Step by step James's imagination had found, had wrought, the healing substance of his art – the strange, bewildering and ambiguous novels in which somehow he had recovered his identity so that he might be again a strong and functioning artist. In this process he had opened himself up – life aiding – to feeling and to love. He had taught himself to accept middle age, and to face great loneliness, and had turned again and again for solace to the discipline and difficulty of his craft. His self-discoveries had not healed every hurt; certain nerves would remain exposed and vulnerable. There would be moments again and again when the depths of his sadness, his inner mourning, and his deepest anger, would blacken the light of day. Nevertheless he could weather storms within himself as never before. In this indirect soothing of his soul, the frigid wall of his egotism had been breached to an enlarged vision of the world, and a larger feeling of the world's human warmth.

During the century's first summer, at the urging of Howells, James picked up again *The Sense of the Past*, but a short struggle showed him clearly that this was not what he wanted to write. He wanted to write the story, long buried in his notebook, about the middle-aged American, who arrives in Paris wondering whether he is rediscovering human experience and life's values 'too late'. With his message of 'live all you can' – his *cri de coeur* that was now Henry James's as well – he was a protagonist who expressed James's new will to life and being, the belief in himself and his old power as artist. 'We open the door to the Devil himself,' he wrote to one literary lady at this moment, describing the act of art and of life he daily performed, 'the Devil himself – who is nothing but the sense of beauty, of mystery, of relations, of appearances, of abysses, of the whole – and of *expression*!'

Beauty, mystery, relations, appearances, abysses! These words seemed to contain all the stages through which he had passed in his six-year purgatorial journey. To Howells he wrote, as he set aside *The Sense of the Past*, 'preoccupied with half a dozen things of the altogether human order now fermenting in my brain I don't care for "terror" (terror, that is, without "pity,") so much as I otherwise might'. He was no longer willing to write his ghost story; he no longer felt trapped by his past. And one day that spring, confronting himself again in the mirror, he had a sudden impulse – he would shave off his beard. It had hidden his face since the days of the Civil War. He was prepared now to shed an old identity, to divorce himself from his youth, his past, to be a new man – and in the new century. On 12 May 1900 he wrote to his brother William that he had been unable to bear any longer his increased hoariness, 'it had suddenly begun these three months since, to come out quite white and made me *feel*, as well as look, so old'.

Now he felt '*forty* and clean and light'. He had made his face correspond to a kind of physical youth he could feel again. A new face for the new century! 'I am told,' he wrote to Grace Norton, 'this shaven me is wholly another person from the old, of all the years.' It was another person. Now the massive forehead, the great dome, the smooth cheeks, the strong line of the nose, the full sensuous lips, and the deep blue penetrating eyes showed to the world another, a stronger visage. The benignity of an Archbishop, the aspect of an elder statesman, formidable in utterance and style – the Henry James whom the younger men now coming up around him would address as *cher maître*, *maestro* – master. And daily now, in the brightening summer that heralded the twentieth century, *The Ambassadors* took its shape in the Garden Room of Lamb House.

BOOK THREE
THE ILLUSION OF FREEDOM
1900–1904

The artist is present in every page of every book
from which he sought so assiduously to eliminate himself.

HENRY JAMES

Part One

Notes on Novelists

55

Vie de Province

I

ON afternoons in the late autumn and early winter, when the roads were sufficiently dry, the clean-shaven master of Lamb House would descend from his hilltop into the High Street. He wrapped himself in a heavy coat. Sometimes he wore a small peaked cap; sometimes a felt hat. There was invariably a touch of colour – in his knotted thick cravat, or, if he unbuttoned his coat, in a show of orange or blue waistcoat. He walked massively, carrying one of his many sticks. Behind him, waddling slowly as if he possessed some of his master's authority, was one of James's dogs, say Maximilian, his dachshund, successor to the long-lived Tosca, of the De Vere Gardens time. When James walked alone, he walked solemnly, unsmiling and grave, greeting old and young alike with deliberate courtesy. Even when he paused and pondered he seemed remote and absent-minded; yet his searching eyes looked everywhere. Sometimes his typist walked with him – there would be three of them and two would keep diaries. Sometimes he was accompanied by a guest. He also had walking companions among his fellow-residents in the ancient port. At the turn of the century, he had for company a former Indian colonial servant, 'whose face I suit and whose reminiscences I invite'. Later there would be A. C. Bradley, Sydney Waterlow, Fanny Prothero, a Mr Tayleure, and others. On occasion James walked to Playden, where he had lived briefly in 1896 and had written The Spoils of Poynton; or along the sea by Camber, past the golf course and the grazing sheep; or he would take the road to picturesque and desolate Winchelsea. Walking across the marshes, he looked on melancholy relics of the past. 'Rye dares to be cheerful,' he remarked, 'Winchelsea has the courage of its desolation.' He still bicycled; on some days he would sweep off to more distant towns, dressed in knicker-bockers and an 'exiguous jacket' of black and white stripes (as David Garnett would remember out of a boyhood glimpse), with the peaked cap which made James seem broader than he was. The walker in the

Alps, the rider on horseback in the Campagna, was now a cyclist on the salt flats of the Cinque Ports.

Passers by going to Rye's church and the Ypres tower on the hill-top, near Lamb House, could hear on any morning after 10 a.m. through the bow windows of the garden room the slow voice speaking to the answering typewriter. James, looking out to the church, saw the burghers 'go in to their righteousness and come out to their dinners'. As owner of Lamb House he had 'an immemorial pew' in the church 'which I have never been in but once'. Still, it made him feel a part of the town. From the first he spoke of himself as if he were a personage in one of Balzac's *scènes de la vie de province*. 'I am learning the lesson,' he wrote to Grace Norton,

that in a small country town where local society is *nil*, fate seems to make the matter as broad as it's long by arranging compensations on strictly domestic lines. In other words, whereas in London the people you know are everywhere, in the country they are all in your own house! This is very ingenious of fate: it is good for everything except reading, writing, arithmetic and the higher branches of solitude.

He listed some of his acquaintances: John Symonds Vidler and his wife Caroline, of Mountsfield, who would remain friendly during all of James's days in Rye; old little Mrs Davies, 'straight out of *Cranford*', whom he found one Christmas day stranded on the road, her conveyance having lost, 'under Christmas influence, *both* its back wheels'. He brought her back to town 'in the frosty moonlight and under her little archaically-sculptured wooden door-canopy of the last century, to the embrace of a rosy maid-servant almost as fluttered as herself and quite as much out of *Cranford*'. Or he dined with the Brookfields of Leasam, Colonel Brookfield being Member of Parliament for East Sussex and elder of the two sons of Thackeray's Mrs Brookfield. As it happened the newer Mrs Brookfield was an American, 'all that there is most of, from Buffalo, N.Y.'

2

Within his first year and a half – that is from mid-1898 to 1900 – James lived himself into the provincial life of Rye. He quickly became a local 'fixture'. The shopkeepers knew him; the local gentry dined him; with characteristic English respect for privacy, he was registered by many of the townsfolk simply as an odd literary gentleman of great courtliness, who walked the roads or bicycled, and who often met his guests at the Rye station himself, accompanied by his gardener wheeling a barrow or cart for the luggage. His was a well-organized establishment; with the Smiths, his husband-and-wife cook and butler, a housemaid, and a houseboy, and George Gammon, the gardener, he was perhaps less servanted than most gentlefolk of the time living in the town's principal houses. The town was more interested in golf than in literature. Neither James nor his guests aroused curiosity; and there was little gossip about them in the town, but there was understandable local pride at having a celebrity in Lamb House. There is only one recorded invasion of James's privacy early in his stay at Rye, and this was done with decorum and tact. In June 1900 Lord and Lady Wolseley came over from their nearby country home at Glynde to visit their novelist-friend. Lady Wolseley, a connoisseur of antiques, had helped James buy pieces of furniture for his house. The word got round quickly that the great soldier was in Rye; moreover, his afternoon's visit coincided with the news of the occupation of Pretoria. A wave of patriotic emotion seized the town, and an informal delegation of officials and leading citizens knocked at the canopied door and asked permission to pay respects to the victor of the Ashantee, who, earlier in the century, had gone to the relief of General Gordon. 'Rye rather lacked history,' Henry wrote to Lady Wolseley afterwards, 'now she *has* it. You didn't leave me where you found me. I am inches and inches higher. I believe I could really do anything with the place.'

This is the only recorded moment when national grandeur touched modest Lamb House. Otherwise the establishment and its tenant blended into the town. Had James been a British citizen he might have been asked to be Rye's mayor, as E. F. Benson was in later days, for Lamb House had been the home of mayors for more than a century, mainly members of the Lamb family. James preferred in any event to be passively civic. He was, however, on good terms with local organizations and generous to local charities. And when the local clergy asked him for favours, he was only too willing to help – for he was on excellent terms in particular with 'a dear little all but Catholic Irish curate'. During the summer of 1900 he billeted a young curate when the Bishop of Chichester came to Rye for certain ordinations. To Lady Wolseley again James wrote that the priest fasted 'on fish, eggs, vegetables, tarts, claret, cigarette, coffee and liqueurs', which the generous Lamb House larder and cellar provided. James was happy to be hospitable. But the problem of finding himself 'face to face with him, at meals', was trying. Remembering his visit to the Wolseleys in Ireland five years earlier, he remarked he would on the whole have been happier to billet a soldier.

These small moments of rural life were sufficiently limited. 'The days depart and pass, laden somehow like processional camels – across the desert of one's solitude.' He felt severed from his old life – 'the blessed Kensington fields'. He had originally planned to live in Rye only half the year; but he had sublet his De Vere Gardens flat and would have to use clubs and hotels in the city. A mild winter led him to remain in Lamb House through 1898-9; but during his second winter in the country, he found himself pining for London lamplight and the sound of its buses. There came to him in twilight vision the colours of the green and red and yellow jars in the chemists' windows and the chiaroscuro of the afternoons. To mitigate his isolation, he constantly urged his friends to come to him; and sometimes they did. 'The youth of the lyrist never was so lonely as the old age of the proser,' he wrote to W. Morton Fullerton. 'I am so alone here at present ... and so nose to nose with the dark, wet country winter, and other still gloomier and embracing conditions, that the presence of a valued friend would be a luxury almost past belief.' And to Howard Sturgis, 'I am lonely and lean and comfortless.' To Edmund Gosse he spoke of going up to London late in 1900 for a real go at town life – 'I shall have been confined to this hamlet for two and a half years on end – save for three or four months abroad. You *must*, all, take me to Madame Tussaud's.' To Mrs W. K. Clifford, one of his oldest and most cherished London friends, he wrote, in May 1900,

But can't you, couldn't you, dearest Lucy Clifford, come down and see me some day next month, some pretty, summery, *possible* day as you did two years ago, and tell me everything that's going and let me drive you to Winchelsea, after feeding and tea-ing and blessing you? Think of it – do, *do*. I will make everything of a comfortable for you! Think of it, plot for it – and let me hear of it. It seems to me as if otherwise I mightn't see you for many a month.

And again, writing of his domestic comforts, 'it would be so infinitely nicer to be sitting by your fire and tasting your charity – and your Benedictine'.

He had made his peace with solitude long ago. But there was an important difference between solitude and loneliness. He had always known how to be alone; he had sought and invited solitude. But he also had always known how to avoid – urban dweller that he was – a feeling of loneliness. The cities, and London in particular, provided people, theatres, tea-talk, the pleasant privacy or gregariousness of his clubs, as he wished. Now in Rye he suffered 'for want of social, domestic, intellectual air'. And yet he was tied to Lamb House even in the winter, because he was tied to his work : his typewriter was not easily movable – the day of the 'portable' was yet to come – and his way of work had changed from his old roving ease. A trip to London meant divorce from his work; his writing was as necessary to him as the social, domestic, intellectual air of which he spoke; indeed it was more than necessary, for he was trying to work off his book-contracts and pay for his house. He had agreed to write three novels, a biography, certain essays, and every now and again he felt moved to write a tale. These were the conflicts of his new 'exile', an intermittent debate between the life of Rye and the life of London. Even after he had created a work-place for himself in the metropolis, as he did within the coming months, he would spend lonely weeks in inclement weather in the sea-town. To an outsider it might have seemed that Rye had been for so urban a man a grave mistake; its simplified life could not meet the needs of so complex a being. On the other hand, the world owes to the long periods of his encaged state, some of his finest writings. Work was his principal refuge and no writer – even the driven Balzac, the prodigiously diligent Walter Scott – applied himself more seriously and assiduously to his craft. The dictation in the morning; the recuperative walk in the afternoon when possible; the re-reading and revision of what had been dictated; the preparation for the next morning's work; the planning of new stories; the writing of scenarios; the long evenings of thought and toil before he was ready to meet his typist once more for renewed endeavour. Out of the hours of Rye's solitude, there took shape and were written within four years, the three last novels, the summit of his creation. It was as if his years of ceaseless wandering and dwelling in cities had prepared him for this final communion with himself, a re-forging out of memory and loneliness of his visions of the civilization absorbed and studied during forty years of cosmopolitan life. In the process he would ask himself what he had really known of life. How much had he *lived*? He had not 'lived' in the common meaning of that word : he had known neither the obsessive passion of a Byron nor the romantic dedication of a Flaubert; he had sought no distant exotic lands, nor indiscriminate sex, the practices of his French con-frères. He had always been quiet, withdrawn, pensive, observant, contemplative: he had fled the society of passionate women. As he put it of Lambert Strether, his hero in *The Ambassadors*, who in so many ways resembled him: 'It was nothing new to him ... that a man might have – at all events such a man as *he* was – an amount of experience out of any proportion to his adventures.' He had put this in another way in his essay on the art of fiction long before, when he had challenged Walter Besant's assertion that young women could not write about soldiers and military life.

The young lady living in a village has only to be a damsel upon whom nothing is lost to make it quite unfair (as it seems to me) to declare to her that she shall have nothing to say about the military. Greater miracles have been seen than that, imagination assisting, she should speak of the truth about some of these gentlemen.

So now, living like his young lady, in what was little more than a village, Henry James could allow his imagination to bring together the essences of the world that he had known.

In the end, after long trial and much work, Rye would cease to be possible as a continual abode. He would say to a friend, 'Little Rye – poor little Rye – I find life there intolerable – yes, Rye has had to be deserted – no, not *permanently* deserted – heaven forbid! – but I have had to make a nest – a perch for myself in London, which in-volves the desertion of Rye for the winter – only temporarily, *hibernetically* speaking.'

3

This was spoken at the end of the Edwardian decade when James had again established an apartment in London. But at the threshold of the decade he found himself a metropolitan perch which served him well and gave him a place for temporary work. On the leasing of Lamb House, he had taken the precaution of putting his name down for a room at the Reform Club. In the autumn of 1900 the vacancy conveniently occurred. He had 'a town-cradle' for his declining years. He refurbished the room, installed his own bed, new blinds, new curtains. He kept enough things in town so that he could come up from Rye with minimal luggage. The room was located high up over Carlton House Terrace: it looked over embassies and lordly houses. 'Nothing could be more *chic*,' he proclaimed. It made him feel less of an outsider. Nevertheless, movement between Rye and London consumed time; and once in London he was divorced from the continuity of his work, even though at the Reform he also installed a typewriter and was able to dictate according to habit. He tended, however, to loiter and ramble and seek mild sociabilities. The general effect of going up to town at first was to make him want his work desk in Rye; and the effect of Rye was to make him pine for London. The city was no longer wholly possible. But neither was the country.

In the better season of the year he forgot the gloom and rustication. Early in his life at Lamb House he set about improving his garden. He had never been a gardener; he would not become one now, any more than he could learn to use his typewriter or ever dreamed of owning, let alone driving, one of the new cars that would soon be depositing visitors at his door. He had, however, committed himself to the upkeep of the Lamb House garden; with his purchase of the house he felt even more strongly that he wanted as much vernal beauty as possible in the private acre outside the french doors of his front parlour and his dining-room. For twenty-two shillings a week he obtained the services of his gardener. It was up to James, however, to provide ideas, and as he looked at the available space he felt himself 'densely ignorant'. He barely knew a dahlia from a mignonette. To Miss Muir Mackenzie, whom he had met once at Winchelsea, he turned for expert advice; and his letters to her tell of his horticultural progress. In his 'poor little tuppenny Rye', his garden looked sad and shiftless. He began by explaining that his temptation was to 'go in for a lawn, which requires mere brute force – no intellect'. Miss Mackenzie was a woman of knowledge and tact; presently she was suggesting that certain kinds of tobacco leaves might be decorative; and then some crocuses at strategic spots in the lawn, for a touch of purple at the right season. James found himself ordering bulbs and roses, and George Gammon industriously carried out his and Miss Mackenzie's designs. James fell into the spirit of the endeavour: his missives went forth addressed to Miss Mackenzie as the 'Hereditary Grand Governess of the Garden' with apologies for offering 'so shabby a government'. He feared that he might become too fascinated. Would the garden become a trap for his hours (which were full) and for his purse (which was empty)? As fuchsias and geraniums were planted, he exclaimed, 'Your touch is magical, your influence infinite,' and 'what a bliss, what a daily excitement, all summer, to see it grow by leaps and bounds' – these were the tobacco leaves [*nicotiana*]. 'We are painfully preparing to become bulbous and particoloured.' Into the lawn went one hundred crocuses, while 'Our Lady of Tobacco' was addressed in letters filled with images of fertility. The novelist sported his growing knowledge in a kittenish way. 'Dear Grand Governess, dear Friend Florist,' he saluted her, and she saluted him back 'Dear Distinguished Author'. In reply he signed himself 'Henry James D.A.' The time would come when his flowers would win prizes in the local flower show. The fig tree kept him in figs, although his grapes left something to be desired; a small kitchen garden provided for his table. The domestic side of Rye had its endearing side.

56

A Letter to Rhoda

'THIS dreadful gruesome New Year, so monstrously numbered,' Henry James wrote on 1 January 1900 to Rhoda Broughton, his fellow-novelist whom he had known for almost a quarter of a century. His ailing brother William, his sister-in-law, his young niece Peggy, were staying at this moment in Lamb House, yet he felt alone – and the last year of the old century had dawned. Miss Broughton was 60; Henry was 57. They had met long ago, during the years of James's conquest of London, at Lord Houghton's, at dinner parties in the literary and social world, where Miss Broughton's sharp tongue and Mr James's wit were prized. Miss Broughton's tongue was sharper than ever, her legend longer. She had found fame as a writer of fiction deemed 'bold' by the Victorians, always about the palpitating young woman who discovers love and defies convention. Her three-deckers were staples of the lending libraries. She quipped that she had begun by being compared with Zola and was ending her career as Charlotte Yonge. In truth she was neither a Zola, nor a Miss Yonge, but simply Rhoda Broughton, a solid British integrity who had known life in Oxford in the days of Pater and Mark Pattison (and had put the much-novelized Pattison and his young wife into a

novel). She had written a widely-read series of fictions with picturesque titles – *Cometh Up as a Flower*, or *Red as a Rose is She*. James
had been sharp about one of her novels in the *Nation* before he met
her. 'A strongly-seasoned literary article,' he had described *Joan* in
1876, 'puerility and nastiness, inanity and vulgarity'. Miss Broughton's 'insidiousness is like the gambols of an elephant ... What
immaturity and crudity of art, what coarseness of sentiment and
vacuity of thought.' Then a year later he met her – and he never
reviewed her again. Having encountered the original, he apparently
had no need for her projection in print. Something in her upturned
nose, her unconcealed asperity, her verbal vitality appealed to
James: she was a reincarnated Mrs Procter, a younger version of old
Mrs Duncan Stewart, the gruff maternal figures of his prime whose
talk he had liked and whose occasional cruel sayings he seemed to
prefer to anything more gentle and feminine. Miss Broughton was
'an old friend ... before whom I even now scarce cease to tremble',
he could write in 1897. 'We are excellent friends, but I really don't
know whether I like her books or not; it is so long since I read one.
She is not in the least a person to whom you have to pay that tribute.'

He knew enough about her love-entangled histories in which
adolescent anguish seemed as eternally fresh as adolescent anger
seemed fresh in Miss Rhoda. She was, moreover, a slight yet
cherished link with Miss Woolson. One evening during his long stay
on Bellosguardo in 1887, when he and Fenimore occupied apartments
in the same villa, Rhoda had climbed the steep hill to dine with them.
She alone of all James's London friends had met his long-dead companion. In 1897 James wrote to Francis Boott that Miss Broughton
was 'too big a subject for the passing phrase, as to which I see, by
the way, that you have an inkling in speaking of your "escape" from
that Bellosguardo dinner that Miss Woolson commemorated to you'.

'That very mature child of nature, my old friend Rhoda Broughton,' James said of her at the end of the century. 'Poor dear heroic
Rhoda,' he was saying as late as 1912, and even later – in the last
year of his life – he spoke of her as delivering 'her appreciations and
discriminations as straight from the shoulder as ever'. In the years
when she had lived at Richmond, he would take the Thames journey
to walk with her in the park; or he summoned her to London to a
play. She would come, refusing to be his guest and belligerently paying for her stall. Above all she seemed to be a figure to whom he
could turn, now that other and older ladies were gone, to pour out

epistolary melancholy and gallantries at decisive moments, as on this occasion when the date on the calendar was changing, and James felt himself lonely, isolated, moving into an unpredictable age.

On this date he found himself turning back

to the warm and coloured past and away from the big black avenue that gapes in front of us. So turning, I find myself, not wholly without trepidation, yet also with a generous confidence, face to face with your distinguished figure – which please don't consider me, rude rustic and benighted alien as I've become, unworthy to greet. The country has swallowed me up, for the time, as you foretold me that it would, but I haven't quite burnt my ships behind me, and I'm counting the months till I can resume possession, for at least half the year in future, of my London habitation.

Then his pen suddenly ceased its ritualized gestures, and gave way to 'I'm so homesick for the blessed Kensington fields that I gloat over the prospect of treading them, finally afresh'. More candour of feeling followed: 'Meanwhile, I've felt remote and unfriended and have lacked courage to write to you almost only (as it might look) to say: "See – from the way I keep it up – how I get on without you!" I get on without you very badly – and worse and worse the *more* I keep it up.'

James wanted her to know 'how poor a business I find it to be so deprived of your society'. He gave her his 'fervent wishes for the dim twelvemonth to come'. With the Boer War raging, the year looked to him 'full of goblins, to be deprecated by prayer and sacrifice – and my incense rises for your immunity, of every kind, not less than for my own ... Think of me, please, meanwhile, as yours, dear Rhoda Broughton, always and always Henry James.'

In the coming years this kind of letter to Rhoda would be repeated again and again. He saluted the hearty and rough woman, almost as if she were some deity to be appeased, some Muse, whose wholesome anger and affection, in moments of despair and loneliness, made his life bearable. 'Our dear Rhoda – our gallant and intrepid Rhoda' she would remain to the end.

57

An Innocent Abroad

IN March of 1900, after almost two years of continual residence in Lamb House – broken only by his Italian trip of 1899 – James had descended on London for a brief holiday. He wrote amusingly of experiencing 'an extraordinary sense of dissipation'. He was surprised to be greeted by friends and acquaintances 'almost as if I had returned from African or Asian exile'. He liked to feel the pavement under foot again; he window-shopped; he wandered into back streets; he browsed in the book shops; he dined out every night. He lunched with Henry White, first secretary of the American embassy, who was entertaining Brooks Adams. Henry Adams's brother was 're-freshingly fundamental and universal – most cosmic and interesting'. He went to see Sargent's large new painting of the Wyndham sisters. The sisters were seated on a sofa, with Watts's portrait of their mother in the background. It was 'vast and dazzling'; there was something about it that reminded James of the feeling he had had in a music-hall or at a fair when a woman was shot out of the mouth of a cannon – its force made him feel 'weak and foolish'. With Sargent he went to call in Tite Street on Edwin Austin Abbey, working on one of his large Shakespearian paintings, 'diabolically clever and effective, with success perched on every banner. I came away biting my thumb, of course, and with my ears burning with the sense of how it's not the age of my dim trade.'

His trade was almost at a standstill. Publishers shook their heads sadly and thinned their lists; the effects of the war were being felt everywhere. London was filled with mourners. Behind the show of patriotism and Empire, James felt the depression. One day he accompanied an army surgeon to watch him check the physical fitness of a batch of recruits. On another day his 13-year-old niece Peggy, with three of her playmates, came to the city from Harrow, and James gave them lunch and took a box at the 'Biograph' to show them the primitive movies of the war. Peggy, true to her father's anti-Imperialism, was pro-Boer. She seemed surprised that her uncle wasn't. His identification with England had been long; he was, however, sufficiently American to decry 'the fetish-worship of the

Queen'. It had 'reached an abasement that makes one wonder if one dreams'. But then Victoria was almost as old as her century.

The novelty of London wore off quickly. Even before James left, he looked forward to 'little restful, red-roofed uncomplicated Rye'. At the end of seventeen days he was back in Lamb House with Jonathan Sturges once more as his guest. However, Rye struck him as 'slightly grim and nude'. So it would be, between London and Rye, during all the Edwardian years.

I

Having broken his spell of absence, James made a second descent on London in mid-May, leaving a Rye in which there had been a dazzling outbreak of spring, after the bleak winter. Tulips and hyacinths, primroses and daffodils, were in bloom; his lawn was 'daisied like a Botticelli picture'. In the interval between his visits he had removed his beard. Writing about his changed appearance he remarked to a correspondent 'still, it will be always I'. Nevertheless it seemed a new 'I' that descended from the train at Charing Cross and now brought his clean-shaven countenance into the familiar drawing-rooms of Mayfair. On a late afternoon James encountered before one of London's tea-hour fires, the grizzled, white-maned Samuel Langhorne Clemens, most famous of America's 'innocents' abroad – rosy as a babe, clear-eyed, clad as always in white and full of rage at the 'damned human race'.

James had gone to call on a friend of his youth, Helena De Kay. The De Kays had been Newport neighbours. Helena was the wife of Richard Watson Gilder, editor of the Century, and a sister of James's old Venetian friend Mrs Bronson. She had a special claim on James's affections: she had been a close friend of Minny Temple. James found himself in a familiar American circle. Mark Twain, moreover, was not new to James; their paths had crossed before.

They faced each other now as changed men. James was bland and cosmopolitan before the brilliant aggressiveness of Clemens. Both were in late middle life, both had passed through long battles with private demons. The nineties had been as hard on the world-seeking prosperous Mark Twain as on the privacy-seeking Henry James. James's clean-shaven face was symbolic of his recovery and awareness of the approaching century. Mark Twain was announcing that 'the twentieth century is a stranger to me'.

The two writers had known each other for years in the way of celebrities who meet at public dinners or in great houses. They had shared the devotion and loyalty of their friend, William Dean Howells – Mark Twain, much more than James, because he was more in America. Twenty years before, in 1879, during the days of James's constant dining out, he had seen Mark Twain a number of times in various London mansions, 'a most excellent pleasant fellow, what they call here very "quaint". Quaint he is! And his two ladies charming!' James and Clemens had been then at the height of their first fame: the one had been writing *A Tramp Abroad*; the other, a great social success of two seasons in London, author of *Daisy Miller*.

They met again – in 1897 – when James was teaching himself to dictate directly to the typewriter. Mark Twain wrote to Howells at the time, 'I was amused when I was in London last fall, to have James tell me that he had taken to dictating all his fiction, because he had heard that I always dictated. He makes it go, but if there could be anything worse for me than a typewriter, it would be a human typewriter.' Mark loved the human race or he would not have had so much fault to find with it; and Henry could not talk to a machine that did not have a human being beside it. A few months before their 1897 meeting Mark Twain, in his preoccupation with the story of Joan of Arc (which had led to his writing a book about her), had told a friend that 'if a master – say Henry James – should translate it [a certain French book about Joan] I think it would live for ever'. To Mark Twain, to Howells, to a newcomer in letters like Conrad, James was now indeed 'master'; he had the largeness of the formidable craftsman who speaks also as an oracle.

2

Mark Twain and Henry James were not by nature destined ever to be intimate; there was a newspaperish side to the humorist, the 'lion' side, and the roar of publicity and a love of broad effects, from which James shrank. 'Temperament' divided them, as it would James and his fellow-novelists in England. Mark Twain was out-going, expansive, capable of great exuberance. James was inward-turned, ruminative, secretive. No two American geniuses were more dissimilar, save in their sense of humour; this in James was highly condensed, epigrammatic, and also private, whereas in Mark Twain it was broad, visceral, and public. Both were lovers of the truth; both critical of their fellow-Americans. Mark Twain had gratified his countrymen by criticizing Europe in *Innocents Abroad*. James had shocked them by making himself a critical analyst of American innocence. Mark Twain had decried the feudal ages, the Roman barbarians, the cant of romance, the violence and brutality of the European centuries. James had discerned the eerie brutality and violence behind the façade of civilization. Nevertheless he had the nineteenth century's belief in 'progress'; he could accept the forms and rituals, the myths and usages men had created in order to be less barbaric. The two writers had great respect for each other, even though Mark Twain had once said he would rather 'be damned to John Bunyan's heaven' than read *The Bostonians*. James, reading Mark Twain's *Life on the Mississippi*, had found in it the presence of 'sublimity'.

Of the particular encounter in London in early 1900 during James's call on Helena Gilder, we know little more than about the other encounters. It was a casual meeting. Mark Twain had been living abroad – Switzerland, France, Austria, Sweden, England, with brief trips to the United States. At this moment he was in a flat in Knightsbridge. He was full of dreams and of rage; he sympathized with the British in the Boer War 'but my heart and such rags of morals as I have are with the Boer'. To Henry James he seems to have talked largely of his symptoms, probably coming to them through Henry's telling him that his brother William had returned to Nauheim for another 'cure'. Mark Twain, who had invested in quack medicines and elixirs as he invested in printing and machinery, was at this phase all for osteopathy. He had recently been to Henrick Kellgren's health establishment in Sweden. Kellgren could cure anything, Mark said. He told Henry he had been in correspondence with William and had offered him medical advice. He also discoursed on 'albumen'. He said he would put William James on to it. The talk was rather confused. When Mark Twain spoke of Kellgren, Henry thought he was referring to Lord Kelvin. 'Why Sweden?' he asked of William's wife, not having apparently related the osteopath to that country. As James put it to Alice, he had met Mark who had given him 'a muddled and confused glimpse of Lord Kelvin, Albumen, Sweden and half a dozen other things on which I was prevented from afterwards bringing him to book'. William James knew Mark Twain more intimately than his brother; the philosopher had met the creator of Huck Finn in Florence, during the winter of 1892. 'A fine, soft-fibred little fellow with the perversest twang and drawl, but very human and good,' William had said. He called him also 'a dear little genius'.

Mark Twain was eight years older than Henry; and his finest work was done. Henry's greatest work was about to be written. In the future they would be archetypal figures in the history of American innocence. Indeed James was now embarked on a novel that would confront America and Europe, provincialism and cosmopolitanism, innocence and experience. Lambert Strether would hardly be a Mark Twain; he would be much closer to Mark's and Henry's friend, Howells, and even to Henry himself – the Henry who listened confusedly to Mark's hypochondriacal babble. But a little touch of this babble would be imported into *The Ambassadors* in the character of the dyspeptic Waymarsh. This hypothesis gains some credence when we discover, in James's original plan for the novel, that the character was first named Way*mark*. The 'sacred rage' of Waymarsh-Waymark would have in it a touch of Mark Twain's 'sacred rage'.

58

A Natural Peculiarity

FORD MADOX HUEFFER, a descendant of peripheral pre-Raphaelites, whose father was a German musicologist enamoured of Wagner and Schopenhauer, had called on Henry James during the summer of 1896 when the novelist first discovered Rye. James had just moved into the Vicarage and Hueffer – who would later be known as Ford Madox Ford – came to lunch one September day with an introduction from Henry's friend, Mrs W. K. Clifford. James received the tall, lean, blond, young man, then 23, with his customary civility. He chatted with him about his relatives – his grandfather on the English side was Ford Madox Brown, a pre-Raphaelite painter – and interrogated him about his literary ambitions. By Hueffer's testimony, Smith, the red-nosed butler, served an efficient meal while markedly tipsy. James sent the young man away with perhaps less than his usual avuncular tenderness for aspirants to literature. Certainly the friendliness is absent in the extant records. And there was no immediate invitation to return.

Hueffer himself only vaguely remembered the Old Vicarage. In his vast recollections a quarter of a century later he recorded a first meeting with the clean-shaven James in Rye, where he had gone with Conrad – but that was in the era of the motor-car. Later he recalled the bearded James of 1896 and the red-nosed alcoholic Smith. His memories of this and other meetings are scrambled. They show proof of that 'copious carelessness of reminiscence' which H. G. Wells described. Hueffer readily confessed to 'a large carelessness', insisting, however, that he was not reporting literal fact. He was, he explained, 'an impressionist'. His impressions, however, were 'absolute'. By this formula, late in life, he composed elaborate portraits which were a strange amalgam of half-truths, vague recollections, anecdotes garnered from reading, and other persons' memories. He could build an entire essay on his having offered Turgenev a chair in his grandfather's studio when he was eight years old. He had fugitive memories of Lamb House: he remembered its colour as grey, and said it was built of stone, forgetting that its characteristic russet was derived from weathered brick. Documents which have survived confirm that he was a literary Munchausen. The famous Baron told tall tales, robust and Rabelaisian. Hueffer contented himself with literary chit-chat, the manufacture of small pastiches out of a blurred imagination. He claimed, for instance, to have been the 'original' of Merton Densher in *The Wings of the Dove*, and this was the slightest of the many identities he constantly borrowed to place himself in a favourable relation to great men. H. G. Wells, who like others saw the humour and the nonsense of Hueffer, called this 'his great system of assumed *personas* and dramatized selves'. Hueffer's tendency to change his own name was symptomatic of a lifelong quest for an identity. He seems not to have been certain at first whether he should make much of his severe German father or pose as his mother's son and an English gentleman. He was actually baptized Ford Hermann Hueffer, but on becoming a Catholic at 18 – still another change of identity – he took two more names, Joseph and Leopold. Then, as if searching for a makeweight for the German nomenclature, he adopted his mother's name of Madox. During another phase, he claimed he was Baron Hueffer von Aschendorf. The final shift to Ford Madox Ford, which wholly eliminated his father, occurred after the First World War when he had for several years worn the guise of 'the good soldier' and wanted to forget his German antecedents. Perhaps a more compelling reason for the change was to avoid a legal struggle with his wife; he was by then living with Stella Bowen. Under this name, the writings of Henry James aiding, he made his long friendship with 'the Master' the very centre of his myth through four volumes of anecdotal self-inflating but genial inventions.

The young man James met in 1896 was not yet the formed myth-maker of the later decades. He was uncertain, confused, romantic and good-naturedly poetic. Whether the American novelist recognized that he had invented Hueffer long before he met him, it would be hard to say. In the early 1880s James had dined in a London house where a lively individual provided 'the woven wonders of a summer holiday, the exploits of a salamander, among Mediterranean isles', and other pleasing tall tales. He wrote an artful tale simply titled *The Liar*, about a Colonel Capadose, who 'lies about the time of day, about the name of his hatter'. It is quite disinterested. He is not in the least a scoundrel, 'there's no harm in him and no bad intention; he doesn't steal nor cheat nor gamble nor drink; he's very kind – he sticks to his wife, is fond of his children. He simply can't give you a straight answer.' This description fitted Hueffer with the exception that ultimately he did not stick to his wife. He was inclined, like James's Capadose, to a mixture of the correct and the extravagant; he had good manners and yet could tell stories in bad taste. Also like Colonel Capadose, he inspired affection. His 'natural peculiarity' was forgiven by many devoted friends because it testified to an overflow of life and genial spirits. Hueffer would be kind and generous to many young writers; and from James and Conrad he borrowed a high seriousness about the art of fiction.

Joseph Conrad, who would collaborate with Hueffer, may have intuitively grasped the protean essence of his friend, for in *Heart of Darkness*, written early in their acquaintance, there is a strange, mysterious character, a man dressed in motley who carries – in the midst of the jungle – a book on navigation. This man, wearing a coat of many colours, a kind of patchwork European, with the wrong book to guide him, seems a premonition of the composite Ford Madox Hueffer, with 'little blue eyes that were perfectly round' and an abiding loyalty to Kurtz, the figure at the 'heart of darkness'. 'Brother sailor ... honour ... pleasure ... delight ... introduce myself . . Russian ... son of an archpriest ... Government of Tambov ... What? Tobacco! English tobacco; the excellent

English tobacco! Now that's brotherly. Smoke? Where's a sailor that does not smoke?' Hueffer, in later years, leaning on grand pianos in the drawing-rooms of England and America, talked in this way. His passages in his memoirs about Henry James have the same kind of discontinuity.

2

It would be a large and ungrateful task to unravel Hueffer's James-ian tales.* A slender thread of fact informs some of them; others were culled from his reading of James's *Partial Portraits* or *Notes on Novelists*, and became a kind of free rewrite of James's own cautious reminiscence of some of the French novelists he had known. They form a part of the false 'image' of Henry James at Rye, but have been adopted by so many as authentic that some characterization of them seems inevitable. The best-known Huef-ferian tale is his claim that James hated Flaubert because the French writer received him one day wearing a dressing-gown. James's actual report on Flaubert's dress is to be found in his late essay on the French writer and it is wholly complimentary. He tells us the French master wore 'up to any hour of the afternoon that long, colloquial dressing-gown, with trousers to match, which one has always associated with literature in France – the uniform really of freedom of talk'. James here was thinking of the ways in which French writers are often described *en pantoufles*. Hueffer joined to his anecdote something he had read in the Goncourt journals. This was that Flaubert had once severely admonished an American, whose initial was given as H. That the H. turned out to be not Henry but Harisse mattered very little. In the repertoire of Hueffer, James had been scolded by Flaubert, and Flaubert had had the indecency to welcome him in a bath-robe. Such is the small talk of Huefferian legend.

Curiously enough, Hueffer read James's critical account of Mau-passant and decided that the Master liked him very much. To be sure, said Hueffer, James had been upset when he arrived at Mau-passant's for lunch and found a naked *femme du monde* seated at table wearing a mask. In Hueffer's myth-making, one gathers the naked Beardsley lady disturbed James less than Flaubert's dressing-

* Simon Nowell-Smith long ago analysed their improvised character in his *Legend of the Master* (1948).

gown. Reading of James's constant correspondence with Mrs Humphry Ward about how novels should be written, Hueffer said James always corrected that lady's manuscripts. Ford probably got this from Violet Hunt who noted in her diary that James complained to her that Mrs Ward occasionally sent him typescripts 'for his corrections'. He pictured James in Rye as practising black magic – or so he said the townsfolk believed. He told how a murderer once confessed his crime to James. He also made James out to have been a financial supporter of the *Yellow Book*; and said *Guy Domville* was booed because the audience did not like to pay for its programmes. A glimpse of the crippled Jonathan Sturges in Lamb House yielded the following reminiscence:

I have attended at conversations between him and a queer tiny being who lay as if crumpled up on the stately sofa in James's magnificent panelled room in Lamb House – conversations that made the tall wax candles seem to me to waver in their sockets and the skin of my forehead and hands to prickle with sweat. I am in these things rather squeamish ... They occurred as part of the necessary pursuit of that knowledge that permitted James to give his reader the 'sense of evil' ... And I dare say they freed him from the almost universal proneness of Anglo-Saxon writers to indulge in their works in a continually intrusive fumbling in placket-holes as Sterne called it, or in the lugubrious occupation of composing libidinous limericks.

One of his most charming inventions was that James telegraphed Wanamaker's to have apple butter and pumpkin pie sent to the dying Stephen Crane. In this way James was given legendary form by Hueffer's shaky ego. He described James as 'the most masterful man I have ever met', and this probably was true. To which he added, with equal truth, that 'I do not think that, till the end of his days, he regarded me as a serious writer'. How this accorded with James's consulting Hueffer, as the latter claimed, 'about his most intimate practical affairs', it is difficult to see. In one of his essays Hueffer, after this kind of self-depreciation, finally remarked, 'I think I will, after reflection, lay claim to a very considerable degree of intimacy.' He did make this claim; and it remains highly at variance with the available testimony. James's secretary recorded that James once made her jump a ditch in order to avoid an encounter with Hueffer on the Winchelsea road; on another occasion he quickly pulled her behind a tree, till Hueffer had walked by. There is also the testimony of a Rye neighbour, a writer, Archibald Marshall. In his memoirs he relates 'how very coldly Hueffer's name was received'. There had been some question of an invitation that would 'bring that young man down upon me again' and James exclaimed to Marshall, 'I said to myself, No! and again No!'

3

There was a certain pathos in Hueffer's need to stand in the good graces of the Master, and his strange swagger and boast of later years. On one occasion he speculated that James 'must have liked' him and Hueffer gave as the reason that this was because he was 'a strong silent man of affairs'. Hueffer boasted that James described him to Conrad as *votre ami, le jeune homme modeste.* If James said this there may have been a certain characteristic irony in the remark. Modesty was not one of Hueffer's outstanding qualities. His decision that James had converted him into the passive Merton Densher was based largely on Densher's being 'longish, leanish, fairish'. From the few letters of James to Hueffer that survive we know that the latter did write to James about *The Wings of the Dove.* In another letter James offered qualified praise for *Poems for Pictures* which Hueffer had sent him. James thanked him for his 'so curious and interesting book of verses'. He found some of them 'terribly natural and true and "right", drawn from the real wretchedness of things. The poetry of the cold and the damp and the mud and the nearness to earth – this is a chord you touch in a way that makes me wonder if there isn't still more for you to get from it.' And he ended this letter, one of his less impersonal missives to Hueffer, by asking him to stop by, if he happened to pass his way.

Flowing into Hueffer's mythology of James was the admiration of Conrad, and the worship of Hueffer's wife Elsie, and of her Garnett friends, especially that of Olivia Rayne Garnett, who wrote novels and had a curious 'fixation' on the American novelist. Two years before she ever set eyes on James, Olivia Garnett recorded in her diary: 'I had a dream this morning: Henry James looked up at me from writing and said smiling: "You know, life isn't ONLY reality, it's a small part of a great whole." I believed him and awoke.' Later we find her working on a story 'of what it would be like to love and be loved by Henry James'. Finally there are glimpses of the Master in an entry of November 1901. Olivia relates how she goes to Winchelsea to visit Hueffer and his wife, and travels on the train with James's new cook. The Great Man is at the station. He greets the cook, 'I have come to meet my doom.' A day or so later the Hueffers and Miss Garnett walk to Rye from Winchelsea; they enter by the Ypres gate, go past the church and then 'a moment for me!' – they pass Lamb House. They have tea at the Mermaid and go to the butcher's and draper's. While at the draper's 'we heard James's voice as he passed with his typist'. A few days later Mrs Hueffer and Olivia Garnett walk to Rye after tea:

It was dark when we got there, and stopping outside a lighted chemist's shop Elsie said 'I have to go in there, but I am not sure, I think that is James inside. What do you say?' I looked, and saw a huge round figure in a light overcoat, and almost sure it wasn't James said 'Oh no, let's go in.' So in we went and in another moment I was being introduced! The figure swung round, seemed to bend an impressive searching look on me, and a voice said, 'I have met you in London.' I said 'Yes,' and seemed to heave my face upwards. The next moment there were inquiries about walking, Ford, etc. 'You did not recognize me. I have scraped my chin.' 'No, I should not have recognized you,' and we were walking up to Lamb House. He asked me if I had known Madox Brown, and what he was like, and talked of the abysmal vulgarity of the British public, coming down the street with us as far as the toy-shop. We parted abruptly. Elsie and I went home by train and lived on the recollection till the return of Ford.

Finally there came the summons to tea in Lamb House. Elsie Hueffer describes to James how Conrad and Hueffer are collaborating on *The Inheritors*. James looks at Olivia Garnett. He speaks of the dissimilar traditions of Hueffer and Conrad, and how 'inconceivable' such collaboration was. 'To me,' said James (and Miss Olivia later records it), 'this is like a bad dream which one relates at breakfast.'

The diarist meekly added, 'we all munched bread and butter and no more was said on the subject'.

59

A Master Mariner

FORD MADOX HUEFFER moved to Winchelsea early in 1901, and during the next two years Joseph Conrad visited him frequently, for they were collaborating on *Romance*. It was during this period that Conrad 'haunted' Winchelsea and, as James said, Winchelsea 'in discretion' haunted Rye. The novelist continued to marvel at this collaboration; he had a certain sense of the unsounded depths of Conrad; he could not reconcile them with the shallows of Hueffer. On occasion, Conrad alone, sometimes with Hueffer, knocked at the canopied portal of Lamb House for a tea-time talk or an afternoon's walk with the Master. James's nephew Billy recalled these visits – and particularly the way in which James would take Conrad's arm and start off with him along the road, leaving Hueffer and Billy to bring up the rear. 'Hueffer babbled,' the frustrated nephew said, 'and I didn't listen. I wanted to hear what the great men were saying up ahead, but there I was stuck with Hueffer. Occasionally a word or two would drift back and what I always heard was – French!' The two novelists, the American and the Pole, discussed the form and future of the English novel in the language of art and diplomacy – and with appropriate gestures. So it would always be between them – a mask of politeness, a kind of guarded 'distance', a mixture of friendliness and anxiety.

Conrad induced a state of malaise in James. It was not his 'foreignness', nor his harsh slavonic accent. James had known and liked many émigré Russians and Poles since the days of his friendship with Turgenev in Paris. Nor were there any difficulties about the professional side : there was great esteem between them. Conrad 'put himself in relation with me years ago, when he had written but his first book or two,' James told Edith Wharton in 1912, adding that his feelings about him were mixed up 'with personal impressions since received'. While he did not specify these, the implication was that they were not entirely favourable. Hueffer insisted that James actively disliked Conrad; but it would be more accurate to say that he was simply troubled by him – by his nervousness, his 'temperament' and the signals James picked up of a deep morbidity.

The Pole and the American exchanged compliments and books. James praised Conrad's early works. The middle period – *Nostromo, The Secret Agent, Under Western Eyes* – he described to Mrs Wharton as 'impossibilities' and 'wastes of desolation that succeeded the two or three final good things of his earlier time'. *Chance* he found 'rather yieldingly difficult and charming'. On his side, Conrad always saluted James as *cher maître* and in the end as 'very dear Master'. James responded by disclosing to him a few of the secrets of his writing desk, something he seldom did. Indeed, when Wells learned that James had shown Conrad a scenario for *The Wings of the Dove*, he did not conceal his jealousy. He had never been given such a privilege. James honoured Conrad the craftsman but was uneasy about the man. He spoke of him as 'curious' and 'interesting', or as 'the interesting and remarkable Conrad'. This juxtaposition of the weak and the emphatic adjective denoted on the part of James a degree of bewilderment. On a later occasion he spoke of Conrad as 'that poor queer man'. This was not condescension. One way of translating these remarks might be 'that poor troubled man – who somehow gives me a queer feeling'. The key to these remarks may be seen in his confiding to Mrs Wharton that he had a 'realizing sense' of Conrad but it was of 'a rum sort'. James was saying – he who prided himself on his insights – that he couldn't quite fathom the gifted Pole.

I

They met when Conrad was 39 and James 53. Both were occupied at that moment with a world that seemed to them 'illusion'. James had been in the depths of despair after his failure in the theatre; Conrad was trying to understand his two decades of seafaring and to find an outlet in the writing of fiction for his inner nightmares of violence. The sea might be the 'destructive element' but he could be sustained by it; it was much more difficult to cope with life on land. James too had spoken of the sea, many times: but for him, as a landlubber, it was 'far shallower than the spirit of man', shallower than man's 'abyss of illusion'. To Conrad all was illusion. Man when born, he said, fell 'into a dream like a man falls into the sea'. Conrad had left Poland in 1874 – when he was Josef Teodor Konrad Nalecz Korzeniowski – 'as a man gets into a dream'. He had been living that dream ever since, attempting to understand and describe as he would later say to James, 'the poignant reality of illusion'. James in his subjectivity had also come to wonder about the phantasmagoria of being, but it led him always back to immediate realities – the 'real, the tideless deep' of man.

The first gesture had been made by Conrad as early as 1896. He debated whether to send James his second book *An Outcast of the Islands*. He feared at first he might be thought 'impudent'. But so strong was the impulse that he finally dispatched the volume, writing on the flyleaf the equivalent of a letter. 'I address you across a vast space,' he wrote to James, and he told him that he had read his novels while sailing many seas. James's characters were 'Exquisite Shades, with live hearts and clothed in the wonderful garment of your prose'. They had stood 'consoling by my side under many skies. They have lived with me, faithful and serene – with the bright serenity of Immortals. And to you thanks are due for such glorious companionship.' The inscription was flowery; yet it seemed deeply felt. James liked it. He also liked the book. He waited for a few weeks, and when *The Spoils of Poynton* was published, he dispatched one of the first copies to Conrad in February 1897 inscribing it 'Joseph Conrad, in dreadfully delayed but very grateful acknowledgment of an offering singularly generous and beautiful.' Conrad had not expected such spontaneous acceptance. 'The delicacy and tenuity' of the *Spoils*, he said, was like 'a great sheet of plate glass – you don't know it's there till you run against it'. The image was apt. There would always be a plate glass between James and Conrad. He discerned in advance the quality of 'distance' James possessed. The American did not let the matter rest with this exchange of books. He was curious about the mariner-novelist and he sent a lively note suggesting that Conrad come to lunch. Conrad's report on it to Edward Garnett was: 'He is quite playful about it. Says we shall be alone – no one to separate us if we quarrel. It's the most delicate flattery I've ever been victim to.' No more delicate, it might be remarked, or flattering than Conrad's inscription of his book to James.

They lunched on 25 February 1897 in De Vere Gardens and the master mariner got a sense of the established power of James's literary life. What Conrad could not know was that he met a James who was at odds with himself. In the midst of his fame, and with his command of the world's respect, the American was going through a difficult phase. What James couldn't know – though he seems to have sensed it – was that he was faced with a powerful and deeply disturbed genius, possessed of 'paranoid trends' (as one psychiatrist surmises) whose strength resided in his perception of the buried violence within himself. Conrad reached out to James with a predatory emotion that made him want on occasion, as he himself avowed, 'to howl and foam at the mouth'. And he couldn't reach James. The plate glass was between them. What they talked about we do not know; but James that very morning had written to Whistler 'with the artist, the artist communicates'. James and Conrad stood on their common ground of art. We can imagine the two face to face. Both were short stocky men. James was all repose and assurance. Conrad, with his head tucked between his shoulders, his strong Polish accent, looked at James with eyes which seemed to live in wild dream and which somehow, for all their penetration, sought the very 'heart of darkness'. The man who would write a tale of such a search faced the man who would write *The Beast in the Jungle*. The two stories speak for the two temperaments. Conrad, making the descent into the irrational jungle of himself, James fearing the irrationality, walking anxiously and warily through the dense growth of human consciousness, on guard against the beasts that might leap – yet knowing that the beasts were those of his own mind. With his slow-moving eyes and settled aristocratic manner he would have listened to Conrad and answered his questions. He had always loved seamen's tales. James may have described on this occasion how he was learning to dictate directly to the typewriter: he had just begun. Conrad would allude to this in an article he wrote some years later. They may have discussed the British Navy for at some point the first volume of Pepys's diary was pulled from the shelf. In turning its pages Conrad came upon the passage describing the boarding of the *Naseby* to bring Charles II back from his exile across the water. 'My lord, in his discourse discovered a great deal of love in this ship.' Conrad copied the sentence. He affixed it as epigraph to the book he had completed that week, *The Nigger of the Narcissus*.

If we do not know the precise nature of their talk we know that James would speak of the 'independent nobleness' in Conrad's work and the 'moral radiance' that he apparently did not find in the man. He got from Conrad a vivid sense of long lonely vigils on ships in distant waters, of the landfall in the dark, of adventures such as he had learned only in books or from men of action. 'I read you,' James would write to Conrad, 'as I listen to rare music – with the deepest depths of surrender.' This would not always be so. Conrad on his side liked the nobility of James's world and the way in which he created characters with 'fine consciences'. He would argue this with John Galsworthy, when the latter called James 'cold'. James's finished, chiselled, carved work might be so called, Conrad admitted, but the perfection of craft did not prevent James from imparting to his readers a full sense of 'flesh and blood'. Above all, Conrad felt that James's people rode always to moral victory: they lost battles, yet never left the battlefield. They renounced, but it was 'an energetic act' – 'energetic not violent'. James's books ended as episodes in life ended; one retained a feeling of life still going on. 'His mankind is delightful,' Conrad would write. 'It is delightful in its tenacity; it refuses to own itself beaten.' And in a supreme passage in his essay on James, Conrad wrote words that would inspire a novelist of a later date (William Faulkner) to proclaim the victories of life over death, of art over chaos:

When the last aqueduct shall have crumbled to pieces, the last airship fallen to the ground, the last blade of grass have died upon a dying earth, man, indomitable by his training in resistance to misery and pain shall set this undiminished light of his eyes against the feeble glow of the sun.

Conrad inscribed *The Nigger of the Narcissus* to James in French – a long inscription in which occurred the phrase *on ne communique pas la réalité poignante des illusions*. Perhaps it was difficult to communicate the poignancy of certain dreams, perhaps this poignancy could never wholly penetrate the soul of the listener – so Conrad mused in his eloquent *dédicace*: and perhaps this was because behind his deep reserve this listener seemed remote, inscrutable, sovereign. But James was not always aloof and Conrad's admiration was not lost on him. In writing to the Royal Literary Fund in 1902 in support of a grant to Conrad he said that 'The Nigger of the Narcissus is in my opinion the very finest and strongest picture of the sea and sea-life that our language possesses – the masterpiece in a whole great class; and *Lord Jim* runs it very close.' His liking for *Lord Jim* was conveyed in a letter which Conrad characterized as 'a draught from the Fountain of Eternal Youth. Wouldn't you think a boy had written it? Such enthusiasm! Wonderful old man, with his record of wonderful work!'

To the Royal Literary Fund James wrote:

When I think that such completeness, such intensity of expression has been arrived at by a man not born to our speech, but who took it up, with singular courage, from necessity and sympathy, and has laboured at it heroically and devotedly, I am equally impressed with the fine persistence and the intrinsic success. Born a Pole and cast upon the waters, he has worked out an English style that is more than correct, that has *quality* and ingenuity. The case seems to me unique and peculiarly worthy of recognition. Unhappily, to be very serious and subtle isn't one of the paths to fortune. Therefore I greatly hope the Royal Literary Fund may be able to do something for him.

The Fund in due course bestowed the sum Conrad needed, £300.

We have a further record of an exchange between the two writers. In 1906 Conrad dispatched *The Mirror of the Sea* to James, and once more filled the end-paper with an epistolary inscription in French. This time he described it as 'a little preface written for you alone'. He tried to explain why he had been self-indulgent, why he had written a book of reminiscences for his own pleasure – 'a dangerous fantasy' for any writer. He was confessing this to James because he was 'very sure of the friendship with which you have honoured me'. And he added: 'Your friendly eye will know how to distinguish in these pages that piety of memory which has guided the groping phrase and the ever-rebel pen.'

James responded by telling Conrad that whatever he might say of his difficult medium and his 'rebel pen', he knocked about 'in the wide waters of expression like the raciest and boldest of privateers'. And he told Conrad,

you have made the whole place your own *en même temps que les droits les plus acquis vous y avez les plus rares bonheurs*. Nothing you have done has more in it ... You stir me to amazement and you touch me to tears, and I thank the powers who so mysteriously let you loose with such sensibilities, into such an undiscovered country – *for sensibility* ... I want to see you again.

He concluded with 'I pat you, my dear Conrad, very affectionately and complacently on the back, and am yours very constantly Henry James'. *Complacently* we must assume, for being so admirable a disciple, so admirably a fellow-artist.

3

Concerning this discipleship perhaps not enough has been said : for dissimilar as the two writers were, and distinctive as Conrad's genius was, James played a much greater role in Conrad's crafts-manship than has perhaps been allowed. No one has noticed that *The Turn of the Screw* and *Heart of Darkness* appeared within a year of each other; and that both tales begin in the same way – the quiet circle, the atmosphere of mystery and gloom, the hint of terrible evil, the reflective narrator, the retrospective method, the recall of crucial episodes. And perhaps from the 'Mr Quint is dead' of the ghostly tale there sounds in Conrad a powerful echo, 'Mistah Kurtz – he dead.' The stories are as different as their authors, but they suggest that Conrad went to school in the works of Henry James – and notably learned James's devices for obtaining distance from his materials. In James this was inevitable, given his own shrinking from the violence of passion. In Conrad it proved a much-needed method; it helped him cope with a great flow of emotion, and 'contained' his 'cosmic' feeling. Of *The Turn of the Screw* Con-rad said James showed how to extract an 'intellectual thrill' from his materials leaving 'a kind of phosphorescent trail in one's mind'. There would come a time, a decade later, when James would criti-cize Conrad's excesses in indirect narration; perhaps the Master felt that his lesson had been too well learned. Conrad resented the rebuke; and on James's part it was ill-considered. It occurred in a two-part article 19 March and 1 April 1914 in *The Times Literary Supplement* called *The Younger Generation*, James's final critical fling at the writers who followed on his heels and whose youth and talent he sometimes resented with all the vitality of his old age. He was kinder to Conrad than to any of the other writers, save Hugh Walpole and Mrs Wharton, to whom however he offered superficial accolades. He paid Conrad the compliment of taking him seriously; and for Conrad alone, in this array of writers, he reserved the title of 'genius'. But when it came to matters of tech-nique, he had some fine-spun observations. Conrad was alone, as regards method, 'absolutely alone as the votary of the way to do a thing that shall make it undergo most doing'. James complained, nevertheless, about the 'prolonged hovering flight of the subjective over the outstretched ground of the case exposed. We make out this ground, only through the shadow cast by the flight' and he took his image out of the recently developed machines of flight, for he had seen, one day at Rye, Blériot's plane over the Channel. Conrad's narration within narration (an extension of James's devices) he likened to a series of aeroplane shadows which create an eclipse upon 'the instrinsic colour and form and whatever, upon the passive expanse'.

In his complex and subtle analysis of Conrad's modes of narration in *Chance*, in forgetting that Conrad (by then 51) was hardly of the 'younger' generation (as he had been when James met him), and in failing to speak of other works which had pleased him more than *Chance*, James understandably hurt Conrad. The latter felt, as he said, 'rather airily condemned'. He added, 'I may say with scrupulous truth that this was the *only time* a criticism affected me painfully.' It must have been extremely painful for it came from a revered source which had hitherto given him the finest praise. In later years Conrad remembered not the rebuke but James's singular kindness. His response to James's gift of the first batch of volumes of the New York Edition shows his depth of feeling:

'*Très cher maître,*' he began, 'they have arrived – the six of them : I have felt them all in turn and all at one time as it were.' He had taken the morning off to browse in them and read the preface to *The American*.

Afterwards I could not resist the temptation of reading the beautiful and touching last ten pages of the story. There is in them perfection of tone which calmed me, and I sat for a long while with the closed volume in my hand going over the preface in my mind and thinking – that is how it began, that's how it was done!

The Pole thanked James for 'the opportunity to breathe in the assurance of your good-will, the fortifying atmosphere of your serene achievement'.

Long afterwards, when James was dead, Conrad one day found himself describing to John Quinn, the Irish-American patron of the arts, how he had felt about the American novelist. He could not bring himself to say positively that James had liked him; perhaps the memory of his hurt over *Chance* made him cautious. He spoke as if he had to infer James's feelings, in spite of the letters James had written to him. And he was right. James's feelings had been mixed. On his own side side Conrad could be affirmative. 'I had a profound affection for him,' he told Quinn, adding that James 'accepted it as if it were something worth having. At any rate that is the impression I have.' Then, almost as if he were ruminating aloud, he said James 'wasn't a man who would pretend' to like some one. What need had he? – even if he had been capable of the pretence?

60

A Ghostly Rental

I

HENRY JAMES met H. G. Wells and Stephen Crane during 1898 and within months both became his neighbours – Wells at Sandgate on the Kentish coast, across Romney Marsh from Rye, and Crane at Brede, in Sussex, an eight-mile bicycle run from Lamb House. Legend has it that Crane and James met at a bohemian party in London, at which a woman named Madame Zipango poured champagne into James's top hat. James protested this affront to the symbol of his dignity. Crane is said to have spirited the offender away from the party and addressed himself tactfully to salvaging the hat and soothing the Master. They had been discussing literary style. Crane may have been alluding to this incident a few days later when he spoke of seeing James 'make a holy show of himself in a situation that – on my honour – would have been simple to an ordinary man'. He added, 'it seems impossible to dislike him. He is so kind to everybody.'

Crane's friend Harold Frederic, a fellow-American, and London correspondent of the New York *Times*, took a less generous view of the rituals of the Master. A down-to-earth, rough-and-ready newspaperman who had written a best-selling novel, *The Damnation of Theron Ware* (about a Methodist clergyman, the flesh and the devil) he characterized James as 'an effeminate old donkey who lives with a herd of other donkeys around him and insists on being treated as if he were the Pope'. He spoke too of James's 'usual lack of a sense of generosity'. Both Crane and Frederic lived 'hard' and died young – Frederic of a stroke that very year. He had maintained two households and left illegitimate as well as legitimate children and he would have been astonished to learn that the man he described as lacking generosity was among the first to sign an appeal for money for the illegitimate children. James wrote to Cora Crane, Shephen's common-law wife, 'deeper than I can say is my commiseration of these beautiful children'. The sentimental and practical Cora wept when she received £50 from James. Historians of the Cranes and the Frederics have described James as disturbed and even shocked by the bohemianism of this group of American journalist-novelists. Cora had been the 'madame' of a 'house of joy' in Jacksonville, Florida, but there was no failure of courtesy on James's part when she became his neighbour. He had known bohemianism in all its forms from the days of his studio hauntings in Rome, Paris, London. He had chronicled the lives of dissolute artists in his novels and tales. If he passed judgement on them it was not that they led bohemian lives but that they made their bohemianism an excuse for poor art. When Cora Crane sent him Frederic's posthumous work, *The Market Place*, he read it 'with a lively sense of what Harold Frederic might have done if he had lived – and above all lived (and therefore worked) differently'.

2

James's meeting with Wells had in it less of the bohemian and more of the dignity of letters. The younger writer had been enjoying increasing prosperity with his tales about man in time and space. Early in the summer of 1898, he had gone on a bicycle trip along the Kentish coast, accompanied by his wife. He found himself, however, increasingly unwell and collapsed at New Romney with a high fever. An old kidney ailment had declared itself, and he spent a number of weeks under medical care. In August there appeared at his cottage two important-looking middle-aged gentlemen, wheeling their bicycles. Wells recognized Henry James. He had seen him on the night of *Guy Domville*. The other visitor was Edmund Gosse. They had cycled over from Lamb House to inquire about his health. Wells was then 32; James 55. The younger writer was touched – and flattered – to have two outstanding members of the literary establishment show such a kindly interest in his welfare. They sat around a table, drank tea, talked sociably for an hour and then the visitors left as unceremoniously as they had arrived. Some years later Wells put two and two together and realized that the visit was not as innocent as it had seemed : James and Gosse had been quietly ascertaining, on behalf of the Royal Literary Fund, whether the younger writer was in financial need.

From the time of this meeting, and through the Edwardian years, Wells and James were excellent friends. James sent Wells *The Turn of the Screw* which was published that year, and Wells sent James *The Time Machine*, and from then on bestowed all his books on the Master. This may have been unwise, for James felt he would insult the younger man if he acknowledged them in a perfunctory way. He invariably offered a full-dress critique. He liked the utopias for their abundance of ideas and originality; but he candidly complained to Wells that he was not concerned sufficiently with art in his fiction. Wells, in an anonymous review, before he had met James, had criticized the American's 'frosted genius'. He spoke of his 'ground-glass style', but admitted that James's characters were 'living men and women'. James's main criticism of Wells was that he failed to create such men and women. 'I rewrite you much, as I read – which is the highest tribute my damned impertinence can pay an author,' James said.

In the summer of their meeting, Wells decided to stay on in Kent. He occupied Beach Cottage at Sandgate, and later built himself a solid brick house, Spade House, symbol of his growing prosperity. Both Wells and James, during the early months of their friendship, would be the spectators of the passage at nearby Brede House of Stephen Crane and his honey-haired Cora. Wells indeed would leave some of the most vivid pictures we have of the ill-fated young American writer.

3

James had known about Crane some time before he met him. He knew that Howells had praised *Maggie: A Girl of the Streets* and he had read *The Red Badge of Courage*, seeing in it qualities he associated with Zola. Crane's subject, we may surmise, touched James – the Civil War had been an anguished memory of his youth, and then Crane – who knew it only from history – had created a young man who was heroic in spite of himself. This was a type of hero James had treated in his story of the young pacifist (*Owen Wingrave*) who proves a good soldier in spite of his pacifism. James quickly appreciated Crane's intensity, his industry, his dedication. He belonged to a new generation; and while James speaks of him nowhere, and no letters to him have survived, we do know how he characterized the new breed of literary journalists. He regarded Richard Harding Davis, Crane's journalistic contemporary, as belonging to 'the possible fatal extravagance of our growing world-hunger' – that 'alert, familiar journalism, the world-hunger made easy, made for the time irresistible'. Crane had ministered to this hunger by going to scenes of war and violence: he was a kind of ancestor of Hemingway. When James met him he had returned from the Greco-Turkish War, and was on his way to the Spanish-American War. It was after his brief and violent experiences in the Cuban war, and the Puerto Rico Campaign – heedless where his personal safety was concerned – that he returned to England.

Crane and Cora Taylor (as she was then known) had been living together ever since the Greco-Turkish War. They had met at her high-class bawdy house, 'Hotel de Dream', in Jacksonville. With her pretensions to literature, her pleasure-loving ways, her managerial abilities, she had attached herself to Crane and followed him to Greece, taking the *nom de plume* of Imogene Carter. She had been one of the earliest of her tribe – a lady war correspondent. Crane edited some of her dispatches and they were published. Cora Howorth had been married twice before; first to a man named Murphy in New York, whom she had divorced; then in her 'siege of London' she married the son of a baronet. James had written *that* story long ago. They had parted early but Captain Donald Stewart would not give her a divorce. Unable to marry Crane, she did not relish trying to live with him as his common-law wife in the United States where his activities were always publicized and where she could have no status as the 'wife' of a celebrity. In England all was different. The English asked no questions and they were more 'accepting'. Crane's writings had made him a large English reputation ahead of his recognition in America. And then Cora had large social aspirations. She was an egotist, a woman slightly overblown, proud of her blonde hair and fleshly charm, and energetic in her pursuit of pleasure and 'society'. James had invented her long ago; indeed everything she did seemed to have been told in his early 'international' tales. Even before Stephen Crane returned from Cuba, she had arranged to rent Brede House from Moreton Frewen (young Winston Churchill's uncle through his marriage to one of the Jerome sisters). Frewen was happy to let the old family house of Brede to the talented Crane, and asked £40 a year. Brede was a massive manor house, begun in the fourteenth century, to which there had been subsequent elaborate additions. It had a large hall, a chapel, great fireplaces; but it was in disrepair, and filled with cold and damp. Its sanitary conveniences were old-fashioned and minimal. Nevertheless the place ministered to Cora's grandiose dreams of social glory; she would play *grande dame* in baronial halls. She showed Brede House to Stephen Crane in January of 1899; in February they moved in and she wrote promptly to Henry James to announce their arrival. But James was on the verge of leaving for Italy. By the time he returned, the Cranes were well established. They had no money; they lived from hand to mouth on the charity of their friends and the credit of the neighbourhood. The unbuttoned and bohemian Crane fell in with Cora's pretensions; he began to dress for dinner. He lived the life of a gentleman and left practical affairs to Cora. People came and went; journalists turned up to interview Crane; relatives appeared from America. The place was meagrely furnished but they strewed rushes on the floors and kept mastiffs in the Elizabethan style. Whole trees were burned in the capacious fireplaces. They were aided by Frewen's servants – a butler named Heather, a brandy-loving cook, a maid. In the grounds romped 'the young barbarians', as James called them, Frederic's illegitimate orphans. Crane had a wagonette and also rode on horseback, wearing riding breeches and a flannel shirt. Hueffer said this costume shocked James – but then Hueffer was always depicting James as shocked by other people's attire. Shortly after James returned from Italy, in July 1899, he cycled to Brede and left his card on which he scrawled in pencil, 'Mr and Mrs Crane: Very sorry to miss you – had a dark foreboding it was you I passed a quarter of an hour ago in a populous wagonette. Will try you soon again.'

The biographers of the Cranes have created an impression that from this time on there was much fraternizing between Brede House and Lamb House. So far as we know the Cranes came to Lamb House for tea on two, perhaps three, occasions during the rest of that summer; and James in turn visited them at Brede perhaps the same number of times. In a word, the deep and 'intimate' friendship between the Cranes and James of which so much has been made never existed: and this in part because James had little opportunity that year to be neighbourly. He was preoccupied with his new friendship with Hendrik Andersen, the young sculptor, who visited him that

August. Then his brother William came abroad after his heart attack. Finally Lamb House at this moment was put up for sale and James bought it, in great nervousness – for he did not have much ready cash. He had promptly set to work to earn the sum needed for the initial payment.

At Brede, Crane daily sat in his study, in the tower, trying to write tales in order to provide money for the improvident Cora. In Lamb House, James was producing throughout that autumn an article or a tale a week, in a fever of writing, in order to provide himself with a home for his old age. He was fascinated – and pained – by the spectacle of the Cranes. They were living out his tales – about old English houses in need of repair let to Americans; about ambitious American women with a 'past'; about talented writers struggling to do the successful thing in order to dress their wives and pay for food and rent. He had satirized in his ironic tales the mixture of pretension to English manners and the flamboyance and ignorance of Americans. The situation at Brede had also a touch of the eerie of James's ghostly tales. There was a legend that Brede had had an ogre, a consumer of children; he had ultimately been done to death with a wooden saw. Other legends said there were underground passages which served generations of smugglers. But more than its ghosts, its draughts, its creaking boards, its tree-consuming fireplaces, Brede was clearly the last place in the world for a malaria-ridden consumptive to spend a cold damp English winter. Wells remembered Crane as 'profoundly weary and ill'. He described him as 'essentially the helpless artist; he wasn't the master of his party, he wasn't the master of his home; his life was altogether out of control; he was being carried along. What he was still clinging to, but with a dwindling zest, was artistry.' And what Cora was clinging to was her love of pleasure. Cora did not notice – what everyone else saw – that Crane was destined to be very soon one of the ghostliest of Brede's ghosts.

4

There are many anecdotes about the Cranes at Lamb House, and these made it seem as if the Cranes were visiting James every other day. One journalist has Mrs Humphry Ward pouring tea during one of Crane's visits; but Mrs Ward did not come to Lamb House during this period. She was busy writing *Eleanor* and Henry James was offering lengthy criticisms by mail. Another journalist describes

Crane as giving James Knut Hamsun's *Hunger*, and their talking about the annual mud-boat regatta, which James refereed in Rye wearing knickerbockers, ghillie-shoes, and a homburg. It is possible that much of the gossip came from the talkative and inventive Cora. There was certainly talk of the Boer War – a subject of common interest to both writers. James gave Crane a copy of *In the Cage* and inscribed *The Awkward Age* to him. He was quoted as saying, 'We love Stephen Crane for what he is; and admire him for what he is going to be.' At Brede, James was reputed to have turned up on one occasion with a party of 'stuffed shirts' and Cora was forced to improvise lunch for the group – but this was not in character; James never organized spontaneous visits of this sort: it sounds like a tale circulated by Hueffer that James sent over a bundle of manuscripts to Crane asking for his opinion and for editorial help. Nothing could have been less likely – that James with his sense of craft should at 56 seek counsel from a 27-year-old. Evidence shows that James that autumn allowed no manuscripts to linger on his desk; he sent them with great rapidity to his agent in London, sometimes in instalments. Many were rapidly placed. Indeed James's earnings during these weeks were substantial. Crane, sickly and straining at his desk, had greater fame and a smaller market.

Late in August James attended a party at the Brede Rectory organized by Cora. Of this occasion two significant snapshots survive: one of James in his trimmed spade-like beard standing beside Cora and another with his mouth wide open – he was snapped in the act of eating a doughnut. When he received 'the strange images' James wrote to Cora that they formed 'a precious memento of a romantic hour. But no surely, it can't be any doughnut of yours that is making me make such a gruesome grimace. I look as if I had swallowed a wasp or a penny toy, and I tried to look so beautiful. I tried too hard, doubtless. But don't show it to anyone as H.J. trying.' He concluded by hoping Frederic's 'young barbarians' were at play 'far from Crane's laboratory'.

His scribbled social notes to Cora are cordial and friendly. She wanted information about a ladies' club at the Mermaid Inn and James gave it to her, telling her how to join. At the end of September there is a telegram accepting an invitation to tea. After that there are no communications, for a full six months. During this period William James was in England after his cure at Bad Nauheim. We are abundantly documented on the activities of the Cranes during this time – for Conrads, Hueffers, Wells and his wife, Garnetts, journalists and literary hangers-on continued to come. For Cora it was a perpetual carnival; for Crane it was a continual sad grind. H. G. Wells has told the story of the great Christmas-week party Cora organized to welcome the year 1900. The guests were asked to bring their own bedding. There were few furnished bedrooms in Brede House and Cora created a dormitory for the ladies and another for the men. They stayed late before roaring fires. Large candles burned in sockets fixed for the occasion by the local blacksmith; guests showed marks of candle-wax on their clothes. There was an acute shortage of toilets. Troubled-looking male guests wandered about the grounds in the early mornings. Crane tried to organize American-style poker games which his English guests did not take seriously. Wells called the house party a 'lark', not all the visitors would have agreed. On Christmas Eve a play was given in the local school house written in part by Crane, who asked James, Conrad, Wells, Gissing, A. E. W. Mason, and others to add a few words to the script, making it the most 'authored' play of the century. It was about the Brede ghost – the child-eating ogre who was sawed in half. James's contribution to the script was part of the name of one character – who was called Peter Quint Prodmore Moreau – Peter Quint from *The Turn of the Screw* and Prodmore from *Covering End* (he is the sharp businessman who holds all the mortgages). The Moreau belonged to H. G. Wells. The party had a painful finale at just about the hour when Henry James, in nearby Lamb House, was invoking the 'gruesome' date of 1900 in his letter to Rhoda Broughton. He had seen the new year in quietly with William and his young niece Peggy. Eight miles away Cora was waking up Wells. Crane had just had a lung haemorrhage. Wells's final memory of the party was a ride into the drizzle at dawn on a bicycle in search of a doctor.

During the first months of the new year, when Crane was ill most of the time, Henry James wrote *The Sacred Fount*. It may have derived some of its poignancy from his vision of Crane visibly dying while Cora thrived, unaware of the tragedy being lived out under her roof. This was a very old theme with James – the way in which men and women prey on one another. Late in May, Cora finally grasped the truth. She had stayed with Crane in the damp old house all winter; with the approaching summer she rushed him off to the Continent, borrowing money on all sides, arranging for a special train, taking the local doctor, Ernest Skinner, along. They paused at Dover and James and Wells planned to drive over to see Crane off. James was detained and Wells went alone. Later Wells told of his last glimpse of the American lying wrapped in blankets before an open window at the Dover hotel 'thin and gaunt and wasted, too weak for more than a remembered jest and a greeting and good wishes'. Wells noted 'a face of a type very typically American, long and spare, with very straight hair and straight features and long, quiet hands and hollow eyes, moving slowly, smiling and speaking slowly'.

Cora got Crane to the Black Forest, and there he died. James received the news of Crane's impending end from the Moreton Frewens who had returned to Brede House; not only had Frewen never been paid his rent, but he had actually sent money to his desperate tenants. In early June 1900 James wrote his longest letter to Cora. He had heard how ill Crane was; he was sorry not to have seen him at Dover; he enclosed a cheque for £50.

I won't pretend to utter hopes about Crane which may be in vain ... but I constantly think of him and as it were pray for him. I feel that I am not taking too much for granted in believing that you may be in the midst of worries on the money-score which will perhaps make the cheque for Fifty Pounds, that I enclose, a convenience to you. Please view it as such and dedicate it to whatever service it may best render my stricken young friend. It meagrely represents my tender benediction to him.

He had barely posted this letter when he read of Crane's death. He wrote to Cora, 'What a brutal, needless extinction – what an un-mitigated unredeemed catastrophe! I think of him with such a sense of possibilities and powers! Not that one would have drawn out longer these last cruel weeks –!' A few days later he told Wells: 'You will have felt, as I have done, the miserable sadness of poor Crane's so precipitated and, somehow, so unnecessary extinction. I was at Brede Place this afternoon – and it looked conscious and cruel.' The word 'cruel' may have been used by design.

5

That autumn James wrote to the Royal Literary Fund at Cora's request, but he doubted whether this British fund could allocate money to Americans or to widows. She wrote to James and asked for more money – but he had sent her the equivalent of what he was paid for one of his stories. He told his agent, 'I can do very little more.' He added, 'my heart, I fear, is generally hard to her'. Pinker warned James that Cora would return to the charge and James replied that he considered her 'an unprofitable person, and I judge her whole course and career, so far as it appeared in this neighbourhood, very sternly and unforgivingly'. He was particularly incensed that Cora had made no effort to pay Dr Skinner. Nevertheless, when Cora sent James Crane's posthumous *Wounds in the Rain*, he answered her that 'if Crane could have lived – success and he would evidently have been constantly, no strangers. The greater the tragedy!' He concluded speaking of Rye, 'it's very much in the minor key here'.

The allusion to Crane's possible success, the reference to 'the minor key', suggests that James may have been recalling a story written some years before, in which he described an author who writes himself to death. One of the novels the fictitious author writes is called *The Major Key*. In the end the writer gives up. He awakens one morning 'in the country of the blue'. The pen drops from his hand. 'The voice of the market had suddenly grown faint and far ... he had floated away into a grand indifference, into a reckless consciousness of art'. Stephen Crane had done just that. He had simply come to a stop.

Cora, at a later time, when she had remarried, tried to call on James. He announced himself unavailable. His heart remained 'hard' to her. This had nothing to do with her 'past'. James had been too close a spectator of the tragi-comedy played out in the old manor house: Crane had been a Jamesian hero – a Ralph Limbert, or the young aspirant who tries to learn 'the lesson of the master'. The lesson had been that a writer must choose between art and worldliness. Crane had not even made a choice. He had been caught passively between the two. 'His short, so troubled, yet also so peaceful passage' at Brede, James wrote, was 'a strange, pathetic, memorable chapter'.

61

The Ambassadors

DURING the last summer of the old century when Henry James was writing *The Ambassadors* – an uncommonly hot summer for England – he sat for his portrait to the gifted member of the 'Emmetry', his cousin Ellen Emmet, familiarly known as 'Bay'. She had been studying in Paris; now she planned to live and work in America. James, to encourage her, insisted that he pay her for a full-length painting although she was to do just head and shoulders. He wanted, in all probability, to put on canvas his newly-shaven countenance. Bay Emmet was talented and skilful. James described her as 'a *pure* painter, a real one, a good one', but added, in a letter to his brother, that she was 'without imagination, a grain'. The finished portrait is a close-up. James looks directly out of the frame : his eyes are veiled; half the face is in deep shadow. The wear and tear of the years is erased and she has given the face an effect of greater length than it possessed. James wore for the sittings a beige waistcoat, a dark suit, and a prominent heavy-knotted white-speckled cravat. In his strong writing fist he has a tight grip on his spectacles. The portrait – its conception – is precocious, for Bay was in her mid-20s; it is also rather 'arty', in imitation of Sargent.

Many years later, when it was being cleaned and repaired, the restorer found beneath it, on a separate canvas, a sketch made by Bay Emmet obviously abandoned before it was finished. She had posed James differently, at an angle, and was looking downward at him. She had applied a great deal of red to the face but had not yet finished painting the flesh; the effect, especially of the nose, resembled the colour of James's alcoholic butler rather than that of the abstemious novelist. The suggestion, in this uncompleted work, is of great ruddiness, a figure as of a country squire, a haunter of pubs. James's shortness is emphasized; his shoulders are out of proportion, the cravat is unfinished. One can see that both painter and sitter were dissatisfied with what was emerging. Nevertheless there is a great deal of life in the face, and the eyes are large, clear, alert, much more than in the 'set' and inanimate finished portrait.

The novelist varnished the painting himself, found an old frame for it, placed it above his sideboard in his dining-room. There it hung for the remainder of his life. Visitors, seeing it, little dreamed that hidden behind the solemn and unsmiling face of the Master there existed a sketch of a more 'bouncy' human being, the relaxed parochial resident of Rye. James never considered the finished portrait a good likeness. He described it to Bay as 'the smooth and anxious clerical gentleman in the spotted necktie'. 'Do you remember,' he wrote to her a couple of years later, 'when you were (more or less vaguely) painting me?' If the gentleman on the wall didn't look like him, he said, he looked immensely 'like *you*, dear Bay, and he reminds me of our so genial, roasting romantic summer-before-last here together, when we took grassy walks at eventide, and in the sunset, after each afternoon's repainting'.

I

The Ambassadors was written as 'the picture of a certain momentous and interesting period, of some six months or so, in the history of a man no longer in the prime of life'. He himself had had such six months from the time in 1899 when he had met Hendrik Andersen, purchased Lamb House, written *The Sacred Fount* and suddenly found himself – after removing his beard – wanting to write things of 'the altogether human order'. The novel he wrote about his middle-aged hero had a single primary message, for himself as for his readers: that one must live in full awareness and 'with sufficient intensity', be a source of 'what may be called excitement' to oneself. At 57 he seemed to be starting his career all over again: and this was suggested by his return, after almost two decades, to the 'international' subject by which he had first established his fame. He came back to it with unconcealed pleasure; came back to a story of an American in Paris, as if he were once more 33 and writing *The American*. His new novel was about the rigidities of New England and the relaxed cosmopolitanism of 'Europe'. In his long-ago romantic novel he had told of Christopher Newman seeking entry into the Faubourg St Germain like a Balzacian young man from the provinces. *The Ambassadors* was to be the story of an elderly hero who, in the French capital, breaks out of the shell of his New England conscience – and discovers how innocent he has been. James felt, as he dictated his work in the Garden Room, as if all his data were 'installed on my premises like a monotony of fine weather'. He finished the book in about eight months. Its twelve parts, one for each month of a year of serialization, were shaped in pictures and scenes, using the techniques he had perfected since his play-writing. 'Nothing resisted, nothing betrayed,' said James, who would speak of this book as 'quite the best, "all round" of my productions.' And it is true that the novel possesses a singular harmony of form and content.

Its story was simple, almost conventional; it told of a young man from New England who lingers too long in Paris; and of a middle-aged 'ambassador' sent out by the young man's mother to bring him home. James named the principal envoy Lewis Lambert Strether after Balzac's hero in the novel *Louis Lambert*. In his opening pages he went out of his way to draw attention to this fact: few authors indeed have ever signalled a 'source' more clearly. When Miss Gostrey, looking at Strether's card, says, 'It's the name of a novel of Balzac's,' Strether replies, 'Oh, I know that!' She rejoins, 'But the novel's an awfully bad one.' Strether's reply is prompt. 'I know that too.'

Balzac's *roman philosophique* is the inflated story of the education of a young man, his inhibited compulsive constricted Latin 'formation' – as constricted as a 'New England conscience'. Louis Lambert is a cerebral prodigy, a near-genius; he writes a portentous *Treatise on the Will* and dies young, after a painful love affair. If there is any connection between *The Ambassadors* and the Balzacian novel it may be in Lambert Strether's struggle to discover the difference between what he sees and what he imagines – between what is 'real' and what is illusion. James's novel tells us that life is willed for us, that each man must make the best of his own fate. He must have felt that he too was writing a 'philosophical' novel – a novel of a certain kind of 'education', in which Strether, strapped tight by his New England 'conditioning', unwinds in the Parisian circle of Chad Newsome's friends, discovering that the flexible cosmopolites 'live' by being open to experience, while the New Englanders keep themselves closed. The book contains a cautious hedonism; and its moral is that high civilization derives from a life – as Balzac might have said – of 'expectant attention'. One learns to see into things; one recognizes that the best freedom man has is the freedom of his imagination – the freedom of his illusions. Lambert Strether refuses to accept the preconceptions of Woollett, Mass. The Newsomes, mother and daughter, have made up their minds that Chad, the son and heir, remains abroad because some woman, some Cleopatra-enchantress, has taken hold of him, as if he were a Caesar or an Antony. Chad is hardly made of such heroic stuff. Strether knew him as a rough, spoiled small-town boy. Now he finds a smooth egotistical young man obviously improved and polished by his life abroad. He lives in a pleasant apartment in the Boulevard Males-herbes; he has cosmopolite friends – among them a young artist named John Little Bilham, who resembles Jonathan Sturges (the writer who had brought James the original idea for this novel) and other friends like Miss Barrace, in whom James drew an accurate portrait of his old friend Henrietta Reubell, the American-Parisian expatriate. Above all there is the presence in Chad's entourage of Madame de Vionnet, an aristocratic French lady who has a grown daughter. She is a *grande dame*, half English and half French, separated from her husband. She embodies French elegance, tradi-tion, discretion; and she has also a certain Anglo-Saxon high-minded-ness. Strether finds her appealing and assumes that she has been the benign influence on Chad; it is she, he believes, who has given the young man his high continental polish. He believes also at first that she is trying to marry her daughter to him.

Mrs Newsome's ambassador is in no hurry about his mission. It is, in the first place, an embarrassing one. Chad is old enough not to be accountable to his mother; and Strether has no relish in making inquiries about his Parisian way of life. He gives himself over to enjoying the city, with the aid of a sophisticated American lady he met in England, at a hotel in Chester. She is Maria Gostrey; very quickly she becomes his confidante. He has told her the details of his mission; she gives him a great deal of useful advice and helps con-stantly to correct his active, romantic imagination. For he is inclined to live in his fancies. The Woollett envoy also has as companion an American friend, Waymarsh, a distinguished Washington lawyer, who is dyspeptic, ill at ease, and always growling against Europe very much in the manner of William James. Abroad, William was always belligerently American; in America he longed for Europe. Waymarsh seems to possess the gloom of Henry Adams, William's dislike of Europe, and the hypochondriacal problems of Mark Twain. He acts as Strether's foil, and like many an American tourist, cools his 'sacred rage' by frequent incursions into shops. Strether finally musters the courage to ask Little Bilham about Chad and Madame de Vionnet. Little Bilham, being a gentleman, answers that theirs is a 'virtuous attachment'. No Jamesian gentleman, as one remembers from *The Siege of London* is supposed to 'tell' on a woman. Strether through the first half of the book has sent detailed dispatches to the 'home office', to Mrs Newsome. He has reached the conclusion that Chad should stay abroad. He feels Madame de Vionnet is good for him. He encounters the grand lady one day in Notre Dame and they have a charming lunch on the quays. Over their *omelette aux tomates* and their straw-coloured Chablis, while Madame de Vionnet's 'grey eyes moved in and out of their talk', he gallantly feels that he must help her. She is fond of the young man – and besides the attachment is 'virtuous'. The result is that in the exact middle of the book, Strether is relieved of his high office. New ambassadors are dispatched – Chad's sister Sarah and her husband, a Woollett mediocrity named Jim Pocock. On arrival Sarah proclaims to Strether that Madame de Vionnet is 'not even an apology for a decent woman'. Pocock goes off to the Folies.

2

The novel has two brilliant climactic scenes, set with classical symmetry in the fifth and eleventh parts of the book. The first is the scene in Gloriani's garden, which had been the original 'germ' for the story. Long ago, James had heard how his friend William Dean Howells had murmured to Jonathan Sturges in Whistler's garden in Paris that, really, one should 'live all one can'. This had caused James to make a long entry in his notebook. He liked the idea of Howells saying this – he who had 'never known *at all* any woman BUT his wife'. James knew Whistler's garden – he knew it very well; he had visited Whistler there; but he had also seen it years before, during 1875–6 when he called on occasion in the house overlooking the garden, and talked with old Madame Mohl, Fanny Kemble's friend, the Anglo-French hostess who had been a friend of Madame Récamier and Chateaubriand. James had stood at her window and observed the adjoining convent for the training of missionary priests. In *The Ambassadors* he endows Strether with his memories:

Strether had presently the sense of a great convent, a convent of missions, famous for he scarce knew what, a nursery of young priests, of scattered shade, of straight alleys and chapel-bells, that spread its mass in one quarter; he had the sense of names in the air, of ghosts at the windows, of signs and tokens, a whole range of expression, all about him, too thick for prompt discrimination.

Charming indeed, an author who allows his principal character to see the ghost of himself at a window. There may be a touch of Whistler in James's image of the artist Gloriani – Gloriani, resuscitated from *Roderick Hudson*, James's Roman novel of 1875. In *Roderick*, Gloriani still had his career to make; he possessed 'the mere base maximum of cleverness'. This was a reproach James had addressed to Whistler in his earlier period in London. Now the fictional character, like Whistler, has matured. Gloriani has acquired greatness. It has come to him by his having the courage to live the passion of his art. Strether is 'held by the sculptor's eyes ... the deep human expertness in Gloriani's charming smile – oh the terrible life behind it!'

In this garden with his sense of the beauty and his anxieties Strether delivers himself of one of the most poignant soliloquies in all of James's fiction. He begins his quiet speech to the artist-expatriate, Little Bilham, by wondering whether it is too late for someone like himself to 'live'. He images himself as having failed to catch the train that waited for him; now he can only hear its distant whistle. 'Live all you can; it's a mistake not to. It doesn't so much matter what you do in particular,' he tells Bilham, 'so long as you have your life.' He adds, 'If you haven't had that what *have* you had?' Later, Little Bilham will change the speech slightly. He will remind Strether that he had said '*see* all you can'. Strether does not contradict him. *Seeing* is accordingy equated with living. After this Strether speaks the words that give the novel its 'deterministic' post-Darwinian philosophy. We are all moulds, 'either fluted and embossed, with ornamental excrescences, or else smooth and dreadfully plain, into which a helpless jelly, one's consciousness is poured'. One takes his form and his shape. You are what you are, James seems to say and you must make the most of it. After this prophecy of 'conditioning' Strether observes, 'still, one has the illusion of freedom; therefore don't be, like me, without the memory of that illusion'.

The second scene which haunts readers of *The Ambassadors* is that of Lambert Strether's relaxed day in the country. This is the crucial moment in which he discovers the affair between Chad and Madame de Vionnet. The Strether of the early part of the novel is always looking at his watch, always patting his pocket to make sure his wallet is in its place. The later Strether sets off casually in search of a certain metallic green in the French landscape that he had encountered once in a painting by Lambinet. To find this he takes a train to a station indiscriminately chosen – the exact terminus isn't needed. What is needed is a general direction. In this chapter James makes us feel the way in which Strether enters the countryside as if he were moving through the very frame of the Lambinet seen long years before in an art shop in Tremont Street in Boston. He gives us first the image of the painting; then, as if a camera were moving towards the picture, he picks up a stream, the greens of the landscape, the church spire. Descending from the train, Strether walks into the painting

the oblong gilt frame disposed its enclosing lines; the poplars and willows, the reeds and river – a river of which he didn't know, and didn't want to know, the name – fell into composition, full of felicity, within them; the sky was silver and turquoise and varnish; the village on the left was white and the church on the right was grey; it was all there, in short – it was what he wanted; it was Tremont Street, it was France, it was Lambinet. Moreover he was freely walking about in it.

Strether has discovered a kind of freedom which can escape rigidities, omniscience and a life conducted like a railway timetable. He can avoid the set journey, the designated place, even the names of places – 'a river of which he didn't know, and didn't want to know, the name'. We are reminded of the mysterious article – never named – manufactured by the Newsomes in Woollett, the source of their fortune. The reader is again being told that in this world we can never know everything. The name of the village is of little importance – although James was fond of esoteric names. What counts is the silver and turquoise, the poplars, the willows, the impressionistic play of light over the enchanted scene. Strether escapes Woollett during these carefree hours; he cultivates his 'illusion of freedom'. He waits for his dinner at the inn, on the bank of the river. He sees a boat, as in a Manet painting. In one of those coincidences Balzac loved, and James emulated, the boat contains Chad and Madame de Vionnet. In the rustic twilight, Strether suddenly experiences the anguish of his disillusion. Woollett has been right after all. Or had it? At any rate, he feels 'sold'. The grand lady is indeed Chad's mistress: their informality, their casual clothes reveal to Strether they must be staying at a nearby inn.

3

No bald sketch of *The Ambassadors* can convey the brilliance and the wit of its comedy, the ironic delicacy of its scenes and conversation, the ways in which James, with the ease and skill of his maturity, dissects America and Europe and re-imagines his international myth. He tells himself that America has always been provincial, that he has been wise to live in the high places of civilization. America is Mrs Newsome, an implacable, immobile force, intransigent and exigent: she is there, in Woollett, or a hundred cities where values are unambiguous, and where everyone pays a price – the price of muffled feeling, the conventional, the prescribed. One doesn't 'live all you can'. Mrs Newsome clings to her children, demands that they remain at home, refuses to allow them to grow up and lead their own lives. She 'hangs together with a perfection of her own'. The only solution – the one James had sought – is casually mentioned in the book, 'you've got morally and intellectually to get rid of her'. The ex-ambassador learns how to ease his moral and intellectual bondage. He will return to Woollett which 'isn't sure it ought to enjoy life', with a recognition that if Europe is amoral (by Woollett standards) it offers him beautiful illusions of freedom. He can live by his illusions – if he remains open to experience and doesn't require life to measure up to the Woollett yardstick.

The Ambassadors was told by James in a complex indirect style he had never attempted before and it revealed that he had at last reconciled himself to diminished omniscience. One could never know everything. He was determined to make his readers feel this, rather than accept the old tradition of the novel which told everything. James paid his price for running against the basic element that made novels the most popular art form of modern times. Instead of allowing his novel to gratify curiosity, James turned it into an instrument of mystification. He allowed his readers to know only as much as one learns in life. And he developed for the first time shifting angles of vision. In terms of old-fashioned storytelling this resulted in a novel without action. The excitement was intellectual, the pleasure resided in the unfolding of minute detail. Characters are glimpsed from particular angles. We are given a feeling that we have access to a series of cameras – and James is writing long before the modern cinema. We first see Miss Gostrey through Strether's eyes, ' a lady ... whose features – not freshly young, not markedly fine, but on happy terms with each other'. We first see Strether through her eyes, and in deliberate shifts and close-ups,

what his hostess saw, what she might have taken in with a vision kindly adjusted, was the lean, the slightly loose figure of a man of the middle height and something more perhaps than the middle age – a man of five and fifty, whose most immediate signs were a marked bloodless brown-ness of face, a thick dark moustache, of characteristically American cut, growing strong and falling low, a head of hair still abundant . . .

Then we look at the two together 'each so finely brown and so sharply spare, each confessing so to dents of surface and aids to sight, to a disproportionate nose and a head delicately or grossly grizzled, they might have been brother and sister'. It has often been said that in *The Ambassadors* the story remains wholly in the 'point of view' of Strether. But we discover soon enough that James brings in clouds of witnesses, first person intruders, spectators, individuals with 'ad-justed' vision; he keeps his camera moving; he asks us to use our imagination and to enjoy the personal relations he is showing us at the very heart of his story.

Seen in the light of its inventions, its original style, its psychology, the novel can be recognized in literary history as a Stendhalian mirror in the roadway, past which Marcel Proust, James Joyce, Vir-ginia Woolf, William Faulkner and so many others have since travelled. It might be called the first authentic masterpiece of the 'modern movement'. Its pattern-structure prefigured *Ulysses*; its long river-like sentences anticipated the reflective novel of Proust. Its quest for 'auras' of feeling foreshadowed the experiments of Virginia Woolf.

4

Beyond 'technique' and its resourceful experiments, beyond its neat symmetrical design, the care with which it is 'composed' – its in-directions, its deliberate withholding of information – that is its refusal to 'specify' as in *The Turn of the Screw* – beyond all this, the novel spoke for the central myth of Henry James's life. James had long before made up his mind that his choice of Europe was wise, that Woollett and Mrs Newsome – that is, the U.S.A. – could not offer him the sense of freedom he had won abroad. Europe was art, manners, landscapes in old paintings, interesting women like

Madame de Vionnet, in whose apartments one found the historical past of the French Empire; or it was relaxed Maupassant afternoons on the banks of the Seine – or the Thames – and wayside inns where civilization composed itself into pictures. Woollett was filled with the parochialisms and narrowness of the Newsomes; it was not a place for freedom of spirit. It was all constraint – it was Puritan. James seems to be struggling still with visions of a powerful, controlling yet beneficent mother – authority figures of his childhood and youth. There is first America itself, the mother sitting, waiting, in Woollett (or Cambridge), asking the son to perform in the great world into which he has ventured – but at the end of a silver cord. He struggles to free himself, to pursue his own life abroad and not be in a perpetual state of ambassadorship. In Europe he acquires other mothers. Miss Gostrey represents the mother – or even the brother – of intelligence; Madame de Vionnet is 'Europe' and passion. Her being Anglo-French gives her the two streams of culture that met in James. She is also the temptress-mother, a mysterious fount of anxiety. James's mother's name was Mary. Miss Gostrey is named Maria and Madame de Vionnet is Marie. In the mythic symbolism of the book the two motherlands of James's life take primary place – beneficient Europe, exigent America. And he had had to choose and accept the idea of exile.

On psychological ground we can see the prolonged struggle in James to cut the silver cord that bound him to Quincy Street, to Boston and New York. He could, at the end of his novel, send Strether back to Woollett – for he was quite prepared to re-visit America himself. From the time of this novel, aided by the sight of his nephews, nieces, cousins, he begins to speak of the need to give a sense of rootedness to American children. Circumstances had provided him with trans-Atlantic roots, but he was no longer sure that native rootedness would not have been better. In effect he is saying also that had he stayed at home, life would have been, for him, less ambiguous. Yet this had made possible his life of art and involved him in a constant balancing of the good and the bad of America and Europe. It had enabled him to be Henry James now the Master – and to write *The Ambassadors*.

Part Two
The Beast in the Jungle

62

A Poor Ancient Lady

WILLIAM JAMES and his wife Alice had been abroad ever since William became ill with heart trouble in 1899. In the spring of 1900 William was in Rome, trying to recover strength and well-being. His daughter Peggy, 13 when they arrived, had been living with an English family, the Joseph Thatcher Clarkes, friends of William, attending an English school at Harrow. Uprooted from the familiar American environment at adolescence, confined to English rural life, homesick, lonely, Peggy vigorously protested to her parents and to her uncle at Lamb House. The latter had large sympathies for her; he remembered out of his early years what it meant to be cast adrift as a child in Europe. From the first – with his long-nourished theories of juvenile education – he had urged William to send Peggy to a school in England; now he pleaded with her mother to worry a little less about inculcating 'moral and spiritual' ideas in the child. This had always been the trouble with the James family, he said; his own father had had that too-exclusive preoccupation. What Peggy could use, he told his brother and sister-in-law, was something more worldly. 'With her so definite Puritan heritage, Peggy could afford to be raised on almost solely *cultivated* "social" and aesthetic lines. The Devil (of the moral and spiritual) can – given her "atmosphere" – be trusted to look out for himself.'

Casting about, Henry James decided that Peggy could be best educated if she were entrusted to the well-known Marie Souvestre, who

has had for many years a very highly esteemed school for girls at high, breezy Wimbledon, near London (an admirable situation) – where she has formed the daughters of many of the very good English *advanced* Liberal political and professional connection during these latter times. She is a very fine, interesting person, her school holds a very particular place (all Joe Chamberlain's daughters were there and they adore her), and I must tell you more of her.

Henry's only objection to Mlle Souvestre's establishment was that it was definitely 'middle-class' – but then, he added, '*all* schools here are that'.

The William Jameses opposed such a school for their only daughter. They wanted her to live in a family environment which was one of the reasons they chose the Clarkes. In retrospect one wonders whether the uncle's perception of Peggy's needs, given the temporary expatriation of the William Jameses, was not more acute than that of her own parents. At Mlle Souvestre's Peggy would have been involved in the active life of a school run with French realism and imagination; she would have found there such young women as the future Eleanor Roosevelt; she would have met among English families, the Stracheys, for Lytton Strachey's sisters were close to Mlle Souvestre. The environment would have been benign for a young American girl who had lived in a family composed entirely of brothers and a celebrated father. Life was difficult for Peggy at the Joseph Thatcher Clarkes, where the exuberant Clarke boys visited various petty indignities on her. The Clarke family was good-natured, prosaic, middle class. Peggy wrote homesick letters to her parents on the Continent and received from her uncle gentle letters of encouragement. James arranged to have Peggy and some of her playmates regularly brought to London and escorted them to the primitive movies being shown then, or to some theatrical show he judged fitting for their tender ages. We find him writing to Peggy early in 1900, 'I hope that your journey home a week ago was comfortable and easy and that some of the rather horrid figures and sounds that passed before us at the theatre didn't haunt your dreams. There were too many *ugly* ones. The next time I shall take you to something prettier.' And again, 'your poor old lonely uncle misses you very much and takes the greatest interest in your new form of life and feeling greatly'. This had a depth of truth in it far beyond what little Peggy could have known.

The lonely uncle asked his lonely niece to come and stay with him at Lamb House that Christmas of 1900. England was in mourning for its dead and dying in Africa; the war had cast a blight over everything. The old Queen's life was running to its end. And Henry was uncomfortable – a troublesome eczema had bothered him ever since the middle of the year and would continue throughout the writing of *The Ambassadors*. In the midst of the general depression, and his own discomfort James acted with his quick empathy for the female young. He gave Peggy the unrestrained affection of which he was capable, plied her with sweets and good food, and planted her in his oak-parlour with the novels of Sir Walter Scott. A serious, solemn, articulate, slightly depressed girl, Peggy was a good reader. She made her way, during the wet and windy days at Lamb House, through *Redgauntlet, Old Mortality, The Pirate, The Antiquary*, and since she could read French, Rostand's *L'Aiglon*. When weather permitted novelist and niece went forth for walks with their little wire-haired fox terrier Nick, one of the Master's most beloved dogs. 'It was very nice,' wrote Peggy to her parents. 'Nothing much happened.' James corrected Peggy's American speech, and expressed confidence in her 'heroism' not to lose what she had learned in resuming life in Cambridge.

It was a little like Mr Longdon and Nanda, although Peggy, now turned 14, was a few years younger than James's grave intelligent girl of *The Awkward Age*. 'We make together a very quiet and cosy couple,' he wrote to Clare, niece of Miss Woolson. On Christmas Day he wrote to another friend, Jessie Allen:

I have just come up to a small upstairs study that I rejoice in here – after a *tête-à-tête* with my niece over a colossal turkey on which we made no perceptible impression whatever; and I have left her alone, by the fire and the lamp in the little oak-parlour – if a young thing may be said to be alone who is deep down in Sir Walter. The sea-wind howls in my old chimneys and round my old angles; but the clock ticks loud and the fire crackles fast within.

And so the uncle and Peggy spent their Christmas as the clock ticked the dying hours of the old century. James retreated to London on 31 December taking his niece with him to restore her to Harrow. Before leaving he wrote quick notes to various friends, wishing them 'a solid slice of the new era'. There was even a little note to Cora Crane, that betrayed no sign that his heart was hard against her. He could imagine 'how little of anything but heaviness' this Christmas had for her, 'in the dark and dreary town and with little but ghosts at your fireside'.

I

The old Queen was dying; with her unusual physical strength she had survived into a new time that was not her own. England at war and in mourning prepared itself for deeper mourning still.

Profoundly American though Henry James was, he experienced to the full the public emotion. Victoria was too much a part of his own life for him not to feel strangely stirred; the public's silver cord and the private were intertwined. He spoke of England feeling 'quite motherless' adding 'and I to some extent have my part in the feeling'. He wrote of her as 'a poor and ancient lady', a tired creature of pomp who had patiently laboured and lasted. Victoria had been an immovable presence when he had reached London in 1855, a boy of Peggy's age. He had seen her riding in her carriage from the time when the Prince Consort still lived; then in her widowhood, and at the last in her final dropsical old age 'throwing her good fat weight into the scales of general decency'.

The tiny figure on the canopied bed in Osborne House took its last breath on the evening of 22 January 1901, surrounded by children and grandchildren in prayer. The novelist, coming out of the Reform Club saw the headline, 'Death of the Queen'. The streets of London seemed to him 'strange and indescribable', the people hushed as if helpless – almost, he wrote, as if scared. It was 'a very curious and unforgettable impression'. He had not thought that he himself would experience grief, for it had been 'a simple running down of the old used up watch'. 'One knew then that one had ended by taking her for a kind of nursing mother of the land and of the empire, and by attaching to her duration an extraordinary idea of beneficence. This idea was just,' he told Bourget, 'and her duration is over. It's a new era – and we don't know what it is.' However there were other feelings and he wrote to Miss Woolson's sister and niece :

The Prince of Wales is an arch-vulgarian ... the wretched little Yorks are less than nothing; the Queen's magnificent duration had held things magnificently – beneficently – together and prevented all sorts of accidents. Her death, in short, will let loose incalculable forces for possible ill. I am very pessimistic.

Edward was an 'ugly' omen 'for the dignity of things', he felt, and his accession would make for 'vulgarity and frivolity'. There would probably be a year's mourning. He told the Woolson relatives they ought to wear mourning at least for a month, as a gesture – Victoria had been 'always nice' to the U.S.A. When he found himself at the Reform Club writing letters on the club's black-bordered stationery, James continued to experience unexpected emotions. They were only partly for Victoria; she had embodied his lifetime experience of governing women. 'It has really been, the Event, most moving, interesting and picturesque. I have felt *more* moved, than I should have expected (such is the *community* of sentiment,) and one has realized all sorts of things about the brave old woman's beneficent duration and holding-together virtue.' Dining amid various Privy Councillors and the leaders of England at his club, Henry James caught the traditional wave of sympathy which always flows towards the new monarch as he heard John Morley say that Edward 'made a good impression' at his first Council. But, James whispered in a letter to William, 'speriamo'.

2

From a window in the home of friends who had once lived in New England, Peggy James watched the procession built around the tiny coffin – it seemed almost a child's coffin – in which Victoria was borne through the streets of the capital she had graced so long, to Paddington Station, to last obsequies at Windsor. Peggy's uncle had fully briefed her; and he had insisted she wear a little black mourning hat which he purchased for her as befitted the occasion. Peggy saw great pageantry. Europe's princes and kings, not least the Emperor of the Germans, rode and marched; bells tolled; the streets were dark with people in black. The slow procession was lit by a break in the cloud-canopy; and within the black-bordered frame of funeral the empire at war asserted its pride and glory in handsome bedecked horses, great lines of soldiers.

Henry James had met his niece the previous afternoon and arranged for her to spend the night at their friend's home. This left him free on the day itself to see the procession from other windows, those of still another friend, at Buckingham Gate. It was a good window; the view was splendid; but the visual-minded novelist was not altogether happy. The ladies wore high plumes and bows and as a 'lone and modest man', (he explained to his niece), 'I had the back seat, as it were, of all. However I saw a good deal and our windows were close to the show.' The formidably large gun carriage on which the coffin was placed 'just grazed the ridiculous' yet he found it all 'interesting and moving and picturesque'. There were he remarked 'no anarchist bomb, no ugliness, nor infelicity of any sort. But strange is the feeling that the door is closed on the past sixty years.' The new King looked well on horseback and James came away from his vantage point with Alice Stopford Green, widow of the historian, who had a lively tongue and quick mind and also wrote history. A loyal Irishwoman, she had strong views on colonialism and the Boer

War. James found her 'troubled about many things – too troubled perhaps and about too many. But on some of them I much feel with her.' He 'loathed' the war; he felt 'that if this dear stupid old Country doesn't stop trying to bite off more than she can chew ... she will sink'.

'I mourn the safe and motherly old middle-class queen, who held the nation warm under the fold of her big, hideous Scotch-plaid shawl and whose duration had been so extraordinarily convenient and beneficent,' he wrote a few days later to Wendell Holmes. She had been for him 'a sustaining symbol'.

Shortly afterwards he found himself mourning another sustaining symbol of his life. Mrs Bronson, who had presided queen-like over the Grand Canal in her charming Ca'Alvisi, also died with the new century. Her death made James feel 'older and sadder', he wrote to her daughter, the Contessa Rucellai. 'It is the end of so many things – so many delightful memories, histories, associations – some of the happiest elements of one's past. From years ever so far back she was delightfully kind to me. Those long Venetian years will be for all her friends a sort of legend and boast.' James would write a memorial to Mrs Bronson, hostess of Browning and himself, and of so many others; and later that year he would begin a novel whose greatest scenes would be set in the city of Mrs Bronson's adoption.

63

Miss Weld

I

JAMES had lost the habit of London, but he came back to the metropolis during the winter of 1901 with all his old energies, and this in spite of the fact that his skin irritation continued to trouble him. He felt a great burning in his face and described it to his brother as 'visible *gout*' – in spite of 'extreme sobriety and abstinence: small, very small, too small, eating and no drinking. The smallest drop of wine or spirits sets my face on fire.' It did not prevent him from dining out strenuously, as of old; and he worked strenuously too. This was the first occasion on which he occupied his newly furnished room at the Reform Club. He was able to have MacAlpine in from mid-mornings until almost two o'clock to receive dictation of *The Ambassadors*. He worked with a certain desperation, for he had decided some weeks before to part with the Scottish typist 'not in anger or as a catastrophe', but simply because 'he's too damned expensive, and always has been – and too place-taking in my life and economy. I can get a highly competent little woman for half, or a less full-blown young man at a great abatement. He had found a new position for MacAlpine, which the latter would assume after Easter. In the interval he sought to get as much of his novel as possible completed before reorganizing 'this branch of my establishment'.

His mornings were consistently given over to work; after a late lunch he was always ready for his renewed town life. The occasions were muted, because of the universal mourning, but they still had a large interest for the novelist. He noticed, in some of the great houses, how much more the diamonds gleamed against the mourning black of the ladies' dresses; and the servants, in ubiquitous black, looked 'as if they were of more exalted station'. He relished the pageantry which went with the public grief, for the new King was to be crowned. He had come back to the capital, he wrote to Wendell Holmes, after two suburban winters to fall on 'pomps and pageants ... We are going to have a pompous king.' Edward would provide circuses, if not bread. 'We grovel before fat Edward.' To Morton Fullerton he repeated that 'the old Queen's death was a real emotion – quite big and fine, but we have dropped again to Edwardism quite unvarnished and Chamberlainism quite unblushing'. He dined with the Humphry Wards, Jonathan Sturges, A. C. Benson, Gosse. He drank tea with Violet Hunt at her club. However, he did not lose sight of his niece. When he could not go out to Harrow on a Sunday to visit her, he made arrangements for her to come into town. Years later she still remembered his courtliness and gentleness. He took her to a performance of *Twelfth Night*; he marched her through museums; and in gentle letters to her guardian he spoke of his search for 'some innocent place of entertainment – say the Hippodrome or the Alhambra'.

In the cold days of March, after little more than eight weeks of London life, he felt 'a yearning for cabless days and dinnerless nights'. The William Jameses were coming north again after their winter in Rome and would arrive at Lamb House after Easter. William had been preparing a series of lectures on 'the varieties of religious experience' – the Gifford Lectures – to be delivered that spring at Edinburgh. His brother and sister-in-law had been abroad for two years and his niece was nearing her 15th birthday. Recognizing that there would be interruptions of his work he addressed himself to a secretarial bureau. He wanted a young woman, he explained, willing to live out in Rye, capable of learning to take dictation directly to the machine. He could promise few distractions for a young person save those of rural charm and the bicycle.

2

Henry James's literary situation at the moment of his change of secretaries was as follows: he had published the previous autumn his volume of tales *The Soft Side*, containing a dozen stories written by him, most of them during the weeks when he was attempting to 'finance' the purchase of Lamb House. At Easter 1901 he had almost completed *The Ambassadors* for which he had not yet signed a contract. He had already begun another novel, and there loomed before him the life of William Wetmore Story promised to Blackwood in Edinburgh. In addition he was to do an introduction to a new edition of *Madame Bovary* and one to a volume of Balzac – these promised to Edmund Gosse, editor of a series entitled *A Century of French Romance*. Also the *North American Review* had asked for some literary essays.

The William Jameses arrived at Lamb House at the end of the first week in April, Peggy coming with them. Just after their re-installation, Mary Weld, young, clear-eyed, round-faced, fresh from a holiday in Berlin, came to Rye to discuss working for Mr James. He interviewed her in the Garden Room where she would do her typing. She had first-class references. Her father had been a classical scholar at Trinity in Dublin and had published English translations of certain of the Greek tragedies. She had attended a college for young ladies; and then, in the emancipatory spirit of the times, she had gone to secretarial school. She seemed modest, willing, and delighted at the prospect of Rye and the bicycle. James was nervous during the interview (she later recalled) and she herself felt anxious. They discussed what she would do during the long pauses that sometimes occurred during dictation. MacAlpine had smoked; it was settled that she might crochet. James escorted her into Lamb House for lunch, where she met the William Jameses. There was a long discussion at table as to what an amanuensis should wear for such duties. Mrs William agreed that a 'suit' – that is, a coat and skirt – would be appropriate. That same afternoon Miss Weld went hunting for a room in Rye. Her diary records that there was snow in the town on 15 April, when she arrived to start work; and the next morning she began. As it turned out, her first task was not for Henry James. What she found herself typing were William James's lectures on religion. Miss Weld would say later that typing for Henry James was like accompanying a singer on the piano. In a letter to a friend she wrote that James's dictation was 'remarkably fluent. The hesitation and searching for the right word people talk about, was simply nervousness and vanished once he knew you well ... when working I was just part of the machinery, but out of school, so to speak, he was extraordinarily kind, courteous, and considerate.' Sometimes in the afternoon he bicycled with her. Sometimes she accompanied him on his walks. It was she who recalled how James hid to avoid encountering Hueffer. She also recalled that a certain woman in Rye came to Lamb House to make sure that everything was 'respectable' – since so young a lady was working for an elderly bachelor. In little more than a month Henry James was writing that 'Miss Weld proves decidedly a *bijou*', and to the Duchess of Sutherland in June of that year, who inquired about her compatriot MacAlpine, James replied the latter had found 'more exalted employment', adding 'he had too much Personality – and I have secured in his place a young lady who has, to the best of my belief, less, or who disguises it more'. Miss Weld did have her own more modest kind of personality. At times it may have seemed mouse-like to the Master, but she was always at ease with him and always helpful and tactful. MacAlpine's 'lady successor is an improvement on him! and an economy!' James wrote. And again: 'Miss Weld continues dressy and refined and devoted.' In later letters he Italianized her name, as he had often done to Lizzie Boott. His typist became 'the little Weldina' – and he was delighted when she took up bookbinding with the help of a friend. 'Little Weldina,' he wrote, 'is still in the foreground – but she has now a background of bookbinding that greatly helps.' He saw that this employment would relieve the monotony of Rye for so young a person. He made available to her the adjacent studio in Watchbell Street, which he had offered repeatedly to Hendrik Andersen. 'The Diversion,' he wrote of the bookbinding, 'seems to have been quite successfully operated.' He allowed Miss Weld to bind certain of his French books and told her 'poor binding is an abject thing, good a divine. Go in for the latter.'

It fell to Miss Weld to receive dictation of the latter part of *The Ambassadors*, *The Wings of the Dove* and *The Golden Bowl*. Her typewriter also took down masses of correspondence, the biography of W. W. Story, some of James's finest late essays, and some of his most remarkable tales, those contained in *The Better Sort*. Her punctuality, efficiency, and good nature contributed markedly to the environment he needed for this sustained period of his labours, the summit of his long career.

64

A Family Summer

I

FROM Peggy James, 14, 26 April 1901, at Lamb House in Rye, to her older brother Billy, 19, in Cambridge, Massachusetts:

Dear old Billy – We are down here at Rye again and it is mighty nice. In the morning I moon around and take pictures ... The elders meanwhile occupy themselves in various ways. Uncle Henry dictating to his typewriter, Papa doing his Gifford lectures mostly and Mama reading, writing or putting our clothes to rights. Uncle Henry, Mama and I used always to go for a long walk in the afternoon, that is to say when Nick allowed us to go, by not chasing sheep or chickens, and having to be brought home again. It is too funny for words sometimes when this happens and it nearly drives Uncle Henry to distraction and he yells in a terribly loud voice 'Oh! oh! oh! oh! oh! you little brute! you little brute! you beast! oh! oh! oh!' Then he hurries home with the unfortunate wretch and leaves Mama and me to follow on at our own sweet pace. Lately however Papa has felt better and we have all gone to drive ... a most picturesque old house came into sight. It was built of gray stone overgrown with ivy in some parts. It had casement windows with tiny diamond-shaped panes of glass in them. A little chapel occupys one wing ... Uncle Henry knocked at a huge iron knocker which was on an iron-studded oak door .. the huge fireplaces were just what one would have expected. You may be interested to hear that Stephen Crane lived there ...

William James, looking at his brother after a winter's absence, wrote to Dr Baldwin 'he works steadily, and seems less well than he did – possibly the result of a London winter'. The London winter had, as a matter of fact, done Henry much good; and what William saw, but could not recognize, was Henry's usual worried state whenever his brother was on the scene. In a letter to Miss Robins, the novelist spoke of 'anxiety-breeding relations in my house'. Part of the anxiety was a concern for William's health. The family party was joined by Harry, his elder son, now grown to young manhood, who came to attend his father's Edinburgh lectures. With four more mouths to feed in Lamb House, James found himself in constant consultation with his cook.

The novelist wanted to get on with *The Ambassadors* but the distractions were numerous. He found himself finally free in May, when his relatives left for the Continent. On 9 May 1901 he dispatched the first nine parts of his novel to his agent in a form destined for serialization. The remaining parts were transmitted shortly afterwards, James warning that in the book form he would restore three and a half chapters omitted in the serial. In the restoration a chapter was misplaced in the American edition, but the English edition was accurate. There is no record that James noted the error.

He enjoyed the early days of summer at Lamb House. Miss Weld arranged flowers in strategic places. 'She does so charmingly – has a real gift,' he told his niece. The novelist would later speak of this summer as 'a family summer', for Peggy stayed with him while the William Jameses were on the Continent. Lamb House was filled with many other guests as well. On a day in June, H. G. Wells brought over George Gissing and the two spent the night at Lamb House. James was fascinated by Gissing, disapproved of his 'amazing' relations with women – 'why will he do these things?' – but approved of *New Grub Street*. However, he deplored its style. He found it colourless and surfaced as with some mechanical gloss. Gissing's best quality, James held, was that he really described the life of the lower middle class; other novelists seemed to prefer the extremes of 'low life or lords'. Gissing had led a life among prostitutes and his face was disfigured by a purple syphilitic scar. He had left his second wife and children to live with a mistress in France. From then on James followed his career through Wells, and was touched by Gissing's sufferings and Wells's loyalty.

On another day James received the Kent contingent, 'Joseph Conrad, wife, baby and trap and pony' who came to tea and stayed all afternoon. The previous day he had had the Winchelsea contingent, the Hueffers, Ford, his wife and guest 'for hours'. Various Bostonians turned up, including Wendell Holmes; and English intimates such as Edmund Gosse, and the old dilettante, Hamilton Aïdé whom James characterized as 'the Diane de Poitiers of our time'. As between Holmes, Aïdé, and Peggy, he was happiest with his niece. Holmes's views 'on the course of Empire and other matters', he disliked, so they confined themselves to a few chosen topics; with Aïdé 'the superficial is imposed by the very nature of his mind'. Peggy imposed no strain; she showed off her continental frocks to her uncle and he approved of her speech and manners. Her two years in England had done much for her. 'She is a most soothing and satisfactory maid, attached and attaching to her (poor old) Uncle,' James wrote to Morton Fullerton.

We are spending the summer days, (amazing for unbroken beauty, but too rainless,) here together in idyllic intimacy and tranquillity ... We take longish late afternoon walks, and this afternoon off – two miles by the Golfists little steam-train – to the beautiful sands of the shore, vast and firm and shining, with the dear old Romney Marsh on one side, and the blue, blue sea of August on the other – where we wandered far and far and missed you awfully and awfully. Ah, you must come.

Fullerton wrote back beautiful and affectionate letters, but remained embedded in his Paris.

2

By the middle of July, Henry James announced the title of his new novel, *The Wings of the Dove*, and said it would be a love story. The idea for the story had been in his notebooks since 1894 and he had made a start on the book in 1900 but had dropped it to write *The Ambassadors*. Before returning to it, he wrote the last of his theatrical articles – he had written a sufficient number during all his years to fill a stout volume. This one dealt with the French neo-romantic, Edmond Rostand. He had seen Sarah Bernhardt in *L'Aiglon* and *La Princesse Lointaine*, and Coquelin in *Cyrano de Bergerac*. He considered Rostand a journalistic Victor Hugo; he liked his theatricality, his swagger, his combination of whimsicality and nationalism, the sentimental with the sublime. As always, something beside his admiration made James write such fugitive essays. What fascinated

him in Rostand was his success; he equated this with the success of
Kipling, finding in both writers 'the patriotic note, the note of the
militant and triumphant race'. As always he pondered the way in
which these men, with one or two works, suddenly captured the
public, suddenly became personalities and, above all, suddenly became wealthy. Rostand's themes were close to his own – Cyrano's
love and renunciation; the frustration of the faraway princess and
the pilgrim; the play about Napoleon II, 'who lives over the vast
paternal legend, the glories, the victories, the successive battlefields,
the anecdotes, the manners, the personal habits, the aspect and trick
of the very clothes'. The Napoleonic story as always had a magical
appeal for James – it was also a story of success – and then of fall,
in the old tragic sense. Above all it spoke for great power and
for *gloire*. *L'Aiglon* was about an 'eaglet' unable to soar – and
James was writing a novel about a dove, which also could not soar.
The poetry, the melancholy, the gloom in Rostand touched James;
although we gather not as deeply as that which he found at this
time in the plays of Maurice Maeterlinck, about whom he did not
write an article but whose works he saw. He very quickly grasped
their crepuscular symbolism, their veiled allegory. There are explicit
references to Maeterlinck in *The Wings of the Dove* and careful
evocation of the mood of *Pelléas and Mélisande*.

The William Jameses sailed at the end of August. Henry gave
them a sad send-off at Euston station. With all the anxieties William induced in him, Henry had a deep love for his brother. And
his attachment to the young 'Peggotina' was now profound. 'I feel
very lonely and bereft,' he wrote to his brother, 'more than ever
eager to borrow a child from you, if you only had the right one.' He
returned to Rye having caught a cold, and feeling seedy. 'The beautiful vanished days ... they have continued here, the beautiful days,
of an exquisite quality.' Lamb House remained, as he ruefully testified, 'an hotel'. Gosse returned from Venice and reported on his
adventures. The annals of the house record that for the first time
young Percy Lubbock 'of long limbs and candid countenance' visited
Henry James that summer; most important of all, Hendrik Andersen was due in Paris and promised to dash over for a few days. James
was expecting Lily Norton, various other Boston ladies, and a writer
friend, T. Bailey Saunders. He warned Andersen they would have
very little time alone; he added, however, 'I shall at the station, take
very personal possession of you.' Andersen's visit, so long and so

eagerly awaited, with all its overtones of affection and love, occurred in the midst of a series of unscheduled events. 'A below-stairs crisis that has been maturing fast for some time, reaches visibly its acute stage,' James wrote to a friend on 19 September 1901. Three words in Miss Weld's diary, the next day, 'the Smith tragedy', tell us that the crisis had – after many years – been reached.

65

A Domestic Upheaval

I

FOR some sixteen years – ever since he had originally settled in De Vere Gardens (in 1886) – James had had as servants an English couple, the Smiths, husband and wife. They had kept house for him with great efficiency, the husband as butler, the wife as cook. The two, with the addition of a parlour maid, and his house-boy Burgess, constituted his total staff in the country. There had been long intervals in the old days when James travelled on the Continent – periods of idleness for his servants – during which the Smiths became increasingly alcoholic. James had been a generous employer. He paid them well. They did not work hard. They had more work, however, at Lamb House than in London, especially with so many visitors, during the summers. And they had never wholly accommodated themselves to their absence from the metropolis. Rural life encouraged their alcoholism. One of Hueffer's memories had been his luncheon with James served by the red-nosed Smith with elaborate control of his tipsiness. Only ten days before Andersen's arrival, James had written to his brother, 'I am living from hand to mouth with the Smiths, who remain exactly the same queer mixture of alcohol and perfection.' The 'perfection' had to give way.

On their side, the Smiths seem to have been content with their distinguished master. In 1892, when James was mourning the death of his sister, he had allowed Mrs Smith to bring into De Vere Gardens her ailing sister during one of his absences. He had returned to discover that the woman was seriously ill. She had cancer and he permitted her to come back to De Vere Gardens after her operation. He brought nurses in, and for a time turned his flat into a hospital.

Finally he had her removed to a nursing home, and paid most of the medical bills. The gratitude of the Smiths had been shown through the years. However, James could also be demanding and irritable and a hard taskmaster.

The collapse of the Smiths was sudden, though fully expected. On 19 September, a Thursday, Lily Norton came to spend the night at Lamb House. The next day she and James were joined at lunch by Ida Agassiz Higginson, an old Boston friend, wife of the financier and patron of the arts, Henry Lee Higginson. In the afternoon T. Bailey Saunders arrived from Eastbourne to spend the week-end. Smith seems to have managed the lunch; but he was out cold shortly thereafter. James got the ladies off to London without their suspecting a domestic crisis. 'Smith,' Henry wrote to Mrs William James 'was *accumulatedly* so drunk that I got him out of the house – i.e. all Friday and Saturday and Sunday.' Andersen arrived on Saturday. James got the local doctor, Skinner, to treat the man, but his employer 'could not really communicate with him to the extent of a word'. In the meantime Mrs Smith anaesthetized herself. James summoned Mrs Smith's sister, whom he knew to be in service at the home of England's poet laureate, Alfred Austin, at nearby Ashford. She arrived, helped to pack their belongings (they still too drunk to help themselves) and on the Monday they left – dismissed at last, and leaving James's house unstaffed, save for 'the gnome' Burgess, as James playfully called his loyal local boy, and the housemaid, Fanny.

'They were, at the end, simply two saturated and demoralized victims, with not a word to say for themselves and going in silence to their doom; but great is the miracle of their having been, all the while, the admirable servants they were and whom I shall ever unutterably mourn and miss.' It was clear at the end that most of their wages had gone into liquor. James thought it an extraordinarily lucky thing he had been able to find their relatives 'otherwise my case would have indeed been queer'. He gave the Smiths 'an almost foolishly liberal' severance pay of two months' wages each, 'till they can turn round'. He added, to Alice James,

They will never turn round; they are lost utterly; but I would have promised *anything* in my desire to get them out of the house before some still more hideous helplessness made it impossible. A new place is impossible to either; they wouldn't keep it three days; and their deplorable incriminating aspect alone damns them beyond appeal. What they looked like going to the Station!

James paid their liquor bill in the town and settled down to make-shift living, taking some of his meals at the Mermaid Inn, while he sent out appeals to his London lady friends for help.

2

In retrospect James wrote good-humouredly to Andersen of 'my little squalid botheration'. The long-awaited reunion of the old Master and the young sculptor however had lost some of its intimacy. James was too upset. 'Saunders and dear young Andersen remained with me through it and were really a comfort,' the novelist reported to Mrs William, who had met Andersen in Rome. The sculptor, however, prolonged his stay into the middle of the week and the two recaptured at the end a few hours of privacy. Once again James found Andersen enormously appealing: once again he offered him tenderness and affection. He had described Andersen to the William Jameses, as 'a sincere and intelligent being, though handicapped by a strange "self-made" illiteracy and ignorance of many things'. The sculptor had had a difficult time in America. He had done a nude, but the statue had been turned down because of the nudity. James was consoling. 'What a dismal doom for a sculptor to work for a great vulgar stupid community that revels in every hideous vulgarity and only quakes at the clean and blessed nude – the last refuge of Honour!' He urged Andersen to leave Rome. 'What I should like is that you should come and stay with me till you are wholly rested and consoled and cheered – no matter how long it takes: the longer the better.' The longest time the sculptor gave him was this brief, and as it happened, interrupted visit.

Their personal relationship was one thing; the matter of art was another – and when it came to a statue of Lincoln, of which Andersen sent James a photograph, the novelist was direct and uncompromising. He reminded Andersen that in his youth he had been 'drenched with feeling' for the President. A seated Lincoln shocked him. 'He was for us all, then, standing up very tall.' He began by saying he liked the head but thought it 'rather too smooth, ironed-out, simplified as to ruggedness, ugliness, mouth, etc.' His principal complaint, however, was that Andersen had not conveyed the sense of a *physical* Lincoln. 'I don't feel the length of limb, leg, shanks, loose-jointedness, etc. – nor the thickness of the large body in the clothes – especially the presence of shoulders, big arms and big hands.' He told Andersen that he had made 'a *softer*, smaller giant than we used to see'. The face lacked 'light and shade', and what was needed was 'more breaking-up, under his accursed clothing, more bone, more mass'. Also he was too 'placid'. The image of history and memory was 'benevolent, but deeply troubled, and altogether tragic : that's how one thinks of him'.

The young sculptor took these criticisms with good grace. They were gently given 'for the love of your glory and your gain'. Moreover, Andersen's self-assurance was impervious to subtleties. When they were together it was Andersen's stature, his shoulders, his arms and hands, the solid physical presence that counted. James escorted him as far as the junction point of Ashford and wrote to him promptly, 'I miss you – keep on doing so – out of all proportion to the too few hours you were here – and even go so far as to ask myself whether visits so damnably short haven't more in them to groan, than to thank for.' He said also 'the memory *is* a kind of beggarly stopgap till we can meet again'. When he got word of the sculptor's safe return to his studio in Rome he imaged him as a young priest returned to his altar – but a pagan priest, for he saw him with 'your idols, bless their brave limbs and blank eyes, ranged roundabout'.

'I wish you, my dear Boy, such a high tide o. inspiration and execution as will float you over every worry and land you in peace and renown.'

With Andersen gone James addressed himself to restoring his household. 'Peace now reigns – I am happy to say – though peace a little sharply distinguished from Plenty,' he wrote to his other recent guest, Bailey Saunders. A charwoman was recruited as emergency cook. With the aid of the 'knife-boy' Burgess and maid, normal life was restored. To Peggy, with whom he now began a fairly regular correspondence, he described his staff and household as reduced to 'picnicking lines'. 'Mrs Bourne, who sleeps here, roasts chickens, fries soles, makes custard puddings, etc. Fanny and the gnome Burgess affect me as a delightful simplification. I have no desire for the present to alter it.' He was glad the catastrophe had been stayed until after the William Jameses had left. Their handsome tips on departure had all been invested in liquor. 'I see now,' he told Peggy, 'how heavily for years, the accumulated (the thousands of gallons of) whisky of the Smiths has weighed on my spirits, how odiously uneasy I had chronically been.'

66

Aunt Lucy

OF the London ladies to whom Henry James appealed for help there was one who entered most into his domestic crisis. This was Mrs W. K. Clifford. He had known her since the 1880s and their friendship had deepened every year. Lucy Clifford, the former Lucy Lane, had been in her youth a golden-haired, red-cheeked art student, who sketched antique statues in the British Museum. She had married one of the greatest mathematicians of the Victorian era, W. K. Clifford, who died at 34. Finding herself a widow – she was then 24 – with two young daughters to support, Lucy turned to writing – journalism, fiction, and later, plays. Her courage, her steadfastness, her alertness, and her abilities won her wide admiration. She was still wearing mourning when James met her in 1880; he was the same age as her husband but she had treated him as if he were one of her young literary protégés who came to her Sunday salon. In the 1890s, when he had been discouraged by the failure of his plays, she had induced the editor of the *Illustrated London News* to publish a Henry James serial – one of the strangest mediums in which the novelist ever appeared. This was *The Other House*. By that time she had become a hearty, mothering, energetic, enveloping woman, direct in her conversation and formidable in her ability to get things done. It was she who helped launch Rudyard Kipling in literary London after reading some of his work published in India. James was an habitué of her home. He liked nothing better than to sip a liqueur by her fireside after an evening at the theatre; or to take tea with her and listen to London literary gossip. Her novel *Mrs Keith's Crime* proved a great success; and also *Aunt Anne*, which still has its place on the shelf of minor Victorian fiction. Because of the latter, James often addressed her in his letters as 'Dearest Aunt Lucy'. She responded by calling him her 'nevvy'. On other occasions she was his 'Beloved girl'. She was brisk, original, loyal, self-assertive, and full of warm feelings.

Unlike the ladies James had cultivated in his younger years, Lucy Clifford did not possess a sharp tongue, or an underlying cruelty that he had accepted and even found attractive in them. Lucy Clifford was genial. She spoke well, she was eminently expressive and generous. One would not have called her a pretty woman. But her irregular features had much charm, and then one always knew where one stood with her. She had loyal friends among London's most distinguished men – Huxley, Tyndall, among her husband's scientific friends; Browning, Morley, Lowell, during his ambassadorial time, and Henry James. Frequenters of her salon encountered Bernard Shaw, when he was still the red-bearded music critic of his nonage. In the twentieth century she was still befriending the literary young, Hugh Walpole, among others, and after him Charles Morgan. Late in life James would speak of 'that admirable Lucy Clifford – as a character, a nature, a soul of generosity and devotion'. She was, in these ways, he said 'one of the finest bravest creatures possible'. Mrs Clifford was one of three London friends who would be remembered in Henry James's will.

2

She had just returned from Vienna when James wrote her of his domestic débâcle, using the language of cataclysm. His letters record a tidal wave, a whirlwind, a shooting 'into space' of the drunken Smiths, a 'domestic cyclone'. One feels in reading his letters to her that she was ready to swoop down on Rye and keep house for him. 'How noble and generous your instant impulse of succour in respect of my disabled house and how deeply I am touched by it! I thank you with all my heart.' She immediately got into touch with a housemaid and she canvassed others for interviews. James reassured her. He was not 'in extreme discomfort; therefore don't pity me or think of me too much'. It was really a relief not to have whiskyfied servants around; it was 'a blissful cessation of nightmare'. He would be in town early in the new year and probably could make do until then. And he told Mrs Clifford that other friends had recommended a certain lady named Paddington, with a record of having held only two posts, nineteen years in one and ten in another. 'Bear with the lonely celibate,' he wrote to loyal Lucy, 'who has, as it were to boil his own pot ... It's horrible not immediately to see you – and to know that you must all the while be letting off steam by which I shan't – or don't – profit. Do bottle a little up for me, and I will come and uncork the wine on the earliest possible day.' Lucy, however, continued to send telegrams; she had a stand-by housemaid readied in case of emergency; and James came to confer with her when he arrived in town for his interview with the matronly Mrs Paddington.

The matron had impeccable references. She seemed to like the idea of a bachelor establishment. She was ready to come for £3 a month. Such was the wage-scale of the time for a good housekeeper-cook. She would not, however, be free until mid-November. James was prepared to go on with his improvised household until then. He was working at *The Wings of the Dove* and the autumn at Rye was exquisite – 'the tree forms grow in beauty as they simplify in dress; the grey sky is streaked with vague pink; peculiar delicacies and poetries abound; and the stillness is like the long gulp or catching of breath that precedes ... a long sob, or other vocal outbreak'. He added, 'May this fine image not fit too closely my own hushed personal condition.' He was writing then to his garden-lady Miss Muir Mackenzie. 'I go down at last, only tomorrow (to the station) to meet the lady of the Gorringe's costume, on whose convenience I have been waiting all this time. She is my Fate! may she not be my Doom. May a "long sob" not have cause to ensue upon this period of quite resigned suspense.'

It will be recalled that Olivia Garnett, she who had dreams of Henry James saying profound things to her, stepped off the train at Rye station on her way to visit the Hueffers the next morning and beheld Henry James approaching a matronly lady and heard him say, 'I have come to meet my doom.' Thus began the long régime of Mrs Paddington in Lamb House, a woman who was severe and auto-cratic with her fellow-servants, but who knew her business thoroughly. Three weeks after her arrival, James was writing of the 'peace' she promised his household –

a *real*, trained, all-round, excellent cook, up to the wildest want, or flight ... a *supreme* economist, manager, mistress of thrift, foresight (my tradesmen's books going steadily down and down;) and an equally ex-cellent, genial, sensible, good-tempered, friendly woman – safe with her fellow-servants altogether ... *The* blessing in Mrs P. is that she clearly likes my service, as much as I cling to *her*.

67

The Wings of the Dove

HENRY JAMES began dictating *The Wings of the Dove* on 9 July 1901; he worked on the book intermittently during August when Peggy was with him; and ..e continued through the domestic interruptions in October and on into the new year. He was away from Rye briefly to visit E. L. Godkin, his old *Nation* editor who had come to England to spend his last days. Godkin died at Torquay shortly after James had his last glimpse of him.

Jonathan Sturges paid one of his long visits to Lamb House through Christmas and the year's end, with the consequence that James stayed on until the end of January before going up to London where he planned to remain during the worst part of the winter. So confident was James of completing his novel that he sent off 500 pages of the manuscript to Constable and was reading proofs of his book even while writing the final sections – the pages – devoted to the rage of the elements in Venice as Milly, his heiress, dies in her rented palazzo. In the Venetian chapter James relived old memories, not only the long-ago death of Minny Temple, but the wasting illness of his sister, and the violent end – in Venice – of Miss Woolson. He reached London on 27 January – the anniversary week of Miss Woolson's death – and had no sooner settled into the Reform Club when he became 'painfully' ill. He described it as an 'inflammation of the bowels'. He continued to have stomach upsets and gout; in mid-February he dashed back to Rye; even in mid-winter Lamb House, with its servants, was preferable to his lonely club room. He could receive better care in time of illness.

During ensuing weeks he had 'botherations, aberrations, damnations of the mind and body'. The subject or central dilemma of his novel, the death in Venice, was a heavy charge on his emotions. Within the year his memories of Miss Woolson's suicide had been stirred by a visit to Rye of Grace Carter, Fenimore's cousin. She had seen Miss Woolson in death, had made the funeral arrangements in Rome; and from that troubled time they had been friends. He had not met her for some years, but now he wrote her a series of letters, cherishing 'our common memory of, and common affection for, dear

C.F.W.' Then he learned from the Benedicts that Miss Woolson's dog, Otello, had died. 'This end of his career,' James wrote to them, 'takes me back in memory to that other end – the melancholy days in Venice.' The dog, James reminded them, stood 'for a particular terrible passage' in their lives. The passage had been terrible in his life as well; and he was in a sense reliving it for he had decided to have his heroine die, as Miss Woolson had done, in an old Venetian palace. He had direct news of the palace he was putting into the novel, from Edmund Gosse, who visited James's friends the Curtises in 'the divine Barbaro, noblest of human habitations'. To Mrs Curtis he wrote that 'Venice ... seems such a museum of distressed *ends*'. They were discussing the disappearance from the scene of many familiar figures. By a coincidence, the news of Miss Woolson's dog was followed by the sudden death of his own beloved wire terrier. Everything seemed to contribute to encroachment on mind and memory of the crowded recent past – not least – publication of Graham Balfour's biography of Robert Louis Stevenson who had died less than a year after Miss Woolson. James's illness delayed the novel; the final pages were written late in May. In June he had a return, in attenuated form, of his winter's illness, but he recovered rapidly. After that Lamb House began to receive its summer quotas of visitors. His novel, delayed by his illness, was published on 21 August 1902 in New York and nine days later in England.

I

The idea for the novel about a doomed young woman had been with him ever since the early death of Minny Temple in 1870. He had seemed almost to welcome her death – if it had to be – because he could take total possession of her in his mind and memory; he had told his mother Minny would be an inspiration to him in years to come. This she had been. She had died of 'galloping' consumption. James, thinking of his own ill-health during the Civil War, had spoken of himself as 'slowly crawling from weakness and inaction and suffering into strength and health and hope; she sinking out of brightness and youth into decline and death'. The death of one or the other partner in love : this had been his theme in tales as early as *De Grey: a Romance* or *Longstaff's Marriage*. In later years, re-worked, it had become the macabre story of *Maud-Evelyn* in which a young man falls in love with a dead girl he has never known, and convinces himself she has been his wife. When James's heroes do not actively renounce marriage, they passively displace love from the living to the dead.

He had published a curious story in 1884 called *Georgina's Reasons*, in which the recurrent theme expressed itself in still another form. In it two women bear names that would be used in *The Wings of the Dove*, Kate and Mildred Theory. Mildred Theory would become Milly Theale. Both Mildreds are doomed, Mildred Theory by consumption, Milly Theale by an unnamed disease. Mildred Theory is 'as beautiful as a saint, and as delicate and refined as an angel'; in short, she too is a 'dove'. Kate must curtail her freedom to her sister's needs. 'So long as Mildred should live, her own life was suspended.' She cannot allow herself to feel love for the handsome naval officer, who comes to see her in their temporary home at Posilippo. He is Raymond Benyon, secretly married to a woman in New York named Georgina, as Merton Densher will ultimately be secretly engaged to Kate in *The Wings of the Dove*. In the earlier tale we find a vivid 'recognition scene' in front of a portrait, foreshadowing the dramatic moment in which Milly Theale faces a Bronzino portrait of a lady who resembles her. Minny Temple – Mildred Theory – Milly Theale – the three belonged to a single line of fantasy. In its essence it was that of the Henry James who could not bring himself to love and marry. He could worship a younger woman in a utopia of the mind. But in life he required the friendship of protective and sheltering females, to whom he could be kind and attentive, but who gave him everything and seemed satisfied that he be 'kind' in return. The ending of the story of the Theory sisters is pure melodrama. Benyon discovers that the woman to whom he is secretly married – she has borne his child and abandoned it in Italy – has remarried. He is free to marry his Kate, when her sister dies; but he is held back by his unwillingness to duplicate the bigamy of his wife. He sails away for another long voyage. Kate Theory will wait. Once again James arranged his story so as to leave his uncomfortable hero unmarried and his heroine also uncomfortably suspended in a void.

The notes for *The Wings of the Dove* were written in the autumn of 1894 in James's notebooks, in the year of the death of Constance Fenimore Woolson, in Venice. She had been the most important of his 'protective' ladies in the twelve years he had known her; only after her death had it occurred to him that she might have loved him more than he knew. He had always been attentive, dutiful, kind because she seemed so devoted to him. What we can read in these repeated fantasies of his inner passional life, is a reflection of the old situation in the James family, present to him from earliest child-hood. It will be remembered there had been two sisters in the Walsh family, in Washington Square; Henry James's father married the older one, Mary. The younger, Catherine, had been quite as spell-bound by the fervour and eloquence of Henry Sr, and she had come to live with the Jameses. The real-life sisters, Mary and Kate, the omnipresent older female figures of Henry James's childhood, may be regarded as the figures behind the Milly and Kate of fiction, the idealized mother and the down-to-earth Aunt – Kate Theory and Mildred, Kate Croy and Milly – the strong and the weak, the good and bad heroines of the various stories, representatives of spirit and flesh. They represented the everlasting vision of a mother who seemed compliant and sacrificial and an aunt who was assertive and perhaps manipulative. In such complex equations resided Henry James's myth of women. The myth had been translated early in life into the apotheosis of Minny Temple as the 'heroine of the scene'. Later, with Miss Woolson, the old triangle of his father's life, and of his own, was redrawn. Minny Temple remained a 'luminary of the mind'. Fenimore was a fellow-writer, with womanly demands. The myths of the ethereal and the fleshly, of spirit and body, in James's equations were converted into art and passion – and in his existence the two could not be reconciled. The solution: renunciation. One renounced love, or was deprived of it. Accepted, it represented ruin.

In returning to these themes now, James was making a supreme attempt to understand and resolve a life-dilemma in which he had feared the love of woman and learned to keep himself emotionally distant from all human relations lest he commit himself to unfore-seen catastrophes. In all his tales about authors this is the semi-humorous, but at bottom deeply serious 'lesson', given by literary masters to their acolytes. Marriage destroyed art; passion destroyed life.

2

To understand James's return to his myth of the 'sacred woman', a kind of personal virgin-worship he disliked when he saw it in the Church, we must remember that he had begun a kind of rewriting of his past. *The Ambassadors* had been a return to *The American*. Now he was re-telling *The Portrait of a Lady* which had been his attempt to construct a story for Minny Temple as if she had gone on living. He had shown that she would have been frustrated by life, that the dancing flame would in any event have been quenched. In his novel he created an 'heiress of the ages' deprived of her patrimony – of life itself. 'Live all you can' had been the theme of *The Ambassadors*; but the question now was, 'What if one can't really live?' The answer would be, in part at least, 'One can still love – and love can endure from beyond the grave.' Renunciation and sacrifice were now however directly coupled with thoughts of fleshly love. In opening himself to feeling in recent months, in allowing himself to experience the touch, the presence, the embrace, of the young sculptor, James had learned the meaning of physical love. Life was at last proving more attentive than fiction. His novel was, he told Howells, 'a prettyish tale ... It's moreover, probably, of a prettyish inspiration – a "love-story" of a romantic tinge'. He had never written such a novel. All his earlier tales had been stories of artists seeking glory and power, and finding passion incompatible with their art; of businessmen seeking to conquer a wife as they had conquered their fortunes; of young American heiresses marrying 'sensibly' because they fear marriage as a form of bondage and an invasion of their sovereignty. In no novel had James pictured a pair of lovers or made love the very heart of his action. In his 60th year he found himself writing about a love affair – and on a large scale. There would be scheming and treachery, as in *The Portrait of a Lady*. Kate Croy, discovering that Milly the heiress is doomed, will tell a civilized lie, a 'constructive' lie: she will deny to the heiress that she loves Merton Densher. The heiress will be free to love him; and Kate will instruct Merton to be 'kind' to the dying girl. Her hope is that the heiress will 'endow' Merton – and so endow their marriage. Milly will have her love in the moments of her fear and trembling over her impending separation from the world. What would have been a meaningless death could become, through Kate's lie, a beautiful journey to an illuminated Paradise. This was Kate's reasoning, and this her 'plot'.

As with *The Ambassadors*, Henry James brought all the resources of his art to bear on this melodrama. He had begun by seeing it as 'ugly and vulgar'. He would gild the ugliness and the vulgarity with his prose and his style. To do so he summoned the full orchestra of his symbolic imagination. He had never paid attention in his critical writings to the symbolist movement in France, he who had otherwise watched closely the art of the novel in the Third Republic. There is no mention of Verlaine in his essays nor of Mallarmé. And his essay of the 1870s on Baudelaire shows how limited was his vision of that artist whom he condemned with the eyes of a 'realist' for his unpleasant concern with 'flowers of evil'. His early reading of Hawthorne to be sure had shown him the uses of allegorical symbolism; but he had enrolled himself instead under the banner of Balzac. James came late to the symbolist movement, even as he had been tardy in accepting impressionism in painting. He discovered it in the theatre, in Ibsen, and even then it had had to be called to his attention by William Archer. Once James had grasped the uses of the symbol he possessed the power and the poetry to assimilate it promptly into his art: to discard the literal realism of Balzac for the evocative realism of Ibsen. We have but to call the roll of Henry James's novels to see the change – the label titles give way first to the ironic-symbolic, and then wholly to the symbolic – *Washington Square*, *The Bostonians*, *The Princess Casamassima*, change to allusive titles such as *The Spoils of Poynton*, or collections of tales called *Terminations* or *Embarrassments*. And now for the first time he finds a new kind of title – *The Wings of the Dove* – as he will find *The Golden Bowl*.

> Oh that I had wings like a dove! for then would I fly
> away, and be at rest.

The 55th Psalm also speaks of 'deceit and guile', and its lines record treachery and despair. We must, however, take note of lines in the 67th Psalm as well, 'yet shall ye be as the wings of a dove covered with silver, and her feathers with yellow gold'. Milly the dove who wants ultimately to fly away and be at rest has gold-covered wings; with her fragility she possesses the gilded power of an heiress. And beyond this suggestive title, James fills his novel with the beating of wings, the sense of the abyss, as if we were in the opening pages of Balzac's *Seraphita*, the novel of the androgynous nature of love (which would fascinate Yeats) with his Swedenborgianism and its use of the fjords of Norway and great Miltonic effects of sky and clouds and mist to suggest the empyrean. Like *Louis Lambert*, the story of *Seraphita* was one of Balzac's *études philosophiques*. Was it a coincidence that in Balzac's novel there should be a Minna – as there was a Minny? And that we should meet Milly perched on a crag in the Alps in Switzerland with the world 'all before her'. (James will repeat the final words from *Paradise Lost* thrice in the novel.) In *Seraphita* James found echoes of the Swedenborgianism of his father. Moreover, during the year of the writing of the *Wings*, Lamb House was filled with talk of William's *Varieties of Religious Experience*, his lectures which sprang out of the depths of James family history – deeply related to the religious passion and mystical revelations experienced by the elder Henry James. *The Wings of the Dove* borrows the symbolism of Judaism and Christianity to clothe the sordid drama it has to tell, to convert the gold-weighted Milly into a seraph and a dove and the predatory Kate into a creature motivated by her poverty to seek a better life for herself. In the novel's imagery, Kate is a panther and she is named Croy – the crow, a blackbird, of which the name in French is *merle* (and Madame Merle in *The Portrait of a Lady* had played a similar role). The bird imagery is sustained in the name Theale – the silver-and-gold dove is also thus a little duck. The realist of the novel, turned poet, seemed to be trying to reconcile the divine and the earthly. Memories of Milton and Blake : his father had edited a volume of Blake's poems – the marriage of heaven and hell. And then Henry James had seen, after Ibsen – with his *Wild Duck* and his *Doll's House* and his *Peer Gynt* – the evocative plays of Maeterlinck, vague, mystical, crepuscular. There are two allusions to Maeterlinck in *The Wings of the Dove* : the Boston lady, Susan Shepherd Stringham, the shepherdess of Milly, has read her Maeterlinck along with her Pater; and in the heart of the novel we are invited to look at Milly as if she were a princess, in her plumes and jewels, with Kate as her handmaiden, circling about in the twilight 'in the likeness of some dim scene in a Maeterlinck play'.

In *The Portrait of a Lady* there had been a physician who was given a brief walk-on part; James had named him Sir Matthew Hope. In the *Wings* he is at the centre of the action and his name is that of the healer, Luke – Sir Luke Strett. There is also Lord Mark, who journeys to the city of St Mark as the *deus ex machina* of Milly's drama. The very introduction of Mark and St Mark brings a new pair of wings into the novel, not those of the dove, but of the winged lion, emblem of Mark, and emblem of Venice. *The Wings of the Dove* seems a riot of symbols, not least that of the ascending dove of the title, whose wings shelter those left behind. Since they are wings of gold, the gold weighs down Merton Densher at the end.

As in the early story of the naval officer who sails away and leaves Kate Theory, Densher turns from Kate Croy. Their cruel gambit has succeeded; but they can no longer be as they were. The solution of *The Wings of the Dove* still finds James rewriting an old equation. The dead interfere with the living; the worship of woman as goddess is a prohibition to human love.

3

This is the deepest flaw within the inventive poetry and form of *The Wings of the Dove*. For all his disguises as active and even coercive lover, Merton Densher, is in reality the classical passive, renunciatory Jamesian hero. He drifts in his passivity into a solution comfortable to himself. He sits back and allows women to be kind, devoted, sacrificial. Kate serves him, and plots for him; Milly is a fine rare creature who loves him; he 'takes the comfort of it'. James has tried to suggest a certain opaque quality within his passivity, as if to provide some reason for it : and his name is interpreted for us when we are told that Kate is 'almost tired of his density'. But there is nothing 'dense' about Merton Densher. In drifting, and accepting, he becomes irritated by his 'so extremely manipulated state'. The result is one of the coolest–hottest scenes in all of James's fiction. He threatens to spoil Kate's plans – as if she were doing everything for herself and not also for him; and exacts as his price for continued passivity that the woman he loves come to his rooms, and sleep with him. It is in this sudden show of active (but also aggressive) male force, that Densher finally differs from all his predecessors. Kate yields; Densher feels himself 'master in the conflict'. Yet there has been no conflict. There have been only the demands of an irritated lover, asking Kate not only to continue to do everything for him, but to surrender to him. She is willing, for she loves Densher.

The effect of this change in the old Jamesian equation, however, is simply to offer a new justification for old conclusions. Densher's physical love of Kate frees him for his spiritual love of Milly. What he has not counted on, and does not recognize, is his guilt. The hand reaching from beyond the grave, offering him continued sustenance fills him with remorse : fills him with an impulsive need to rush to the altar in the Brompton Oratory. In the final scene Densher has withdrawn into greater passivity than ever. Kate now believes that

Densher is in love with Milly's memory. Yet it has been clear throughout that Densher does not love the sick girl. If Milly's wings cover him from beyond life, his freedom has been diminished; he chooses to live with a ghost rather than with the strong and living woman, like the young man in *Maud-Evelyn*. The renunciation is as complex as all of James's renunciations; nevertheless it is touched by the exquisite delicacy with which James describes the final meeting of the lovers. And for the first time in all his fiction James writes believably of sexual passion. Kate and Merton are aware of one another as physical beings. And he writes with an awareness of love's vulnerability. He muses at one point on the impatience of love, 'how ill a man, and even a woman could feel from such a cause'. He complains that men have been unimaginative in their vocabulary of love. Nowhere in his novels is there a stronger sense of the physical than in the account of Densher left alone in his rooms after Kate's visit. The entire place is changed. Eros has touched everything. Densher can lay on Kate 'strong hands almost in anger' and she closes her eyes 'as with the sense that he might strike her but she could gratefully take it'. James had come face to face at last with 'the great relation'. But he had not been able to banish his other ghost – the ghost of doubt, of guilt, the double-love of the heroine of the spirit and the heroine of the flesh; they were still the 'good' and the 'bad' heroines of all his stories. The resolution would have to be attempted once again : and James did, the following year, and for a last time.

4

James would speak later of his quest for a 'compositional key' to the structure of *The Wings of the Dove*. This was made necessary by his subject. 'The way grew straight,' he wrote, 'from the moment one recognized that the poet essentially can't be concerned with the act of dying. Let him deal with the sickest of the sick, it is still by the act of living that they appeal to him, and appeal the more as the conditions plot against them and prescribe the battle.' To depict the stages of Milly Theale's illness, as in the doleful last act of some opera, was merely to create a novel of the 'graveyard' school or a 'soap opera'. Death resulting from the accidents of life is sad, but not tragic. James had a subject likely to cause an unmotivated flow of tears rather than provide the catharsis of tragedy. His solution was to omit the tearful scenes, the very scenes which the sentimental novelists put in so as to wring every possible emotion out of the audience. Venice in the *Wings* remains the Venice of Othello or of Volpone. But the reader is kept out of certain rooms; he may not be present at certain encounters. We remain with the living – their greed, their guilt, their anguish. The *expected* moments do not materialize. We are allowed to see Milly in thought and action so long as she is physically strong: or as James put it in his preface, he had been reduced, out of 'tenderness of his imagination' to watching her 'through the successive windows of other people's interest in her'. We see her in her passionate scene before the Bronzino, proclaiming that the woman in the picture is 'dead, dead, dead', and as she looks she holds in her hand a cup of iced coffee, chill reminder of her mortality. We see Densher in the autumn downpour in Venice; the winter winds lash the lagoon, all the elements enter into the climax. We are present at the confrontation – one of James's greatest moments of drama – in the National Gallery when Milly comes upon Kate and Densher. We accompany Densher in the gondola, as he goes for his 'last interview' with Milly. We expect to see her on her couch, to hear her words, to listen to Densher's explanations. He is received at the palace. The doors close in our face. When we turn the page we are no longer in Venice. We will never know what passed between the hero and the heroine, although Densher will later have brief moments of memory. It was to this that Ford Madox Hueffer alluded when he inquired why the Master had deprived him of the 'last interview'. James's answer had been that the book had had to be 'composed in a certain way, in order to come into being at all, and the lines of composition, so to speak, determined and controlled its parts and account for what is and isn't there; what isn't e.g. like the "last interview" of Densher and Milly'. In a parenthesis he inserted 'Hall Caine would have made it large as life and magnificent, wouldn't he?'

This is a part of the strange organization of *The Wings of the Dove*. The Master plays with fire but does not burn his fingers. He creates a novel in which all the 'great scenes' – all the *expected* ones are omitted. He substitutes other scenes which belong to Kate and Densher – 'the subject,' he told Hueffer, 'was Densher's history with Kate Croy – hers with him, and Milly's history was but a thing involved and embroiled in that. I fear I even then let my system betray me, and at any rate I feel I have welded my structure of rather too large and too heavy historic bricks.' By this he meant that he had developed each section of his structure with great solidity until the novel was four-fifths finished; and had then had to foreshorten in the fifth. He spoke of the *Wings* as suffering from a 'misplaced pivot', or he humorously described its structural flaw, in a letter to Mrs Cadwalader Jones, as having too big a head for its body. He said the book was 'too inordinately drawn out and too inordinately rubbed in. The centre, moreover, isn't in the middle, or the middle, rather, isn't in the centre, but ever so much too near the end, so that what was to come after it is truncated.' To Lucy Clifford he wrote that *The Ambassadors*, which still remained unpublished – and would not appear until more than a year after the publication of the *Wings* – was 'much better and less long'.

Whatever its defects, the latter novel has the strong interest of its subject and the scenic structure by which the subject is rendered. A new generation of dramatizers and opera writers would be attracted to the book, and would insert the very scenes James purposely left out. In other words, they made it into the 'tear-jerker' it was not supposed to be. In his text, James makes direct allusion to his intention. Densher, returning to London, talks with Kate and 'she sat before the scene ... very much as a stout citizen's wife might have sat during a play that made people cry'. Seeking popularity, James nevertheless worked very hard to fashion his book in the way of art; he did not intend it, apparently, for stout citizen's wives. If James resorted to omission and indirection, thereby further disposing of the omniscient author, as he had done in *The Ambassadors*, he gives full play to those scenes in which we are allowed to see Milly resisting her fate. The novel is never more in command of itself, nor of its existential materials, than in the quiet give-and-take of Sir Luke Strett, the physician, and his doomed patient. There are many things in Sir Luke which suggest the authority and the bedside manner of Dr W. W. Baldwin who had been doctor of Henry, William, Alice, and in Florence of Miss Woolson. Moreover, in naming the Italian doctor who substitutes for Sir Luke in Venice Taccini, James was using the actual name of Baldwin's Falstaffian friend, the Italian-teacher, with whom the novelist and the American doctor had gone on a walking tour in Tuscany in 1890. Once again James is careful not to specify. The only medical word he uses in these scenes is 'auscultation'. There is never a hint of the nature of Milly's illness. We are present rather at a comparatively modern therapeutic session, as if James were predicting, two years after Freud's book on dreams, the future of psychoanalysis. Sir Luke is 'supportive'; he emphasizes the immediate, the real. Milly has had only premonitory symptoms; she is still in possession of her faculties and her strength; the physician is determined not to allow her to be sorry for herself, nor to convert self-pity into pity for him. She speaks of her isolation. He is not convinced. Who had accompanied Milly on her first visit? A devoted friend – well then, 'doesn't that make another friend for you?' And he amusedly reminds her that her being American makes her a member of a large national gregarious family, 'it puts you with plenty of others – that isn't pure solitude.' We are also made party to Milly's fancies. She dreams of offering her doctor a gift; she suggests that she is kind to him by being so easy to treat 'since you've already done me so much good'. He refuses to play her game. 'Oh no, you're extremely difficult to treat. I've need with you, I assure you, of all my wit.' He dismisses the past – her past of dead parents, dead relatives, her being alone in the world. 'Don't try to bear more things than you need ... Hard things have come to you in youth, but you mustn't think life will be for you all hard things. You've a right to be happy. You must make up your mind to it. You must attempt any form in which happiness must come.'

Milly feels as if she has been to confession and been absolved. She faces the world with renewed hope. She rents a palace in Venice and invites her friends to join her. And in Venice life and art are deeply mingled for James. He embodies in these beautiful chapters memories of his visits at the Palazzo Barbaro. The palace itself is described, with its *piano nobile* and the shuttered light playing across its floors. He had stayed there with the Curtises (he was in correspondence with them during the writing of this novel), and he had been there during Mrs Gardner's rental of the palazzo early in the '90s. There is a recall of Mrs Gardner and her famous strings of pearl, in the scene in which Kate studies Milly's pearls, and recognizes that the weak dove has the strength of her wealth.

... the long priceless chain, wound twice round the neck, hung, heavy and pure, down the front of the wearer's breast – so far down that Milly's trick, evidently unconscious, of holding and vaguely fingering and entwining a part of it, conduced presumably to convenience. 'She's a dove,' Kate went on, 'and one somehow doesn't think of doves as bejewelled. Yet they suit her down to the ground.'

Densher, listening, knows that Kate is 'exceptionally under the impression of that element of wealth in her which was a power, a great power, and which was dove-like only so far as one remembered that doves have wings and wondrous flights, have them as well as tender tints and soft sounds'.

The centre of emotion in this novel is fixed in Merton Densher, a figure not unlike James's Parisian friend W. Morton Fullerton, who was a passive, sentimental man. Fullerton spent his days writing cables for the London *Times* and lived a life similar to James's hero. On reading the book he asked whether Densher was modelled on a man named T. A. Cook. '*Ah, que non!*' James responded, 'he was *not* my poor distinguished Densher. I never dreamed of him.' He did not say, however, of whom he had dreamed. Certainly it was not Ford Madox Hueffer. The personality of Morton Fullerton and the use of the name Merton, permits us to speculate that the Parisianized journalist had ground for his inquiries. We must recognize nevertheless that there is much of James's own moral feeling in Densher, his own reticences, his own fear of women. In writing this novel he touched the mystery of Fenimore and the painful weeks of questioning and mourning when he had lived in her Venetian apartment – above all the great riddle of death. This is suggested in the closing pages of *The Wings of the Dove* and may explain James's uneasiness and uncertainties – and troubled health – during these months. If he could not find an answer to the riddle of death he would try to answer the riddle of life – and this may to some extent explain why he could not stop writing, even though he had published three volumes between 1900 and 1902 and had written still another that awaited publication.

68

Billy

FROM Billy James, 7 October 1902, in Lamb House, to his parents in Cambridge, Massachusetts:

I arrived here last night and am drunk – with Rye, and Lamb House, and Uncle Henry. By Jove! isn't it great? Uncle Henry's welcome to me, and his treatment of me in general, is kinder than that of a mother, if such a thing can be, and as for the place, I could rest right here for the rest of my days and be perfectly happy. The length of my stay will only be a question of my boring Uncle Henry, Dad, the thing will never work the other way as far as I am concerned. The crooked red roofs and the chimney pots, and the water-colors that hang about Uncle Henry's walls make me itch to draw, and curse myself that I cannot do it, but I will learn to yet, at least to the extent of giving myself pleasure, or die in the attempt.

I

When Billy James, William's second son, had been told in his boy-hood that his uncle was a famous writer, he remarked a trifle en-viously, 'I suppose there's nothing that Uncle Henry can't spell.' Now 20, an enthusiastic oarsman and a fine tennis player, he was being sent abroad to spend a year on the Continent. His turn in the family hierarchy had come for exposure to his uncle. Henry James had last seen him when he was 8. He was now a tall slender youth, well turned out by his tailor, and wearing a small military mous-tache. He had an elegant upright carriage and manner, and a certain hesitancy of speech; he possessed a well-modulated voice and an in-tensity and sincerity that endeared him promptly to James. Billy was distinctly unlike his elder brother Harry, who had visited Lamb House four years before and spent his time writing a diary wonder-ing what his uncle thought of him. The younger nephew was in-terested in what went on around him; he seemed to have his father's early addiction to sketching although he was at the moment not des-tined for art – and the novelist reported to Cambridge, 'we have had the happy inspiration of his taking lessons in water colours from a modest but skilful little artist who is living here – so that he may simply learn how to use colour'. Perhaps this 'inspiration' contri-buted to Billy's decision later to abandon medical studies and go to Julien's in Paris to study painting.

Billy was unlike his elder brother in many respects. Harry was deeply serious, unsmiling, thoughtful; he had the cognitive and in-tellectual qualities of his father, but not his easy spontaneity. Harry also had none of the liveliness of the Jameses, and little of their 'Irishness'. The novelist was fond of him and in later years greatly valued his help in practical matters, particularly in financial affairs. It would be Billy and Peggy who would have the largest share of their uncle's affection. William's youngest son, Alex, arrived much later on the scene.

Billy reached Rye early in October 1902. He was on his way to Geneva and planned to spend a fortnight in Lamb House and then a few days in Paris visiting the Louvre. 'I congratulate you all on him,' James wrote to Billy's elder brother, 'so beautiful he is, and so attaching; so formed to charm and interest and, as it were, repay. I *knew* well enough that I should take satisfaction in him, but I take ... still more than I expected.' Billy little dreamed that the voice he heard in the morning in the Garden Room, during his brief stay, was dictating what were to be two celebrated tales, *The Birthplace* and *The Beast in the Jungle*. His vision was of a short, rotund man, with a quick sensibility and a boundless capacity for affection. He carried away from his elderly uncle a memory of hearing him say 'three things in human life, are important. The first is to be kind. The second is to be kind. And the third is to be kind.' He always remembered the days of his first stay at Lamb House, spent on the bicycle, with long walks in between, and with the central drama revolving around the arrival of his Emmet cousins, Bay and Leslie, whom he found 'devastatingly' beautiful and who made a great fuss over their handsome cousin. He remembered, too, how the age of the motor-car came to Lamb House – the Rudyard Kiplings driving up in their new £2,000 machine, an object of curiosity and wonder. There had been a lively lunch in which Rudyard was talkative, anecdotal, poetic. Kipling greatly liked Billy, as his subsequent letters to James showed. Then, when they got into the car to return to Burwash, twenty miles away, the vehicle 'in the manner of its kind' wouldn't start. Rudyard grew increasingly angry over its behaviour. He had baptized it Amelia. It behaved as he believed all women behaved. The Kiplings had to take a train. There followed a long letter from the author of *The Jungle Book* describing the struggle of the successive 'engineers' to get Amelia started. 'It's not as easy as it looks, a sick motor,' Kipling wrote to James. The factory finally sent another 'engineer' from Birmingham who 'vowed that the accident which had befallen her was unique in all mechanics and motoring'. Kipling ended by inviting the novelist and his nephew to lunch, urging them to take the train which 'tho' slow is safe' and promising Amelia would take them home.

Billy left for the Continent, but he was not a letter-writer, and his uncle became worried. He had visions of the innocent nephew 'swindled or bamboozled in Paris', or even 'robbed and murdered in your night train in Geneva'. He sent an uneasy wire to Geneva.

All was well though the doting uncle wondered 'when you *did* mean to write!' And he expressed pleasure that his nephew was 'under a human roof, and at a nourishing board and in a coherent curriculum'. Remembering his own days in Geneva, Henry James added he had found the city attractive 'all except the Slavonic females, who I should think *would* be a great thorn in the flesh'. The Uncle was being maternal. To William James he wrote that he had 'rejoiced' in Billy, and found him 'an ornament to my life'. At a later stage he expressed the belief that Billy's 'personal charm' smoothed his path through life and invited 'general good-will'.

Billy stayed briefly at Geneva and then spent the winter at Marburg, where he attended classes at the university. In emulation of his father he returned to study medicine in Cambridge, after another stay at Lamb House. Ultimately he would be back in Europe studying art. In the coming years uncle and favourite nephew would see each other on many occasions; and Henry would watch and encourage his work. As he had advised Bay Emmet to 'beware of finding yourself not able to feel your subjects at your ease and with true inwardness', so he one day gave Billy advice that remained fixed in the young man's memory for the rest of his life. What he recalled was his uncle standing behind him as he was struggling with a canvas. After a long period of silent watching, the voice slowly and with characteristic deliberation said : 'Bill, remember that no captain ever makes port with all the cargo with which he set sail.' A long pause. 'And Bill – remember – there is always another voyage.'

69

In the Workshop

THERE were eight writing tables or secretary-desks in Lamb House. Henry James could write comfortably in almost every room, although he worked largely in his upstairs Green Room during the winters and in the detached Garden House as soon as warm weather permitted. Visitors used to hear him dictating from 10 a.m. until 1.45. What they did not know were the hours spent in revising what had been dictated, the close attention he gave to proofs, the number of notes he made, the amount of reading he did, and the time he devoted to letters, which he often preferred writing in longhand since he deemed many of them too personal to share with his typist. Also he did not want to waste time on correspondence during Miss Weld's working hours. As he grew older and wrote less – in the years to come – he began to dictate the long letters of his late years as if he were writing epistolary fiction.

Life in Lamb House had a certain military regularity. At eight every morning Burgess mounted the stairs to the Master's bedroom, and brought him hot shaving water. There followed the hot bath, the meditated choice of what to wear and finally the descent of the sartorially neat and bright-cravatted novelist, wearing an equally colourful waistcoat, into the dining-room. The typical breakfast consisted of cereal with cream, followed by three shirred eggs. It was always served at 9 a.m. and while James slowly ate this repast he issued his instructions and complimented the housekeeper on her wise economies. At 10 a.m. Miss Weld arrived and work began. Visitors knew they could never see the Master before lunch. The voice dictated rhythmically – with long pauses – in the workshop. They could hear James pacing constantly with the quality of a restless animal, and in rhythm with the familiar response of the typewriter. When various friends suggested that dictation affected his style – which to a degree it did – he was vehement in his denial.

The value of that process for me is in its help to do over and over, for which it is extremely adapted, and which is the only way I can do at all. It soon enough becomes *intellectually*, absolutely identical with the act of writing – or has become so, after five years now, with me; so that the difference is only material and illusory – only the difference, that is, that I walk up and down; which is so much to the good.

There was a difference. In the old days he had not been able to 'do over and over'. His novels of the middle period had all been written with little revision and dispatched in longhand to the magazines. There had been revision in proof, and from magazine to book. In his tale *The Middle Years* (1893) his famous writer's ideal would have been 'to publish secretly, and then, on the published text, treat himself to the terrified revise, sacrificing always a first edition and beginning for posterity and even for the collectors, poor dears, with a second'. The typewriter in his own study gave James this 'better chance'. Now he revised constantly; and while revising, new metaphors, large similes, were inserted into the text. Miss Weld repeatedly retyped the manuscript – James could as it were read proof on his work continually, from day to day. The late style is a 're-vised' style, a building of the prose page by a process of accretion. In this process certain mannerisms crept in – attempts to get away from old familiar forms of expression: displacement and splitting of verbs, the emergence of unexpected adverbs, the removal of the given phrase from that part of the sentence where the reader expected to find it, into another part. And then James's prose was now spoken prose. Writing had become a matter of controlled speech.

Dictation also enabled James, as never before, to work at several things at once. He had tended, when he wrote in longhand, to push ahead with a given piece of work. The brief but illuminating record kept by Miss Weld of her work-days shows us how James would start a story one day, drop it for other work the next, go on with still another story, return to the first, start still another: there were always several hares running at once. The physical effort of penmanship would have slowed James down as he grew older; the method of dictation enabled him to be as productive as ever – indeed more productive – with the aid of his crowded imagination. An illustration of simultaneity of work on various stories occurs immediately after completion of *The Wings of the Dove* during the summer of 1902. While James is reading the final proofs he is already assembling a collection of tales to make up a book called *The Better Sort*. He discovers the volume will not be of proper length. Two or three more stories are needed. On 1 July 1902 he begins a story titled provisionally *John Marcher*, the tale destined to be known as *The Beast in the Jungle*. The start apparently was made on that day; there is then no further reference to it for three months, to be exact not until 12 October. In the interval James has been working on three other stories. They consisted of a story first called *Maud Blandy* later the very long tale of *The Papers*; the story called *The Birthplace*, and a tale known in Miss Weld's record only as *The Beautiful Child* never completed. This may have been a development of a fragment among James's papers written in longhand, a tale based on an anecdote of Bourget's, of two parents who ask a painter to paint a portrait of their non-existent child. The following will suggest how James moved between one tale and another, between his various tasks and the usual interruptions of his gregarious social life:

Beast	Papers	Birthplace	Child
1 July	24 July	14 August	11 July
12 October	1 August	30 September	22 July
16 October	11 August	10 October	
	11 October		
	16 October		
	5 November		
	13 November		

Miss Weld's entries say very clearly when each tale was completed – *The Birthplace* on 10 October, *The Beast in the Jungle* 16 October, *The Papers* 13 November. This would suggest that the tale of John Marcher, a remarkably unified tonal picture and perhaps James's finest story, was written in three sessions, due allowance made for manual revisions. There were days when Miss Weld was allowed to idle: an entry of 8 August 1902 tells us 'no work, Mr James revising'. There were other days when the typist was pressed into overtime: thus in 1903 the record shows that to meet a deadline for an article, Miss Weld worked 'nine hours with Mr James on D'Annunzio to finish'.

During the summer of 1902 James finally disposed of the lease of his flat at De Vere Gardens. It had been his home for more than ten years, from 1886 until 1898. The flat had been let for the past three and a half years; it still had in it many fine pieces of furniture and many of James's books. The novelist turned over some of the furniture to the William Jameses and it was shipped to America; other pieces found their place in Lamb House, and some time was consumed in finding a place for the hundreds of books that arrived. Three entries made by Miss Weld give the elements of the story:

Saturday, July 19 – Furniture arrives. Assist in stowage and lunch at Lamb House.
Sunday, July 20 – Books!
Monday, July 21 – Hanging of pictures. Lunch and tea at Lamb House.
Tuesday, July 22 – Work again, continue *The Beautiful Child*.

In between work on these tales, Henry James was sorting out the papers of William Wetmore Story and Miss Weld typed such letters as he would use in the long-postponed memoir. This was the next large piece of work he intended to do, and an entry of 22 September records that she had finished copying the letters 'so really begin W. W. Story'.

Within his workshop Henry James found himself studying closely the working methods, the large creative designs, of his predecessors. During the opening years of the new century the Master began his revaluation of the writers who had meant most to him, those who, as he put it, have 'done something for us, become part of the answer to our curiosity'. Circumstances aiding, he was led to write the series of papers on George Sand, and large explanatory essays on Balzac, Flaubert, Zola. He had dealt with them in the past, often in piece-meal fashion, either by reviewing them or discussing various editions of their works. But now he found himself looking at their total achievement. Criticism had always been, for Henry James, an extension of his creative act: one always felt, in what he wrote of other novelists – and he rarely discussed poets – that he was asking himself 'What are they trying to do? What has been their intention?' and this was a surfacing of a buried question, 'Is there anything I can learn for the work I have to do?' His essay of 1902 on Balzac begins with his asking himself what he had learned from the French master: and the answer would be given in his later lecture *The Lesson of Balzac*. He had read him in his youth. Now, re-reading him on the threshold of his old age, he recognized that Balzac had passed long ago into the very texture of his life. 'Endless are the uses of great persons and great things,' he told himself, and what he discerned, in each of these large 'cases' was the manner in which his ultimate literary monument had been erected.

At 60 James could well ask himself – looking back at all the books he had written, and in the very midst of this period of extraordinary fertility – where he stood in the history of the novel? He had asked himself this question at the beginning of his play-writing. He had sought always to win success, and had always remained an ambiguous figure in the market-place. What future did he have? What would be the fate of his 'reputation?' Thus he embraced the new opportunities given him by Edmund Gosse to preface a Balzac novel and a new edition of *Madame Bovary*. He had watched the growth of this classic from the day when, as a boy in Paris in 1856, he had read the first instalments in the *Revue de Paris*. He had also watched, since the death of Balzac in 1850, the slow growth of a formidable reputation, the way in which the *Comédie Humaine* had established itself in the mind of Europe – and the world. And he remembered Zola, just beginning his fame, and their talks during Flaubert's Sunday afternoons in 1876.

In his essay on Balzac we find James writing of that novelist's 'mass and weight', his 'scheme and scope". From this he is led to 'the question of what makes the artist on a great scale'. This was what interested Henry James above everything: what had made James an artist – perhaps on the grand scale? Balzac's imagination had encompassed all his experience. He had created with enormous fertility. He had in his 'active intention' tried to read 'the universe, as hard and as loud as he could, *into* France of his time'. He had been 'a beast with a hundred claws', hugging his material close to him with enormous energy. 'He is the only member of his order really monumental, the sturdiest seated mass that rises in our path,' wrote Henry James and he added 'we are never so curious about successes as about interesting failures ... the scale on which, in its own quarter of his genius, success worked itself out for him.' James might have been trying to work this out for himself. So in his essay on Flaubert, also of 1902, he discusses, in a final survey, the uneven work of that master to the end of discovering how he 'built himself into literature'. Flaubert was the opposite of Balzac. He did not have abundance in him. He was not on the 'monumental' scale. But then one could hardly have wanted, James implied, more books of the type of *Madame Bovary* or *Salammbô*. 'When the production of a great artist who has lived a length of years has been small,' wrote James, '... the case is doubtless predetermined by the particular kind of great artist the writer happens to be.' George Sand, James wrote, had had great abundance, but she had produced much less *literature* than Flaubert. 'She had undoubtedly herself the benefit of her facility, but are we not left wondering to what extent *we* have it?' The omniscient Balzac had created a world. Flaubert had created a single classic. Zola, in his particular and grosser way, had established a 'massive identity'. And George Sand, in her fluency, her liquid qualities, had been 'a supreme case of the successful practice of life itself'.

Thus in the midst of his great fertile years, when he summoned to his work the powers of his maturity, James interrogated the literary reputations of the great novelists of France, in the interest of his own literary reputation. He was like a Napoleon of literature surveying conquered territories. His exploration would lead him to shore up, against the ravages of posterity, a great part of his *œuvre* – in the New York Edition, the 'definitive edition' he had planned for years.

In his exploration of what made the artist 'on the grand scale' the Master was led to the question of biography. What distinctions were to be made between the man and the artist? He was about to write a biographical memoir, the only one he had ever undertaken; and in his stories there had for a long time been an increasing interrogation of the question of the private life of art and the public life of the work issuing from that art. At this moment, however, on the evidence of his stories, a more fundamental question seemed to trouble James. He had never been a great success on the scale of Kipling – or of Rostand. He had a small general reputation even if a formidable authority among other novelists. He knew too well how artists create during all their lives only to go down, in death, into oblivion. He had, very early in his career, written in *The Madonna of the Future* the record of the impotent artist, who wishes for fame and can only struggle helplessly in front of his canvas. He had had his own show of fame; he had certainly never been impotent. But what if he had lived all his life for his great moment, for that *gloire* in which he believed – and what if the moment in the decades of the future, in the annals of literary history and of the novel, would never come? Out of this troubled emotion, the 'ferocious ambition' to which he had early testified, he now fashioned two tales, one tragic and mysterious, the other comic and ironic. Both were parables of the artist-life. *The Beast in the Jungle* was about a man who thinks himself destined for a role 'rare and strange', and who ends up being someone to whom nothing happens – save his having had a negative life. *The Birthplace*, satirizing the rituals of Stratford-on-Avon, has in it the corollary to this: it is the story of 'the human character the most magnificently endowed, in all time, with the sense of the life of man, and with the apparatus for recording it'. The man is almost invisible; yet he is luminous in his work. In this way, after a lifetime devoted to novelists of his time, James came to the question of the supreme poet and dramatist; he came to William Shakespeare.

70

The Impenetrable Sphinx

THE BEAST IN THE JUNGLE, as we have seen, was begun in July of 1902 but seems to have been written largely in two sessions that autumn, during the first days of Billy James's stay in Lamb House. Miss Weld's diary tells us, 'October 12, return to John Marcher or The Beast in the Jungle.' The next day she notes that Kipling lunched at Lamb House. Three days later 'Finish the Beast in the Jungle. Back to The Papers'.

Presence of the author of The Jungle Book in Lamb House at the moment of the writing of The Beast in the Jungle was a coincidence. However, James had mentioned Kipling when he was writing, earlier, about Rostand; he had evoked him as a figure who, like the French dramatist, had had a phenomenal public success. Henry James himself had had, in the English-speaking world, what might be termed a private success, a succès d'estime. In The Beast in the Jungle we can discover a remarkable coalescence of this theme with themes which the novelist had been unable to resolve in the just-completed Wings of the Dove – the question of men who in this world believe themselves reserved for a special destiny only to discover that their name is writ in water. Or the one who believes – like Keats – that he is condemned to oblivion – yet in his posthumous life becomes a hero of culture and civilization. Corollary to this, James used the theme of egotism : the man so absorbed in his ultimate destiny, that he fails to live the life given him; worse still, he fails to discover the meaning of love. The eerie passion of The Beast in the Jungle resides in a consummate threading of these themes into a parable in which James finally casts the woman in the story in the role of the eternal keeper of man's riddles – casts her and visions her, as a Sphinx.

It was as if, in his own life, after wandering about the world seeking the answer to the mysteries of his life – as the frantic narrator had done in The Sacred Fount or the little critic in The Figure in the Carpet – he at last had decided to confront, in her awesome majesty, the mythic figure, Theban or Egyptian, her who was half lion, half woman, guardian of the needed answers. In all his work there is no tale written with greater investment of personal emotion. The un-lived life of so many of his heroes is embodied in John Marcher, the great Anonymous Man, who in thinking of his fate blinds himself to his anonymity.

There may be a link between this majestic tale and a little story of Maupassant's called *Promenade*, which James marked when he read it in the 1880s. It is a tale of a drudge-clerk in Paris who on a spring evening goes out to dinner and pleasantly content, strolls into the Bois only to be overcome suddenly by the emptiness of his life.

He thought of the life he had led, so different from the lives of others, this life so sombre, so dull, so flat, so empty. Some people simply have no luck. And suddenly as if a thick veil was being rent, he saw the infinite misery, the monotonous misery of his existence: past misery, present misery, future misery; recent days, no different from earlier days, noth-ing lying ahead, nothing behind, nothing around him, nothing in his heart, nothing anywhere.

The story ends with the police finding the man's body. He has hanged himself.

The Beast in the Jungle, sustained in its mood and in its evocative poetry, is a tale of melancholy and loneliness. The passage of an entire lifetime is told in six neatly balanced sections. Thirty pages encompass years of futility. John Marcher feels 'lost in the crowd' at the start of the tale; and he finds this anonymity unbearable. In a house called Weatherend, filled with art objects out of the centuries, he meets a woman named May Bartram. They have met before – ten years earlier, at Naples; and one day at Sorrento (she reminds Marcher), he had confided to her his secret: he believed himself reserved for an unusual experience. What it is to be, or its strange-ness, he does not know. The prophesied occurrence is imaged as a beast tracking him in the jungle, waiting for its moment to spring. He is not sure whether the climax will be beautiful or horrible. He is certain that it will come.

Marcher and May are 35 and 30 when they renew their acquaint-ance at Weatherend. May says she believes in Marcher's haunted vision and is ready to participate in his life's vigil. He has the thought that 'a man of feeling didn't cause himself to be accompanied by a lady on a tiger hunt'; he nevertheless allows her to share in his fantasy – in which he is not at all sure whether he is hunter or hunted. Their encounter occurs on an October afternoon, when the sky is sombre and flushed with red; and in the next two sections of the story Marcher and May keep company – and the years pass. He goes with her to art galleries; he takes her to the opera. He is devoted to her as Henry James had been to Miss Woolson, in the first days of their friendship when they had been tourists in Florence during a certain April and May in the early 1880s and had sought each other out almost daily. The first of the two crucial episodes in the story is set in April. Half a lifetime has passed; Marcher now is aware that May is ill; and for the first time he begins to recognize that they have both grown old waiting for the beast to spring. In this climactic section we are told of the 'long fresh light of waning April days which affects us often with sadness sharper than the greyest hours of autumn'. May stands before a fireless hearth. She wears a green scarf, but like her life it is faded. As in the story *The Aspern Papers*, in which Juliana sheds her green eyeshade, and the narrator sees for the first time the bright intensity of her eyes, so here Marcher looks once more into May's eyes and finds them 'as beautiful as they had been in youth, only beautiful with a strange cold light – a light that somehow was a part of the effect, if it wasn't rather a part of the cause, of the pale hard sweetness of the season and the hour'. At this moment before the cold hearth and the Dresden china on the mantelpiece, and with a sense of 'the odd irregular rhythm of their intensities and avoidances', John Marcher images her as 'a serene and exquisite but impenetrable sphinx, whose head, or indeed all whose person, might have been powdered with silver'. We are at last face to face with the supreme keeper of the Riddle, the possessor of 'the figure in the carpet'.

May Bartram keeps the riddle of John Marcher's life. She tells him that the beast has sprung, that his fate – or doom – has already occurred. 'You were to suffer your fate,' she says. 'That was not necessarily to know.' It is an agony for Marcher. He has been deprived of the one anchor to which he has clung all his life. Suddenly his jungle is empty and 'poor Marcher waded through his beaten grass, where no life stirred, where no breath sounded, where no evil eye seemed to gleam from a possible lair, very much as if vaguely looking for the Beast, and still more as if acutely missing it'.

At this moment, Marcher joins another image to that of the Sphinx. He sees May, in her whiteness of age, as a lily under a bell of glass, the green of her scarf forming the leaves. Thus John

Marcher's dream of woman mingles with the eternal dream of Henry James; she is sphinx, matron, virgin, beast, all in one – artificial and safely preserved under glass, like an artefact. The novelist had long ago imaged the virginal Minny Temple, when he mourned her death, as shut within the 'crystal walls of the past'.

'You've had your experience,' Marcher desolately says to May – 'you leave me to my fate.' May can do nothing else. They have a final interview, almost as if James, avoiding the last confrontation between Milly and Densher in his just-completed novel, still had to get the scene out of his system. We are given the last confrontation between Marcher and May, and May's last words come to him as 'the true voice of the law; so on her lips would the law itself sound'. The Sphinx has spoken. He never sees her again. She has left him with the unsolved riddle. He must live with it for the rest of his life, as James lived with the unsolved riddle of Fenimore's death. As the grave closes over her he stands looking at the gravestone, 'beating his forehead against the fact of the secret' kept by the name and date, 'drawing his breath, while he waited, as if some sense would, in pity of him, rise from the stones. He kneeled on the stones, however in vain; they kept what they concealed; and if the face of the tomb did become a face for him it was because her two names became a pair of eyes that didn't know him.'

2

In *The Figure in the Carpet* everyone who knew the secret died and the secret remained untold; in *The Friends of the Friends* the woman who could tell about the ghost remains silent in death; death turns the key on something the jealous narrator is concerned to know. The time had come when James could no longer stand such eternal frustration; and his imagination gives John Marcher a final scene, one of the most intense and dramatic he ever wrote in any of his tales. It occurs at the cemetery. In the interval between his visits to this cemetery Marcher has travelled to the East, to Asia, India, to Egypt – to the lands of the Sphinx. But the riddles of history offer him nothing that doesn't seem 'common' compared with the dream he has nourished of being one of the elect. Turning from the great temples and sepulchres he comes back to his private sepulchre. In a sense James here revisits the tale he wrote immediately after Miss Woolson's death, *The Altar of the Dead*. In that tale a woman had deprived a man of his altar – and of the secret of his life. Now, face to face with May Bartram's tomb, Marcher happens to notice a mourner at another grave. He suddenly allows himself to see not his own grief, but the grief of another, an 'image of scarred passion'. Insight comes at last. He witnesses the grief of love. He realizes what the Sphinx had wanted him to see on that April day beside May's cold hearth, when he had turned her into an artificial flower and put her under glass. 'No passion had ever touched him, for this was what passion meant ... He had seen *outside* of his life, not learned it within.' The expected climax in Marcher's life is an anti-climax. The event is a non-event. He had been singled out – such might be his consolation – as someone to whom 'nothing on earth was to have happened'. He had not allowed himself to 'live' or to love. He had circled perpetually in his little private jungle – a hunter hunted – and haunted – by the beast of his own blindness and narcissism. He had not recognized love when it had been offered to him. The final passage in James's story rises to heights of passion, of tenderness, of guilt, of self-accusation. It is as if Marcher's revelation were his own.

The escape would have been to love her; then, *then* he would have lived. *She* had lived – who could say now with what passion? – since she had loved him for himself; whereas he had never thought of her (ah, how it hugely glared at him!) but in the chill of his egotism and the light of her use. Her spoken words came back to him – the chain stretched and stretched. The Beast had lurked indeed, and the Beast, at its hour, had sprung; it had sprung in that twilight of the cold April, when pale, ill, wasted, but all beautiful, and perhaps even then recoverable, she had risen from her chair to stand before him and let him imaginably guess. It had sprung as he didn't guess; it had sprung as she hopelessly turned from him, and the mark, by the time he left her, had fallen where it *was* to fall.

In the final sentences the passionate words James was setting down seemed to carry with them the deepest message of his own egotism, the blindness he had ironically written into *The Aspern Papers* which he now saw as if in some vast hallucination, like his father's 'vastation' long ago.

This horror of waking – *this* was knowledge, knowledge under the breath of which the very tears in his eyes seemed to freeze. Through them, none the less, he tried to fix it and hold it; he kept it there before him so that he might feel the pain. That at least, belated and bitter, had something of the taste of life. But the bitterness suddenly sickened him, and it was as if, horribly, he saw, in the truth, in the cruelty of his image, what had been appointed and done. He saw the Jungle of his life and saw the lurking Beast; then, while he looked, perceived it, as by a stir' of the air, rise, huge and hideous, for the leap that was to settle him. His eyes darkened – it was close; and instinctively turning, in his hallucination, to avoid it, he flung himself, face down, on the tomb.

These are the last words of the tale. In a moment of perception Henry James was, it would seem, revisiting the grave in the Protestant cemetery in Rome, near the grave of Keats, where Constance Fenimore Woolson's name and her dates were simply carved on the stone embedded in violets. Long ago James had imaged the frosty Winterbourne, a predecessor of John Marcher, standing on this spot unable to answer the riddle of Daisy Miller: the continuity of his imagination may be seen in the two frosty names, Winterbourne and Marcher. Marcher has deciphered his riddle. What he had lost would have made him mortal; to be mortal – that is, to live one's life – is the real escape from anonymity.

And so, into this strange and haunted story, James translated universal symbols of the riddle of man's life, his struggle against annihilation and anonymity, his belief that love makes existence possible and preserves man from the dark abyss. In its use of myth, its mood of desolation, its portrait of alienated man, it is James's most 'modern' tale.

71

The Real Right Thing

THE BEAST IN THE JUNGLE had provided a catharsis for Henry James: it was a moment of insight such as his brother, William, described in The Varieties of Religious Experience. The novelist, we know, was reading this book when he wrote the tale. He was recognizing anew – and more intensely than ever – the ways in which people 'use' one another, and this may have helped lighten some of his old feelings of guilt which had coloured the ending of The Wings of the Dove. Miss Woolson had killed herself in Venice for reasons of her own. Her death had been her decision and no one else's. It had been her fate and her mystery; and it would remain a mystery. In The Beast in the Jungle James seems to have reached a moment when he could say to himself that he must occupy himself with his own mysteries, light up the gloom in his own soul. He had behaved with Miss Woolson like one of his vampire-people in *The Sacred Fount* – and like John Marcher with May Bartram. His recognition that he was capable of love and was vulnerable, enabled him now to revisit his past and ease his soul.

His perceptive and sentimental friend in Paris, Morton Fullerton, reading the story of 'the Beast' with some attention questioned James's underlining of the emotion in the final section of the story. The novelist admitted he had been over-insistent, 'as of the school-slate and the column of figures'. And yet 'I did it, consciously, anxiously, for the help of the unutterable reader at large, who would have been incapable, down to his boots, of your discrimination'. But James rarely made concessions to the reader. He had been over-insistent because it was his need; he was searching out the riddle of the 'impenetrable Sphinx'. Long ago he had reminded his friend Grace Norton that every life was a special problem 'which is not yours but another's', and he had urged her to content herself with 'the terrible algebra' of her own. He was well on the way to working out some of his own 'terrible' algebra. *The Wings of the Dove* and the tale of John Marcher had provided insights; the 'deep well of unconscious cerebration' had sent up a series of signs and symbols. The answers always seemed simple – yet he had had to wait until he was ready to understand them. Strether's 'live all you can' had been answered by Milly's fate; one really hadn't lived until one had learned to love. The story of Marcher and May implied that one could love only when one ceased to love oneself. James had treated Miss Woolson as if she had been his Aunt Kate. And he had expended his love for years on ethereal heroines of the mind. Now, on the edge of 60, he had had this profound revelation which freed him for the things he had to do. First was the great sustaining question of his life's work. Scattered in the magazines, arrayed on the bookshelves, were the works he had written in his early chamber in Cambridge, in dim lodgings in Bolton Street, in half a hundred hotels on the Continent, amid the affluence of De Vere Gardens – some with passion of art and intensity of intellectual effort – his whole life, all the adventures of his soul, were in these works. Was he to leave these to the vulgarizing multitude, to the newspaper critics who were interested in chatter not in art, to the biographers who might exploit him not for what he had written, but for the irrelevant 'facts' of his daily life? He had said this in his little tale of *Sir Dominick Ferrand*, about a bundle of letters found in an old desk and the newspaper that wanted to publish them; in *The Aspern Papers* and its history of the 'publishing scoundrel'; in *John Delavoy*, in which the artist was 'the most unadvertised, unreported, uninterviewed, unphotographed, uncriticized of all originals. Was he not the man of the time about whose private life we delightfully knew least?' The artist was what he did – he was nothing else. And there was the great question 'what makes the artist on the grand scale?' He had written these words about Balzac. He felt that he had been such an artist – on the grand scale, astride two continents, writing out personal histories, exploring the underside of the human tapestry. The time had come for him to take stock – to pay attention to his own legend. A writer on the grand scale had to shore up all that was worth preserving out of his years of endeavour. No one else could do it for him. He thought, as the French did, of his personal *gloire* – had he not always really thought of it, in those early days when he had confessed to his mother that he had a 'ferocious ambition?' The great men of the earth lived by the legend they left behind them; their tangible works were their monument. Time had spilled itself out for Henry James: the spinning years had brought him to the moment when he could reflect on the lessons of literature – the example of Balzac, the mystery of Shakespeare – and make the decisions that would lengthen his own shadow beyond the grave. He had always said that an artist should not leave his personal papers to accident. In the coming time he would act on this. He burned his manuscripts and hundreds, thousands, of letters received from the men and women he had known. What he could not destroy were the letters he had written to others; and it does not seem to have occurred to him that these letters – so full were they of style, individuality, eccentricity – had been saved by everyone.

Two years before his death he would take another step. He issued instructions to his literary executor, his nephew Harry, William's oldest son:

My sole wish is to frustrate as utterly as possible the post mortem exploiter – which, I know, is but so imperfectly possible. Still one can do something, and I have long thought of launching, by a provision in my will, a curse no less explicit than Shakespeare's own on any such as try to move my bones. Your question determines me definitely to advert to the matter in my will – that is to declare my utter and absolute abhorrence of any attempted biography or the giving to the world by 'the family', or by any person for whom my disapproval has any sanctity, of any part or parts of my private correspondence. One can discredit and dishonour such enterprises even if one can't prevent them, and as you are my sole and exclusive literary heir and executor you will doubtless be able to serve in some degree as a check and a frustrator.

I

The Shakespearian curse, recalled in this letter to his nephew, written as late as 7 April 1914, eight days before James's 71st birthday, was implicit in the Shakespearian story *The Birthplace* James wrote while he was writing *The Beast in the Jungle*, and also a brilliant if long-drawn-out prophecy of modern 'public relations', a story called *The Papers* also written during the autumn of 1902. The novelist at that moment was embarking on his biography, the life of William Wetmore Story. His actions could have been predicted from his tales of letter-burning or the story *The Real Right Thing* published in December 1899. It deals with a young biographer who works in his subject's study. Ghostly hands move the papers away from him; they turn the pages of certain books; they seem to warn him to leave privacy alone. In the end the biographer tells the widow – who wants to do 'the real right thing' – that the right thing is to leave the dead alone. As if to drive the lesson home, the biographer (to whom James gave the symbolic name of Withermore) one day finds the ghost of his subject standing on the threshold of the chamber. Shakespeare's curse had been stated explicitly enough in James's tales.

His discussion of biography is nowhere more brilliantly sustained than in an 1899 essay on George Sand: indeed that essay and *The Real Right Thing* both seem to have been products of the Story venture. It was as if James, about to join the ranks of biographers, wondered whether this was the real right thing for a novelist to be doing. George Sand offered the 'special case'. She had always lived in public. She had made of her work 'the affirmation of an unprecedented intensity of life'. Long after she died the revelations had come: her violent 'love-life' with Musset, her affair in Venice with Pagello, the endless train of men she had taken in bold assertion that a woman had as much right to lovers as men had to mistresses. If all this seemed to make George Sand a 'rueful denuded figure' on the broad highway of life, it raised the deeper question of what was to be done when the figure was encountered. Modesty caused one to avert one's eyes, James supposed, but after all 'we have *seen* ... and mystery has fled with a shriek'. The disappearance of mystery was like turning down the incandescent light of genius and substituting the light of common day. The heroic figure of the artist shrank, was diminished, ceased to be the transcendent figure of the imagination; the unearthly voice of great poetry and divine inspiration became an ordinary human voice. Reading at this time the life of Robert Louis Stevenson by Graham Balfour, James had a new glimpse of his beloved Louis, who had vanished into the South Seas like some mysterious bird of passage. His beloved friend had become merely a picturesque figure in literary history. James had praise for Balfour; but he wrote him with affectionate candour that Stevenson's books were now 'jealous and a certain supremacy and mystery (above all) has, as it were, gone from them. The achieved legend and history that has *him* for subject, has made so to speak, light of *their* subjects, of their claim to represent him.' The biographer had made Stevenson too '*personally* celebrated'. Of course Stevenson himself had been picturesque – and to that extent he was 'in some degree the victim of himself'. James reminded Balfour he was saying all this 'from the literary vision, the vision for which the rarest works pop out of the dusk of the inscrutable, the untracked'.

In writing of George Sand, James suggested that perhaps the artist, the subject, should organize the game of biography on his own terms, rather than leave it to the biographer. 'There are secrets for privacy and silence, let them only be cultivated on the part of the hunted creature with even half the method with which the love of sport – or call it the historic sense – is cultivated on the part of the investigator. They have been left too much to the natural, the instinctive man.' The thing was indeed to burn papers, keep secrets, challenge the biographer to dig harder for his facts, demand a genuine effort of inquiry and research. It was all too easy to leave a massive archive. 'Then,' wrote James,

the cunning of the inquirer, envenomed with resistance, will exceed in subtlety and ferocity anything we today conceive, and the pale forewarned victim, with every track covered, every paper burnt and every letter unanswered, will, in the tower of art, the invulnerable granite, stand, without a sally, the siege of all the years.

2

Shakespeare had withstood the siege of the years; he had survived as invulnerable granite : even generations of actors, raving and ranting, could not spoil him. There had been, to be sure, some of the subtlety and ferocity of which James spoke; critics and biographers had had their say; they continued to build a great library around the First Folio and the Quartos. Yet Shakespeare seemed immune – immune as no other artist in literary history. In *The Birthplace* James wrote still another of his parables – he had written so many – about the life of art. He had always mocked the legends of Stratford-on-Avon. He had spoken of 'the lout from Stratford' and had been dressed down by his acerbic friend Rhoda Broughton – 'A lout – me divine William a lout! I won't have yer call me divine William, a lout. Me beloved Jamie calling Shakespeare a lout!' But James had not intended condescension or depreciation. He argued that the facts of Stratford did not 'square' with the plays of the genius. The facts spoke for a commonplace man; the plays for the greatest genius the world had ever known. This was 'the most attaching of literary mysteries'. And James wrote to a friend, 'take my word for it, as a dabbler in fable and fiction, that the plays and the sonnets were never written but by a Personal Poet, a Poet, and Nothing Else, a Poet, who being Nothing Else, could never be a Bacon'. James refused to accept the Baconian theory, or the parochial *bêtise*, as he called it, of the Ciphers. The Baconians would overlook this and claim him as their own.

To Violet Hunt, James reiterated that he was

haunted by the conviction that the divine William is the biggest and most successful fraud ever practised on a patient world ... I can only express my general sense by saying that I find it *almost* as impossible to conceive that Bacon wrote the plays as to conceive that the man from Stratford, as we know the man from Stratford, did.

Miss Hunt compared Shakespeare's genius to a passenger on a liner who has a cabin and great reserves of luggage in the hold. The analogy did not satisfy James. The point about genius he replied was that 'it gets at its *own* luggage, in the hold perfectly (while common mortality is reduced to a box under the berth) but it doesn't get at the Captain's and the First Mate's, in *their* mysterious retreats'. In a word the artist knows only his own consciousness. When James was 22, and writing an early book review, he had formulated this very clearly: 'To project yourself into a consciousness of a person essentially your opposite requires the audacity of great genius; and even men of genius are cautious in approaching the problem.' In his answer to Miss Hunt, James remarked that 'William of Stratford (it seems to me) had no luggage, could have had none, in any part of the ship, corresponding to much of the wardrobe sported in the plays'.

All of Henry James's work shows that he had been saturated with Shakespeare from his earliest days. He had known him as a boy in Lamb's re-telling of the plays; he had seen him acted in many forms – not only the Shakespeare of old New York theatres, but the Shakespeare of Dickensian London, and the Shakespeare of the Lyceum, the heavily costumed creatures of Henry Irving. He had written about these productions, often quite sharply and he had made his pilgrimage long ago – in the days when he had been a 'passionate pilgrim' – to Warwickshire, to the Shakespeare country. He had revisited Stratford five years later, in 1877, on the eve of *Daisy Miller*. The densely grassed meadows and parks were perhaps not as prettily trimmed in Shakespeare's day; yet this had been the Bard's 'green picture of the world'. Even then, at Stratford, he found a 'torment' in Shakespeare's 'unguessed riddle'. If it was 'the richest corner of England', it was also the most mysterious.

James expanded his view of 'the lout', or as he put it with greater gentleness in writing, 'the transmuted young rustic', on only two occasions. The first was in the form of *The Birthplace*, published in *The Better Sort* of 1903; the second was in a preface to *The Tempest* of 1907 written for an edition of Shakespeare edited by the Bard's biographer, Sir Sidney Lee. James had met Lee during visits to Sir George Otto Trevelyan, the historian, at Welcombe, near Stratford, where we find him writing 'it's lovely here – and awfully Shakespearian–every step seems somehow, on William's grave and every word a quotation'. He knew the grave well; he admired the spire and chancel of the church in which the Bard was buried; and he knew by heart the cryptic doggerel bespeaking the curse on anyone who would disturb Shakespeare's bones. Long ago, when he had spent a Christmas with Fanny Kemble, at Stratford, they had gone to service in this church – Fanny Kemble, whom James in his boyhood had heard in her readings and whose talk was so saturated with the language of the plays that she made the Bard 'the air she lived in'. Hawthorne had visited the Birthplace and described it in a touching essay. He had felt, he said 'not the slightest emotion while viewing it, nor any quickening of the imagination'. For 'the Shakespeare whom I met there took various guises, but had not his laurel on'. And one suspects that Henry James, knowing this essay, must have very early accepted Hawthorne's view, so close was it to his own – that 'it is for the high interests of the world not to insist upon finding out that its greatest men are ... very much the same kind of men as the rest of us, and often a little worse'. Hawthorne also said that

when Shakespeare invoked a curse on the man who should stir his bones, he perhaps meant the larger share of it for him or them who should pry into his perishing earthliness, the defects or even the merits of the character that he wore in Stratford, when he had left mankind so much to muse upon that which was imperishable and divine.

In Henry James this view was filled with the ambivalence he always showed when faced with the 'facts' of biography. The artist in him was curious about the life of art: if an artist were careless enough to leave his papers and they were not destroyed the world could hardly ignore them. Moreover, one supposes, James believed that it was proper for artists to write about artists. It was the public, and the penny-catching journalists, who never understood.

3

James's little-known preface to *The Tempest* tells us, in many subtle ways, and with all the *finesse* of his late prose, that he could under no circumstances swallow the legend that Shakespeare wrote *The Tempest* and then gave up writing. This was not the way of a genius with so much abundance in him. *How*, James asked,

did the faculty so radiant here contrive, in such perfection, the arrest of its divine flight? By what inscrutable process was the extinguisher applied and, when once applied, kept in its place to the end? What became of the checked torrent, as a latent, bewildered presence *and* energy, in the life across which the dam was constructed?

Recorded circumstances were of course dim and sparse. They indicated at any rate, James wryly remarked, 'that our hero may have died – since he did so soon – of his unnatural effort'. Shakespeare, the man, did not exist. What existed was simply the Artist – 'the monster and magician of a thousand masks ... so generalized, so consummate and typical, so frankly amused with himself, that is with his art, with his power, with his theme, that it is as if he came to meet us more than his usual halfway', gave us the illusion of 'meeting and touching the man'. But the man was 'locked up and imprisoned in the artist'. In an exquisite passage of summary James elaborated what he had meant in his private letter about the Personal Poet:

The subjects of the Comedies are, without exception, old wives' tales – which we are not too insufferably aware of only because the iridescent veil so perverts their proportions. The subjects of the Histories are no subjects at all; each is but a row of pegs for the hanging of the cloth of gold that is to muffle them. Such a thing as *The Merchant of Venice* declines for very shame, to be reduced to its elements of witless 'story'; such things as the two Parts of *Henry the Fourth* form no more than a straight convenient channel for the procession of evoked images that is to pour through it like a torrent. Each of these productions is none the less of incomparable splendour; by which splendour we are bewildered till we see how it comes. Then we see that every inch of it is personal tone, or in other words brooding expression raised to the highest energy.

If energy were pushed far enough – 'far enough if you can!' – then, said Henry James, what you had was Character.

Tone, energy, character – the chemistry of Shakespeare which Henry James described, as he described that of Balzac – showed his belief that artists live in the ways in which they express themselves. They were not – Shakespeare was not – a sensitive harp set once for all in a window to catch the air: he had descended into the street in quest of every possible experience and adventure. And he was to be grasped as a questing spirit, not as a static harp – 'the genius is part of the mind, the mind a part of behaviour, so that, for the attitude of inquiry, without which appreciation means nothing, where does one of these provinces end and the other begin? We may take the genius first or the behaviour first, but we inevitably proceed from the one to the other.' James was prepared to accept the art of biography only if it became 'a quest of imaginative experience'. In such circumstances it could be 'one of the greatest observed adventures of mankind'.

4

This was Henry James's prophecy of the criticism of the future, and of the future of biography. His tale of *The Birthplace* is of a piece with the stories he had written in which he scoffed at newspaper-made fame, and placed himself wholly on the side of the imagination. The tale does not mention Shakespeare; nor does it mention Stratford. But the birthplace is 'the Mecca of the English-speaking race'. The story follows closely the original idea given James in May 1901 during one of his visits to Welcombe. Lady Trevelyn had told him of a man and his wife who had been placed in charge of the Shakespeare house. They were 'rather strenuous and superior people' from Newcastle. They embraced the job eagerly, only to find at the end of six months that they could not stand the 'humbug' imposed upon them by the tourists. Morris Gedge, in the story, the newly appointed keeper, realizes soon enough that the birthplace is a lot of humbug. He would have liked to stick to hard facts, but the visitors impose upon him their desire for homely detail. He finds, in a visiting American couple, kindred spirits. And to them he confides 'there *is* no author ... There are all the immortal people – *in* the work; but there's nobody else.' And then, when he realizes that he may lose his job, he is able to yield to his own reconstructing imagination. He starts to embroider the legend; he becomes a creator himself. His wife now fears he will be discharged for weaving too much romance. Apparently the visitors cannot have too much. When the appreciative American couple return, he gives them an example of his delicate improvisations as he stands in the Birthroom :

Across that threshold He habitually passed; through these low windows in childhood, He peered out into the world that He was to make so much happier by the gift to it of His Genius; over the boards of this floor – that is over *some* of them, for we mustn't be carried away! – his little feet often pattered, and the beams of this ceiling (we must really in some places take care of *our* heads!) he endeavoured, in boyish strife, to jump up and touch.

In this vein Gedge creates a fanciful fabric. He is now a success. The directors vote to double his pay. The creative imagination triumphs over the mundane. In the tale James gives us the levels of art-appreciation – that of the flat-footed public, which merely wants to know how like itself greatness is; the sensitive appreciators, like the American couple, who represent higher criticism, and finally the keeper of the shrine, who pays his tribute to art by being imaginative himself.

Part Three
The Better Sort

72

Goody Two Shoes

THE crowded years had fled; but the new years, the approach of old age, had their own crowdedness, and the traveller to the Continent – the tourist in France, the voyager in Italy – now had his beaten path from Rye to London. Henry James might pose amusedly as a rural aristocrat, a member of the landed gentry; he had his eye nevertheless on the metropolis that had sheltered him most of his expatriation. It was his little joke that he lived a dutiful life among his 'peasantry' in 'the solitudinous and silent nature of Lamb House'. These only sharpened his appetite for London. 'You have no idea,' he wrote to the distant Grace Norton, 'what a small personal world I live in, in having come to live so much as I do in the country.' He had thought he knew how to live alone; he was learning better each month. But was this kind of life good for him? He asked the question of Miss Norton and answered it promptly – yes, it was beautiful – for three quarters of the year! For the remaining quarter he needed the amplifications of the capital. The *impersonal* life, he explained, 'is provided for among my Sussex yokels'. Various neighbours were dutifully dined at the Yule-time – the parochial, golf-playing, walking, gardening, tea-drinking retired generation with whom he was 'gorged to such repletion that I am heavy even as with their heaviness'. And if his friends would ask, 'Why have them?' his answer would have to be, 'What will you have? The Squire – ! One's "people".' He had such a sense of being 'looked to' from humble quarters, 'that one feels with one's brass knocker and one's garden-patch, quite like a country gentleman, with his "people" and his church-monuments'. *Noblesse oblige.*

I

Two of his paths in London led him to certain ladies. When he was younger the ladies he had cultivated were older, they reached backward to the eighteenth century. Now they were closer to his own years. One path always led to Lucy Clifford's – that was the road to the literary salon, a hearth where one talked of old friends and met the children of the New Novel and the New Poetry over whom Aunt Lucy fussed hen-like and devoted. The other path led to Eaton Terrace, to Jessie Allen's, and the echoes of the grand world offered by his newer friend, two years younger than himself, whom he had met in Venice in 1899. He had begun by going to her small corner house at No. 74 by invitation, but increasingly was allowed to turn up at the tea-hour, uninvited; although he sometimes risked the absence of his hostess. Thus he could write to her on one such occasion in 1903

on Saturday *week* last the 14th – or was it Friday 13th – when being in town for three days and near Eaton Terrace, a gentleman of distinguished though faded, appearance, with the remains of once remarkable beauty distinguishable under the flickering street lamps, might have been seen to hurry, all intent to No. 74 (about five o'clock) and then, at the sight of its darkened windows and closed shutters, stop short, smite his still noble brow, glare wildly about him, murmur a deep imprecation and stride gloomily away.

The artisan of the 'modern' wasn't above mocking the platitudes of Victorian fiction.

James found Elizabeth Jessie Jane Allen lively and amusing from the first. They had met under the noble roof of the Curtises in the Palazzo Barbaro (renamed Palazzo Leporelli in *The Wings of the Dove*) and thereafter Miss Allen, who was very *écrivassière*, as James put it, sent him thirty-page letters filled with news of castles and country houses. She couldn't, for her life, as James said to Mrs Curtis, write a simple note. Her letters were filled with 'the bright pageant of her pen'. She came of the Allens of Cresselly. Her great-grandfather had been the Earl of Jersey, and in the way of distinguished British families, various relatives in various generations married Wedgwoods and Darwins. Raised by devoted aunts and trained in the hope, it was said, that she might become a lady-in-waiting at Court, she had, however, lacked the requisite lineage. But she moved through the world as if she were a noble attendant bent on the highest service. She was always on the move, to Wales, to the castles of the Scottish border, to great English homes. In Eaton Square, with her two loyal maids, her cat, her delicate Victorian water-colours, her choice miniatures and fine antiques, she served tea or dinner to Henry James usually in her upstairs drawing-room. She might have been in earlier years a Madame Merle, though less calculating. Now she was more like Maria Gostrey. Indeed James compared her to that lady of *The Ambassadors* in a letter in which they gossiped, as they invariably did, of the Curtises of Venice who 'see all the greatness of the earth and bestrew their path with anecdotes and witticisms'. The Curtises, James told Jessie, had a kind of 'dim theory that we, you and I, sort of daily conspire together – if only, as it were, towards an indiscreet alliance, in which we communicate over *their* heads!' And he went on to tell her (he was actually reading proof of his novel) that he had been writing 'some stuff in which a woman who has in certain circumstances' – and his pen slipped at this moment and in wanting to write the word 'rather' James wrote 'Strether' instead. He corrected this, and went on, 'who has in certain circumstances rather launched a man, has occasion to say to him afterwards: "Ah, I did it all, but now you can toddle alone!"' The Curtises had made him acquainted with Miss Allen. Now the two toddled alone 'in a manner that their sponsors have possibly a vague, uneasy, conception of'.

They toddled charmingly for the last seventeen years of James's life; and the more than 200 letters he wrote and Miss Allen saved, are filled with ardent anecdote, now ancient, of the Curtises and others of the cosmopolite-English world. Miss Allen used to write her letters in a low chair with a small table at her side. Her penmanship was beautiful and as each letter was ready for the post she dropped it on the floor to be mailed by one of her maids. She affected a cape and bonnet when she went to the theatre with James. She attached great importance to her little glass of port at lunch. Her voice was deep and low. She was above all an old-fashioned Lady Bountiful. James had begun by saying to her that her letters brought him 'something of the rattle and the fragrance – as of a thousand expensive essences – of the great world' and exclaiming 'how much good you must do and how many people you make happy!' But soon his letters were filled with warnings and with dismay at the way in which she spent herself doing good deeds for vampires. He spoke of her 'hungry genius for relieving humanity', of 'the sad and dreary things – things of woe and wretchedness – that you seem always condemned to be doing.'

Very early Henry James found himself included in Miss Allen's largesse. On the first Christmas of their friendship, in 1899, Jessie sent her new friend a Venetian *cinquecento* taper. James gracefully thanked her with full euphemism: it would be the joy of his eye – 'the flower of my collection, and the pride of my house'. The following Christmas, Miss Jessie's gift consisted of two fine brass Venetian candlesticks. James told her he bowed his head very low in gratitude. All Venice – the Salute, San Giorgio, the Dogana – was in her gift; but he also had an uneasy feeling he said that 'the positive frenzy of your altruism' required close watching. The Christmas after that, still keeping up the Venetian memory, it was a fine casket, doubtless like one of Portia's. In the fourth Christmas, and perhaps because it was a winter of blizzard at Rye, Jessie departed from the Venetian mood. What descended on Lamb House, in the midst of the deep snow, were two large bearskin rugs.

2

Henry James had addressed her as 'Dearest and unspeakable Miss Allen' for her earlier gifts. Now he wrote to 'Dearest and worst Miss Allen'. He told her he would have to bring the bearskin rugs back to Eaton Square. They were 'impossible, unspeakable, unforgivable'. He refused to regard them as his. 'I really, dear lady, can *not* again receive *any* object of value from your hands, of value or even of *no* value.' What was more, he said, he wouldn't even 'growl' his 'thank you' for the bearskins. To such ungraciousness was he reduced by her perversity. He wanted a solemn promise she wouldn't do it again.

And even thus the bearskins will be deposited at no distant date either on the top of your house or at its foundations, or thrust into one of its windows or down one of its chimneys; for I thought I had made all this plain last year. There! – And do you see what a Pig you make of me. And a Pig that I shall *remain*, that I shall continue to be, elaborately, inexorably, always, *always*!

He added: 'See, too, what you compel me to sit up nights writing about, when I might be either reducing my oil-bill or at least writing about Shakespeare, and the musical glasses, or ... the crimes of the aristocracy.'

A day or two later, James went up to London. There was a confrontation in Eaton Square between the Great Novelist and the Altruistic Lady. Whether he carried the bearskins with him on this occasion we do not know. But he seems to have faced utter defeat. A letter of 15 December 1902 shows him in a mood of compromise. He agrees to keep the gift. 'I promise,' he wrote, 'to wear the bearskins in bed in the blizzard that I feel to be now again preparing; but all on one condition.' The implacable, great condition was that from this time on he would address Miss Allen as 'Goody Two Shoes'. This was an allusion to the eighteenth-century moral tale attributed to Oliver Goldsmith and written for the edification of the young about Little Goody Two Shoes otherwise called Mrs Margery Two Shoes

> who from a state of rags and care
> and having shoes but half a pair
> Their fortune and their fame would fix,
> and gallop in a coach and six.

Miss Allen was hardly an orphan and she had all the shoes she needed. But she had Goody's addiction to generous deeds and noble sacrifices. The descendant of the Allens of Cresselly became, in the Jamesian mythos, for all her future 'dear generous Goody' or 'my dear Goody – best of goodies'. Books were inscribed to her thus by James. Sometimes she was 'Dear St Goody', or 'my eternally martyred and murdered Goody'. She was indeed too good – 'wherever I look, in your existence, it strikes me as bristling with merciless monsters, with devouring dragons. I would like to St George them all into the bottomless pit.'

John Singer Sargent, who was both James's friend and Miss Allen's, and also a friend of the Curtises, characterized Miss Allen's letters to James – which the novelist burned with his other papers – as 'mischievous tattle about James's friends, whom she always tried to alienate from him'. He said that James's letters were 'sympathetic replies'. Shorn of their associations, this abundant correspondence remains a monument of elegant, ironic persiflage and personal reference; many of the details have been rendered meaningless by time; but in them one finds a comedy of old-fashioned manners, that of the latter-day Goody Two Shoes and her Novelist, humblest, yet most Napoleonic of her friends.

73

A Queer Job

I

HENRY JAMES called his book about William Wetmore Story 'a queer job'. It was a mixture of biography, documents, reminiscence. The tone of reminiscence dominated the book. The two thick volumes published late in 1903 at the same time as the long-delayed *Ambassadors* – held back by Harpers who doubted the success of the novel – were distinctly autobiographical. The novelist had found that he had to eke out the scant history of his subject with 'my own little personal memories, inferences, evocations, and imagination'. James was not in reality a biographer; he had no intention of becoming one. Moreover, he had never liked Story. Faced with bundles of letters and certain diary notes he had neither the time nor the inclination to do the required 'research' which would have provided him with a full background; nor did he have the patience of the scholar accustomed to using 'given' material. His own creative and organizing imagination played around the impersonal and inanimate documents and sought constantly to 'novelize' them. He had undertaken the book in a moment of financial need and under the pressure of Story's children. He had known Story, the Bostonian-Roman, not intimately, but had seen him long ago in his forty-room apartment in the Barberini Palace; he had visited his studio, where morsels of marble shone in the yard and expert Italian stonecutters carried out Story's ideas. Story had lived in general grandeur in the artistic ambiance of *Roderick Hudson*, which had dealt with an American sculptor in Rome – though he had by no means been the 'original' for Roderick. The novel had no original; it was based on James's friendship with a group of painters and scuptors in the Holy City in the early 1870s. Story himself, a consistent amateur – he sculptured, wrote verses, plays, essays, staged theatricals – James had considered a case of 'prosperous pretension'. He became famous in Victorian England with a statue of Cleopatra. All his sculptures were narratives; and American businessmen visiting Rome in quest of 'art' purchased them. The world had been more than kind to

Story. Set against his time and his generation, he was an archetypal American subject, a Jamesian subject – the American expatriate with a penchant for the artist life. Story had originally been a lawyer and a professor of law; he had never learned the law of the artist.

This James said at several points in his book with delicate tact which enabled him to speak the truth – a felicitously varnished truth. 'How could he be, our friend, we sometimes find ourselves wondering, so restlessly, sincerely aesthetic, and yet, constitutionally, so little insistent.' By 'insistent' James meant the act of 'throwing the whole weight of the mind' into what an artist is doing. With artists this was instinctive. 'They feel unsafe, uncertain, exposed, unless the spirit, such as it is, be at the point in question "all there". Story's rather odd case, if I may call it so, was that when he wrote, prose or verse, he was "there" only in part.' Having in this passage, as in others, clearly shown Story's amateurism, James turned to the other question that must have made him originally interested in the biography – Story's expatriation. Had Story paid in his art for having chosen to live abroad – and in a seductive country that beguiled, tempted, distracted the artist? Robert Browning, Story's friend, had lived in the same country and produced some of his finest work. 'Italy, obviously, was never too much,' for the author of *Men and Women*. 'That weight of the whole mind which we have speculatively invoked was a pressure that he easily enough, at any point, that he in fact almost extravagantly, brought to bear. And then he was neither divided nor dispersed. He was devoted to no other art.' Story had been divided and dispersed; he was more social than artistic, and much too worldly.

Out of such mixed elements, James produced this book; he was already thinking of *The Golden Bowl* as he wrote it, and he disposed of his 'queer job' in about two months, dictating eloquent commentaries around a series of letters to Story from the Brownings, from Norton, Lowell, and others. He gave the book a careful title: *William Wetmore Story and His Friends: From Letters, Diaries and Recollections*. The key word was 'recollections'. He always fell back on memories; speaking always in the first person he created a series of exquisite pictures of the old Roman time. To start remembering was to run away from his material. The digressions were numerous. An instance of this was James's coming on a reference to the thick ankles of the ballerina Taglioni in one of the letters. There ensues in these pages a passage in which James reminds himself of dining in the great houses of London with Taglioni when she was old and her ankles were no longer visible on the stage of the world. So too, a reference to Mrs Procter enabled him to yield to an old desire to commemorate that caustic old lady, whom he had liked so much, when he had known her in his early London days. Small wonder certain of James's critics in the United States described the life Story as the 'sacrifice' of a fine subject to Henry James's egotism. The statement was true. Yet one must recognize, in the fullness of time, that the Story volumes now stand as a separate work of art, filled with lessons for the modern biographer – hints from a powerful creative intelligence how to use significant detail, the organizing imagination, the transfiguring touch. It also suggests how style and evocation can illuminate inanimate documents. The loosest kind of biography, the life of Story suggests to us how fine an historian James might have been had he not been a novelist. Houghton Mifflin editors, reading the book, promptly asked James to do a life of Lowell. His reply showed how well he understood the biographer's task. The interest of a biographical work, he wrote,

must depend on intrinsic richness of matter. If a man has had a quiet life, but a great mind, one may do something with him; as one may also do something with him even if he has had a small mind and great adventures. But when he has had neither adventures nor intellectual, spiritual, or whatever inward history, then one's case is hard. One becomes, at any rate very careful.

This was the lesson learned by James. In the history of biography the Story volumes should be given a particular place : not only do they show the struggle of the free imagination within the documentary prison; they illustrate how a work of art can be created about a subject the biographer dislikes. The Story life is not a 'debunking' biography. James addresses himself instead to extracting such richnesses as he can : and the richness he ends up with comes from his own discipline, his own experience, his own mind. The writing had proved a 'damnedly difficult job – to make an at all lively and shapely and artful little book – which should not give poor dear W.W.S. simply clean away'. Or as he put it to the Duchess of Sutherland late in 1903, he had, in this biography made bricks without straw, he had chronicled 'small beer with the effect of opening champagne'. Story was the dearest of men, but he wasn't massive, his artistic and literary baggage were of the slightest, and the materials for a biography *nil*. Hence (once I had succumbed to the amiable pressure of his children,) I had really to invent a book, patching the thing together and eking it out with barefaced irrelevances – starting above all *any* hare, however small, that might lurk by the way. It is very pleasant to get from a discriminating reader the token that I have carried the trick through. But the magic is but scantly mine – it is really that of the beloved old Italy, who always *will* consent to fling a glamour for you, whenever you speak her fair.

The two artful volumes represent still another instance of the power of the artist to illuminate whatever crosses his path. Story's sculptures rest in the deepest basements of the art museums; few pause to look at his public statues. But in the pages of Henry James he is enshrined in the grandeur of a style – decidedly not his own.

2

Henry James's old friend Henry Adams read the Story volumes during a stay in Paris in the autumn of 1903. The two had not met since the period of the Spanish-American war, five years earlier. Adams was moved by the book and, with his asperity and melancholy, he read a deeper message in it. The result was a remarkable, and very personal, letter to Henry James. His New England generation, Adams told James 'were in actual fact only one mind and nature; the individual was a facet of Boston'. Henry James had chronicled, in writing Story's life, the history of a generation. 'Harvard College and Unitarianism kept us all shallow,' wrote Henry Adams. 'We knew nothing – no! but really nothing! of the world.' Adams went on to say that one could not exaggerate

the profundity of ignorance of Story in becoming a sculptor, or Sumner in becoming a statesman, or Emerson in becoming a philosopher. Story and Sumner, Emerson and Alcott, Lowell and Longfellow, Hillard, Winthrop, Motley, Prescott and all the rest, were the same mind – and so, poor worm – was I!

Turning the lens of history on himself, Adams said he and the others had been the '*type bourgeois bostonien!*' Doubtless a type as good as another, but

What you say of Story is at bottom exactly what you would say of Lowell, Motley and Sumner, barring degrees of egotism. You cannot help smiling at them, but you smile at us all equally. God knows that we knew our want of knowledge! the self-distrust became introspection, nervous self-consciousness, irritable dislike of America, and antipathy to Boston. *Auch ich war in Arcadien geboren.*

Adams concluded by saying James had written 'not Story's life but your own and mine – pure autobiography, the more keen for what is beneath, implied, intelligible only to me and half a dozen other people still living'. He ended, 'You make me curl up, like a trodden-on worm. Improvised Europeans we were, and – Lord God! – how thin!'

James could have replied that *he* certainly wasn't an 'improvised European' and certainly not a Bostonian. Yet in the long historical perspective Adams had touched an important truth. The Bostonians, products of a puritan tradition, Story, Sumner, Emerson, Alcott, Lowell, Holmes, Longfellow had all been intellectuals, to a degree writers of disguised sermons; they had lacked the larger imagination. One might speak of the 'flowering of New England' but the flowers were tame and confined to a well-ordered churchly garden. It had been New York that supplied the largest imaginations in American literature – in Melville's reach to the South Seas, in Whitman's demo-cratic 'barbaric yawp', and in the super-civilized psychology of Henry James who went to Europe as Melville had gone to the Pacific, in quest of himself and of freedom.

What James thought of Adams's reaction to his book we do not altogether know. We can only read between the lines of his reply, which was gentle and mild and quietly reproving, for he could not join Adams in his pessimism. There was, said Henry James, 'a kind of *inevitableness* in my having made you squirm'. But he himself had been pushed 'to conclusions less grim'.

The truth is that any retraced story of bourgeois lives (lives other than great lives of 'action' – *et encore!*) throws a chill upon the scene, the time, the subject, the small mapped-out facts, and if you find 'great men thin' it isn't really so much their fault (and least of all yours) as that the art of the biographer – devilish art! – is somehow practically *thinning*. It simplifies even while seeking to enrich – and even the Immortals are so helpless and passive in death.

James had wanted, he said, to invest old Boston out of which Wil-liam Wetmore Story came with a mellow and a golden glow and he

had succeeded only in making it bleak for Henry Adams. He ended
by telling Adams he had not yet heard from the Story family. 'I
think they don't know whether they like it or not! They are waiting
to find out – and I am glad on the whole they haven't access to *you*.'

74

The Master at 60

THE book on Story was at the printer's and Henry James was
making a fresh adjustment to London in his annual winter flight
from Lamb House. If he had in the metropolis his usual distractions
– his tea ceremony at Eaton Square, his visits to the Gosses at Dela-
mere Terrace, his quiet hours with Lucy Clifford – he at the same
time maintained his ceaseless industry in his comfortable room at
the Reform Club. *The Ambassadors* was being serialized at last and
he was reading proof; and he had promised the *Atlantic Monthly*
an article on Zola, who had died of carbon monoxide poisoning the
previous autumn. James had written his summing up of Balzac and
of Flaubert a few months earlier. It was fitting that he should now
call on his memory, and his reading, to offer a final tribute to the
author of *Les Rougon-Macquart* and the courageous defender of
Dreyfus. The essay is of a piece with its predecessors and those he
had written earlier on George Sand; in effect he was rewriting his
1878 book *French Poets and Novelists*. He had then at the threshold
of his middle years recorded his appreciation and his debt to the
French writers. Now he was revisiting them, looking at them from
the distance of his maturity. He had begun by being fascinated by
Zola, but had disliked his subject-matter; 'a combination of the cess-
pool and the house of prostitution', he had said of *Nana*; at least
officially, in the journals of the New World, he had deprecated
Zola's tendency to deal with 'dirty' subjects, his pronounced physi-
cality. But he had always shown in these criticisms that he also liked
the determination and persistence, the dogged seriousness of the
man – ever since he had heard him one day at Flaubert's describe
how he was compiling for himself a dictionary of coarse language
to write *L'Assommoir*. He had been struck 'with the tone in which
he made the announcement – without bravado and without apology,
as an interesting idea that had come to him and that he was working,

really to arrive at character and particular truth, with all his con-science'. James remembered how the novel's audacity had got it banned. Now it was judged a masterpiece. As in his other late essays, his concern at maturity was no longer with the power of individual works. He looked at the total work, the figure, the legend, the making of a 'classic'. In a few passages of reminiscence, in this essay, in which he allowed his admiration for Zola to be expressed at last, he remembered their talk when the French novelist had come to London : and the factitious side too, of his creation, Zola's account of how he intended to do a series on Lourdes, Paris, Rome. James was prepared to allow Zola the first two: but Rome! Zola con-fessed to having been once in Italy, in Genoa.

It was splendid for confidence and cheer, but it left me, I fear, more or less gaping ... he was an honest man – he had always bristled with it at every pore; but no artistic reverse was inconceivable for an adven-turer who, stating in one breath that his knowledge of Italy consisted of a few days spent at Genoa, was ready to declare in the next that he had planned, on a scale, a picture of Rome. It flooded his career, to my sense, with light; it showed how he had marched from subject to subject and had 'got up' each in turn – showing also how consummately he had reduced such getting-up to an artifice.

James thought of his own 'frequentations, saturations' – a history of long years in his adored Rome. And here was Zola giving Rome away 'before possessing an inch of it'.

So James mused, recalling also how in his talk with Zola in the 1890s the French writer appeared to him to have lived only for the writing of his great series of novels. He had wondered what else he had lived for. It was almost 'as if *Les Rougon-Macquart* had written him as he stood and sat, as he looked and spoke, as the long, con-centrated, merciless effort had made and stamped and left him'. But then something fundamental had happened. Zola had been shaken to his roots. *J'Accuse* had happened – and Zola's defence of Dreyfus was that of a man who finally found his commitment to life as well as to art – 'a man with arrears of personal history to make up, the act of a spirit for which life, or for which at any rate freedom, had been too much postponed, treating itself at last to a luxury of ex-perience'.

2

Henry James was 60; but this birthday, which placed him now in the autumn of life, came and went on 15 April in a heedless London. Moreover James himself would have liked to forget it. He wrote to Grace Norton, 'Any age is in itself good enough – even the latest.' The devil of it was that its identity was so brief; it passed so quickly. Landmarks of time there were, on all sides, and in the faces of American and English and French friends, those who had survived out of earlier years. Grace Norton's brother, Charles Eliot Norton, loomed one day, on James's horizon, at Lamb House, but he was distinctly a figure in an ancient gallery; he belonged, James felt, to 'some alien epoch of my youth'; even Norton's critical terminology, filled with echoes of the days of Carlyle and Ruskin, seemed quaint. He was of another age, and James felt he had 'travelled thousands of miles from the order and air' of Cambridge and Shady Hill. 'It takes one whole life,' he wrote to Miss Norton, in the vein of his hero of *The Ambassadors*, 'for some persons *dont je suis*, to learn how to live at all; which is absurd if there is not to be another in which to apply the lessons.'

Another Cambridge friend of the old days seemed indestructible and had just crowned his career by being named to the Supreme Court. Henry James had predicted long ago, when they were mere youths, that the younger Oliver Wendell Holmes would some day rise to eminence 'in a specialty, but to a high degree'. Holmes visited James in Rye during the summer of 1903, and the novelist continued to marvel at the associate justice's 'faculty for uncritical enjoyment and seeing and imagining'. What struck him as unusual about Holmes was that he remained himself, in all his integrity, unmodified by time. 'The people of such perfect sameness are usually those who *haven't* lived.' Wendell moved through life 'like a full glass carried without spilling a drop'. To the new associate justice Henry wrote not without a touch of irony 'you were *born* historic'. Holmes, he said, would remain 'solidly seated ... a beautiful great portrait, as it were, hung up in the chamber of my life'.

Norton, and Holmes – and then, there was Howells, 'the dear man'. He too belonged to James's old Cambridge. Miss Norton told Henry James that Howells, in an intimate moment, had confided to her his feeling that he had lived his life under the dominion of fear. James, commenting on this, said he had always felt the depression in Howells. He hadn't felt this in his verses – but then he hadn't much cared for these. Real as Howells's depression was, however, James believed he was able to disconnect it from his '*operative* self'. It had never been, said James 'the least paralysing, or interfering, or practically depressing'. On the contrary, Howells had arrived at compensations 'very stimulating to endeavour'. The melancholy wasn't to be found in his prose 'and he has in short been so inordinately and cheeringly and cheerfully "successful".' Still James had always known that Howells had a strange, sad, 'kind of crepuscular *alter ego*, a sort of "down cellar" (where they keep the apples of discord) gloom and apprehension'. He could quite believe that Howells had tried to explain the merits of James's later work to Miss Norton. Henry James said he would enjoy Howells's

zeal and deplore your darkness even more had I not reached a state of final beatitude in which one cares not a fraction of a straw what any one in the world *thinks* of one. How they *feel* for one, yes – or even against one; that as much (almost!) as ever. But how they *judge* – never again, never! And it is a peace worth having lived long and wearily to have attained.

In James's letters of his 60th year we obtain new glimpses of old faces. Late in the year he sums up Edmund Gosse

our immortal Gosse – the grand features of his career and character reproduce themselves from month to month in the most punctual and genial way. He is only rather *more* a child of the World and a presider at the Table than hitherto, and his World and his Table and his relations to the same and his pursuit of society and conversation, and of the Great – and of the Small – and of everything and everyone, remain the same bewildering and baffling enigma as ever to me (in respect to their compatibility with the cultivation of Letters, and with the interests of the Board of Trade.)

Gosse was still translator at the latter institution; and James's quick sketch of him, written for W. E. Norris, did not alter the fact that they remained excellent friends.

Time had also brought distancings. Jules Jusserand, the diplomat, James's walking companion of London in the 1880s, had long been away, in other scenes, serving at other embassies. James felt 'the little able and ambitious, contracted and concentrated (*in* ambition) demon that he is' would return to his orbit. Jusserand was now

France's Ambassador to Washington; and there he had become one of the intimates of President Theodore Roosevelt.

Perhaps because he had written of Zola and Dreyfus, James's mind turned in one of his letters to Paul Bourget whose deep-seated conservatism and anti-semitism had revealed itself during the Dreyfus affair. Bourget's 'views and convictions, obsessions and fanaticisms', these were, in the French novelist's brilliant talk, 'perverse', but animated, characteristic.

It is his form, manner and general laxity and monotony in the novel, that I regard as a greater menace to his prosperity, and that make his future doubtful and darksome to me ... However, with an intelligence so great, a literary sense so great, and a humanity, after all, by no means exhausted, a man, at his age, ought still to have a large margin. *Patientons!*

But Bourget would never use that margin. Presently he and James ceased altogether to correspond.

If at 60 we see James glancing at the ageing countenances of some of his contemporaries, his own face remained the brooding unsmiling countenance that Max Beerbohm described; and if James's life was peopled alike with ghosts of the long-dead, it had wide room for the newer generation. Late in 1903 we find him in the presence of Virginia and Vanessa Stephen, now fully grown, daughters of his old friend, Sir Leslie Stephen. He had known Sir Leslie longer than most of the other Londoners; Stephen had published *Washington Square* and had befriended James during the novelist's first adult journey to England in 1869. Now old, weak, Sir Leslie was slowly dying. Henry visited him and talked with him, although their communication had always been more in silence than in speech. Stephen's first wife had been Thackeray's daughter; and to her sister, Anne Thackeray Ritchie, another friend out of the late Victorian London, James wrote of one of his last visits to Leslie in the house at Hyde Park Gate. He had found him brighter and firmer than he had hoped. 'He is as infinitely touching and backward-reaching, and particularly beautiful in his humorous kindly patience with his long ordeal.' His dying seemed to James 'very handsome, noble, gentle and, full of all the achievements behind it and surrounded with such beauty in present and past – beautiful ghosts, beautiful living images (how beautiful Vanessa!) beautiful inspired and communicated benevolence and consideration on the part of everyone'. James found Stephen lying on his couch reading; and told him of some new French books that might interest him.

3

He lived now on a new plane; after the long desolation of the 1890s he had greeted the new century with an outburst of writing. Since 1900 he had published three novels, two volumes of tales, a series of articles; and the life of Story was in the press. He might complain during the winter stretches in Rye of solitude, but no writer of his age was more productive, and no American author had ever, so late in life, written with such power and such serene command of craft. James could look back to the Victorian creators – in France, Flaubert and the *cénacle*, and his beloved old friend Turgenev; in England, the wide circle of the late Victorians. Now the young Edwardians were emerging. Among them he stood, still a presence in the bookshops and the magazines, and a great authoritative voice that spoke of old and new, past and present, a voice awesome and uncompromising on the subject of art. His presence was a living force – still providing new works, and works strange in style and 'difficult', a figure mysterious to the literary world beside the ubiquitous Gosse, or those who wrote for the newspapers. Distinctly one of the élite, his private life unknown, his rare public appearances always portentous, he was pointed to in clubs and sought after by hostesses; he remained aloof and oracular. His speech had grown slower and more elaborate. His short frame had become heavy. When he spoke he delivered himself with a kind of dramatic wit, in sedate, austere phrases, phrases that amplified, described, touched, retouched. There was something Johnsonian about him – a Johnson who spoke not with the voice of dogma, but with irony, the essence of wit. He was always clothed elegantly but sometimes – as the Bay Emmet portrait shows – with a certain extravagance of colour. Henry Dwight Sedgwick glimpsing him in 1901 in the New Forest, saw him as a figure of vaudeville – tight check trousers, waistcoat of a violent pattern, coat with short tails like a cock sparrow – and none matching; and this topped by a cravat in a large, flowery bow.

Gosse was reminded of a canon he had seen preaching in the Cathedral of Toulouse – in the unction, gravity, yet vehemence of his speech. James had about him the suggestion of an actor; there was a theatrical look in the extravagant costume, and the skin of his face seemed blue, from his close shave, as Clive Bell remembered. Whatever the costume, or the tone of speech, the effect was, as Gosse also said, of 'a radically powerful and unique outer appearance. The beautiful modelling of the brows waxing and waning under the stress of excitement,' dwelt in his memory. An American publishing lady, Elizabeth Jordan, on first meeting him at a dinner saw someone who might have been a successful lawyer or banker; and it was not until the dinner was half over that James suddenly turned and looked at her very closely. Then she realized 'the strange power of Henry James's eyes. They made me feel in those instants as if he had read me to the soul and I rather think he had.' An English journalistic lady, Ella Hepworth Dixon, described his eyes as 'not only age-old and world-weary, as are those of cultured Jews, but they had vision – and one did not like to think of what they saw.' Lady Ottoline Morrell in her memoirs said 'they were unlike any other eyes I have ever seen'. Conrad's were 'tragic and worn and suffering', James's, she wrote, 'were of a fluid quality'. They seemed to absorb and distil what they apprehended. Hueffer quoted his servants as saying, 'It always gives me a turn to open the door for Mr James. His eyes seem to look you through to the very backbone.' Thomas Hardy was distinctly in the minority in speaking of James's 'nebulous gaze' – but then this may have been the Master's way of looking at the author of *Tess*.

As we turn the pages of volumes of Victorian and Edwardian reminiscence, James is there, in this drawing-room or that, and the images invoked for him are usually images of power – he recalls Caesar or Napoleon, or he reminds one of a Rothschild, or the Catholic 'Lacordaire in the intolerable scrutiny of the eyes.' His sentences have become labyrinthine; sometimes he seemed to carry over his literary dictation into the salon. And he could be 'as ceremonial as an Oriental'. The dramatist Alfred Sutro recalled, 'one had to wait a long time for the thought to be expressed; one watched the process of its germination and development; but when it came one felt that it had been tremendously worth waiting for, and that it was a thought peculiarly his own and expressed as no other man could have expressed it.' It depended often on the listener. There was in this behaviour, without doubt, a form of aggression – this coercing of the listener's attention. Edith Wharton called the elaborate hesitations a cobweb bridge flung from James's mind to the listener 'an invisible passage over which one knew that silver-footed ironies, veiled jokes, tiptoe malices, were stealing to explode a huge laugh at one's feet'. It was, she said, a 'unique experience'.

Anyone who rummages through the memoirs – they are endless – is led to the conclusion that James was a bore to the bores; but when he found his intellectual peers he could relax; the 'front' of the Master dropped, the sentences became shorter, the give and take easier. The image of James at 60, the common denominator of these multiple pictures, is that of a man who, if he seemed at moments idiosyncratic, eccentric, even comical, exuded aggressive strength. He was assertive and uncompromising, a formed figure, shaped by two continents and many journeys, a tireless observer with an ability to see behind the frail and doubting, the conflicted and am-biguous façade of humanity. Gloriani's eyes in *The Ambassadors* are James's – and we remember how Strether is 'held' by them. He thinks of them as 'the source of the deepest intellectual sounding to which he had ever been exposed'. 'Was it the most special flare, un-equalled, supreme of the aesthetic torch, lighting that wondrous world for ever, or was it above all the long straight shaft sunk by a personal acuteness that life had seasoned to steel?' One wonders whether in the case of Henry James this power of vision was not both – the aesthetic torch, the 'long straight shaft'.

4

In the midst of his work in London James had to rush back to Rye for 'a tiresome little episode, one of the sorrows of a proprietor'. He found himself having to purchase a large piece of garden, next to his own, which had been acquired by an individual named J. H. Gasson, a 'blatant tradesman and scourge of Rye'. Gasson could have built on the lot and ruined James's view. Gasson offered it to James at what was then a high price – £200. 'The danger poisoned my rest, and would have ruined my one view and all my little place, practically – so that there was nothing to do but to buy – and save the situation,' he wrote to William James. Then a little while later another townsman named Whiteman threatened to tear down two 'little old-world whitey-grey cottages' at the end of his garden wall, in the direction of the church. James's gardener lived in one of them. Both had their old gables, and a silvery surface, and were often sketched and painted by artists. New negotiations ensued. James consulted his architect and the destruction was averted, at what cost we do not know.

As always in such matters, James moved quickly to rectify depletion of his bank account. He received from Blackwood £250, the balance of his advance on the Story biography; but he also signed a contract for a new book – over and above two contracts he had signed to produce two novels during the ensuing year. Macmillan had for some time wanted James to write a book about London. It was to be one of a series for which F. Marion Crawford had just done a book on Rome and would be illustrated by Joseph Pennell. James told Macmillan he would need space to turn around in, at least 150,000 words. He agreed to a royalty of 20 per cent and an advance of £1,000 to be paid on publication. The book would never be written, but the traces of what it would have been can be found in a series of pencilled scrawls in a small red pocket notebook, as he visited old corners of London; and in his annotated volumes on London in his library. Too many other things intervened, not least a journey to America. But with the Blackwood money, and assurance of the Macmillan advance, James had a renewed sense of margin.

He returned to Rye in the early summer of 1903, with his productions of the past two years on the press. He returned also with the most famous of his dogs, Max, 'a very precious red Dachshund pup – hideously expensive but eight months old – and undomesticated; but with a pedigree as long as a Remington ribbon. So I have work cut out.' Thus to Miss Weld.

A few days later he was enjoying his garden, his flowers, the late spring 'the last whistle of the blackbirds sounding in the trees and a wonderful red hawthorn ... quite glowing and flaming in the sunset'. The typewriter ticked again in the Garden Room. James had begun a new novel. It was called *The Golden Bowl*.

75

The Reverberator

FIFTEEN years earlier James had written a witty comedy of manners called *The Reverberator* (it was the name of a newspaper), about a young American girl whose romance in France is almost ruined by a snooping American gossip writer named George Flack. James had foreseen – as he measured the future of America – how freedom of the press would lead to licence; how responsibility would cease – and so would privacy. As Mr Flack, who is a more extreme version of Henrietta Stackpole of *The Portrait of a Lady*, or Matthias Pardon of *The Bostonians*, put it with reportorial vehemence;

The society news of every quarter of the globe, furnished by the prominent members themselves (oh, *they* can be fixed – you'll see!) from day to day and from hour to hour and served up at every breakfast-table in the United States – that's what the American people want and that's what the American people are going to have.

There came a moment, in the wake of his novel *The Wings of the Dove*, when James himself, lover of privacy, student of private lives, was served up on the American breakfast-table as a 'lover' (at 60) of a young scandal-creating beauty, mistress of a tycoon, who barged into British society like one of James's early heroines. Once again – he might ruefully tell himself – his fiction had a way of coming true.

I

That spring of 1903 in London, at a tea party, a young woman, dressed in white, fresh and radiant, detached herself from those present and confronted the author of *The Wings of the Dove*. She was small, plump, alert, and had beautiful red hair. Her smile revealed a row of even teeth. She fluttered, a vision of white skin and Titian hair. 'Oh, Mr James, everyone says I look like Milly Theale. Do *you* think I look like Milly Theale?' The anecdotes do not record Henry James's reply. But if he was hesitant and qualifying, he was also pleased. She seemed to have read his novel. The fictional Miss Theale and the real-life Miss Grigsby had one thing in common; they pos-

sessed red hair and a great deal of wealth. It little mattered to Miss
Grigsby that she was meeting James almost a year after publication
of the novel. With a fine disregard for chronology, she would always
give herself out as the 'original' of James's heroine. She had probably not read the book. She may have taken her cue from a charming
article Howells had devoted to *The Wings of the Dove*. He had
spoken of Milly Theale's 'lovely impalpability'.

There was nothing impalpable about Miss Emilie Busbey Grigsby.
Her vague earlier history records that she was the daughter of a Confederate officer and a certain Sue Grigsby of Kentucky; a writer of a
later generation would speak of the mother as a kind of 'super Scar-
lett O'Hara'. Emilie was said to be convent-bred; but all her history
is a tissue of rumour and publicity. Her wealth came from her 'protector', the Chicago traction magnate Charles T. Yerkes, 'an elderly
platonic infatuate' as one commentator put it, or her lover. He had
installed her in a five-storey mansion at 660 Park Avenue in New
York, which the press called 'The House of Mystery'. At 17 she had
described herself as having 'a tingling ᴊense of a young pulsating life.
I loved my hands because they were so fine of touch and tint and my
long firm untried limbs, which could dance all night and hardly know
it; in fine, I loved the body of me with a hearty animal relish and yet
I was not sensuous.' Sensuous she was, as these words suggest; and
she was worldly, and socially ambitious. James met her when she
was 23. Her 'natural history' was known to him; had he not been
the historian of the American girl? Miss Grigsby's siege of London
was conducted from the Savoy; later she would acquire a house and
still later a flat in Mayfair, where Sir Rupert Hart-Davis recalled seeing walls covered with military mementoes, chiefly of Sir John
French and some of Lord Kitchener. James knew of her from his
friends the Henry Harlands, and from Meredith's daughter. Miss
Grigsby would claim in due course that Meredith, seeing her, had
said he had at last met the heroine of *The Ordeal of Richard Feverel*.
She had an image of herself as heroine in many novels; and in her
pursuit of literature as well as 'society' she resembled an earlier
adventuress, Blanche Roosevelt, who had made friends in America
with Longfellow and in France with Victor Hugo and Maupassant;
in England she had sought, but had not conquered Henry James.
Emilie Grigsby, later annals would record, dined Yeats; and one
legend said that Rupert Brooke 'spent his last night in England at Old
Meadows' where Miss Grigsby lived. Indeed the lines he wrote in her

visitors' book were afterwards engraved in bronze over Miss Grigsby's door. But then she also turned up in Westminster Abbey for the coronation of George V, and claimed an acquaintance with Princess Mary, later Queen. The press established that her acquaintance was with someone backstairs in Buckingham Palace.

She was a woman who created her own legend. When she was old, and lived in a fine house in New York, she spoke of Henry James as an intimate friend, who had admired her when she was young and had put her into his novel. By James's account he saw her only four or five times. She invited him to various parties. He declined. Then feeling that he at least should be civil, he paid a formal call on her at the Savoy, and spent ten minutes chatting with her. This was all that Miss Grigsby needed : the Master had actually called on her. The only allusion to the ambitious Emilie in his correspondence of this year is to be found in a letter of 5 May 1903 to Goody Allen. 'Grigsbina is, thank the Lord, in her natural dressmaking Paris – but I *have* seen her too. But of her and every thing anon.' Miss Grigsby is not reported to have sent James such gifts as Goody Allen's bearskins; there was, however, a story that she dispatched to the Master at Christmas a fine ham, cooked in champagne.

2

She would always pass as 'a mysterious and beautiful' figure who, like so many young Americans, had been a part of the Mayfair of the Edwardian years. Her meeting with Henry James would be a matter for scant attention had not her subsequent history proved so lurid. Two years after that London springtime, Miss Grigsby's patron, Charles T. Yerkes, the very prototype of an American tycoon, died at the Waldorf and Miss Grigsby was with him at the time. The indomitable Emilie was projected from the society pages into the front pages of all the scandal sheets of America. She carried with her among many names the name of Henry James – and the name of Milly Theale. In the fullness of time she would get herself into a novel, indeed a series of novels. Yerkes became Theodore Dreiser's 'financier' in his trilogy; and Emilie Grigsby figures in *The Titan* of that series as Berenice Fleming.

Logan Pearsall Smith, an inveterate polisher and amplifier of Jamesian anecdote, long after used to say that the ham cooked in champagne was at the heart of the story. His version was that Henry

James one day, in 1905 or 1906, after Yerkes's death, entered the Reform Club and joined a group of men who were gossiping idly. One among them at a given moment suddenly remarked, 'Whatever became of that Grigsby woman?' In the ensuing silence, Pearsall Smith used to say, James began to issue denials, like a Foreign Office. He denied he had ever known her, save to meet her on a few impersonal social occasions; he denied that she was the original of Milly Theale; he volunteered, and then denied, saying that it was simply a *canard*, that she had sent him a ham cooked in champagne.

This was Pearsall Smith's way of building up from slender threads his elaborate stories about the Master. There are two documents, however, which testify to the extent of the legend. For the story finally reached the Hearst press. 'Heroine in Master's Novel; Grigsby in Language of Love.' The *New York Evening Journal*, which published it on 4 January 1906, carried a caricature of a long-faced, lecherous-looking bald-headed Henry James seated at his writing desk looking at a bust on a pedestal and at a portrait on his wall of Miss Emilie Grigsby. The caption read 'Henry James and his Shrine: This is the celebrated author, reported to be in love with Emilie Grigsby, who is Mildred Theale, heroine of his novel *The Wings of the Dove*, whom he describes in terms of adoration, has placed on a pedestal as an object of adoration, an image of Miss Grigsby.' A subheading pushed harder: 'Famous Author, some say, has Romantic Attachment for Girl he idealized as Mildred Theale.'

The story began, with the usual qualifications of journalism:

Out of the pages of fiction from the pen of one of the greatest master geniuses that America has given the world in modern years – Henry James – comes a wonderful, a close and detailed psychic and physical portrait of Emilie Grigsby, the girl whose wondrous beauty and strange, startling personality, fascinated Charles T. Yerkes, a foremost financier of the world, fascinated foremost society men and women in England, and in turn, it is also declared, absolutely entranced men of such amplitude of genius and almost uncanny intuitive gifts as George Meredith and her portrayer, Henry James.

It may or may not be true that Henry James was, as report has stated of him, at one time deeply in love with Emilie Grigsby – that at 65 he sneered at conventionalities and in full knowledge of her past laid his great fame at her young feet and asked her to marry him. Men who came to him warning him that there was in the girl's career and antecedents that which would turn his romance over to the sneers of the world, are said to have been sent away from him with crackling words of anger and scorn. It is further said that when she left England and travelled to the Isle of Wight he followed her, and his recent return after years and years of absence to America was solely because of her return also to America.

The reporter went on:
'Friends of Miss Grigsby, while not denying that Henry James honoured her with his admiration, declare as fiction itself the tale of his love for her and his proposal of marriage to her. James himself is simply silent on the subject.' There followed lengthy passages from the *Wings*, those in which James had described Milly Theale. These were prefaced as follows:

There can be little doubt that the remarkable girl who had the devotion of Yerkes, the millionaire, was also the inspiration for the great writer's character-drawing of the strange, intense, fascinating girl, Mildred Theale ... So much of Emilie Grigsby's life is like that of Mildred Theale, her voyage in Europe in the hope of securing the communion with cultured people that was denied her by her peculiar position in New York, her half successes, her trials in London life, and, so much in his actual description of the heroine's appearance and temperament coincide, that reading the splendid novel one feels of a certainty that Mildred Theale in real life was none other than Emilie Grigsby.

The second document in the case is Henry James's letter to his brother William, dated 6 May 1904. William had inquired whether it was true that he had proposed marriage to Miss Grigsby.

Dearest William. Your 'Grigsby' letter, which has just come in, would be worthy of the world-laughter of the Homeric Gods, if it didn't rather much depress me with the sense of the mere inane silliness of this so vulgarly chattering and so cheaply-fabricating age – the bricks of whose mendacity are made without even as many wisps of straw as would go into the mad Ophelia's hair. My engagement to *any one* is – as a 'rumour' – exactly as fantastic and gratuitous a folly as would be the 'ringing' report that Peggy, say, is engaged to Booker Washington, *ouf*! or that Aleck is engaged to Grace Norton. There *is* a Miss Grigsby whom I barely know to speak of, who has been in London two or three June or Julys.

He had seen Miss Grigsby, he said, half a dozen times in all.

She is, I believe, a Catholic, a millionaire and a Kentuckyian, and gives out that she is the original of the 'Milly' of my fiction *The Wings of the Dove*, published before I had ever heard of her apparently extremely silly existence ... *She* must have put about the 'rumour' which, though I thought her silly, I didn't suppose her silly *enough* for. But who – of her sex and species – isn't silly enough for *anything*, in this nightmare-world of insane *bavardage* ... When you 'deny', deny not simply by my authority please, but with my explicit derision and disgust.

He signed himself as 'always your hopelessly celibate even though sexagenarian Henry'.

76

An Exquisite Relation

DURING the spring of 1903, when the sexagenarian bachelor was still in London, he received a letter from the famous Mrs Sitwell, who had been the 'muse' of Robert Louis Stevenson's early days. She told Henry James that she and Sidney Colvin would marry that summer, and invited him to the wedding. Theirs had been a romance of forty years' standing. Colvin, keeper of prints and drawings at the British Museum, was 58 – almost a sexagenarian; and the bride was six years older. Henry James had known the two since the days of his friendship with Stevenson, when he saw Louis regularly at Skerryvore, near Bournemouth. Mrs Sitwell was then separated from her clergyman husband, who was now dead. Colvin had had to support an aged mother. Now they were free to marry. Mrs Sitwell was a plump white-haired lady with a large nose and soft eyes; she wore large hats and feather boas. She had always maintained a literary salon, especially for young writers; Stevenson had been her great celebrity. She had been hostess for Colvin when he entertained in his British Museum residence, and all Victorian London knew that they had been in love for decades. 'How charming and interesting your note, and how deeply touched I feel at having your news from you in this delightful way,' James replied to Mrs Sitwell. 'Besides being good, your intention is beautiful, which good intentions always aren't. It has a noble poetic justice.' Just before the wedding James sent his old friends a small silver salver 'big enough to hold a glass of wine or a vase of flowers'. He little dreamed that the wedding, a quiet, almost a secret one in view of the ages of the bride and groom, would prove an extraordinary occasion in his own life.

Only four guests were invited to the Marylebone Church, on 7 July 1903; Browning, whom they had all known, had romantically married Elizabeth Barrett in this church so many years before. James went in the company of Lucy Clifford. The Sitwell–Colvin party consisted of the Bishop who married the couple, a cousin of Robert Louis Stevenson named Mrs Babington and his one-time friend Basil Champneys. Stevenson was an invisible presence and his memory linked everyone on this occasion. The ceremony was soon over and the party went on foot to the Great Central Hotel a quarter of a mile away for luncheon. Lucy Clifford reported 'no one would have suspected six sedate middle-agers in everyday clothes, of anything unusual. We sauntered casually into the hotel, where a quiet little luncheon party had been arranged.' It was very quiet indeed. The Colvins were obviously full of happy embarrassment, the guests were afraid to laugh and spoke in low tones lest the waiter should suspect it was a marriage feast. 'We did not even drink their health,' said Mrs Clifford, 'till someone, Basil Champneys I think, suggested that it ought to be done; then a bottle of still white wine was brought, our glasses were filled, and when the waiter was out of sight and hearing we drank to the bride and bridegroom with little nods and whispers.'

The party was joined at the hotel by a young friend of Mrs Sitwell's, a handsome, elegant man, who seemed a dandy, and who looked younger than his years. Amid the elderly guests he seemed young indeed : but he was actually 30. His name was Dudley Jocelyn Persse. He was a Persse of Galway, a nephew of James's friend, Lady Gregory. Jocelyn carried himself with ease; he was gentle, self-assured, yet with a touch of shyness. He laughed a great deal. James found him attractive from the first. The novelist would speak later to Mrs Sitwell of Jocelyn's 'constituted *aura* of fine gold and rose-colour'. Persse on his side was drawn to the stocky elderly man, who looked at him in so friendly a way with his piercing eyes, and spoke with so much humour and had such an avuncular manner. We are left with the impression that the Master's eyes were always on Jocelyn. They found each other irresistible. A week later Henry James wrote to Mrs Colvin of the presence in Lamb House 'of your delightful young Irish friend Jocelyn Persse. I feel as if I ought to thank you for him.'

I

Two days after the wedding Jocelyn called on the Master at the Reform Club. That same week-end he journeyed to Rye, where the two spent three days together, not unlike the long week-end four years earlier when Henry James had discovered how much he loved the young sculptor, Hendrik Andersen. He loved Persse one judges quite as much – if not more. The first letter from James to Persse, nine days after their meeting, is addressed from the Athenaeum Club to 'my dear, dear, Jocelyn'. James was snatching a minute, he said, to scribble a few friendly words. 'You were as happily inspired to write me so humanely as when you had that other inspiration – days ago – of coming to see me at the Reform.' The 'days ago' were exactly a week. 'Cultivate always, in the future, inspirations as happy and as generous.' He was, he said, lunching, tea-ing and dining out, 'but finding it all less good, by a long shot, for soul and sense, than the least moment of that golden westward walk and talk of ours on Monday afternoon. A blessing rested on that, still rests, will ever rest.' James added that it would 'rest better still if you will remember that you promised to send a photograph to yours always and ever' and he signed his name with his customary grand flourish. He added an exhortation: 'Let me find the photograph at Lamb House when I go back.'

When four days later James returned, Jocelyn's photograph 'welcomed me home to my empty halls and made them seem for the moment less lonely'. The novelist evicted another picture from a frame to make room for his new friend, wishing Jocelyn had autographed it – 'for you are one of those of whom the beholder asks who you are'. James added, possessively, 'You are not for the staring crowd.' Alluding to Persse's social life, he added, 'may these things not float you too direfully far – far, I mean, from the virtuous *grind* of life and the sober realities that a homely friend can hope to share with you!' He ended by enjoining Jocelyn to remember – 'and never doubt of it' – that 'no small sign of your remembrance will ever fail even of its most meagre message to yours, my dear Jocelyn, always Henry James.'

This was the note, the consistent tender note, of a friendship that would grow in warmth and feeling and remain devoted and loyal to the end – into the time when James grew old and ill and Jocelyn's golden hair turned white. The refrain was that of the young man-about-town, who moves in the great wide world and brings tidings to the elderly writer, in his Rye hermitage – the great wide world of country houses, visits to Ireland and Scotland, and the Riviera, dinners and parties, which had been James's life during the period of his conquest of London. Even more than Andersen, Jocelyn Persse became a kind of image in a mirror of James's younger days. Jocelyn was half James's age; he made James feel as if he were still 30. Andersen had helped break the plate-glass front of James's life and Persse and the novelist were able to approach one another with an ease and directness James had not allowed himself in his earlier and more reserved years.

2

The more than seventy letters Persse kept – there probably were others – had been hastily thrown into drawers of old desks; their pages are mixed up; some are partly torn; some sheets are missing; some have cigarette or cigar holes burned in them. Their condition suggests that Persse lived much in the moment; that his friendship with James depended on their direct meetings rather than on the written word. Through these letters, in their tattered state, shines the constancy of James's affection and the evidence of Jocelyn's loyal response. The letters have none of the desperation, or anguish, or ache of passion that occurs periodically in the letters to Andersen (these by contrast preserved meticulously, perhaps with a sense of their future value as autographs). There was for James 'something admirable and absolute' between him and Jocelyn. This was true. He would speak also of 'this exquisite relation of ours'. Jocelyn wasn't the least bit 'literary'. He was a finely-turned-out specimen of the Anglo-Irish gentry – addicted to good manners, food and drink, fine cigars, and brandy, hunting, flirtation, romance, the 'fun' of living. Very early in their friendship James wrote to Jocelyn:

I seem to see you roll, triumphant, from one scene of amiable hospitality and promiscuous social exercise to another; and, sitting here, on my side, as tight as I can, with a complete avoidance of personal rolling, I quite rejoice in the bright brave vision of you, who are willing to do these things (that I can't do) for my mind, and to take me with you, so to speak in thought – so that, even while I crouch in my corner, I get through you, more or less, the vibration of adventure and the side-wind of the unfolding panorama. May you to the end of the feast, retain a stout young stomach! which is a manner of saying – may you suffer yourself to be pelted with as many of the flowers of experience as you can (we won't talk just now of the thorns;) so that when we next meet you shall have at least some of the withered leaves to show me and let me sniff.

And James told him that

the record of your eternal Bacchanalia (do you know what Bacchanalia are?) continues to excite my vague envy, or at least my lively admiration, of your social genius, social good health, the mysterious genial power that guides and sustains you through the multitude of your contacts and the mazes of your dance. What I do envy is the magnificent *ease* with which you circulate and revolve – spinning round like a brightly-painted top that emits, as it goes, only the most musical hum. You don't *creak*.

Or again: 'I rejoice greatly in your breezy, heathery, grousy – and housey, I suppose – adventures, and envy you, as always, your exquisite possession of the Art of Life which beats any Art of mine hollow.'

Others – Hugh Walpote for instance – who watched James's friendship with Persse wondered what the two talked about, how this young man whose spelling wasn't up to scratch and whose talk was social and gossipy, could hold the formidable Master. But then Hugh stood in awe of James; Jocelyn didn't. Hugh mentioned this once to James (for he was jealous of Jocelyn) and asked what 'subjects in common' they found to talk about. He got a clear answer. 'One gets on with him in a way without them, and says to one's self, I think, that if *he* doesn't mind, well, why should one either? At any rate I am glad you were gentle with him. I am infinitely and gladly so.' Hugh Walpole was often intensely bored by Jocelyn, who had none of Hugh's ambition or his literary and social pretensions. But Walpole did write in his diary that he found Jocelyn 'nice, eager to be liked, easily pleased' and again 'very agreeable – a good creature', 'the kindest and nicest of creatures'. One entry as late as 17 March 1914: 'Spent evening with Jocelyn who was perfectly delightful with his simplicity and charm.'

His simplicity, his charm, his good looks, *these* mattered for James much more than any high intellectual talk. Jocelyn, faced with a literary question, usually ducked it. 'Well, I think there are things to be said *for* – and *against* – don't you?' So Walpole remembered. James had had enough of that sort of thing in the *grand monde* of literature. Early in their friendship Jocelyn was off to Greece and James wrote him:

God grant that I be here when you turn up with the rich glow of travel on your manly cheek and the oaths of all the Mediterranean peoples on your moustachioed lips (as I hope, at least, I should like to hear you rip them out.) But I yearn, dear Jocelyn, for all your sensations and notations, and think with joy of your coming to me for a couple of days, near at hand a little later on, shaking the dews of Parnassus from your hair. When I think you are living with Phidias and the Hermes, with the divine race, in short, I am ashamed of writing you a prosy Pall Mall note. *Je t'embrasse bien tendrement*.

James was 'peculiarly *touched* by every letter of yours that reaches me'. What existed between him and Jocelyn was one of those friendships in which neither friend makes large demands on the other. Jocelyn wandered in 'society', visited, travelled – and eventually came to Lamb House. James went to America and was away for many months. When they met they did so with a fullness of appreciation of one another and a great joy in their companionship. When Jocelyn was in London, in his flat at Park Place, James periodically issued one of his elaborate invitations to the younger man to join him for dinner and a theatre in town. 'Can you miraculously dine with me either tonight or tomorrow *here* – at 8.15 – and perhaps "go" somewhere; or at any rate *talk*? – when I will tell you many things – most of all how indeed I remember last year.' James was writing on the first anniversary of their first week-end together at Lamb House. He had been to the British Musem 'where, between Colvin and Colvina, our meeting of last summer always comes romantically back'. When Jocelyn considerately wondered whether he wasn't keeping James from work and from doing important things instead of simply gossiping with him, James replied, 'Don't, my dear boy, afflict me again by talking of my "sacrifices." There is, for me, something admirable and absolute between us which waves away all that. But these things are beyond words – words almost vulgarize them. Yet the last ones of your note infinitely move me.' They went to see the new Shaw plays at the Court Theatre. They saw Gerald du Maurier, son of James's old friend, in *Raffles*. They went to plays given by the Stage Society – Persse remembered one such occasion when they saw Gertie Millar and James was 'bored to distraction'. 'The humour of a country circus', he exclaimed and they walked out at the end of the first act. Then for lighter entertainment there were always the music-halls. James was a devotee and so was Jocelyn. The younger man remembered taking James 'to the low' Middlesex, which Walter Sickert painted, and where 'the primitive audience appealed to him'. James sent Persse *The Ambassadors* when it was published – 'if you are able successfully to struggle with it try to like the poor old hero, in whom you will perhaps find a vague resemblance (though not facial!) to yours always Henry James'. He knew that Jocelyn probably wouldn't read him. Jocelyn wasn't bookish. But this mattered not at all to James. What mattered was the air of charm and enchantment they seemed to weave for one another. 'Why he liked me so much I cannot say,' Persse would write many years later. He said also James was 'the dearest human being I have ever known'.

3

James found himself, in his 61st year, with two attachments to ease the loneliness and melancholy of ageing. He continued to write passionate letters to Andersen – although letters increasingly critical – even while he enjoyed his periodical meetings with Jocelyn. The letters to Jocelyn do not contain the quantity of verbal embracings and laying on of hands that we find in those addressed to Andersen. Perhaps the intimacy with the young Irishman was close; it did not need so much verbalizing – 'words almost vulgarize them,' James had said to Persse. But for Andersen words were available. We may speculate, in trying to read between the lines, that James's involvement with Andersen had in it a part of his passion as artist. Andersen was trying to become a great sculptor. He had a strong touch of megalomania that James, with his own Napoleonic drive, would recognize : and on that 'wave-length' their feelings were deeply enmeshed, or at least James's seemed to be, so that when Andersen did not measure up to James's high standards and codes of art, there was strong and poignant disillusion. With Jocelyn no such tensions seem to have existed. Percy Lubbock, whose involvement with James as the first editor of his letters, would be posthumous rather than actual, would write a novel called *The Region Cloud* about a great artist and his disciples, picturing the artist as a powerful vampire, who needed young admirers to feed his incredible egotism. Whether he was thinking of himself and James we do not know : but in the very style of the novel, with its Jamesian imitations, and hinged and dramatized sentences, Lubbock created a portrait-caricature of James of considerable power and a certain amount of truth. The artist in the novel is both vampire and cannibal: he is so creative that he 'makes his own life, every hour of it – he is the author of it all; and when he has made an hour of it his life is not what it was before, it is changed by the value of that hour; and so it's a new man, a new author, who passes on to the next hour and the next, and each of his days is a creation as fresh as the first'. In a very Jamesian passage, Lubbock describes his character's charm –

he dazzled the intruders with his mirth, or he flattered them with his grandeur, or he caressed them with his irony – always according to his mood, giving them what he was pleased to give; for they mightn't choose, they had to take what he offered them, the greatest with the least. Sometimes he bullied and trounced them without mercy, and on this mood, too, they thrived as well as ever ... he overruled the intruders, one and all, with that lordly possession of himself.

This is the extreme of discipleship. It has in it some of the flavour of James's letters to Andersen, to Persse and later to Hugh Walpole. Lubbock's fictional recreation suggests a ruthlessness and a lack of a sense of reality. But if James could be ruthless with others he was no less ruthless with himself. And he never lost sight, even in his moments of love and loftiness, of the realities in his personal relations.

We capture such a moment – it is the only one recorded – in a letter written by James to Persse in 1910 from America. The previous year he and Jocelyn had visited Ockham, Lady Lovelace's, and James remembers the occasion:

In spite of these grim notes of absence, dearest Jocelyn, I want you to feel with what a rush, a passionate yearning rush, I shall return. The time – this *time* – will pass – I find that even in darkness and pain it does insistently pass – and we shall recover something, as nearly as possible everything, of our beautiful *other* time. We shall make it live again. Before long will come round the anniversary of our rather odd and melancholy, but also exquisite Sunday at Ockham – November 27–29th, 1909 – in those fantastic contiguous apartments. When I think of such scenes and occasions from *this* point of view I grind my teeth for homesickness, I reach out for you with a sort of tender frenzy.

Years later Hugh Walpole spoke of James's 'inevitable loneliness' and of the conflict in James's temperament, between his 'reticent puritanism' and his 'intellectual curiosity'. He believed the loneliness in James came from his remaining an exile in Europe, while never at peace with America. In America 'he longed for the age, the quiet, the sophistications of Europe'. And his young friends, the young men who clustered around him, whether disciples in letters or caught up in the magnetism and egotism of the artist, fed his powerful feelings. 'His passion for his friends – Lucy Clifford, Edith Wharton, Jocelyn Persse, Mrs Prothero, among others – was the intense longing of a lonely man. It was most unselfish and noble.' Walpole was partly right; it was noble in its grandiosity, but not always unselfish; there was in it some of the egotism James himself had described in *The Beast in the Jungle*; but it had in it also the nobility of his art.

In referring to James's Puritanism Walpole may have sought to varnish the eroticism of the novelist's letters to his acolytes. The exact nature of James's friendship with Jocelyn, as that with Andersen, is difficult to describe. Sir Rupert Hart-Davis recalls meeting Persse while walking down Piccadilly with Wapole and Hugh saying, after they left him, 'Believe it or not, Henry James was madly in love with him.' The evidence is tenuous: we have so little beyond the affectionate language of James's letters. We must remind ourselves that if on the one hand there was a buried life of sexual adventure among some Victorian men, there were also many friendships which were romantic rather than physical. The Victorian world was a man's world: men met in clubs; there were very few women in offices or in business. The women had their world of the home and of society. Whether the homo-erotic feeling between Persse and James was 'acted out' is perhaps less important than the fact that an intimate affection existed between them. We must remind ourselves that James was old, stout, Johnsonian. He probably loved Persse in some ways as Johnson had loved his Boswell. But Boswell was a 'publishing' individual who consumed his life in his diaries – and planned to write the life of Johnson. Persse simply lived his life; and his memories of James remained unrecorded; they were absorbed into one great memory – that of an abiding affection. James's date-books, and the letters, tell us all we know of their meetings. We are left with the impression that James's love meant more to Persse than James's greatness. They both possessed a fund of hedonism. It was the love of an ageing man for his lost youth, and the evocation of it in a figure of masculine beauty, as with Hendrik Andersen. He found in his relationship with Persse what he did not find with Andersen, the serenity that enabled him to make *The Golden Bowl*, a work unique among all his novels: it is James's only novel in which things come out right for his characters – the marriage survives, there is progeny, and the hero has an unique strength and masculinity. James's feelings of the moment were always incorporated into what he was writing. Prince Amerigo may have in him some touches of Jocelyn – but he has much more the strength and self-assertion of James himself. In his relation with Persse, James finally freed himself from the prolonged innocence of his earlier years. Persse helped complete the process begun four years earlier when James had met Andersen in Rome. And while James tried to write more novels after *The Golden Bowl*, he no longer needed to do so: he had finally resolved the questions, curious and passionate, that had kept him at his desk in his inquiries into the process of living. He could now make his peace with America; and he could now collect and unify the work of a lifetime.

77

Lessons of the Master

HE had become a presence, an oracle, a legend. Not only the increasingly conferred title of 'Master', but the awe he seemed to inspire in the drawing-rooms, the adulation of the young men, the way in which he was publicly quoted, the fact that he was now imitated, parodied, caricatured – all this spoke for the imprint of a style and a personality. The very headlines in the New York newspapers – or their reverberations – had in them the overtones of a reputation. If there was laughter at James's oddness, or complaint that he was 'difficult', this suggested he was read and discussed. People took sides. Articles appeared, *The Queerness of Henry James*, or *In Darkest James*. Frank Moore Colby, taking his readers on a tour of the jungle of James, would speak of chapters in *The Wings of the Dove* 'like wonderful games of solitaire, broken by no human sound' except for the author's 'own chuckle when he takes some mysterious trick or makes a move that he says is "beautiful".' But Colby also said that James produced 'very strange and powerful effects' even when he was 'wearisomely prolix'. People had cared for Browning not because he had a 'message', but because of his presence in his poems; 'part of the obscurity of Henry James,' Colby said, 'springs from the same pleasing and honorable egotism.'

Young writers began to write like him. Henry James received a sample of this in late 1902. His friend Morton Fullerton's cousin, Katherine, who would later be a successful magazine writer, (Katherine Fullerton Gerould), had written a tale which James read with strange feelings of embarrassment and pleasure. 'Am I so much that *as* that?' he queried Morton, 'it *is*, but too sensitively, too insanely *me* ... She may see a little where she's going, but I see where she's *coming* – and oh, the dangers scare me.' He himself, he said, would much sooner have written like Anthony Hope or F. Marion Crawford, naming the authors of the hour, 'and I think she ought accordingly to ask herself if the real tribute shouldn't be to do what the accident of myself only has prevented me from doing. Let her apply my inclination, my yearning, as I can't apply it.'

I

He had a particular and even painful instance of the effect of his personality and his literary power in the autumn of 1903 when Howard Overing Sturgis brought him the galleys of a long-planned novel. Sturgis was a very particular friend whose name sometimes got him confused with James's other friend, the crippled 'little demon', Jonathan Sturges. Howard visited Lamb House rarely, but James stayed quite often in Howard's comfortable oversize Georgian villa, Queen's Acre – called by everyone 'Qu'Acre' – on the edge of Windsor Park. Here at various times during the coming years James would be at the centre of Sturgis's entourage, Benson, Lubbock, the young American historian Lapsley who taught at Trinity College, Cambridge, Rhoda Broughton, and a bit later Edith Wharton who had known Sturgis at Newport. Howard was the youngest son of the American banker Russell Sturgis, whom James had known since the 1870s. James remembered the youthful Howard, but he had not really got to know him until the young man completed his education at Eton and Cambridge. He inherited considerable wealth and settled promptly into Victorian domesticity. As George Santayana later put it, Howard Sturgis believed that there was nothing women did that men could not do better. Howard's most characteristic eccentricity was his addiction to embroidery and knitting. He would sit with his thick golden hair – which later became silvered – beautifully brushed, his small feet daintily crossed, in the middle of a square carpet on the lawn, or by his fireside, with his basket and his dogs about him, working on some large golden-threaded design. He lived with a friend, a younger man, William Haynes Smith, known to the Qu'Acre circle as 'The Babe'. He might have been the child Howard might have borne if he had been of the opposite sex; or the younger brother he never had, for he himself had been the youngest. His mother's boudoir had been Howard's nursery; she had clung to him in her widowhood. Santayana said Howard was 'her last and permanent baby'. The philosopher added that Howard became in due course 'a perfect young lady of the Victorian type'. There are more friendly characterizations, for in spite of his eccentricities, 'Howdie' – even his nickname carried with it a flavour of the nursery – had had a very successful career at school; he had embodied his Eton experience in a sentimental novel called *Tim*, long before he met James. He was witty, poetic, sociable, gentle, and not at all intellectual. We can see him through the eyes of one of the younger Etonians admitted to his circle, Percy Lubbock. 'He sat at home,' wrote Lubbock, 'wound his wool and stitched at his work; he took a turn on the road with his infirmary of dogs; with head inclined in sympathy and suavity he poured out tea for the local dowager who called on him.' His villa had a quiet domestic air, with its white-panelled walls hung with water-colours, its furniture of faded slippery chintz, its French windows opening on an old-fashioned large American-style verandah. Edith Wharton remembered the view from the windows – a weedy lawn, uneven shrubbery, a neglected rose garden, a dancing faun poised above an 'arty' blue-tiled pool. Small wonder that Qu'Acre, and its homey atmosphere provided such a warm hearth for Howdie's intimates who weren't bothered by his feminine traits. Howard attracted dandies, distinguished dames, the *literati*. And over his salon he presided, a passive nature lodged in the sturdy frame of a moustachioed and vigorous male. The atmosphere was a mixture of the maternal, paternal and the matriarchal. Perhaps this was why James once told Howard he could find it possible to live with him – an unusually affectionate declaration from a novelist who lived so proudly alone. It would have been for James a little like living with his mother – and the American females he had described in his early Civil War tales seated knitting by the fire. James spoke of 'Howard in his infinite Howardism' – finding no other way of defining his friend except in his own terms. His other image for him recalled childhood goodies. Howdie was like a richly-sugared cake, said James, always available on the table. 'We sit round him in a circle and help ourselves. Now and then we fling a slice over our shoulders to somebody outside.' Henry James, during his Qu'Acre visits, would pad about the room in his comfortable bulk, or stand hugely by the fireside, 'listening, muttering, groaning disapproval or chuckling assent to the paradoxes of the other tea drinkers'. And he would talk when tea was over – about Paris, or his earlier London, or some novel he had read, or play he had seen, or about Balzac, Tolstoy, or Meredith. This was one of the stranger and more home-like salons of the many he had frequented; and its frequenters were all amusing and brilliant, and all of 'the better sort'.

2

Howard Sturgis had long before this time told James of the novel he was writing, and had received strong encouragement. After *Tim* he had published a short fiction with a Trollopeian title, *All That Was Possible*, written in the old-fashioned epistolary style. Now he had completed his long work, *Belchamber*. It was about a young English marquis, of an extremely passive nature, who marries a pushing young woman more out of chivalry than affection, flattered that she should be interested in him. She wants his title and his wealth, but despises him and the marriage is never consummated. She takes lovers and he continues his bachelor existence. In due course she presents him with an heir. The young nobleman remains passive. Howard thus provided himself in his novel with a babe, without having to sleep with any woman. The best part of the novel is the affection Sainty – Howdie's hero – bestows on the infant.

'Bring your book and read it aloud!' James told Sturgis, inviting him to Lamb House early in October 1903. Jocelyn wanted to come at this time but James postponed his visit. Then Howard postponed his, and his stay overlapped with a visit long planned by Hendrik Andersen, who came over to Rye for four or five days from Paris. Howard seems not to have read his novel aloud to James, but he left behind a batch of galleys. In a matter of days he received the first report. The novel was going 'very solidly and smoothly,' James wrote. Having delivered a series of compliments, James settled down to the essentials. After all he was 'a battered producer and "technician"' himself, and could read only critically, constructively and 'reconstructively'. James was up to his old tricks; this was the way he always dealt with Mrs Humphry Ward, or H. G. Wells; he would do the same to the young Hugh Walpole. Critical though he was, he said he was ready to 'pass' Howard's book. The one detail over which he paused was Howdie's choosing as his main character a member of the English nobility and of such high rank, a Marquis. 'When a man is an English Marquis, even a lame one, there are whole masses of Marquisate things and items, a multitude of inherent detail in his existence, which it isn't open to the painter *de gaieté de cœur* not to make some picture of.' James was sure however other readers wouldn't notice this. 'No one notices or understands *any*thing and no one will make a single intelligent or intelligible observation about your work. They will make plenty of others.' And James applauded the way in which Howdie had stayed with the inner world of Sainty.

These observations were mild enough, but Howard Sturgis was understandably sensitive about his work; he was worried by James's implying that an American, like himself, however much identified with England, could hardly know the inner world of the nobility. What James perhaps overlooked was that Howdie had recorded, with great accuracy, the natural history of a passive male. James, however, came to the question of the passivity in his second letter, after he had read a further batch of galleys. It wasn't only Sainty's aristocratic 'point of view,' said James, it was that he was '*all* passive and nullity'. Where was the *positive* side? James suddenly expressed the wish that he might have talked with Sturgis while 'the book was a-writing' in the interest of producing a Sainty 'with a constituted and intense imaginative life of his own'. He did not question the existence of so virtuous and innocent a young man, who came through to the reader in so negative a way : this was however because Sturgis gave Sainty '*no state of his own* as the field and stage of the vision and the drama'. The novel didn't seem to happen to Sainty, but *around* him. When Sturgis replied that after Sainty's marriage 'nothing happens to him' James replied as from Olympus :

Why, my dear Howard, it is the part in which *most* happens! His marriage itself, his wife *herself*, happen to him at every hour of the 24 – and he is the only person to whom anything does ... If he had only felt everything else as he feels his wife's baby ... the subject would have been fully expressed. But it is the baby, as a baby, that he actually feels – for a pleasure – most.

James pointed out to Howard that to have Sainty living with his wife day after day as if he were a bachelor who had no thoughts or feelings on the subject was to have nothing 'happen' in the novel – 'to whom *is* it happening?' To have married this young woman in the belief that she cared for him and to find her then wholly avoiding him 'would be really for him an experience of some kind of Intensity. There was something in him (at the worst!) to which this was to be *shown as happening* – horribly, tormentedly, strangely – in some way or *other* happening.' James's unveiling of the work's central weakness overwhelmed Howard. We do not have his letter, but we know that he announced to the Master he was withdrawing his novel from publication. James, clearly upset, wrote in haste of

your too lamentable letter, in which you speak of 'withdrawing' your novel – too miserably, horribly, impossibly, for me to listen to you for a moment. If you *think* of anything so insane you will break my heart and bring my grey hairs, the few left me, in sorrow and shame to the grave. Why should you have an inspiration so perverse and so criminal? If it springs from anything I have said to you I must have expressed myself with strange and deplorable clumsiness.

Lessons of a Master, however close to the sanctity and integrity of art, could overwhelm. He reassured Howdie: 'Your book will be the joy of thousands of people, who will very justly find it interesting and vivid, and pronounce it "disagreeable," etc., vivid, and lively, curious and witty and *real*.' James said his own 'esoteric' reflections would occur to no one else 'at all, and the whole thing will excite marked attention'. If Howdie loved him, said James, 'let your adventure take care of itself to the end'.

There exists an independent report of the Master's essentially uncompromising attitude towards the novel, in the diary of Arthur Christopher Benson. The latter, in April 1904, was cross-examining James at the Athenaeum, on how ideas came to him for a book. James replied 'It's all *about*, it's about – it's in the air – it, so to speak, follows me and dogs me.' At this point Thomas Hardy came and sat on the other side of Benson, so that he felt 'like Alice between the two Queens'. The conversation flowed to Cardinal Newman, and then to Flaubert about whom James was oracular. 'Then Hardy went away wearily and kindly. Then H.J. and I talked of Howard's *Belchamber*,' just published – for Howdie had been mollified. James said it was a good idea, a good situation. He had read it and 'Good Heavens, I said to myself, he has made nothing of it! ... Good God, why this chronicle, if it is a mere passage, a mere ante-chamber, and

leads to nothing.' He had tried, he said, 'with a thousand subterfuges and doublings such as one uses with the work of a friend' to
indicate the fault.

This was harsher than anything James had written to Sturgis. But
even with the 'subterfuges and doublings' James's criticisms came
through to his friend with distinct clarity, and Howdie felt the disapproval all the more profoundly because he loved the Master. Edith
Wharton, contending that James was never to be trusted about the
value of any fiction 'not built according to his own rigid plan', said
that Sturgis – his 'native indolence and genuine humility aiding' –
accepted James's verdict and 'relapsed into knitting and embroidery'.
But in the privacy of his study Sturgis wrote out his painful feelings
in an unpublished tale called *The China Pot* – about a great writer
who demolishes the work of a younger man. The younger man takes
this so to heart that he commits suicide; and in a scene at the cemetery, the Great Author and another friend discuss why the young
man has taken his life. He had had everything to live for, youth,
good looks, freedom from care, intelligence. The Great Author says
he finds his death 'amazing, mysterious and inexplicable'. But the
other man 'could see that he knew as well as I did, and that he knew
that I knew'. This was an ending worthy of James himself, and one
that would have given the deepest pain to the Master, which is perhaps why Howdie never published the story. James had had a signal,
however, of how powerful his effect on others could be.

A few months after the *Belchamber* incident, James received a
novel by Forrest Reid – *The Kingdom of Twilight*. It was an offering
of homage from a young admirer. James promptly read the book
'with interest and attention'. The attention was weighty. 'Up to the
middle at least, you see your subject where it *is* – in the character
and situation of your young man.' But – the invariable *but* –

I confess however, that, *after* the middle you strike me as *losing* your
subject – or, at any rate, I, as your reader, did so. After the meeting with
the woman by the sea – certainly after the parting from her – I felt the
reality of the thing deviate, felt the subject lose its conditions, so to
speak, its *observed* character and its logic.

And then the final flourish and the accolade – 'it's not of your young
(as I take it) your airy and enviably young inexpertnesses that I
wished to speak – for many of these you will obviously leave behind

you. There are elements of beauty and sincerity in your volume that remain with me.' Thus the doctrinaire lessons of the Master : much kindness, much truth, great integrity – yet often the weighty foot stepping on tender toes.

78

An Agreeable Woman

FOR some years the Master had been quietly pursued by another American writer, an elegant lady, more professional in her work than Howard Sturgis, more determined, more ambitious. Her name was Edith Wharton. She came out of James's 'old New York', although born two decades later. His locale had been essentially Washington Square (before the city had moved uptown), with its prosperous upper middle-class merchants and doctors. Mrs Wharton's was the higher reach of the then residential Fifth Avenue, and the aristocracy of wealth and tradition that had developed from the days of the 'patroons' during the Dutch régime. She had Joneses, Schermerhorns, Rhinelanders, Pendletons, Gallatins, and Ledyards for ancestors. Her maternal ancestor, General Ebenezer Stevens, had served under Lafayette in the defeat of Cornwallis. She had a large inheritance and had grown up to 'a life of leisure and amiable hospitality', as she put it. Edith Newbold Jones came to maturity in a small and wealthy Manhattan society that was now threatened by the new industrialism, the *arrivistes* James had only tentatively sketched in his fiction. She herself would describe her group as having 'a blind dread of innovation, an instinctive shrinking from responsibility'. Edith Jones met her responsibilities. She knew to the core this small world, with its old decencies, its stratified codes, its tradition of elegance, and the daily life within its brownstone mansions already fenced in by tall buildings.

She had been reared in a masculine family circle. Her two brothers were grown men when she was still a child, and she was deeply attached to her father. In her memoirs she sketches an intimate portrait of him but adopts towards her mother a tone of condescension, an aloof tolerance for her love of fashionable clothes and the life of 'society'. Edith herself would insist later in life, not successfully, that her name be dropped from the 'Social Register'. The male circle which framed her childhood would lead Edith Jones to have more men friends than women and they were always men high in the life of the country. It was said of her that she brought a man's strength to the sympathy and solicitude of a woman, and a man's organizing power to a woman's interest in dress and the decoration of houses. James would put it in another way, comparing her with the volatile and 'liquid' George Sand and the intellectually powerful George Eliot. In her novels he found 'the masculine conclusion' tended 'so to crown the feminine observation'. She was, in James's life, one of the 'queenly' women he had studied closely in earlier years. Mrs Gardner's assertiveness had attracted him to her – but Mrs Wharton did not have to assert her queenliness in the eccentric ways of Mrs Jack. It was instinctive, inbred – and what endeared her to James was that she possessed also a civilized mind and an artist's style. Indeed her 'set' never forgave her devotion to her art. And it took her many years, as her novels show, to free herself from the fetters of her class.

I

She would later recall that she had crossed Henry James's path twice in the 1880s and the early 1890s : but she was then too shy and in awe of the Master to speak to him, and he paid no attention to her. The first occasion had been at the home of the Edward Boits in Paris, where Mrs Wharton had sported a specimen of the *haute couture* in the hope that she might catch the attention of the pensive bearded novelist. She failed. She tried again one day in Venice in the Curtis entourage, where she made a point of wearing a particularly fetching hat. To this display of finery he seems to have been impervious : or perhaps to Edith's assertion of personality through dress. She had not, then, published anything and was living with her socially prominent husband, Edward Robbins Wharton, largely at Newport, and paying extended visits to Europe. In the closing years of the century, the Bourgets began to speak to James of their valued American friend, Madame Whar-ton. He heard of her also from Mary Cadwalader Jones, the divorced wife of Edith's older brother, whom he had known for some years and liked. Through the Bourgets, Mrs Wharton sent James a message of good-will at the moment of *Guy Domville*. And in 1899 she sent him her first book of tales, *The Greater Inclination*. James told Bourget he had received 'a fruit of literary toil' from Mrs Wharton and a note that she expected to be at Claridge's – 'the sojourn of kings'. As the remark implied, James had no intention of calling on her in such a royal place. Towards the end of that year he wrote Bourget he had read Mrs Wharton's stories. What was best in them was 'her amiable self'. What was 'not best was quite another person'. He had recognized himself, his style, 'I should like a quiet hour with that almost too susceptible *élève*. In which of the hemispheres does she happen for the moment to be?'

Almost a year elapsed before he acknowledged the tales. What prompted him finally to write was a story in *Lippincott's*, called *The Line of Least Resistance*. He found Mrs Wharton's tale 'brilliant'. It possessed 'an admirable sharpness and neatness and infinite wit and point'. And in his most charming law-giving vein he continued, in his first letter to her, dated 26 October 1900:

I applaud, I mean I value, I egg you on in your study of the American life that surrounds you. Let yourself go in it and *at* it – it's an untouched field, really: the folk who try, over there, don't come within miles of any civilized, any 'evolved' life. And use to the full your remarkable ironic and valeric gifts; they form a most valuable, (I hold) and beneficent engine.

Still her irony and her 'valeric' quality needed moderating. The *Lippincott* tale was 'a little hard, a little purely derisive'. He hastened to tone this down by his usual invocation to Youth – 'you're so young, and with it, so clever. Youth is hard – and your needle-point later on will muffle itself in a little blur of silk. It *is* needle-point!' The allusion to her youth was generous: she was by now almost 40. He ended by urging Edith Wharton to send him what she wrote. 'I'll do the same by you!' he promised. He asked her also to come to see him some day.

She had finally made a distinct impression. But she was then writing a long novel and creating one of the finest of her houses in America (her first book had been a collaboration with an architect, *The Decoration of Houses*). The house was The Mount, at Lenox, Massachusetts. They had not yet met when in 1902 she sent James her two-volume historical fiction, *The Valley of Decision*, which she dedicated to Bourget; and Mrs Cadwalader Jones sent Mrs Wharton's new collection of tales, *Crucial Instances*, and her short novel *The Touchstone*. James acknowledged the historical novel and told Mrs Wharton he had read it with sympathy, 'high criticism, high consideration' and 'generally most intimate participation'. He did not tell her that he disliked this kind of novel; instead he returned to the charge of his earlier letter. He wanted 'crudely' but

earnestly, tenderly, intelligently to admonish you, while you are young, free, expert, exposed (to illumination) – by which I mean while you're in full command of the situation – admonish you, I say, in favour of the *American Subject*. There it is round you. Don't pass it by – the immediate, the real, the ours, the yours, the novelists' that it waits for. Take hold of it and keep hold, and let it pull you where it will.

He drove home the lesson. 'Profit, be warned, by my awful example of exile and ignorance. You will say that *j'en parle à mon aise*, but I shall have paid for my ease, and I don't want you to pay (as much) for yours.' Pausing to apologize for his 'impertinent importunities' he still returned to the charge with 'All the same DO NEW YORK! The first-hand account is precious.'

The Master saw, with great clarity, where Mrs Wharton's talent and subject lay. A few days later he sent to Mrs Cadwalader Jones his famous statement that Edith 'must be tethered in native pastures, even if it reduce her to a backyard in New York'. He further told the authoress's sister-in-law, that he was 'very taken with Mrs Wharton – her diabolical little cleverness, the quantity of intention and intelligence in her style, and her sharp eye for an interesting *kind* of subject'.

2

They actually did not meet until December 1903, when James had passed his 60th birthday and Mrs Wharton her 40th. In the interval she had installed herself in The Mount. She came abroad that year, and when she arrived in London, James called on her, one day just before Christmas. He seems then also to have met her husband. James saw a woman of about his own height, dressed with taste and distinction; she spoke in the civilized manner of her tales. Her husband was genial and wholly non-intellectual. Mrs Wharton was all the blue-stocking, with a range of literary knowledge and quotation, a saturation in German – part of her childhood had been passed in Germany – and a thorough knowledge of things French. She was cosmopolitan like himself. She had lived much in her imagination during her European childhood. Yet she was grounded in New York;

and she was concrete and observant. On her side, she saw a different James from the bearded 'Penseroso' of Mrs Boit's Parisian drawing-room, or the light-jacketed James of Venice. For the first time she looked upon his shaven countenance, 'the noble Roman mask' of his face and 'the big dramatic mouth', and she noticed well-tailored clothes which now loosely enveloped the considerable embonpoint. James was massive and masterly. Her report of her meeting, to her editor at Scribner's, spoke of his looking, without his beard, like a blend of Coquelin and Lord Rosebery. Thus she caught the histrionic aspect of James as well as the aristocratic. He seemed to her 'in good spirits' and she said he talked 'more lucidly than he writes', for she did not like his later manner. The once-shy young woman had herself changed to matronly middle age. She no longer stood in awe of the Master. But he remained, and would remain, a figure of magnetic charm and force – her greatest literary friend. His first impression of her was, as he put it to Henrietta Reubell, that she was *sèche*, although agreeable and intelligent. The word 'dry' continued to characterize her in his letters for some time. He would grow to ad-mire her, with careful qualifications, but she would never occupy in his existence the role that Goody Allen then occupied, or Lucy Clifford, or his friend in Rye, Fanny Prothero. He and Mrs Wharton had their common American background, their friends abroad, their 'international' feeling. Their sense of irony and humour was tuned to the same key and on this ground Mrs Wharton said that 'Henry James was perhaps the most intimate friend I ever had though in many ways we were so different'. James would not have used the word 'intimate'. Mrs Wharton was always for him the *grande dame*; but he admired her intellectual and literary qualities and her style. His affection was genuine; his reservations were strong. One writer has attempted to inject a feeling of romance saying they should be portrayed 'almost as though they were a married couple or acknow-ledged lovers'. This was hardly the case; nor can their friendship be considered 'one of the unique attachments of literary history'. Mrs Wharton was inclined to be 'possessive', and James kept his friendly distance. She was right, however, in remembering that 'suddenly it was as if we had always been friends'. The friends of the friends – the Bourgets, Mary Cadwalader Jones, the Edward Boits, Howard Sturgis, a wide circle of common acquaintance – had prepared the ground. 'I mustn't omit to tell you, though you probably by this time know it,' James wrote to Mrs Cadwalader Jones, that Mrs Wharton has gone and come – gone, alas, more particularly, fleeing before the dark discipline of the London winter afternoon. I was in town for a day or two during her passage, and I lunched with her, with very great pleasure, and had the opportunity of some talk. This gave me much desire for more – finding her, as I did, *really* conversible (rare characteristic, *par le temps qui court!*) and sympathetic in every way.

To Mrs John La Farge, formerly Margaret Perry, he wrote a few days later that he found in Mrs Wharton 'a slightly cold but quite individual grace'.

3

The following spring, at Whitsuntide, Edith Wharton and her husband, familiarly called Teddy, hired a motor – they did not then own one – and were chauffeured to Rye where they spent twenty-four hours with the Master. By that time Henry James had no doubt of Mrs Wharton's role in her marriage. He treated her as if she were Teddy's husband. 'The Edith Whartons,' he told Howells, had been with him 'in force'. In her late reminiscences, written long after James was dead, she would describe Lamb House with careful and observed detail and with the eye of one accustomed to living in much larger and more palatial establishments. The Garden Room with its Palladian windows pleased her; the general air of amiability and the constantly bubbling wit and acerbity of the Master delighted her. He would always be candid with her and even aggressive in his criticism. And it is clear from her account of the ways in which he spoke to her that he assumed his best 'courtier' style, the style he had used with Mrs Gardner, even though Edith's aristocratic tone was genuine and Mrs Jack's assumed. James reacted against the wealth of both these ladies – that is, he felt that a condition of chronic luxury tended to insulate and to produce a certain blindness in them. He had long before expressed his suspicion of 'the great ones' of the earth; he had complained that they lacked imagination. This was true sometimes of Mrs Wharton. It can be discerned in the things she noticed in Lamb House and her description of Jamesian hospitality. She alone of all his guests would speak of his 'anxious frugality', would comment on the 'dreary pudding or pie of which a quarter or a half had been consumed at dinner' and its reappearing on the table the next day 'with its ravages unrepaired'. She who had gardens and gardeners – and woe to them if a protruding twig or two were discovered on the trimmed hedge – remarked on the 'unkempt' flower borders of James's small Lamb House plot. From her point of view James – whose servants called him a martinet and 'an old toff' – did not know how to give them orders. She also would speak of him as being helpless in choosing items of dress or making travel arrangements. These comments were strange. James had travelled alone since the last days of the stage-coach in the middle nineteenth century; and he had always been smartly turned out by his tailors. It is clear that when James visited Edith Wharton she took command; and before a commanding woman – as with his older brother – James withered and passively surrendered. She made him feel powerless – he who otherwise exuded power. Mrs Wharton's remark that James 'lived in terror of being thought rich, worldly or luxurious' must be understood as stemming from his continued ironies about his inability to live up to *her* style. She tells us he was for ever 'contrasting his visitors' supposed opulence and self indulgence with his own hermit-like asceticism and apologizing for his poor food while he trembled lest it should be thought too good'. There is a singular failure in this on the part of Mrs Wharton to understand what James was doing. James's visitors usually testified to the solid bourgeois comfort of his house and the quality of his table; his claret had been praised and the efficiencies of his small household staff. What Mrs Wharton did not grasp – she could be very literal in such matters – was that James amusedly posed as a country squire and treated her with great flourishes as a visiting lady of high estate. In the same way, he would refer later to his penny royalties and compare them with Mrs Wharton's large earnings in the literary marketplace. James was in fact, especially during these years when his maturing annuities increased his income, decently well off; he had about £2,000 a year as against Mrs Wharton's £10,000. Moreover, James liked to mock forceful ladies. To his friends he spoke of her 'devouring, burning and destroying energy'. That was why she was sometimes 'the Firebird' and sometimes the 'Angel of Devastation'. Mrs Wharton's failure to understand James's candid if ironic declarations that he simply could not offer her customary luxuries is exemplified in her saying years later that James 'denied himself (I believe quite needlessly) the pleasure and relaxation which a car of his own might have given him, but took advantage, to the last drop of petrol, of the travelling capacity of any visitor's car'. This was ungenerous.

The last thing James wanted, or could afford in the early days of motoring, was a car. He had poked fun at Kipling's large motor-monster, and had mused on the large royalties that made such a machine possible; and while he greatly enjoyed motoring with Mrs Wharton, his complaints are numerous. A little motoring with her went a long way. Yet there was no stopping her when she arrived on his horizon for what James called 'the eagle pounce and eagle flight'.

James was writing of Mrs Wharton's world in the novel he was finishing when she and Teddy came for their first visit to Lamb House. The Whartons were on their way back to the United States and he promised Edith he would visit her at Lenox later that year – for by this time it was settled that the native would return after his twenty-year absence. To Mrs La Farge he described how Mrs Wharton had been presented by Miss Weld with one of James's books, beautifully bound in her little bindery. It had been an act of homage 'to no less a *raffinée* than Mrs Wharton'. He had seen 'more of them – of her – than ever before, and greatly liked her, though finding her a little dry'. He added these significant words 'she is too pampered and provided and facilitated for one to be able really to judge of the woman herself, or for *her* even, I think, to be able to get really *at* things'. The judgement would be muted in later years. Her energy would enable her to get at some things; but when James wrote of the Prince in *The Golden Bowl* that 'below a certain social plane, he never *saw*' he was describing in effect Edith Wharton's failures in perception. These misunderstandings between Mrs Wharton and Henry James would reach an ultimate climax. But it would occur at a later time, after James had become also her counsellor and comforter in her marital difficulties and complicated affairs of the heart.

79

The Golden Bowl

DURING the Christmas season of 1902, in that busy year in which he had published *The Wings of the Dove* and written the life of Story, Henry James had an opportunity to view an *objet d'art* which belonged to the descendants of the Lambs, the family that had built the house he now owned. It was a golden bowl, presented by George I after his ship had put in to the Sussex coast during a storm. The King had slept in Lamb House; and during his stay he attended the christening of a recently born baby in the Lamb family. The bowl was the King's gift to the child. James saw the vessel at a local bank, where it was kept in the vault. To one of the Lamb descendants, he wrote he had been 'delighted to rest my eyes on this admirable and venerable object'. It had 'a beautiful colour – the tone of old gold – as well as a grand style and capacity'. He added that he was eager for 'every ascertainable fact' about Lamb House and felt 'personally indebted to your peculiarly civilized ancestor who kindly conceived and put together for my benefit, so long ago, exactly the charming, braceful, sturdy little habitation (full of *sense*, discretion, taste) that suits alike my fancy and necessity, and in which I hope in time (D.V.) to end my days'.

King George's Bowl was more than an 'ascertainable fact' about Lamb House. It gave him the title for his last novel.

I

He had written *The Ambassadors* and *The Wings of the Dove* each in less than a year: but he spent more than a twelvemonth over *The Golden Bowl*, rewriting almost every page, as he had done long ago with *The Portrait of a Lady*. When he sailed in August 1904 for America the manuscript had been delivered to Scribner's for autumn publication. In England it was scheduled for the following spring.

The idea for *The Golden Bowl* had been in his notebooks for more than ten years: that of a father and daughter who both become engaged, the daughter to an Englishman and the father, a widower, still youngish, to an American girl of the same age as his daughter. 'Say he has done it to console himself in his abandonment – to make up for the loss of the daughter, to whom he has been devoted.' Then and there (it was on 28 November 1892) he sketched his plot for what he thought would be a short story. The marriages would take place 'with this characteristic consequence' that father and daughter would continue to see one another and in fact maintain their old interest, while the husband of the one and the young wife of the other would in turn be thrown together – with the father's second wife becoming 'much more attractive to the young husband of the girl than the girl herself has remained'. The subject for James resided in 'the pathetic simplicity and good faith of the father and daughter in their abandonment. They feel abandoned, yet they feel consoled with *each other*, and they don't see in the business in the least what every one else sees in it.' It was a kind of crisis of mutual abandonment and consolation. A necessary basis 'must have been an intense and exceptional degree of attachment between the father and daughter – he peculiarly paternal, she passionately *filial*!' James originally thought he would make the daughter's young husband a Frenchman; and the father and daughter would be 'intensely American'. He returned to the idea in 1895 just after *Guy Domville*. At the end of that year, he reminded himself of 'the Father and Daughter, with the husband of the one and the wife of the other entangled in a mutual passion, an intrigue'. It was the kind of story that would be attractive for Harpers, except for its 'adulterine element', but he asked himself, 'may it not be simply a question of *handling* that?' At the time the other element in the plot, the 'incestuous' element, did not constitute a difficulty. The Victorian daughter was expected to be devoted to the father; she was expected to sacrifice her own interests. From the days of *Washington Square*, James had written stories of 'dutiful' daughters in various stages of revolt. Or of daughters so 'fixated' on their fathers that they ruin the paternal chances of remarrying, as in *The Marriages* in which a daughter tells the fiancée a lie, while persuading herself that she is being faithful to the memory of her dead mother. James's sister Alice had been a dutiful and invalid daughter, who had remained at home, and kept house for her father after their mother's death. Even more, there remained with him the image of Lizzie Boott who had grown up in Italy under the care and education of her father, the amateur composer Francis Boott. Old Boott was dying at the moment that James was completing *The Golden Bowl*; he remembered Henry in his will, for the novelist had been an old and loyal friend. What had struck James long before, had been the way in which Lizzie and her father, in the Villa Castellani, on Bellosguardo, had led a self-sufficient life: this image gave him earlier Pansy and Osmond. Then Lizzie had fallen in love with her art teacher Frank Duveneck, the bohemian painter. She had married him in the late 1880s. Nevertheless life with her father had gone on as before and Duveneck seemed to James very much of a third party. At the time of this marriage the novelist had seen Boott, suddenly bereft of the single interest of his life.

It is doubtful whether James himself could know how much of his life was in this novel, the richest of all his creations. *The Golden*

Bowl seemed indeed a final attempt to resolve the problems treated from so many approaches in his earlier works. The adulterous couple forced to make marriages of 'convenience' rather than of love: Charlotte and the Prince in this novel had been foreshadowed by Madame Merle and Osmond, by Kate Croy and Densher or even by Christina who had married Prince Casamassima and later taken lovers. Maggie Verver had appeared earlier as Pansy Osmond; and Adam Verver as a whole generation of fathers. But in the close-knit family constellation James created in *The Golden Bowl* he was dealing with the deepest part of his own inner world – his father's having had in the house not only his wife Mary Walsh, Henry's mother, but her sister Catherine, the loyal Aunt Kate. There had always been triangles in James's life. In the little tale of *Georgina's Reasons* which anticipated some of the themes of *The Wings of the Dove*, there had been the young man and the two sisters, one dying of consumption. But there was also in that story another triangle, the strange situation resulting from the young man's marriage in New York to Georgina, who had kept the marriage secret, and had given their secretly-born child away for adoption. Georgina blandly committed bigamy, creating another triangle. Moreover she urged her husband to feel free to marry again – that is to commit bigamy, too. Strange fantasies, these of triangular human relations, and they culminated, in this ultimate work, in two joined triangles: father, daughter, and daughter's husband; and the husband's mistress, who then marries the father and so becomes the stepmother of the heroine, and mother-in-law of her lover. The implication of emotional 'incest' is not as significant in this work as the fact that in the situation everyone begins by having his cake and eating it. The daughter marries but remains close to her father. The father acquires a bride, but still possesses his daughter. The Prince acquires his Princess, but doesn't have to give up his mistress. The mistress makes the marriage she had waited for, a marriage of wealth and position, but keeps her lover. In an Elizabethan tragedy such situations could lead to a sanguinary end. In *The Golden Bowl* the energies of the characters, and of the work, have as their goal an extraordinary attempt to maintain a balance – without rocking the boat.

2

There is little doubt that, in addition to the memory of King George's offering to the Lambs, James had in mind Ecclesiastes 12:6-7 – 'Or ever the silver cord be loosed, or the golden bowl be broken, or the pitcher be broken at the fountain, or the wheel broken at the cistern, Then shall the dust return to the earth as it was: and the spirit shall return unto God who gave it.' He may also have remembered Blake's lines, 'Can wisdom be kept in a silver rod, Or love in a golden bowl?' The golden bowl is seen originally by Charlotte and the Prince in a London curiosity shop; she wants to offer it as a marriage gift, but the Prince, whom James names Amerigo, is deeply superstitious; he discerns a flaw in the bowl: it is not made of gold, but is gilded crystal; and it contains a crack, like the porcelain cup handled by Osmond one day during a crisis with Madame Merle in *The Portrait of a Lady*. The symbol was an old one in Henry James – but in this novel the flawed artefact is emblematic not only of the marriage of the Prince and Maggie (he too is a discoverer of America) but of the entire civilization in which this marriage has been consummated. The Prince, Maggie, and her father belong to the world exemplified for James by Edith Wharton. The Prince's aristocratic lineage, and the American aristocrats of wealth were insulated – and therefore blinded – from certain truths of life within their charmed circle. This world is also imaged for us in the metaphor of the pagoda with which the second half of the novel begins, an 'outlandish' artefact, 'a structure plated with hard, bright porcelain, coloured and figured and adorned, at the overhanging eaves, with silver bells that tinkled, ever so charmingly, when stirred by chance airs'. The great surface remains 'impenetrable and inscrutable' to Maggie. It might have been a Mahometan mosque, 'with which no base heretic could take a liberty'. She has never really sought admission. She has remained outside, living in proximity to this artificial hard-surfaced, beautiful but lifeless, object. And it will be the plebeians who will break the artificial world: the dealer in antiques will reveal inadvertently the liaison between the Prince and Charlotte to Maggie; she will come into possession of the flawed golden bowl; and it will be another plebeian, Fanny Assingham, who will perform the single act of violence in the novel; she will deliberately drop the Bowl on the polished floor and it will split neatly into three pieces.

James was writing, in this strange and heavily loaded symbolic drama, a story of the education of a princess, an American princess. Nothing in Maggie's life has prepared her for her crisis – her discovery that the person closest to her, the aristocratic husband she has acquired as if he were still another artefact, is treacherous and unfaithful; and that he is being unfaithful with her friend, Charlotte, whom she had induced her father to marry, in order to 'console' him for the loss of herself. Maggie's insulated life had provided her with no means to deal with such a situation; the loss of innocence is violent, a complete collapse of her pagoda-life. What she possesses is the knowledge of her power : and the innate strategy of her insulation. She has learned long ago that one does not upset boats; there is a risk of everyone drowning; and where in a hundred novels such a heroine would have torn her passion to tatters, raged, threatened, exposed, made grand scenes, James remains true to Maggie's delicate upbringing and also her state of innocence and ignorance. He is writing the story of her growing-up. In the process of her education, and by her recognition of the elements of power in her predicament, she is able to get rid of the disequilibrium in her life. She comes to recognize that the Prince, having married wealth, will hardly wish to renounce it; that Charlotte in turn has gained the position of comfort and ease she has wanted. With the coolness of an heiress of the ages, she brings about a 'palace' revolution that gives her full command. By degrees she recognizes that a daughter is supposed to grow up; that she has involuntarily – through the conditions of her life – thought that she could be both a wife and a daughter. She now sees that if she is to remain a wife she must indeed cease to be a daughter. She dispatches her father to America to lead his own life. Charlotte, the adulteress, is thereby banished from Europe. And the Prince, who has wanted a wife instead of an immature father-attached girl, finds that he now has one. They have a child, a boy, and for the first and only time in all of James's fiction this novel ends with a family in which the offspring is allowed to live. Many lies are told to save the marriage, but they have been, as in *The Wings of the Dove* and *The Ambassadors*, 'constructive' lies – the lies or myths by which civilization holds together. The whole truth, James suggests, could destroy civilization, for everything, as the Prince is made to say, is 'terrible in the heart of man'. All the more reason, this novel seems to imply, that the terrors of the heart should not be translated into life. They would be unbearable. As James had felt, in his early days in Rome, that the dead past must be kept buried, that the primitive uncovered, becomes too dangerous to continuation of life, so in the last of his 'philosophical novels' he places himself on the side of the 'illusions' by which man lives. Like Marlow, in Conrad's *Heart of Darkness*, James's characters tell lies because the truth can serve no useful purpose. Certain lies however can be extremely useful.

A few critics, reading this novel, have tried to see Maggie as evil and destructive; in their sympathy for the cool and admirable Charlotte, who is one of James's most remarkable 'bad heroines', they have blinded themselves to the fact that at the end of the novel the latter is better off than she was at the beginning. At the beginning she had lost the Prince; he has preferred to marry a rich heiress rather than continue a love affair that reduces him to poverty. Charlotte ends with the wealth and power and freedom of her marriage to an American tycoon; and if Adam takes her back to America, this does not mean that she is necessarily being taken to prison. We know she will be free, like James's other American wives, to travel, to build houses, to acquire art treasures, or lovers. She can become Mrs Touchett or resemble the real-life Mrs Gardner. And Maggie, far from being a 'witch', has simply learned that a revolution cannot restore the *status quo ante*. By thinking she could live in a fool's paradise of perpetual daughterhood – that is a perpetual child – she had lost her husband. By acquiring her maturity, she recovers him. She shows herself capable of facing realities in the great scene of the novel, when she paces the terrace and watches the game of bridge played by her father and Mrs Assingham with the two lovers.

... meanwhile the facts of the situation were upright for her round the green cloth and the silver flambeaux; the fact of her father's wife's lover facing his mistress; the fact of her father sitting, all unsounded and unblinking, between them; the fact of Charlotte keeping it up, keeping up everything, across the table, with her husband beside her; the fact of Fanny Assingham, wonderful creature, placed opposite to the three and knowing more about each, probably, when one came to think, than either of them knew of either. Erect above all for her was the sharp-edged fact of the relation of the whole group, individually and collectively, to herself – herself so speciously eliminated for the hour, but presumably more present to the attention of each than the next card to be played.

It is one of Henry James's great fixed scenes, in its fine-toned 'awareness', in the revealed sensibility of Maggie Verver, and in its open theatricality. James had finally been able to bring into the open the deeply buried scenes of his childhood – that of the curious little boy who has to contend with triangular enigmas of father, mother, aunt – and having to make choices, not always knowing to whom exactly he belongs – like his Maggie, who belongs to her father and to her husband, and yet must surrender one, if she is to have the other. In some dim and difficult way James, having tried the Vionnet–Strether–Chad combination in *The Ambassadors*, and the Kate–Densher–Milly combination in *The Wings of the Dove*, had finally found the combination that could unlock the secrets of his life. The Prince–Adam–Charlotte combination seemed to work. Everything in this novel is at last – and for the only time in Henry James – resolved; above all the marriage – which had seemed impossible in all his other fiction – is consummated. He had written nineteen novels and in many of them he had affirmed that no marriage was possible between the Old World and the New – that America and Europe were irreconcilable. Now in his twentieth he brings the marriage off. Prince Amerigo, descendant of explorers, can as it were 'marry' the continent of their journeyings; and Maggie – and America – can with the proper will respond not in ignorance but in awareness.

In terms of another of his favourite symbols – that of the cage – Henry James in this novel is able at last to set free the young female adolescent imprisoned within his spirit and his imagination. She had grown from childhood with his growth; she had been Daisy and Maisie, and the governess, and Nanda, she had tried to deduce the outer world studying the telegrams passed to her in the branch post office; or she had revolved in the glass cage of *The Sacred Fount*. Now she emerges from the pagoda-cage. She has ceased to observe actively while remaining physically passive; she refuses to 're-nounce'. She can act – with strength, with resolution, even when necessary with hardness and cruelty. The fable is at last complete.

3

The symbolic statement of *The Golden Bowl* is most personal and autobiographical, not in the artefact but in the crack in the artefact. In the earlier work of the novelist society was accepted as a *status quo* and James was interested in personal relations within that society. In this philosophical novel, he finds answers to the questioning of society which had begun with *The Awkward Age* in 1898 and had continued into the final three novels. Having put together the strange pagoda of Maggie Verver's life – for such is the central image in the novel next to the golden bowl itself – the novelist is able to face the truth reflected by the image. The golden bowl contains a crack; moreover it is only a *gilded* bowl. One can live a life of artifice; but it will always have a crack in its seemingly smooth and metallic surface. The pagoda's bells tinkle when brushed by 'chance airs'; but they give off a remote sound. The flaws must be discovered, the correct values re-established. In his questioning James re-expresses what he had once asserted as an epigram : that life could get by sufficiently without art; but that 'art without life is a poor affair'. The Ververs are patrons of the arts, collectors of discrimination and taste; they possess sufficient wealth to endow large museums; even Prince Amerigo, a work of art of the ages, can be acquired as husband and son-in-law. One can possess a pagoda, and it can be exquisite, yet in the end it is no substitute for life, for living; it remains an ornament of life. The golden bowl may have great beauty of form, but in reality it is a fake. The crack in the bowl stood thus for the cracks in James's life : as in the life of the Ververs. He had for too long cast his life exclusively with art; he had not allowed himself to experience the force of life itself. In *The Golden Bowl* Prince Amerigo becomes the strongest and most assertive of James's heroes : he possesses a long and corrupt family history; and he faces life without illusions. He wants the genuine, not the fake. In adumbrating a hero who no longer rationalizes away the claims of love, of physical love, James reflected the presence in his life, at the moment that he began to write this book, of Jocelyn Persse, whom James adored. 'Live all you can,' had been central to *The Ambassadors* : man had to learn to live with the illusion of his freedom. Life without love wasn't life – this was the conclusion of *The Wings of the Dove*; and having found love James had come to see at last that art could not be art, and not life, without love. He had become his own Sphinx; he was answering his own riddles. Step by step he had discovered the crack in the beautifully contrived British society originally admired but finally attacked in *The Awkward Age*; he had discerned the crack in the purely artistic object, the artefacts of the centuries, the museum world that fascinated *within* the museum but had no place in the daily drawing-rooms of life. And he had worked through the crack in his relationship with Fenimore which revealed itself in the writing of *The Beast in the Jungle*. In the larger experience, he saw the crack in civilization, which has to contend with human force and human frailty and the grandeurs and terrors of the human heart. The 'sinful' relations of Chad and Madame de Vionnet, Densher and Kate, the Prince and Charlotte were no longer the essence of the matter; each had had to make the most of the process of living and the vulnerability of love – and of life itself. Civilization might be a subtle deceit, a façade, a series of myths created by man – yet it was one of man's greatest creations. Behind the smile, the experience, the ravage in the countenance of Gloriani there had been the sense of the lived life. To be sure, one could not always have the best of all worlds. Maggie had to lose her father to keep her husband; the Prince had to lose his mistress to keep his wife. Henry James had had to give up America in order to have Europe. But in all such decisions, civilization alone assured equilibrium and a rule of law and a code of decency by which man sought to subdue primordial violence. A few decent lies or 'sins' mattered very little, if ultimate truths were to survive. Such would seem to be the conclusions of Henry James in the three pragmatic novels with which he ended his career as novelist. *The Golden Bowl* is the summit of that career.

4

As he wrote his novel, Henry James believed (so he told his agent and his publisher) that he was 'producing the best book I have ever done'. He had worked on it, day after day, for thirteen months and written 200,000 words 'with the rarest perfection'. To Scribner's he wrote, as he was reading proof, 'it is distinctly, in my view, the most *done* of my productions – the most composed and constructed and completed, and it proved, during long months, while it got itself step by step, endowed with logical life, only too deep and abysmal an artistic trap'. He added, 'by which I don't mean an abyss without a bottom, but a shaft sunk to the real basis of the subject – a real feat of engineering'. He concluded by saying he would shamelessly repeat, and his publisher could quote him, that 'I hold the thing the solidest, as yet, of all my fictions'.

Some of his readers would say that it was too solid, too compact, too filled with suggestions and associations, too crowded and imaged. Reviewers would call it 'detached', 'cold', 'cruel', and 'a psychological dime-novel'. They would find it over-intellectual, and overloaded.

But few denied its greatness in 1904. Read with the kind of leisure that went into its writing, *The Golden Bowl* on every page shows clarity of intention and consummation. The prose is dense, yet fluid, and the surfeit of architectural and museum-world imagery, the gathering of social and artistic materials to suggest the fabric of civilization, combined the art of realism James had learned long ago from Balzac, with the old art of the fable. The novel, in its 'story-line', is a fable, a moral tale built out of symmetries and patterns, and a tissuing together of organic materials – emotional sensibility, taste, 'spiritual' quality, into a charged and subjective narrative. James divided the book into two parts: the first half belongs to the Prince, the second to the Princess. These are the two 'points of view'. The Prince's story begins with his arrival in London to arrange his marriage and his feeling – this descendant of an old *Imperium* – how much the centre of the Empire had shifted to the British capital. James makes us see him and the civilization that has produced him in architectural terms, the spaciousness of old palaces and formal gardens, the thousands of years of human endeavour that moulded him into a certain kind of heir of the ages. The prevailing imagery is that of voyage and exploration; the descendant of Amerigo Ves-pucci is created out of allusions to ships and quests, harbours and searches for the North-West Passage or Golden Isles, or even the narrative of Arthur Gordon Pym and his macabre polar journey. He is seen also in architectural terms – his dark blue eyes 'resembled nothing so much as the high windows of a Roman palace, of an historic front by one of the great old designers, thrown open on a feast-day to the golden air'. Grandeur and history, lead the novelist to the ironic marriage that unites this descendant of one kind of Imperium to the daughter of the still newer Empire created out of exploration and voyage, which even bears the name that originally belonged to the family of the Prince. The symbolic statement of exploration, wealth, conquest, hard masculine adventure is com-pounded into the sense the Prince has of achieving at last the life he wanted, a life of ease and affluence: and then we see his gradual isolation and his turning for companionship to the woman he had known before meeting the innocent Maggie, the American Charlotte, who is imaged for us, in many ways, not least in the form of James's familiar evocation of Diana the huntress. The imagery changes when we come to the second half of the novel, in which Maggie must face the crack in her life and her phantoms – 'the horror of finding evil seated, all at its ease, where she had only dreamed of good; the horror of the thing hideously *behind*, behind so much trusted, so much pretended nobleness, cleverness, tenderness'. For the first time the insulated American innocent learns that life has its treacheries and that the pagoda, with its pleasant bright surfaces and the gentle sound of its tinkling bells can conceal the ominous and sinister, as in a nightmare – 'it had met her like some bad-faced stranger surprised in one of the thick-carpeted corridors of a house of quiet on a Sunday afternoon'. The terror behind the bland surface of common day – this had always been James's most powerful evocative instrument: the latent horror that had made *The Turn of the Screw* one of his most deeply felt creations. Animal imagery, the prowl of predatory creatures, is felt in the gradual unveiling of Maggie's inner world; she must live through her jealousy, her sense of the collapse of her world, her re-education, and do it with calm duplicity; she remains ironically close to the tinkling bells and the pagoda-existence. James makes us feel the power of her subdued passion – the power of the 'really agitated lamb'. Lions are as nothing compared to them, 'for lions are sophisticated, are blasé, are brought up from the first to prowling and mauling', as the cynical Fanny Assingham remarks to her husband.

Within the houses of London – Portland Place of the Prince and Princess, Eaton Square of the Ververs, and the lowlier Cadogan Place of the Assinghams – moves Adam Verver, the enigmatic, poker-faced, check-suited American tycoon. James treats him as a mystery figure, a kind of 'Uncle Sam' whose thoughts are never known, but who represents American indulgence where his daughter is concerned, and American shrewdness in the gathering in of Europe's creations. If he is Adam, the first man, he seems often in this novel to be still living in the Garden, 'in a state of childlike innocence', as the Prince observes. He is that great anomaly, the American who has inherited the ages without having had to suffer; things have fallen into his lap. Other nations suffered. He has reaped the rewards of suffering. However, he has his insights. When Maggie tells her father she doesn't believe he is selfish, he rejoins, 'But we're selfish together – we move as a selfish mass. You see we always want the same thing and that holds us, that binds us, together. We want each other, only wanting it, each time, *for* each other. That's what I call the happy spell; but it's also, a little, possibly, the immorality.' And when she questions 'the immorality' he acknowledges 'we're tremendously moral for ourselves – that is for each other'. Yet he finds too 'there's something haunting – as if it were a bit uncanny – in such a consciousness of our general comfort and privilege'. Father and daughter throughout the book 'protect' one another, and also understand one another. In silence, and with calm, they work out their problem with the calculations of a game of chess. The imagery in the book of the Princess is filled with the sense of her pagoda-claustrophobia; it gives way to the confrontation with Charlotte and the mounting tension in which the Prince discovers he is no longer married to a passive little girl, clinging to her father, but to a determined woman, a woman of character, who exercises her power without 'making a scene'. In the final meeting of the two women, the 'bad heroine' and the 'good', James cannot resist piling up his mythic allusions and artefact-images. Maggie waiting and wondering whether she and Charlotte will meet, feels herself to be like Io, in the old legend, goaded by the gadfly, or Ariadne, who having helped Theseus find his way out of the labyrinth, is left 'roaming the lone sea-strand'. She is 'some far-off harassed heroine'. The final artefact is the work of the printer, a book, a three-decker novel, of which Charlotte has in error picked up the second volume instead of the first. As they meet, Maggie can say, 'You've got the wrong volume, and I've brought you out the right.' Order, sequence, chronology are restored. Maggie has her husband, Charlotte hers. Each has the right volume. Charlotte too cannot have her cake and eat it.

In the last of his novels, as in the earliest, James is concerned with the dynamic of power. What is new here, as in *The Wings of the Dove*, is a quality of eroticism, an awareness of love, absent in the earlier works. We witness only one passionate encounter between Charlotte and the Prince. It suffices. Once we have seen, we know. The lovers have been saying to one another that they must protect the happiness of father and daughter – and by this see themselves protected in their adultery.

And so for a minute they stood together, as strongly held and as closely confronted as any hour of their easier past even had seen them. They were silent at first, only facing and faced, only grasping and grasped, only meeting and met. 'It's sacred,' he said at last.

'It's sacred,' she breathed back at him. They vowed it, gave it out and took it in, drawn by their intensity, more closely together. Then of a sudden, through this tightened circle, as at the issue of a narrow strait into the sea beyond, everything broke up, broke down, gave way, melted and mingled. Their lips sought their lips, their pressure their response and their response their pressure; with a violence that had sighed itself the next moment to the longest and deepest of stillnesses they passionately sealed their pledge.

This is perhaps not characteristic James: and at this distance from its time there is something cloying in the prose. However, read with a backward view, it tells us how far the author of this passage had come in his treatment of the relation between man and woman. One has only to recall the kiss – the only kiss – in *The Portrait of a Lady*.

Of such passages Stephen Spender has said – discerning the latent biographical meaning as no other critic has done – that they were written by 'a person who, profoundly with his whole being, after overcoming great inhibition, has accepted the *idea* of people loving ... after a lifetime of deep human understanding, has arrived at a stage where in suffering and pity he could accept the physical fact of love'.

80

A Passion of Nostalgia

ONE day in November of 1903 while in London, James went to the Tilbury dock to see Mrs John La Farge and her daughter off to America. He seems to have told the story of this little adventure to Ford Madox Hueffer who described James as returning to Rye 'singularly excited, bringing out a great many unusually uncompleted sentences'. Hueffer quoted him as saying 'And once aboard the lugger ... And if ... Say a toothbrush ... and circular notes ... and so something for the night ...' We have, however, James's own account. He went to the dreary dock because his friends were 'rather helpless and alone'. He did go aboard the ship, the *Minnehaha*, 'almost into their very bunks in the electric-lighted dark of the day'. And he said to himself: 'Now or never is my chance; stay and sail – borrow clothes, borrow a toothbrush, borrow a bunk, borrow $100; you will never be so near to it again. The worst is over – the arranging: it's all arranged *for* you, with two kind ladies thrown in.' His fantasy had been lively: if he had only had a thicker overcoat and the ladies had had an extra bunk 'I would have turned in *with* them and taken my chance'. As it was, he experienced a sudden acute wish to be in America again, resisted it, and shoved his way 'out of the encumbered tubular passages'. He 'turned and fled, bounding along Tilbury docks in the grimy fog and never stopping till I clutched at something that was going back to London'.

I

Behind the humour and exaggerations of this little episode lay a profound emotion. He had become aware of it during the writing of *The Ambassadors*; it had made him urge Edith Wharton to stay with her American subject. He found himself remembering the leaves he had kicked in the autumn along the lower reaches of Fifth Avenue, 'as I can to this hour feel myself, hear myself, positively *smell* myself doing'. But perhaps there were 'no leaves and no trees now in Fifth Avenue – nothing but patriotic arches, Astor Hotels and Vanderbilt Palaces'. He had in his younger years known only the eastern seaboard and had made a single foray as far as Wisconsin in 1883. Now the land of his birth extended to California. It seemed quite as 'romantic' as the Europe of his younger dreams. Visits from Justice Holmes, the La Farges, the Edith Whartons, his recent exchange of letters with Henry Adams – all spoke of an America no longer known to him. It was time to go back. When he had turned 60, in April of 1903, he had begun to feel as never before the memories of childhood and youth. 'I must go before I'm too old, and, above all, before I mind being older,' he wrote to William James. To Howells he gave further proof of his longing, 'I *want* to come, quite pathetically and tragically – it is a passion of nostalgia.' On the eve of his birthday he wrote a long letter to his brother describing his inner debate between desire for the journey and the practical obstacles – the letting of his house, the unaccustomed voyage, the proper itinerary, the financing of the trip. 'The desire to go "home" for six months (not less,) daily grows in me,' he wrote, 'before senile decay sets in.' He felt he should look after his long-neglected literary interests and examine what opportunities there might be in order to 'quicken and improve them, after so endless an absence'. But the process would be so 'damnedly expensive'. There would be six months of American hotels. He couldn't 'stay' with friends; he wanted to move about. He could finance the trip by writing a book of 'impressions' – it would have to be 'for much money'. He wanted to *see* the country at large, yet 'I don't see myself prowling alone in

Western cities and hotels, or finding my way about by myself and it is all darksome and tangled'.

William's reply was characteristic. He said he could imagine 'the sort of physical loathing with which many features of our national life will inspire you'. William listed the things in America that displeased him and he thought would displease Henry – the sight of Americans having boiled eggs for breakfast with butter on them and the *vocalization* 'of our countrymen'. Couldn't Henry have his copyrights and literary matters taken care of by an agent? In effect he seemed to urge him not to come. Of course Henry might lecture at the Lowell Institute. On the other hand, there was the American out-of-doors. If Henry would avoid the *banalité* of the eastern cities and travel to the South, to Colorado, across Canada, possibly to Hawaii, he might find the journey rewarding, but he would have to pay the price. William advised him to come in spring and to stay till October. He invited Henry to spend the hot months with his family at Chocorua, their summer home. He would even go with Henry to certain places if he wished. But he was busy, and he urged his brother not to take the trip before the spring of 1904. The letter was friendly and helpful, but it had a certain diffidence in it and the younger brother had his usual emotional response. There was no possibility, he said, of a trip before August of 1904. William had been very 'dissuasive – even more than I expected'. It was all very well for him to speak in this way: he had moved around America at his ease, but Henry had always travelled very little; there was only the well-beaten path to Italy, that had been all. He had never been to Spain, or Greece, or Sicily; he had had no glimpse of the East. He could not see himself writing little travel articles in these countries as he had done in his younger years. If he couldn't bring off his American trip he would have to settle down to his shuttle between Rye and London, with nothing left for him 'in the way of (the poetry of) motion'. He regarded this as 'a thin, starved, lonely, defeated, *beaten* prospect: in comparison with which your own circumgyrations have been as the adventures of Marco Polo or H. M. Stanley'. Thus spoke the younger brother, in his perpetual sense of 'deprivation and rivalry'. The trip to America would represent 'the one big taste of travel not supremely missed'. An American agent wouldn't begin to do for him what he could do for himself. As to the boiled eggs and the 'vocalization' and 'the Shocks in general', all this was irrelevant. The ways in which Americans ate their eggs were just the sort of thing that interested him as a novelist. 'I want to see them, I want to see everything. I want to see the Country, scarcely a bit New York and Boston, but intensely the Middle and Far West and California and the South.' He did not want to spend the summer in America; arriving in August, he would have the American autumn, which he had always loved, and he could go to the warmer areas in the winter months. It is clear that the plan for his journey was complete in his mind. He had asked for a brotherly blessing and it had not been given. There remained only the practical matters. Goody Allen was already on the alert for tenants for Lamb House. He had discussed with his agent, Pinker, the idea for the collective edition to be negotiated in America, probably with Scribner.

What astonished him was that friends and relatives seemed to have a picture of him as likely to get lost in America and to hate everything he would see. They did not reckon with Henry's eagerness for experience. Grace Norton wrote that she talked with Mrs William James of Henry's 'dislike' of his native land. He admonished her in his reply: 'Never, never, my dear Grace: you must have misunderstood Alice – or she herself – as to the fabled growth of my still more fabled "dislike".' On the contrary,

I have never been more curious of it, nor more interested in it, nor more sensible of loss by absence from it (in certain ways,) than in the light of so much talk with her and William ... The idea of *seeing* American life again and tasting the American air, that is a vision, a possibility, an impossibility, positively romantic.

The possibility, he explained, was his wish to return and revisit. The impossibility was that it would be 'a very expensive and bewildering luxury and amusement, and a very difficult and complicated one to organize. But if I *could*! – if I *can*!' How take care of his servants? his typist? the unfinished books?

Miss Norton spoke, he later said, in Cassandra tones and with Cassandra warnings. His answer was that 'the thought of breathing my native air again for a few months (at the latest decent date before I may begin to cease to breathe at all) strikes me as a singularly normal and natural impulse, round which no cloud of complications or other bedevilments should be *allowed* to settle'. To another friend he wrote, 'I think with a great appetite in advance, of the chance, once more, *to lie on the ground*, on an American hillside, on the edge of the woods, in the manner of my youth.' He wasn't sure he could lecture – he was about as capable of that, he said, as of doing a trapeze act. 'If I do achieve a few months in the country at large,' he told Miss Norton, 'the thing will have been the most private and personal act of my very private and personal life.' By the autumn of 1903, the nostalgia had become a challenge. It would be 'ignobly weak' not to find solutions to his problems. Presently all his friends seemed involved. The peripatetic Benedicts, Miss Woolson's relatives, wrote as if a voyage were as routine as a bus trip in London. James had crossed the sea in the days when the potential rage of the ocean was a constant anxiety. The Benedicts described the luxury of the new 'liners'. He could go with them, when they returned in August 1904 from their annual jaunt to Italy, to Bayreuth, to Vienna.

In January of 1904, with the end of *The Golden Bowl* in sight, he accordingly paid his deposit on an upper promenade deck cabin on the *Kaiser Wilhelm II*, sailing from Southampton in August. In spite of the long inner debate there had never been any real doubt from the first. 'I should greatly like before I chuck up the game,' he wrote Howells, 'to write (another!!) American novel or two – putting the thing *in* the country; which would take, God knows – I mean would require – some impressions.' He was ready to have his impressions.

2

He had said he would not lecture in America. But the question kept coming up. His sister-in-law asked whether he would be interested in doing the Lowell lectures in Boston, and he answered, 'I am 60 years old, and have never written a lecture in my life.' It would take much time. Would it pay? 'You impute to me, alas, a facility that I'm far from possessing.' Nevertheless, he kept an open mind. The proposal had been, that he deliver eight lectures on 'The English Novelists'. Overtures began to be made the moment the word got around that he was going. Colonel George Harvey, head of Harper and Brothers, agreed to serialize James's American impressions in the *North American Review* and make a book of it afterwards. Both Harvey and Howells, who was literary adviser to Harper, were in London that spring, and James had direct aid in making his plans. Also abroad was one of the Harper editors, an energetic young woman named Elizabeth Jordan. She was asked to canvass lecture possibilities. James became interested from the moment he learned that he could command substantial fees. Colonel Harvey spoke of

$500 a lecture; Howells mentioned $150 or $200. 'He ought to lecture very, very few times,' Howells wrote to Miss Jordan, 'and *not* on any terms of public vastness. He should read as I have done, in drawing-rooms, country-club rooms, and the like, and the public should be more or less invited, and made to feel itself privileged.' James had intimated that he was prepared to lecture but not 'if the personal exposure is out of proportion to the tip'.

More pressing than the American arrangements was the problem of Lamb House and the servants. The irrepressible Goody had come up with some possible tenants, the Miss Horstmanns, one of whom was in England to marry John Boit of Boston. Lamb House would be a 'honeymoon' house. James asked for a rental of £5 a week that would include 'the servants, the forks and spoons, and house linen and books, and in short everything that is in the house except my scant supply of clothing'. Also the care of the dachshund, Maximilian. The rent would just cover the wages of his servants. He hoped that 'the Young Things' would be 'bribeable by frantic cheapness'. A bare four weeks before sailing, he was able to telegraph Goody Allen, 'Little Friends accept for six months hooray and glory to immortal Goody.'

His letter to his prospective tenants outlined his domestic arrangements. There were five servants including the gardener, and Burgess, the house-boy. Mrs Paddington, the cook-housekeeper, was 'an absolutely brilliant economist' and a very orderly person. The parlourmaid, Alice Skinner, had been with James for six years, 'a thoroughly respectable, well-disposed and duly competent young woman'. The housemaid was 'very pretty and gentle – and not a very, *very* bad one. The house-boy, Burgess Noakes, isn't very pretty, but is on the other hand very gentle, punctual, and desirous to please.' He cleaned shoes, knives, doorsteps, windows, and took letters to post and so forth. Burgess was then 19.

'Lastly,' James wrote,

I take the liberty of confiding to your charity and humanity the precious little person of my Dachshund Max, who is the best and gentlest and most reasonable and well-mannered as well as most beautiful, small animal of his kind to be easily come across – so that I think you will speedily find yourselves loving him for his own sweet sake.

The servants would take care of his welfare and he wasn't to be fed between meals. But he would appreciate being taken for walks. If indulged in this way 'all the latent beauty of his nature will come out'.

James bought a new steamer trunk. He visited his London tailor. He made last-minute calls. From America invitations poured in – Mrs Gardner expected to see him; also the Secretary of State, John Hay in Washington and his friend Henry Adams; so did the Emmets at their farm in Connecticut; and then Peggy wrote, and the William Jameses. It was settled he should go first to Chocorua. His nephew Harry would meet the liner at Hoboken. Edith Wharton sent him her volume of tales, *The Descent of Man*, and he praised her 'wise and witty art'. He would be seeing her at Lenox.

Miss Weld, not involved in James's domestic arrangements, and employed on an hourly basis, sought other employment during James's absence. But before his return from America she had become engaged and married and had left his employ.

On 19 August he said good-bye to his servants, buried his nose in Max's little gold-coloured back, 'wetting it with my tears'. As he made his way to the boat-train at Waterloo Station he was conscious of 'a pandemonium of uncertainties and mysteries'. He sailed 24 August 1904, having said his farewell to Jocelyn a few days before, and written also a long letter to Hendrik Andersen, the first of a series in which he began to express misgiving about Andersen's statues, of which he had received photographs. 'They terrify me so with their evidence as of a *madness* (almost) in the scale on which you are working.' Andersen was planning an enormous fountain – it was magnificent, heroic, sublime, said James, but where would it have any practical use? 'I yearn for the *smaller masterpiece*; the condensed, consummate, caressed, intensely filled-out thing.' He patted Hendrik 'lovingly, tenderly, tenderly' and sailed with the sense of further 'dreary and deadly postponements' of their meetings.

Henry James's lifetime had been spent in adapting his Puritan heritage to the more flexible – and more realistic – standards of Europe. He had been unable to make his peace with his native land; and in his choice of exile had, like Lambert Strether, to accommodate himself to 'Europe'. At the end of *The Golden Bowl* he resolved the situation by sending Charlotte and Adam back to the United States. It is a cruel fate for the interesting Charlotte, the Europeanized American. Once the novel was written, and this resolution found, James had been able to book his own passage home. He was quite as free, indeed freer, than his Charlotte. His was a voluntary voyage; hers had in it elements of coercion. James, pacing the deck of the *Kaiser Wilhelm II* as it left Southampton, felt himself acting out a significant part of his destiny. He had been abroad too long; he needed to recover a sense of his homeland. 'I feel my going not only as a lively desire but as a supreme necessity,' he wrote Howells. He had lived a great part of the past two decades between two worlds and in a cosmopolitan world of his own making. He had said that he felt the romance and curiosity of his journey – the return to the landscapes of his childhood and youth – as if it were a new voyage of discovery. The vision was expressed by Mrs Assingham in the passage he had written towards the end of *The Golden Bowl*. 'I see the long miles of ocean and the dreadful great country, State after State – which have never seemed to me so big or so terrible.'

Just before leaving, he instructed his agent to inform Charles Scribner that the time had come for a definitive edition of his works. 'Mr James's idea is to write for each volume a preface of a rather intimate character, and there is no doubt that such a preface would add greatly to the interest of the books.' What would contribute to the intimacy of the prefaces would be the seeing again of scenes and places in which his great adventure – in art, in life – had begun. The 'passionate pilgrim' was returning to the New York of his boyhood, the Cambridge of his youth, the new America of which he had had so many hints and glimpses for twenty years.

BOOK FOUR:

THE AMERICAN SCENE

1904-5

81

The Jersey Shore

A REPORTER covering the waterfront in Hoboken found Henry James guarding his luggage on the pier in the big shed, waiting for a customs inspector. Some 3,000 persons were milling about, passengers who had crossed on the North German Lloyd liner *Kaiser Wilhelm II*, many of them German-American Jews. The reporter noted James's 'regular and sharp' features; he described him as an 'immensely robust figure' with a firm elastic step. His nephew Harry had met him, and a representative from the firm of Harper and Brothers. James seemed unruffled and relaxed amid the confusion attending a late summer docking. For a celebrity, he appeared 'remote', inconspicuous. But then the author of *The Reverberator* seldom talked to reporters. And his coming had not been heralded. After the baggage was cleared, James personally supervised its removal to a carriage; but he was in no hurry to start. As he came out into the sunshine he turned and surveyed the New York skyline. Detaching himself from the little group he paused, and said the reporter, 'almost gasped for breath'. He walked to a railing; he looked for a long time, 'deaf to the questions of his friends'. He might have been Rip Van Winkle awakening out of a twenty-year sleep. He had last seen New York in 1883. It was now 30 August 1904.

Henry James had skipped two decades of his country's life. And yet certain things were unchanged. Crossing to Lower Manhattan he saw New York from the ferry as held in the embrace of its two good-natured rivers; he likened the city to an overblown beauty held in the arms of a not-too-fastidious gallant. The new buildings, called skyscrapers, seemed stuck in here, there and everywhere like extravagant pins in an extravagant pincushion. There were recognizable smells. As the ferry approached the terminal he saw that the waterfront was true to a 'barbarism it had not outlived'. All the ugly old items – loose cobbles, unregulated traffic, big drays pulled by struggling long-necked sharp-ribbed horses. Corpulent constables stood in high detachment with helmets askew. There were huddled houses from the older time; red-faced in their glazed paint, and off balance amid an assortment of newer buildings.

The light of the end-of-August day was clear; the sun of New York rested lazily on the crimson buildings. James rode uptown, discovering familiar things among the unfamiliar. At Washington Square he noted the truncated arch; it was wholly without suggestion of grandeur or 'glory'. He saw a few of the buildings of his childhood, and suddenly found himself recalling old empty New York afternoons in waning summers. He continued to Gramercy Park where apparently he paused for rest in the home of a friend. He had planned to leave that evening for Boston with Harry, to join William James at Chocorua in New Hampshire. However, Colonel Harvey, president of Harper, had sent a pressing invitation – almost a summons. James was expected at his country place on the Jersey shore. Having agreed, when they met earlier that year in London, to publish James's American impressions, Harvey was also taking James under his wing during this visit. James felt that he was falling into some kind of a social 'trap'; nevertheless he yielded. His nephew took most of his baggage on to New England; James, in Gramercy Park, piled into another four-wheeler and returned to the docks. There were a great many suburban 'young men of business' aboard the ferry, going to the Jersey shore at the end of their day's work in downtown Manhattan. James listened to their talk and looked at the breezy bay, 'the great unlocked and tumbled-out city on the one hand and the low, accessible mystery of the opposite State on the other'. What struck him most about the young men was their 'unconscious affluence'.

Presently he was being driven along a straight road, following a blue band of sea, between the sandy shore and a chain of big villas. They appeared like a bunch of white boxes. Each villa presided over a small bit of bright green lawn that looked like a skirt sharply pulled down over the knees. They passed through Long Branch. Someone pointed out the cottage where Grant had lived; and the cottage where Garfield had died. The little dwellings were outclassed by a general expensiveness surrounding them.

Colonel Harvey's cottage was spacious and substantial. It stood near the sea, at Deal Beach, N.J. The tall sociable host and a plump Mrs Harvey greeted the distinguished visitor. He discovered a fellow-guest awaiting him – the grizzled, white-suited, cigar-smoking 'natural' Samuel Langhorne Clemens, archetypal innocent abroad and quintessential American. Colonel Harvey had gathered in his two literary lions. 'Poor dear old Mark Twain beguiles the session on the deep piazza,' Henry James scrawled in a hasty pencilled note to William James.

2

Colonel George Harvey was a symbol of the new America, as Mark Twain represented the old. A native of Vermont, he was the epitome of the advertising, newspaperism and public relations James detested; but the novelist knew he could take the smooth, efficient colonel in his stride. Harvey had been a 'boy-wonder', one of Joseph Pulitzer's lieutenants. Forced by his health to leave the *World*, he had, with the aid of William Whitney and J. P. Morgan, amassed a fortune in Wall Street and purchased the *North American Review*. When at the century's turn Harper and Brothers went into receivership, Morgan had him appointed administrator. Howells remained its principal literary adviser, Mark Twain its lucrative author, and Henry James its principal ornament. It was probably because of these various connections that James decided to pay this visit, although he shrank from the clear signals he received that the colonel would make the most of his presence. Harvey was already talking of the big public dinner he planned for James. The novelist swept the idea aside. He was off to New England; he had no intention of staying in the city's end-of-summer dust and grime. He would come back after he had seen the leaves turn to russet and gold.

James's remark about 'poor dear old Mark Twain' sounded condescending, but it was in reality sympathetic. Clemens had lost his wife a few months earlier, during a stay in Florence; James had heard about this in some detail, not only from his friend Dr Baldwin, who was Mrs Clemens's physician, but from Howells. The author of *Huckleberry Finn* was now at loose ends; he was living for the moment in a hotel in lower Fifth Avenue, and behind his volubility and wit he was more depressed than ever. Four years had elapsed since the two had met in London, when Mark Twain had talked to James about Swedish health cures. With his halo of white hair, his brilliant aggressive loquacity, he continued to charm, as he had always done. The repatriated novelist enjoyed his brief interlude in New Jersey although he stayed only the next day. The weather was good and he took pleasure in the air, and the play of light over the coast. 'The basis of privacy was somehow wanting,' he would write in the opening pages of *The American Scene*, quite secure in the feeling that the extrovert Colonel Harvey would miss his allusions.

The white boxes seemed to say, 'We are only instalments, symbols, stop gaps; expensive as we are, we have nothing to do with continuity, responsibility, transmission, and don't in the least care what becomes of us after we have served our present purpose.' James was driven to various places during this day and on the roads saw 'the chariots, the buggies, the motors, the pedestrians – which last number, indeed, was remarkably small'. The thirty-six hours at Harvey's was summed up in his allusion to 'the air of unmitigated publicity, publicity as a condition, as a doom, from which there could be no appeal'. On his arrival in New Hampshire his thank-you note to Harvey spoke of having 'a bushel of Impressions already gathered'. The note of affluence and advertising, of impermanence, of a civilization created wholly for commerce, had been struck for him.

82

A New England Autumn

HE had a strange feeling the evening he stepped out of the South Station in Boston, a sense of 'confused and surprised recognition'. He rode through the warm September night to Cambridge without so much as seeing a single policeman between the depot and Harvard Square. The town seemed vacant. The immediate Cambridge impression was its 'earth smell'. In the darkness it 'fairly poetized the suburbs, and with the queer, far, wild throb of shrilling insects'. Cambridge was still faithful to its type – but the rustle of the trees had a larger tone and there was more lamplight. New and strange architecture loomed through the dark. Harvard stretched acquisitive arms in many directions.

James drove to 95 Irving Street, the large shingled house William James had built ten years before, which Henry had never seen. Here he spent the night. The next day he took the train into the White Mountains, to Chocorua where he found – so he wrote Edith Wharton – 'the Domestic circle blooming for the poor celibate exile'.

I

William James's summer home at Chocorua was a low rambling two-storey bungalow on the edge of a forest-fringed slope. From the high ground on which it stood, Henry James looked at a great sweep of country, a chain of small lakes, and off to the right the grey head of Chocorua mountain. He had a warm reunion with his brother and sister-in-law, his nephews, his niece. The family installed him in a suite of rooms at one end of the L-shaped house. He liked the spacious verandahs and the smell of the woods. He had a sense of total privacy. Later he spoke of the 'Arcadian elegance and amiability' of this part of New England. It reminded him of an old legend, an old love story, one of those written by Mademoiselle de Scudéry in fifteen volumes – an allusion to the way in which she had travestied her time by disguising her personages as Greeks and Romans. The place was Arcadian because it was poetic, romantic, and unburdened with too much history. Such history as it had he saw soon enough – the 'old, hard New England effort, defeated by the soil and the climate and reclaimed by nature and time'. He had seen the great ruins of the centuries in old European cities; but here he looked on crumbled chimney-stacks, overgrown thresholds, dried-up wells, vague cart-tracks of another time. There was the immediate richness of the leaves turning to crimson. He liked the hush of the landscape; he found an elegance in common objects, the silver-grey rock showing through thinly grassed acres, the boulders in the woods, 'the scattered wild apples ... like figures in the carpet'. He found everything 'funny and lovely'. The loveliness resided in nature. The 'funny' element was represented by the people, their incongruities and manners – and absence of form. In *The American Scene* there are beautiful verbal landscapes; James obviously went on long rambles, and he had always been a student of nature in a pictorial way. There is also a great deal of social criticism. He was troubled by what he saw – the 'sallow, saturnine' people driving teams, carts and conveyances, their slovenliness of dress and careless articulation; there was a kind of general 'human neglect' surrounding farmhouses and towns. With his old interest in comparing Old World life and American, he felt the difference 'in a land of long winters' made by the suppression of the two great factors of the familiar English landscape, the squire and the parson. The shrill New England meeting house was no substitute for 'the seated solidity of religion', which in England provided so much social furnishing. James would write of the villages, their lack of civic pride, their absence of standards. He wondered at the high wages paid unskilled 'hired' men and servants, not because he grudged them their earnings but because there was no matching of skill with remuneration. He disliked the attitude of the employed. They seemed to feel that everything was 'owed *to* them, not to be rendered, but to be received'.

Henry James thought too many roads were being built in New England. He wasn't happy when he was driven in buggies or wagons behind ostrich-necked horses at breakneck speed. However, he enjoyed the domestic life in William James's house; he had an enormous appetite for the country butter, cream, eggs, chickens, and the delectable home-baked loaf, such as he had not eaten in years. Shortly before leaving England he had decided to try the new fad of 'Fletcherism'. An American, Horace Fletcher, was teaching the virtues of slow and lengthy chewing of food. James's deliberate mastication seemed to go hand in hand with his slow ruminative conversation.

He had boasted of his escape from interviewers in New York, but one young woman, armed with a letter from Scribner's, made her way to Chocorua. James, who had never given an interview, felt it would be unkind not to see her. He stipulated, however, that she must send him no clippings. She described a man of middle height, bald, his black hair turned to iron grey at the sides, wearing a plain rough sack suit of dark grey, and not as 'different from other people as his fiction is different from other fiction'. His face was 'long and strong, broad of cheek-bone and jaw, narrower in the high doming forehead'. James's blue-grey eyes had 'seen, rather than seemed to see' – perhaps testimony of his lack of interest, for he described his interviewer as 'a pathetic bore'. Her account however has a certain documentary value. 'His nose is massive and fine, his mouth large and tender', she found a 'delicate, young expression of the chin'. Superficially, she said, one would not count the whole as striking, but the distinction lay in the play of expression – strength, mellowness, shyness, kindness. His manner was more American 'than it might have been considering his long residence in England'. They talked in a low-ceilinged room 'where the dreamy space of grass surmounted by a rim of trees' provided a natural panorama. James throughout was simple and relaxed.

'One's craft, one's art, is his expression,' he told his interviewer, 'not one's person, as that of some great actress or singer is hers.' He said that

after you have heard a Patti sing why should you care to hear the small private voice of the woman. One rather discounts mere talk. In such a matter, too, the artist is practically helpless, practically at the mercy of the hearer. The author in his work has meant something perhaps, but if he had to express this meaning in a different way it would never have been written.

The young woman asked the Master about the 'moral purpose' in his way of ending his stories leaving everything up in the air. 'Ah, is not that the trick that life plays?' James rejoined. 'Life itself leaves you with a question – it asks you questions.'

Perhaps the most interesting part of the interview, which was heavily interlarded with appreciative references to certain of his novels, was James's description of the reading public. He called it 'dissolute'; he said it was omnivorous, gulping, either ignorant or weary, reading to soothe or indulge. He felt that people in America did not like to think. In older civilizations there were more defined differences of public desire, 'conditions that have had time to accumulate and so to be observed'. James said that the French writers he had known wrote of a strong tradition 'and I wish to say that an author for whom I entertain a great esteem is Balzac'. James would have a great deal to say about Balzac during his journeying in America.

2

The novelist seems to have been restless at Chocorua. He had always been active; he liked to move about; and he made three trips within a matter of days after his arrival. The first involved Balzac. He went to Jackson, New Hampshire, to spend a day with the 74-year-old Katherine Prescott Wormeley, who had devoted her life to translating and writing about Balzac. She was a sister of Ariana Curtis, his hostess in Venice at the Palazzo Barbero. He had spoken of Miss Wormeley in his 1902 essay on Balzac as an 'interpreter, translator and worshipper', an example of 'the passionate piety' that the novelist could inspire. He arrived at nightfall, high in the White Mountains, and was reminded of a Swiss village; he stayed at the inn next to the Wildcat River and climbed to Miss Wormeley's house the next morning where he found five verandahs for the view, and 'images of furnished peace, within, as could but illustrate a rare personal history'.

His second journey was to Howard Sturgis on Cape Cod. James had visited the Cape twenty years before, and had described it in *The Bostonians*. This time he went, by the slow jogging train from Boston, to West Barnstaple and thence to Cotuit by horse and buggy, driven by 'a little boy in tight knickerbockers'. The horse 'was barely an animal at all ... a mere ambling spirit in shafts on the scale of a hairpin'. The drive was long and James enjoyed 'the little white houses, the feathery elms, the band of ocean blue, the strip of sandy yellow, the tufted pines in angular silhouette, the cranberry swamps, stringed across, for the picking, like the ruled pages of ledgers'. The place looked for him like a pictured Japanese screen; and the communities were locked up tight, as if painted on Japanese silk. He had three pleasant days with Sturgis; otherwise he found little human company. He carried away a glimpse of a young man, waist high, prodding the sea bottom for oysters. He saw a mute citizen or two packing oysters in boxes for shipment to Boston; he listened to 'the unabashed discourse of three or four school-children at leisure, visibly "prominent" and apparently in charge of the life of the place'. As during his visit twenty years before, he was convinced that America in its 'permissiveness' was surrendering its culture to the uncultivated young.

His third trip was farther away, a sally into Connecticut to visit his Emmet cousins, whom he hadn't seen since 1900 when Bay Emmet had painted his portrait. They were now living on a farm near Salisbury – the mother, Mrs Hunter and Rosina, Leslie, and Bay. Going there James suddenly realized that every trip in America involved distance, compared with the easy little journeys in and out of London he had been making for years. He found Connecticut 'a ravishing land', and he was pleased particularly by the fine houses, the elms, the general aspect of Farmington. Here he found 'the note of the aristocratic in an air that so often affects us as drained precisely and well-nigh to our gasping, of any exception to the common'. In one house he was shown an array of impressionist paintings, 'wondrous examples of Manet, of Degas, of Claude Monet, of Whistler'. It made him realize, he said, that he had been starved of such things in his early weeks in America. Everywhere he had discovered a desire among people for 'sameness' rather than difference. When he asked about the conditions of life, even at Farmington, the answer he got was 'The conditions of life? Why, the same conditions as everywhere else.' James bowed his head to this kind of 'monotony of acquiescence'.

3

He explored, that autumn, as the colours of the trees continued to change and the leaves began to fall, the no-longer familiar contours of Cambridge, the mysteries of expanded Boston. He revisited Newport, scene of his younger self, as well as Concord and Salem. The personal America of his earlier years seemed shrunken; the new America, and the new racial mixtures, confronted him everywhere. In William James's spacious house in Irving Street he had his anchor; here there were memories of his father and mother, including the striking sketch, in oils for the paternal portrait by Duveneck, and objects of furniture, such as his father's old large work-table which William now used. These referred him back to a remote past. William's house was spacious with a smallish verandah, a square garden at the side, a long and wide study-sitting-room, behind the front parlour, in which the family could gather round the fire in the evenings. The novelist had his isolated quarters in the upper reaches of this house and worked in the mornings as usual, but without a typist. Accustomed always to talking and observing, he strolled in the afternoons, he read, he took notes. Just across the way from William's home lived the ageing Grace Norton, his confidante of many years. He found her much less the personage he had made of her; he still felt an old affection for her, in her spinsterish aloofness; but she was 'intellectually inaccessible' and this fact destroyed his old desire to write to her, once he was abroad again. But in her possession were some of the finest letters he had written, many more than he remembered.

In October he paid a long visit to Mrs Wharton in the Berkshires. He visited also that other *grande dame*, the indomitable 'Mrs Jack' Gardner at Green Hill in Brookline, and saw the all-but-completed and already inaugurated Venetian *palazzo* she had built in the Fenway, admiring her gift in shoring up the fragments of her far-flung purchases abroad. He had once spoken of 'the age of Mrs Jack'; that age had now composed itself into a set form, a museum-mould, as he had imagined in his creation of Adam Verver, and his dream of an art centre in American City. He wrote to Paul Bourget that Mrs Gardner's *palais-musée*

is a really great creation. Her acquisitions during the last ten years have been magnificent; her arrangement and administration of them are admirable, and her spirit soars higher still. Her spirit is immense, and proof against time and fate. It has greatly 'improved' her in every way to have done a thing of so much interest and importance – and to have had to do it with such almost unaided courage, intelligence and energy! She has become really a great little personage.

4

James's inspection of Cambridge began, as might be expected, with Harvard, where he found himself musing anew at the shape of the Harvard Yard and the fact that it was still not sufficiently enclosed. With his novelist's need for shape and form, the unenclosed gave an effect for him of extemporization and thinness. And he remembered the high grills and palings at Oxford, and the sense of mystery these created for him. His nephew Harry, so lately a graduate, guided him to the various buildings; and the novelist, thinking back on the small Harvard of his own youth, and the few brief months he had spent at the old law school in Dane Hall, looked at each item of the new 'pampered state' of the students – 'multiplied resources, faculties, museums, undergraduate and postgraduate habitations ... pompous little club-houses'. He went into the Law Library and saw in the distance, John Gray, whom he had known in his youth when they had both admired his cousin Minny Temple – but 'to go to him I should have had to cross the bridge that spans the gulf of time.' He kept his distance.

He stepped into the student union, admiring the Sargent portrait of the donor, Major Henry Lee Higginson; he paused before the tablets carrying the names of members of the university who had died in the Civil War. He felt in all this 'the too scant presence of the massive and the mature'. Walking about the yard he scanned the faces of the young men. Many of them already seemed to have for James a 'businessman' face; he was speaking of facial cast and expression alone, leaving out of account questions of 'voice, tone, utterance, and attitude'. The American women seemed to be 'of markedly finer texture' than the men; and this led James to wonder how American men could satisfy American women, or as he put it 'this apparent privation, for the man, of his right kind of woman, and this apparent privation, for the woman, of her right kind of man'. Such were the inquiries of 'the restless analyst'. They were social, psychological, historical, based not on any scientific method or any dialectic but rather the intuitions, the feelings, the soundings, of an artist who had the deepest trust in his own senses and faculties, not least the supremacy of his intellect.

Meanwhile, however, his concern was most often with the relation of the past – his personal past – to what he saw in the America of 1904 and 1905. One of his first pilgrimages in Boston was to Ashburton Place, in quest of the house in which he had lived during the two far-away years of his youth, the last two years of the Civil War – the house of his early 'initiations'. He found it isolated behind the State House in an area already much cleared-out; some of the little old crooked streets had disappeared. Here had come the news of the death of Lincoln, the end of the war, and word of Hawthorne's death. Here he had counted the first greenbacks earned by his book reviews. He seemed to hear ghostly footsteps, 'the sound as of taps on the window-pane heard in the dim dawn', the place held old secrets, old stories, 'a saturation of life as closed together and preserved in it as the scent lingering in a folded pocket handkerchief'. Yet when he returned a month later, for another look, the old house was gone – every brick of it – 'the brutal effacement, at a stroke, of every related object, of the whole precious past'. He had a vivid impression of the impermanence of American life.

Beacon Hill was full of memories. There was Mount Vernon Street where his father had died and where he had stayed, in the house of death, through the spring of 1883 with his sister Alice. And here he speaks with intensity of habitations built of brick as against those of wood he found in so many of the New England towns. 'Oh, the wide benignity of brick, the goodly, friendly, ruddy fronts, the felicity of scale, the solid *seat* of everything ... to walk down Mount Vernon Street to Charles was to have a brush with that truth ... the preservation of character and the continuity of tradition.' But what he saw in great measure was 'the lapse into shabbiness and into bad company'. In Charles Street he passed the house which had been the centre of culture in his day – the home of J. T. Fields and his beautiful wife, where Dickens and Thackeray and the Brahmins had been entertained, even himself as a young aspirant – where he had met Mrs Stowe and listened to Julia Ward Howe read the *Battle Hymn of the Republic*. Behind the effaced anonymous door he could remember the long drawing-room looking over the water towards the sunset, like the finished background of a Dürer print. In the same locality he passed the spot where Dr Oliver Wendell Holmes had lived and remembered the August emptiness, the closed houses, the absent families, and how he had in his youth come to ask for news of Wendell Holmes 'then on his first flushed and charming visit to England and saw his mother in the cool dim matted drawing-room of that house and got the news, of all his London, his general English success and felicity, and *vibrated* so with the wonder and romance and curiosity and dim weak tender (oh, tender!) envy of it'. He had remounted Mount Vernon Street to the Athenaeum on that occasion filled with longing for London 'humming with it, and the emotion, exquisite of its kind'. He never seems to have forgotten the hour as 'a sovereign contribution to the germ of that inward romantic principle which was to determine so much later (ten years!) my own vision-haunted migration'.

In Back Bay he revisited Marlborough Street, comparing it to Wimpole and Harley Streets. He remembered the winter winds and snows and the eternal dust; he studied the individual house-fronts, finding too many bow windows and suddenly recalled a phrase from Tennyson, 'long, unlovely street'. Yet Marlborough Street, unlike the English street, did not have a monotony of leasehold brick and there was evidence of architectural experiment. Nevertheless Harley Street had character and depth : Marlborough Street was thin with the tone of a precocious child.

He looked closely at the Florentine palace that was the new public library in Copley Square; he had watched Abbey paint some of its murals. He inspected those of Puvis de Chavannes and noted the comings and goings of readers, and yet found – it was his common complaint – that the majesty of such a place was diminished by the absence of 'penetralia'. One failed to get the feeling in these American buildings that there was an innermost shrine, some sacred centre. His feeling of this was increased by the ubiquity of the American child, '*most* irrepressible little democrats of the democracy'. Even works of art in the city, like Saint-Gaudens' noble monument to Robert Gould Shaw and the Fifty-fourth Massachusetts Regiment in which James's brother Wilky had served, seemed placed with a casualness that was a disrespect both to art and memory. There was an absence of majesty. America could scatter emblems of things far and wide; it seemed to pay no attention to their meaning.

Much of James's progress through America during these intensely-felt weeks is recorded, with swelling phrase and large metaphor, in his book. In Newport he experienced the bitter-sweet of finding little corners full of old recall and the work of the real estate operators and American wealth and pretension, that had superseded old views and old values. There is a beautiful tenderness in which James describes the topographical contours of Newport – 'a little bare, white, open hand, with slightly-parted fingers' and remembers the days of his youth on its lonely beaches. He visits the villas and palaces 'into which the cottages have all turned' as if he were living in a fairy-tale – or the ancient story of King Midas. The place seemed heaped with gold 'to an amount so oddly out of proportion to the scale of nature and of space'. He would locate here the opening scene of the American novel he started to write seven years later, *The Ivory Tower.*

At Concord he remembered Emerson in his orchards; he had attended Emerson's funeral during his visit twenty years before. He found less change here; and he saw anew the Old Manse. He hung over the Concord River and looked closely at the scene of Concord's single historic event, where the minute men had made their stand. Thoreau, Hawthorne, and Emerson had expressed 'the sense of this full, slow, sleepy, meadowy flood'; he imaged it as setting its pace and taking its twists 'like some large obese benevolent person'. His youngest brother, Robertson James, who had fought in the Civil War, was living in Concord with his family. Bob had aged much; but he talked as brilliantly as ever. The three years that separated them in age, and the war experience, had made great differences between them; and then Bob had had spiritual struggles, and never found a focus in his life. Henry James could remember when Robertson, and their long-dead brother Wilky, had gone to school in Concord. Personal memories ranged deeply under the elms and in the sleepy streets; and yet what prevailed above all was the sense of the two geniuses of the place, Hawthorne and Emerson. James went in quest of Hawthorne also, in Salem; he found the birthplace, set in an area taken over by industry; he looked at what was said to be the house of the seven gables. He did not venture into it – he had a horror of 'reconstituted antiquity'. And for the same reason he paused before the Salem Witch House with a kind of 'sacred terror' and a 'sacred tenderness'. The wooden houses 'look brief and provisional at the best – look, above all, incorrigibly and witlessly innocent'. His entire visit left him wondering how this place had nurtured Hawthorne, and how 'merely "subjective" in us are our discoveries about genius. Endless are its ways of besetting and eluding, of meeting and mocking us ... we recognize ruefully that we are for ever condemned to know it only after the fact.'

83

The Lady of Lenox

I

As might be expected of a woman who had written a book on the decoration of houses, Edith Wharton had built her new home at Lenox, Massachusetts, in the Berkshires, with a sense of style and comfort. The Mount stood on a slope; it was spacious; it was dignified. It overlooked the dark waters and wooded shores of Laurel Lake. In the French style, its drawing-room, dining-room and library opened through large glass doors on a terrace beyond which was a stretch of formal garden. Henry James sank into the house as into a bed of luxury. He had come to the United States, he explained to Goody Allen (to whom at intervals he reported on his American progress) 'with a neat little project of paying no visits' and he was carrying this project out 'still more neatly, by having spent but two nights at an hotel, and done nothing but proceed from one irresistible hospitable house to another'. The Mount was 'an exquisite and marvellous place,' he wrote to Howard Sturgis, 'a delicate French Chateau mirrored in a Massachusetts pond' and a monument to 'the almost too impeccable taste of its so accomplished mistress'.

'Everyone is oppressively rich and *cossu* and "a million a year" (£200,000) seems to be the usual income,' he explained to Miss Allen. He was having 'a most agreeable and absorbing adventure and this golden glorious American autumn (such weather, as of tinkling crystal, and *such* colours, as of molten topaz and ruby and amber!) a prolonged fairy-tale'. The country was 'too terrifically big – and yet all this New England is but the corner of a corner of a corner'.

Mrs Wharton motored constantly, with her handsome heavily mous-
tached husband, a poodle, and the increasingly absorbed and fascinated distinguished visitor. Henry James was won over to this form
of travel in spite of bad roads, and 'the mountain-and-valley, lake-
and-river beauty extends so far, and goes so on and on, that even the
longest spins do not take one out of it'. They visited every accessible
part of Massachusetts and crossed into New York to large Hudson
vistas. James in the horse-and-buggy days of his earlier years had
known but limited areas of the eastern seaboard. To find himself in
the heart of New England and of New York State, was to make him
feel as if a great deal of freshness was breaking through old staleness, 'when the staleness, so agreeably favoured with hospitality,
and indeed with new ingredients, was a felt element at all'. They
drove through the great Lebanon bowl and the Shaker settlement –
skirting on the wide hard floor of the valley rows of gaunt windows
that resembled parallelograms of black paint, criss-crossed with
white lines, as in Nuremberg dolls'-houses. The place wore 'the
strangest air of active, operative death ... the final hush of passions,
desires, dangers'. Mrs Wharton must have provided an active commentary also on the New England villages through which they
passed, for James would write of 'those of the sagacious who had
occasionally put it before me that the village street, the arched um-
brageous vista, half so candid and half so cool, is too frequently, in
respect to "morals," but a whited sepulchre'. It had been put to him,
he said, that 'the great facts of life are in high fermentation on the
other side of the ground glass that never for a moment flushes, to the
casual eye, with the hint of a lurid light'. This caused the novelist,
who had seen sex in the open in Europe, who had written of Maupassant, D'Annunzio, and Serao, and French morality, to wonder
profoundly whether American 'realism' had really had 'veracity and
courage'. The village street and the lonely farm, as he looked at
them from the moving motor, 'became positively richer objects
under the smutch of imputation'. He had heard not only of desire
but of incest under the elms, for he wrote that

twitched with a grim effect, the thinness of their mantle, shook out of its
folds such crudity and levity as they might, and borrowed, for dignity,
a shade of the darkness of Cenci drama, of monstrous legend, of old
Greek tragedy, and thus helped themselves out for the story-seeker more
patient almost of anything than of flatness.

Edith Wharton would write of these subjects in *Ethan Frome* and *Summer*.

They found themselves one day foraging for dinner in a town by the Hudson, with the dim Catskills in the distance. The car had broken down. They walked the long straight street to the hotel where they were barred from the dining-room because of Mrs Wharton's poodle. They found a quiet cook-shop instead, where there was little denial of 'the superstition of cookery'. What remained was the memory of the long straight street. The Hudson stretched back 'with fumbling friendly hand, to the earliest outlook of my consciousness'. The river had been a link in the lives of the Jameses between their parental Albany and their own New York – 'small echoes and tones and sleeping lights, small sights and sounds and smells that made one, for an hour, *as* small, – carried one up the rest of the river, the very river of life, indeed, as a thrilled, roundabouted pilgrim, by primitive steamboat, to a mellow, medieval Albany'.

2

The days at the Mount, both that autumn, and the following summer, when James revisited it, had a great calm, a luxurious ease. Hostess and guest spent their mornings writing; Teddy Wharton smoked his cigars and came and went. Lunch was late; they motored afternoons and spent evenings by the fire, in talk and in jest. When Howard Sturgis was there they might as well have been at Qu'Acre or Lamb House. Edith Wharton had considerable 'style', and grace; she appreciated a good story and could tell her own stories very well; and she had a love of poetry even though her published verses are indifferently stiff and solemn. Her admiration for James was profound – he was becoming one of the largest figures in her life. And her account of his various remarks to her, about her work, convey a feeling of a certain sharpness on his part that may have been mitigated by his voice, and complete acceptance, on her part, of their barbed quality. On one occasion Teddy Wharton made some remark about 'Edith's new story' just published in *Scribner's*, and the Master's answer was prompt: 'Oh yes, my dear Edward, I've read the little work – of course I've read it. Admirable, admirable; a masterly little achievement.' And turning towards her,

Of course so accomplished a mistress of the art would not, without deliberate intention, have given the tale so curiously conventional a treatment. Though indeed, in the given case, no treatment *but* the conventional was possible; which might conceivably, my dear lady, on further consideration, have led you to reject your subject as – er – in itself a totally unsuitable one.

Mrs Wharton recognized in this the characteristic tendency of James, to begin with praise and then find himself 'overmastered by the need to speak the truth'. He had done the same to Miss Jewett in a letter in which he suddenly cast aside 'the mere twaddle of graciousness' and criticized her historical novel, *The Tory Lover*, as a falsified pastiche. So on another occasion, after praising *The Custom of the Country*, he burst forth to Mrs Wharton: 'But of course you know – as how should you, with your infernal keenness of perception, *not* know? – that in doing your tale you had under your hand a magnificent subject, which ought to have been your main theme, and that you used it as mere incident and then passed it by.' Mrs Wharton recorded still another instance of this kind of cushioned cruelty of criticism. She had written a tale in French for the *Revue des Deux Mondes*, and when someone spoke of this as 'remarkable', James came crashing in with, 'Remarkable – most remarkable! An altogether astonishing feat. I do congratulate you, my dear, on the way in which you've picked up every old worn-out literary phrase that's been lying about the streets of Paris, for the last twenty years and managed to pack them all into those few pages.' He then added, thoughtfully, 'a very creditable episode in her career. *But she must never do it again.*'

Small wonder Mrs Wharton found such comments 'withering', even though she joined in the laughter and spoke good-naturedly of 'our literary rough-and-tumble'. The sharpness of James's remarks, as she recorded them – so stark when compared with the tone of similar strictures made in letters to Mrs Humphry Ward, or some of the young writers – suggests that there existed between the Master and the lady novelist a directness, an openness and freedom – and truth – that gave to their friendship a rare quality of mutual 'ease'. This, at any rate, is what Mrs Wharton tries to suggest in her reminiscences. At the same time we may imagine that James's tone of voice could have softened the harshness of his Johnsonian dicta. Perhaps too, in remembering them, Mrs Wharton was recalling the 'message' in all its nakedness, and not the surrounding euphemisms.

3

Mrs Wharton would remember James's reading poetry by her fireplace in Lenox, remembered his taking up Emily Brontë's poems and 'with some far-away emotion' his eyes filled and in his rich flexible voice chanting

> Cold in the earth – and the deep snow piled above thee –
> Far, far removed, cold in the dreary grave!
> Have I forgot, my only Love, to love thee,
> Severed at last by Time's all-severing wave?

His reading she felt was 'an emanation of his inmost self, unaffected by fashion or elocutionary artifice'. On another evening, they began to quote Whitman. In his young manhood James had been sharply critical of old Walt; he had published an uncompromising review attacking his 'flashy imitation of ideas'. Recently he had mentioned this article to an old friend who threatened to dig it up: James's recantation was vigorous. The review had been, he said, 'a little atrocity'. Nothing would induce me to reveal the whereabouts of my disgrace, which I only recollect as deep and damning.' If it were to cross his path he would not look at it; wherever he encountered 'the abominations of my early innocence' he destroyed them. He had indeed made his peace with Whitman in the long years since the Civil War. Perhaps it was a result of his renewed vision of America, the touching of old emotions; or Whitman's homo-eroticism. At any rate 'his voice filled the hushed room like an organ adagio as he read from *The Song of Myself* and *When lilacs last in the dooryard bloomed* and *Out of the Cradle* which he crooned rather than read. We talked long that night of *Leaves of Grass*,' Mrs Wharton remembered, 'tossing back and forth to each other treasure after treasure.' At the end, the Master flung his hands upward, a characteristic gesture, and with eyes twinkling said: 'Oh yes, a great genius; undoubtedly a very great genius! Only one cannot help deploring his too-extensive acquaintance with the foreign languages.'

On another evening, when they had sat late on the terrace, there was some allusion to his Emmet cousins, at Salisbury. A member of the party said, 'Tell us about the Emmets – tell us all about them.' James began and suddenly he seemed to forget where he was, the place, the surrounding friends; he was lost in visions of his youth.

Ghostlike indeed at first, wavering and indistinct, they glimmered at us through a series of disconnected ejaculations, epithets, allusions, parenthetical rectifications and restatements, till not only our brains but the clear night itself seemed filled with a palpable fog; and then, suddenly, by some miracle of shifted lights and accumulated strokes, there they stood before us as they lived, drawn with a million filament-like lines.

It was 'a summoning to life of dead-and-gone Emmets and Temples, old lovelinesses, old follies, old failures, all long laid away and forgotten under old crumbling gravestones'. The artist in Edith Wharton responded warmly to the Master's sense of his personal past.

4

At Lenox, Henry James met Walter Berry whom he would see intermittently during the ensuing years, and would like – his conversation, his logical mind, his general enjoyment of life. Berry would be a peripheral friend of the two masters of the modern subjective novel – Marcel Proust in France and Henry James in England and America; and he was already, and would continue to be, one of the closest of Edith Wharton's friends. James corresponded with him playfully, amusedly, ironically, and the handful of letters printed when Mrs Wharton was still alive, disguised her presence in them, although allusions to 'the Lady of L –' could hardly escape the notice of those who knew her. She is also 'the Princesse Lointaine' and 'the Angel of Devastation' in these letters; and there are allusions to the rue de Varenne where she later lived and the 'sarabandistes' of that *rue*, as James came to call Mrs Wharton's attendant friends. One postscript has contributed to the legend that Walter Berry was Edith Wharton's lover, for James wrote to Berry 'it adds to my joy *de vous savoir* in such bowers of bliss, abysses of interest, labyrinths of history – soft sheets generally *quoi*'. This allusion need not be read too literally. In private James found Berry very much a man of the world and a familiar cosmopolite figure – one of the characters he had invented. Berry came out of old New York – his full name was Walter Van Rensselaer Berry. He was in his forties when James met him. Born in Paris, educated at Harvard, admitted to the bar, he was at one time president of the American Chamber of Commerce in Paris, and practised as an international lawyer. Mrs Wharton has described how Berry filled an intellectual void in her life and he motored with her in many parts of Europe in later years. There survive joint postcards, written by them to James during their travels. Of Mrs Wharton's love for Berry we know a great deal: of Berry, the confirmed bachelor said to have been interested in Mrs Wharton's intellect, and in young dancers at the Folies (as one who knew him said) we know perhaps less. He was handsome, tall, a bit stiff, a bit dry – so some saw him – deeply committed to the cause of France against Germany. Percy Lubbock would describe Berry's effect on Mrs Wharton's art as nothing less than disastrous; Nicky Mariano, Bernard Berenson's companion, would remember how radiant Mrs Wharton was in Berry's presence. But all this was of a later time. In James's letters to Mrs Wharton he is 'the brave Berry' and James speaks of him as having 'greatly endeared himself to me' with his mixture of his 'gifts and his unhappinesses', his alertness, and his melancholy. He writes on occasion, 'I hope you've not wanted for the sight of Walter Berry.'

From Lenox, Edith Wharton wrote to Minnie Bourget in France of the visit of her distinguished guest. The self-effacing Minnie responded with words that showed how deeply the Bourgets loved Henry James. 'Nobody,' wrote Minnie in Gallic-tinged English,

who has not actually lived with him will ever completely appreciate this *great artist*, the wonderful companion, the charm of whom resides in that perfect simplicity and adaptation of everyday life with the ever-springing source of comprehension and keen sensitiveness. There are early Italian days in my memory when I became for ever attached to what I must call his genius, in an antique sense of that word.

Minnie also spoke of Mrs Wharton's having discovered 'the compatriot' in James – 'he loves his country, perhaps even when he does not know himself to what extent'.

'I am immensely touched,' James wrote to Mrs Wharton when she sent him this letter. But the Bourgets didn't *really* know him, he added. He did not comment on Minnie's observations concerning his patriotism.

84

The Medusa Face

ONE Sunday in Cambridge he went in search of the Fresh Pond of of his personal past. In his youth, when Howells was also young and learning to edit the *Atlantic*, the two used to walk beside the pond and speak of the novels they wanted to write and what a novel should be. He found the muses of the place had fled, 'the little nestling lake had ceased to nestle'. Still, James remarked that he could 'at this day, on printed, on almost faded pages, give chapter and verse for the effect, audible on the Sunday afternoons' of those Fresh Pond muses. Which was to say that he and Howells had not simply talked; certain of their early writings had issued from these promenades. A charming Country Club now stood on the ground towards Watertown, all verandahs and golf-links, 'all tea and ices and self-consciousness'. And there was a great deal of highway 'the arms of carnivorous giants' across the rural scenery. The old haunt, 'desecrated and destroyed', could no longer be a place for 'shared literary secrets'. Henry James spoke of 'angrily missing' among the ruins the atmosphere he had gone to recover – 'some echo of youth, the titles of tales, the communities of friendship, the sympathies and patiences, in fine, of dear W.D.H.' With the tact and reticence of the time he reduced Howells to his initials in *The American Scene* since the latter still lived, and Henry was determined to stay with impressions and not go 'smash on the rock of autobiography'.

I

He reserved, however, one stroll in Cambridge for a special time. It would have to be a 'favouring hour', when he was in the right mood, when he could face his long-dead personal past that lived in him alone. The moment came one evening in November, some time after his return from Lenox. He set out on foot. There was a wintry pink in the west, the special shade of late autumn 'fading into a heartless prettiness of grey' – heartless because it silhouetted in gaunt and grim tracery the bare trees of November. James walked past Longfellow's house, admiring its ample style and its symmetry, thinking of it before it had become a tourist-haunted spot, when he used to visit the poet and talk of his travels. He walked past high, square, sad, and silent Elmwood, and lingered around it, remembering his best-loved Cambridge friend, James Russell Lowell, whom he mentions also only by initials – remarking it was difficult to put him into the past tense. The passage in *The American Scene* describing this walk is charged with autobiographical feeling even if it avoids autobiographical reminiscence. He thinks of Lowell as 'the very genius of the spot'. He had been a 'rustic'; James had often said this, and he said it now with gentle words. Lowell had been 'without provision, whether of poetry or of prose, against the picture of proportion and relations overwhelmingly readjusted'. Even more than Longfellow, however, Lowell had given Cambridge its literary cachet. And James could not say whether in this new time Harvard, looking 'very hard at blue horizons of possibility, across the high table-land of her future' could offer as much as Lowell had offered when James visited his classroom. 'The light of literary desire is not perceptible in her eye' – this was James's verdict on the new Harvard. Lowell had had a perhaps humorous thesis that 'Cambridge, Mass., was, taken altogether, the most inwardly civilized, most intimately humane, among the haunts of men'. James's friends had committed themselves to cultivating the *genius loci*.

His lonely walk was carefully planned. Presently he was making his way among the graves in the Cambridge Cemetery, slowly and deliberately, until he came to the James family plot, on its little ridge – an 'unspeakable group of graves'. There were four then – those of his mother, his father and his sister Alice, and near by that of one of William's children who had died young. When he had last visited America, James had come here (in December 1882) in heavy snow to see his father's newly dug grave, and had read aloud William's letter of farewell.

It seemed to James as if he had returned to America precisely for this vision and for this moment. So he said, at any rate, in the moving words he scribbled in a notebook some weeks later when he was in California – 'I seemed then to know why I had done this; I seemed then to know why I had *come* – and to feel how not to have come would have been miserably, horribly, to miss it. It made everything right – it made everything priceless.' The moon was rising, early, white, young and seemed reflected in the white face of the great empty stadium where a few days before he had witnessed the Harvard–Dartmouth game and 'the capacity of the American public for momentary gregarious emphasis'. The stadium formed the boundaries of Soldiers' Field that 'stared over to me, through the clear twilight, from across the Charles'. James carefully took in the scene, noting the quality of the air, the stillness, the waning light. The place 'bristled with merciless memories'. Turning back to look at the graves, he felt the recognition, stillness, the strangeness, the pity, the sanctity and the terror, the breath-catching passion, and the divine relief of tears'.

Through his tears he read the words from Dante on the little marble urn of his sister's ashes, which William had had carved in Florence: *ed essa da martiro e da essilio venne a questa pace*. The line 'took me so at the throat by its penetrating *rightness*'. It was as if he had sunk on his knees before the symbols of family past and family history 'in a kind of anguish of gratitude before something for which one had waited with a long, deep *ache*'.

James stood there a long time; he looked again across the Charles. It was the old Cambridge – and he had moved past ghosts of friendship to reach ghosts of family. This was 'the cold Medusa-face of life'. He thought of 'all the life *lived* on every side'. He remembered 'the old thinner New England air and more meagre New England scheme'. 'But why do I write of the all unutterable and the all abysmal?' he asked himself as he sat with these autumn memories beside the Pacific. 'Why does my pen not drop from my hand on approaching the infinite pity and tragedy of all the past? It does, poor heipless pen, with what it meets of the ineffable.' And he exclaimed – 'Oh, strange little intensities of history, of ineffaceability; oh delicate little odd links in the long chain, kept unbroken for the fingers of one's tenderest touch! Sanctities, pieties, treasures, abysses! ... Basta, basta!'

85

City of Conversation

BETWEEN the time of his visit to Lenox and his travels at the beginning of 1905, Henry James went through 'an interminable and abysmal siege of American dentistry'. This lasted during the greater part of November and December, 'a monument of technical art but a bottomless gulf of physical and financial ruin'. He slipped away from Boston to New York, however, in November to keep his promise to Colonel Harvey; the dinner, long-planned, was a modest one in spite of the publicity-loving colonel – only thirty guests and not at Delmonico's, but at the Metropolitan Club. Mark Twain, Booth Tarkington, G. W. Smalley, Hamlin Garland, and the journalist Arthur Brisbane, were among the guests. The novelist sat between Mrs Harvey and Mrs Cornelius Vanderbilt. His dental difficulties deprived him of full enjoyment of the food; moreover he disliked Harvey's ostentation, mentioning in particular the floral decorations which cost $500. After Christmas, when the Boston dentist released him, he returned to New York, first staying at Mrs Cadwalader Jones's, at 21 East Eleventh Street, in that part of the city most crowded with boyhood memories. He moved uptown after the new year to visit at Mrs Wharton's flat, 884 Park Avenue – 'a bonbonnière of the last daintiness naturally,' he told Howard Sturgis, 'but we were more compressed than at Lenox and Teddy more sandwiched between, and we gave a little more on each other's nerves, I think, and there was less of the Lenox looseness.' Still, James added, 'she was charming, kind, and ingenious, and taste and tone and the finest discriminations, ironies, and draperies mantelled us about'. After eight days uptown he returned with relief downtown to Mrs Jones's in the Village, just before going to Washington where he had been invited to stay with Henry Adams and to attend a dinner in his honour to be given by the Secretary of State, John Hay. From this time on he made Minnie Jones's place on East Eleventh Street his headquarters, in his comings and goings in Manhattan. She provided privacy and quiet, and her daughter Beatrix showered attention on him. He felt himself 'half-killed with kindness'. Mrs Jones had a pet name for James out of a French farce by Labiche – Célimare – perhaps because the central character *le bien aimé* inspires universal affection (he carries on love affairs with two ladies whose husbands also dote on him, and manages to keep their love when he marries a young woman half his age). James was not capable of the comedy – Célimare's prodigalities of *amour* – but he seems to have been the centre at Mrs Jones's of an adoring circle.

En route to Washington, the novelist stopped in Philadelphia to see his old friend Mrs Wister, Fanny Kemble's daughter, and to deliver the first of what would prove to be a series of lectures – or as one critic who watched him closely described them, 'oral essays'.

He had finally decided to ask $250 as his fee for speaking to a ladies' group in Boston; the honorarium was designed to discourage them. It did; but the Contemporary Club of Philadelphia was not easily discouraged, and had the money for such occasions. James read a lecture on *The Lesson of Balzac*. More than one hundred elegantly dressed ladies and gentlemen stood during the lecture which was attended, said the press, by the most distinguished representatives of letters, art, the learned professions, and public life in Philadelphia. James read his paper without a trace of embarrassment, holding the loose sheets in one hand and keeping the other in his pocket 'save', said the newspaper, 'where two or three times there came an involuntary gesture'. There was no emphasis; the delivery was bland. Agnes Repplier, the cultural leader of Philadelphia, well known for her familiar essays, presided with style and charm. And James, who had suffered stage fright, was elated. 'A dazzling success,' Célimare reported to his New York circle, 'a huge concourse, five or six hundred folk, a vast hall, and perfect brazen assurance and audibility on Célimare's part. *Il s'est révélé conférencier*.' The novelist was put up at the Rittenhouse Club by Sargent's friend, the eminent surgeon Dr J. William White, who supported James before the ordeal and gave him a triumphant supper afterwards. Carey Thomas, president of Bryn Mawr, had also invited James, offering him the standard $50 given to lecturers. James replied he did not have anything suitable for young girls but then, having tasted triumph, he added, 'to be lucid, the honorarium you offer is not sufficient'. He reduced his fee, however, to $200 and agreed to double back from Washington to speak at the college before proceeding south.

I

Washington seemed mild and soft. Henry James was pleasantly surprised. He remembered it from his visit in 1882 as a gossipy but masculine town; now the women dominated the social scene while the men legislated – a town devoid of industry or trade, indeed of any distinctive economic life. But then he had known it in the days when it was still a rather nude capital, with the dome and the shaft presiding over much parochialism, and the President visiting in various houses as if he were a local – rather than a national – celebrity. James had encountered President Chester Arthur in a private home during his former visit and even put the encounter into one of his stories. This time everything was on a much grander scale. He stayed with Henry Adams in his big house on Lafayette Square, next to Adams's bosom friend, Secretary of State Hay, with whom James shared common memories of Miss Woolson. As fellow-guest, James found at Adam's his friend of his youth, John La Farge. Old circles, old familiarities were briefly re-established. As in 1882, Adams's house was a hotbed of Washington gossip; but James missed Clover Adams, who had committed suicide in the 1880s. She had always been a lively companion. Adams seldom spoke of her; and James hesitated to ask him about her tomb for which Augustus Saint-Gaudens had carved a much-talked-of mourning figure. In his prolonged grief and shock Adams had left to John La Farge and Saint-Gaudens most of the artistic decisions. At lunch at Adams's one day James whispered to Mrs Winthrop Chanler that the one thing in Washington he wanted to see was this statue in Rock Creek Cemetery, but he felt he could not make the wish known to Adams. Mrs Chanler took him there in her brougham immediately after lunch. It was a mild wintry day and the trees around the tomb had snow on their boughs. James stood uncovered for a long time before the bronze symbolic figure, with its draperies shrouding its head. 'He seemed deeply moved.' Marion 'Clover' Hooper, whom he had known long before she married Adams, had been a 'Voltaire in petticoats' to him; she belonged to a remote past. Mrs Chanler remembered that on their return to Lafayette Square James talked of Clover's career as a Washington hostess, and her command of the capital's social strategies. There had always been good talk at Clover's table – indeed James had ever after that visit spoken of Washington as a 'city of conversation'.

2

In 1882, although he was the author of the much-discussed *Portrait of a Lady*, Henry James had received no official recognition during his Washington visit, nor had he expected it. Washington had then hardly discovered the arts, save those of architecture and monuments. In January of 1905, thanks to the Secretary of State, and the artistic entourage at Adams's, James was welcomed as a literary Master, so that even President Theodore Roosevelt – who disliked and had even denounced the novelist as 'effete' and 'a miserable little snob' – opened the White House to him. Henry James had quite as low an opinion of Roosevelt. He considered him 'a dangerous and ominous jingo'. The amenities were observed to the last letter of the alphabet, and the novelist was flattered. With his Napoleonic propensities, he was fascinated by power – particularly power in the American style.

'Theodore Rex,' the gentle Célimare informed East Eleventh Street, 'is a really extraordinary creature for native intensity, veracity, and *bonhomie* – he plays his part with the best will in the world and I recognize his amusing likeability.' To William James he wrote that the President 'did me the honour to cause me to be placed' – the precision of this statement, the monarchical 'cause' could not have been lost on William – 'at his table (of eight) and on the right of the lady at *his* right ... It was very curious and interesting ... The President is distinctly tending – or trying – to make a "court".' James sounded less impressed in his report to Edith Wharton.

I went to Court the other night, for the Diplomatic Reception, and he did me the honour, to put me at his table and almost beside him – whereby I got a rich impression of him, and of his being, verily, a wonderful little machine : destined to be overstrained perhaps, but not as yet, truly, betraying the least creak. It functions astonishingly, and is quite exciting to see. But it's really like something behind a great plate-glass window on Broadway.

As for Washington itself, it was 'oddly ambiguous'. It seemed to James to sit 'for ever saying to your private ear, from every door and window, as you pass "I am nothing, I am nothing, nothing!" and whose charm, interest, amiability, irresistibility, you are yet perpetually making calls to commemorate and insist upon'. It had a kind of 'spacious vacancy'. Secretary Hay gave an impressive dinner for James; so did his old friend Ambassador Jusserand. He lunched with Senator Henry Cabot Lodge. And then, at the invitation of Charles McKim, he went with La Farge and Saint-Gaudens to a dinner of the American Institute of Architects at which official and artistic Washington was present in force. The dinner was 'a big success and beautifully done – but the Eagle screamed in the speeches and I didn't know that that fowl was still (after all these years and improvements,) *permitted* to do. It was werry werry quaint and queer – but so is *everything, sans exception*, and the sensitive Célimare absorbs it at every pore.'

President Roosevelt did not forget Henry James. Some years after the death of John Hay he spoke of the latter as 'not a great secretary of state'. Hay's close intimacy with Henry James and Henry Adams – 'charming men but exceedingly undesirable companions for any man not of a strong nature – and the tone of satirical cynicism which they admired ... marked that phase of his character which so impaired his usefulness as a public man'.

To Henry James, Roosevelt had been 'the mere monstrous embodiment of unprecedented and resounding noise'.

3

James spent eight days in Washington, enjoying his role of literary lion, but was bewildered when Admiral Dewey, hero of Manila, left his card. A call from a naval personality seemed the last thing he expected; perhaps it was a case simply of one celebrity paying respects to another. If James was amused by the glitter of Roosevelt's Washington it left him with no illusions. 'To *live* here,' he wrote to Mrs William James, 'would be death and madness –' and doubtless, he added, one would pay calls forever 'in one's delirium'. He found Washington's size 'dreary' as of 'a great sunny void furnished only with a drizzle of paste-board'. He returned to his civilized friends in Philadelphia, and enjoyed his night at Bryn Mawr. He was put up at the Deanery; the audience of young women was enchanted by James's charm and delicacy. James found the occasion so felicitous that he promised to return as Commencement speaker in the spring.

He spent several days in Philadelphia, visiting with the Whites and Mrs Wister, and seeing something of Dr J. Weir Mitchell, the medical-novelist, who was perhaps a little sensitive because James refused to take him seriously as a writer, treating him with respect but apparently with the coolness of a professional addressing an amateur. Mitchell was a friend of Mrs Wharton and was credited with having started her on her career as a writer (prescribing it as a kind of 'occupational therapy'). James found Philadelphia to be, after Washington, a city of culture and refinement; but even more a city which was a 'society' in the sense of having 'human groups that discriminate in their own favour'; he liked its serenity, the fact that it was 'settled and confirmed and content'. In that sense New York was 'not a society at all', and Chicago, he would later judge, was still less. Neither had been able to recognize and maintain its identity. If Boston, as it was said, was 'a state of mind', Philadelphia was a 'state of consanguinity'. And James clearly indicated what he meant when he used the word 'society' – he meant 'the number of organic social relations' it represented. Philadelphia in 1905 satisfied James more than other cities 'of all goodly villages, the very good-liest, probably in the world; the very largest, and flattest, and smoothest, the most rounded and complete'. His less official view was that Philadelphia was 'kind, plenitudinous, promiscuous'.

We can obtain a glimpse of James through the eyes of a Canadian, the distinguished Dr George Robert Parkin, who happened to be visiting Dr S. Weir Mitchell in Walnut Street during the week James was in Philadelphia. A staunch imperialist, he had been principal of Upper Canada College and was now the organizing secretary of the Rhodes Scholarships. He was taken by his host on a round of visits and in one residence found himself introduced to a 'Mr James'. Mr James, not realizing Parkin's involvement, listened as the idea for the Rhodes scholarships was explained and promptly denounced it as 'deplorable'. What, the Master asked, in his most law-giving manner 'does Oxford want of men from Nebraska and Canada?' His next logical step was to inquire, 'Why should we all be asked to fall down and glorify Rhodes?' Dr Parkin defended his mission, unaware who was his interlocutor. 'He was and is an absolute surprise to me. I had always thought of him as an alert, versatile man. In looks and talk he seems much more like a heavy, opinionated, self-satisfied English businessman of exceedingly contracted views. But the whole affair was too absurd.' However, facing Henry James at dinner at Dr Mitchell's, Parkin discovered that he could be 'quite different from yesterday'. At the dinner, James, in a mood of persiflage, began 'in some absurd connection' to explain how he would elope with his hostess; the elaborateness of his plan, as he worked it out seems quite to have charmed away the Canadian's ruffled feelings. 'We got on capitally,' he wrote.

In the midst of these sociabilities, a series of minor difficulties suddenly developed. James's dental siege apparently wasn't over; an upper front tooth came out, 'and I look like a "fright" but I am cynical, indifferent, desperate – I don't mind it,' he told William. And then, when he would have sought local dental help, snow came, more than a foot; deep drifts were under his window at Mrs Wister's 'and you may therefore imagine the temperature of the room I write in ... The trolleys don't run, I can't get to the station; high drifts and a polar hurricane bar the way.' He restlessly waited in his 'fatally (and oh so "complacently"!) uncomfortable house'. Philadelphia now seemed a 'fearsome ordeal'. He took train for Richmond – 'the southern sun, for which I fairly sicken, will re-create me'. A night in the Pullman shook his faith still more. There was snow at Richmond and 'the ugliness appals'. He put up at the Jefferson Hotel, discovered that he had run out of linen and shirts, and waited for his laundry to be done before going on to visit the George Vanderbilts in North Carolina. While here he received word that he had been elected to the newly founded American Academy of Arts and Letters. On 3 February, his laundry done, and feeling thoroughly rested, he set out for Biltmore, the palatial Vanderbilt home. There was a new, driving snowstorm; but he was confident that he would be expensively sheltered from it.

4

He was sitting in front of a large picture window – 'a hideous plate-glass window like the door of an ice-house'. It had no curtains, no shutters, no blinds; north light shone cold and intense, reflected from a vastness of snow. His room was icy. He had gout in his left foot. When he rang the bell for a servant none came. He found himself hobbling and hopping down long corridors to a remote bathroom to fetch hot water. In a moment of sociability and curiosity he had accepted the invitation to stop en route in the fantastic Biltmore – 'the chateau of Biltmore' he called it – built by George Vanderbilt, culture-seeking youngest son of the railroader. The place was 'impractically spacious'. His room was 'a glacial phantasy'. He estimated it to be half a mile from the 'mile-long library'. 'We measure by leagues and we sit in Cathedrals,' he wrote to Mrs Cadwalader Jones.

He had arrived at the dream castle in the North Carolina mountains on 3 February 1905, from Richmond in the midst of a snowstorm. The land was buried, bleak, dreary. The first thing that happened was this sudden flare-up of his gout. He needed bran footbaths; he was taking pills. He was minus a front tooth. In an agony of pain he hopped about – alternating between anger and despair, furious at the circumstance that had brought him into deeper cold than any he had fled, 'helpless snow-congested New York like a huge baffled machine roaring at a standstill *did* simply (as a place of convenience and *agrément*) appal me'. Biltmore appalled him no less; his gout brought him to a standstill. He was trapped in a chateau set 2,500 feet in the air – the Château de Blois enlarged and glorified. 'Roll three or four Rothschild houses into one, surround them with a principality of mountain, lake and forest, 200,000 acres, surround *that* with vast states of niggery desolation and make it impossible, through distance and time, to get anyone to stay with you, and you have the bloated Biltmore.' The place was the *gageure* of 'an imperfectly aesthetic young billionaire'. Magnificent, imposing 'and utterly unaddressed to any possible arrangement of life, or state of society'.

After the first pain subsided, and his foot was reduced to manageable proportions, Henry James took in his surroundings with less violence of feeling, but with continuing bewilderment. He would later ironically call Biltmore 'a castle of enchantment'. In *The American Scene* he saluted the will, purpose, patience, knowledge, involved in creating a composite castle-cathedral in a mountain wilderness. He put in the better part of a week there. 'There are five or six different tapestried cathedrals (of size) to sit in, and 36 empty guest rooms – wondrously appointed – besides the small, chill (with a vast glacial window) retreat in the "bachelor wing" to which I am relegated.' Moreover 'the climate stalks about in the marble halls in default of guests'. His stay was lonely. There were a Mrs Hunt of Washington, and a British military personage, Sir Thomas Fraser, as fellow-guests. He had come at the wrong season.

When he was able to put a normal shoe on his gouty foot at the week-end, he made the night-long journey to Charleston. Owen Wister met him. After that he went to Palm Beach where the subtropical landscape, such as he had never seen before, the green palms, the flaming hibiscus, the oranges and grapefruit, the general softness, restored him to a more comfortable state of mind.

86

The Blighted Invalid

HENRY JAMES'S visit to the South was brief: the few days at Richmond, in the snow, the pleasant interlude at Charleston, with Owen Wister as his guide, a glance at Jacksonville; then the stay in Palm Beach, and three days at St Augustine where he went to see his brother Roberston's wife and their daughter Mary, later Mrs Vaux. Four decades had elapsed since the Civil War: but the old muffled ache, the anguish of fratricidal struggle remained. James looked upon the South with time-wearied eyes – also with eyes that had seen the ravages of history in Europe. The hurts and wounds, the stirred feelings of defeats and victories, had shrunk now to paper mementoes, hollow-eyed statues and renovated ruins. In Charleston, visiting an old cemetery, he seems to have walked with memories of Miss Woolson. An allusion to Venice, in the midst of his description of the place, suggests that he remembered Fenimore's *Rodman the Keeper*; and then she had talked to him of these very places – for she had lived in the post-bellum South and had been its modest fictional historian. He strolled in an old cemetery, by the lagoon, and he remembered 'the golden afternoon, the low, silvery, seaward horizon, as of wide, sleepy, game-haunted inlets and reed-smothered banks, possible site of some Venice that had never mustered the luxury, in the mild air, of shrub and plant and blossom that the pale North can but distantly envy'. He found in this place a certain 'proud humility'.

The South was a 'society still shut up in a world smaller than what one might suppose its true desire, to say nothing of its true desert'. He looked at Fort Sumter, and the other forts at Charleston, remembering the far-off historical moment: the forts in the twinkling blue sea seemed not like military bastions but simply vague marine flowers. Owen Wister, standing beside him, remarked, 'I never at Charleston look out to the old betrayed Forts without feeling my heart harden again to steel.' Wister's was perhaps not the most authoritative voice, even though he lived in the South and felt its sadness and sorrow; for he wrote about the West and had had a boyhood abroad. His grandfather, however, had been a famous slave-owner and his grandmother had been James's old friend, Fanny Kemble, who had written an anti-slavery book, describing her life on a Georgia plantation. In the Richmond Confederate museum, where James looked at framed letters, orders, autographs, tatters of paper currency, together with faded portraits, emblems of woe and glory, he found another kind of witness. He got into conversation with a young Southern farmer who had come to the city for the day, and was reliving the war between the States. James paid close attention to his southern accent, and followed him about as he pointed out certain relics preserved also in his family. He seemed thoroughly familiar with his father's exploits; he related a war adventure 'which comprised a desperate evasion of capture, or worse, by the lucky smashing of the skull of a Union soldier'. James 'complimented him on his exact knowledge of these old, unhappy, far-off things', and received in return the candid remark, 'Oh, I should be ready to do them all over again myself.' Then with a smile, the younger farmer added, 'That's the kind of Southerner I am.' James 'allowed that he was a capital kind of Southerner, and we afterwards walked together to the Public Library, where, on our final parting, I could but thank him again for being so much the kind of Southerner I had wanted'. He wouldn't hurt a Northern fly – as Northern; but his consciousness James felt 'would have been poor and unfurnished without this cool platonic passion'. James reflected too that though he wouldn't hurt a Northern fly, there were things – for they had talked of the blacks – that 'all fair, engaging, smiling, as he stood there, he would have done to a Southern Negro'.

The blacks in the South struck James as 'ragged and rudimentary', unlike Northern Negroes he had known; and he recognized that there was no way to preach 'sweet reasonableness' to the South about them. The novelist had been reading W. E. B. Du Bois' *The Souls of Black Folk* which he characterized as the only Southern book of any distinction that he had ever read. He wondered at the way in which the Confederate world had pinned everything on the institution of slavery. Deprived of this, a great vacuity remained. He saw the South as in an eternal false position –

condemned as she was to institutions, condemned to a state of temper, of exasperation and depression, a horrid heritage she had never consciously invited, that bound up her life with a hundred mistakes and make-believes, suppressions and prevarications, things that really all named themselves in the noted provincialism.

At the end he imaged the South as 'a figure somehow blighted or stricken, discomfortable, impossible seated in an invalid-chair, and yet fixing one with strange eyes that were half a defiance and half a deprecation of one's noticing and much more of one's referring to, any abnormal sign'.

2

Part of his small 'historic whiff' he got by looking out of 'the Pullmans that are like rushing hotels and the hotels that are like stationary Pullmans'. In Palm Beach he put up at the Breakers, enjoying the hotel luxuries and concluding that one might live in the soft climate 'as in a void furnished at the most with velvet air'. One might even live in Florida with an idea, 'if you are content that your idea shall consist of grapefruit and oranges'. He enjoyed the sea and the air; he liked the little golden fruit-ranches, but he shrank from the human picture – 'decent, gregarious, and moneyed, but overwhelmingly monotonous and on the whole pretty ugly', and 'unacquainted with the rudiments of tone or indeed with any human utterance'. In St Augustine, wearing a recently purchased derby too large for his head, he stayed at the hotel Ponce de Leon, and wrote to his brother William of his pleasure in meeting his niece Mary, 'very matured and very agreeable', and 'highly susceptible, I think, of culture'. They went sightseeing together to look at the little Spanish fort and the old Spanish cathedral, 'these poor little scraps of Florida's antiquity so meagre and vague'. But his true impression of Florida was conveyed to the matron in whom he was now confiding most, Mrs Cadwalader Jones:

Florida is a fearful fraud – a ton of dreary jungle and swamp and misery of flat forest monotony to an ounce or two of little coast perching-place – a few feet wide between the jungle and the sea. Nine-tenths of this meagre margin are the areas of the hotels – the remaining tenth is the beauties of nature and the little walk of the bamboozled tourist. It's really *mauvaise plaisanterie*.

Ten days sufficed for his sole venture into the South. He turned North again, for word of his Philadelphia performance had spread and he now knew he could pay his way with 'The Lesson of Balzac'. He was due in St Louis, Chicago, South Bend, Indianapolis, San Francisco. Other places beckoned. Indianapolis, thanks to Booth Tarkington, had arranged a double-audience of two cultural organizations with the result that he was offered $400 and could have had $500.

With a grand gesture he accepted the lower sum, murmuring 'bloated Indianapolis!' He wrote to Edmund Gosse: 'If I could come back here to abide I think I should really be able to abide in (relative) affluence: one can, on the spot, make so much more money – or at least I might.' He added: 'But I would rather live a beggar at Lamb House – and it's to that I shall return. Let my biographer, however, recalled the solid sacrifice I shall have made.'

87

A Western Journey

HENRY JAMES had chosen to lecture to his fellow-Americans on – of all subjects – 'The Lesson of Balzac'. He talked to them as if they were novelists like himself. He did them this honour, even though America was addicted then to 'molasses fiction' as critics used to say. *The Golden Bowl* consorted in the bookshops with the current best-sellers – *The Little Shepherd of Kingdom Come, Mrs Wiggs of the Cabbage Patch, Rebecca of Sunnybrook Farm*. James was not concerned with what the public might want. He had always argued (even in his theatre days) that the artist must try to lead – and go his own way. He chose to speak out of the full life of his art. He had no illusions as to why men and women – and especially women – came in such numbers to hear him. He was aware that they came to see the lecturer rather than hear the lecture. He had been a name so long in America; now they could look upon his face and form. Everywhere people still remembered *Daisy Miller*. Her spirit went marching on even though a quarter of a century had elapsed since he had captured her stylish figure in the hotel corridors at Vevey. One waggish Chicago reporter, however, with more literary sense than most, wrote his account of the novelist's arrival as if James were Lambert Strether casting a weary eye on 'the bleak parks, the jumbled gray masses of tenements and the engulfing avenues of warehouses and freight sheds'. He imitated James's technique of putting the reader into the character's angle-of-vision:

Mr James gave himself up to the little dreary pictures of Chicago life, which framed themselves on either hand in the square of cab door glass. It came home to him in the orthodox Jamesian manner that all he had heard of Chicago was stockyards and boards of trade and dirt and coarse fearful exploits in the getting of money.

It was flattering to be reported in one's own style. But James paid little heed to the chattering press. Most of the newspapers were not quite as caressing. They spoke of James as 'a novelist of the aristocracy', a condescending expatriate who talked of 'the advance of civilization' in America as if he were still in the world of Fenimore Cooper. Americans did not seem to want to be described as still advancing. An Indiana editor angrily rejoined that if there was an 'advance' it surely could not have been stimulated by reading Mr James's 'inane' fictions.

I

James left Boston on 4 March 1905 and travelled for forty hours across great tracts of snow to the banks of the Mississippi – to St Louis. 'Oh the dreariness of getting here.' He had covered a thousand miles – 'a single boundless empty platitude'. The middle west was friendly but 'featureless', and 'the ugliness, the absence of any charm, is like a permanent plague – chronic and miserable'. St Louis was 'a vast grey, smoky, extraordinary *bourgeois* place' and 'as languid and dreamy as the possession of coal-smoke and skyscrapers will permit'. A soft gentle rain fell most of the time he was there. He read 'The Lesson of Balzac' before the Contemporary Club of St Louis on 7 March. There was first a long stifling dinner; and before that he had stood in line shaking anonymous hands. He felt depleted from the start. He did not like to meet people *en masse*. He had a feeling as he read his lecture that it was 'too special, too literary, too critical'. But the audience was enthusiastic; and he also experienced a sense of embarrassment when, *coram publico*, the chairman handed him the cheque of payment – almost before he had said the last word. Business was distinctly business in America. People smothered him with hospitality. He went to lunch at the 'Noonday Club' and to a reception held in his honour at the University Club of St Louis. The reception was to be without his making any speech, but he found himself seated at a large table with some forty club members around him, relaxed and eager for literary gossip. The occasion resulted in one of those rare documents in which we catch the aphoristic flavour of James's talk; a minute of the occasion, written afterwards by a lawyer, in question and answer form.

Among the questions James handled, with delicacy and tact, were some relating to the work of Mrs Humphry Ward and whether she could be compared with George Eliot. James carefully replied, 'George Eliot was a great woman. I have the profoundest respect for the cleverness of Mrs Humphry Ward.' Someone asked what Matthew Arnold had thought of his niece Mrs Ward's work. James said that Arnold's reply to this question used to be that if any Arnold could have written a novel 'I would have done it long ago'. He was asked if he had ever met Ruskin. He said he had found him 'un-happy' and also 'despondent and sentimental'. Asked who was the most agreeable Englishman he had ever known, James named Sir Leslie Stephen, 'a purely literary man of the very best type, an ideal literary man; and no one could know him without feeling a warm affection for him'. Gladstone, James said, 'qualified too much' but his speeches 'sounded grandly', his voice was delightful and his manner imposing. Oscar Wilde he called 'one of those Irish adven-turers who had something of the Roman character – able but false'. He considered Whistler 'a much more interesting man' and told some Whistler–Wilde stories. He said that Wilde had returned to 'the abominable life he had been leading' as soon as he got out of prison and his death was 'miserable'.

One other matter was discussed, a novel close to the mid-westerners. This was *Ben Hur* by Indiana's Lew Wallace. James said he could not account for its success 'except that there are multitudes of people who have little taste; or upon the ground that religious sentiment is more prevalent here than elsewhere'.

2

In Chicago he stayed with Higginson cousins at Winnetka, and later at the University Club. From here he swung over to Notre Dame where he spoke to two Catholic groups in one day; then he returned to Chicago and went to Indianapolis, where he spoke before the massed culture-groups.

We get glimpses of James in Chicago. One day he returned from a luncheon engagement on the far south side by way of a suburban train, along the wintry shore of the Lake, accompanied by Robert Herrick, the Chicago novelist. They rode through 'the smudged purlieus of the untidy city into the black gloom of the Loop'. James sits huddled on the dingy bench of the suburban car, draped in the loose folds of his mackintosh, his hands clasped about his 'baggy' umbrella, 'his face haggard under the shuttling blows of the Chicago panorama'. 'What monstrous ugliness!' he murmurs in a tone of pure physical anguish. (Three years later, an English diarist would record that James, recalling this trip, spoke of 'ugliness, ugliness' – 'he repeated it in a kind of groan!' On the other hand he said it was interesting to meet men in America 'who had never thought of themselves as belonging to any class – a thing impossible in feudal Europe'.)

In Chicago he visited the studio of the sculptor Lorado Taft; and he dined at Hamlin Garland's studio. Garland, novelist of the 'middle border' and friend of Howells, brought together some of the local literary and artistic folk. He went to the University Club to pick up James, and noted, when the novelist came down the elevator, how 'worn and haggard' he looked. 'His derby was too large for him, his vest being a little awry and his collar was a trifle wilted, but his face was kindly and his greeting warm. He met the people at the studio with entire friendliness but with only an abstract interest so far as most of them were concerned.' Among them was Henry Blake Fuller, the Chicago novelist. One gets the impression from Garland's notations that James was depressed and dissociated. 'He had forgotten many of his books and spoke of them rather vaguely as though they represented another phase on various planes of his life. He has lost his enthusiasm but still has his intellectual interests. He is going on now out of sheer momentum.' What these diary notes tell us is that James was exhausted – and bored.

3

'The Lesson of Balzac' was decidedly not the lecture of a man who had lost his enthusiasm; and apparently James's delivery of it was an admirable piece of conversational reading. Edna Kenton, a magazine writer who would spend a lifetime reading James, remembered him as massive and clear-eyed on the Chicago platform, speaking with a total absence of oratorical effect, in a voice filled with subtle tones. Van Wyck Brooks, who heard James that spring at Harvard, recalled his voice rolling 'like an organ through a hall that could scarcely contain the aura of his presence'. One listener who heard the novelist in Brooklyn wrote that if James's sentences were long they were perfectly clear and 'the average high school boy of today would have been able to grasp all that he said'. This listener found a dry shrewd humour in the lecture; James's speech was 'that of a sincere man with something to say, and he says it delightfully'. The listener found also 'scarcely a trace of English accent despite the fact that he was born in New York and has lived twenty years or more in England'.

James read his lecture before the assorted audiences quietly. He was always deliberate; when his witticisms were appreciated and the audience laughed, he nodded and smiled. Otherwise he was solemn. There was never a lapse into insistence. Everything was low keyed and 'evenly modulated', although some listeners noted a falling inflection 'so often heard in pulpit delivery'.

In the content of the lecture there was no compromise with popular standards. James was his Jamesian self. He spoke of Balzac as 'the master of us all' – no novelist but had learned something from him. The opening sentences suggest his strategy of formal informality:

I have found it necessary, at the eleventh hour, to sacrifice to the terrible question of time a very beautiful and majestic approach that I had prepared to the subject on which I have the honour of addressing you. I recognize it as impossible to ask you to linger with me on that pillared portico – paved with marble, I beg you to believe, and overtwined with charming flowers. I must invite you to pass straight into the house and bear with me there as if I had already succeeded in beginning to interest you. Let us assume, therefore, that we have exchanged some ideas on the question of the beneficent play of criticism, and that I have even ingeniously struck it off that criticism is the only gate of appreciation, just as appreciation is, in regard to a work of art, the only gate of enjoyment.

No audience in America, we might speculate, had ever been so ingratiatingly approached; the tone was confidential; the suave assumption was that the listeners were the speaker's peers, and they all had deep and intimate matters to deal with. James went on to deplore the absence of a genuine criticism. Readers needed help when literary production was 'uncontrolled' and 'untouched by criticism, unguided, unlighted, uninstructed'. He resorted to his favourite pastoral imagery. American readers were the biggest flock straying without shepherds and 'without a sound of the sheepdog's bark'. Worse still, 'the shepherds have diminished as the flock has increased'.

From this it was a direct step to Balzac as a novelist who offers example and invites criticism. There followed an amusing passage on Jane Austen, who left readers hardly more curious about her process, James said, 'or of the experience in her that fed it, than the brown thrush who tells his story from the garden bough'. These preliminaries led James to say that 'even in this age of superlative study of the cheap and easy' Balzac stood as an extemporizer whom closeness and weight had preserved. 'I speak of him,' said James,

and can only speak, as a man of his own craft, an emulous fellow-worker, who has learned from him more of the lessons of the engaging mystery of fiction than from anyone else, who is conscious of so large a debt to repay that it has had positively to be discharged in instalments, as if one could never have at once all the required cash in hand.

The lecture repaid that debt. Balzac was all prose, 'with huge feet fairly ploughing the sand of our desert' yet he was 'the very type and model of the projector and creator'. With many subtle strokes James sketched Balzac's qualities but with constant reference to novelists more familiar to his audiences. Perhaps the most beautiful passage in the lecture was the following:

Why is it that the life that overflows in Dickens seems to me always to go on in the morning, or in the very earliest hours of the afternoon at most, and in a vast apartment that appears to have windows, large, un-curtained, and rather unwashed windows, on all sides at once? Why is it that in George Eliot the sun sinks for ever to the west, and the shadows are long, and the afternoon wanes, and the trees vaguely rustle, and the colour of the day is much inclined to yellow? Why is it that in Charlotte Brontë we move through an endless autumn? Why is it that in Jane Austen we sit quite resigned in an arrested spring? Why does Hawthorne give us the afternoon hour later than any one else? – oh, late, late, quite uncannily late, as if it were always winter outside?

Such passages provoked charmed murmurs from certain members of his audience and brief stirrings of applause. Balzac's plan, said James, was 'to handle, primarily, not a world of ideas, animated by figures representing these ideas; but the packed and constituted, the palpable, proveable world before him, by the study of which ideas would inevitably find themselves thrown up'. Taking a hint from Taine, he showed how Balzac loved his men and women even when they were horrible; how he identified himself with them, all the more to make us see them as they were. Balzac's handling of Valérie de Marneffe he contrasted with the way in which Thackeray sat in judgement on Becky Sharp. Valérie is given enough rope to act herself out. 'Balzac loved his Valérie then as Thackeray did not love his Becky.' A great part of the lecture was devoted to a close analysis of Balzac's way of painting the conditions and environment of his characters, his possession always of all the elements of his picture, his ability to 'foreshorten' and in the midst of detail stay with his 'principle of composition' and convey, as few novelists have done, the lapse and duration of time. 'It is the art of the brush,' said James, 'as opposed to the art of the slate pencil.' He interpolated a long passage in which he praised Zola, but showed exactly where that disciple of Balzac had lacked his master's art of 'representation'. Balzac, 'with all his faults of pedantry, ponderosity, pretentiousness, bad taste and charmless form', still achieved his subject 'the complicated human creature or human condition'. Only at the end did James artfully take notice that he was speaking 'as if we all, as if you all, without exception were novelists, haunting the back shop, the laboratory, or, more nobly expressed, the inner shrine of the temple'. His lecture terminated with the language of primitive religion. Balzac was in the sacred grove, the idol, 'gilded thick with so much gold – plated and burnished and bright, in the manner of towering idols'. And his final sentence – 'it is for the lighter and looser and poorer among us to be gilded thin!'

4

With $1,350 in his pocket and complaining of 'the fatigue of the good kind but too boresome people', Henry James boarded a Pullman in Chicago for the west coast. He had made a side-trip to Milwaukee for a brief visit with the wife and children of his long-dead brother Garth Wilkinson. 'I am just escaping with my life,' he wrote to his sister-in-law in Cambridge. 'The visual ugliness of it all ... the place a desolation of dreariness.' He went straight to Los Angeles: three days and three nights, 'through unspeakable alkali deserts', across Kansas, Arizona, and New Mexico. He almost broke down, he said, from tension, sickness, and weariness; he did not find the clattering of the train and the chattering 'Pullman civilization' helpful. He would never again, he said, attempt a journey 'of that confined and cooped up continuity'. The train arrived many hours late, and the old backache of his youth threatened to return; but a night in bed restored him. Also the soft California light and the warmth.

'This country is too *huge* simply, for any human convenience,' he wrote to Jocelyn Persse, 'and so unutterably empty that I defy any civilization, any mere money-grabbing democracy, to make on it any impression worthy of the 'name.' The great green Pacific, the golden orange groves, the huge flowers, and Southern California 'manners and human forms' gave promise of interest. Nevertheless, he was 'well-nigh *rotten* with the languishment of homesickness'.

He received promptly an invitation to lecture to a ladies' 'culture club' in Los Angeles and decided to give himself a holiday in the interval. He moved into the Hotel del Coronado at Coronado beach near San Diego in a room hanging over the Pacific, to work at his American travel essays. The days were of 'heavenly beauty'. He was reminded of Italy. A series of entries in his notebooks shows him organizing the materials published in *New England: An Autumn Impression*. 'Everything sinks in,' he wrote, 'nothing is lost; everything abides and fertilizes and renews its golden promise.' After the strain and tension of the winter he felt his heart 'uplifted'; and he dreamed of the time when in Lamb House he would plunge 'my hand, my arm *in*, deep and far, and up to the shoulder – into the heavy bag of remembrance – of suggestion – of imagination – of art – and fish out every little figure and felicity, every little fact and fancy that can be to my purpose'. Sitting by the 'strange Pacific', he found himself thinking of what he would say about Cambridge in his American sketches, but soon his memory wandered to his youth in Boston – the time of his 'obscure hurt' during the Civil War and he wrote a vivid passage on the '*initiation première* (the divine, the unique)' when in Ashburton Place in 1865 he had begun his career as writer. These memories would only be hinted at in *The American Scene*, but he would return to them in his later autobiographies.

Some 800 ladies came to his Los Angeles lecture; one, aged 95, spoke to him familiarly of his mother and father whom she had known in New York, and of her memories of Margaret Fuller. After this James spent a few days at Monterey and journeyed to San Francisco. He wandered up and down its primitive hills (it was before the earthquake) but enjoyed being fêted by the Bohemian Club, where he talked with Charles Warren Stoddard, author of books and sketches about Hawaii and Tahiti, and met the tenor Enrico Caruso. He had more talk of Polynesia with his old friend,

Mrs Robert Louis Stevenson, in her house in Hyde Street. He warned her not to prepare a repast; a plate of oranges would suffice. They had not seen each other since the day when she and Louis had sailed on their romantic journey, in the 1880s. Mrs Stevenson remembered James's enthusiasm for the flowery hill-slopes and the green canyons. 'Poor lady, poor barbarous and merely instinctive lady,' he would murmur later to a cultivated San Francisco bachelor, a man of artistic taste and wide culture named Bruce Porter, whom he met during this visit. James little dreamed – and would never know – that this man was destined to become the husband of his beloved niece, Peggy. Porter was a distinguished amateur of the arts. He had a flair for architecture, landscape gardening, verse-making. He would ultimately design the Stevenson memorial in Portsmouth Square in San Francisco. He was addicted to the theory of the Shakespearian ciphers, a matter in which he received no support from Henry James. They became, however, good friends at once. James was critical of San Francisco; he found in it 'a poverty of aspect and quality' and he left it, he said, without a pang. Nevertheless he experienced a touch of western openness when the owner of St Dunstan's, the hotel where he stayed, refused to render him a bill – it had been a privilege to have so distinguished a guest. 'Brave golden California, more brave and golden for *such* possibilities surely, than any other country under the sun!' James took a train for Seattle, passing through the beflowered valleys of Oregon and spending a night in Portland. In Seattle he visited his brother Robertson's eldest son, Edward Holton James. Ned James would be one of the most eccentric of the novelist's nephews and would later be cut out of his uncle's will because he espoused attacks against George V, who he alleged had made a morganatic marriage. But this occasion was genial, and we have Ned James's account written years later for his children.

When Uncle Henry came to see us, he found the west rather crude. I sat by the hour, with wide open mouth, drinking in his wonderful exotic conversation. He was bored by the west, by the 'slobber of noises', which we call our language, by the stream of vacant stupid faces on the streets and everywhere the 'big ogre of business'.

James stayed at a club where he was put up by a son of his old friend John La Farge; but he was in a hurry to return to the east. His nephew got him a comfortable Pullman bedroom and arranged for a break in the journey at St Paul. At Chicago his Higginson cousin guided him to the night train to New York. The next morning, when he reached Albany, scene of so much of his childhood, he had 'the absurdest sense of meeting again a ripe old civilization and travelling through a country that showed the mark of established manners'. He seemed now back in history. There was 'thicker detail'; and then there was the familiar Hudson whose shore the train followed into New York. The river's face was veiled by the mists of a premature spring. James gave himself up to romantic feelings, remembering old night journeys to grandmotherly Albany. Once again in Manhattan he relapsed into the safety and comfort of Minnie Jones's house in Eleventh street, and wrote of his bliss in 'having (approximately) done with Barbarism'.

88

The Terrible Town

HENRY JAMES left to the last his exploration of New York, his home-city, and during May and June, when his stay in America was nearing its end, he inspected what he called, half-lovingly, half-seriously, 'the terrible town'. He had had a panoramic vision of it one day, arriving from Washington. He was bound for Boston and he remained in his Pullman while his car was taken by barge around the tip of Manhattan, descending the western waters and remounting to Harlem. It was a vision 'of the most extravagant of cities, rejoicing, as with the voice of morning, in its might, its fortune, its unsurpassable conditions'. What he studied, once he had settled into his first-floor back rooms in Eleventh Street, was its planning, its architecture, its institutions, its ethnic groups. He had looked, from his Pullman window, at New York's 'pin-cushion profile', noted the cool assurance of the Bay, the impersonal harbour which had 'no item of the romantic, or even of the picturesque', and pondered the 'depressingly furnished and prosaically peopled' shore. New York had made no use of the natural beauty of its surroundings, the little islands, the farther shores. There was space and light and air at the open gates of the Hudson, but the city seemed to defy these with vehemence. Everything 'rushed and shrieked'. He felt as if he were looking at 'some colossal set of clockworks, some steelsouled machine-room of brandished arms and hammering fists and opening and closing jaws'.

The tall buildings were 'impudently new – and still more impudently novel'. They had this in common 'with so many other terrible things in America' – they were 'triumphant payers of dividends'. He had compared them to pins stuck irregularly into a pincushion; but now he saw the skyline as a jagged up-ended comb, a 'loose nosegay of architectural flowers'. The buildings were like 'American beauty' roses that possessed an 'interminable stem', and were grown to be picked in time with a shears; nipped short off, as soon as American science, applied to gain, 'has put upon the table, from far up its sleeve, some more winning card'. James's prose, as he surveyed 'the thousand glassy eyes' of the giants, was sufficiently blunt:

Crowned not only with no history, but with no credible possibility of time for history, and consecrated by no uses save the commercial at any cost, they are simply the most piercing notes in that concert of the expensively provisional into which your supreme sense of New York resolves itself. They never begin to speak to you, in the manner of the builded majesties of the world as we have heretofore known such – towers or temples or fortresses or palaces – with the authority of things of permanence or even of things of long duration. One story is good only till another is told, and sky-scrapers are the last word of economic ingenuity only till another word be written.

This would be the theme of all his poetic pictures of Manhattan as he viewed the city during the spring of 1905 – the new city spreading itself into the modernity of the new century. It was a city created on a foundation of impermanence. America seemed to build only to re-build. Remembering the beauty of Giotto's tower in Florence, James shifted his attention to the beauty of Trinity Church in downtown New York, which he had known when its simplified Gothic towered over Wall Street. Now it was submerged, surrounded, smothered, caged, dishonoured. James wrote of it as if he were endowing it with a physical hurt. Trinity Church seemed to say, 'Yes, the wretched figure I am making is as little as you see my fault – it is the fault of the buildings whose very first care is to deprive churches of their visibility.' And New Yorkers seemed to take this for granted 'with remarkable stupidity or with remarkable cynicism'. The skycrapers towering over the spire created an effect of a mountain wall; one usually expected an avalanche to drop from such a wall on village and village spire at its foot.

He looked at Castle Garden, doomed to extinction; here he had heard Patti warble like a tiny thrush when she was a child. He had, for that matter, been scarcely older. He visited Ellis Island and felt that the aliens, flooding into New York, were taking full possession of it. James, the old New Yorker, who had known the city when it seemed a village, felt dispossessed. Would the racial mix achieve a 'whole national consciousness as that of the Switzer and the Scot?'

I

He went first in search of personal memories, in the lower Fifth Avenue neighbourhood. On East Eleventh Street or West Tenth Street he felt as if he were still keeping clear 'of the awful hug of the serpent'; he studied an old house on Waverly Place that had survived and the 'lamentable little Arch of Triumph' built into the Square since that time – suggesting in its truncated form so little the glories it was supposed to celebrate. The author of *The Birthplace* walked over to Washington Place, to that part of the street leading from the Square to Broadway, where his father's house had stood and where he had been born sixty-two years before. The house was gone. In its place had been built a high, square, impersonal structure, proclaiming its lack of interest in the past with a crudity all its own. James felt 'amputated of half my history'. There was no original wall left on which a tablet might commemorate the fact that Henry James, novelist of New York, had been born here on 15 April 1843.* Such tablets swarmed thickly in Europe. Henry James would find a solution to this neglect. He would bestow on the collective edition of his works the name of his birth-city. The sense of personal affront was perhaps not so powerful as the thought that the city lacked self-confidence; it didn't really believe in itself. Otherwise it would not tear itself down so often. Its mission seemed to be 'to gild the temporary with its gold, as many inches thick as may be, and then, with a fresh shrug, a shrug of its splendid cynicism, give up its actual work, however exorbitant, as the merest of stop gaps'. James walked through streets 'to which the rich taste of history is forbidden'. He mused that the few landmarks, like the

---

*In 1966 such a tablet was unveiled on the spot where the Brown Building of New York University now stands.

City Hall, illustrated exactly his feelings that multiplied floors and windows hardly represented 'any grace of building'. Only in the uptown reaches did he feel that some attempt was being made to inject a human note: to build certain homes with feeling for Style.

2

The record of Henry James's energetic exploration of Manhattan is to be found in three closely written and evocative chapters in *The American Scene*. 'New York and the Hudson; A Spring Impression', 'New York: Social Notes', and 'The Bowery and Thereabouts'. These pages, filled with nostalgia and shock, surprise and resignation, reflect both James's delight in the poetry of the urban and despair at the sordid works and self-doom of the city. New York had created not a social order but an extemporized utility life that substituted the glamour of technology for the deep-rooted foundations of existence. He cared for 'the terrible town', cared for it deeply, as one born in it; and it therefore hurt him all the more that man could create so blindly and so crudely the foundations of inevitable 'blight'. Long before the word gained currency in the language of urban decay, Henry James used it as he wandered in the Italian and Jewish neighbourhoods. He was struck by the alienation of the Italian immigrants when compared with those he had known during his many trips to Italy. In Italy one could address them in a give-and-take of traveller and native; here they seemed to have suffered a sea-change; they seemed remote and melancholy. On the other hand he found the Jewish ghetto, on the lower east side, animated and bewildering. His view of the Jews in the mass had always been distant; he had repeated the clichés by which their national distinctness was marked in the English novel, very much as Dickens had depicted them in *Oliver Twist*. He saw them swarming over the fire-escapes attached to the tenements and wondered what would become of them in the New World. He went to a Jewish home, in a converted tenement, for dinner.* The windows looked on a teeming little square. He noted the overtowering school that dominated the ghetto, harbinger of its education. He listened to the babel of children in great numbers, and the old, with marked distinctive faces, occupying doorstep and pavement, kerbstone and gutter. The

---

* James's correspondence does not disclose the names of his Jewish acquaintances except for the mention of Jacob Gordin, the Yiddish playwright.

'individual Jew' was for James 'more of a concentrated person, savingly possessed of everything that is in him, than any other human, noted at random'. He commented on 'the unsurpassed strength of the race'; it had withstood the forces of history that sought to chop it into 'myriads of fine fragments'. An array of Jews resembled in this 'diffused intensity' a 'long nocturnal street where every window in every house shows a maintained light'. With their reverence for intellect, he would have toasted them as 'an intellect-ual people', but America seemed to do its work and he saw the 'hard glitter of Israel'. Pondering the abundance of the ghetto shops, James wondered whether the United States wasn't inventing 'a new style of poverty'. To be sure, he had not had a chance to see all the elements of the sordid and squalid in New York; but he saw enough to feel that 'there is such a thing, in the United States, as freedom to grow up to be blighted'. And he reflected that this 'may be the only freedom in store for the smaller fry of future generations'.

Under the wing of his Jewish friends he was taken on a round of beer houses and cafés. At the Café Royal, on the lower East side where Jewish literati and café-philosophers mingled, James listened to the accents of Europe as they fractured the English language. Language for the novelist was sacred, and in especial the language with which he worked. In these warm-lighted cafés he felt himself in 'the torture rooms of the living idiom'. What would this do in America to 'the Accent of the Future?' It might become of course the most beautiful in the world, James mused, but 'we shall not know it for English'.

He inspected Riverside Drive, bemoaning the unimaginative name given to the avenue that provided such fine Hudson vistas; he paused at Grant's tomb, liking its situation, and its direct democratic acces-sibility to spectators who didn't remove their hats in the shrine. He wandered in upper Fifth Avenue and looked at the palatial houses of the rich seeing them as a 'record, in the last analysis of individual loneliness'. They never became seats of family; they were as dis-continuous as much else of American life, reduced to 'the present, pure and simple'. This present squared itself 'between an absent future and an absent past'. He wandered in Central Park and found it filled with 'eruptive and agitated effect' and afraid 'to be just vague and frank and quiet'. He likened the park to an actress desti-tute of talent, ranging in the course of a given week from roles such as the tragedy queen to the singing chambermaid. The intention of beauty in the Park was too 'insistent'. In the Metropolitan Museum he winced

at the expense which, like so much of the expense of New York, doesn't educate ... There was money in the air, ever so much money – that was, grossly expressed, the sense of the whole intimation. And the money was to be all for the most exquisite things – for *all* the most exquisite except creation, which was to be off the scene altogether.

Seeking to recapture fragments of the past, he went to a Bowery theatre; he remembered old Bowery evenings, 'the big bare ranting stupid stage, the grey void smelling of dust and tobacco-juice'. The new audience was filled with alien faces, Moldavian, Galician, Hebraic. It sat munching candy – the Cult of Candy, he commented, seemed prodigious in the United States. The play was a farce melo-drama. There was a wonderful folding bed on the stage. The villain of the piece pursued the virtuous heroine round and round the room trying to leap over the bed; and the heroine closed the bed so that the villain was engulfed in it 'as in the jaws of a crocodile'. After a while James left 'perhaps from an excess of suspense'. It all seemed to him 'a queer, clumsy, wasteful social chemistry'. He visited also the Yiddish theatre, guided by the reigning Jewish dramatist, Jacob Gordin. The place was convivial; the ventilation left much to be desired, and after looking at some broad passage of a Yiddish comedy of manners he walked out – 'it was a scent, literally, not further to be followed'. He was happier in an upper east side bowl-ing alley and billiard room, a German beer-hall which however served no beer, but where in the shadows he remembered the faint click of the moved domino, and the quiet honest men, playing silently. This little temple of relaxation seemed a triumph amid all the 'surrounding triumphs'. The host had omitted learning 'the current American'. He did not fracture the English. He spoke but a dozen words – and since he talked little, James felt the stillness to be friendly. In this dingy place James found a conception 'of de-cency and dignity' – a few tables and chairs, a few coffee cups and boxes of dominoes. And James concluded that the 'charm of the place in short was that its note of the exclusive had been arrived at with such a beautifully fine economy'.

89

The Brothers

HENRY JAMES'S incursion into the orbit of his elder brother, after a three-decade absence, revived the long-buried struggle for power that had existed between the two – ever since their nursery days in Washington Square. The infant Henry had made his original incursion by the very act of birth and caused William to flee instinctively from the threat to his dominion. William had been the only son of his young parents for more than a year; and suddenly this uniqueness had ended. The rivalry, in its childish essence, may seem altogether too remote and too simple; but in the development of two geniuses, malaise and avoidance, reinforced over the years, had become a prevailing mode of existence. In their youth they had been like Jacob and Esau. In the language of that myth Henry James now spoke of his return as 'taking up again my birthright'. Mutual guilt had made them feel as if each were encroaching upon the other's birthright. Henry had felt most free in his young days when William was away. William had felt free only when he could escape – to Brazil, to Germany. Both relapsed into petty illnesses when they had to be together for too long a time. But between 1875 and 1905 each had carved out his own empire. Henry James had made himself the culture bearer of America in Europe. William had made himself the hero of American pragmatism. George Santayana would see them in still another light, as classic and romantic. Henry, as the analyst of American manners, overcame the genteel tradition – 'in the classic way, by understanding it'. William, whose student Santayana had been, overcame it 'in the romantic way, by continuing it into its opposite' by his prophetic sympathy 'with the dawning sentiments of the age, with the moods of the dumb majority'. Both brothers with their early exposure to Europe and their father's mixture of mystical feeling and hard-headed realism, were grandchildren of the romantic movement. Henry, however, had become a formalist in art. Composition alone was 'positive beauty', he would say, and art preserved life. William, as Santayana saw, had a spontaneity and vitality which made him scatter words that 'caught fire in many parts of the world'. What Santayana could not foresee was that Henry's large glimpse of the American myth would capture a still later imagination in the West. The differences between the brothers was never more marked than in 1904–5 when Henry, all power and drive, came as a 'restless analyst' to study William's America, and suddenly caught the public eye in a country where the philosopher's public image was large. The two brothers had renewed their ties in the autumn of 1904 in Chocorua and for a brief period there were walks and talks and the old communion of their youth. 'It is a pleasure to be with anyone who takes in things through the eyes,' said William. On his side Henry wrote 'whenever one is with William one receives such an immense accession of suggestion and impression'.

Henry did not spend much time with his brother. He was in New York; he was in Lenox; he went south; and then that spring when he arrived in the middle west and the press began to pay increasing attention to him, William quite suddenly set sail for the isles of Greece. He went on an impulse. He had never been in Athens or for that matter southern Italy. His reason for departure at this moment seems curiously flimsy: he wanted to escape the 'influenza season' in Cambridge, although other such seasons had come and gone without his seeking flight. He was apparently escaping something else, and perhaps in part, his brother. Henry applauded his desire for travel; Mrs William was relieved to have him escape from some of his academic burdens. The departure of the elder brother, during the time of Henry's presence in the country was, on the surface, understandable enough. Each had his own destiny to fulfil; and then they often grated on one another. 'He and I are so utterly different in all our observances and springs of action, that we can't rightly judge each other,' William had written a couple of years earlier. Henry would write that autumn to William, in response to William's criticism of *The Golden Bowl*, 'how far apart and to what different ends we have had to work out, (very naturally and properly!) our respective intellectual lives'.

Although William always attacked Europe and pleaded with Henry to 'drop your English ideas and take America and Americans as they take themselves', he was, during his trip to Greece, in a somewhat different mood. The end of middle age, his heart attacks, his years of work, seemed to make him conscious of missed opportunities; and his letters to his wife during his journey had in them strains of his brother Henry's early romantic discoveries of Italy. 'I have come here too late in life,' he wrote, 'when the picturesque has lost its serious reality. Time was when hunger for it haunted me like a passion.' Was it the sense of 'too late?' – the theme his brother had written into *The Ambassadors* and *The Beast in the Jungle* that made William – in defiance of his heart condition – journey through rugged Greece and stand before the Parthenon, as so many romantics had done before, with tears in his eyes? *J'ai vu la beauté parfaite*, he wrote, lapsing into the language he criticized his brother for using so often. Turning to Rome, he attended a philosophical congress, and with great spontaneity read a paper in French on 'consciousness'. He rejoiced to find that his ideas had sparked a whole group of European pragmatists. He was quite the hero of the meeting. And then he went on a long motor drive with his former student Bernard Berenson, and an Austrian Princess – Pisa, Genoa, Cannes. He returned in May to Cambridge, strengthened, refreshed, to find his brother Henry in Irving Street full of impressions of old New York. They saw each other briefly. Henry went off to stay with Mrs Wharton at Lenox just before sailing. William left for Chicago to deliver a series of lectures. Irving Street seemed like a railway station with all the comings and goings. The brothers did not meet again during Henry's American trip. William sent Henry a cheerful letter of good-bye. Henry waved back one of his regular epistolary flourishes.

I

What Henry did not know – and would never know – was that William had just accomplished one of the most unusual epistolary flourishes of his life – with Henry as object if not subject. The brothers were both members of the National Institute of Arts and Letters, having been elected in 1898 when the Institute was founded. During 1905 the Institute began procedures for establishing an Academy of Arts and Letters of limited membership, like the French Academy, its members to be chosen from the ranks of the Institute. In effect the Institute became the parent body of the otherwise autonomous Academy. A group of seven academicians was elected – among them Mark Twain – and these members in turn proceeded to the election of the full complement, ultimately limited to fifty. Henry James was among those elected during the second ballot in February 1905; William was elected during the fourth ballot in May and found the notification of election awaiting him on his return that month. He seems to have brooded over the matter for a month and then, in a letter dated 17 June 1905 informed the Academy secretary, Robert Underwood Johnson, that he could not accept the honour. He began by giving as reason that he never accepted honours in academic bodies which did not have some work cut out for them, and this Academy seemed to him purely honorific. His second reason was that it would be contrary to his preachings of a lifetime 'against the world and its vanities'. His third reason was that with his brother also a member, the James influence in the Academy might be held excessive. He phrased this part of his letter as follows:

I am the more encouraged to this course by the fact that my younger and shallower and vainer brother is already in the Academy and that if I were there too, the other families represented might think the James influence too rank and strong.

The gesture was private, and Johnson wrote, years later in his memoirs:

I have always regretted that I did not go to Cambridge to explain to Professor James more fully the character and purpose of the new organization to which he would have been a distinguished and appropriate addition. I mention his selection lest it should be thought that a man of such admirable scholarship and style had been neglected.

There were two matters in which William was not being consistent or truthful – with himself – in writing this letter. The first was that he had not considered there was a redundancy of Jameses when he and Henry had been elected to the Institute in 1898. He was having this afterthought only now, when Henry was elected ahead of him to the new body. His letter rectified this inconsistency by adding, 'I think I ought to resign from the Institute (in which I have played so inactive a part) which act I here also perform.' And then he quietly overlooked the fact that he had accepted a number of honours in spite of his claim that for 'a philosopher with my pretensions to austerity and righteousness' the only 'consistent course is to give up this particular vanity and treat myself as unworthy of the honour, which I assuredly am'. He had not taken such a position in accepting honorary membership in the Institut de France in 1898; and he accepted a number of honorary degrees – from Padua, Princeton, Edinburgh, and his own Harvard before he wrote this letter, and would accept others from Durham and Oxford three years later, and Geneva as late as 1909.

A deeper and more palpable reason existed than those he gave for his refusal to accept election to the Academy chair. He had in effect articulated it by his characterization of his 'younger brother'. The Academy had elected Henry James – 'younger, shallower, vainer' – ahead of the older brother, who considered himself wiser, more serious-minded, and without vanity. The letter seemed to imply once again that it was impossible for Jacob and Esau to live under the same roof, to be in the same room – or Academy – and occupy seats side by side. The adult William admitted in his letter that his act was 'sour' and 'ungenial'. In fact he added a sentence 'if you knew how greatly against the grain these duty-inspired lines are written, you would not deem me unfriendly or ungenial, but only a little cracked.' The philosopher of pragmatism sensed he was committing – under some strange impulse – an irrational and inconsistent act. Still, under the guise of modesty and consistency, he bowed himself out of the American Academy of Arts and Letters and its parent, the Institute.

2

In the ensuing months William James would express this hidden rivalry in the most consistent barrage he had ever laid down against his brother's work. He launched a measured critique of *The Golden Bowl* which he had not read earlier and when, in 1907, *The American Scene* was published he displayed his own great verbal virtuosity by writing his sharpest words against his brother's 'later manner'.

Reading *The Golden Bowl* had put him 'as most of your recenter long stories have put me, in a very puzzled state of mind'. The method of elaboration went 'agin the grain of all my own impulses in writing, and yet in spite of all,' he acknowledged, 'there is a brilliancy and cleanliness of effect, and in this book especially a high-toned social atmosphere that are unique and extraordinary'. Such stricture and praise were not new; William had done this many years before when Henry was having his first successes. The philosopher now added:

Why don't you, just to please Brother, sit down and write a new book, with no twilight or mustiness in the plot, with great vigour and decisive-

ness in the action, no fencing in the dialogue, or psychological commentaries, and absolute straightness in style. Publish it in my name, I will
acknowledge it, and give you half the proceeds. Seriously, I wish you
would, for you *can*; and I should think it would tempt you, to embark
on a 'fourth manner'.

Henry James's answer was sufficiently direct, and he fell in with
William's barbed aggression. He would write

some uncanny form of thing, in fiction, that will gratify you, as Brother
– but let me say, dear William, that I shall greatly be humiliated if you
do like it, and thereby lump it in your affection with things of the current age, that I have heard you express admiration for and that I would
sooner descend to a dishonoured grave than have written.

William wanted him, he suggested, quoting from his lecture on
Balzac, to take up the art of the slate pencil instead of the art of
the brush.

I'm always sorry when I hear of your reading anything of mine, and
always hope you won't – you seem to me so constitutionally unable to
'enjoy' it ... I see nowhere about me done or dreamed of the things
that alone for me constitute the *interest* of the doing of the novel – and
yet it is in a sacrifice of them on their very own ground that the thing
you suggest to me evidently consists.

Always the younger brother, Henry softened his firm response by
assuring William he was reading him 'with rapture'.

William returned to the charge in 1907. *The American Scene*
seemed 'supremely great'. He went on to remind Henry, how
opposed 'your whole "third manner" of execution is to the literary
ideals which animate my crude and Orson-like breast'. William's
were

to say a thing in one sentence as straight and explicit as it can be made,
and then drop it forever; yours being to avoid naming it straight, but by
dint of breathing and sighing all round and round it, to arouse in the
reader who may have had a similar perception already (Heaven help him
if he hasn't!) the illusion of a solid object, made (like the 'ghost' at the
Polytechnic) wholly out of impalpable materials, air and the prismatic
interferences of light, ingeniously focused by mirrors upon empty space.
But you *do* it, that's the queerness!

William the scientist, added : 'Say it *out*, for God's sake, and have
done with it.' He accused Henry of having become a 'curiosity of
literature'. 'For gleams and innuendos and felicitous verbal insinua-

tions you are unapproachable, but the *core* of literature is solid. Give it to us *once* again! The bare perfume of things will not support existence, and the effect of solidity you reach is but perfume and simulacrum.' He enjoined Henry not to answer 'these absurd remarks'. Henry obliged. He went his own way as he had always done.

By now Henry James had outlived the hurts he used to experience at such attacks. His rejoinder to William was simply that he found the critical letter 'rich and luminous'. He promised he would have 'a reply almost as interesting as, and far more annihilating than, your letter itself'. He then said that perhaps William needed to read the book in handsomer print than the American edition and promised to send him the English edition. The younger brother let it go at that. In the intervening weeks William had a change of heart towards the book. He read the chapter on Florida and was delighted with it. Henry's ultimate rejoinder took the form simply of an inscription in the English edition: 'To William James, his incoherent, admiring, affectionate Brother, Henry James, Lamb House, August 21st 1907'.

3

In attacking his brother's style William James was adding a private fraternal voice to hostile voices raised in the press throughout Henry James's visit to the United States. Not a Sunday passed without a letter to the New York *Times* about the form or moral content of Henry's books. Jokes went into circulation in cultured circles – the lady who knew 'several languages – French, New Thought, and Henry James', or the lady who boasted she could read Henry James 'in the original'. When James delivered 'The Question of Our Speech' at the Bryn Mawr Commencement in the Spring of 1905 the press paid scant attention to the fact that James's remarks were addressed to the slipshod ways in which American girls spoke. It assumed James was attacking the American language itself, and Dr Woodrow Wilson, the president of Princeton, defended newspaper English against the 'laborious' style of the novelist. One letter-writer to the *Times* said James's style would 'drive a grammarian mad'. Another 'wished he would not put the tail of his sentences where the head belongs and the head where the body should be or the body where one naturally expects to see the tail'.

His 'morality' seems to have offended even more than his style. *The Ambassadors* was described by one correspondent as a 'notably warped situation'. Did not Lambert Strether advise the nice clean American youth to cleave unto the questionable married woman in Paris? and to harden his heart to the tender claims of his mother and sister in far, humdrum, inartistic Massachusetts? 'Which Henry James ending do you like best?' queried the lady who wrote this letter, 'the one which turns to the left and says nothing – or the one which turns to the right and says "So there we are".' Obviously the woman had read much of James; she reminded him that in *Transatlantic Sketches* he had disapproved of the liaison between Rousseau and Madame de Warens; and yet in *The Ambassadors* he had written 'in these places such things were'.

One reader was unhappy that in *The Golden Bowl* he had allowed Charlotte to be 'dragged over to exile in dreadful California'. The 'dreadful' proved ironic, however, for the writer added 'if only Mr Henry James would migrate with Adam Verver to California and there make us one of his old-time magic books under clean blue American skies'. The writer of this letter spoke of James's 'politely vicious literary behaviour'. There was no doubt that James was a man of genius, she said, who 'sees far into hearts and minds of men and women' but the substance of his books was 'like a beautiful and radiant soul' in a 'deformed body'. A letter-writer signing 'Optimist' asked 'is not the world worse for the decadence shown on the pages of Henry James?' A Brooklyn correspondent reported that in a reading club of 1,000 only three out of every hundred read Henry James. The popular novelist Alice Duer Miller, who was reaching a large audience, said that James, within *The Golden Bowl*, indulged in 'a situation only scandalmongers are supposed to discuss'. On the other hand Claude Bragdon defended James's extended metaphors and the way in which 'intellectuality overpowers the sensuous'. Others found the novelist 'detached', 'cold', 'cruel'. One correspondent linked James and Edith Wharton.

Is a delicate dissector like Edith Wharton, writing *The Sanctuary*, to spoil us? Is Henry James writing about that loveliest of all women Milly Theale in order to pollute us young Americans? ... if James, Wharton and their disciples be decadents, then may I join the choir invisible that sings where they will sing in what's beyond.

4

Things moved at an accelerated pace as the day of James's departure approached. He had never been a public figure on this scale. There were more caricatures and editorials in the press; he was recognized in the street and in the shops. One observer, Robert Cortes Holliday, then a book salesman in Scribner's, recorded a meeting at the foot of the elevator of W. C. Brownell, Scribner's senior editor, Henry James, and Mrs Wharton. Teddy Wharton sat in the bookshop waiting and smoking a cigar. Holliday remembered James stepping out of the store, 'overhauled by Mrs Wharton under full sail' and then the three moving down the avenue, James on one arm, Teddy on the other, and 'in this formation, sticks flashing, skirt whipping, with a somewhat spirited mien, the august spectacle receded'. Holliday watched James browse in the bookshop. 'He ran his nose over the tables, and inch by inch along the walls, stood on tiptoe and pulled down volumes from high places, rummaged in dark corners.' Not knowing he was recognized he explained, 'I live in England myself and am curious to know this,' and he asked what percentage of the novels on the fiction table was the product of English writers. He barely glanced at a high pile of *Golden Bowls*.

Le Roy Phillips, a cousin of James's friend Morton Fullerton, wrote to inform the novelist he was compiling a bibliography of his writings. He asked for help to identify certain anonymous pieces. James's reply was Olympian. He discouraged 'the pick-axe and the spade'. To another bibliographer he wondered 'why and how any such wretched little question can matter, at this hour, to any human being endowed with the responsibility of intelligence'. But he added kindly that 'your great good-will in the matter almost brings to my eyes tears of compassionate remonstrance for misapplied effort'. James said he would rather with his own hand heap mountains of earth on his old writings and so bury them deeper, 'beyond any sympathetic finding-out'. Phillips was not discouraged; by looking up old magazine account books he unearthed a large body of James's unsigned early writings; for the accounts named the articles for which James was paid.

At the end James found himself involved in a series of visits. Hendrik Andersen turned up in Boston and the two went briefly to Newport. He journeyed to Kittery Point in Maine to say farewell to Howells and also saw Miss Jewett. Mrs Wharton beckoned emphatically from Lenox. James, remembering her knowlege of German, replied, '*Ich kann nicht anders*. Be indulgent and don't shoot. I am doing my best.' He managed to squeeze in a few days with her. Teddy was in Canada fishing. She had a 'big, commodious new motor' and they swept through the countryside. It was a fine way to rope in 'a huge netful of impressions at once'. They went to Ashfield to see Charles Eliot Norton, covering eighty miles between lunch and dinner. During the last days Pinker arrived from London and in a series of conferences with Scribner's worked out the initial plans for a 'definitive edition' of James's novels and tales. Things were sociable to the last. Walter Berry, Europe-bound, booked a cabin on James's ship, the *Ivernia*; so did Elizabeth Robins, the actress, who had been revisiting her homeland. On 5 July James bade farewell to America. He had spent ten busy months. His journey had been a minor triumph. He had renewed contact with his kin-folk and he had crossed a continent. Tired, stimulated, his expenses covered by his lectures, he would now try to sort out his impressions. The voyage was lively. James sat on deck revising *Roderick Hudson* for the Scribner edition. Berry and Miss Robins played a game called 'hunt the adjective' – they tried to see how many adjectives could be eradicated from whatever they were reading. James hunted superfluous commas in his own past writings. Miss Robins remembered James 'sending that melancholy look of his out over the Atlantic waste' and protesting against light-minded flittering of Americans back and forth across the sea. James was eloquent on the segregation of the sexes in the United States 'beyond anything existing out of the Orient' – the men always in their offices, the women 'uptown' or at Newport. He had long ago described this in his tales. The *Ivernia* docked at Liverpool after a nine-day voyage. Restored to his London club, James briefly saw Jocelyn Persse. Then he was in Lamb House facing a vast accumulation of books, papers, magazines, letters – and a staff in revolt. The servants had not been happy with the tenants. His housekeeper threatened to leave. She was comforted by an increase in wages and the prompt discharge of two superfluous maids. Young Burgess was promoted from house-boy to valet, 'a very improved little auxiliary'. 'The situation is clearing – Rye and my four-square little garden better and sweeter than they ever were,' James reported to Mrs Williams in far-away Cambridge. The Master was home again.

BOOK FIVE:
THE MASTER
1905–16

Art *makes* life, makes interest, makes importance.
HENRY JAMES

Part One

Estimates and Revisions

90

The Supreme Relation

IN his earlier years Henry James had longed for Europe when in America, but in Europe had felt himself a claimant to kingdoms not his own. In Quincy Street he had always been a second son, except when William was away; in Bolton Street he was for a long time an 'observant stranger'. Now, in the fullness of time, he had reclaimed his birthright. He had re-annexed lost provinces of his life. He had re-possessed America. It was 'cruelly charmless', to be sure. The wreckers had destroyed the physical landscapes of his youth. Everything seemed to proceed 'by cataclysms and violence and enormity – leaps and bounds from one kind of excess to another kind'. James ached with this vision; he winced, he said, with the very noise of it. He wanted to crouch for ever in Lamb House. He 'couldn't do it all *again* and survive'. He winced; he ached; he crouched; and yet 'my ten months among you renewed my curiosities and sympathies and possible understandings'. In some way his visit had answered an old riddle, resolved a double-exile. He had thought of America as having rejected him: now he found that even when it laughed at him it loved him. He recognized, as he said in his book of impressions, that 'one's supreme relation, as one had always put it, was one's relation to one's country'.

He talked of that 'supreme relation' one evening in June 1906 with Hamlin Garland, the son of the 'middle border' who had entertained him in Chicago, and who came to Rye to spend a night. James found Howells's friend simple, provincial, dull. He spoke of his being both American and cosmopolitan. He had long ago suggested that this was a highly civilized state, even if the ideal were to be a 'concentrated patriot'. Garland quoted James as saying, 'The mixture of Europe and America which you see in me has proved disastrous. It has made of me a man who is neither American nor European. I have lost touch with my own people and I live here alone.' This has been read by many as Henry James's acknowledgement that his expatriation was a large mistake. Garland's notebook of the time shows, however, that James did not speak as positively. It has him saying 'if I were to live my life again I would be American – steep myself in it – know no other'. He then added that the 'mixture of Europe and America is disastrous' – so Garland originally noted – but he did not use the words 'which you see in me'. These were inserted by Garland. James always felt that he was a consistent cosmopolitan. He made this point to Edith Wharton; she lacked, he said, 'the homeliness and inevitability and the happy limitation and the affluent poverty of a Country of your Own'. To which he added 'comme moi, par exemple'.

I

Two months after Garland's visit, during the night of 3–4 August 1906, Henry James found himself kept awake by an idea for a story – a story about a repatriated American who goes in search of himself in a house in New York – himself *as he might have been* had he stayed at home. He wrote to his agent, 'I have an excellent little idea through not having slept a wink last night *all* for thinking of it, and must therefore at least get the advantage of striking while the iron is hot.' He called the story at first *The Second House*; presently it was renamed *The Jolly Corner*. James seems to have written it during the next few days. He felt he was robbing his unfinished novel *The Sense of the Past*. That work dealt with an American who inherits a house in London, and finds himself, on entering it, within the past of his English ancestors. The reverse of this idea was the tale of Spencer Brydon, who has lived abroad for thirty years. He returns to rebuild a Manhattan house for rental purposes; but also finds himself wandering in his own private past, in his other house on a corner in Lower Fifth Avenue, the house of his birth and childhood – the house of Family. Brydon wanders through the rooms night after night, restlessly, hauntedly, carrying a sputtering candle. He is haunted by the thought of what he might have been had he not gone to live in Europe. He has discussed this with his friend Alice Staverton, who had remained a spinster in her old house in Irving Place. It becomes an obsession with him – 'how he might have led his life, and "turned out", if he had not so, at the outset, given it up'. To Miss Staverton he says: 'What would it have made of me, what would it have made of me? I keep for ever wondering, all idiotically, as if I could possibly know! I see what it has made of dozens of others, those I meet, and it positively aches within me, to the point of exasperation, that it would have made something of me as well.'

This 'rage of curiosity never to be satisfied' is expressed by Brydon as he looks through his monocle at Alice Staverton and drinks tea by her fireside. He had been, at 23, too young to judge what kind of American life was possible to him. He doesn't admire those who remained; he isn't sure what charm the country has exerted on them 'beyond that of the rank money-passion'; yet he feels he had, in his early American years 'some strange *alter ego* deep down somewhere within me'. He had transferred this other self to a strange climate in which it didn't have a chance to grow. Alice Staverton says she feels that if Brydon had remained in America he would have had 'power'.

> 'You'd have liked me that way?' he asked.
> She barely hung fire. 'How should I not have liked you?'
> 'I see. You'd have liked me, have preferred me, a billionaire!'
> 'How should I not have liked you?' she simply again asked.

His nights of curiosity and meditation in 'the jolly corner' become a quest for the *alter ego* – the self that might have been. The tale is a kind of active *Beast in the Jungle*; Brydon unlike John Marcher goes in pursuit of the 'beast' instead of waiting for it to spring. The story is more than a revisiting of a personal past; it becomes a journey into the self, almost as if the house on 'the jolly corner' were a mind, a brain, and Spencer Brydon were walking through its passages finding certain doors of resistance closed to truths hidden from himself. On one occasion he notices with a *frisson* that a door hitherto closed is open; someone must have opened it. Descending the staircase to the vestibule he sees dark shadows taking material form. A figure rises before him rigid, conscious, spectral, yet human – a man of his own substance and stature awaits him. Brydon sees

... his planted stillness, his vivid truth, his grizzled bent head and white masking hands, his quiet actuality of evening dress, of dangling double eye-glass, of gleaming silk lappet and white linen, of pearl button and gold watch-guard and polished shoe. No portrait by a great modern master could have presented him with more intensity, thrust him out of his frame with more art.

The apparition stands there with its hands over its face, 'splendid covering hands, strong and completely spread!' But two fingers are missing from the right hand, as if they had been 'accidentally shot away'. Then the hands move and the answer Brydon has sought is revealed. He sees a face of horror.

Then harder pressed still, sick with the force of his shock, and falling back as under the hot breath and the roused passion of a life larger than his own, a rage of personality before his own collapsed, he felt the whole vision turn to darkness and his very feet give way.

Alice Staverton arrives to rescue him from his fainting spell. She has seen the same figure in a dream; she confirms her occult experience by her knowledge of the two missing fingers. But she doesn't agree with Brydon that the figure is a 'horror'. 'I had accepted him,' she says.

In this tale James's imagination completed full circle from 1871, when he wrote *A Passionate Pilgrim* about an American claimant in Europe, through *The Sense of the Past* about an American heir in Europe. Like Peer Gynt, the hero has returned to his own land after endless wandering to find that his Solveig has waited for him, was always there, the accepting mother in the accepting motherland. Personal myths seem bound together in this strange tale by which James announced to himself that had he stayed at home the hand that held the pen might have been crippled, but that he might also have been a titan of finance, a re-modeller of old houses, a builder of skyscrapers – even as this enterprising side of himself was about to re-model his writings in the New York Edition. Beyond Henry James's incorporation in this mythic tale of the memory of his father's amputation, associated with the New York of his childhood, we can read in *The Jolly Corner* the recognition of his own ambivalence about his Americano-European legend. He sees at last his own dual nature – the self of intellect and power and the self of imagination and art; the self that for so long had tried to live in his brother's skin, but could now shed it, and the self that reflected his creativity. Spencer Brydon and Alice Staverton – James had given her his sister's and his sister-in-law's name – agree that if Brydon had remained at home he would by now be a millionaire. *The Jolly Corner* embodied James's recurrent dream of pursuing a ghost or other self – a haunting creature – and defying and conquering it. He was always more powerful in his night-dreams than in his waking thoughts. He would tell Lady Ottoline Morrell one such dream, a version of his dream of the Louvre which he also had during these late years. He walks into a house filled with antiques, cabinets, tables, chairs, a veritable *Spoils of Poynton* house. He feels vaguely there is a strange presence in one of the rooms. Upstairs he finds an old man sitting in a chair and he calls out to him 'you're afraid of me, you coward'. The man denies this. James contradicts him. 'You are, I know it. I see the sweat on your brow.' Always his dreams begin with a sense of foreboding and terror; an anxiety that seeks relief. Threatened, he then turns the tables; it is *he* who suddenly frightens the *alter ego*. James would never forget this – the idea that a haunted person's fright can also frighten others. This was what he tried to put into *The Sense of the Past*. In *The Jolly Corner* Spencer Brydon is frightened by his own creation – the Self he has materialized, the thought of what his life might have been. The resolution of the story is that he had had to fulfil his destiny; that he must accept himself even as America accepted him. By the same process he was laying the ghost of his old rivalry with William. He did not have to be William; he could be himself. The myth of Past and Present, of the conquest of brothers and mythical worlds – worlds of enterprise and art – and of 'the supreme relation' – are embodied in this low-keyed, tense little tale. Its elements seemed to compose themselves in some magical way out of unconscious depths where they had lain hidden for years. James called it 'a miraculous masterpiece' in writing to his agent. The thrill for him was that it settled the whole question of his American journey. He had always banished his own ghosts by writing about them. The next four years would be years of great fertility in spite of his advancing years; and they would be Henry James's 'American years', more American even than the years of his lost youth. The decade that remained to the Master would assert his recaptured self. Out of them would emerge the edition of his novels and tales – his personal monument – designed as the 'New York Edition'. His late tales would be set in New York; his last unfinished novel would be on an American subject and would open in Newport. His memoirs would dwell on his New York childhood, on Newport and Boston. He was ready to complete *The American Scene*; to write papers about American manners. All that he did from now on was intimately related to his American self. And he would return once again to his homeland – for a last look, for last visits, for a final embrace.

2

The American Scene, published in 1907, was written with all the passion of a patriot and all the critical zeal of an intellectual who could not countenance national complacency and indifference. Civilization meant order, composition, restraint, moderation, beauty, duration. It meant creation of a way of life that ministered to man's finest qualities and potential. Using this standard of measurement, James found America terribly wanting. The country was founded on violence, plunder, loot, commerce; its monuments were built neither for beauty nor for glory, but for obsolescence. It was science and technology in the service of the profit motive; and in this there resided an inherent decay of human forms and human values. Older nations had known how to rise above shopkeeping; they had not made a cult of 'business' and of 'success'. And then James hated the continental 'bigness' of America. Homogeneity, rootedness, manners – modes of life – these were his materials and everywhere James looked he found there had been an erosion of the standards and forms necessary to a novelist, necessary also to civilization. The self-indulgence and advertisement of the plunderers were carried over to the indulging of their young. Americans had interpreted freedom as a licence to plunder. This was the burden of the impressions James set down, in the days when they were still vivid, and in the light of his native, his early emotion. He wrote in a vein of poetry: buildings address him; monuments meditate; he offers us a continual monologue, sometimes rhapsodic, often reportorial. He looks everywhere with scrupulous attention – and with passion. He touches the America of his own past with great personal tenderness and melancholy. The book is both elegy and oration. The stages of his journey are told as they might have been painted by an impressionist painter; but the accompanying script might have been written by a documentary poet, like Zola. The book ends with a peroration on the rape of the land that makes him a prophet of the pollutions of the future. He put his words into the mouth of an Indian, looking at what the white man has done. 'Beauty and charm would be for me in the solitude you have ravaged, and I should owe you my grudge for every disfigurement and every violence, for every wound with which you have caused the face of the land to bleed' in the name of 'your pretended message of civilization'. He made him say also 'you touch the great lonely land – as one feels it still to be – only to plant upon it some ugliness about which, never dreaming of the grace of apology or contrition, you then proceed to brag with a cynicism all your own'. Perhaps feeling that the passage might be jarring to American self-assurance Harpers simply left it out. It is to be found in the English edition. James apparently did not read the American proofs.

'I would take my stand,' wrote James, 'on my gathered impressions.' Then, perhaps remembering how he had been pilloried in America for his little study of Hawthorne a quarter of a century before, he added he was prepared to 'go to the stake' for what he had written. The American critics had no violent reaction. They spoke of James's 'antipathy' and they complained about his style. At the same time the usual compliments were paid to his 'fastidiously probing mind'. H. G. Wells, who had written a book on *The Future in America* published almost at the same time, wrote James – 'you take the whole thing as an ineffectual civilization and judge it with so temperate and informed a decisiveness'. He added, 'I wish there was a Public worthy of you – and me ... How much will they get out of what you have got in?'

3

He could not resist an opportunity offered him shortly after his book was done to discuss further the ways in which American women sacrificed the tone and the form of their inherited speech. Asked by Elizabeth Jordan to write three articles for *Harper's Bazar* he ended by doing eight, four on American speech and four on American manners. These he did not try to publish in England. They were intended for Americans. Bad speech bred bad manners. He blamed American men for cultivating and fostering a state of 'queenship' in the women; and he blamed the women for their failure to meet the responsibilities of sustaining and moulding the young. The essays were written in haste and with great looseness. James had spent his best efforts on *The American Scene*. The chips from the workshop are fragmentary and prolix; yet they reflect the same critical spirit, the same indignation; and the same energy. The American language was undermined by 'the unequalled potency of advertisement'. He remembered the older time when speech in New England had been 'an interesting, a really tonic form of English utterance' – touched always 'with a certain Puritan rusticity, as by the echo of the ox-team driven, before the plough, over stony soil, and of the small and circumspect town-meeting'. What hurt James in a country with so large a heritage was 'the apparently bland acceptance of the rising tide of barbarism by those who had so many reasons to "know", and who would have had so many rights to protest'.

His papers on manners were of a piece with those on speech. He amusingly characterized the strange feminine diets 'slobbering up a dab of hot and a dab of cold, a dab of sweet and a dab of sour, of mixing salads with ices, fish with flesh, hot cakes with mutton chops, pickles with pastry and maple syrup with everything' and all the while reading newspapers – 'the vast open mouth, adjusted as to the chatter of Bedlam'.

'We have, as a people, no sense of manners at all,' said James, and by manners he meant the totality of the forms of human relations. This reflected 'an absence of discipline'. His conclusion was that manners were above all 'an economy; the sacrifice of them has always in the long run to be made up, just as the breakages and dilapidations have to paid for at the end of the tenancy of a house carelessly occupied'.

He had planned a second volume of American impressions. He wanted to write a paper on the middle west; another on 'California and the Pacific Coast'; there would be one on the universities and the colleges, for he had lectured at almost a dozen from Bryn Mawr to Harvard, from Notre Dame to Berkeley, and had even visited an eccentric 'School of Antiquity' of theosophical orientation at Point Loma, California. By the time he had completed *The American Scene* and the articles on speech and manners he found his impressions fading; he felt also he had sufficiently exploited his trip. His nephew Harry believed that the San Francisco earthquake of 1906 'made such a large hole in what he would have written'. William James and his wife were at Stamford when it occurred, and Henry experienced several days of deep anxiety about his brother's fate. And then more important work needed to be done. The western journey was never written.

91

The Better Chance

THE next four years were spent by Henry James preparing the collective edition of his novels and tales. 'I should particularly like to call it the New York Edition if that may pass for a general title of sufficient dignity and distinctness,' he wrote to Scribner's, adding that it 'refers the whole enterprise explicitly to my native city – to which I have had no great opportunity of rendering that sort of homage'. The months of unrelieved toil James expended in the preparation of the Edition (its full title was *The Novels and Tales of Henry James*, New York Edition) shows beyond question that he regarded this as his literary monument. With a courage and zeal few writers had shown, he rewrote his early works to bring them up to the level of his maturity. He did not adhere to their chronological order, but grouped them according to themes and subjects; he wrote a series of prefaces, discussing publicly for the first time the history and theory of his work, the 'poetics' of his fiction. And he embarked with great enthusiasm on a quest to discover the right symbolic scenes to serve as frontispieces. He was ruthless in his omissions. As his publisher announced, the New York Edition contained 'all of the author's fiction that he desires perpetuated'.

I

From the very beginning James had decided the set should consist of twenty-three volumes. 'I regard 23 volumes as sufficient for the series and have no wish to transcend it. I shall make what I wish to "preserve" fit into the number and only desire to sift and re-sift, in selection – so as to leave nothing but fine gold!' Later, James would shift ground and say the number of volumes was imposed by his publisher; the preliminary correspondence shows however that Scribner was ready to print James's total work. The 'complete' novels and tales would have come to thirty-five volumes. The idea of making the edition *selective* was entirely James's, and was emphasized by him in a long memorandum to his publisher. The choice of twenty-three was not arbitrary. There seems to have been a special reason for it. The figure seems indeed to have had a certain magic for James; when he needs a date, a youthful age, a general number, he often fixes on twenty-three. One recalls in particular a scene in *The Awkward Age* when Vanderbank explores Nanda's library: 'I see you go in for sets – and, my dear child, upon my word, I see *big* sets. What's this – "Vol. 23 : *The British Poets*." Vol. 23 is delightful – do tell me about Vol. 23.' We might speculate about the significance of the combination of 2 and 3 – and we might recognize that James had always been the 'third person' in his relations with his mother and his brother; and then his Aunt Kate was the third person in a combination with his parents. But we need not go so far afield in seeking an answer to the arcane number. James's first essay on Balzac in 1875 was inspired by the issue of the collected edition of that novelist and in it we find him saying, 'Balzac's complete works occupy 23 huge octavo volumes, in the stately but inconvenient *édition définitive* lately published.' The Master, who regarded Balzac as 'the father of us all', paid homage not only to New York in his Edition. He bowed respectfully to the *Comédie Humaine*. His edition would be the '*comédie humaine*' of Henry James.

2

The figure 23 offers us a key to its organization. As Balzac had grouped his scenes of provincial, Parisian, political and private life, we can discern that James planned the New York Edition as a series of 'scenes of the international life', to which he added a group of 'scenes of English life'. In his correspondence with Scribner's he fell into Balzacian designations, referring to his 'stories of the literary life' and his 'tales of the quasi-supernatural and "gruesome"' grouped in separate volumes. The effect of this limitation was that the novelist did not give himself room to turn around. Six of his novels were of such length that they required two volumes. With the addition of three single-volumed novels, he used up fifteen of his twenty-three volumes at the very start. He then had to fit his shorter novels, and a selection of his tales, into the remaining eight volumes. Thus of the 108 short stories he had written up to this time, only sixty-six found their way into the definitive edition.

This kind of selection and arrangement meant that James had to juggle with stories according to their length as well as their subject or theme. Chronology, he had to admit, was 'absolutely defeated' not only by thematic arrangement but by still other 'adjustments' such as making sure the title stories matched the frontispieces. In the Scribner papers are preserved loose sheets on which James listed the contents of his volumes of tales. The tales were considerably shuffled. In the end part of his scheme collapsed. He had not counted his wordage carefully: his volumes of tales proved too long. They spilled over into a twenty-fourth volume. James did not reply to Scribner for a week. Then he wrote a long letter in which we can read his deep irritation and disappointment. The arcane plan was spoiled. 'My groupings had been, of course, affinities much observed, so that each volume should offer, as to content, a certain harmonious physiognomy; and now that felicity is perforce – I abundantly recognize – disturbed.' If this was true of two or three of the volumes containing tales, it nevertheless did not affect the fundamental structure of the edifice. The architectural form of the monument was preserved; it constitutes, in the totality of Henry James's work, a work of art in itself.

3

In preparing the New York Edition James seems to have had an image of himself as the 'American Balzac'. The language of the prospectus accords him this kind of position.

He is *par excellence* the American novelist. In the words of no other writer have American types of character and ideas appeared in such high relief and been characterized with such definite reference to *nationality*. He is the representative cosmopolitan novelist, also. And it is because of the frequent foreignness of his scene, which serves as a background, and of the society that peoples it, which affords a contrast, that his American characters and American point of view are set off with such marked effect.

The prospectus went on to say in similar Jamesian sentences that in this notable aspect James was the true successor to Fenimore Cooper and shared

with the greatest of our earlier novelists the distinction of performing a patriotic service in the world's field of letters. But for his novels America would figure far less importantly in this domain than it does. And but for his exquisite literary art, developed in a degree hardly con-

ceived of a generation ago, America would stand far lower in the cosmopolitan scale of artistic literary production. As a matter of fact, owing
to Mr James, America holds the world's primacy in fiction.

The New York Edition was designed 'to give Mr James's work the
material form and presentment proportionate to his literary fame'.

Balzac had 'read the universe, as hard and as loud as he could,
into the France of his time,' James had said. He set himself a comparable task – he read America and Americans into the world – the
European world – read them back into the civilization from which
they had seceded. The first three novels deal with three pilgrims
abroad – Roderick Hudson, the artist, Christopher Newman, the
man of business, Isabel Archer, the archetypal American woman.
The next volumes contain James's English novels. There follow the
short novels and the long tales which are arranged thematically :
and then the volumes of short stories, those of the artist life, the
ghost stories, and the international scene. What James left out is
abundantly clear. He omitted his 'Scenes of American Life' – *The
Bostonians, Washington Square, The Europeans*, and nearly all of
his American short stories. They would have required too much
revision especially in the light of his recent travels in America; he
seems to have set them aside to be a later extension of the original
edifice, in the way that Balzac's twenty-three volumes were aug-
mented so that the set of Balzac on the Master's shelves consisted
finally of fifty-two volumes. 'I treat certain portions of my work
as unhappy accidents (many portions of many – of all men's works
are)', he explained to one inquirer. He had tried to re-read *Washington Square* but couldn't 'and I fear it must go'. Also set aside was
the early pot-boiler *Confidence*.

Of the Edition's size James said to Howells,

Twenty-three do seem a fairly blatant array – and yet I rather surmise
that there may have to be a couple of supplementary volumes for certain
too marked omissions ... I have even a dim vague view of reintroducing
with a good deal of titivation and cancellation the too-diffuse but, I
somehow feel, tolerably full and good *Bostonians* of nearly a quarter of
a century ago; that production never having, even to my much-
disciplined patience, received any sort of justice. But it will take, doubtless, a great deal of artful redoing, and – and I haven't now had the
courage or time for anything so formidable as touching and retouching it.

4

In his tale *The Middle Years* Henry James had described an elderly writer who dreams of 'a better chance' in which to do the supreme writing of his life. He is 'a passionate corrector, a fingerer of style'. In creating the New York Edition James got his better chance. Not only could he alter his old texts, but he could apply the varnish of his late style. James used the imagery of picture-restoration to describe his process. Going over old work affirmed a 'creative intimacy'; 'critical apprehension' became active again. James 'nowhere scrupled to rewrite a sentence or a passage on judging it susceptible of a better turn'. Revision for James was not a matter of choice but of 'immediate and perfect necessity'. Even much-revised older work found itself revised again. *Roderick Hudson* had been retouched in its progress from magazine to book in 1875. Preparing the English edition four years later James added a note saying the book had received 'a large number of verbal alterations'. Several passages had been rewritten. Now in 1905 he was rewriting portions of it again. *The Portrait of a Lady* was wholly renovated since it occupies so large a place in his canon. His emendations strengthen his characters and eliminate ambiguities. Isabel Archer is so altered as to be almost a new personage. In this 'fingering' of his text, James did not alter the substance of his story; he introduced no new scenes or new incidents. The essential structure remained. His method was to use reinforcing imagery to overcome earlier failures in explicitness. If erotic feeling was absent in the earlier work, the Master now made amends. The best-known example is that of Caspar Goodwood's kiss in the closing paragraphs of *The Portrait of a Lady*. In the first edition James described the kiss in a single sentence. 'His kiss was like a flash of lightning; when it was dark again she was free.' In the New York Edition this becomes a paragraph :

His kiss was like white lightning, a flash that spread, and spread again, and stayed; and it was extraordinarily as if, while she took it, she felt each thing in his hard manhood that had least pleased her, each aggressive fact of his face, his figure, his presence, justified of its intense identity and made one with this act of possession. So had she heard of those wrecked and under water following a train of images before they sink. But when darkness returned she was free.

The earlier Isabel was incapable of this kind of feeling. Her fear of passion is now made explicit – and in the language of Eros.

The American which James revised after the *Portrait* is the most rewritten of all the novels. It had originally been set down in a hurry to support the novelist during his first winter's residence in Paris; re-reading it, twenty-eight years later, James said he was 'stupefied' by his failure to create an atmosphere of feeling between his American hero and the French noblewoman, Madame de Cintré. In the first edition of 1877 Newman says to Madame de Cintré, 'Your only reason is that you love me!' and James makes him murmur this 'with an eloquent gesture, and for want of a better reason Madame de Cintré reconciled herself to this one'. James now altered this:

'Your only reason is that you love me!' he almost groaned for deep insistence; and he laid his two hands on her with a persuasion that she rose to meet. He let her feel as he drew her close, bending his face to her, the fullest force of his imposition; and she took it from him with a silent, fragrant, flexible surrender which – since she seemed to keep back nothing – affected him as sufficiently prolonged to pledge her to everything.

In revising *The American* James made a certain number of significant substantive changes. He added five years to Christopher Newman's age – made him 40 rather than 35. By this stroke he altered the time-scheme of the entire novel. He wanted a more mature Newman. He had originally given Newman too little time in which to make his fortune between the end of the Civil War and his going abroad. The general effect of most of the revisions is in the direction of verbal precision, clarification of motive and a strengthening of the fibre of the work. James took care of certain overworked words like 'picturesque' and 'romantic'. He seems to have been less inclined to drop his much-used 'dusky'. He simplified conversation, substituted more direct language for pompous words and introduced fresh colloquial utterance. Some of his revisions went in the opposite direction; new pomposities and verbal eccentricities were set down. The classical example is a change made by James which substitutes the verbal baroque for direct statement. In the first edition of *The American* James described Newman – 'his eye was of a clear, cold grey, and save for a rather abundant moustache, he was clean shaved'. In the New York Edition this became: 'His eye was of a clear cold grey, and save for the abundant droop of his moustache he spoke, as to cheek and chin, of the joy of the matutinal steel.' James had been experiencing this joy ever since he had shaved off his beard. The change of text adds a note of comedy not intended by the author.

The paste-up of *The Portrait of a Lady* has been preserved and it can be noted that James freely mixed editions. He used leaves from both the Boston edition of 1882 and the one-volume London edition of the same year. Sometimes even his trained eye had missed errors which were carried through most of the earlier editions to be corrected now in the New York Edition. Thus Palazzo Roccanera is called *Piazza* Roccanera in all but the first serial version, the London 1883 edition and the New York Edition. In six other printings the error is uncorrected. Such technical matters aside, the net effect of James's revisions, and particularly in the *Portrait*, is to enhance the text and in this instance, the rewriting has been so subtle and skilful, as to create almost a new novel. A striking alteration was James's omission of two pages in the twenty-ninth chapter devoted to the nature of Osmond and the egotism of bachelorhood. Perhaps his own years as a bachelor and his concern with egotism made him feel that his reflections on this subject at 38 were superficial. At any rate, for some ninety-four lines of early analysis of his character James substituted ten lines in which he simply tells the reader that Isabel has discerned Osmond's 'style' and that this has a certain uniqueness. As James elsewhere put it, Osmond suggests 'the elegant complicated medal struck off for a special occasion'.

James's revisions – of the *Portrait* in particular – pose a complicated problem for textual editors. The editions cannot be harmonized into a single text; to do so would be to create still another version of the novel not of James's making. James created a situation in which the early text must be regarded as having its own validity quite distinct from that of the later text. The New York Edition becomes a separate and unique entity.

'How sickly I used to write!' James exclaimed to Brander Matthews who wanted to reprint an old James essay in an anthology. Max Beerbohm must have heard of this, for he one day drew on the flyleaf of a volume containing another revised Jamesian essay, a caricature of the obese Master, clean-shaven, facing the slimmer bearded James of the middle years. The cartoon could have figured in Max's famous series of 'the old and the young self'. In a balloon over the heads of early and late Henry James, Max wrote the words 'How badly you –' the Old James ending the sentence with 'wrote' and the Young James with 'write'. Beside James's footnote, saying the essay had been published originally in 1887, Beerbohm scribbled 'and was very obviously – or rather, deviously, and circuitously – revised in the great dark fulness of time, for republication in 1915'.

5

The prefaces – eighteen in number – which Henry James created for the Edition enabled him to say what he had hoped all his life critics would say for him. He defined his exploration of the novel form, discussed his belief that the novelist must create an organic whole, and explained his innovations, particularly his addiction to 'point of view'. The novel in English had long been taken for granted as simple storytelling. James, arriving on the English scene late in century, had taken the novel-machine apart in a very American way, given it a technology it had not possessed, and like the Americans of the future, practised his craft strenuously and professionally, whereas most of his English confrères practised it in a relaxed and spontaneous way, often as amateurs. James's joy lay in the skill, the craft, the pride of invention. He valued craft even beyond *gloire*. In his prefaces, to list but a few of the subjects, James discussed the extent to which the sense of place has to be created; the way in which a novelist must make his reader feel the passage of time; the need, as he felt it, for placing the novel's vision in a 'central intelligence', so that the world is perceived through a Hamlet or a Lear and not through some 'headlong fool' who can only see so much less of it. He discussed the use of first person narration, and the 'fluidity of self-revelation' resulting from this kind of storytelling. He himself was willing to use the first person only in shorter tales; not one of his long novels is told by a character involved in the action. In perhaps the finest of the prefaces, affixed to *The Portrait of a Lady*, James discussed the way in which a novel must be considered an 'organic' structure – quite like the human body – in which everything is related to everything else. He discussed also the secrets of the imagination, the 'deep well of unconscious cerebration', recognizing like Coleridge – and Freud – that within the unconscious the deepest and richest part of man's art invisibly grows and finds its shape. He talked of form, and the way in which it is substance; he described how some of his characters began as *ficelles*, that is as puppets drawn by a string, placed as 'the reader's friend' in stories from which the omniscient author with-draws and lets the narrative unwind by itself; and how a *ficelle* can take on flesh, cease to be a puppet, become a part of the action. He talked of indirection in storytelling, and how to arouse terror in the reader by artful ambiguity; he had clearly analysed, long before modern psychology, the ways in which a novelist involves his reader in the story and plays on the reader's feelings. He dealt with the plasticity of the novelist's medium and the use in alternation of 'picture' and 'scene'; he described his way of turning narrative into drama – and how he used to say to himself 'dramatize! dramatize!' These were but a few of the subjects he dealt with on the level of craft, using vigorous imagery and highly condensed verbal state-ment. And then there were definitions and 'terms' – a whole termin-ology of fiction which critics have since borrowed and made universal. This does not exhaust the complexity of the prefaces; woven into them was also a meditation on his own themes – the 'Americano-European legend' he had created, the variant situations of the myth he had explored. Playing through the prefaces is the human light by which James worked – the situations he chose to develop and explore. In his preface to *The Aspern Papers* there is an eloquent excursion on the uses of the past, the 'visitable' past, in which the artist can still recover the human fact and the human dilemma, instead of the broken artefacts of the early centuries, whose creators are out of reach of the modern mind. A great sense of poetry is infused into the prefaces; and then they are touched by a gentle mood of reminiscence. James begins by recalling the occa-sion on which the first idea came to him; a dinner-table conversa-tion, a sudden flash of inspiration while riding in a horse-car in Boston, an anecdote told by a lady in Rome (of a young girl from America whose brashness shocked the Roman 'set'), or how Tur-genev, talking to him long ago in Paris, made him feel that plot isn't important – that what counts is the novelist's seeing his charac-ter. Then the character itself possesses and provides its 'story'. In the prefaces, James recalled the places in which his stories had been written, how the chattering waterside life had floated in through his hotel window in Venice as he composed certain pages of *The Portrait of a Lady*; or how he had written parts of *The American* in elaborate rooms in Paris; or how one day on a pottering train in Italy, in the hot summer, he whiled away the time listening to an American doctor speak of his practice, and got the theme for *The*

Pupil. He spoke of the fog-filtered Kensington mornings, when he had worked in De Vere Gardens in that comfortable bourgeois flat with its sky windows; or his hotel bedroom during the centenary exhibition in Paris in 1889. Into this mixture of memory and theory he dropped the names of the novelists and poets who had meant most to him – and to the art of fiction – the lessons learned not only from Balzac but from Browning, Cervantes and Coleridge, Dickens, Turgenev, and George Eliot – she who had written of the 'frail vessels', the young women who also became James's subject – and Flaubert and Ibsen, Maupassant and Meredith, Shakespeare and Stendhal, Stevenson and Thackeray, Trollope and Tolstoy – the Russians whose works he called 'large loose baggy monsters' because they did not shape their materials, but gave the readers great chunks of life 'with their queer elements of the accidental and the arbitrary'. James would always argue that Tolstoy's greatness lay not in his art but in his vision of life – and that no one could learn anything about novel-writing from him.

In these crowded pages Percy Lubbuck quarried the essence of his book *The Craft of Fiction*; and in studying the prefaces Richard Blackmur developed his recondite critical style. James's declaration to Howells that his prefaces were 'in general, a sort of plea for Criticism, for Discrimination, for Appreciation on other than infantile lines – as against the so almost universal Anglo-Saxon absence of these things' was accurate. Less than a treatise, these prefaces, in their colloquial ease and flow, dictated at intervals between 1906 and 1908, show the embodied truths of the art of fiction as James had practised it and the distillation of a lifetime of close reading of major and minor novelists in the West. There is a noble peroration which sums up James's belief in the 'religion of doing', that is the life of action in art – by which he meant 'the imagination in action'. The prefaces were James's supreme gift to criticism: and at the same time they elucidated what criticism in its chronic blindness had failed to perceive in his work. It would take fifty years of hindsight for criticism to catch up with the lesson of Henry James.

6

From the first, James had taken it for granted that each volume of his definitive edition would have a frontispiece. A long line of illustrators, not least Cruikshank, had added pictures to prose fiction.

However, he looked askance at any effort 'to graft or "grow" at whatever point, a picture by another hand on my own picture'. He accordingly took the precaution of telling Scribner that he would appreciate 'a single good plate, in each volume'. To make certain there would be no mistake about it he added 'only one, but of thoroughly fine quality'. Twenty or more frontispieces were needed – 'some scene, object or locality, and associated with some one or other of the tales in the volume. To obtain this would be costly. Scribner underwrote the cost.

In the United States early in 1905 Henry James had been approached by a young photographer named Alvin Langdon Coburn, an artistic young man of 23 who photographed him for a New York magazine. James had the idea of trying him out on some of the scenes needed for the edition. In spite of his youth, Coburn was considered a pioneering figure in the new art of the camera. At his one-man show in London he had been praised by Bernard Shaw, as 'one of the most accomplished and sensitive artist-photographers now living'. James had seen his work; not only his portraits but his pictures of London, his landscapes, photographs of docks at Liverpool and arches in Rome, all attempting, in the fashion of the time, to give a painter-like texture to photographic surface. During Coburn's visit in 1906 to Rye, James gave Coburn his preliminary instructions and out of Coburn's photographs evolved the principle that satisfied James completely. His illustrations would be 'optical' symbols. They would be photographs of general scenes, material objects. They would enhance, but in no way intrude irrelevant images upon, his own literary images. Photographs would have a total 'objectivity', an impersonal quality necessary for illustrating the edition.

James entered into the plans with a zest the photographer would always remember. He dispatched Coburn to the Continent, to the cities of his fictions, and promised that he would himself guide him in London. In a series of letters he gave Coburn his instructions – as if he were an envoy on a delicate mission. First James wanted a portal of an aristocratic hotel in the Faubourg St Germain – a *porte-cochère*, 'a grand specimen of the type for *The American*.' 'Tell a cabman that you want to drive through every street [in the Faubourg St Germain] not but that there are there plenty of featureless houses too.' After the drive James urged Coburn to 'go back and walk and stare at your ease'. He asked Coburn to look out in the

Place de la Concorde 'for some combination of objects that won't be hackneyed and commonplace and panoramic; some fountain or statue or balustrade or vista or suggestion (of some damnable sort or other) that will serve in connection with *The Ambassadors* perhaps'. James wanted a photograph of the Théâtre Français; also 'go into the sad Luxembourg Gardens, and, straight across from the arcade of the Odéon, to look for my right garden-statue (composing with other interesting objects) – against which my chair was tilted back. Do bring me something right, in short, from the Luxembourg.'

Early in December 1906 Coburn went to Venice. For guidance James sent the photographer to his old friend Constance Fletcher, the American writer who lived in the Palazzo Capello on the Rio Marin, diagonally opposite the railway station. It had that rare thing in Venice, a garden. This was the Palazzino James had had in mind in 1887 for *The Aspern Papers*. The novelist fell into the language of the story itself.

It is the old faded pink-faced battered-looking and quite homely and plain (as things go in Venice) old Palazzino on the right side of the small Canal, a little way along, as you enter it by the end of the Canal towards the Station. It has a garden behind it, and I think, though I am not sure, some bit of a garden-wall beside it; it doesn't moreover bathe its steps, if I remember right, directly in the Canal, but has a small paved Riva or footway in front of it, and *then* water-steps down from this little quay. As to that, however, the time since I have seen it may muddle me; but I am almost sure ... You must judge for yourself, face to face with the object, how much, on the spot, it seems to lend itself to a picture.

The other Venetian picture was a photograph of the Palazzo Barbaro, scene of so many of James's visits to Venice in his later years. James referred to 'the beautiful range of old *upper* Gothic windows' and it was these Coburn photographed for *The Wings of the Dove*. 'And do any other odd and interesting bit you can, that may serve for a sort of symbolized and generalized Venice; preferring the noble and fine aspect, however, to the merely shabby and familiar ... yet especially *not* choosing the pompous and obvious things that one everywhere sees photos of.'

London subjects were searched out together – the front of the old antique shop for *The Golden Bowl*, the front of the grocery shop for *In the Cage*, a house in St John's Wood where James's memories went back to his boyhood. On another occasion they went to Hampstead Heath in search of a bench needed for the 'tales of the literary life'. The photograph appears there labelled 'Saltram's Seat' – Saltram being the Coleridge figure in James's tale *The Coxon Fund*. This was the bench on which James had sat, long ago, with George du Maurier, during their rambles on the Heath, talking of Paris and French novels. For the last of the series Coburn took a memorable and much-reprinted picture – that of a slightly blurred Portland Place, used in the second volume of *The Golden Bowl* – the rear view of a hansom in the broad thoroughfare, the distance fading into a haze.

There was one other London picture which James wanted specifically. He arranged with Claude Phillips, keeper of the Wallace Collection, for Coburn to photograph 'a divine little chimney piece, with all its wondrous garniture, a couple of chairs beside it, and a piece on either side, of the pale green figured damask of the wall'. This was to be the frontispiece to *The Spoils of Poynton*. The Master introduced a hidden autobiographical note when he had Coburn photograph the entrance to Lamb House to serve as frontispiece to *The Awkward Age*.

In his preface to *The Golden Bowl* the novelist paid tribute to Coburn's art but he was precise about the danger of the visual to the verbal. 'Anything that relieves responsible prose of the duty of being good enough, interesting enough, and pictorial enough does it the worst of services,' James wrote. The quest for the small antiquarian shop was in reality a quest for 'a shop of the mind'; for this reason nothing would induce James to say where they had found their picture. They had sought always 'certain inanimate characteristics of London streets' and London always ended by 'giving one absolutely everything one asks'.

Long before he had finished his work on the New York Edition, Henry James was exhausted and even bored with it. The volumes began to be issued, in December 1907 and continued into 1909. To his nephew Harry, James wrote of

the Nightmare of the edition ... my terror of not keeping sufficiently ahead in doing my part of it (all the revising, rewriting, retouching, Preface-making and proof-correcting) has so paralysed me – as panic fear – that I have let other decencies go to the wall. The printers and publishers tread on my heels, and I feel their hot breath behind me.

There were in reality only certain moments when this pressure was intense. James gave himself an excellent head start, and the issuing of the novels – that is, the first fifteen volumes – proceeded with great regularity. The overflow into twenty-four volumes meant dismembering some of the prefaces already written to suit the new story-arrangements. The rearrangement meant that he had to put the tale of *Julia Bride* into his volume of ghost stories; and certain later tales on other themes consorted with *Daisy Miller* in the 'international' volume. Chagrin gave way to indifference. The re-arrangements were awkward; he wasn't sure that the prefaces now alluded to the stories in the volumes they prefaced (most of them did) 'but at any rate let matters stand as they are, please, in spite of any such small irregularity'. Long afterwards – in the last year of his life – he would describe the Edition as 'really a monument (like Ozymandias) which has never had the least intelligent critical justice done to it – or any sort of critical attention at all paid to it –' He added that

the artistic problem involved in my scheme was a deep and exquisite one, and moreover, was as I held, very effectively solved. Only it took such time – *and* such taste – in other words such aesthetic light. No more commercially thankless job of the literary order was (Prefaces and all – *they* of a thanklessness!) accordingly ever achieved.

92

The House of Mirth

BY the spring of 1907, after almost two years of unremitting labour, Henry James began to feel restless. *The American Scene* was in the press. He had given himself a long head start on the New York Edition and was revising *The Princess Casamassima*, the fifth and sixth volumes. He had written *The Jolly Corner* and several fugitive pieces, and had just finished a chapter for a novel by several hands, *The Whole Family*, a literary stunt originated by Harpers. He longed to be out of his Rye-cage. For some weeks the 'Angel of Devastation' had been beckoning. Mrs Wharton had leased an apartment in Paris at 58 rue de Varenne. Would Henry come and stay? Would he go on a motor trip to the south of France? Eight years had elapsed since the novelist's last visit to the Continent, two since his return from America. The Master spoke of 'pampered Princesses', and the Whartonian 'eagle pounce and eagle flight'. He squirmed at the pounce; he loved the flight. Mrs Wharton's energy was 'devouring and desolating, ravaging, burning, and destroying'. She destroyed by taking him away from his work. But he wanted to be taken away. New imagery began to creep into his letters. Now the eagle had become a 'Firebird'; she rode in 'a chariot of fire'. When she looked at him, in her serious way, with a touch of smile at the edge of her lips – looked at him out of her hazel eyes – Henry James found it difficult to say 'no'. 'The rich, rushing, ravening Whartons' – this they might be, yet James at 64 was not yet prepared to give up the social pleasures of his prime. 'I won't deny,' he wrote to his Gallo-American friend, Edward Lee Childe, 'that for the charm of Mrs Wharton's society I would go far.' He didn't have to go far. Early in March of 1907 he crossed the Channel; in the rue de Varenne, he announced himself in 'gilded captivity'. He came for a week or two. He remained in Paris a fortnight and then they went for the tour Mrs Wharton celebrated in *A Motor-Flight through France*; after that there was a further stay at No. 58 which James called 'the house of mirth' – an allusion to Mrs Wharton's successful novel. James felt this might be his last visit to the Continent and he prolonged it. It was the longest visit he ever paid. He may not have had a 'pure' holiday because Scribner proofs kept catching up with him. But when had he not worked as he travelled?

I

Mrs Wharton respected James's working hours; she had hers as well. Both novelists – the inventor of the American–European legend and the dissector of 'old New York' – remained in their rooms until lunch, sometimes into the afternoon. Mrs Wharton scribbled little messages and sent them by her servants to divert the Master. There were no serious interruptions. James had never penetrated the life of the Faubourg St Germain and now he found himself agreeably ensconced in it, not far from the Invalides. Mrs Wharton, an American aristocrat, had little difficulty encountering the newer French aristocracy – an aristocracy less rigid than that described by Honoré de Balzac. She moved with ease and elegance among countesses and duchesses. James's old friend Paul Bourget, now an 'inflamed academician' gave Mrs Wharton *entrée*. 'Our friend is a great and graceful lioness,' James told Howard Sturgis; keeping up the image he said he had 'come in for many odd bones and other leavings of the Christians (if Christians they can be called) who have been offered to her maw in this extraordinary circus'. There were charming small dinner parties in the rue de Varenne. Mrs Winthrop Chanler remembered 'the guests were carefully chosen for their absolute compatibility'. When the parties were over and the guests were gone, James would draw his chair to the fire, invite his American friends to approach and opening his eyes wide would murmur: 'Now let us say what we really think.'

Mrs Wharton remembered James's 'schoolboy's zest'. Her friends told her they had never met an Anglo-Saxon who spoke such admirable French. He was not only correct and fluent; he translated the Jamesian style into it. The schoolboy's zest of which Mrs Wharton speaks is to be read in his letters. He reported he had had 'an indigestion of Chères Madames' – he who had always wanted to meet French society. The most attractive woman he met wasn't French, but she had been absorbed as a graft in the Faubourg St Germain. Descended from Viennese Jewish bankers, the widowed Comtesse Robert de Fitz-James entertained and amused him. Then there was the Comtesse d'Humières, with her 'pretty salient eyes and her pretty salient gestures', whose husband had translated Kipling; and there were such old Faubourg names as de Béarn and D'Arenberg and others, like Madame Waddington, once Mary King, the American wife of a French foreign minister. 'Mrs Wharton has been exceedingly kind – she is a dear of dears,' James told Sturgis. 'It has really been lovely,' he wrote on the eve of their motor tour to the South of France.

2

They left on a bland March morning, the first day of spring, in the Wharton's new Panhard, with the Yankee chauffeur Charles Cook at the wheel, and various servants dispatched ahead with the luggage as for a royal progress. The car climbed the hill to Ville d'Avray and proceeded to Versailles. They were 'on indiarubber wings'. They visited Rambouillet, they paused in Chartres, they looked at chateaux, they lingered in churches. It was leisurely; it was princely. They went to Blois, to Poitiers, to Bordeaux, and thence to the Pyrenees. There were local stops and lunches at various inns. 'The motor is a magical marvel,' James wrote, and 'this large, smooth old France is wonderful'. He had never seen France in such a beguiling sequence of panorama and close-up. At Pau, Teddy Wharton was ill for several days, and Henry and Mrs Wharton made a series of neighbourhood excursions. Then they went to Carcassonne and Toulouse; remounting the valley of the Rhône they paused at Nîmes, Arles, and Orange. The stop at Pau enabled James to write some letters. A long one to Goody Allen reveals the only serious discomfort he experienced in this otherwise cheerful journey. He had always stayed at first-class hotels but had never cultivated the hotel de luxe: and he discovered that the delights and comforts of this kind of travel drained his modest purse. He was living, as he put it, 'an expensive fairy-tale', proof again of the old saying that it was 'one's rich friends who cost one!' He blushed, he told Goody Allen, 'for such sordid details in the face of my high entertainment'. The loyal Jessie Allen kept this letter, but pasted strips of paper over the sordid details.

They stopped at Nohant to visit the home of George Sand. James was enormously curious about it. They wandered through the old country mansion, inspected the family graves, James reading every word on the tombstones; then after looking at the marionette theatre they went into the garden. James surveyed the plain house which had harboured so much ancient passion: 'And in which of those rooms, I wonder, did George herself sleep?' Edith heard him muse. He looked at her with a twinkling eye. 'Though in which, indeed, in which indeed, my dear, did she *not*?' Years later James would write of

that wondrous day when we explored the very scene where they pigged so thrillingly together. What a crew, what *mœurs*, what habits, what conditions and relations every way – and what an altogether mighty and marvellous George! – not diminished by all the greasiness and smelliness in which she made herself (and so many other persons!) at home.

The Master and Mrs Wharton had a great community of interest: it was Teddy Wharton who was the 'third person' in this party. And it is clear that when the Panhard turned again into the Parisian traffic, after three exciting weeks, the Master and the lady novelist felt they had had a charming adventure together, a little tour of high intelligence and perception and for James a great deal of luxurious living. The Master complained to the end that it had been costly: there would have been seven servants including the chauffeur to tip. But, 'Ah, the lovely rivers and the inveterately glorious grub.'

And to friends at Rye, 'Ah, the good food and good manners and good looks everywhere!' Followed by 'Ah, the poor frowsy tea-and-toasty Lamb House.'

He was in no hurry to return to his tea-and-toast. Waiting in the rue de Varenne were piles of Edition proof. He settled down to the galleys. The life of the Faubourg continued. 'We *déjeunons* out, and we dine, and we visit countesses in between.' James was writing to their friend Gaillard Lapsley. 'The Teddies are divinely good – and their inflamed Academician lunches here Sunday.' James continued to be shocked by the changes in Bourget. He had once admired him; now he spoke of his 'almost *insane* bad manners, snobbishness, and folly', a talent spoiled by social pampering and worldliness. He found a great alienation in him, 'a detachment and irrelevancy of attitude, tone, and direction'. His old friend Thomas Sergeant Perry turned up; they had been at school together in Newport; Perry had married a Cabot; the years had passed; they had drifted apart. They met almost as if there had been no gap; they took long walks, and went to a concert. Perry's version was, 'I saw Harry James several times when he was here, tho' his hostess, Mrs Wharton kept a pretty tight clutch on him, and didn't let him stray far out of sight.' James spent agreeable hours with his nephew Billy, who painted at Julien's when he wasn't playing tennis or rowing. The novelist's letters to William have a little of the tone of Lambert Strether talking about Chad Newsome as he urges his brother to allow Billy to remain in Paris and keep at his painting. 'He ought absolutely to stay another year and not *retomber* to the art-desert of home, before, like a camel, he has filled his stomach-pouch with water to see him through.' Henry James was thinking of his own art-starved condition in Cambridge forty years earlier.

James remained in Paris for three more weeks, well into May, 'steeped up to my chin in the human and social imbroglio', even though he felt himself to be 'rather keyed up' by ten weeks of the *grand monde*. He had enjoyed his weeks with the Whartons. They had marked a difference 'from one's promiscuous boulevardian quarters of the past', and he continued on this theme to Jocelyn Persse: 'I have had a very interesting agreeable time – one of the most agreeable I have ever had in Paris, through living in singularly well-appointed privacy in this fine old Rive Gauche quarter, away from the horrible boulevards and hotels and cosmopolite crowd.' He had 'come in for a great many social impressions of a sort I hadn't had for a long time – some of them of a more or less intimate French sort that I had *never* had; mixed, all, with a great deal of wondrous and beautiful motoring'. In most of his letters to his younger friend, it had been James who pleaded with Persse to bring him news of the great world. Now he had

plenty to tell you on some blest Sunday, after my return, when you come down and stroll with me in the alentour of poor dear russet Lamb House; which appears to me from here so russet and so humble and so modest and so British and so pervaded by boiled mutton and turnips; and yet withal so intensely precious and so calculated to rack me with homesickness.

The homesickness was a mere spasm. Italy called. He had made plans for a little trip south – it would be the twelfth of his lifetime. Howard Sturgis was in Rome; Hendrik Andersen beckoned. He travelled in a sleeper to Turin, pausing to revise certain pages of the *Princess Casamassima*; it was a way of ministering to his constitutional need for a few – even if very few – days 'of *recueillement* and solitude'.

3

He kept speaking of this as the 'last continental episode of my aged life', which it was not. A year later he would visit Mrs Wharton in Paris once more. Yet he felt quite correctly that he would never see Italy again. It was grossly changed from the time he had known it – the time when the Colosseum was still filled with earth and flowers grew out of the ruins. He spent seventeen days in Rome. Here he found Alice Mason, whom he remembered as young and beautiful in the days when they had gone riding in the Campagna. She was now 'very gentle and easy and coherent' – a 'silvery ghost' of the strong and passionate woman he remembered. He had some hours with Howard Sturgis whom he found rather depressed; they would meet again at the Edward Boits at Cernitoio. He spent much time with Hendrik Andersen who did a bust of the Master making him look like a Roman senator, but with much less life in his face than is to be found in the relics of the times of the Caesars. On one day James went to the Protestant Cemetery; he had visited it long ago to look at Shelley's grave and at Keats's; and here he had described the burial of Daisy Miller. He returned this time to see once more the violet-covered grave of Miss Woolson. Thirteen years had passed since her mysterious death. James communed silently there – feeling this to be his last farewell. His only reference to this personal pilgrimage was in a letter to Fenimore's niece, in which he spoke of the grave as 'the most beautiful thing in Italy – almost' and 'tremendously inexhaustibly touching'. He added 'its effect never fails to overwhelm'. The old emotion remained – and the old mystery.

Rome no longer had its old charm. 'The abatements and changes and modernisms and vulgarities, the crowd and the struggle and the frustration (of real communion with what one wanted) are quite dreadful,' he wrote to Billy. 'I quite revel in the thought that I shall never come to Italy *at all* again.' He dined one evening with his old friend Henry Brewster, one of the most perfect examples of the cosmopolitan-American type James had ever met. He had been fond of him of old; this was the last time he saw him, for Brewster died shortly afterwards. The latter, in a letter, described the dinner: 'I had an impression of great goodness and kindness, almost tenderness; of an immense *bienveillance* and yet of fastidious discrimination; something delicate and strong morally.' He noted James's 'puffy vegetarian look, and the spring, the flash of steel has gone'. He also said 'all joys, sorrows, hopes, trials, and strivings find a prompt and delicate echo in him'.

James enjoyed his renewed meetings with Hendrik Andersen – they had seen so little of each other during the eight years of their friendship. One gets a feeling, however, that his original ardour had cooled; yet a certain tenderness remained. James's memories were of his hours with Andersen in 'the cool arched workshop' fraternizing with the sculptor's models and posing for his bust; there were sessions at a restaurant, visits to a foundry where some of Andersen's work was being cast, and a long last evening on a terrace. Andersen lived with his sister Lucia and several of her snapshots have survived in which the sculptor, thin, bony, tall but no longer handsome, looms beside the portly obese novelist.

James was to have the novelty of motoring in Italy with Filippo de Filippi, an Italian explorer and traveller who had married an American wife. Filippi had the English manner of hospitality; he gave fine dinner parties over which he presided with his dark southern features and powerful voice. The Filippis, with the explorer himself driving, took James on two or three Roman excursions, including a crossing of the Tiber 'on a medieval raft', and then a picnic on the edge of the sea; there was 'a divine day' at Subiaco and then a two-day jaunt to Naples, going down by the mountains, to Monte Cassino, and returning by Gaeta, Terracina, the Pontine Marshes, and the Castelli, 'quite an ineffable experience. This brought home to me,' James wrote to Mrs Wharton later, 'with an intimacy and a penetration unprecedented how incomparably the old *coquine* of an Italy is the most beautiful country in the world – of a beauty (and an interest and complexity of beauty) so far beyond any other that none other is worth talking about.' James spoke out of the limitations of his journeyings. In his busy life he had not known Greece, or Africa, or the tropical parts of the world. Italy had sufficed. The 'dishevelled nymph' of his youth, however, was now an 'old *coquine*'. Of the Naples journey James told Mrs Wharton 'the day we came down from Posilippo in the early June morning is a memory of splendour and style and heroic elegance I never shall lose – and never shall renew!' This journey was memorialized in a vein of beautiful nostalgia in certain pages James added to his old writings about Italy when he assembled *Italian Hours* – that book in 1910 was his way of saying farewell to the Italy of all his years. The added pages were titled 'A Few Other Roman Neighbourhoods'. In them we find the delight he took in the ferrying of the Filippi car over the saffron-coloured Tiber 'on a boat that was little more than a big rustic raft', the visit to Ostia, to Castel Fusano with the massive Chigi tower and 'the immemorial stone-pines and the afternoon sky and the desolate sweetness and concentrated rarity of the picture'. These 'all kept their appointment, to fond memory, with that especial form of Roman faith, the fine aesthetic conscience in things, that is never, never broken'. James saw the ubiquitous bicycles of the Roman youth who had 'a great taste for flashing about in more or less denuded or costumed athletic and romantic bands and guilds'. He harboured special memories of Subiaco – a plunge into 'splendid solitary gravities, supreme romantic solemnities and sublimities, of landscape'. The Benedicine convent, clinging to vertiginous ledges and slopes of a vast gorge within that setting, was for James 'the very ideal of the tradition of that *extraordinary in the romantic*, handed down to us, as the most attaching and inviting spell of Italy, by all the old academic literature of travel and art of Salvator Rosas and Claudes'. As always, in his pictorial travel sketches, James brought in the hints of the personal – his exploration of 'sordidly papal streets' in the heterogeneous city 'in the company of a sculptor friend'. And he ended the pages of memory with an allusion to the last dinner with Andersen

an evening meal spread, in the warm still darkness that made no candle flicker, on the wide high space of an old loggia that overhung, in one quarter, the great obelisked Square preceding one of the Gates, and in the other the Tiber and the far Trastevere and more things than I can say – above all, as it were, the whole awkward past, the mild confused romance of the Rome one had lived and of which one was exactly taking leave under protection of the friendly lanterned and garlanded feast and the commanding, all-embracing roof-garden. It was indeed a reconciling, it was an altogether penetrating, last hour.

4

He had long ago said farewell to Florence. We have no record of this final visit. He had known so much of the old Americano–Florentine life, the days when Bellosguardo had been familiar with its drama of Frank Boott and his daughter Lizzie, and Duveneck, and the days he had spent with Fenimore. We know only that he lingered briefly and spent four days with Howard Sturgis and 'the Babe' who were in turn staying with James's old friend, the painter, Ned Boit at Cernitoio, over against Vallombrosa 'a dream of Tuscan loveliness'. A photograph of James, cigarette in hand on the long terrace of the Boits, with Sturgis in the foreground, offers us a less bloated figure than the Roman snapshots, and a more characteristic one. James had 'a really adorable *séjour*' and went on to Venice to the familiar Palazzo Barbaro and the Curtises.

Venice was his old Venice, unique, exquisite, beloved of all his years. 'Never has the whole place seemed to me sweeter, clearer, diviner,' and this in spite of a sirocco that blew during part of the time. He found the Curtises restrictive, formal, rigid, bound up by their prejudices and with 'such a terror of the vulgar' – but perhaps this was because he himself had so considerably 'loosened up'. They had grown older – Daniel Curtis indeed would soon die and Ariana would leave Venice for perpetual visits to friends and a lonely life chronicled by James to their mutual friend Goody Allen. The Curtises made James feel 'they discriminated so invidiously against anyone I might weakly wish to see, of my little other promiscuous acquaintance in Venice that I felt I could never again face the irritations and the inconvenience of it'. So it was farewell to Venice, too.

Yet it was the most difficult farewell of all. 'I don't care, frankly, if I never see the vulgarized Rome or Florence again,' James wrote that summer to Edith Wharton – 'but Venice never seemed to me more lovable.'

Late in June he turned north again. He spent three days at Lausanne at the Hotel Gibbon visiting a relative. On 4 July he was in Paris where he stayed at the Hôtel du Palais d'Orsay. Edith was no longer in the rue de Varenne. A few days later he was back at Lamb House. This was one of the rare occasions when his little English home seemed to him after the glories of Rome and the delights of Venice 'flat and common and humiliating. But here I am – and in my little deep-green garden, where the roses are almost as good as the Roman, and the lawn is almost as smooth beneath the feet as your floors of No. 3 – I try to forget what I've lost.' Thus to Henrik Andersen.

5

His farewell to Italy had been unmistakable. His farewell to Paris was more tentative. After a busy autumn and winter James repeated, in the spring of 1908, his visit of the year before. This time Mrs Wharton was in a rented apartment at 3 Place des États Unis. James came with the understanding that his stay would be brief. The Olympian world still fascinated and Mrs Wharton was possessive, to judge by T. S. Perry's again remarking that James was 'in her clutch', and that she 'very unwillingly relaxed her hold'. The great lady had arranged for the Master to have his portrait painted by the *littérateur*-painter Jacques-Émile Blanche, who had an enormous facility, was a great social lion and usually worked in his studio before an audience of Faubourg ladies – it was always a performance. He posed James full face. When the portrait was finished it turned out to be in profile. It is a good likeness of the Master. Mrs Wharton always considered it the best portrait of James ever painted. Writing to Bay Emmet, who had painted him in 1900, James described himself as looking 'very big, and fat and uncanny and "brainy" and awful'. He characterized Blanche as a 'do-you-any-way-you-like sort of painter'. It is not clear whether Mrs Wharton paid for it. When James saw the painting in London he could not recognize it. It was a *chic'd* thing, but had 'a certain dignity of intention'.

Paris was 'wonderful' but a 'fatal and prostrating vortex'. 'I am kept here in gilded chains, in gorgeous bondage, in breathless attend-ance and luxurious *asservissement*,' he wrote to Henry Adams, who had sent him his privately printed *Education*.

The visit was soon over and James rushed back to his Edition. By this time he had had a larger vision of Mrs Wharton. She was 'the wonderful, the unique Edith Wharton' to James, and also, in a variant on his earlier characterization 'the angel of beautiful ruin' – the devastation 'of one's time and domestic economy'. He spoke of 'her frame of steel' and of 'the iridescent track of her Devasta-tion'. She was 'an amiable and highly imperative friend' but also 'a very great person'. He imaged himself as a 'poor old croaking barn-yard fowl' pitted against 'a golden eagle'. If we discount the euphe-misms and playful ironies, we may still accept one designation as carrying the essence of his feeling about her – she was, he re-marked, 'almost too insistently Olympian'.

93

The Velvet Glove

HENRY JAMES wrote a bit of history – literary history – after his two visits to the world of Edith Wharton. He incorporated her high life – of society, of literature, her grand style, and Princess-like existence – in a tale, incorporated it with such flourish of fine-spun allusion that few have recognized his elaborate joke and the deeper criticism it contains. Mrs Wharton saw the joke at once, but seemed to close her eyes to the meanings that might be read in it. Years later she drew attention to the tale in her reminiscences – perhaps a way of throwing dust in readers' eyes – saying it originated one night in Paris when she had taken James on a long drive in the 'chariot of fire' – so called in the tale – 'high above the moonlit lamplit city and the gleaming curves of the Seine'. That drive is told in the Master's high style in the last part of the tale. Its origin was more complicated than Mrs Wharton knew. An agency in New York wrote to James saying that Mrs Wharton had suggested he write an article about her. Its stationery carried a Marxian motto, 'from each according to ability, unto each according to need'. Apparently a socialist publication was interested in Mrs Wharton's discussion of labour–management relations in her new novel, *The*

Fruit of the Tree. 'She has indicated,' the letter told James, 'that if the leading opinion could be from your pen, it would be gratifying to her.'

From the first James did not believe Mrs Wharton would, in this fashion, ask for a 'puff' from him. Mrs Wharton denied any knowledge of the matter. However she did say (James told his agent) 'that she would be sorry to stand in the way of my writing the little article – or *a* little article – if I am moved to it'. He added, 'I seem to make out that the thing would give her pleasure indeed – *should* I do it.' He thought it would be 'amiable' of him to produce 3,000 words and was tempted to use her new novel as a peg for such a tribute. He added, however, 'I rather detest the man's false statement – unless he can account for it.'

Perhaps behind his willingness was a feeling that there was practically no other way in which he could reciprocate Mrs Wharton's extended hospitalities. It was largely a matter of gesture; but such gestures had always been a challenge. He had long ago written an ambiguous tribute to Mrs Humphry Ward, a mixture of caution and generosity, which he could make with a clear conscience. For Mrs Wharton's art, even with its limitations, he had a much higher regard. He put the matter to her with candour. A seed had been dropped in his mind he said, 'by however a crooked *geste*', and he was now conscious of 'a lively and spontaneous disposition to really dedicate a few lucid remarks to the mystery of your genius'. Mrs Wharton expressed proper caution to her editor at Scribner's. She asked him to send *The Fruit of the Tree* to Henry James who wants to write 'a few words on the mystery of my genius'. This sounded 'as if he meant to make mince-meat of me'.

James told Mrs Wharton he was writing 'to the inquirer whose letter I sent you that if he can explain his so highly imaginative statement about your expressed wish (really, evidently, a barefaced lie, and as I judge, a common trick of the trade,) I will send him 3,000 words'. He did not receive a satisfactory answer; by the time he got a reply he had read *The Fruit of the Tree*. He had no desire to write about it. The novel was simply not good enough. It was of 'a strangely infirm composition and construction'; he said as much to Mrs Wharton, praising, however, 'the element of good writing in it'. It had 'more *kinds* of interest than anyone now going can pretend to achieve'. Still 'I don't feel that I can "enthuse" over you in a hole-and-corner publication.'

I

There was, however, an idea for a story in the incident. What if a great lady – of the world and the pen – did ask a great writer for a puff? How amusing the irony? to have a writer ascend to her Olympus and then have her forget her goddess-state and invite, from a mere mortal, a particular tribute? He seems to have written the tale in an open spirit of mockery; his first title was *The Top of the Tree*. In the end he decided to be more cautious. The story was given a mysterious title, *The Velvet Glove*.

In the tale James resorted to the Balzacian 'going on with a character'. He resurrected Gloriani out of *Roderick Hudson* and *The Ambassadors*. At a great reception in Gloriani's studio in Paris a young English nobleman approaches a novelist-playwright who has written 'a slightly too fat volume' called *The Heart of Gold* – a Jamesian allusion perhaps to the size and shape of *The Golden Bowl*. The author of that book is named John Berridge, perhaps an allusion to Walter Berry. The young English lord is an intermediary – like the inquirer from New York; he asks whether Berridge wouldn't take a look at a book by a friend of his. He would value his opinion. Berridge happens to find life more interesting than literature – 'what was the pale page of fiction compared with the intimately personal adventure?' He prefers 'the grand personal adventure on the grand personal basis'. He is an outsider in Society, a mortal on Olympus enchanted with the romances of the Olympians. The word Olympian is sprinkled with great regularity through the pages of the tale, and allusions to Endymion, Hebe, Apollo, Astarte are made together with a reference to *The Winter's Tale* and to Claude Lorrain – in a word to elements of the pastoral, great personages masquerading as shepherdesses and shepherds. Berridge meets a glamorous Princess and is astonished, after admiring her elegance and beauty, to discover that her disguise is that of plain Amy Evans (a name as plain as Edith Jones) a writer of novels. He has read her recent novel *The Top of the Tree* in its 'tawdry red cover', an allusion to the binding of *The Fruit of the Tree* and other fictions of Mrs Wharton's.

The Princess is a figure of Romance; she floats through Gloriani's studio as a creature of magic. Berridge is delighted when she suggests they leave together; she will take him away for a ride in her 'chariot of fire'. In the cushioned vehicle Berridge feels himself carried on wings of Romance. It is a soft April night; they hang over Paris from vague consecrated lamp-studded heights and taking in, spread below and afar, the great scroll of all its irresistible story, pricked out, across river and bridge and radiant *place*, and along quays and boulevards and avenues, and around monumental circles and squares, in syllables of fire, and sketched and summarized, farther and farther, in the dim fire-dust of endless avenues; that was all of the essence of fond and thrilled and throbbing recognition, with a thousand things understood and a flood of response conveyed, a whole familiar possessive feeling appealed to and attested.

This beauty so touching to John Berridge seems not to touch the Princess. She pursues her purpose relentlessly. Her new novel 'The Velvet Glove' would benefit greatly from a preface by John Berridge. It 'would do so much for the thing in America'. She says this 'with the clearest coolness of her general privilege. "Why, my dear man, let your Preface show, the lovely, friendly irresistible log-rolling Preface, that I've been asking you if you wouldn't be an angel and write for me"' – and she also says '" of course I don't want you to perjure yourself; but –"' and the Princess 'fairly brushed him again, at their close quarters, with her fresh fragrant smile' – '"I do want you so to like me, and to say it all out beautifully and publicly."'

And Berridge had thought she valued him for himself and the successful play he had written! He wonders what

could lead a creature so formed for living and breathing her Romance, and so committed up to the eyes, to the constant fact of her personal immersion in it and genius for it, the dreadful amateurish dance of un-grammatically scribbling it, with editions and advertisements and reviews and royalties and every other futile item.

He meditates on 'the really great ease of really great ladies, and the perfectly perfect facility of everything once they were great enough'.

In effect James seems to be saying that Princesses should not step off their pedestals; they cease to be Princesses. It is deeply dis-illusioning; it hurts his pride and his self-esteem. John Berridge re-plies to mere 'Amy Evans' by breaking the barriers between himself and her exalted state – since she has broken them first. He kisses her hand; and then unceremoniously presses his lips against hers. 'You are Romance,' he tells her with a show of gallantry. 'Don't attempt such base things. Leave those to us. Only live. Only be. We'll do the rest.'

There was something deeply mocking and hostile in the tale in spite of its verbal gauze; as if James still resented the very idea of Mrs Wharton approaching him indirectly through a New York hole-and-corner publication for a puff – even though he had established her innocence. James put the icing on the story as thickly as he could. Berridge is aware of 'these high existences', of 'the Olympian race' and 'the affairs, and above all the passions, of Olympus'. The Princess strikes him as 'some divine Greek mask overpainted say by Titian ... she might have been, with her long rustle across the room, Artemis decorated, hung with pearls, for her worshippers, yet disconcerting them by having under an impulse just faintly fierce, snatched the cup of gold from Hebe'. 'The cup of gold' may be still another allusion to *The Golden Bowl*, and perhaps to the fact that the author of *The Fruit of the Tree* had been critical of that novel. Mrs Wharton once remarked to James, 'What was your idea in suspending the four principal characters in *The Golden Bowl* in the void? What sort of life did they lead when they were not watching each other, and fencing with each other? Why have you stripped them of all the *human fringes* we necessarily trail after us through life?' James answered in a disturbed voice, 'My dear – I didn't know I had!'

Within the story James extended his mockery – but it would be visible only to those who had read *The Fruit of the Tree* with some closeness. In her novel Mrs Wharton writes of a character as 'with *all the ardour* of her young motherliness', or of a young man roused 'with *all the boyhood* in his blood' or '*all the spirit* in him rode' or longing 'with *all the warm instincts of youth*'. The embracing word was resorted to again and again by James in his references to Amy Evans's 'The Top of the Tree':

... which all the Amy Evans in her, as she would doubtless have put it ...
... all the conscious conqueror in him, as Amy Evans would again have said ...
... while all the conscientious man of letters in him, as she might so supremely have phrased it ...

He is also parodying Mrs Wharton's writing in this book in a sentence such as: 'It was too much for all the passionate woman in her, and she let herself go, over the flowering land that had been, but was no longer their love, with an effect of blighting desolation that might have proceeded from one of the more physical, though not more awful convulsions of nature.' He seems also to be rapping Mrs Wharton over the knuckles for some awkward sentences in the following passage from 'The Top of the Tree' :

The loveliness of the gaze, *which** was that of the glorious period in *which* Pheidias reigned supreme, and *which* owed its most exquisite note to that shell-like curl of the upper lip *which* always somehow recalls for us the smile with *which* wind-blown Astarte must have risen from the salt sea to *which* she owed her birth and her terrible moods.

The allusion to Astarte may have greater meaning than meets the eye. Astarte was a deity of fecundity whose rites were celebrated by men dressed as women. It was not the first time James had looked at the element of the transvestite in popular literary circles – his tale of *The Death of the Lion* had featured men who wrote under women's names and women who wrote under men's. Amy Evans may herself be an echo of Mary Ann Evans who had written as George Eliot, or a reminder of George Sand. The allusion to Astarte may sound the fundamental theme of disguise in *The Velvet Glove* in which lords and ladies convert themselves into nymphs and shepherds and princesses became commoners by writing novels. Behind this over-elaborate joke there is a suggestion of trust betrayed, of the mighty who cease being mighty when they scribble, of hostility against that *grand monde* James admired and studied but also criticized. In a letter to Grace Norton, on the eve of his first visit to the rue de Varenne, he had spoken of getting news of the Nortons from Mrs Wharton, adding 'so far as the Pampered Princesses of this world, can when very intelligent and very literary and very gracious, *ever* arrive at real news of anything!'

James seems to have been sure that his joke would not offend – that its fun would be treated simply as fun. He had perhaps noticed a sentence in *The Fruit of the Tree* about characters 'blent in that closest of unions, the discovery of a common fund of humour'. When the story appeared in the *English Review* of March 1909 Mrs Wharton apparently told him it was 'really good' and queried him about it. He had a ready answer. Two periodicals had declined the tale of John Berridge and the Princess 'which was a good deal *comme qui dirait* like declining *you*: since *bien assurément* the whole thing *reeks* with you – and with Cook, and with our Paris

*The repeated *which* has been underlined by me to emphasize the parody.

(Cook's and yours and mine:) so no wonder it's "really good".'
Asked about this tale years later, Mrs Wharton rejoined with a
smile, 'Oh but I would never have asked Henry to write a preface
for me.' And she told of 'a very beautiful young English woman of
great position and unappeased literary ambitions' who had once
tried to beguile James 'into contributing an introduction to a novel
she was writing – or else into reviewing the book, I forget which'.

Whatever further 'sources' there may be for the story, its theme
and the expression of it suggests that James's compliments to Mrs
Wharton had their barbed side: that he stood his literary ground as
Master and law-giver, and that he felt Edith Wharton should stand
on her ground, that of a great and perceptive lady. She clearly swallowed the story as she accepted all of James's criticisms: their
friendship was strong: it could withstand Olympian satire. Mrs
Wharton was prepared to make allowance for anything in the
Master. On his side, his admiration for her grew with the passing
years.

94

Miss Bosanquet

WHEN Miss Theodora Bosanquet went that summer's day in 1907
to Miss Petheridge's secretarial office and employment agency, she
had no notion that this would be one of the most eventful days of
her life. She felt somewhat slack and headachy. She was disinclined
to brave the noise of the tube, and took a bus to Conduit Street. For
some time she had been proof-reading an index to the Report of the
Royal Commission on Coast Erosion. She was wearing her usual
office outfit, a white blouse and green skirt, a belt and a tie, a 'busi-
ness-like and, I hoped, becoming costume'. At about noon she
learned that Mr Henry James was in the office. She had expected
an interview but had not known on which day. She fidgeted nervously; she felt cold. She was a young, slim woman in her early 20s,
rather boyish, with bright blue eyes and a shy manner. After a
childhood on the Isle of Wight and at Lyme Regis, she had gone to
Cheltenham Ladies' College and then to University College where
she had taken a degree. She had, thus, much more education than
Miss Weld, who had married while the novelist was in America

and left his employ. He had required no typist during the revising of the New York Edition. Miss Bosanquet had no intention of parading her education, or her 'literary' interests. Her precaution was confirmed later when she learned that Mr James liked his typists to be 'without a mind' – and certainly not to suggest words to him, as some had done during pauses in dictation. It is doubtful whether he ever learned that Miss Bosanquet had trained herself especially to be his amanuensis. Earlier that summer she had heard chapters from *The Ambassadors* being dictated at one end of the office. She knew the novel and wondered why James's prose was being put to this service. On inquiry she had learned James needed a typist. Miss Bosanquet promptly set herself to learn typing.

She was intelligent and observant. She had learned long ago to take mental notes. Her diary of that August day gives us a distinct picture.

He is like Coleridge – in figure – one feels that he ought to be wearing a flowered waistcoat – very expansive – 'unrestrained' in the lower part. He wore green trousers and a blue waistcoat with a yellow sort of check on it and a black coat – that was rather a shock. I'd imagined him as always very correctly dressed in London. He is bald – except for tufts of not very grey hair at the sides. His eyes, grey I think, are exactly what I should expect – but the rest of his face is too fat. He talks slowly but continuously – I found it hard to get in any words of my own. But he is *most* kind and considerate.

James seems to have paid little attention to Miss Bosanquet. He was interested in two or three essential things. Rye was remote; would she find it too lonely? She must come to lunch and look for satisfactory lodgings. He would lend her books to read. He told her about walks and bicycle rides. He asked no questions. He informed her he was slow at dictating; she would have to amuse herself while he was evolving a sentence. 'He was careful,' Miss Bosanquet noted, 'to impress on me the danger of boredom.'

Miss Bosanquet remarked that he did not have 'the self-possession I should have expected'. He seemed, however, 'most kind and nice – and so absolutely unassuming'. They could start in the autumn. This would give Miss Bosanquet time to make the move from London.

2

Miss Bosanquet arrived in Rye on 10 October 1907 and James met her at the station. His grimy gardener took her luggage. James apologized, 'he ought not to have shown himself like that'. He walked her to her rooms 'the talk being slightly constrained'. He talked of the days when he used to see 'dear old Burne-Jones' in this neighbourhood. He left his new employee in the care of her landlady, telling her to come to Lamb House later and inspect the new Remington. This she did. She felt 'horribly desolate'. Her rooms were nice but she missed her London flat.

Miss Bosanquet rose early the next morning and took a stroll after breakfast. She was struck by the pretty view across the levels reclaimed from the sea and the masts in Rye harbour. Sharp at 10.15 she mounted the cobbled street to Lamb House. James let her in. He began by showing her shelves of books and telling her she could borrow anything she pleased. Then he led her to the Green Room upstairs, a little square room with two windows. There were more books, easy chairs, a table for the typewriter. Dictation began. James was working on a preface to *The Tragic Muse* 'in a tone of personal reminiscence'. Her diary records,

he dictates considerably – slowly and very clearly – giving all the punctuation and often the spelling. I was abominably slow and clumsy – but he was very kind – even complimentary though he admitted that he hoped I should soon go a little faster. He sat in a chair at first – then paced about, smoking – finishing soon after half past one.

Miss Bosanquet then helped herself to a topical book and a volume on Meredith's poetry given to James by Meredith himself 'so presumably worth reading'. She ended her diary of her first day, 'Mr James assumes complete ignorance of any literary knowledge on the part of his amanuensis. He told me that *The Newcomes* was in one word and that it was by Thackeray!'

Things were easier on the second day. She was less nervous and typed more rapidly.

The preface to *The Tragic Muse* continues and grows ever more interesting now that he is dealing with the interrelations of the characters. I mentioned that I had read it quite recently – and, after a moment of some murmur of 'oh – my rubbish', said deprecatingly, he seemed, on the whole, pleased – and remarked that his former amanuensis had never at all fathomed what he wrote and made many 'exceedingly fantastic mistakes'.

Miss Bosanquet herself was worried, for once or twice she had written down the wrong word. She left on this occasion with Howells's *Heroines of Fiction* under her arm. She discovered also that the novelist worked on Sundays. The diary entry for 13 October, a Sunday, reads

Mr James was more – to use a quite inappropriate word – 'sharp' this morning, at least much engrossed. He dismissed me at half past twelve, as he had by then completed the preface to *The Tragic Muse* and only wanted to look through it. I could wish he weren't extremely likely to find it crowded with my careless mistakes.

Miss Bosanquet need not have worried. In a very short time James knew that he had an accomplished amanuensis. A week after she had begun work for him he was writing William James

a new excellent amanuensis, a young boyish Miss Bosanquet, who is worth all the other (females) that I have had put together and who confirms me in the perception afresh – after eight months without such an agent – that for certain, for most, kinds of diligence and production, the intervention of the agent is, to *my* perverse constitution, an intense aid and a true economy! There is no comparison!

James did not keep his feelings from Miss Bosanquet. Nine days after her arrival 'at the close of the morning, Mr James looked out of the window and said "Ah – it's coming better today – I don't mean the dictation – though as to that I have great pleasure in saying that I'm extremely satisfied Miss Bosanquet. You seem to have picked things up so quickly and so intelligently."' Miss Bosanquet replied in her shy way that the work was so interesting it was natural she should do her best. James replied, 'Among the faults of my previous amanuenses – not by any means the *only* fault – was their apparent lack of comprehension of what I was driving at.' So, added the amanuensis 'we parted quite pleased with each other'. James might have been less pleased had he read her diary on the day on which he started dictating his preface to *The Awkward Age* – 'The nervous tension of the situation when he is "agonizing" for a word is appalling – but may grow less. I hope it will ... He goes in, more than I had noticed, for alliteration, and I didn't *quite* like "a fine purple peach' which occurred this morning. Peaches have too *mellow* a colour to be called purple.'

Miss Bosanquet would become increasingly worshipful of the Master, yet it was not blind worship. She retained a strong sense of her own identity. She was often critical of his social weaknesses and his occasional duplicities. She sometimes protested, to herself, over his orotund sentences. Her diary of 15 October 1907 records that she was much flattered 'to notice that one or two sentences I had thought rather obscure were the very ones he had picked out for revision'. On another day James made her observe how he altered 'a second-rate phrase' to 'a first-rate one'. She doesn't, however, give us the phrase. He dictates a letter to Gertrude Atherton about hotels in Paris prefacing it by saying 'I abominate the woman' and, Miss Bosanquet adds, 'at frequent intervals he groaned about having to write to her'. On one occasion she glimpses the Master's bedroom while he is in London. 'I was allowed hot water and washed my hands in Mr James's room – *such* a nice room, panelled, all quite simple, photographic reproductions on the walls. Two *charming* little silver candlesticks by the bed. A very good old mirror against the wall.'

When James was away she found other employment and stayed in her flat in London. From this time on, with certain gaps (some of her diaries were lost during the Second World War) James is mirrored almost daily in the lucid prose of his typist. Miss Bosanquet was always discreet, always tactful, always efficient. Her subsequent career would be distinguished. She wrote books – one on Paul Valéry – and an admirable pamphlet for the Hogarth Press describing James's working methods. She was for a number of years secretary to the International Federation of University Women. One of the early feminists, she was associated with *Time and Tide* as its literary editor and for years was known to the young writers in Bloomsbury. In her work for Henry James she was submerging her own distinct personality and cultivated literary tastes. When he was dead she was able to enter on her own career.

Miss Bosanquet received twenty-five shillings for her first fifteen hours of work, that is just a little more than a shilling an hour. It was the regular pay at the time; and it was, she told James, the first money she had ever earned. There were certain gallantries between them. On a day when Miss Bosanquet would be indisposed, he usually turned up at her lodgings with a bouquet of roses; if he kept her overtime and she grew hungry he would strip the silver foil off and place a chocolate bar beside her typewriter. At Christmas he had her to dinner at Lamb House and gave her a glove-box as a gift, which the boyish side of her did not appreciate; especially when on a later Christmas James duplicated this gift. After a while she stopped recording details of her routine in her diary, but she made a point of setting down any incidental remarks made by the novelist. In this respect the diary offers us many little touches, a kind of 'work-table-talk' of the Master that could not otherwise have been preserved. What James did not know was that Miss Bosanquet was writing as well. She tried her hand at verse, an occasional essay for such publications as *Hearth and Home* and even a bit of fiction. She took part in literary contests in the *Westminster Gazette*.

3

One day James dictated a letter to his brother William and Miss Bosanquet wrote in her diary 'I *am* in luck's way – fancy *me* being in a sense the *medium* between Henry James and William.' Her diary records during the summer of 1908 what James meant when he said to a friend 'I am deep in family'. The William Jameses came abroad in the spring of that year. William was to give the Hibbert Lectures at Oxford; and he accepted – quite forgetting one reason for resigning from the American Academy – an honorary degree of Doctor of Science. These were the lectures which became *A Pluralistic Universe*. The typist's diary reveals what a complex life James led during such family visits. He was on the fifteenth volume of his Edition and writing his preface on tales of the supernatural. He worked every morning. But thereafter he was with his brother and Alice. Three of William's children also came to Lamb House at various times. During the summer the figures of Kipling, H. G. Wells and Chesterton moved through the Rye streets. At the summer's end Mrs Wharton was there 'fairish-bright hazel eyes, brown much-wrinkled skin – looks tired – quite pleasant,' Miss Bosanquet records. Her own shyness bothered her. She adds 'I was an awkward fool as usual.' She seemed, however, comfortable with the James family and liked William. 'He *is* a charming man – there's something so simple and fresh about him somehow.' In another entry – 'a delightful man – small and thin – he looks about ten years older than Mr Henry James but it's only one more, I believe'. William walked with her down the road one day as he was going to post a letter, commenting on the picturesqueness of Rye; on another day she found him using the typewriter and enjoyed having him dictate part of a page to her. There were moments when she was less happy. 10 September 1908: 'Saw Professor James and told him of my interest in the Society of Psychical Research report [on automatic writing]. He said I evidently had a logical mind! He found it hard to keep the threads clear! Horrid sarcasm.' On another occasion seeing that Miss Bosanquet was reading a book on spiritualism he told her a 'new era' was dawning in these matters. Miss Bosanquet discussed psychical research with Peggy, now 22. Peggy often sought Miss Bosanquet's company and they went on walks together. 'Miss James hasn't much sense of humour, which makes her just a bit heavy in hand.' She described Peggy as swarthy-complexioned, pleasant and intelligent-looking with a lot of literary taste. James took his niece to a suffragette lecture in Rye. Miss Bosanquet reported the occasion was 'very inspiring'. She found Mrs William James 'most pleasant' – 'a fine strong face framed with white hair. Her daughter is just like her.'

On 27 July 1908: 'In the course of the morning Mr James made me go and peep through the curtain to see "the unspeakable Chesterton" pass by – a sort of elephant with a crimson face and oily curls. He [James] thinks it very tragic that his mind should be imprisoned in such a body.' Chesterton's presence in Rye produced an incident which H. G. Wells remembered. William James climbed the gardener's ladder to peep over the wall at Chesterton. Henry apparently felt it proper to look out of his window at Chesterton as passer-by, but that it was wrong to invade privacy by peeping over a wall. They quarrelled about this, Wells remembered, when he arrived in a car to fetch the William Jameses and Peggy for a visit to his home at Sandgate. James appealed to Wells. 'It simply wasn't done, emphatically, it wasn't permissible behaviour in England' – this was the gist of Henry's appeal. 'Henry had instructed the gardener to put away that ladder and William was looking thoroughly naughty about it.' To Henry's relief Wells carried William off in his car. They passed Chesterton, so the pragmatist met him after all – and Chesterton invited William to come and see him. Henry and William paid a call. William's diary records 'at nine to Chesterton's where we sat till midnight drinking port with Hilaire Belloc'.

Harry, William's oldest son, now 29, visited briefly at Lamb

House that summer and was interested in his uncle's methods of dictation. A successful executive, he had taken the Syracuse properties of the Jameses in hand and improved their yield. When Henry James began to receive more substantial sums he tended to impart occult financial powers to his nephew. Harry had the dignity and the distinction of the Jameses and the same 'heavyness' that Miss Bosanquet noted in Peggy. He would stand all his life in the shadow of a distinguished father and a celebrated uncle. But he would achieve a quiet eminence of his own. From William he picked up a certain condescending air towards his uncle which appears in his letters to his parents. But his uncle loved him and admired his financial skills, and made him his executor. During this summer William's youngest son Alex, aged 17, came to Lamb House also and Henry found him shy, silent, too withdrawn, but 'a dear young presence and worthy of the rest of the brood'.

William wrote their younger brother Robertson that he found Henry stolid and grave, the natural result of the years; he seemed to have lost none of his early pleasure in the possession of Lamb House. Henry on his side was impressed by William's vitality. In spite of several heart attacks, William refused to obey the doctors. He took long walks, insisted on vaulting over gates and stiles and was 'in general better, I think, than I have of late years *ever* seen him'.

95

Theatricals: Second Series

IN the midst of his work on the New York Edition, Henry James received new overtures from the theatre which he had abandoned in such pain twelve years earlier. To be sure, in 1895, immediately after *Guy Domville*, he had written a one-act play for Ellen Terry. She had never produced it: one more proof for James that the stage was an 'abyss'. Yet it was this very play which now returned to haunt him. In 1897 he had remade it into a short story called *Covering End* and published it as a companion piece to *The Turn of the Screw*. Suddenly actor-managers were writing to tell him the story would make a good play! Two managers approached James in 1899; he turned them down. He had had enough of the treacherous stage.

Now, in 1907, Johnston Forbes-Robertson returned to the charge. *Covering End*, he told James, would be an ideal vehicle for himself and his American wife, Gertrude Elliott, sister of the famous Maxine. James was more receptive now; he found himself 're-aching and re-brooding and re-itching for the theatre in a manner very uncomfortable to other concentrations'. With Miss Bosanquet installed behind the big typewriter and his work on the Edition going smoothly, it seemed to James he could try once again – it was after all simply a matter of re-writing *Covering End* into its original form. Moreover, Forbes-Robertson had asked him to expand the one act into three; the thought of enlarging rather than cutting a play appealed to James. To his friend Lucy Clifford he wrote 'I assented, for the lust of a little possible gold.' It was to be played 'without one bloody cut (which is bribery and balmery to me)'. It would be like doing something in three Cantos or Stanzas with 'two very short curtain drops without fiddles – in which case I get three-act terms for it'. To which he added, as of old, the injunction that it was a deep secret, 'I breathe the weird tale into your ear alone.'

The language of his dramatic years was again on his lips – he would do it for gold; it had to be kept a secret; he hated the conditions of the theatre – but he would participate in the rehearsals. His old distinction between drama-stuff and theatre-stuff was suddenly voiced again, this time to another confidante, Edith Wharton. 'I loathe the Theatre, but the Drama tormentingly speaks to me.' It spoke sufficiently for James to write *The High Bid* (as *Covering End* was now called) in twenty days; and then to go on to a scenario of one of his old short stories *The Chaperon*, (Pinero had told him it would make a fine comedy), and then a one-act play based on his tale *Owen Wingrave*. After that he began revising *The Other House*, which he also had converted to fiction, and now returned to its original form. Miss Bosanquet found herself typing scripts and James began attending rehearsals. He was repeating his old experiences. He was charmed; he was sanguine. 'Whatever happens,' he wrote to Lucy Clifford, 'it is a very *safe* and neat and pleasing (orthodox-pleasing) little invention – which no monstrous doom can overtake.' This was his way of saying that he did not fear a repetition of *Guy Domville*.

The try-out took place in Edinburgh in March 1908. James had joined the troupe at Manchester, 'I travelling with the animals like the lion-tamer or the serpent-charmer in person and quite enjoying the caravan-quality, the bariole Bohemian or *picaresque* note of the affair'. The omens were good. The little play was 'pretty and pleasing and amusing and orthodox and mercenary and *safe* (absit omen!) – cravenly, ignobly *canny* : also clearly to be very decently acted'. James was so confident that he invited Lucy Clifford to the first night and when Jocelyn Persse, then travelling in Algeria, expressed an interest, he invited him also. Jocelyn made the long journey and was James's guest throughout the first-night festivities. The production was well received. James cautiously disappeared at the curtain calls. As with *The American*, he felt the play needed a London production. He liked the way in which Gertrude Elliott played Mrs Gracedew, the American widow who arrives as a tourist in an English country house and pleads with its owner, Captain Yule (Forbes-Robertson) for the house's preservation on grounds of tradition, history, art, a cherishing of the past. James's central irony was that the American woman should turn out to be more English than the English. It was the sort of thing that might have been expected from him before *The American Scene*, but hardly after. The play would have been fine in the 1890s; in the Edwardian period it was out of date. Audiences had had a great deal of Bernard Shaw; they were 'socially-minded'. To the embarrassment of Gertrude Elliott they applauded the 'radical' speeches of her husband in the play rather than her own romantic–historic flights. When she delivered an emotional appeal, 'Look at this sweet old human home, and feel all its gathered memories,' the audience did not share her feeling. But when Captain Yule, a liberal and socialist-tinged member of parliament answered, 'I see something else in the world than the beauty of old show-houses and the glory of old show families. There are thousands of people in England who can show no houses *at all*,' the audiences burst into applause. Gertrude Elliott asked James to do something about this. It was after all *her* 'vehicle'. The Master could do nothing, short of scrapping the entire play.

Forbes-Robertson sensed this. He felt the play was far too delicate for the theatre audiences, it had too much 'literary elegance'. His actor's instincts told him that a script he had received from Jerome K. Jerome titled *The Passing of the Third Floor Back* – about a stranger in a lodging house, who seemed to be a reincarnation of Christ – might have greater success. James was derisive and angry. He predicted to Lucy Clifford instant failure or at least an 'imperfect success'. Then remembering that strange things could happen in the theatre, he also said that it might have a 'most rapturous success'. To Miss Bosanquet he remarked that 'Jesus Christ is the main character and of course one has to realize that He's a formidable competition'. The play ran for four years; it made Forbes-Robertson's fortune. The best the actor and his wife could do, to keep their commitment to James, was to perform *The High Bid* for five matinées. This attracted a Jamesian type of audience and got him excellent notices from ardent followers like Max Beerbohm and A. B. Walkley. Max's review began by describing Forbes-Robertson making his exit in *The Passing of the Third Floor Back* with enough of a halo of light to suggest there had been something sacred about his presence in the Bloomsbury lodging house; then it seemed as if the stage had revolved and Forbes-Robertson re-entered the old English house, in his street clothes. It was 'rather a long way for an actor to travel', said Max but Forbes-Robertson accomplished the journey with distinction. One moment he was the Christ-figure and the next he was a radical member of parliament saying, 'What are you exactly?' to an old family butler – 'I mean, to whom do you beautifully *belong*?'

'There, in those six last words,' wrote Max,

is the quintessence of Mr James; and the sound of them sent innumerable little vibrations through the heart of every good Jacobite in the audience ... The words could not have been more perfectly uttered than they were by Mr Forbes-Robertson. He realized at once to whom *he* beautifully belongs. It is to Mr Henry James ... In his eyes, as he surveyed the old butler, and in his smile, and in the groping hesitancy before the adverb was found, and in the sinking of the tone at the verb, there was a whole world of good feeling, good manners, and humour. It was love seeing the fun of the thing. It was irony kneeling in awe. It was an authentic part of the soul of Mr James.

To which Max added, from the authority of his critical position and out of his adoration, 'little though Mr James can on the stage give us of his great art, even that little has a quality which no other man can give us; an inalienable magic'.

2

James's renewed confidence in the theatre in spite of the limited production of *The High Bid*, sprang in part from the evolution of the English stage since the 1890s. The battle for Ibsen had been won. Arthur Pinero and Henry Arthur Jones had demonstrated in strong social dramas, that British audiences did not need to be fed trivialities. The new repertory theatres had followed. The plays of Bernard Shaw, aided by the directorial art of Harley Granville Barker, taught audiences to accept a discussion of ideas if properly seasoned with a certain amount of clowning and a measure of Irish wit. There were new men and new audiences; and if they did not wholly satisfy the Master, they were the sort of people he could talk to – they were closer to art and letters than the old stage-tinkers. James had seen the Shaw plays, usually with Jocelyn Persse – *Man and Superman, Major Barbara, The Doctor's Dilemma*; he had gone to Barker's *Voysey Inheritance*. He met Barrie and Galsworthy and joined them in their attack on the censorship of British plays, writing a letter which was read into the proceedings of a Royal Commission and is buried in an ancient blue book – a letter almost Miltonic in its phraseology. Censorship tended to deprive the theatre, James wrote, 'of intellectual life, of the *importance* to which a free choice of subjects and illustrations, directly ministers, and to confine it to the trivial and the puerile'. Censorship in England had the effect of relegating drama 'to the position of a mean minor art, and of condemning it to ignoble dependencies, poverties, and pusillanimities'.

If James stood now with the dramatists, and was received in their midst with respect, he found himself engaged in an unexpected debate with the wittiest and most didactic of the new men. The Master had converted *Owen Wingrave*, his old ghost story about a young pacifist in a military family, into a one-act play *The Saloon*, in the hope that the Forbes-Robertsons would use it as curtain-raiser to *The High Bid*. Another play was used and James was induced by St John Hankin to submit it in 1909 to the Incorporated Stage Society which gave subscription performances of non-commercial plays. The script was read by the board members and rejected. The minutes of the board of 12 January 1909, record that 'Mr Bernard Shaw undertook to write to Henry James with reference to *The Saloon*'. Five days later Shaw carried out his undertaking beginning, in anticipation of the era of broadcasting: 'Shaw's writing – Bernard Shaw.'

He had read *The Saloon* he wrote and it had been 'sticking in my gizzard ever since'. That play needed another act – by James's father, an allusion by Shaw to the elder Henry's general optimism.

Shaw found the play too deterministic. 'What do you want to break men's spirits for?' he queried. 'Surely George Eliot did as much of that as is needed.' The dramatist then developed a Shavian version of the play. Did James think his hero would have been seriously beaten by the ghost? He was referring to the fact that Owen Wingrave is killed by his military ancestor, punished for his strong pacifism. James had tried to establish the irony that the military 'conditioning' Owen had received enabled him to fight and die for his pacifism like a young soldier. To Shaw, arguing as a socialist, this kind of determinism was anathema. He spoke of 'that useless, dispiriting, discouraging fatalism which broke out so horribly in the 1860s at the word of Darwin, and persuaded people in spite of their own teeth and claws that Man is the will-less slave and victim of his environment'. As a Marxist he knew 'the enormous power of the environment as a dead destiny', but 'we can change it: we must change it: there is absolutely no other sense in life than the work of changing it'. In effect Shaw argued that the play should be rewritten – Owen Wingrave should kill the ghost, not the ghost Owen. And Shaw quoted Dr Johnson's 'I, sir, should have frightened the ghost.' Instinctively Shaw touched a deep part of James's life. Had not his dream of the Louvre been just that? In his dreams James succeeded in frightening his ghosts. It was in his waking state that he found them terrifying. Shaw ended his letter:

It is really a damnable sin to draw with such consummate art a houseful of rubbish, and a dead incubus of a father waiting to be scrapped; to bring on for us the hero with his torch and his scrapping shovel; and then, when the audience is saturated with interest and elated with hope, waiting for the triumph and the victory, calmly announce that the rubbish has choked the hero, and that the incubus is the really strong master of all our souls. Why have you done this? If it were true to nature – if it were scientific – if it were common sense, I should say let us face it, let us say Amen. But it isn't. Every man who really wants his latchkey gets it. No man who doesn't believe in ghosts ever sees one. Families like these are smashed every day and their members delivered from bondage, not by heroic young men, but by one girl who goes out and earns her living or takes a degree somewhere. Why do you preach cowardice to an army which has victory always and easily within its reach?

People needed, Shaw said, 'encouragement' and he repeated that word five times and signed his name. Thus spoke Shaw, espousing in effect the idea that art should be didactic, a vehicle for a social idea.

James pondered the letter for a week. It must have given him some trouble: for Shaw had the same wit and a native irrationality akin to James's father's. There was indeed much in common between the Irishness of the two. To answer Shaw was a little like trying to answer the father in Quincy Street. Which explains why Henry dictated 3,000 words of reply to Miss Bosanquet, beginning with a long explanation of 'why' and 'how' he had written the play. James chose, however, not to argue with Shaw's Marxism. On this point he simply answered

you strike me as carrying all your eggs, of conviction, appreciation, discussion etc. ... in one basket, where you put your hand on them all with great ease and convenience; while I have mine scattered all over the place – many of them still under the hens! ... You take the little play socialistically, it first strikes me, all too hard.

Shaw has asked him why he did such things and James's answer was:

I do such things because I happen to be a man of imagination and taste, extremely interested in life, and because the imagination thus, from the moment direction and motive play upon it from all sides, absolutely enjoys and insists on and incurably leads a life of its own, for which just this vivacity itself is its warrant ... Half the beautiful things that the benefactors of the human species have produced would surely be wiped out if you don't allow this adventurous and speculative imagination its rights.

James went on to say the only way in which *The Saloon* could be 'scientific' would be that it be done 'with all the knowledge and intelligence relevant to its motive'. As for people wanting not works of art but 'encouragement', James could only reply that works of art were 'capable of saying more things to man about himself than any other "works" whatever are capable of doing'. He added he had been 'touched and charmed by the generous abundance' of Shaw's letter.

Shaw answered briefly and militantly. James was trying to evade him.

The question of whether the man is to get the better of the ghost or the ghost of the man is not an artistic question: you can give victory to one side just as artistically as to the other. And your interest in life is just the very reverse of a good reason for condemning your hero to death. You have given victory to death and obsolescence: I want you to give it to life and regeneration.

James's second rejoinder pointed out to Shaw that he was quarrelling with the subject itself and that every artist had to be allowed his subject. Criticism had to criticize what was *done*; the subject itself belonged to the artist. One could dislike it, but that was another matter. There was no competition between man and ghost in the play. Owen Wingrave actually wins the victory, James argued, even if he pays for it with his life. What sort of play would it be if there were no danger and no resistance? It was Owen's resisting this danger and doing so with the courage of a soldier that constituted the drama. So James argued. 'You look at the little piece, I hold, with a luxurious perversity; but my worst vengeance shall be to impose on you as soon as possible the knowledge of a much longer and more insistent one, which I may even put you in peril of rather liking.'

This ended James's first debate with one of the new men: a debate which foreshadowed the entire question of didactic art in the twentieth century – art in the service of a theory or a state. In reality it was also a debate between a writer concerned with the psychological truths and one whose art rested on satire and intellectual humour. 'Almost all my greatest ideas have occurred to me first as jokes,' Shaw said to James. Implicit in this debate was James's taking the world as he found it, and seeking to demonstrate its realities and existential absurdities. Shaw took the world as a place in which art had to serve revolution. There is no doubt that Shaw could have written a diverting play on the same theme, but it would not have touched the conflict and ambivalence of James's hero, whose energies and courage derive both from his constituted temperament as well as his pacifistic ardour. In a word James was saying to Shaw there was the question of 'human nature'. Shaw was brushing this aside and saying 'let's change the system'.

3

In this second series of theatricals – a mere skirmish in the theatre compared with the old struggle – James had in effect two failures. *The High Bid*, written ostensibly for revenue, had its five matinées and was on the shelf; *The Saloon* yielded only a pleasant exchange on the high plane of 'the purposes of art'. James was, however, not discouraged. He rewrote *The Other House*. He had sketched it in 1894 as an 'Ibsen-type' play. In novel form it was all dialogue and stage-scene. In June of 1909 Herbert Trench, the Anglo-Irish poet-scholar, planned a repertory at the Haymarket and paid James £100 for an option on this play. James pocketed the money. The play was not produced.

Early in the same year Charles Frohman, the American producer, began to plan a repertory season in London at the Duke of York's Theatre. The moving figure behind the plan was J. M. Barrie, who enlisted the help of Granville Barker. Allan Wade, a former actor associated with the Abbey Theatre's season in London, joined Frohman's staff; Wade believed that the theatre was suffering a serious loss in not finding a place for the work of so great an artist as Henry James. Granville Barker and Barrie agreed. James was invited to write a play especially for this season. During the spring of 1909 he read *The Other House* to Harley Granville Barker one morning at the Reform Club. 'But what we wanted from him was an original play, not an adapted novel,' Granville Barker wrote. The other dramatists in the repertory were Shaw, Galsworthy, Granville Barker, Somerset Maugham, John Masefield, and Barrie. This time James found himself dealing not with a 'managerial abyss' but with fellow-craftsmen. Shaw wrote *Misalliance*, Galsworthy *Justice*, Barker *The Madras House*, Barrie contributed *The Twelve-Pound Look*, and James wrote *The Outcry*. Wade later recalled his excitement in reading the manuscript 'and my conviction that it would be far over the heads of our rather stupid audiences'. He added:

It is true that James's dramatic sense was more in tune with the French than the English theatre of his day – but had he been given more occasion for actual and practical work in the theatre he would probably have been able to modify his tendency to excessive length and our theatre would have gained a really fine dramatist.

The Outcry was long and required cutting. Granville Barker remembered 'he had to be induced to part with first one bit; then after a while another. But it was really necessary.' The play was 'topical'. James made a comedy out of connoisseurship and the moral question involved in selling works of art. In its quiet way it satirized Bernard Berenson and the question of art expertise. The young amateur art historian of the play, whose appearance, though not his personality, is almost an exact description of Hugh Walpole – he is called Hugh Crimble – recognizes in a great house a classic work of art. The owner decides to sell it to Breckenridge Bender, (the initials are Berenson's) an art dealer from America, a hard-headed and predatory Christopher Newman, not unfavourably drawn, but a man with a 'really *big* Yankee cheque'. The young art scholar and his fiancée, who is the daughter of the owner of the picture, decide to raise an 'outcry'. The picture must be kept in England. Then the Berensonian experts are called in. Was the picture a Moretto or a Mantovano? There was Pappendick, of Belgium, who says it isn't a Mantovano; and then Caselli is called in from Milan. He contradicts Pappendick.

James had never met Berenson and would meet him on only one occasion when he would describe him to Mrs Wharton as a 'concentrated little commentator'. But he had heard about the young Harvard precocity from Grace Norton as early as 1903. 'I read over your letter and I come upon the Berensons, whom I don't know,' he had written, 'and as to *him* confess to him by others' – meaning he had heard about the young Berenson from Mrs Jack Gardner. James added that he knew him only by his association with that 'writing upon art' which he had

long since come to feel as the most boring and *insupportable* identity a man can have. I am so weary, weary of pictures and of questions of pictures, that it is the most I can do to drag myself for three minutes every three years into the National Gallery. If *you* are not it is only because you live at Cambridge, Mass. You *would* be if you lived – at Rye, Sussex.

Berenson would later say he didn't get along very well with James because James didn't like Jews. But the evidence seems to be that James was not interested in art experts. At any rate his comedy on the subject seemed thoroughly manageable in the hands of another kind of expert, Granville Barker, who defended it from attacks on its 'inhumanly literary' dialogue – Shaw's phrase. He said it was no more difficult to produce than a play of Chekhov's 'and we long ago found out how to do that'. The real problem with *The Outcry* was finding a cast capable of speaking James's lines. As Granville Barker put it the dialogue was 'artificial – very; but that is legitimate. It might be hard to speak but I think that most of it could be made very effective once the right method had been found.' Actors certainly could not blend it with 'melodramatic' acting, this was probably the fault with *The Saloon*. He suggested that if *The Outcry* were placed 'beside a Congreve and a Wycherley' it might 'not be so good as the first but I believe you'd find more style and bite in it than in the second'.

At the moment when the last volume of James's New York Edition came off the press, late in 1909, Harley Granville Barker was seeking a cast for *The Outcry*.

96

The Tone of Time

HENRY JAMES was 62 when he began his work on the New York Edition and 66 when it was completed. During these four years he had given continuous proof of his undiminished creativity – he had worked and taken holidays, written plays, and lived his social life – to be sure at a reduced pitch, yet with a liveliness of spirit that showed him to be mentally and spiritually younger than his ageing body. He commented on this in one of his new year's letters to W. E. Norris.

I am engaged in a perpetual adventure, the most thrilling and in every way the greatest of my life, and which consists of having for more than four years entered into a state of health so altogether better than any I had ever known, that my whole consciousness is transformed by the intense alleviation of it and I lose much time in pinching myself to see if this be not, really, 'none of I'.

The value of it still outweighed 'the formidable, the heaped-up and pressed together burden of my years'.

His sense of well-being had been evident ever since publication of *The Golden Bowl*. That novel represented some kind of resolution of old unconscious stress; and his subsequent trip to America smoothed the sharper edges of his years'-long quarrel with his homeland, as well as the buried sensitivities of his relation with his brother. William's heart attacks which blighted his ageing, reduced some of Henry's tension. The Master, however, had the normal revolt of a powerful individual who feels his powers shrinking. To Mrs Clifford he spoke with philosophical resignation of having left behind the period of 'the Passions'. He likened this to 'the quiet Atlantic liner alongside the wharf after the awful days out in the open'. Long ago he had written in his notebooks that 'youth' was the most beautiful word in the language.

He had not accustomed himself to the dropping away of old friends. It was always a wrench. Henry Harland died in 1905, comparatively young, of tuberculosis. He had had an easy talent which James praised; he considered him a supreme case not of the expatriate – *that* case was himself – but of the *dis*patriate. Harland had genuinely detached himself from America. He had worshipped James, maintaining the novelist's intellect ranked with Aristotle's; and he insisted also that James was as great as Tolstoy and Balzac. James glowed in his praise. Then the Master lost Hamilton Aïdé, whom he had met in endless drawing-rooms of late Victorian London. Aïdé had been a supreme dilettante : he wrote novels, verses, plays, composed music, gave interesting parties, was a cultivated man-about-town. James went up to London for his requiem service and was deeply moved. He looked about the church for the faces of certain common friends. For a while he wondered why they had not come; and then it occurred to him that they weren't there 'simply because they were dead'. Writing to several ladies of their common generation – Anne Ritchie, the Ranee of Sarawak, Rhoda Broughton, James said Aïdé's death made him feel as if the room 'of the dusky p.m. of our common existence' had become greyer and poorer. One of its pink lampshades was gone.

In 1908 he lost one of his oldest friends, Charles Eliot Norton, who had published James's first book reviews, taught him to look at early Italian art, introduced him to Ruskin, Darwin, Leslie Stephen. Norton had been a votary of culture in a barren America. James pictured him as a transmuted puritan who 'could still plead most for substance when proposing to plead for style, could still try to lose himself in the labyrinth of delight while keeping tight hold of the clue of duty, tangled even a little at his feet'. This had been Norton's ironic New England role.

2

His country life, with all its limitations, offered much solace to the ageing novelist. 'I have lived *into* my little old house and garden so thoroughly that they have become a kind of domiciliary skin, that can't be peeled off without pain.' The time would come when he would shed his skin; but between 1905 and 1910 he found in Rye a new circle of friends whose firesides offered him tea and conversation at the end of his long walks; he also found certain ideal walking companions. He could enjoy many of the consolations of old age, not least his garden. His flowers won prizes at the local exhibitions. And also there were perpetual teas and motors pulling into the cobbled street with unexpected visitors. The prevalence of the motor-car began to trouble him – 'the realization of what, in a country as small as England, the motor may come to mean for people in quiet intended hermitages'. He lost his dachshund Max and buried him sorrowfully in the small row of dog-graves at one end of his garden. He decided he would have no more pets. One hot summer a chameleon turned up on his lawn as from nowhere; it blushed and flushed black and brown and blanched to pinkish grey ten times a minute. James found him an exquisite little temporary pet. And one night in a rage against a too-audible feline, he killed the creature on the lawn with a blow of his stick – and promptly was sick at the stomach.

To these years belonged a series of friendships in Rye itself. He had complained earlier of the dullness of his neighbours. Now he found an excellent walking companion in Sydney Waterlow, a brilliant graduate of Cambridge and contemporary there of Strachey, Woolf, Keynes, and others who would be part of the later 'Bloomsbury'. Waterlow was in the Foreign Office and married then to Alice Pollock, daughter of the eminent jurist. James had known her since her childhood. At a cottage called The Steps, James could stop for tea with an 'elfin' lady named Alice Dew-Smith, who believed in psychical phenomena and wrote a book called *The Diary of a Dreamer*. She had a witty pen and published miniature essays in the *Pall Mall Gazette*. One of her books was called *Soul Shapes*. James liked The Steps; on clear days it offered a view of Cap Gris-Nez. His characterization of Mrs Dew-Smith's dog as 'a positive emetic' was long remembered in Rye. Miss Bosanquet described Mrs Dew-Smith as having 'a rather plaintive face and weird brown eyes ... I can well imagine her to be gifted with psychic powers.' Above all James found in Fanny Prothero, wife of George Prothero, editor of the *Quarterly Review*, a new and lively woman companion. She was 'Irishly amiable'. They lived in Dial Cottage. Small, bird-like, direct, Fanny Prothero had easy access to Lamb House; she gave James advice unceremoniously about simple household matters; she used to go below stairs, put her feet up on a chair and chat with James's servants. They liked her easy democracy, little realizing that this was her way of keeping an eye on them. There is a kind of high euphoria in James's letters to her, a mixture of formal domesticity and easy affection. Fanny Prothero – later Lady Prothero – understood Henry James very well, and especially his ability to focus intensely on persons and things in their immediacy. She had been sitting with the novelist one day when he was ill and Miss Bosanquet remarked Henry James would miss her after she went up to London. 'Well, Miss Bosanquet,' Fanny answered, 'Henry James is very fond of people when they are here, but I don't believe he cares a bit when they aren't. Anyone else who would sit by his bedside would do just as well. I've often noticed that, friendly and charming as he is, he is really quite aloof from everyone.' She added: 'It's the artist in him.' It was also the Henry James who preferred to be alone rather than be bored. Fanny was never boring.

Leonard Woolf remembered Waterlow as an 'infant prodigy' at Cambridge; E. M. Forster recalled him as 'affectionate and kind' but also apt to alternate 'the dictatorial with penitence'. To Waterlow, who had the precision of his diplomatic training and kept a lively diary, we owe a vivid account of James's characteristic talk during the long walks they took in and around Rye. James talked about current affairs, his immediate reading, his literary friends, his old memories. *On politics:* 'He often wondered how so complete and cumbrous a thing as the British Empire managed to go on at all; there must be some mysterious tough element in it; perhaps it was simply easier for it to go on than to stop . . . He felt tempted to call himself a rabid Socialist.' *On the Suffragettes:* 'all the signs of the beginning of a great movement, in spite of the ease of ridiculing them for desiring martyrdom on such cheap terms, "for the terms *are* cheap".' *On Christian Science:* 'A new religion growing before our eyes, just like Christianity or Mohammedanism, but (stroke of genius) addressed only to the comfortably rich.' *On taste:* 'James said his taste grew more and more delicate and sensitive. I said I found I attached less and less importance to taste. A foolish remark, but it drew the reply: "Attach importance: that isn't what one ever does or did to it. Why it attaches importance to one".' *On Ibsen* – James had been reading Gosse's book on the dramatist: 'What a bare, poor, miserable existence he had! What absence of contacts! That horrible café life . . . when he would sit day after day on the red plush benches, glowering at every one and drinking – champagne of all things, and more of it than was good for him. What a way of establishing a contact with life!' *On Meredith:*

You give these men of genius an inch and they take an ell ... *Vittoria* was like the opening of a series of windows on history ... But H.J. is always beset by a sense of the immense difficulty of being really inside things ... Then again what are we to make of the England which Meredith draws: an England of fabulous 'great' people, of coaching, and prizefighting and yachting, flavoured with the Regency, yet incapable of precise location anywhere in space or time.

On Lord Acton: 'He was an intellectual dillettante – wallowing in curious intellectual luxury. An interesting figure from his social station and his cosmopolitan ... There must have been a great fund of stupidity in anyone who could write such long letters to Mary Gladstone.'

One day James improvised a possible dissertation that could be written about 'the vulgarity of modern French literature'. He defined the vulgarity of the French

as consisting not in the absence, but in the badness of their moral standards ... They are blind to all real distinction of good and evil: hence that emptiness and thinness in their work which is what we mean by vulgarity. And it is just as real, he insisted, in France as in England tho' masked in France by perfection of form. In England there is constant vulgarity of form in addition to other vulgarities.

On Flaubert: James described him as head and shoulders above the other members of his group.

His letters to his niece, indiscreetly published, are a wonderful picture: they show him *en pantouffles*, with trousers loose – unbuttoned – sitting on his w.c. – scribbling away to her. He was a gentleman – tho' sometimes not without a touch of *cabotinage*. None of the others were gentlemen; De Goncourt was only a *gentilhomme*.

Waterlow noted that James had 'an extraordinary faculty of creating vivid pictures of persons in words. He adds, quite slowly, always taking his time about getting it precisely, the right epithet, one touch after another, until the whole portrait stands out clearly.' What emerges from the diary of the diplomat is a sense of James's conversational improvisation, his continually skilled exercise in finer discriminations.

3

If a new circle of friends replaced the dead – friendships formed all in the new century, among Edwardians – James still kept in touch with certain old American friends; in his later years Howells crossed the Atlantic more frequently than before; and on each occasion, in London and in Paris, James saw him and revived in their talk many memories; in private and in print, his old friend, by now the *doyen* of American critics, remained loyal to his original admiration of James. James had also kept up a strange friendship out of his old 1874–5 New York days with the Manton Marbles – a Jamesian name if there ever was one. Marble was a famous bi-metallist; he had been an editor of the *World*; and James used to disappear for week-ends into their home near Brighton. It was a little corner of America which James could visit. Edith Wharton said that she and her friends had a theory James 'luxuriated' in the Manton Marble bathroom, rumoured to be one of the best-appointed in England. Marble's interests were only peripherally literary; he and James wrote doggerel to one another, and in the large batch of letters to Marble which survives, is to be found James's recantation of his early criticism of Walt Whitman and a fine letter expressing his doubts about the Shakespeare of legend.

Lady Ottoline Morrell became a friend and James's visits are recorded in her diaries. There remained his old attachment to the crippled Jonathan Sturges, who was increasingly ill. 'Sturges, poor unspeakable little demon, is at present at an hotel at Eastbourne with a nurse (and more or less without a bottle!). He has charming rooms over the sea, he motors a little; and this bland summer (I went over the other day to see him, and shall renew the pilgrimage) will have done something for him.' But at Christmas of 1908 James made the journey again and found Jonathan 'at the best, more and more, but the ghost of his former self'. It was 'pure tragedy – unrelieved'.

A less chronicled friendship was with Antonio de Navarro and his actress wife Mary Anderson. She had retired from the stage on her marriage in 1890 and lived in Broadway, which James had often visited in the past and where he still maintained his friendship with the American painter Frank D. Millet. They had friends in common, particularly Sturges. Navarro was the son of an engineer who had created a steamship line to Cuba; he often wrote candidly to

James about himself and his idleness. One answer suggests the tone of this friendship and the tenderness James could bring to his relations with friends:

I am very sorry to hear of your depressions and lassitudes, I scarcely know what to say to you about them. The want of a commanding, that is of an imperative occupation is a fertile source of woe – to an *âme bien née* – and you are in some degree paying the penalty of your 'material' advantages themselves, your freedom of expatriation, your fortune, your living in a terrific 'modernity' of cosmopolite ease (which has the drawback of not working you actively into the scheme of things here.) My own conditions resemble yours – that is as to ease of expatriation, and putting aside fortune and other *agréments*! – but I am luckily possessed of a certain amount of corrective to our unnatural state, a certain amount of remedy, refuge, retreat, and anodyne! From the bottom of my heart I pity you for being without some practicable door for getting out of yourself. We all need one, and if I didn't have mine I shouldn't – well, I shouldn't be writing you this now. It takes at the best, I think, a great deal of courage and patience to live – but one must do everything to invent, to force open, that door of exit from mere immersion in one's own states.

4

Max Beerbohm belonged to an older generation of James worshippers. He was of the 1890s and he had caricatured James first as a bearded Victorian and later as the clean-shaven ecclesiastical-looking Edwardian. Still later he would parody his style. His parodies had in them a great affection for the Master, a veneration for his use of words. Max was also slightly afraid of the massive overpowering personality – he having remained the eternal mischievous small boy who mocked his elders. Max's notes suggest what he saw – 'priest – fine eyes – magnificent head – strong voice'. Max also noted:

Henry James took a tragic view of everyone, throwing up his hands and closing his eyes to shut out the awful vision. Rocking his chair and talking with tremendous emphasis ... His talk had great authority; there was a great deal of hesitation and gurgitation before he came out with anything: but it was all the more impressive, for the preparatory rumble.

One of Max's most charming anecdotes was how one day, after lunching with Somerset Maugham, he strolled along Piccadilly debating whether to see an art show or go to the Savile Club to read Henry James's new story in the *English Review* – *The Velvet Glove*.

While engaged in this debate he met Henry James himself, who asked about the art shows and expressed regret Beerbohm was walking in the other direction. 'Now if only you were coming in *this* direction, and if we two together could visit the collection you recommend.' Beerbohm always wondered why he lied: 'Ah, if only I could! But I have to be in Kensington at four!' and went instead to the Savile and read James's story. It was a case, he used to say, of his 'preferring the Master's work to the Master'. This was true.

Perhaps the reason Max walked away from James on this day in 1909 was that he sensed a certain reserve. Henry James was of two minds about Max. He liked his praise and his wit; at the same time he experienced the hostility implicit in caricature and parody even when it also contains affection. This he explained during a walk with Sydney Waterlow. He had just read Max's *The Mote in the Middle Distance.* James was 'delighted with Max's parody of himself, only it affected him in a curious way: whatever he wrote now, he felt that he was parodying himself. He said the book was a little masterpiece, but deplored the cruelty of some of the attacks.' James went on to say there was 'something unpleasant about a talent which turned altogether to exposing the weaknesses of others. It was indelicate.' And, said the Master, 'the older I get, the more I hate indelicacy'.

During these later years his public appearances were few; he avoided them as always, in spite of his calculated display during his American tour. But buried in the London newspapers is an account of a rare occasion in which James presided at a French lecture, by André Beaunier. The visitor spoke on Madame Récamier, and the reporter for the London *Times* seems to have captured the tone of James's remarks.

Mr James intimated the sphere in which French literature delights, but where Anglo-Saxon literature, not possessing the precious secret, falls heavily. This was the sphere of 'the complex relations between the sexes; of the subtler shades of passion; of the mysterious justice, of sensibility in regard to give and take.

James, said the reporter, deplored the Anglo-Saxon's lack of appetite for the finer and deeper meanings. 'The position of the person called "lady friend" in Anglo-Saxon was ambiguous – she was either in Byron's company " the unlady" or in Carlyle's "the lady" – she was not herself.'

97

The Younger Generation

AFTER forty-five years of 'the literary life' Henry James's reach could now go far beyond the memory of the young. He could evoke Thackeray out of his childhood, Dickens out of his youth, Flaubert and Turgenev out of his maturity. He remembered Tennyson and Browning, Trollope and George Eliot. And then there was his trans-Atlantic reach as well: he talked of Emerson and Lowell as friends and neighbours. He was that strange 'relic' – unique and larger than life because he had become legendary – an Anglo-American Victorian. Now he was meeting the young of the unpredictable future, and 'Bloomsbury' in particular. At one time or another his path crossed that of every member of 'Old Bloomsbury', as Leonard Woolf would characterize the first generation of the gifted men and women dedicated to the overthrow of the Master's world – who sought the New at the very moment he cherished the Old; and yet who looked at him with a mixture of affection and awe. It was strange that Lytton Strachey, in full revolt against the Victorians, should scan the windows of Lamb House and there see – as large as life – Henry James, looking into the street. The New faced the Old for one brief minute, the, as yet, beardless Strachey and the clean-shaven Master who had once worn a beard. Strachey wrote to his friend Virginia Stephen that the face he saw through the glass seemed like 'an admirable tradesman trying to give his best satisfaction, infinitely solemn and polite'. Strachey wondered how such an individual, with his large embonpoint, could be the author of *The Sacred Fount* or those late novels to which he had thrilled as an undergraduate at Cambridge. 'Perhaps if one talked to him one would understand.' The next day James walked into the Mermaid Inn, in Rye, where Strachey was staying, to show the antique fire-place to a Spanish painter named Gustave Bacaresas, a friend of Hendrik Andersen's. Strachey described James as looking 'colossal'. 'I long to know him,' he wrote to Virginia. They never met. This was in 1907.

E. M. Forster had tea with the Master once in 1908 in Lamb House. James mistook him for G. E. Moore, the Cambridge philosopher whom he had met with that other future friend of Bloomsbury, his neighbour Sydney Waterlow. Forster's diary records, 'we sat in a detached room – glimpse of fine study as we passed. H.J. very kind. Laid his hand on my shoulder and said: "Your name's Moore".' Forster also noted, 'Head rather fat, but fine, and effectively bald. Admired the Queen's letters.' (A. C. Benson's edition of Queen Victoria's letters had been recently published.) James remarked, 'She's more of a man than I expected.' When one of the guests said that the Queen 'underlines her words so', James rejoined, 'Well, she's an underlined man.' Forster also remembered James talking of Mrs Eddy. James believed Mrs Eddy must have said to herself, 'hitherto things have been done *gratis* for the poor. I will provide for the rich and charge enormously.' Forster's diary note concludes, 'He was very anxious one should eat and drink. First great man I've ever seen – not alarming but that isn't my road.' He would always be affectionately critical of the Master.

Desmond MacCarthy would be the most admiring of the group. He met James in 1901. The Master left a profound impression on the sensitive and critical young man, who was a novelist *manqué*. MacCarthy became one of the great conversationalists of his time. James had long been a master of that art. The younger man remembered the unhurried quality of James's talk and his thought; he recalled fumbling the first time he met him. He asked James if he thought London 'beautiful'. The Master gave this casual question the deepest cerebration. 'London? Beautiful?' Then, 'No, hardly beautiful. It is too chaotic, too –' A discourse on London followed that contained a remark about 'craving for a whiff of London's carboniferous damp'. James also said 'my books make no more sound or ripple now than if I dropped them one after the other into mud'. MacCarthy assured the Master that in Cambridge he had been religiously read. James was sceptical. 'I doubt if he believed,' said MacCarthy, 'that anybody thoroughly understood what, as an artist, he was after.' He said that women seemed to open up to James 'as though they were sure of his complete understanding'. The Master disliked poverty and was a seeker of comfort, remarking after visiting what seemed to MacCarthy a reasonably prosperous home, 'Poor S., poor S. – the stamp of unmistakable poverty upon everything.' It is possible, however, that James may have caught certain tell-tale signs not seen by MacCarthy, to whom James also remarked, 'I can stand a great deal of gold.' They were at that moment in an exceptionally gilded drawing-room. MacCarthy once expressed to James a thought about his problems as a writer. Perhaps, he said, writing made him feel 'absolutely alone'. James's answer was, 'Yes, it is solitude. If it runs after you and catches you, well and good. But for heaven's sake don't run after *it*. It is absolute solitude.'

A late visit to James was recorded by MacCarthy in an unpublished letter to Virginia Woolf. James had been ill. MacCarthy was admitted to the Cheyne Walk flat into which James had recently moved by the diminutive 'rock-faced' Burgess who said the Master was unwell. MacCarthy turned to leave but James summoned him. He found him sitting in an armchair with a foot rest, his eyes half-shut. He seemed to speak with difficulty, 'as though whenever his lips closed, they were stuck together and the wheels of his mind turned with a ponderous smooth difficulty, as though there was not steam enough to move so large an engine'. James asked MacCarthy not to smoke; he rang for tea. 'If I take tea it will either kill me or do me good, what shall I do?' MacCarthy refused to take so moment-out a decision. The conversation laboured.

Gradually I became aware, however, that we were making progress. We began to talk about the power to visualize memories and imaginary scenes. He seemed to think that a novelist's power depended on it. I admitted that in his own case the dependence was masked, but in that of others was not the ocular nerve of the reader often positively starved – and with admirable results? Fielding for example – there wasn't a picture on a single page of him! Then we went through the novelists with this idea in our heads, and he read to me. All the time he was getting brisker and brisker till at last from a semi-comatose condition he began to grow positively lively – shovelling on coal and eating cold tea cake and sweet buns. I enjoyed my afternoon extremely.

2

Through Thackeray's daughter Lady Ritchie (whose sister had been the first Mrs Leslie Stephen) Henry James occasionally had news of the Stephen girls, Virginia and Vanessa – the first destined for literature as Virginia Woolf, the second for art as Vanessa Bell and both at the centre of Old Bloomsbury. He had known them as children. James had mourned the passing of their mother, the beautiful Julia Duckworth; and more recently of their father, whom he had esteemed most among the Victorians. In 1906 he was touched by still another death in that much-bereaved family, that of a brother. To Lady Ritchie he wrote:

I haven't really borne to *think* of the bereavement of those brave and handsome young Stephen things (and Thoby's unnatural destruction itself) – and have taken refuge in throwing myself hard on the comparative cheer of Vanessa's engagement – quite as if it were an escape, a happy thought, I myself had invented. So I cling to it and make grossly much of it.

He would make much more than he had anticipated; for when he met the young Clive Bell he actively disliked him. He found him crude, bohemian, earthy, wholly out of key with his image of the beautiful Vanessa and the ethereal Virginia. These opinions he confided to his old friend, Lucy Clifford.

Oh yes, I went to see Vanessa Stephen on the eve of her marriage (at the Registrar's) to the quite dreadful-looking little stoop-shouldered, long-haired, third-rate Clive Bell – described as an 'intimate' friend of poor, dear, clear, tall, shy superior Thoby – even as a little sore-eyed poodle might be an intimate friend of a big mild mastiff.

He presumed Vanessa knew what she was doing. She seemed very happy and eager and 'almost boisterously in love (in that house of all the Deaths, ah me!) and I took her an old silver box ("for hairpins,") and she spoke of having got a "beautiful Florentine teaset" from you'. Virginia, James reported, had 'grown quite elegantly and charmingly and almost "smartly" handsome'.
He added:

I liked being with them, but it was all strange and terrible (with the hungry *futurity* of youth;) and all I could mainly see was the ghosts, even Thoby and Stella, let alone dear old Leslie and beautiful, pale, tragic Julia – on all of whom these young backs were, and quite naturally, so gaily turned. I heard afterwards that the Vanessas, so to speak – for she is the whole housefront – almost missed their marriage altogether (for the time) by scrambling into the Registrar's after their hour and just as he was about to close. What a nuptial 'solemnity!'

The Clive Bells spent the month of September in the year of their marriage at Playden, in that part of Rye where James had lived ten years before. His further view never reconciled the Master to Bell – and as late as 1912 he told Sidney Waterlow he could not cultivate the Stephens, because of the presence of 'that little image'. Waterlow recorded, 'Tell Virginia – tell her – how sorry I am that the inevitabilities of life should have made it seem possible even for a moment that I would allow any child of her father's to swim out of my ken.'

Virginia Stephen, during the 1907 summer at Playden, went to tea with the oracle. She described her progress down the High Street with James. He 'fixed me with his staring blank eye, it is like a child's marble', (so would she years later describe the eye of Shakespeare in *Orlando*) and she then caricatured one of James's sentences:

My dear Virginia, they tell me, they tell me, they tell me, that you – as indeed being your father's daughter, nay your grandfather's grandchild, the descendant, descendant of a century – of a century – of quill pen and ink, ink, in, pots, yes, yes, yes, they tell me ahmmm, that you, that you, that you write in short.

This went on, said Virginia, while 'we all waited, as farmers wait for the hen to lay an egg, do they? nervous, polite, and now on this foot now on that'. The future novelist said she felt 'like a condemned person'. If this made her uneasy it did not prevent her from noting the way James

made phrases over the bread and butter, 'rude and rapid' as it was, and told us of the scandal of Rye, 'Mr Jones has eloped I regret to say to Tasmania leaving twelve little Jones's and a possible thirteenth to Mrs Jones, most regrettable, most unfortunate, and yet not wholly an action to which one has no private key of one's own so to speak.

Leonard Woolf would wryly comment on James's dislike of Clive Bell and Saxon Sydney-Turner, two who 'understood and admired him' far more profoundly than Sydney Waterlow and Hugh Walpole. Yet 'all that the sensitive antennae recorded was that the young man was small, silent, and grubby'. There was no accounting for antipathies; Woolf did not see that young Bell was bumptious and Sydney-Turner a bore: while Waterlow was a good listener and Hugh was 'loveable', and Woolf did not know how much there was of admiration for 'the crushed strawberry glow of Vanessa's beauty and credibility and the promise of Virginia's printed wit'. To his old friend, Sara Norton, James recorded his glimpse of these fair visitors to Rye of that year.

Leslie Stephen's children (three of them – the three surviving poor dear mild able gigantic Thoby gathered in his flower) have taken two houses near me (temporarily) and as I write the handsome (and most lovable) Vanessa Clive-Bell sits on my lawn (unheeded by me) along with her little incongruous and disconcerting but apparently very devoted newly acquired *sposo*. And Virginia, on a near hilltop, writes reviews for *The Times* – and the gentle Adrian interminably long and dumb and 'admitted to the bar' marches beside her like a giraffe beside an ostrich – save that Virginia is facially most fair.

Some sense of his lost youth, his distant days with the parents of these girls, the feeling of the 'generation gap', seems to have touched him deeply at this moment. He had written to Lucy Clifford of 'the hungry futurity' of youth. Now, with a flourish of the pen, he added in this letter to Sara Norton: 'And the hungry generations tread me down!'

3

The future Bloomsbury males were of the generation of the turn of the century at Cambridge. Almost a decade later a new generation at Cambridge was still reading Henry James and worshipping him. On New Year's eve in 1907 Geoffrey Keynes, then at Pembroke, Charles Sayle, under-librarian at the University Library, and Theodore Bartholomew, an assistant librarian, decided to send a card of greeting to the Master. To their surprise he replied: 'I am extremely touched and very grateful and all responsively yours, Henry James.' Emboldened, they invited James to visit them at Cambridge. He was then involved in his second series of theatricals. They tried again on the eve of 1909. This time the answer was, 'Yes, I really will come this year – about the May time I promise myself.' They were strangers to him, but the Master entered into the fun and admiration, which he found 'most sustaining'.

To his American friend Gaillard Lapsley, who was a don at Trinity, James wrote: 'I literally go to Cambridge to stay for forty-eight hours, at 8 Trumpington Street with my bevy of "admirers" – Charles Sayle, Geoffrey Keynes and the elusive Bartholomew (none of whom I have ever seen). I feel rather like an unnatural intellectual Pasha visiting his Circassian Hareem!' The minutely-planned occasion began on 12 June 1909 and James returned to London on 14 June. Again to Lapsley he reported,

My Cambridge adventure was the lively exemplification of a leap in the dark – I having absolutely no données on my hosts, or host. But they were as kind to me as possible and I *liked* it, the whole queer little commerce, and *them*, the queer little all juvenile gaping group, quite sufficiently; so that the leap landed me on my feet and no bones are broken.

His hosts arranged a strenuous programme. He was given dinner on arrival, taken to a concert – Parry, Stanford, Mendelssohn, Wagner. James did not conceal his boredom. Back in Trumpington Street, they talked until late. One subject was Walt Whitman. James maintained that it was impossible for any woman to write a good criticism of Whitman or get near his point of view. The host, Charles Sayle, made one serious mistake: like James's typists, he tried to supply a word during a long-pondered sentence. James waved it aside. Sayle continued to try. The members of the triumvirate suffered. Breakfast, the next morning, was pleasant. James was escorted to King's Chapel and the University Library. At Pembroke, Keynes gave them lunch and guests included Sydney Cockerell, director of the Fitzwilliam Museum and Rupert Brooke. There was no question that the future war poet 'made' the occasion memorable. James visited the Fitzwilliam and talked of Byron and Tolstoy to Cockerell; he met Francis Cornford, later professor of Greek; he lunched with John Maynard Keynes (Geoffrey's brother) and H. J. Norton. Desmond MacCarthy, arriving late at this luncheon, remembered James sitting 'with a cold poached egg in front of him bleeding to death upon a too large, too thick helping of bacon, and surrounded by a respectful circle of silent, smoking, observant undergraduates'. MacCarthy claimed that James cross-examined him about Rupert Brooke. The youth wrote poetry, MacCarthy said, which was no good. James was relieved 'for with *that* appearance if he had also talent it would be too unfair'. James advised Brooke 'not to be afraid of being happy'. This was Lambert Strether talking to Little Bilham. Other memories are of James discussing Carlyle's manner of lecturing and the Russian ballet, and describing Anne Ritchie 'her style, all smiles and wavings of the pocket handkerchief'. The Master dismissed J. K. Huysmans and Pierre Louÿs 'with opprobrium'. 'Excrement,' he said of Louÿs. And he called *Kipps* 'the best novel of the last forty years'. The best-remembered episode was James reclining in a punt on velvet cushions – the image of the Pasha had come true – 'gazing up through prominent half-closed eyes at Brooke's handsome figure clad in white shirt and white flannel trousers'. Cockerell recalled James later saying he had been entertained 'by young men whose mother's milk was barely dry on their lips'. To Sayle James wrote a formal letter of thanks. He recalled he had been made to 'loll not only figuratively but literally on velvet surfaces exactly adapted to my figure'. He sent thanks to all 'with a definite stretch towards the Rupert – with whose name I take this liberty because I don't know whether one loves one's love with a (surname terminal) *e* or not'. In Brooke James had found one friend during that week-end. One of the last sentences the Master would write, after Brooke's death in the war, was in the preface to Brooke's *Letters from America* – recalling how he 'unforgettably' met him early in June 1909.

98

Hugh

HUGH WALPOLE occupied a place apart among the younger generation in the Master's life. Leonard Woolf had wondered what James saw in Hugh when he could have admired the intelligence and perceptions of Clive Bell. James hardy admired Hugh as an intelligence. There was something else which drew him to this young man who descended on London in 1909 hungry for success and invited the literary establishment to love him. He was ingenuous, good-looking and a bit pathetic in his reaching-out to people. 'A nice boy, full of anxiety and good feeling,' A. C. Benson wrote in his diary. Hugh continued to be anxious, and nice, and to possess good feeling. He had had a fragmented childhood. Born in New Zealand, uprooted when his clerical father moved to New York to teach theology, Hugh was sent to school in England at a tender age and had experienced the cruelties which older boys are apt to visit on the younger. His schooldays were a nightmare of pain and loneliness, during years when many children are accustomed to parental love. Things were better at Cambridge; Hugh went through exultations, agonies, a religious crisis. Now he faced the world, with a forward-thrusting chin and a boundless need for love. Sir Rupert Hart-Davis, in his admirable biography of Hugh, suggests this in the epigraph from Jean Paul : *Er liebte jeden Hund, und wunschte von jeden Hund geliebt zu sein.*

Hugh was unashamedly 'on the make' as he settled into his small rooms in Chelsea. He got work as a reviewer; he clipped and sent his reviews to authors he wanted to meet. He nearly always succeeded. His letters were candid and naïve. To Henry James he wrote late in 1908 invoking Benson's name. James found the young man's candour appealing. He responded with a characteristic mixture of kindness and caution. 'I rejoice that you were moved to write it.' On the verge of accepting the invitation of the Cambridge group James added 'I always find myself (when the rare and blest revelation – once in a blue moon – takes place) the happier for the thought that I enjoy the sympathy of the gallant and intelligent young.' He warned Walpole on the dangers of 'the deep sea of journalism' and concluded 'let me believe that at some propitious [hour] I may have the pleasure of seeing you'. A. C. Benson had written him, he said, 'that I shall not make a mistake in attempting, within my compass of the safely combustible to feed your flame'. Unable to resist a touch of irony, he added that 'so dancing and aspiring' a flame scarce required 'more care than you yourself can give it'. He encouraged the young aspirant,

write me the letters and send me Books and pay me the visits; and above all keep as tight hold as you can of the temper and the faith of your almost unbearably enviable youth. I am a hundred years old – it's my one merit – but the breath of your enviability (that name says all for it,) quickens again, after all, yours with every good wish Henry James.

James had sized up his young man, for he also would write him 'you bleat and jump like a white lambkin on the vast epistolary green which stretches before you co-extensive with life ... I positively invite and applaud your gambols.' Thus began the friendship of Hugh Walpole and the Master.

I

They faced each other for the first time in February 1909 when James came up to London to attend a matinée of *The High Bid*. He gave young Hugh dinner at the Reform Club. A bout of ill-health, his new involvement with the theatre, his sense of the passing years – James would be 66 that April – made him particularly receptive to the ardent worship of the young man. Walpole's diary records: 'Dined with Henry James alone at the Reform Club. He was perfectly wonderful. By far the greatest man I have ever met – and yet amazingly humble and affectionate – absolutely delightful. He talked about himself and his books a good deal and said some interesting things. It was a wonderful evening.' Never one to be shy, young Hugh also talked a great deal about himself.

The invitation to Rye followed. 'Can you come some day – some Saturday – in April? I mean after Easter. Bethink yourself.' And referring to Hugh's novel *The Wooden Horse* about to be published James added:

I am tender-hearted enough to be capable of shedding tears of pity and sympathy over young Hugh on the threshold of fictive art – and with the long and awful vista of large production in a largely producing world before him. Ah, dear young Hugh, it will very grim for you with your faithful and dismal friend Henry James.

It wouldn't be in the least grim for the success-hungry Hugh. To be sure James would always be critical; but he gave Hugh a very large measure of tenderness and affection. This was what the young man wanted. And if the Master was critical, the public was less inclined to be so. Hugh was a born storyteller. His novels flowed with the same steadiness as they had flowed from his model, Sir Walter Scott. In future years, Walpole would be two or three novels ahead of his publisher; the printers could hardly keep up with him.

The aspirant came to Rye towards the end of April 1909. 'I shall be here, at your carriage door with open arms (and with my handy man for your bag). Bring a love-scene or something, and read it to yours immensely Henry James.' The love-scene Hugh brought was his own responsive affection and his bright habit of demanding total commitment from those who showed any inclination to give it. As with Hendrik Andersen, as with Jocelyn Persse, the first visit and the chance for private communion in the Rye setting, had its effect on both Master and disciple. Youth responded to affection; age and loneliness to youth. Hugh's diary offers its testimony – 'a wonderful week-end with Henry James. Much more wonderful than I had expected. I am very lucky in my friends. The house and garden are exactly suited to him. He is beyond words. I cannot speak about him.' If he did not speak in his diary, Hugh would later record in *Fortitude*, one of the most successful of his early novels, the lessons of the Master; still later we can find the emotion of their meeting – Hugh's unbounded admiration and worship, James's unbounded delight in Hugh's brashness – in a tale called *Mr Oddy*. James would always seem odd to Hugh, who felt overpowered by him. He named his fictitious novelist, both in novel and tale, Henry Galleon; James, in his obesity, his large Johnsonian body set on his short legs, must have seemed like some great old ship – and like those ships he was also, to Hugh, a great prize or catch. In *Fortitude*, Galleon talks to the young aspirant in simplified Walpolian sentences, but we catch the reverberation of the great style; the feeling rings true. The invocation to 'the sacredness of your calling', the discourse on the treacheries of the market-place. 'Some will tell you that you have no style – others will tell you that you have too much. Some again will tempt you with money and money is not to be despised.' There would be publicity, lecture offers, dinners

... Worst of all there will come to you terrible hours when you yourself know of a sure certainty that your work is worthless. In your middle age a great barrenness will come upon you. You have been a little teller of little tales, and on every side of you there will be others who have striven for other prizes and have won them. Sitting alone in your room with your poor strands of coloured silk that had once been intended to make so beautiful a pattern, poor boy, you will know that you have failed. That will be a very dreadful hour – the only power that can meet it is a blind and deaf courage. Courage is the only thing that we are here to show ...

and again

Fortitude is the artist's only weapon of defence ... I have hurried, I have scrambled, I have fought, cursed and striven, but as an Artist only those hours that I have spent listening, waiting, have been my real life ... You are here to listen ... There must be restraint, austerity, discipline ... the Artist's life is the harshest that God can give to man ... I am at the end of my work. I have done what I can. You are at the beginning of yours. You will do what you can. I wish you good fortune.

Some such words sealed their friendship. As with the young sculptor, James would have been glad to have the young writer stay on at Lamb House indefinitely. James talked of Thackeray and Dickens, Carlyle and Stevenson. 'And then all his talk about the Novel and his own things is quite amazing,' the ebullient Hugh informed his mother. 'It is a wonderful thing for me and will of course alter my whole life. He is, I think, really a great man.' On another occasion, Hugh's diary again offers, 'Such a day! H.J. talking all the time. Described Daudet's meeting with Meredith, smashed *Mrs Tanqueray*, argued with Robbie about the drama, long walk with me during which I told him about *Fortitude* and he approved. Final summing-up of everyone to me in the small hours of the morning.' Robbie was Robert Ross, Oscar Wilde's friend, and the occasion for this diary entry was a week-end spent by James and Walpole at the home of Lady Lovelace.

To Benson, James wrote that he felt for 'the delightful and interesting young Hugh Walpole ... the tenderest sympathy and an absolute affection'. He said that he was inclined to be sorry for 'the intensely young, the intensely confident and intensely ingenuous and generous' but this was not the case with Hugh. 'I somehow don't pity *him*, for I think he has some gift to conciliate the Fates. I feel him at any rate an admirable young friend, of the openest mind and most attaching nature.' This was in June 1909. A month later he told Benson, 'We have become fast friends; I am infinitely touched by his sympathy and charmed by his gifts ... I wish him no end of ardent existence – feeling as I do that he can handsomely and gallantly carry it.'

2

It must be recorded that in matters of craft very few of the Master's lessons rubbed off on young Hugh. He had talent and a kind of invincibility of desire, an impulse to self-indulgence and gratification. He had need of the fortitude but not of the courage that James preached. James was talking from the high places of art and from his arduous career in which his passion had been so largely present. We can quite believe Hugh's record in his diary of James's saying, 'I've had one great passion in my life – the intellectual passion. What that has been for me I cannot say. Make it your rule to encourage the impersonal interests as against the personal – but remember also that they are interdependent.' Hugh tended to do the reverse. He followed the personal rather than the impersonal. His nature spilled out everywhere and he found universal goodwill. He possessed neither James's sense of craft, nor his dedication; he was always active, always spontaneous. Success came to him easily. Perhaps it was his uncomplicatedness that appealed to James. Hugh would find love – the love of men, for he feared women, though he was attractive to them – and wealth, and be knighted, and lecture in America and have an honourable career and a loyal public. Of his relation with James he would write, a dozen years after the novelist's death,

I knew him only during the last ten [it was actually the last seven] years of his life. I loved him, was frightened of him, was bored by him, was staggered by his wisdom and stupefied by his intricacies, altogether enslaved by his kindness, generosity, child-like purity of his affections, his unswerving loyalties, his sly and Puck-like sense of humour.

He also said,

I was a young man in a hurry, ambitious, greedy, excitable. I was not really vain. When he told me gently that I was an idiot and that my novels were worthless, I believed that, from his point of view, it must be so, and that if the world had been peopled with Henry Jameses I should certainly never publish a line. The world was not.

The letter James wrote to Hugh after his first visit to Rye suggests a kind of pact of affection between them. To 'my dear, dear, Hugh', James writes that his 'confidence and trust and affection are infinitely touching and precious to me, and I all responsibly accept them and give you all my own in return. Yes, all "responsibly", my dear boy – large as the question of "living up" to our splendid terms can't but appear to loom to me'. James seems to be speaking of his age, as he would speak in a later letter of his yearning for Hugh 'in the most motherly, not to say grandmotherly, way'. But now he wrote:

Living up to them – for *me* – takes the form of wanting to be more sovereignly and sublimely – and ah so tenderly withal! – good for you and helpful to you than words can well say. This is, in vulgar phrase, a large order, but I'm not afraid of it – and in short it's inspiring to think how magnificently we shall pull together, all round and in every way. See therefore how we're at one, and believe in the comfort I take in you. It goes very deep – deep, deep, deep: so infinitely do you touch and move me, dear Hugh. So for the moment enough said – even though so much less said than felt.

Hugh had asked James how he might address him and the novelist replied that 'for the present' he might call him *très cher maître* or 'my very dear Master'. Hugh complied. The Master on his side was less solemn. He wrote 'belovedest little Hugh', 'beloved boy'; on one occasion 'dearest darlingest little Hugh' which in the same letter he laughingly abbreviated to 'd.d.l.h.' There were moments in which his passion overwhelmed him and the letters (very early in their friendship) spoke of his loneliness and betrayed a curious dependency. 'I only want to be *in* your mind, and not a whit grossly "on" it, while you can always believe and know that you're in mine quite as entirely. I am yours, yours, yours, dearest Hugh, *yours*! H.J.'

From Hugh's own remarks, and a later novel he dedicated to James's memory, one gathers that the young man saw the Master as a figure of physical as well as artistic power and sensed the masculine side of James within the 'grandmotherly'. A strong possessiveness is to be found in these letters as well. James pictures himself on occasion as an 'old ponderous Elephant' reaching out to grasp Hugh with an embracing trunk. On another occasion the Elephant 'paws you oh so benevolently'; still another assures him that the Master is 'a steady old beast'. James could however turn the Elephant into a faithful canine. 'The old grizzled and blear-eyed house-dog looks up, that is, and grunts and wags his tail at the damaged but still Delectable Prodigal Son' – this when Hugh had written James of some bout of illness. There are all kinds of hints and allusions and bursts of jocular jealousy as when James chides Hugh for a dedication. 'Who the devil is the Dedication-wretch of "Mr Perrin" who has – the brute – "more understanding and sympathy than any one you have ever met".' James most assuredly thought himself Hugh's most 'understanding' friend. The Master proceeded then to dissect the novel, *Mr Perrin and Mr Traill*, mercilessly. Hugh did not have an 'operative centre' in it; Mr Traill came through as someone with no capacity for experience. As with his critiques of Howard Sturgis, James brought heavy critical artillery into play, after which there followed an expression of love. 'Don't feel that your infatuated old friend discriminates only to destroy – destroy, that is, the attachment to him that it is his very fondest dream all perpetually and intensely to feel in you.'

He might flatter, praise, smother Hugh with affection; yet he gave him no quarter as a writer. In that respect he was the law-giving Master. His love was earthly; his philosophy of craft Olympian. They had been friends but a few months when Walpole sent James his second novel *Maradick at Forty*. James's answer was to say he had 'in a manner' read it. He reminded Hugh he was 'the grim and battered old *critical* critic'. As always he complimented the young man on his love of life. However he found the book 'nearly as irreflectively juvenile as the Trojans' – an allusion to Hugh's first novel *The Wooden Horse*. Hugh had written, said James, about 'the marital, sexual, bedroom relations of Maradick and his wife' but

you don't tackle and face them – you *can't*. Also the whole thing is a monument to the abuse of voluminous dialogue, the absence of a plan of composition, alternation, distribution, structure, and other phases of presentation than the dialogue – so that the *line* (the only thing *I* value in a fiction, etc.) is replaced by a vast formless featherbediness – billows in which one sinks and is lost. And yet it's so loveable – though not so *written*. It isn't written *at all*, darling Hugh.

Then James was contrite. 'Can you forgive all this to your fondest old reaching-out-his-arms-to-you H.J.?'

Hugh did not betray the hurt. This he buried very deeply, and it did not surface until long after James's death when he wrote out a primordial fantasy in which a slayer becomes the man he slays and dedicated the book to the memory of the Master. This suggests the extent to which Hugh identified with James. It suggests also the inner mechanisms by which Hugh had learned to cope with the school bullies of his childhood – by becoming the bullies.

James's letters, even the most critical, breathe a cheerful affection, that of a man who enjoys Hugh's company enormously – whenever he can have it – loves his easy enthusiasms and his prattle and wants to do everything he can for him. He sent Hugh a large desk for his seaside cottage; he inscribed books; he insisted that Hugh pocket a £5 note during the first Christmas of their acquaintance. Hugh himself told the humorous incident of James's insistently giving him his top hat at the Reform Club in which Hugh felt uncomfortable and did not wear until middle age. On one occasion at Rye, when Hugh kept asking the Master what time it was (he wanted to catch a train), James took his watch from his pocket and gave it him. He always dined him in London. Hugh's diary tells us 6 July 1909; 'Had a ripping dinner with H.J. on Friday night. That is a quite perfect affair in its way and one begins to feel that the *one* thing that one really demands of the friend is perfect comprehension.' The three-score letters which testify to this relationship are among the finest James ever wrote, in their playfulness, their mixture of affection and literary doctrine, their shrewdness, their breadth of feeling. At times these feelings become intense, although there is never quite the same 'tactile' quality, the laying on of hands, which is to be found in the letters to Hendrik Andersen. James wrote with freedom both to Hugh and Hendrik, apparently on the assumption they were destroying his letters. 'Chuck this straight into the fire,' writes James at one point to Hugh, mainly because the letter is full of gossip. He adds, 'I count on that being, by the way, where you *always* chuck me.' Hugh no more could have chucked a James letter into the fire than could Hendrik. James's letters to

Jocelyn Persse offer us a distinct contrast: they are less effusive and the affection in them seems to run deeper, it does not require articulation. With James and Hugh the correspondence is of writer to writer. The verbalization of love was important to both.

3

Hendrik Andersen was 27 when James met him; Jocelyn was 30; Hugh was 24. James had loved Hendrik when he himself was in his 50s. He had reached his 60s and was increasingly ill when he met Hugh. They saw very little of each other during the first year of their friendship. The Master's illness of 1910 culminated in his going to America for a year, and the friendship was not resumed until late in 1911; by that time Hugh was in the first great whirl of success; and the best part of their friendship, and James's finest letters, belong to the short time when James was turning 70 in that season of the century soon to be betrayed by 1914. Of these three significant late friendships, only that with Jocelyn seems to have had a genuine continuity; the friendship with Hendrik was doomed to be distant and James made an image of the sculptor that did not correspond to the reality. James saw brightness where there was dullness; and intelligence where there was mediocrity. With Hugh there was intelligence and the community of literature. With Jocelyn there seems to have existed a permanent sense of comradeship and unquestioned love. Still James could write to Hugh in the autumn of their first year of 'our admirable, our incomparable relation', and echo the words he had used of his relation with Jocelyn, 'we are in such beautiful, such exquisite, relation'.

What that relation was must remain – beyond the evidence of the letters and the testimony of Hugh's diaries – a matter for conjecture. With James there is always a touch of 'too late, too late' as with Lambert Strether, in his meetings with the young man. 'I think I don't regret a single "excess" of my responsive youth,' James wrote on one occasion to Hugh, 'I only regret in my chilled age, certain occasions and possibilities I *didn't* embrace.' According to Hugh there was one occasion which James did not embrace. In his later years Hugh told the young Stephen Spender that he had offered himself to the Master and that James had said, 'I can't, I can't.' Somerset Maugham, as we have earlier recorded, also told this story. It is interesting however to note how often Hugh, in later times, would emphasize James's 'puritanism'. Thus in his most important reminiscence of James, he wrote:

He was curious about everything, he *knew* everything, but his Puritan *taste* would shiver with apprehension. There was no crudity of which he was unaware but he did not wish that crudity to be named. It must be there so that he might apprehend it, but it must not be named. I was, alas, too crude myself to present anything without naming it, and I learnt to dread that shy look of distress that would veil his eyes as he apprehended my clumsy intrepidities.

A striking incident throws doubt on this. Hugh went regularly to Edinburgh, where his father was Bishop. There he met the Catholic priest, John Gray, who had been a friend of Oscar Wilde. He also met André Raffalovich, a European-Russian, author of a book on homosexuality, who was said to have wooed John Gray away from Wilde. Raffalovich had contributed to the building of St Peter's in Father Gray's parish and maintained a ritualized cultural salon in Edinburgh. To some it seemed as if the friendship of Gray and Raffalovich had been translated into religious emotion. Not to Hugh. In his life, religion and homosexuality had been carefully separated. He disapproved of Gray and Raffalovich but instead of saying this to James, or offering any gossip, he simply wrote – rather angrily – of 'immorality on stone floors'. Hugh said he couldn't say more: it made him suffer so. James's rejoinder was a mixture of laughter and affection. 'That's the very *most* juvenile logic possible,' wrote the Master. '*There* was exactly an admirable matter for you to write me *about* – a matter as to which you are strongly and abundantly feeling; and in a relation which lives on communication as ours surely should.' Thus prodded, Hugh seems to have offered a fuller account. James was still not satisfied.

I could have done even with more detail – as when you say 'Such parties!' I want so to hear exactly what parties they are. When you refer to their 'immorality on stone floors', and with prayerbooks in their hands, so long as the exigencies of the situation permit of the manual retention of the sacred volumes, I do so want the picture developed and the proceedings authenticated.

James was curious and saw 'fun' where his younger friend's clerical background interfered.

The novelist met Raffalovich shortly after this exchange, for in a note to Hugh he writes 'Raffalovich of Edinburgh ("immorality on stone floors!") comes on Tuesday.' And it was Raffalovich who told of an incident reflecting what Hugh called James's 'puritanism'. According to Raffalovich James once called on the Beardsleys

and Aubrey's sister (a beautiful and charming girl) pointed out to him on the stairs a Japanese print which shocked him. He called it a 'disconcerting incident' and always afterwards fought shy of her, though the print on the stairs was nothing startling. I remember once teasing him with a friend to know what the Olympian young man 'in the Cage' had done wrong. He swore he did not know, he would rather not know.

Clearly James's 'puritanism' puzzled those who knew him: behind it there was the laughter of *What Maisie Knew*.

4

Henry James once said to Hugh about a friend, 'I not only love him – I *love* to love him.' This was the way in which he loved Hugh. Years later Hugh would write: 'His tenderness of heart was unequalled in the world.' This he described as 'a power of generosity, of loyalty and forgetfulness of self. It had a quality of sweetness quite unmistakable.' James lived, Hugh said,

deeper down than the rest of us ... had had experiences that he could communicate to no one ... He was also a sick man during a great part of the time that I knew him, and I was then extremely healthy and as filled with vitality as a merry-go-round at a fair. It was this vitality that attracted and bewildered him. How could I have so much eagerness, so much real curiosity about life, so much interest in so many *different* things and yet penetrate life so thinly? Why, if I wanted to know so much, didn't I see that I knew more? When I visited Lamb House I must give, in every detail, the full account of every adventure. There he would sit, listening, his head on one side like a stout and very well-dressed robin. But at the end of it I had omitted, it seemed, every essential.

This testimony rings true.

In the year of his 70th birthday James wrote a letter to Hugh, filled with deep emotion. 'Cultivate with me, darlingest Hugh, the natural affections, so far as you are lucky enough to have matter for them. I mean don't wait till you are eighty to do so – though indeed *I* haven't waited, but have made the most of them from far back.' In another passage the letter says:

Don't say to me, by the way, apropos of jinks – the 'high' kind that you speak of having so wallowed in previous to leaving town – that I ever challenge you as to *why* you wallow, or splash, or plunge, or dizzily and sublimely soar (into the jinks element) or whatever you may call it: as if I ever remarked on anything but the absolute inevitability of it for you at your age and with your natural curiosities, as it were, and passions. It's good healthy exercise, when it comes but in bouts and brief convulsions, and it's always a kind of thing that it's good, and considerably final to *have* done. We must know, as much as possible, in our beautiful art, yours and mine, what we are talking about – and the only way to know is to have lived and loved and cursed and floundered and enjoyed and suffered.

He went on to say to Hugh that the advice he was giving was bad doctrine for 'a young idiot or a duffer; but in place for a young friend (pressed to my heart,) with a fund of nobler passion, the preserving, the defying, the dedicating, and which always has the last word'.

99

A Passion on Olympus

HENRY JAMES had spoken of Mrs Wharton as being 'almost too insistently Olympian'. It is doubtful, however, whether he would have written *The Velvet Glove* had he known how troubled and difficult – and passionate – life had become on Olympus. Her high life of the intellect had been her way of escaping from a frivolous and imprisoning society, and from a stifling marriage with a good-natured easy-going man who felt ineffectual, particularly when faced with his wife's strong will and her ethical, moral and artistic intensities. Teddy was handsome, a perfect gentleman of his Boston world, a bit eccentric, a hunter, a fisherman, a lover of animals. He was bored by Edith's artistic friends; and both he and his wife were usually depressed, especially when together, for the communion of love and the bed had not been achieved in their marriage. He once remarked to Henry James that 'Puss' (as Mrs Wharton was known in the earlier New York society) 'wants to come over, but I feel much too well to stand her crowd'. James replied, 'But, my dear Teddy, what's the use of a 40 horsepower Pierce Arrow if you can't fly away in it from any high-browed crowd.' Teddy and his wife were constantly in flight from one another.

For years Mrs Wharton closed her eyes to Teddy's indifferences. She took him for granted. It had been pleasant earlier to have him around as a sort of consort, a gentleman and cavalier, who let her go her own way without making insistent demands. Otherwise she would not have registered with so great a shock in 1908 – when she was 46 – a small episode which suggests that she had had an illumination. Reading a book on heredity she was 'struck by a curious and rather amusing passage' and she held it out to her husband, saying 'Read that!' Teddy dutifully looked at the page. 'Does that sort of thing amuse you?' he asked.

Such moments had probably occurred many times before, and Mrs Wharton had shrugged them off without pain. Now, however, she seems to have listened with her whole being. 'I heard the key turn in the prison lock,' she confided to a new diary which she began to keep at this time. 'Oh, Gods of derision! And you've given me twenty years of it! *Je n'en peux plus.*' A breaking-point had been reached. For she had finally faced the truth of her marriage. What revealed it was her having – after these many years – fallen in love. She was experiencing a kind of 'quiet ecstasy' in the presence of Henry James's soft and sentimental friend, the American journalist William Morton Fullerton, who lived and worked in Paris. An epicurean son of a New England clergyman, Fullerton had graduated from Harvard and gone abroad distinctly as a lover of the life of letters, and of women; and he was capable of intimate male friendship as well. He had known Oscar Wilde; he had been a friend too of the sculptor, Wilde's friend, Lord Ronald Gower. He had had a passionate love affair with James's friend, Margaret Brooke, the statuesque Ranee of Sarawak; Blanche Roosevelt, the wooer of literary celebrity, had crossed his path, and there were others. James had always – from their meeting in the 1880s – found Fullerton appealing and sought his company; they were constantly together when the novelist was in Paris. Although Fullerton was a successful correspondent of the London *Times*, he cultivated in a leisurely way the Gallic spirit – and personal relations. Most of his friends did not know of his unfortunate brief marriage to a singer at the Opéra Comique; nor of his French mistress – Henrietta Mirecourt – with whom he was deeply involved. Or the complexities of his relation to an enamoured cousin, Katherine, who had been adopted by his parents and reared as his sister. By the time Edith met him, Fullerton was more French than the French. He wrote in French. French poetry was constantly on his lips; he was in every way an *homme de coeur*, a discriminatingly promiscuous Victorian-American, who dressed with dignity and lived the life of an egotist as if he were a mixture of a Restoration rake and (in his verbal solemnities) Dr Johnson himself. Wilde had indeed accused him once of writing a Johnsonian letter: but it could have been called Jamesian as well. Morton had some of the stance of Edith Wharton's intellectual friend of many years, Walter Van Rensselaer Berry, but he was softer, more gentle; there was a touch of the feminine in his make-up to which Edith deeply responded. As Berry had been in tune with Mrs Wharton's hard, clear finely-tempered intelligence, Fullerton could be in tune with something even more important – certainly more profound: her long-deprived femininity. Or, as she put it in her love-journal, 'the wasted driven-in feeling of the past!'

Fullerton was more than responsive. He could be an ardent and devoted lover, but never a faithful one: he found women irresistible. Mrs Wharton would write in her memoirs that Berry had found her 'when my mind and soul were hungry and thirsty, and he fed them till our last hour together'. Of Fullerton, who fed much more, though for a briefer time, there is no mention. Fullerton, she might have written, found her a vessel of passion eager for sensual and erotic experience. Excerpts from the particular journal she devoted to this love affair of her middle life, have long been known and were read as if they were addressed to Walter Berry; but during the time of her first passion for Fullerton, Berry was in Egypt as member of an international tribunal; and he was (so everyone felt) a cold dispassionate man. R. W. B. Lewis, the authoritative biographer of Mrs Wharton, has shown that she was in reality addressing, in her journal, not the friend of her mind but the lover of her body. Her journal is unique in the impoverished 'love annals' of America; at moments it is written as if Edith Wharton were Hortense Allart, the candid mistress of Chateaubriand and Sainte-Beuve; or George Sand sounding the depths of her life with Chopin or Alfred de Musset.

Edith had suddenly become aware that Eros lived on Olympus. Henry James understandably did not have access to these recorded passages of intense emotion, otherwise he would have known that the proud Diana – or Astarte – was no longer on her pedestal. 'I am a little humbled, a little ashamed, to find how poor a thing I am, how the personality I had moulded into such strong firm lines has crumbled to a pinch of ashes in this flame!' She had said that 'There is a contact of thought, that seems so much closer than a kiss.' Now she discovered that 'thought may be dissolved in feeling'. It was a terrible – and a joyful – discovery. She told herself that she had endured her marriage 'all these years, and hardly felt it, because I had created a world of my own, in which I had lived without heeding what went on outside'. Henry James had spoken of this to certain of his friends and had characterized it as the blindness of those who have been too 'facilitated'. Mrs Wharton once said to herself that one hour of love 'ought to irradiate a whole life'. Now she exploded, *Eh bien bon, ce n'est pas assez!*

Teddy was actually more ill than Mrs Wharton knew; he would eventually have to be committed to a sanatorium. Berry would remain a valuable intellectual friend. The world wondered at Edith Wharton's admiration for this smooth, impersonal, handsome and handsomely turned-out chamber-of-commerce man. Percy Lubbock would speak of Mrs Wharton's 'surrender' to a man 'of a dry and narrow and supercilious temper'. 'Life is not a matter of abstract principles,' she had lately written in *The Fruit of the Tree* 'but a succession of pitiful compromises with fate, of concessions to old tradition, old beliefs, old charities and frailties ... that was the word of the gods to the mortal who had laid a hand on their bolts. And she had humbled herself to accept the lesson.' It was a hard lesson : and it was the central drama in the life of this brilliant woman who had fascinated and irritated Henry James, and who now, bit by bit, began to discover, like her heroine, new realities within the house of mirth. Edith began to confide in the Master only after his second visit in 1908. Fullerton now appears in company with Mrs Wharton – they turn up at Lamb House together. James goes on excursions with them; and Morton's name begins to figure in the Master's letters to Mrs Wharton. James would say that in her novels 'the masculine conclusion' tended 'so to crown the feminine observation'. Having grown up in a houseful of males with her father and two brothers much older than herself, she was most at ease in the company of men; her intellectual masculinity made it possible for a man of Berry's temperament to accept her almost as if she were a man. But Fullerton's component of femininity may have made him, in turn, highly acceptable to her. Some such chemistry of personality was at work among Edith's friendships – certainly at Qu'Acre where the rite of Astarte was symbolically performed by a circle of younger men, not least the embroidering host, Howard Sturgis.

I

When Edith Wharton began to tell her troubles to Henry James he offered her the advice he had always given his friends – that one must 'live through' an experience and try not to avoid it; that in life it was better to give way to tears than to hold them back; and also that one had to continue with the everyday things of existence – in a word, keep a hold on reality. He warned Mrs Wharton against acting impulsively. The letter he wrote to her has long been known. Mrs Wharton herself allowed it to be published; but she removed certain passages from it. She seems to have frankly confided to him her unhappiness in her marriage. 'Only sit tight yourself and *go through the movements of life*,' James replied, 'live it all through every inch of it ... waitingly.' She must not, he said in a passage she withheld, let herself conclude anything in a hurry. 'Anything is more creditable – conceivable – than a mere inhuman *plan*.'

Edith Wharton had by no means fully confided in James; for the Master remained curious as well as concerned. 'I suffer almost to anguish for the darkness in which I sit,' he wrote to her in April 1909, the month in which *The Velvet Glove* was published in a magazine.

I haven't for a long time known as little of you as these weary weeks – in fact *never* known as little probably in proportion to what there is to know. You must have been living very voluminously in one way or another – and however right it may serve me not to possess the detail of that, I have to invoke a terrible patience – which precludes no gnashing of teeth.

To this Mrs Wharton seems to have responded with greater candour. For in his next letter James told her he now saw 'with all affectionate participation' that her anxiety had been 'extreme'. He added, 'Poor dear Teddy, poor dear Teddy, so little made by all the other indications as one feels, for such assaults and such struggles! I hope with all my heart his respite will be long, however, and yours, with it, of such a nature as to ease you off.' He urged her to 'live in the day – don't borrow trouble, and remember that nothing happens as we forecast it – but always with interesting and, as it were, refreshing differences'.

Edith Wharton having had her conquest of Paris, came to England late in 1908 – to English hospitality and rounds of country visits.

She also came and went in Lamb House. Writing to Walter Berry in Cairo, James said she had been having

after a wild, extravagant, desperate, detached fashion, the Time of her Life. London, and even the Suburbs have opened their arms to her; she has seen everyone and done everything and is even now the occasion of some grand houseparty away off in the Midlands whence she comes back to more triumph and will, I imagine, be kept on here, in one way or another, till the New Year or the arrival of Teddy.

He went on to say that with Edith's 'frame of steel it has been remarkably good for her. But what a frame of steel and what a way of arranging one's life! I have participated by breathless dashes and feverish fits, but then had to rush back here to recuperate and meditate.'

2

To the young Cambridge men who gathered round the Master in Trumpington Street in June 1909 and listened to his suavities, James seemed a quiet, dispassionate, sedentary, slightly prickly figure. And Hugh Walpole spoke of James's 'puritanism'. It little occurred to the young that this same Henry James was at the centre of a series of *liaisons dangereuses*. Edith Wharton's biographer has described how James dined with Edith and Morton at the Charing Cross Hotel on the eve of a swift voyage Morton was making to America, and left the lovers there for their farewell night of love. The dinner is discreetly recorded in James's date-book under 4 June 1909: 'Dine with Morton Fullerton and E.W. Charing Cross Hotel.' Edith's biographer describes it as 'champagne, dim red lamps, laughter and lively talk and very considerable passion'. The next morning, James saw Morton off at Waterloo. He consoled the novelist-lady during her lover's absence. 'Went by motor with E.W. to Guildford and thence by beautiful circuit to Windsor and Queen's Acres.' They spend two days with Howard Sturgis and then motor to Wallingford.

James was at Cambridge from 12 to 14 June. On the 15th he dined with Minnie Jones, Edith's sister-in-law and on the next 'Dine with Mrs Wharton at Lady St Helier's.' However, Jocelyn Persse and Hugh Walpole have to be squeezed into the crowded schedule. He lunches with Hugh, dines with Mrs Wharton; goes again to Queen's Acre on 26 June with Mrs Wharton and motors the next day with her to see Mrs Humphry Ward at Stocks; on 28 June he motors with her and Howard Sturgis to Hurstbourne. During the first week of July he is at the Reform Club and then retreats to Lamb House where Jocelyn Persse spends the week-end of 10 July. On the 12th Persse leaves and 'E.W. and Morton Fullerton arrived to dinner and for night.' (Fullerton's trip to America had been brief.) On the next day Mrs Wharton motors James to Chichester and en route they stop at Eastbourne for lunch with Jonathan Sturges. On 15 July 'Motored with Edith Wharton and Morton Fullerton to Folkestone and thence Canterbury where we lunched. They return to Folkestone for France – I returning to Lamb House by train.' Two days later Hugh Walpole arrives to spend the week-end.

What these bare entries do not reveal is a drama within the drama. While Edith Wharton was living out furiously her crisis of middle age with Morton Fullerton, the Gallo-American was working out a crisis of his own – with the intimate participation and help of his friends. Some of the details are to be found in a series of letters Fullerton separated from his personal papers and entrusted to his enamoured cousin, Mrs Gerould. Fullerton had finally broken a long reticence and confessed to James late in 1907 that he had been having a complicated love affair with Henrietta Mirecourt in Paris. He had rarely been available to come to Lamb House when the Master beckoned, and this had been a source of chagrin to James. James told him he stirred 'my tenderness even to anguish'. In language of reproach and caress, he told Morton to have no compunction or apology for having 'so late, so late, after long years, brought yourself to speak to me of what there was always a muffled unenlightenment and ache for my affection in not knowing'. He had guessed at 'complications' in Morton's life, yet had been 'utterly powerless to get any nearer to'. He was certain he might have been able to offer some moral help

and I think of the whole long mistaken perversity of your averted *reality* so to speak, as a miserable *personal* waste, (that of something – ah, so tender! – in *me* that was only quite yearningly ready for you, and something all possible, and all deeply and admirably appealing in yourself, of which I never got the benefit).

The 'clearing of the air', said James, 'lifts, it seems to me, such a load, removes such a falsity (of defeated relation) between us'.

The plot was thicker than a mere love affair in Paris. Fullerton had been driven to speak to James, who now offered so much fatherly love, because Morton's mistress was blackmailing him. She had taken possession of some of his papers, perhaps Edith's letters. It was like the plot in a Sardou play. Morton was the old-fashioned 'journalist' and a 'voice' of the august Thunderer, and he felt himself vulnerable. The woman apparently could be bought off. And Morton had no money. He did not appeal for financial help to James – he simply seems to have conveyed to the Master his anguish and his dilemma.

James consoled him, suggested he was suffering from 'exacerbated and hypnotized nerves', urged him to get away from his 'damned circle' in Paris; in a word, as with Mrs Wharton, James urged Morton to 'keep very still and very busy and very much interested in things'. 'Throw yourself on your work, on your genius, on your art, on your knowledge, on the Universe in fine (though letting the latter centrally represent H.J.) – throw yourself on the blest *alternative* life which embraces all these things and is what I mean by the life of art.' The life of art would see Morton through everything, James said. 'She has seen *me* through everything and that was a large order too.' But Morton was not an artist, he was simply a journalist – even though it was flattering to be accorded parity with the Master.

Further letters elicited information that Morton was living in the same house, if not the same apartment, as the blackmailer. James regarded her as 'a mad, vindictive, and obscure old woman' who was angry because Morton hadn't married her – or, we might observe, who was jealous of Mrs Wharton. The latter devised an intricate gambit. She had been asked by Macmillan to write a book on Paris; she now suggested to the publisher that he should give Morton a contract for this book, which she said she was too busy to do. Meanwhile she intrigued with Henry James to have him induce the publisher to give Morton a larger advance than usual; to keep herself out of the picture she said she would give James the money, which he in turn would give to Macmillan for Morton. Apparently these complexities – worthy of a Marivaux comedy – were the subject of the discussions between Edith and James, during their motor jaunts in 1908. Edith may have been more involved than James knew, since it was a question not only of rescuing her lover from his mistress, but possibly *her* love letters as well. James agreed to 'play my mechanical part in your magnificent combination with absolute piety, fidelity and punctuality'. Later he wrote to Macmillan explaining the 'combination'. He was willing to send the publisher £100 that Fullerton 'may profit to that end, *without his knowing it comes from me*'. Macmillan simplified matters considerably by telling James it wasn't necessary; *he* would pay the £100 (a considerable sum at the time, about the equivalent of more than £1,000 now) and James would simply act as guarantor. In telling Edith of this, James expressed the hope the blackmailer would not demand too much. We know none of the details save that by late summer of 1909 the two novelists could congratulate one another on their rescue operation, and Mrs Wharton told James that Fullerton was a changed man. James said this brought home the tensions under which he had lived. 'It's you absolutely who have so admirably and definitely pulled him out.' The matter disappears from the correspondence; but we might add that Morton never delivered the book, and that Macmillan generously decided to forget about the matter. James, so far as we know, was never asked to pay back the large advance, although he had stood surety for it.

3

In all this there was a side-plot as well. While Edith Wharton intrigued with James, and James intrigued with Macmillan, she was urging and helping Morton Fullerton perform an act of friendship for Henry James. The New York Edition had been completed. The last volume had now been published. But it had passed almost unnoticed among reviewers. Morton wrote a long and full article on the Edition and on the significance of James's career in the history of the novel. He had no difficulty placing it in the *Quarterly Review*. Mrs Wharton tried to induce *Scribner's Magazine* to publish it in America; the journal was not interested and her own editor at Scribner's told her the reception of the Edition was 'disappointing'. 'I have had a hand – or at least a small finger – in the Article, and I think it's good ...' Edith Wharton wrote to the magazine. 'I long so to have someone speak intelligently and resolutely for James.' This Morton had done. James was shown the article in manuscript. He kept it for some time; he said he was 'embarrassed ... fairly to anguish'. It reads indeed as if the Master had inspired it : but he had talked often enough with Morton and Edith for them to have imbibed a great deal of his doctrine. If certain sentences sound as if James himself wrote them, we must also remember that Fullerton had long been accused of writing his dispatches for *The Times* in a Jamesian style. The article appeared in April 1910 and was reprinted in America in the *Living Age*. It points directly at James's discoveries in the handling of 'the states of mind of the actors *through whom his story became a story*' and discerned his having found a solution 'in the art of passing, at the inevitable moment, from the consciousness of one character to that of another'. Fullerton discussed the prefaces and James's late style. He defended it as providing tone, richness, depth, and 'completeness'. He speaks of James's subjects and the hundreds of characters he had created in his tales – seeing him as

the historiographer of that vast epic – the modern Iliad, when its peripatetic and romantic elements do not make it more like an Odyssey – the clash between two societies, the mutual call of two sundered worlds, with not one Helen but a thousand to create complications and to fire the chivalry of two continents. As a sociological phenomenon, no "Return of the Heracleidae" mythic or real, is comparable to the invasion of Europe by American women, backed by their indispensable heads of commissariat, the silent, clean-shaven American men. The emigration required its Homer,

said Fullerton, 'and Mr James was there.'

James may have felt uneasy over the fulsome Fullertonian journalese. However, the sentiments were genuine and its insights make of this essay an important contemporary document, one of the few to speak of the high originality of James's work.

Thus in an ironic way Edith Wharton reversed the situation of *The Velvet Glove* and secretly repaid James with kindness. If the Master hesitated to 'puff' his acolytes, the acolytes could, with energy and sincerity, puff the Master. The essay James liked best was written by Percy Lubbock. It appeared anonymously in the *Times Literary Supplement*, on 8 July 1909. James soon learned the identity of the author and wrote to Mrs Humphry Ward that the article 'does that gentle and thoroughly literary and finely critical young man great honour, I think – but it does me no less; and I somehow feel as if it drove in with an audible tap a sort of shining silver nail and marked, in a manner, a date'. Unfortunately there were few such dates.

100

Woman-About-Town

FROM the passions of Olympus to sordid blackmail – Henry James had dealt with both during 1909; and in the same year he was himself at the centre of a pathetic minor comedy, a comedy of mere mortal passion involving his old acquaintance of Winchelsea, Ford Madox Hueffer and his friend Violet Hunt. Since the days at the turn of the century when he had waylaid the Master on his daily strolls, Hueffer had had a troubled time. He had had a breakdown in 1903 and gone to Germany for a cure. James had written sympathetically to his wife. He recognized her difficulties. 'You had, together, the sad fortune, inevitable at certain moments of life, that things – things of hard friction – accumulated on your exposed heads and spent their fury.' Germany was just the place 'to muffle and pacify ... intenser and finer vibrations ... Give him my friendliest remembrance ... but don't be precipitate even about that.' The letter has in it James's ironic detachment. The world seemed to find too much comfort in him and he had often to protect himself against its weeping too profusely on his shoulder.

James had known Violet Hunt since she was a young girl. She was the daughter of Alfred Hunt, an Oxford don, who at the urging of Ruskin had become a water-colourist. James had visited his artistic-bohemian house on Campden Hill. Violet Hunt's girlhood memories were of a silken-bearded Henry James with 'deep, wonderful eyes', who looked as if he might have worn earrings and been an Elizabethan sea captain. In her youth she possessed a certain pre-Raphaelite beauty; she was pursued by men and she pursued them. She wrote tales and novels, and James occasionally invited her to Lamb House and listened to her sex-charged gossip. Her diaries show that he shied away from listening to her love affairs. During 2 and 3 November 1907 she recorded her attempt to tell James how she had loved Oswald Crawfurd, whom James had known, 'and poor H.J. got up from the table like a dog that has had enough of his bone and closed the discussion'. She wrote 'he always wants my news but never more than half of it, always getting bored or delicate'. On this particular week-end we receive an image in the diary of

Miss Hunt's seductive approach even to the Master – she speaks of 'drifting as I know how' in her 'white Chinese dressing gown', into the Lamb House drawing-room. She had been unwell after dinner, and James was 'all solicitude and I do believe pleasure' – but un-approachable; the best Miss Hunt could do was to have a conversation with him about Mrs Humphry Ward's novels. James's letters to her are coy and telegraphic. He poses as a 'man-about-town' who will be happy to see the 'woman-about-town' when he is in London. He called her his 'Purple Patch'.

The Purple Patch was eleven years older than Hueffer; she was almost 50 in 1909, he not yet 40. They had becomes lovers; and the discrepancy in their ages made Miss Hunt wish ardently for marriage. Elsie Hueffer, however, was unwilling to give Hueffer a divorce, claiming she was Catholic (actually she was Anglo-Catho-lic). In due course she sued for 'restitution of conjugal rights'. The case got into the newspapers. James happened to have invited Miss Hunt to visit him at Lamb House just before the scandal broke – 'I am more and more aged and infirm and unattractive, but I make such a stand as I can ... We can have a long jaw (with lots of arrears to make up) and, weather permitting, eke a short walk.' That was on 31 October 1909. Two days later, with strange para-graphs appearing in the press, James apparently decided that it would be wise to avoid possible publicity as a third party in the Hueffer family feud. He may have had memories of Miss Grigsby. He wrote to Miss Hunt:

I deeply regret and deplore the lamentable position in which I gather you have placed yourself in respect to divorce proceedings about to be taken by Mrs Hueffer: it affects me as painfully unedifying, and that compels me to regard all agreeable and unembarrassed communication between us as impossible. I can neither suffer you to come down to hear me utter those homely truths, nor pretend, at such a time, of free and natural discourse of other things, on a basis of avoidance of what must now be most to the front in your own consciousness and what in a very unwelcome fashion disconcerts mine.

The letter sounds cruel, and Miss Hunt understandably resented having the door of Lamb House slammed in her face. She felt James was 'disloyal' and proving a fair-weather friend. She argued that he was passing judgement on her private life. James replied that he hadn't 'for a moment tried to characterize her relationship with Hueffer'. This was 'none of my business at all'. He had merely spoken of her 'position, as a result of those relations'. And we may judge that by this he meant essentially the fact that she had got herself into the newspapers. His old abhorrence of the publicizing of private life seemed to be at the heart of his seeming rudeness. He did not speak of this, however. He confined himself to insisting that hospitality for Violet Hunt would involve him with Hueffer's 'and his wife's private affairs, of which I wish to hear nothing whatever'.

To Hueffer, who wrote in remonstrance, James reiterated 'what I wrote to her that I deplored and lamented was the situation in which ... her general relations with you had landed or were going to land her – the situation of her being exposed to figure in public proceedings. I don't see how any old friend of hers can be indifferent to that misfortune.' He denied that he had 'pretended to judge, qualify or deal with any act or conduct of Violet Hunt's in the connection ... that whole quantity being none of my business and destined to remain so'.

The affair developed further complications when Hueffer went to Germany, claimed German nationality and pretended to get a divorce there. Violet promptly began to use the name of Mrs Hueffer. Elsie Hueffer sued for libel. She was the only legitimate Mrs Hueffer under English law, having no bill of divorcement. She won; and the effect was to involve Hueffer and his common-law wife in new scandal. James was in America much of this time and by his return the affair was ancient history. He continued to correspond with Violet Hunt; and he saw both her and Hueffer in London on at least one occasion, in April 1912, for a note in his pocket diary records: 'Met Violet Hunt and F. M. Hueffer and went home with them for half an hour.'

Two facts remain to be recorded in the story of Henry James's relations with Hueffer. One was that during Hueffer's editorship of the *English Review* in 1908 and 1909 he published four of James's late tales, including *The Jolly Corner* and *The Velvet Glove*. The publication was arranged by James's literary agent and there was no contact to speak of between editor and author. Hueffer paid James the regular rate from £50 to £75 for each tale, according to its length; and James wrote to his agent that he was pleased with the typography and presentation of his stories. Then, in 1913, Hueffer brought out a book on James, the first 'critical' study of the novelist to appear, although an earlier expository book about him

by Elisabeth Luther Cary had been published in the United States.
'Mr James is the greatest of living writers,' Hueffer wrote in his introduction, 'and in consequence, for me, the greatest of living men.'
The volume is as discursive as most of Hueffer's critical writing;
but he showed his literary judgement by singling out the works in
which James had developed his late techniques, notably *The Spoils
of Poynton*, *Maisie*, and the tales published in the *English Review*.
A few weeks after its appearance Archibald Marshall asked the
novelist how he felt about Hueffer's book. James replied:

You commiserate me for my exposure to the public assault of F. M.
Hueffer, but I assure you that though I believe this assault has been perpetrated I have not had the least difficulty in remaining wholly unconscious of it. I am vaguely aware that his book is out, but he has at least
had the tact not to send it to me, and as I wouldn't touch it with a ten-
foot pole nothing is simpler than for it not to exist for me.

Part Two
The Finer Grain

101

The Bench of Desolation

THE first royalty statement for the New York Edition reached Henry James in October of 1908 while the final volumes were still in preparation. These figures knocked James 'rather flat' – 'a greater disappointment than I have been prepared for'. After his long labour he experienced 'a great, I confess, and bitter, grief'. 'Is there anything for me at all?' he asked. 'I don't make out or understand.' James had not recognized that his earnings would be reduced by heavy permissions fees due to the publishers participating in the edition – Houghton Mifflin Company, Harper and Brothers, and The Macmillan Company, who had published him before Scribner's. His agent explained this to him. But the Master had had his shock. His four years of unremunerated labour, the gathering in of his work of a lifetime, on which he had counted to yield revenue for his declining years showed signs of being a complete failure. Three days later James wrote that he had recovered a bit since 'the hour of the shock, but I think it would ease off my nerves not a little to see you'. He had built up high hopes on the strength of the 'treasures of ingenuity and labour I have lavished on the amelioration of every page of the thing'. His new fling at the theatre moreover had brought him no great returns. 'The non-response of *both* sources has left me rather high and dry.'

It left him, emotionally, higher and drier than he knew. The effect, though delayed for a few months, was as if he had faced a hostile audience again, and was being told that his life-work was vain and perishable. He had written his way out of depression thirteen years before – it had been a long and difficult ordeal – but now he tumbled back into it. He had then been 52; he was now almost 66. Re-reading the royalty figures he discerned that his first payment would total $211. 'And I have *such* visions and arrears of inspiration.' A brief note in Miss Bosanquet's diary tells us the naked truth. 'Mr James depressed,' she wrote. 'Nearly finished *Golden Bowl* preface – bored by it – says he's "lost his spring" for it.' Some of that depression crept into a letter to Howells on the last day of 1908. 'It will have landed me in Bankruptcy', he said of the Edition. 'It has prevented me doing any other work.' Later he would say it had been 'the most expensive job of my life'.

I

The shock of *Guy Domville* had brought James long ago to the verge of a nervous breakdown. He had staved it off by discovering within himself the themes which resolved his anxieties and restored his self-confidence. This time the breakdown occurred and we can record its stages. Early in 1909, little more than three months after the news had 'knocked me flat' he noted that he felt sharply unwell for the first time in six years. Miss Bosanquet's diary of 17 January says simply, 'Mr James unwell (heart trouble).' At least that was what he thought he had. There were some palpitations, a little short-ness of breath, but no pain to speak of. The doctor prescribed digi-talis. He found nothing ominous and urged James to take more exercise. The Master had become too fat. Henry James seems to have decided he was having, or about to have, a heart condition such as William had lived through, in Lamb House, almost a decade before. In writing to his brother and describing his symptoms Henry also said he was 'a little solitarily worried and depressed'. As in the old days he appealed to his brother's knowledge of medicine, even though William had never practised.

In due course, with increasing anxiety, Henry James wrote to Sir William Osler, who had examined William at the time of his attack. The great doctor recommended that Henry see the renowned heart specialist of the time, Sir James Mackenzie. The novelist paid his visit 25 February 1909. We have access to this consultation since Sir James wrote it up in his book *Angina Pectoris* as Case 97, after the novelist's death. He did not name his patient; yet he gave away his identity by describing him as author of a ghost story about mys-terious occurrences to two children, one of whom 'died in the arms of the narrator'. The physician's notes tell us that he found the patient 'stout and healthy-looking'. His heart was slightly enlarged but 'there is no murmur present'. 'The blood pressure varied curi-ously. He was a nervous man, and on one visit I noticed that when I first took the blood pressure it was 190 mm Hg. After a few minutes it was 170 and later 160 mm Hg.' He prescribed exercise and moderate eating, and addressed himself to James's anxieties. Sir James Mackenzie used the novelist as a case history because he wished to demonstrate how (in a manner that would today be called psychotherapy) he reassured a patient who imagined he had a heart condition. He made James explain what he had tried to do in his ghost story (*The Turn of the Screw* wasn't named) and when the Master admitted his use of ambiguity to make the reader's imagination 'run riot and depict all sorts of horrors', the learned doctor tapped Henry on the chest and said: 'It is the same with you, it is the mystery that is making you ill.' The doctor continued,

You think you have got angina pectoris, and you are very frightened lest you should die suddenly. Now, let me explain to you the real matters. You are 66 years of age. You have got the changes in your body which are coincident with your time of life. It happens that the changes in the arteries of your heart are a little more advanced than in those of your brain, or of your legs. It simply follows that if you be more judicious in your living, and give your heart less work to do, there is no reason why you should not reach the ordinary span of human life.

The doctor reported his patient was 'greatly cheered by this', and that he remained in good health. But apparently James did not believe Sir James Mackenzie. He continued to speak of having had a 'cardiac crisis'. He had apparently decided he was as ill as his brother. Still, he followed the doctor's orders and during the rest of 1909 found himself much improved. He worked, he entered into the casting of *The Outcry*, and he was preoccupied with the affairs of his Olympian friends. In October came the second royalty statement for the Edition. This time it yielded $596.71. He told his agent that in no year had he so 'consummately managed to make so little money as this last'. Notes in the back of his date-book indicate that he reported his earning to the income tax as £1,096 in 1908, £1,020 in 1909, and £1,309 in 1910. His income was thus adequate for his bachelor needs, but offered him slim margin if his powers should fail. His property in America yielded him $3,500 in 1910 and in that year he reported earning by his pen of $2,500. He makes no note of savings; there is simply a note of his having a balance of $2,089 at Brown Brothers, and some £89 in his bank at Rye.

One day, shortly after this, in a fit of sadness, perhaps prompted by fantasies of death, he gathered his private papers – forty years of letters from his contemporaries, manuscripts, scenarios, old notebooks – and piled them on a rubbish fire in his garden. He was ruthless. A great Anglo-American literary archive perished on that day. His act was consistent with his belief that authors were themselves responsible for the fate of their papers. 'I kept almost all my letters for years,' he wrote to his old friend Mrs Fields, on 2 January 1910, 'till my receptacles would no longer hold them; then I made a gigantic bonfire and have been easier in mind since.'

He had, preceding his illness, a lonely and sad Christmas at Rye. An old friend 'considerably lone and lorn' passed the holiday with James, 'a little lugubriously'. And then he went over to Eastbourne to see sick Jonathan Sturges 'ever a stiff bit of discipline for me'. He spoke of Sturges, with whom he had passed so many cheerful Christmases in the past, as 'that tragic and terrible little figure', and 'the ferocious nature of his deeply congenital little egoism now so exasperated by disease and suffering'.

His last effort to work off his depression occurred on 4 January when in the early morning, he began to make notes in pencil, in a large scrawl, for a new fiction which the Harpers had asked him to write. It would be his last recorded invocation of the Muse:

I must now take up projected tasks – this long time *entrevus* and brooded over – with the firmest possible hand. I needn't expatiate on this – on the sharp consciousness of this hour of the dimly-dawning New Year. I mean, I simply invoke and appeal to all the powers and forces and divinities to whom I've ever been loyal and who haven't failed me as yet – after all: never, never yet! ... Momentary sidewinds – things of no real authority – break every now and then to put their inferior little questions to me; but I come back, I come back, as I say, I all throbbingly and yearningly and passionately, oh, *mon bon*, come back to this way that is clearly the only one in which I can do anything now ... *Causons, causons, mon bon* – oh celestial, soothing, sanctifying process, with all the high sane forces of the sacred time, fighting through it, on my side.

It seemed to him he was emerging from his recent 'bad days' and 'the prospect clears and flushes, and my poor blest old Genius pats me so admirably and lovingly on the back that I turn, I screw round, and bend my lips to passionately, in my gratitude, kiss its hand'.

The 'sane forces of the sacred time' – that time when he could write scenarios and plan novels – refused to stay with him. Shortly after writing this supreme appeal to his 'blest Genius' he collapsed. Some vague discomfort in the stomach: inability to take food, a certain amount of nausea. It was indeed difficult to swallow the fact that his work of a lifetime had not met with a greater reception and brought him the recognition he craved and the money that would have given him a greater sense of security. After some weeks he admitted to being attacked by 'the black devils of nervousness, direst damndest demons'.

2

Henry James's illness had been signalled also just before the new year by two bad attacks of gout, first in one foot and then the other. This was followed, early in January by his 'food-loathing' and general debility; he lingered in bed mornings, dozing in a kind of withdrawal from his daily existence. Hugh Walpole asked to come to see him and he answered, scrawling his letters in pencil on his knee, 'I am not fit company for you.' His state was 'obscure'. He was Hugh's 'dilapidated friend'. He would announce improvement for forty-eight hours and then relapse. The local doctor, Ernest Skinner, still found nothing seriously wrong except his loss of appetite and his general weakness. Miss Bosanquet was laid off for the time. She had, however, regularly answered queries addressed to her by James's friends and in particular, at Mrs Wharton's in-sistence, sent daily bulletins. After some three weeks of recurrent illness of this sort the doctor put Henry to bed, insisted on great regularity in his life, and induced him to have a nurse. 'I am so glad that he has decided to submit to the Doctor's orders,' Mrs Wharton wrote to Miss Bosanquet. On 25 January he penned a postcard to Mrs Wharton,

Your beautiful letter this a.m. welcomed. I am doing admirably, mending fast, though sitting up but an hour for the first time (these several days) this afternoon. Beseech you kindly send me *Tales of Men [and Beasts]*. I I want so awfully to see how you do it. More very soon. Am forbidden 'style'. Yours H.J. P.S. All my sympathies in your immersion – which must be grand and horrible.

The Master could be brief when he had to be. 'A digestive crisis making food loathsome and nutrition impossible – and sick inanition and weakness and depression,' he wrote to Bailey Saunders. 'I lie here verily as detached as a sick god on a damp Olympus,' he wrote to Miss Robins. Dr Skinner had him fed every two hours. He was re-duced to an infantile regimen. Mrs Wharton discreetly asked if he was in need of funds. He replied he was on a decent financial basis 'with a margin of no mean breadth and most convenient balance at my bank and a whole year quite provided for even if I should do no work at all'. She made him promise that if he should be in need he would let her know. Once he was a on a regular regimen Mrs Wharton sent him great clusters of grapes. By early February the doctor, treating James as essentially a case of 'nerves', began to take him out daily in his car as he made his calls – to provide an airing and change of scene. Henry wrote a full account of his illness to William and blamed his condition on his having for so long 'Fletcherized' his food – the fad involving lengthy mastication.

Although Henry had cabled cheerfully to Irving Street, William James dispatched his eldest son, Harry, to visit the novelist. Harry crossed the mid-winter seas promptly and arrived at Lamb House on 24 February. Henry was touched. By that time the novelist had begun to speak candidly of his 'black depression' and his 'beastly solitudinous life'. He welcomed the 'priceless youth' with open arms. Harry, firm and managerial, sized up the situation at once and wrote a letter to his father and mother which gives us a vivid picture of the Master's condition. Two things were required, he said: get James out of Rye to London; and have him thoroughly examined by an eminent medical authority. He turned to Sir William Osler.

Harry described his uncle as having been, on his arrival, on an 'upward wave' but secretly Fletcherizing again, feeling he had 'got hold of something'. Then there was a new collapse. At this moment Henry talked freely and it is possible to see what his deeper anxieties were. He remembered his sister's protracted illness; he remembered William's heart attack. Harry described how he found him both depressed and excited one day. The nurse gave the Master some bromide but after supper she hurried to Harry and said his uncle wanted him. He found him in the little oak bedroom in a state of complete despair:

There was nothing for me to do but to sit by his side and hold his hand while he panted and sobbed for two hours until the Doctor arrived, and stammered in despair so eloquently and pathetically that as I write of it the tears flow down my cheeks again. He talked about Aunt Alice and his own end and I knew him to be facing not only the frustration of all his hopes and ambitions, but the vision looming close and threatening to his weary eyes, of a lingering illness such as hers. In sight of all that, he wanted to die ... He didn't have a good night and the next day the same thing began again with a fear of being alone.

When Harry announced he was writing at once to Osler, the Master 'stopped panting and trembling, and from that moment began to revive'. There was a change of mood. In the evening he was vivacious and jocular. Harry realized the great authority and solemnity of the Johnsonian dictator who co-existed with the death-haunted mortal lying there on his bed. With a truly Jamesian touch, Harry called his uncle 'a portentous invalid'.

The magnificent solemnity of process that marks as momentous even the taking of his temperature overwhelms one. This afternoon I watched him begin to stir a cup of beef tea with an expression like a judge about to announce an opinion, and a gesture by which he ladled teaspoonfuls eighteen inches into the air and poured them splashing back again. His mind running off on something else, he continued this splendidly wasteful process unconsciously until I made a movement that brought him back to earth. Nothing is too small to be given its fullest measure and emphasis. Yesterday while taking some milk he handed an open envelope to Burgess, who was to mail some letters, and told him to lick it and close it. Burgess did so, not copiously but promptly, and quite well. 'Oh!' cried Uncle Henry, 'Oh-oh! Burgess not that way; you must wet it *more*.' 'Iss-sir,' said Burgess and applied himself to the more abundant insalivation of the envelope until I was afraid its contents would be drowned. Luckily Burgess is entirely incapable of reflection when he is in Uncle Henry's presence.

The nephew understood the immediate realities of the case, but not the intensities of the Master or the megalomania of genius. They came up to town together to Garland's Hotel in Suffolk Street, and on 14 March Sir William Osler gave Henry James the most complete physical examination he had ever had. He found nothing seriously wrong. He thought him 'splendid for his age'. The novelist's eating habits had done no damage to his stomach; what was needed was reform. Heart, lungs, arteries, were fine, and he said that Henry had 'the pulse of a boy'. William had written to Henry that perhaps he ought to recognize that what he had was something in the nature of a 'nervous breakdown'. The novelist, telling William of Osler's examination, denied this. 'My illness had no more to do with a "nervous breakdown" than with Halley's comet.' He insisted it was a stomach condition. William continued to call it 'melancholia', and after a while Henry accepted the idea, writing to Edmund Gosse that he had had 'a sort of nervous breakdown'. Hugh Walpole, who came to see the novelist at Garland's hotel found him 'most frightfully depressed – most melancholy conversation'. But life in a hotel was no solution for the nervous Master (who nevertheless managed to see Galsworthy's *Justice* in London before Harry took him back to Rye). Osler prescribed massage and walks, and a general routine intended to make James take an interest in everday occupations.

3

Even before Harry returned to America, satisfied with Osler's examination, William and Alice James had sailed to be with Henry. They had decided from Henry's letters that he needed family, distraction, company, and William knew how fond his brother was of Alice. He planned himself to take a further cure at Bad Nauheim, for his heart was troubling him again. They arrived in April and Alice took over in Lamb House. What William would not face, and Alice did not sufficiently perceive, was that the older brother had a serious bodily illness while Henry's illness was one of the spirit. From this time on we have a guide, the daily sentence or two Mrs William James wrote in a little date-book. It is a sad little document – oscillating from day to day in its description of William's increasing debility and Henry's constant changes of mood, from deep depression, to partial calm, and then a relapse into depression. An entry she set down in June is eloquent: 'William cannot walk and Henry cannot smile.' Mrs Wharton provided a motor that spring for Henry and William and they went on long drives. In May Edward VII died; and in the period of mourning and the funeral all the London theatres were closed. This proved a death blow to Frohman's repertory and the impending production of James's play. Frohman paid James $1,000 forfeit as agreed. By this time Henry was indifferent to his work in the theatre. He talked of his 'nervous upsets'. 'But I am emerging,' he wrote to his agent.

To Jocelyn, who was in Ceylon, he wrote of his 'nervous condition – trepidation, agitation, general dreadfulness'. Things had been 'in short, dismally bad'. William with his psychiatric eye judged his brother's case 'more and more plainly one of melancholia, "simple", in that there are no fixed or false ideas,' apart from Henry's belief the cause had been diet. 'He fluctuates a great deal from day to day.' He had complete confidence in the local doctor. In due course, William and Alice convinced Henry that the best thing for him to do would be to return to America with them. William would go to

Nauheim first. Alice would remain in Lamb House with Henry. They would then join William and travel in Switzerland. Henry and William both had memories of their youth in that country; and while such a trip might be helpful to Henry there seems to have been no realization on Alice's part that her husband was too ill for such a journey.

They carried out their plan. In Lamb House Alice tried to distract Henry. On one day, when he could not read, and sat in glum despair, she tried to teach him to knit. He was beyond occupational therapy. Yet he was able to gather his most recent tales into a volume to be called *The Finer Grain*. He led off with *The Velvet Glove* and concluded with a long tale of passivity and despair called *The Bench of Desolation*. Scribner and Methuen agreed to do the book and each paid him $1,000 advance. By now he was taking more food; and walking almost daily. For a fortnight in May Alice took Henry to visit Mrs Charles Hunter, the hostess of Hill Hall and patroness of the arts, in the hope that in a great establishment and with the comings and goings of guests Henry would be distracted. It was only a partial success. Sargent was there; one of his sisters, Mrs Ormond and her husband; Percy Grainger, the pianist; Viola Tree; there were assorted peers and James posed for his portrait which was painted by Mrs Swynnerton. James had 'dark and difficult days' in the 'vast, wondrous, sympathetic house'. 'I am unfit for society,' he wrote to Goody Allen; however, he recognized that the visit on the whole was beneficial.

Early in June they made the trip to Bad Nauheim. William had not benefited by the cure; he was much weaker. From Nauheim the novelist wrote to Mrs Wharton that he was going to America. 'I am wholly unfit to be alone – in spite of amelioration.' They stayed a while in Nauheim. They went on excursions. One gets glimpses of these two tired sick brothers trying to keep up a show of activity and wearing on Mrs William's nerves. William was having the last of his 'curative' baths. Again to Mrs Wharton, the Master wrote, 'I eat, I walk, I *almost* sleep – and what I shall most have done, if things go on as I hope, will be to have walked myself well.' 'Your noble image,' he told Edith, 'is cherished by your affectionate H.J.' To his friends the Protheros in Rye Henry James wrote, 'I have really been down into hell and stayed there for months since I saw you ... I keep hold of my blest companions, I intensely clutch them, as a scared child does his nurse and mother.'

They went to Zürich; they visited scenic views and palaces, William dragging himself along. Then to Lucerne, and the Geneva of their youth; here the news reached them that Robertson James, the Civil War veteran, had died in America in his sleep of a heart attack. Alice told Henry and they agreed to withhold the news from William for the time being. 'Dark troubled sad days,' wrote Henry in his little date-book, recording an attack of gout. Early in July they reached London; Henry went to stay at the Reform Club and was visited by Jocelyn, back from his eastern trip. William and Alice stayed in a hotel. Henry began to note 'William great source of anxiety.' Dr Mackenzie cared for him in London. He mustered enough strength to do some London shopping with Alice. But he had several sharp attacks of chest pain and several times took to his bed.

4

On the morning of 21 July 1910 Henry James awoke in his room at the Reform Club from a good night's sleep. He felt well again. The only clues we have to this moment of experience are in his date-book in which he scribbled 'woke up in great relief'. Then two months later, on 12 September he wrote 'woke up with a return of the old trouble of the black times, which had dropped comparatively, yet as markedly on red-letter day July 21st with that blessed waking in my London room'. We may ask ourselves what there was about that summer's awakening that made it a 'red-letter day' and also 'blessed'. The date-books for that year guard their secret, but they contain a certain amount of mysterious ritual. It begins in October with Henry James using red and black crosses in great profusion. Thus on 24 October there are no less than fifteen red crosses instead of his usual record of engagements, and on 25 October there are twenty-seven such crosses. Various numbers are marked in the book from 26 to 30 October but on 31 October the colour changes to black: there are four black crosses on that day and from 2 to 10 November the crosses continue to be black, most often five in number. On 11 November a variation occurs: they are alternately red and black – thus on this day there are five in all and the second and fourth are red. On 12 November the system changes. He starts with red and then changes to black, the first, third and fifth crosses are in red. Throughout the remainder of November the markings are exclusively red save on 21 November when he makes four black ones. They are red again on 14 December and the system of alternation again occurs. And so on, with variations until the end of the year when the ritual is abandoned.

We have no clues to this personal code save the fact that he spoke of the red-letter day, and then of 'black times'. This would suggest that the red crosses marked the days on which James felt comparatively well and the black recorded his more depressed days. The variations in number may or may not have significance or may simply record the extent of his well-being or discomfort. One other speculation : the day of the splendid awakening in the Reform Club may have been the morning of his dream of the Louvre which he commemorated vividly in A Small Boy and Others. Indeed his account of his dream begins 'I recall to this hour, with the last vividness, what a precious part it [the Galerie d'Apollon in the Louvre] played for me ... on my waking, in a summer dawn many years later, to the fortunate, the instantaneous recovery and capture of the most appalling yet most admirable nightmare of my life.' It can only be conjecture, but the dream was of the sort – in its components of fear, anxiety, and frustration, and then its triumph – that might indeed have resolved his long weeks of depression. Certainly from the time of that awakening, recorded in so enigmatic a form, we may date his gradual recovery from his severe illness of 1910. The dream contained a vigorous moment of self-assertion and putting to flight of a frightening other-self (or brother). It may indeed have helped restore to James that confidence and faith in himself which had crumbled when he received the news of the Edition.

After this stay in London, Henry, William, and Alice went briefly to Rye to enable William to have several days of complete rest before sailing. Henry noted 'Poor – very bad, nights and days for William. Difficult days – dreadful gloomy gales – but I feel my own gain in spite of everything. Heaven preserve me.' And again, 'Ah these dark days of farewell to this dear little old place – saturated now with all associations. William just a little better.' Mrs Wharton arrived with her motor, accompanied by Walter Berry; they took Henry to Windsor, stopping for lunch at Tunbridge Wells. They visited Howard Sturgis at Qu'Acre. 'The dark cloud of William's suffering state hangs over me to the exclusion of all other consciousness – though I am struggling back to work. The weather hot and magnificent; the house ample and easy; the "pathos" of the whole situation wrings my heart.' Henry wrote this on 11 August.

The Jameses sailed on 12 August on the *Empress of Britain* for Quebec, Henry accompanied by Burgess. In his date-book he wrote, extraordinarily peaceful and beautiful voyage with no flaw or cloud on it but William's aggravated weakness and suffering – to see which and not to be able to help or relieve is anguish unutterable; now more and more'. The voyage lasted six days. At Quebec Harry was on hand to help his parents and uncle. They then took the day-long journey to Chocorua. Billy James, William's second son, would remember how he met the voyagers at North Conway in a car and drove them to Chocorua. He was appalled at his father's weakened condition. At first the philosopher still sat at table finding it easier to breathe while erect. On one occasion Henry expatiated on the dreariness of that part of Canada through which they had passed 'that flat desert of fir trees broken only here and there by a bit of prehistoric swamp!' William mustered enough strength to reply 'better than anything in Europe, Henry – better than anything in England'. The end was not in doubt. William James was suffering too much to want to live. On 26 August his younger brother wrote to Grace Norton 'my own fears are of the blackest, I confess to you and at the prospect of losing my wonderful beloved brother out of the world in which, from as far back as in dimmest childhood, I have so yearningly always counted on him, I feel nothing but the abject weakness of grief and even terror'. Grief made James reopen this letter after he sealed it to add a postscript: 'I open my letter of three hours since to add that William passed unconsciously away an hour ago – without apparent pain or struggle. Think of us, dear Grace – think of us!'

102

Notes of a Brother

WILLIAM JAMES died on a Friday and on Monday Henry rose at four-thirty and journeyed from Chocorua to Cambridge where in Appleton Chapel the Harvard University service was held – or as Henry, in a less painful moment would say, Harvard 'meagre mother, did for him – the best that Harvard can'. The philosopher was cremated and his ashes were placed in a grave beside his parents in the Cambridge Cemetery. 'Unutterable, unforgettable hour – with those that have followed ... all unspeakable,' the son and brother wrote in his date-book when they were back in Chocorua.

In the setting of mountain and valley and lake, Henry and Alice, his niece Peggy and his nephews, spent the following days. Henry's mourning was profound. He had always loved his brother with a strong devotion and admiration in which he diminished himself in his belief in William's superiorities; he had been also the rejected one, for William always held and maintained his status of elder brother – 'ideal Elder Brother' as Henry now wrote in answer to condolences. 'I was always his absolute younger and smaller, hanging under the blest sense of his protection and authority.' Henry James was now sole survivor of that branch of the James family which had given America two remarkable men, a philosopher-psychologist, and an artist. Like one of his heroes in many of his stories, he now wore the mantle of Family; he was the last heir, the final voice; his would be the last word. Out of this came, indeed, during the next three years, the Master's autobiographies, *A Small Boy and Others* and *Notes of a Son and Brother*. A third volume, *The Middle Years*, which had himself for subject, and the beginning of his career abroad, was never completed, although Henry lived long enough and had the vigour to write it. He had achieved solitude in his art; but the subject of his art had always been family relations, and personal relations. In reality there was no personal autobiography that he wanted to write, once removed from the frame of Family.

I

The letters Henry James wrote during these weeks were filled with an intense grief, a powerful emotion of helplessness but also of strength. 'My beloved brother's death has cut into me, deep down, even as an absolute mutilation,' the Master wrote to Edith Wharton. As with his 'other-self' in *The Jolly Corner*, the mutilation only gave him a larger sense of power. He could 'only feel stricken and old and ended', in the first moments and the American landscape seemed haunted with associations. William's 'extinction changes the face of life for me', he wrote to their oldest friend, T. S. Perry. It changed his life in quite another sense from that which Henry believed. His strength was returning, even if he still had 'black', depressed days.

He had always found himself strong in William's absence. Now he had full familial authority; his nephews deferred to him; his brother's wife now became a kind of wife to him, ministering to his wants, caring for him as she had cared for the ailing husband and brother. Henry had ascended to what had seemed, for sixty years, an inaccessible throne.

The Master was deeply touched by the world's tributes and particularly by words written by H. G. Wells. 'That all this great edifice of ripened understandings and clarities and lucidities should be swept out of the world leaves me baffled and helplessly distressed,' Wells wrote and James commented to his friends 'a really beautiful eloquence – and he is not often beautiful'. Henry (and Burgess with him) stayed on and in due course moved back into Irving Street where life was resumed on a normal basis. Henry began work again. He would spend the winter in America, he announced, to give support to his brother's family; and there was another purpose in his remaining, for Mrs William James had promised her husband that she would hold seances and try to communicate with his spirit. William's lifelong interest in extra-sensory and extra-human experience had prompted him to tell her that he would seek, from the Outer World, to continue research beyond the grave. What attempts were made in Irving Street are not known, although the matter was not kept secret. Somerset Maugham, who dined with Henry James and Mrs William during that winter, was told that Henry and his sister-in-law were available as 'two sympathetic witnesses on the spot' for any spiritualist messages, if they should come. None came. When Henry received a document describing a seance at which William's voice was heard, he denounced it as 'the most abject and impudent, the hollowest, vulgarest, and basest rubbish ... utterly empty and illiterate, without substance or sense, a mere babble of platitudinous phrases'.

In Irving Street James converted *The Outcry* into a novel and read the last proofs of *The Finer Grain*. He walked a great deal. Maugham quoted him as saying, 'I wander about those great empty streets of Boston and I never see a living creature. I could not be more alone in the Sahara.' He was bored. 'This is a hard country to love,' he wrote to Emily Sargent, the painter's sister. And to Rhoda Broughton he spoke of 'the tedium of vast wastes of homesickness here'. Better, he said 'fifty years of fogland – where indeed I have, alas, almost *had* my fifty years'.

After a number of weeks in Irving Street – in mid-October – it was a relief to hear the sound of 'the silver steam-whistle of the Devastating Angel'. Mrs Wharton had crossed the Atlantic to spend a fortnight in America. She was staying at the new and splendid Hotel Belmont in Times Square. Emerging from his period of retirement, the novelist took train for the city of his birth.

2

On 17 October 1910 John Quinn, a wealthy Irish-American lawyer and patron of the arts, friend of Yeats and Lady Gregory, future friend of Conrad, Joyce, Eliot, Pound, and collector of their works and manuscripts, dining at the Hotel Belmont, suddenly had one of the 'moments' of his life which he recorded. An enthusiast, a lover of literary celebrity, he recognized Henry James, massive, slow-moving, awe-inspiring, at dinner with two gentlemen and a lady. He would never know that he was witness to an unusual gathering of the Angel of Devastation's acolytes. It was not so much James dining with these three, as Edith Wharton, dining with three men of great importance in *her* life. With her at the Belmont were Walter Berry, on one of his holidays from his post in Egypt and W. Morton Fullerton – and the Master, who was friend and party to those other friendships. It was almost like the story by Mrs Wharton of the much-divorced lady who is able to achieve her ambition of having to tea at one time all of her former husbands.* Mrs Wharton was, as it were, with two major characters – and Henry James had joined the party in hotel quarters 'that were as those of the Gonzagas, as who should say, at Mantua'. Henry was delighted that he had answered the summons of the Angel – 'the being devastated', he wrote to Howard Sturgis 'has done me perceptible good'. Edith he said was 'as sublime and as unsurpassable' as ever.

He enjoyed Manhattan, although he would tire of it and say it was 'the eternal Fifth Avenue'. He found 'the rhythm and beat and margin were all scant and inadequate' compared with 'the vast circular Babylon' of London. Still, it was infinitely more interesting than Boston 'so far as either of them is interesting'. New York was 'a queer mixture of the awful and the amusing, the almost interesting and the utterly impossible'. He had a sneaking feeling of kindness for it – for its 'pride and power'. As for the United States (he

* 'The Other Two' in *The Descent of Man* (1904).

wrote to his walking mate, Sydney Waterlow) the country was 'prodigious, interesting, appalling'. To Dr J. William White he spoke of 'this babyish democracy'.

During this year in America, in which he avoided all publicity and refused to lecture, James kept Irving Street in Cambridge as his base and periodically came to New York, usually staying with Mrs Cadwalader Jones in familiar lower Fifth Avenue. He was given a guest membership at the Century Club and there among painters, writers, and amateurs of the arts he often lunched: he visited art galleries; he attended the business meetings of the American Academy held at the University Club and the impression was 'simply sickening'. Everywhere in America he deplored the absence of standards, the lack of ritual. Above all he saw great affluence, great waste, and he was disturbed by the life of the rich who seemed to have no sense of *noblesse oblige*. He was revolted by the growth of advertising and publicity; and it seemed to him that a great national selfishness existed in America from which all kindness had been banished. His nephew took him to visit the Rockefeller Institute, where he met the director Dr Simon Flexner, and certain of the research scientists. Harry was then the business manager of the Institute. Dr Peyton Rous remembered this visit. He remembered James's serious face and the 'banker's eyeglasses', large lenses held together by a black horizontal bar, with a black ribbon arching from them, past a black waistcoat striped with white. His boots were 'almost arrogantly British', very thick-soled. Dr Flexner introduced Dr Rous as in charge of cancer research. Henry laid a heavy hand on his shoulder and said: 'How magnificent! To be young and to have divine power!' The Master paused before the mouse cages. 'May I ask, has the individuality, I might say the personality, of these little creatures impressed itself upon you?' Dr Rous told James that one of the female mice had breast cancer and that a strange thing had happened recently. He had given the young to a healthy mouse to be suckled; she had accepted them as if they were her own. Stimulated by curiosity, Rous had supplied a second litter. Then a third. She patiently nursed these till they were about an inch long. Then 'during a single night she killed them all. It was an act of self-preservation; the urge to live had overcome maternal feeling.'

Dr Rous, who in his old age would be given the Nobel Prize for his researches, told the story in a matter-of-fact way. The Master stood deeply thoughtful. He was about to speak when Dr Flexner put his head through the door and called. Dr Rous ever after told the anecdote with a sense of frustration.

In the spring James accepted an honorary degree from Harvard 'with deference to William's memory – though he was so infinitely more to Harvard than Harvard ever was to, or for, him'. He visited his Emmet cousins in Connecticut. He revisited Newport. He was still in the hands of doctors. In Boston he consulted Dr James Jackson Putnam, a neurologist, and seems to have had what might be called today a number of 'therapeutic sessions'. Dr Putman was in touch with Freud and Ernest Jones and the psychologist Morton Prince. He had known William James. In his office in Marlborough Street the discussion seems to have been – to judge from a letter written by the novelist – about Henry's depression and ways of eating sensibly and walking a great deal. The novelist had made the mistake of trying to reduce by starving himself; in keeping up his walks on so slender a diet he had exhausted himself. This in part seems to have contributed to his 1910 illness. 'You tided me over three or four bad places during those worst months,' James wrote to Dr Putman. In New York he consulted the fashionable Dr Joseph Collins, who seemed as much interested in writing a popular series of books on 'the doctor looks at . . .' life, literature, and so on, as in medicine. After the novelist's death, Dr Collins wrote an account of James's calls on him. This was included in *The Doctor Looks at Biography*. 'He put himself under my professional care and I saw him at close range nearly every day for two months; and talked with him, or listened to him, on countless subjects.' Dr Collins's conclusion was that Henry James had

an enormous amalgam of the feminine in his make-up; he displayed many of the characteristics of adult infantilism; he had a singular capacity for detachment from reality and with it a dependence upon realities that was even pathetic. He had a dread of ugliness in all forms . . . His amatory coefficient was comparatively low; his gonadal sweep was too narrow.

Dr Collins's therapy consisted of 'baths, massage, and electrocutions'. James found Dr Putnam much more helpful.

He spent pleasant hours with Howells; he had long talks with his old friend Grace Norton. Somerset Maugham, during his dinner in Irving Street, found the Master nervous and ill at ease; and while

Maugham is not always a reliable witness – for he disliked James and envied him his vogue as theorist of fiction – he told how Henry escorted him to the street-car on Massachusetts Avenue and described his obsessive concern that Maugham get safely aboard. Henry told Maugham that American street-cars were of a savagery, an inhumanity, a ruthlessness beyond conception.

The early summer brought intense heat and Henry fled to the cooling breezes of a house at Nahant, that of an old friend, George Abbot James. Near here James, who had glimpsed Blériot in flight over the Channel, saw a Wright bi-plane and found it of 'extraordinary thrilling beauty'. Mrs Wharton was back at The Mount trying to decide whether to sell it or not and whether to part from Teddy. James spent a very hot week-end there; Gaillard Lapsley was also a visitor. 'You must insist on saving your life by a separate existence,' James told Mrs Wharton. The heat was intense and Mrs Wharton remembered 'his bodily surface, already broad, seemed to expand to meet it, and his imagination to become a part of his body, so that one dripped words of distress as the other did moisture'. Electric fans, iced drinks, cold baths, didn't seem to help, but motoring did, and Mrs Wharton drove him across miles of landscape, in order to provide coolness. She felt a great desire to pack James off to Europe on the next ship, he seemed so miserable. To have an idea was, for Mrs Wharton, to translate it into action. She got James a booking on a liner sailing from Boston but he had planned his sailing and wasn't going to change it with great suddenness. 'Good God, what a woman – what a woman! Her imagination boggles at nothing! She does not even scruple to project me in a naked flight across the Atlantic.' It was of a piece with his remark, quite in the manner of *The Velvet Glove*, in a letter to Lapsley that he could not help regretting 'that an *intellectuelle* – and an Angel – should require such a big pecuniary basis'.

James made his farewells in Irving Street; he said good-bye to Grace Norton, now one of the very few left out of his distant past. He felt it was their last meeting. He sailed for England on 30 July 1911. He had been in his native land for almost a year. Shortly before sailing he learned that the crippled Jonathan Sturges, 'the little demon', companion of his earlier days at Lamb House, whom he had known so long and cared for so deeply, had died in England. John La Farge had died while he was in America.

On the *Mauretania* he saw 'the great bland simple deaf street boy'

Thomas A. Edison and talked with him. The smooth ocean liner of the new century lifted James across the sea 'as if I had been carried in a gigantic grandmother's bosom and the gentle giantess had made but one mighty stride of it had from land to land'.

3

Re-established in Lamb House, he promptly recognized the realities of his situation. Rye had been splendid for the time of his big novels and the retreat from London. But its loneliness had a great part in his depression; and he found himself slipping again into despair. His remedy was to leave at once, for his perch at the Reform Club. He began also to look for a flat in Bloomsbury. 'Dear old London and its ways and works, its walks and conversations, define themselves as a Prodigious Cure,' he wrote. He feared the 'immobilization, incarceration' of Lamb House; his early sense of being 'caged' in Rye had distinctly returned. His problem was what to do with his servants, who remained in idleness – and how to arrange his work. The Reform Club allowed him to have a typist in his rooms, but not a female, and he was in touch with Miss Bosanquet. She was willing to resume work on the old basis. She had two rooms available at one end of her flat at No. 10 Lawrence Street in Chelsea. These could be furnished; one of them had a bathroom and James could use it as a dressing-room. There was a separate entrance. James was enchanted; he very quickly organized his 'Chelsea cellar' as he called it – because the workroom was long, narrow, and dark. He found he could take a taxi in the morning at the Reform Club, and in ten minutes be at work. He came to call the rooms his 'little Chelsea temple, with its Egeria'. Here he began dictating his notes of a son and brother. He soon found himself writing instead the story of his earliest years – the book that would precede his tribute to William, *A Small Boy and Others*. Miss Bosanquet has given us a vivid picture of this dictation. Each morning, after reading the pages he had written the day before, he would pace up and down

sounding out the periods in tones of free resonant assurance. At such times he was beyond reach of irrelevant sounds or sights. Hosts of cats – a tribe usually routed with shouts of execration – might wail outside the window, phalanxes of motor-cars bearing dreaded visitors might hoot at the door . . . The only thing that could arrest his progress was the escape of the word he wanted to use. When that had vanished he broke off the rhythmic pacing and made his way to a chimney-piece or bookcase tall enough to support his elbows while he rested his head in his hands and audibly pursued the fugitive.

In a certain sense the recall of his childhood in that dim Chelsea room, to the accompaniment of the familiar typewriter, ministered to further physical recovery. He experienced release from discouragement and depression as when a decade earlier he had written out of his fantasies a series of novels and tales about children. Now he could draw directly upon the experiences of the little boy who had played in the streets around lower Fifth Avenue, travelled in the river steamer to visit his grandmother in Albany and eaten peaches from remembered trees in her large yard. An old America of small brick and frame houses and muddy streets, arose out of the past; he found himself remembering Emerson and Thackeray in Fourteenth Street and his one-legged father with his long beard and his hours at his writing desk and the name of Swedenborg constantly spoken in the James's household. There came back to him the London of Dickens and du Maurier, the Paris of the Second Empire, hours in the National Gallery, the first visit to the Galerie d'Apollon. He saw himself and his brother as pious little American 'pilgrims' abroad, decked out in their best, discovering the paintings of Delacroix, or attending old melodramas in the Bowery. The memories may have seemed like anachronisms in a new London but they danced vividly before his eyes and found shape and rhythm in the resonances of his style – quite like Proust, who was making similar discoveries of the 'lost time' of his childhood. One reads *A Small Boy and Others* and hears the personal voice in every line; by degrees what is built up for us in this unique autobiography is the development of an artistic sensibility and the growth of an imagination, that capacity for observing 'by instinct and reflection' with irony 'and yet with that fine taste for the truth of the matter which makes the genius of observation'. The James family with its innumerable cousins and their blighted lives, its galaxy of eccentric uncles and aunts, came to life again. Where other writers remember by simply recounting a curriculum of their lives, James embroidered a *petit point* of memory that showed the weavings to and fro across the Atlantic of the Jameses and the way in which they became – the younger members at least – citizens of two worlds.

He wrote now in the voice of his father and his brother. When he quoted from their letters he freely revised, as if their texts needed the same retouching given his own work in the New York Edition. When his nephew protested, after *Notes of a Son and Brother* was published, at this violation of William's language, Henry explained that he was showing it a marked respect. He could hear the voice of William saying to him, 'Oh, but you're not going to give me away, to hand me over, in my raggedness and my poor accidents, quite unhelped, unfriendly : you're going to do the very best for me you *can*, aren't you?' His goal was to make the documents (and his own text) 'engagingly readable and thereby more tasted and liked'. He admitted that 'I did instinctively regard it at last as all my truth, to do what I would with'. And while he pleaded that he retouched only form, he subtly altered content as well. Part of the family history had to be written as art : life in its raw state was inartistic. This was why James blended two trips to Europe into one, and made his father write a letter to Emerson in stronger language than was in the manuscript. The novelist's visual memory for ancient detail was extraordinary; he calls up the size, shape, and appearance of objects; he remembers the essential physiognomical characteristic of long-dead personages; he is aware of old smells and sounds and when it comes to food he has all the taste of a hungry little boy. His 'dive into the past' was hardly 'free' association – but it was a return to a very old reservoir of experience. And if the old man pacing the narrow room superimposed himself on the bright-eyed small boy or the meditative youth, it was through insights into the stages of his growth, the process that had made him artist and ultimately Master. He recreated as he said 'the vivid image and the very scene; the light of the only terms in which life has treated me to experience' – in a word 'the fine substance of history' – personal history.

The autobiographies evolved by stages. *A Small Boy* took James to his 15th year, when he had typhoid at Boulogne-sur-Mer. He then embarked on a second volume calling it at first *Early Letters of William James with Notes by Henry James*. When Harry sent him from America letters of the elder Henry James, he added – as the manuscript shows – a long section on his father, and in this fashion there evolved *Notes of a Son and Brother*. To his nephew, the busy Uncle kept explaining that he worked 'expensively'; he was writing much more than he would use; that ultimately the 'Family' book would be carved out of this material. In reality Henry James, in accordance with the imperious impulses of his nature, was pre-empting the family scene. Ultimately Harry James himself would edit his father's letters in two volumes. But the Master's enterprise yielded two volumes of rare autobiography in his most original vein. James gave the volumes to the Macmillans – he had owed them a book ever since his promise of the never-written work on London. In America the autobiographies were published by Scribner's, appearing successively in 1913 and 1914. He was paid £500 in advance by each publisher.

Late in 1911 James found a solution for his 'lonely' servants in Rye. His favourite nephew Billy married that autumn in America Alice Runnells, daughter of an affluent railroading family. The Uncle very promptly offered them Lamb House as a honeymoon house, an idea the young couple accepted with delight. James could remain at the Reform Club, his house tenanted by the attractive young people, who were there to take care of him when he stayed in Rye, and even to nurse him through a brief illness. He worked happily in London; and when the honeymooners came to the city the Uncle opened up for them all the avenues of English life. Billy, with his interest in painting, was taken to museums, to studios and to see the royal Holbeins at Windsor. The newest Alice in the James family – now the third – enjoyed meeting James's writer friends. Henry went shopping with them for furniture for their American home – 'two hours of expensive acquisition'. They went to the British Museum. He took them to see Pavlova, in all the freshness of her genius, and they saw the Princess Bariatinsky in a production of *Thérèse Raquin*; one evening when the Irish players came to London they saw *The Playboy of the Western World*. Long remembered by both was a week-end at Mrs Hunter's in Hill Hall, with notables of art and music present, and George Moore at the dinner table insisting on the interest of adultery. Out of this time there remained an anecdote of the Master's going for a stroll with Moore. He was asked on his return whether he had enjoyed his walk. James made a long speech – he talked of the many people he had known, and the delightful women, but he had never met, he said – never in all his experience – anyone who was quite so 'unimportantly dull' as George Moore.

Billy and Alice remained in Lamb House throughout that winter and Henry remained happily in London. The couple returned to America in June; and James re-settled in Lamb House for the summer. Summers were never lonely in Rye; it was the winters he feared. They brought their own moments of terror and the 'eagle pounce' of the Angel of Devastation, and his usual ambivalence. During this particular summer he wanted to finish *Notes of a Son and Brother*. The result was a period of large-scale diplomacy to which James brought all the power of his pen and all the energies of his mind.

103

The Firebird

HENRY JAMES had been seeing Russian ballet – and he had a new name for Edith Wharton. She had been an eagle and an Angel; now she was a Firebird – with 'iridescent Wings'. Bird imagery combined with motor imagery – the Firebird and her Chariot of Fire. She had been in touch with the Master throughout his illness. In 1911 she commissioned a charcoal drawing of him by John Singer Sargent. The artist was delighted to have his old friend for a sitter; but things did not go well. The painter tried once or twice; finally he created a stern, heavy-lidded, accusing-eyed Master. James felt he could not regard the portrait objectively. Mrs Wharton did not like it. Sargent first thought of destroying it. It survives, however. It ended up in the Royal Collection in Windsor Castle, where neither Henry James nor Mrs Wharton ever expected it would be. It was acquired to figure with portraits of holders of the Order of Merit, which would be bestowed on the Master.

I

Henry James had hardly re-settled into Lamb House when he wrote a beguiling – and also a cunning – letter to Mrs Hunter, hostess of Hill Hall. There had been some question of his visiting there with Mrs Wharton and motoring in the surrounding countryside. He suggested tactfully and firmly that Mrs Hunter should try to stay her hand a little 'as regards marked emphasis or pressure' in urging Mrs Wharton to come. He would be 'a little in a false position ... if one puts out a very persuasive hand to draw her over'. If she came, there would be the motor, and he was busy with his writing.

'Pleading with her to come does imply such a pledge – her motoring habits and intentions being so potent and explicit.' In sum : 'I think that what my little plea really amounts to is that you should most kindly not appear to throw *me* into the scales of persuasion.'

It didn't help. Little more than a fortnight later James was wiring Mrs Hunter that the Firebird was about to sweep 'and to catch me up in her irresistible talons'. To Mrs William James he explained 'the pressure on me is great, and I am going and probably shall enjoy it as much as I *can* enjoy it with an irritated and distressed sense of interruptions and deviation'. The question of this motor episode became for him, a matter of comic urgency. Dispatches were sent to Edith's friends and his own, describing the inexorable advance of the authoress on Lamb House. The first in this series is dated 'Reign of Terror, *ce vingt juillet*, 1912' to Howard Sturgis. It was a 'sort of signal of distress' thrown out confidentially

at the approach of the Bird o'freedom – the whirr and wind of whose great pinions is already cold on my foredoomed brow! She is close at hand, she arrives tomorrow, and the poor old Ryebird, ... feels his barn-yard hurry and huddle, emitting desperate and incoherent sounds, while its otherwise serene air begins ominously to darken.

Bref, said James, the Angel – 'half-angel and half-bird' as Browning had prefigured her – 'has a *plan* of course'. They would go to Qu'Acre, then dine with Lady Ripon. The Master was dissociating himself from this in advance. He had wired the Angel in Paris to say so. 'I foresee that on Edith's arrival the battle will be engaged.'

To his Rye confidante, Fanny Prothero :

I clutch at anything to hang on by – Mrs Wharton being due in her motor-car half an hour hence, straight from Paris ... and designing, with a full intensity, to whirl me away for several days – into the land at large. Nothing could suit me less ... Ah our complicated mo-dernity! Yes, pray for me while I am hurried to my doom.

To Goody Allen in London :

An hour ago there arrived Mrs Wharton from Paris, by motor car from Folkestone – it is now 7 p.m. and she left this a.m. and she stays till Tuesday. I shall not get off without *some* surrender; when a lady has motored straight across the channel to ask one to oblige, one must go some little part of the way to meet her – even at the cost of precious hours and blighted labours and dislocated thrift and order.

What particularly troubled James was that Miss Bosanquet had gone away for a holiday; she had provided a temporary substitute, Miss Lois Barker, who would now collect pay while her employer had to go off with Mrs Wharton. 'I feel better,' he told Goody Allen, 'for this (intensely *private*, please,) howl already. But oh one's *opulent* friends – they cost the eyes of the head.'

2

The comedy of the Firebird resolved itself into a series of compromises. James sent her off alone; he promised to go with her to Howard Sturgis and to spend four or five days at Hill Hall. 'The horrible thing about it is that it will be most interesting and wonderful and *worth while* and yet even this won't solve effectually my inward ache.' Meanwhile Miss Barker, the typist, a parson's daughter, would have 'elegant leisure' and James would be doing 'the charmingly right thing at the hideously wrong time'.

July 27, 1912 – Queen's Acre. Motored to Cliveden with Edith Wharton after lunch; had tea there and promised Mrs Waldorf [Astor] to come back on Tuesday till Thursday.

July 29 – Motored with E., Howard and Babe over to tea with Ranee [of Sarawak] at Ascot. Vernon Lee there, with whom I had a good deal of talk.

It was his first meeting with Vernon Lee since she had caricatured him in a novel almost twenty years earlier.

July 30–31 – Afternoon run to Cliveden. Three New Yorkers (*such* New Yorkers!) staying for night with Nancy Astor. Beautiful walk on the slopes down to and by river 6–8 with E.W. Americans left – day wet.

Aug. 1 – Agreed to stay over today Thursday ... Second stroll with E. but had pectoral attack after lunch – through too much hurry and tension on slopes and staircase. Quiet till dinner – but second attack on mounting room 10.30. Lord Curzon at dinner.

Edith was understandably upset by Henry's heart flurries – apparently induced by his conflict between duty and pleasure and the Firebird's importunities. They left on 2 August and went back to Howard Sturgis's where they lunched. Then she sent James back to Lamb House.

... had admirable car and dear Cook lent me by Edith for most beautiful and merciful return, by myself, across country, back to Rye, where I write this. Admirable afternoon; admirable run through so lovely interesting land from about 2 to 6.30. Gave Cook forty shillings. Went straight to bed on arriving last night.

James stayed in bed the following day, but felt he needed 'movement'. He renewed his long walks and experienced immediate relief. 'The only proper place for me is home,' he wrote Mrs Hunter.

James's impression of Nancy Astor, the future hostess of the 'Cliveden Set' and Member of Parliament were that she was 'full of possibilities and fine material – though but a reclaimed barbarian, with all her bounty, spontaneity and charm, too'. He thought Cliveden 'a creation of such beauty and distinction that the mere exposure of one's sensibility and one's imagination to the effect and the "message" of such a place (in itself) becomes a duty if the opportunity arises'. Thus he justified to himself his absence from his work.

Mrs Wharton came to Lamb House early in August just before taking flight for the Continent. 'The firebird perches on my shoulder,' James wrote to Howard Sturgis on 12 August. She had held James and two other visitors 'spell-bound, by her admirable talk. She never was more wound up and going, or more ready, it would appear, for new worlds to conquer.' The only thing was what new worlds were left for her? To Mrs Cadwalader Jones he gave the ultimate summary of 'Edith's prodigious visit'.

She rode the whirlwind, she played with the storm, she laid waste whatever of the land the other raging elements had spared, she consumed in fifteen days what would have served to support an ordinary Christian Community for about ten years. Her powers of devastation are ineffable, her repudiation of repose absolutely tragic, and she was never more brilliant and able and interesting.

Lois Barker, Miss Bosanquet's substitute, remembered vividly her summer's work in Lamb House. She turned up at Lamb House each morning where Burgess ushered her into the Green Room, and occasionally the Garden Room. James was often late. More than once on arriving she met him in the hall dressed only in pyjamas, carrying a large bath sponge. He beamed at her reassuringly in his informality with his 'large blue eyes'. He dictated his autobiographies without notes, though occasionally he darted to a drawer to return with a letter or other document. He wrote that summer the passage in *A Small Boy* in which Thackeray admired the buttons on James's boyhood jacket; he held in his hand the daguerreotype by Brady of the small boy wearing the jacket which would later be the frontispiece to the book. Suddenly in the midst of dictating the passage he left the room and returned. He was carrying the original jacket, buttons and all – those buttons which had fascinated Thackeray more than half a century before in New York.

104

A Browning Centenary

THE Master had avoided public appearances during all the years of his residence in England. *Guy Domville* had been an exception and a mistake for which he had paid a heavy price. He had done nothing abroad comparable to his lectures on Balzac in America. Nevertheless, in the fullness of age, during that spring of 1912 in London, James faced a distinguished audience to deliver a commemorative tribute to his old friend of the London drawing-rooms, to the poet of his youth – Robert Browning. The occasion was Browning's hundredth birthday, 7 May 1912. James had long ago enshrined the double-personality of Browning in his small tale *The Private Life*; now he offered a full-length paper, and read it himself. He called it 'The Novel in *The Ring and the Book*.' He spoke in an upper chamber of Caxton Hall with its pictured windows recording famous events in Westminster. Edmund Gosse presided. The other speaker was Arthur Pinero, the playwright, whose subject was Browning as a dramatist. The ceremony was under the auspices of the Academic Committee of the Royal Society of Literature to which Henry James had been elected some years before. It was one of those occasions relished by men of letters, proud of their craft, with the full sense of their profession and their status. It was also an odd occasion. In celebrating the centenary of Browning the two speakers were each dealing with him through their particular art – Pinero's address, long, loud, delivered with oratorical flourish and booming voice, was designed to show that Browning had been in no way a playwright; Henry James's tribute analysed *The Ring and the Book* to show how it might have been written as a novel – a novel, to be sure, by the author of *The Golden Bowl*.

'Pinero who thunderously preceded me,' said James afterwards, 'spoke twice as long as I had been told he was to; and this made me *apprehensive* and hurried and flurried and worried and faint through the sense that we were all *spent* – and the hall vast.' It was too vast to carry James's voice when he let it fall, so that his talk was intermittently inaudible to some parts of the audience. And yet the audience never became restless. It sat indeed as if hypnotized. It murmured approval. As at the Balzac lectures there were bursts of applause; and when the Master came to a particularly fine passage describing the sense of place – Tuscany and Rome – in Shelley, Swinburne, and Browning, a great stir and a great flutter greeted his words:

Shelley, let us say in the connection, is a light, and Swinburne is a sound – Browning alone is a temperature.

He compared Browning's recreation of history with *Romola*. Browning stirred up 'a perfect cloud of gold dust' whereas George Eliot 'leaves the air about us clear, about as white, and withal about as cold, as before she had benevolently entered it'.

Then James began to rewrite *The Ring and the Book* into a novel; he would bring the Canon Caponsacchi on earlier, 'ever so much earlier, turn him on, with a brave ingenuity, from the very first', and in the city of Rome perhaps, 'place him there in the field, at once recipient and agent, vaguely conscious and with splendid brooding apprehension, awaiting the adventure of his life, awaiting his call, his real call (the others have been such vain show and hollow stopgaps), awaiting in fine, his terrible great fortune'. With delicate touches James also painted the background 'my Italy of the eve of the eighteenth century – a vast painted and gilded rococo shell roofing over a scenic, an amazingly figured and furnished earth, but shutting out almost the whole of our own dearly-bought, rudely-recovered spiritual sky'.

James was clear throughout – as he expounded doctrine out of the New York Edition prefaces – that his was an act of homage to Browning. 'We move with him but in images and references and vast and far correspondences; we eat but of strange compounds and drink but of rare distillations; and very soon, after a course of this, we feel ourselves ... in the world of Expression at any cost.' He compared poets and novelists by saying the reader of fiction walks with the novelist on the same side of the street, whereas the poet is always 'elegantly' walking on the other side, across the way 'where we greet them without danger of concussion'.

James singled out one quality in especial in Browning's work – 'the great constringent relation between man and woman at once at its maximum and as the relation most worth while in life for either party'. This remained, said James, the thing of which 'his own rich experience most convincingly spoke to him'. He had figured it 'as never too much either of the flesh or of the spirit for him, so long as the possibility of both of these is in each, but always and ever as the thing absolutely most worth-while'. Was it worth-while for *them* or for the reader? 'Well, let us say worth-while assuredly for us, in this noble exercise of the imagination.' But there wasn't a detail of the 'panting' flight of Caponsacchi and Pompilia over the autumn Apennines 'the long hours when they melt together only *not* to meet – that doesn't positively plead for our perfect prose transcript'.

The lecture had elegance; it had authority; it spoke for a powerful directing mind. James created seemingly impossible sentences and made them meaningful to the audience. Lord Charnwood, biographer of Lincoln, said there was an 'extreme point-lace kind of refinement and elaboration of phrase and thought which makes me, personally, sick when I see a page of Henry James in cold print', but listening that afternoon it was 'fascinating, soothing, elevating, even in parts intelligible to me when I heard it from the living voice of a quite living man'. And then Lord Charnwood was arrested by the way James left him aware in his talk of Browning, 'of one thing that might really satisfy a man's desire of life, namely to love a woman'. A reporter present spoke of the 'visible movement of enjoyment' in the listeners 'over some more than usually musical and in every way beautiful sentence'. When James stopped and sat down it seemed 'as if the applause would never cease'.

He had richly paid his debt to the remembered Browning, who had taught him so much about 'point of view' long ago; about entering into the thoughts of characters. But now the audience of literary England, of his peers and of his readers, paid its homage to him. It had never had such a chance in all the years of his English life; and it did so with a fullness of measure that perhaps James, in his flustered state, and high nervousness, did not appreciate – until he read the reports in the papers. One journalist spoke of sentences so musical and 'so charged with criticism and insight that one would strive to fix it in the memory; and then, just as one thought one had succeeded, another as significant and as rhythmical, would sound forth, and drive the predecessor away'. James began by reading the expository part of the lecture rapidly; then he slowed down. His tone was conversational, his voice mellow. 'All true charm is indescribable, and that of Henry James is more indescribable than most,' the reporter wrote. The press spoke of his 'magic' very much as Max Beerbohm had described it. 'I noticed,' wrote Filson Young in the *Pall Mall Gazette* 'that even the most experienced reporters gave it up in despair, laid down their pencils, and sat hypnotized ... One merely listened to the voice of this charming old artist as though in the enchantment of a dream.'

I was sitting near him and could hear every word; I am afraid that at least half of the audience could hear nothing at all; but such was the charm in the voice, such was the magic of this dear old man's personality, and such were the affection and regard in which he was held by his audience, that not a sound or movement disturbed the silence of the room during the whole of that long and infinitely complicated address.

The Master to the Firebird:

It might indeed have diverted you to be present at our Browning commemoration – for Pinero was by far the most salient feature of it (simple, sensuous, passionate – that is artless, audible, incredible!) and was one of the most amusing British documents we had had for many a day. He had quite exhausted the air by the time I came on – and I but panted in the void. But dear Howard and dear Percy held each a hand of me – across the width of the room – and I struggled through.

James was pleased nevertheless; he clipped Filson Young's comments and sent them to Cambridge, Massachusetts.

105

La Folie des Grandeurs

THE years had passed and Hendrik Andersen had produced no professional work to speak of, certainly nothing that could be considered a masterpiece. He had been young, ambitious, full of promise, when James met him. He was now 40 and dull, complacent, impractical. James had had great expectations, for he endowed

Andersen with his own feelings about the role of an artist; and from time to time, in his letters of love, he had admonished the sculptor to work within the realities of his 'trade'. But Andersen went on multiplying, as James ruefully specified, buttocks and breasts and penises, in the massive fountains he designed, with no visible sign that America was interested in such a quantity of nudity. After their brief meeting in 1905, when James and Andersen had gone to Newport together, James had written to him 'it's all pretty wretched, this non-communication – for there are long and weighty things about your work, your plan, your perversity, your fountain, your building, on and on and up and up, *in the air*, as it were, and *out of relation to possibilities and actualities*, that I wanted to say to you'. He went on to urge him once again to '*make the pot boil, at any price, as the only real basis* of freedom and sanity'.

What American community, James wondered, 'is going to want to pay for thirty and forty stark-naked men and women, of whatever beauty and lifted into the raw light of one of their public places. Keep in relation to the *possible* possibilities, dearest boy.' He returned frequently to the charge. He spoke of 'your horribly expensive family of naked sons and daughters, of all sizes, and ages ... And then I reflect that you are always (terrible fellow!) begetting new ones as fast as possible – and I do lie awake at night asking myself what will become either of them or of you.'

In 1906 Andersen sent James a photograph of a statue of two lovers in embrace. James said the work was the finest of the long 'and interminable' series. He went on to analyse the statue's qualities:

I don't think I find the *hands*, on the backs, *living* enough and participant enough in the kiss. They would be, in life, very participant – to their fingertips, and would show it in many ways. But this you know, and the thing is very strong and (otherwise) more complete. There is more flesh and *pulp* in it, more life of *surface* and of blood-flow *under* the surface, than you have hitherto, in your powerful simplifications, gone in for. So keep at *that* – at the flesh and the devil and the rest of it, make the creatures palpitate, and their flesh tingle and flush, and their internal economy proceed, and their bellies ache and their bladders fill – all in the mystery of your art.

Thus the artist who had once described a parsimonious kiss in one of his famous novels and lately revised it in the sense in which he now wrote. His words fell, however, on emptiness. Andersen neither understood, nor did he listen. In another letter of this year James is again wondering 'where this colossal multiplication of divinely naked and intimately associated gentlemen and ladies, flaunting their bellies and bottoms and their other private affairs, in the face of day, is going, on any *American* possibility, to land you'. He complained that Andersen's figures were too stocky, 'the faces too blank and stony'. Andersen's women and men were also too undifferentiated – '*the* indispensable sign apart'. There was a statue of a ballerina : he had not allowed her 'a quite sufficient luxury – to my taste – of hip, or to speak plainly, Bottom. She hasn't *much* more of that than her husband and I should like her to have a good deal more.' He adjures him to 'stop your multiplication of unsaleable nakedness for a while and hurl yourself, into the production of the interesting, the charming, the vendible, the *placeable* small thing'. He urged him to get at busts,

for it is fatal for you to go on infinitely neglecting the Face never doing one, only adding Belly to Belly – however beautiful – and Bottom to Bottom, however sublime. It is only by the Face that the artist – and the sculptor – can hope *predominantly* to live and steadily to live – it is so supremely and exquisitely interesting to do.

Such passages usually ended with 'dear, dear Hendrik, have patience with my words and judge of the affection that prompted them'.

2

In a letter of 1908, after he had his reunion in Rome with Hendrik and watched him work in his studio, Henry James resumed his warnings. He had seen the great impractical fountains, the lifeless nudes, *tutti bravi signori*, brave men, and beautiful women; and he remarked ironically 'we shall have to build a big bold city on purpose to take them in'. He added, not realizing how thoroughly he had diagnosed Hendrik Andersen, 'I daresay you would take a contract for that, too, yourself.' James probably forgot that he had written this. Yet he could not have put his finger more accurately on Andersen's vaulting fantasy, his megalomania of the colossal.

Early in 1912, Hendrik sent the Master plans, circulars, appeals for funds, which he was distributing throughout Europe. He wanted to build a 'World City', a 'world centre of communication'. The motto for it would be 'Love – Equality – Peace.' His idea was that nations separated by oceans and mountains, language and custom, politics and prejudice, religion and culture – these phrases were in the prospectus – might here 'imbibe living and vibrating knowledge at a great fountain, and offer of their best'. To that end Hendrik envisaged, and had elaborate architectural drawings made by forty architects, of a Paris-like metropolis, a long mall, resembling the Tuileries, with a Palace of Nations, like the Louvre, with an Olympic athletic area at one end and a vast Palace of the Arts at the other, with a tremendous tower – a kind of mixture of the leaning tower of Pisa and the Eiffel Tower – presiding over the whole show. It was an architect's and sculptor's dream of a kind of permanent, super-World Fair. The buildings were all of the Grand Palais style, Graeco-Roman; one has a feeling that Hendrik Andersen planned this city around the huge fountains he had been designing for years. The photographs of the fountain-figures quite fit the descriptions of them in James's letters. One might add that both men and women look like heavyweight boxers – the women formidable with only the slightest of breasts, and their limbs set and masculine, poised in their frozen ballet. The plan would later elaborate the economy of the city down to the central heating. Andersen's idea was that it could be placed anywhere, he had no particular site in mind. He finally got up a big two-volume printing of three hundred copies of his plans and sent them to the millionaires of the world. And he travelled about Europe soliciting help for his idea. The King of the Belgians received him and gave him his blessing. The statues continued to multiply in Rome. The sculptured utopia remained still-born.

The whole scheme was too much for the Master. James's reply 14 April 1912 had a portentous beginning.

Not another day do I delay to answer (with such difficulty!) your long and interesting letter ... Brace yourself ... though I don't quite see why I need, having showed you in the past, so again and again, that your mania for the colossal, the swelling and the huge, the monotonously and repeatedly huge, breaks the heart of me for you.

His only answer to this waste of money and time on 'a ready-made City' was to 'cover my head with my mantle and turn my face to the wall, and there, dearest Hendrik, just bitterly *weep* for you – just desperately and dismally and helplessly water that dim refuge with a salt flood'. He warned him of 'dread Delusion' – medical science had a name for it, MEGALOMANIA, and Henry wrote it in capital letters adding 'look it up in the Dictionary'. He also gave it to him in French, *la folie des grandeurs*. The dictionary wasn't necessary, for James went on to explain it was 'the infatuated, and disproportionate love and pursuit of, and attempt at, the Big, the Bigger, the Biggest, the Immensest Immensity, with all sense of proportion, application, relation, and possibility madly *submerged*'. The idea of a city built *de chic* filled the Master 'with mere pitying dismay, the unutterable Waste of it all makes me retire into my room and lock the door to howl! Think of me as doing so, as howling for hours on end.' He would continue to howl, he said, until he heard that Hendrik had chucked the whole thing into the Tiber. Cities he explained to Andersen, were 'living organisms'. They grew from within, piece by piece. There could not be a 'ready-made city, made-while-one-waits'. He closed asking Hendrik to understand 'how dismally unspeakably much these cold hard, desperate words, withholding sympathy, cost your ever-affectionate, your terribly tender old friend'. The world, James explained to Andersen, was no place for castles in the air given 'this terribly crowded and smothered and overbuilt ground that stretches under the feet of the for the most part raging and would-be throat-cutting and mutually dynamiting nations'. He also said that 'things struggle into life, even the very best of them, by slow steps and stages and rages and convulsions of experience, and utterly refuse to be taken over ready-made or *en bloc*'.

When Hendrik wrote again a year later, James had to recognize that 'evidently, my dear boy, I can only give you pain'. He repeated he did not understand 'your very terms of "world" this and "world" the other'. He told him 'you take too much for granted, and take it too sublimely so, of the poor old friend who left you such a comparatively short time since in all contentment, as he supposed, in a happy Roman studio'. The Master went on to say that he would feel quite the same about such vague immensities 'even if I were not old and ill and detached, and reduced to ending my life in a very restricted way'. Hendrik had dragged it out of him; he had to say to him,

I simply loathe such pretentious forms of words as 'world' anything – they are to me mere monstrous sound without sense. The World is a prodigious and portentous and immeasurable affair, and I can't for a moment pretend to sit in my little corner here and 'sympathize' with proposals for dealing with it. It is so far vaster in its appalling complexity than you or me, or than anything we can pretend without the imputation of absurdity and insanity to do to it, that I content myself, and inevitably *must* (so far as I can do anything at all now), with living in the realities of things, with 'cultivating my garden', (morally and intellectually speaking) and with referring my questions to a Conscience (my own poor little personal), less inconceivable than that of the globe.

With the words of Voltaire, this curious friendship of the Master with the no longer young sculptor more or less came to an end. James referred again to 'the dark danger' of megalomania, 'that way, my dear boy, Madness simply lies. Reality, reality, the seeing of things as they *are*, and not in the light of the loosest simplifications – come back to *that* with me, and then, even now we can talk!' And James signed himself 'your poor old weary and sorrowing and yet always so personally and faithfully tender old Henry James'.

We must recognize that in the inner world of the Master some deep dream of grandeur also existed – a dream of triumph amid the art works of the great world – as in the Galerie d'Apollon of the Louvre where he could defeat fear and feel the exaltation of power. It may be that Hendrik Andersen, in addition to having been an image in a mirror of youth in 1899, when James was reaching the farther limit of middle age, was also James's 'secret sharer' of those drives of craft and glory. James had been able to control and channel his drive to greatness into the realities of his time and his world. Andersen would live to old age in Rome and leave his great unsold collection of statues; some would be used in buildings projected by another individual with a *folie des grandeurs*. Andersen's art was that kind of blind cold frozen art that could adorn great Mussolini manifestations of public frenzy and national megalomania. The ornaments of an intended city of peace became the ornaments of a government of war. This, however, was beyond the lifetime of the Master.

106

A Determined Woman

ONE of the consequences of the Firebird's view of Henry James during the motor tours of 1912 was her growing belief that he needed money. He had complained to her once too often of his low royalties; his ironies about his unprincely scale of life were taken very seriously. During 1912 Walter Berry sent James a beautifully fitted leather suitcase lined with morocco. James had written an elaborate thank-you telling Berry how the beautiful object made everything else in Lamb House seem poverty-stricken. The letter was a bit overdone. James found the conceit too enticing to let go without an even more than customary recourse to hyperbole. '*Très cher et très-grand ami!*' he began, and after referring to Berry's '*ineffable procédé*' he spoke throughout the letter of the suitcase as 'him' and said 'I can't live with him, you see, because I can't live up to him'. With his customary irony he went on to speak of

his claims, his pretensions, his dimensions, his assumptions and consumptions, above all the manner in which he causes every surrounding object (on my poor premises or within my poor range) to tell a dingy, and deplorable tale – all this makes him the very scourge of my life, the very blot on my scutcheon ... I simply can't afford him, and that is the sorry homely truth. He is out of the picture – out of *mine*

and so on for nearly 2,000 words. Mrs Wharton saw this letter. She probably noted the phrase 'I simply can't afford him'. She had heard James say this often enough. James was in reality telling Berry that he didn't need so grandiose an article but Mrs Wharton must have received quite another message.

In the preceding year she had quietly organized, with the help of Edmund Gosse in England, and with that of William Dean Howells in America, a vigorous campaign to obtain the Nobel Prize for Henry James. It had never been given to an American and would not be until 1930. The Swedish Academy was thoroughly documented; appropriate letters were written emphasizing the Master's supreme position in Anglo-American letters. But the northern judges of the world's literature had not read Henry James and had not read about him in the newspapers; he was an intensely private figure; moreover, they tended then to be influenced by the degree to which foreign writers were popular in other countries than their own and the extent to which they were translated. James had been very little translated. He did not permit it. He considered himself – and most translators agreed – untranslatable. In a word James was not as 'visible' as Kipling, who had received the prize in 1907. Even the Firebird, with her tremendous energy and enthusiasm, could not convince the Academicians that a writer who belonged so intensely to the Anglo-American world deserved the great prize. It was much easier to award it that year to Maurice Maeterlinck.

Edith Wharton was not to be frustrated. She remembered the highly successful device by which she – and the Master himself – had provided much-needed funds to Morton Fullerton when he was being blackmailed. She accordingly entered into secret correspondence with Charles Scribner who was her publisher in America – and also Henry James's. She and Scribner agreed that $8,000 could safely be diverted from her royalties to the Master's account without arousing suspicion. They could hardly falsify the earnings on the New York Edition. Scribner accordingly wrote a letter to James which the novelist read with a certain amount of surprise, pleasure, and suspicion. The letter was a model of discretion. The publisher expressed delight at the chance to do the autobiographies. James's agent had, moreover, said that the Master was working on a novel of American life – an allusion to his sketching out of *The Ivory Tower* just before his 1910 illness. 'As the publishers of your definitive edition we want another great novel to balance *The Golden Bowl* and round off the series of books in which you have developed the theory of composition set forth in your prefaces.' Such a book would be of great advantage both to publisher and author; it should be written as soon as possible. It obviously would demand much time, and Scribner's had decided therefore to make an 'unusual proposal'. If James could begin the book soon, the publisher was prepared to pay him an advance of $8,000 (£1,500), perhaps half on signing the contract and half on delivery of the manuscript. The novel would be added to the New York Edition.

James had never received so handsome an offer. It was settled that he would be given a 20 per cent royalty and Scribner would have world rights and would thus arrange publication in England. Also that James would write the novel as soon as possible after the completion of the autobiographies. James B. Pinker, the novelist's agent, was not fooled; he ultimately fathomed the intrigue, for a note in Miss Bosanquet's diary, after James's death, tells us that Pinker 'has been convinced by his recent communications with Scribner's that his guess as to Mrs Wharton having subsidized the Scribner novel contract was quite correct'. The agent was discretion itself. James remarked he could hardly believe in the bounty of publishers, but that he should certainly make the most of this opportunity.

Mrs Wharton was disturbed that James handed the matter over to his agent. It meant that almost $1,000 of the sum – or to be exact $800 – would be paid to Pinker as his fee. She did not see why Pinker should get anything; and caused Scribner to suggest to James that since the initiative had been the publisher's the agent was not needed. James, however, insisted that Pinker receive his due. The first intalment of the advance was $3,600 – which James happily pocketed, still surprised, but also delighted.

2

Mrs Wharton's initiative, while meddlesome and not required, helped to give James's morale a lift at a crucial moment. For in the autumn of 1912, when he seemed to have fully recovered from his depression and illness of two years earlier, he suddenly came down with the painful systemic virus disease known as *herpes zoster* – in a word 'shingles'. The evenly spaced skin eruption, from which the ailment takes its name, appeared across the chest and round to his back; since it follows the line of a cutaneous nerve, it is painful in the extreme. James had a very bad case of it – it laid him low for the next four months and while he could have been ambulatory, he spent much time in bed since he found that his clothing irritated his skin. A consequence of this was that he did not get the exercise he required, given his obesity. His letters of this time, some scrawled in pencil in bed, betray his intense irritation and suffering. And yet he kept up his friendships and his interests; he managed to do a considerable amount of reading and planning, and even dictation, so that *A Small Boy and Others* was completed, and *Notes of a Son and Brother* got under way. In the midwinter, in February of 1913, the prolonged inactivity produced an accumulation of fluid at the bottom of James's lungs. This was not at first diagnosed, and as

James's breathing became more difficult, and his discomfort acute, alarms went out to his friends. Mrs William James offered to come from America. Mrs Wharton was prepared to 'rush over for two or three days at once' from Paris.

James's loyal housemaid, Minnie Kidd, at this moment was called to her aged mother who was ill and the doctor brought in a nurse. The Master regarded her as 'a mild dragon'. Mrs Wharton secretly provided funds for a nurse for Kidd's mother and restored the faithful maid to James's bedside – this being arranged through Miss Bosanquet. The nurse was dismissed. Once diagnosed, James's oedema was readily treated and he rapidly recovered. 'My vitality, my still sufficient cluster of vital "assets,"' James wrote to his nephew Harry, 'to say nothing of my *will to live and to write*, assert themselves in spite of everything.' This was true. There was little depression in this illness. The prospect of doing a new novel for Scribner, the handsome sum advanced, the progress of the auto-biographies, prevailed over the ills of the flesh. James went through the siege surrounded by friends, and after the first eight or ten weeks was able to move about during the daytime though quite eager to tear off his clothes and get into bed as quickly as possible. For a while in the later stages massage was prescribed but it coincided with the onset of the oedema and was not successful. There is an interesting footnote to the massage by way of a remark made by a Swedish masseur to a lady in Sweden who incorporated it in her memoirs. The Swedish authoress, Mia Leche Löfgren, recorded a conversation with a 'medical gymnast' who said he had worked for Henry James and 'didn't like him'. Wasn't he friendly? the authoress asked, and the answer was, 'Yes, he was *too* friendly.'

3

In the weeks preceding his illness, Henry James had been extra-ordinarily active. He was delighted that his old friend Edmund Gosse had become librarian of the House of Lords and had tea with him in the lordly surroundings. At the beginning of 1912, dining at Edmund Gosse's, he met the young French writer André Gide, 'an interesting Frenchman', James noted. It was their only meeting.

James's date-books show that during this period he met May Sinclair, attended a reception at Sir Edward Elgar's, saw again his old friend Lady Gregory, with whom he shared in common an interest in Paul Harvey, now having a distinguished career in the diplomatic service. William Lyon Phelps, the Yale *literatus*, turned up in London. James described him as 'the boring and vacuous (though so well-meaning) Yale chatterbox Phelps'. The Master took a lively interest in suffragette activities. He saw something of Lady Ottoline Morrell 'always touching and charming; and yesterday (8 May 1912) she was very interesting; and also beautiful. But I wish she didn't run so much to the stale, but a little more to the fresh, in costume.' He referred to her 'window-curtaining clothes'.

On 26 June 1912 Oxford bestowed the honorary degree of doctor of letters on the Master and he may have remembered how years before he had given a dinner in London to celebrate bestowal of that honour on Turgenev. Attired in the academic gown he heard himself described as 'fecundissimum et facundissimum scriptorem, Henricum James'.

He wrote during that year a long and warm letter of praise for William Dean Howells's 75th birthday to be read at one of Colonel Harvey's great dinners in New York. It was almost as long as an essay and surveyed Howells's work with affection and friendliness out of their lifetime of friendship. He reminded Howells that Taine had once greeted him as 'a precious painter and a sovereign witness', and he told him that 'the critical intelligence – if any such fitful and discredited light may still be conceived as within our sphere – has not at all begun to render you its tribute'.

Reading that autumn the letters of George Meredith, just published, he was led to reflect on the way in which greatness is reduced in the posthumous world. He complained at the letters chosen by Meredith's son, their scantiness and their failure to convey the charm and magic of the Meredith he had so long known. In a series of letters to Gosse, James wrote

what lacerates me perhaps most of all in the Meredith is the meanness and poorness of the editing – the absence of any attempt to project the Image (of character, temper, quantity and quality of mind, general size, and sort of personality,) that such a subject cries aloud for; to the shame of our purblind criticism. For such a Vividness to go a-begging.

On further acquaintance with the volumes he grew critical; he complained that the 'aesthetic range' of the letters was meagre; Meredith had lived, James felt 'even less than one had the sense of his doing, in the world of art – in that whole divine preoccupation ... His whole case is full of anomaly ... He was *starved*, to my vision, in many ways – and that makes him but the more nobly pathetic.' It was Meredith's lack of 'aesthetic curiosity' that bothered James most.

The Master's date-books do not record his encountering a young American with thick fluffy brown hair growing back from a very straight line along his forehead and a little pointed moustache and beard, and as Miss Bosanquet would note 'slightly aesthetic clothes'. Ezra Pound spoke with a drawl; he lowered his voice so as to become inaudible. This may have been the awe in which he stood of the Master. Pound wrote home that he and Henry James 'glared at one another across the same carpet' and he remembered James's saying of America, that it was 'strange how all taint of art or letters seems to shun that continent'. In Pound's *Cantos* years later was recorded a memory of the Master, a glimpse at the Reform Club:

> And the great domed head, *con gli occhi*
> > *onesti e tardi*
> Moves before me, phantom with weighted motion,
> *Grave incessu*, drinking the tone of things
> And the old voice lifts itself
> > weaving an endless sentence.

This was indeed Henry James; and on 15 April 1913 he would be 70.

4

Shortly before the onset of his attack of the shingles, Henry James had found a flat in London, in Cheyne Walk, in Chelsea. His room at the Reform Club had served him for more than ten years; now, with his intermittent illnesses, and his need to have Miss Bosanquet available, and above all remembering how his 'hibernation' at Rye bred loneliness and depression, he had decided to return to the metropolis. He would use Lamb House only in the summers. No. 21 Carlyle Mansions suited him in every way. It was an L-shaped apartment, with two large rooms hanging over the Thames; these could serve as study and dining-room. Off the long corridor there was a series of smaller rooms, a master bedroom for himself and further down rooms for his cook, a maid, and the indispensable Burgess. There were five bedrooms in all. It would cost him only £60 a year more than his pied-à-terre at the Reform. He was a little touchy about the fact that the landlord hadn't heard of Henry James and asked for references; but Edmund Gosse, with his address at the House of Lords, provided the kind of *cachet* that seemed to be needed. He would have as a neighbour his old friend, Emily Sargent, sister of the painter. The rooms over the river gave him a southern view: they had a great deal of sun. The view had been painted by Whistler, whose studio had been in nearby Tite Street where Sargent now lived. James had fond memories of the area; in 1869, during his first adult trip abroad, he had been taken here to visit Dante Gabriel Rossetti. He liked the pompously-embanked river which offered him a walk all the way to Westminster; and the neighbourhood was associated with Carlyle, Turner, Leigh Hunt, George Eliot.

Since he was still ill in January 1913, when he took possession of the apartment, the move was made by his servants, who brought various pieces of furniture from Lamb House, and settled everything for the Master. He arrived to a tolerably organized domestic establishment; Fanny Prothero had supervised the move with great efficiency.

And so Henry James formerly of 34 De Vere Gardens, Kensington, who had forsaken London in the late 1890s, now returned to the metropolis. He was again near his clubs and a new generation of friends. He could watch the boats on the river; and feel himself once more in harmony with the rumbling city. He now had a telephone; the days of 'calling' and leaving cards were being supplanted by that device. Taxi-cabs were handy. He was ready to settle down to work again. But he knew – he felt – that this was his last harbour.

107

The Master at 70

LATE in 1912 or early in 1913 Edith Wharton caused to be circulated a form letter among figures of society and finance in the United States proposing that a substantial sum be raised in honour of Henry James's 70th birthday. She regarded the secretly diverted royalty as a stop-gap: she wanted the Master to receive a large purse. If the Swedish Academy would not give him the Nobel Prize his own countrymen should do something quite as handsome. The circular letter suggested that a series of large contributions would be welcomed and named a bank into which the sums should be paid. It was a characteristic example of the generous – and thoughtless – impulses of the Firebird; she had acted quickly and imperiously, but without sufficient attention to Henry James's feelings. One of her thoughts seems to have been that James might purchase a car from the proceeds of this subscription.

While the appeal was private and wholly unpublicized, word of it reached Henry James's nephews Harry, at the Rockefeller Institute in New York, and Billy, who had settled in Boston after his honeymoon. Billy cabled his uncle at once. The reply could not have been more prompt. 'Immense thanks for warning taking instant prohibitive action. Please express to individuals approached my horror money absolutely returned. Uncle.' This was followed by a letter to Billy saying he wanted the appeal for funds 'stamped out by any violent means (not, of course, of the newspaper)'. He added: 'A more reckless and indiscreet undertaking, with no ghost of a preliminary leave asked, no hint of a sounding taken, I cannot possibly conceive – and am still rubbing my eyes for incredulity.' He wanted it given out, privately and socially, 'to all it may concern, this my all but indignant, and my wholly prohibitive protest'. The money was returned. Among the papers of Mrs Wharton there is no letter from Henry James on the subject; the chances are he said not a word to her. Their friendship continued unchanged; however misguided the attempt, her motive had been generous. She had been guilty of a failure in empathy – and in strategy.

I

Henry James's friends in England, practised in the arts of homage, had quite another scheme. Percy Lubbock, Hugh Walpole, Edmund Gosse, Lucy Clifford, and others, a small informal committee, issued an appeal to the Master's friends and admirers. His seventy years of art and distinction should be honoured, and in a fitting public fashion. James got wind of this initiative from loyal Goody Allen and asked very promptly they put a stop to it. He explained to Miss Bosanquet he didn't want it bruited abroad 'that I'm a fabulous age when I'm trying to put forth some further exhibition of my powers'. Lucy Clifford flatly told him he was 'cold, callous and ungracious'.

He capitulated. No one was allowed to contribute more than £5. Nearly 300 persons subscribed, and with this sum a silver-gilt Charles II porringer and dish was purchased for £50 to be presented to the author of *The Golden Bowl*. The balance was offered to John Singer Sargent to paint a portrait of the Master. Sargent, as a friend of many years, refused to take the honorarium; and the sum was used to commission a bust by a young sculptor chosen by Sargent, Derwent Wood. In this way, and with all the niceties observed, the Master awoke on 15 April to discover himself, at least for a day, a great public figure.

The bell at No. 21 began to ring early; by forenoon the apartment was filled with flowers; cables and telegrams arrived from everywhere. On behalf of friends and admirers the Golden Bowl was presented and accepted by James with his customary elegance. Inscribed on the bowl were the simple words 'To Henry James from some of his friends'. He announced he would sit for the portrait (and later consented to sit for the bust) but that he would not accept the painting as belonging to himself; it belonged to his admirers. He agreed to be its custodian and publicly willed it to the National Portrait Gallery; if it should be judged unacceptable by that institution, he suggested it be offered to the Metropolitan Museum in New York. He thus gave the country of his adoption 'first refusal', but he did not forget the city of his birth. The portrait hangs today – one of Sargent's masterpieces – in the National Portrait Gallery in London.

He had felt so many times in his life that the world did not want his art and did not recognize his genius. But on this day he was given a full measure of the world's affection. Lucy Clifford, one of James's most cherished friends, wrote to Scribner's,

we have just had a high jubilation over Henry James's birthday, given him an address, a really beautiful golden bowl. I went to see him on the great morning and found him bewildered – his staircase a sort of highway for messengers and telegraph boys carrying messages, wonderful flowers arriving, the telephone bell going like mad; his faithful servants standing on their heads, and a general effect of joy, congratulations, and delightful lunacy. I happen to adore him very much, so after an hour of it, I carried him off to lunch peacefully at my club and then returned him to the rejoicings at his flat.

Opening the *Pall Mall Gazette* on that day the Master found in it an editorial entitled 'Henry James'. The newspaper spoke of the 'spontaneous impulse' of James's innumerable friends in England and on the Continent but 'thousands of others who will only hear of it today, will be with the participants in their hearts'. The editorial referred to James's 'immense achievement' and the appearance at this moment of *A Small Boy and Others*. It expressed the wish that 'this keen observer, very great artist, and brilliant and generous critic of men and manners, may, in the best of health and the fulness of power, enjoy many more birthdays; and that that great delight, "a new book by Henry James," may be often in store for the public in the future'. In an age of 'much hurry, superficiality, and meanness', said the editorial, it had been shown that 'a great and deliberate artist and a generous spirit can still win its proud and affectionate recognition.'

The name of Edith Wharton was not in the list of subscribers because the committee had known of her separate initiative and had not approached her; but James added her name afterwards and that of Walter Berry, and he quietly added the names of a few others who had been informed too late or who were not known to the committee when the appeal went out. He did this because he had decided to print and send to the donors a formal letter of thanks, and added all the names at the bottom of the letter. Later he arranged for the donors to receive a photograph of the Sargent portrait signed on the left by Sargent and on the right by himself. Sargent's name has all but faded from such of these as survive; but James's name, with its customary largeness and boldness, remains visible.

All of James's epistolary art is in the letter of thanks. 'Dear Friends All,' he began, 'let me acknowledge with boundless pleasure, the singularly generous and beautiful letter, signed by your great and dazzling array and reinforced by a correspondingly bright material gage, which reached me on my recent birthday, April 15th.' It had moved him 'as brave gifts and benedictions can only do when they come as signal surprises. I seem to wake up to an air of breathing good-will the full sweetness of which I had never yet tasted.' He had been drawn to London, he wrote, long years before, by the sense 'of all the interest and association I should find here, and now I see how my faith was to sink deeper foundations that I could presume ever to measure.' It was wonderful to count over 'your dear and distinguished friendly names, taking in all they recall and represent, that I permit myself to feel at once highly successful and extremely proud'. His friends and admirers 'making one rich tone of your many voices', told him 'the whole story of my social experience ... there is scarce one of your ranged company but makes good some happy train and flushes with some individual colour'.

The list of names is a roll call of splendour in the annals of the arts, politics, and the social life of the time. The nobility of England and the Rye neighbours; James's physicians; the personalities of the stage, a great many novelists; one notes the absence of Conrad and Hardy, who may have been overlooked when the appeal went out. His French friends, however, were not forgotten.

2

James posed that spring for Sargent in his studio, about a dozen times. Sargent painted him in a characteristic pose, his left thumb catching his striped and elegant waistcoat. He is wearing a bow tie and starched collar, and the watch chain dangles across the ample embonpoint at the lower end of the picture. On the strong hand holding the waistcoat may be seen the topaz ring James had worn for many years, an American ring, probably a family heirloom. For the rest, the picture fades into chiaroscuro, since Sargent painted always from dark to light; the full highlight accentuates the great forehead, as Pound describes it in the Cantos, the eyes half closed as if in the middle of thought, but with all their visual acuteness, which so many of his contemporaries had described; and the lips are formed as if the Master were about to speak. In every way it was a portrait of power and mastery so that some disliked it, feeling that it looked more like a painting of a corporation president or a titan of finance. Beyond the portliness Sargent has conveyed the sensitivity of the Master. James is caught in one of the moments of his greatness – that is a moment of 'authority'. He felt this as he saw himself take form on the canvas. He was a patient sitter but Sargent had him invite friends to talk to him and distract him while he was being painted 'to break the spell of a settled gloom in my countenance'. Jocelyn Persse was summoned; and also the young Ruth Draper, freshly descended on London from America to do her inimitable monologues at that time in some of the great houses. James was fascinated by her from the first. 'Little Ruth is a dear of dears,' he wrote, 'and her talent has really an extraordinary charm.' Inspired by her work he wrote a monologue for her which, however, she never performed, for she always created her own. James greatly enjoyed his sittings in Sargent's high cool studio which opened on a balcony and a green Chelsea garden. He found himself saying that he looked more and more like Sir Joshua's Dr Johnson, and others who saw the picture had the same impression – certainly it was true of the massiveness of the figure if not of the features – James's having a delicacy not visible in the coarser face of the eighteenth-century's literary dictator. To Rhoda Broughton, James wrote that the picture was

Sargent at his very best and poor old H.J. not at his worst; in short a living breathing likeness and a masterpiece of painting. I am really quite ashamed to admire it so much and so loudly it's so much as if I were calling attention to my own fine points. I don't, alas, exhibit a 'point' in it, but am all large and luscious rotundity – by which you may see how true a thing it is.

Since the picture had been commissioned, in effect, by some 300 persons, Sargent held a special showing of it in his studio in December 1913 during three consecutive days. This provided the novelist with an opportunity to thank the donors personally. They flocked to see portrait and subject in great numbers and 'I really put myself on exhibition beside it,' James wrote to Gosse, 'each of the days, morning and afternoon, and the translation (a perfect Omar Khayyam, *quoi*!) visibly left the original nowhere'. It had been an 'exquisite incident ... most beautiful and flawless'. The work was acclaimed 'with an unanimity of admiration, and literally, of *intelligence*, that I can testify to'.

108

The Ebbing Time

THE following spring – early in May 1914 – an elderly white-haired woman, placid-looking and wearing a loose purple cloak, entered the rooms of the Royal Academy in London. It was the opening day of the spring show. She walked from room to room until she came to Room III. Here she found the portrait by John Singer Sargent of Henry James. It was attracting much attention in the press. Suddenly those in the room heard the sound of shattering glass. The peaceable-looking lady was wielding with vigour a meat-cleaver she had concealed beneath the purple cloak. Several women pounced on her – but already Sargent's masterpiece had in it three ugly gashes. She had cut through the left side of the head, the right side of the mouth and below the right shoulder. A man who attempted to defend the violent lady from the irate women had his glasses broken. The police arrived promptly.

At the station the woman gave her name as Mrs Mary Wood. She had never heard of Henry James. Her assault on the picture was for reasons that had nothing to do with the novelist or with Sargent. She was explicit in police court that day. A militant suffragette, she said that she had read that the picture was valued at £700. A woman painter, she said, would not have received anywhere near such a sum. She wished 'to show the public that they have no security for their property, nor for their art treasures, until women are given their political freedom'.

'Academy Outrage,' the newspaper headlines screamed. In jail Mrs Woods went on a hunger-and-thirst strike and after a few days was released. Edmund Gosse wrote a letter to *The Times* saying it had been a 'horrible' outrage since the picture had been 'the emblem of private affection and regard' for a great artist – a great man 'who has nothing to do with politics'.

'Most gentle friend,' Henry James wrote to Goody Allen after the onslaught, 'I naturally feel very scalped and disfigured, but you will be glad to know that I seem to be pronounced curable ... The damage, in other words, isn't past praying for, or rather past mending, given the magic of the modern mender's art.' His table was strewn, he said, with 390 kind notes of condolence. The suffragette had only caused him to receive, less than a year after his 70th birthday, still another ovation. To William Roughead, the Edinburgh jurist, with whom James had been having a lively correspondence about old Scottish murder trials, the Master wrote that it was a sad fact that all that could be done was 'to lock the stable door after the horse is stolen'. The 'smash of an object really precious to the general mind' should be acclaimed only 'for the light and wisdom and reason that they shall bring to our councils'.

To Howells, James was less urbane. 'Those ladies really outrage humanity, and the public patience has to me a very imbecile side.' Another portrait had been hacked with a chopper on the day he was writing – such events being contagious – 'and the work goes bravely on'. The Sargent portrait was repaired before the end of the month and exhibited under watchful guard.

I

Henry James remained in London until late in the spring of 1913 in order to pose for his bust. A few days before his scheduled departure for Rye, he felt ill, went to bed and lost consciousness. He had never had a fainting spell and it frightened him. 'I was *consciously* sure I was dying,' he said. His doctor brought in a nurse; within twenty-four hours the Master – after a 'wretched time' – was able to have lunch at home with his nephew Harry; Peggy James and Fanny Prothero came at once to give him support. His specialist, Dr Des Voeux, was 'very reassuring and interesting' James noted in his date-book. He said the novelist had '*very* great powers of recuperation'. Heartened James left as he had planned for Lamb House accompanied by his niece. He had begun to restrict his activities even before this brief illness. He had once described the predicament of a novelist who feels the world shrinking (in *The Middle Years*); the novelist muses that 'he was better of course, but better, after all than what? He should never again, as at one or two great moments of the past, be better than himself. The infinite of life was gone, and what remained of the dose was a small glass scored like a thermometer by the apothecary.'

'The evening of life is difficult,' James wrote. He tried to see it 'as much as I can by exemptions and simplifications'. He told his niece that if he let himself go, he would find it sad to think there were well-loved places on this earth 'that I have said good-bye to forever, shall never see again'. To Hugh Walpole he wrote, 'I grow relentlessly older and you shamelessly younger,' but he added 'let us keep the possibility just enough *ahead* of the difficulty'. He maintained his old way of life in Rye. He spent his three hours in the garden room every morning; with Peggy James he took his long walks in the afternoon, even if the pace was less lively. And visitors came and went. Peggy met Mrs Wharton and Mrs Cadwalader Jones and found both 'formidable'. She wrote to her mother that her uncle had no illusions about Mrs Wharton 'he merely takes the good part of her and is thankful'. Amy Lowell, representative of the new poetry, came in her massive weight, smoked her cigars and was 'very noisy and amusing'. Logan Pearsall Smith had a week-end at Lamb House.

They had never known each other well. Logan would greatly exaggerate their friendship. 'The tide of gossip between us rose high, he being a great master of that effect,' said James. Logan was especially lurid about the elderly stout Constance Fletcher, James's old friend, and he would have an elaborate anecdote about her adventures in a bath-tub in Lamb House from which, because of her obesity, she could not extricate herself. On another occasion, in the last year of James's life, Pearsall Smith arranged for the Master to lunch with Santayana; he quoted James as saying he would walk barefoot through the snow to meet the philosopher. Actually what James had written was that he 'prized' Santayana's mind and style and 'I wish greatly he sometimes came to London'. Santayana spoke of the meeting. 'In that one interview,' he wrote, James 'made me feel more at home and better understood than his brother William ever had done in the long years of our acquaintance. Henry was calm, he liked to see things as they are, and be free afterwards to imagine how they might have been.' Other visitors that summer were Joseph Conrad, 'poor queer man', who came to Lamb House for lunch, and Bernard Shaw and Granville Barker. James shocked Shaw by kissing him on both cheeks. Shaw in turn impressed Peggy by telling her 'never do unto others as you would that they should do unto you; their tastes may not be the same'. G.B.S. was quoting himself out of his handbook for revolutionists.

Wells's new novel *The Passionate Friends* arrived and James read it. His letters of criticism was as sharp as always. He had for a long time been giving Wells private full-dress reviews of each book. Almost as if he were addressing young Hugh, and not the experienced Wells, James said he found him 'perverse' and 'on a whole side, unconscious, as I can only call it, but my point is that *with* this heart-breaking leak even sometimes so nearly playing the devil with the boat your talent remains so savoury and what you do substantial. I adore a rounded objectivity.' James objected to Wells's use of the autobiographical form. He had said this many times before – the use of the first person led to too much fluidity, brought in too many extraneous elements. Wells, whether in irony or truth, replied that

my art is abortion – on the shelves of my study stand a little vain-gloriously thirty-odd premature births ... But it is when you write to me out of your secure and masterly *finish*, out of your golden globe of leisurely (yet not slow) and infinitely *easy* accomplishment that the sense of my unworthiness and rawness is most vivid. Then indeed I want to embrace your feet and bedew your knees with tears – of quite unfruitful penitence.

To Walpole James said that this reply showed Wells 'profusely extravagantly apologetic and profoundly indifferent'. He added that artistically Wells had 'gone to the dogs. They all seem to me money-grabbers pure and simple, naked and unashamed; and Arnold Bennett now with an indecency, verily, an obscenity of nudity!'

Toward the end of the summer Peggy became mildly critical of her uncle – he seemed to her concerned too much with people and had not sufficiently 'Dad's quality' of giving a 'spiritual or speculative turn' to things. 'For the first time,' Peggy (now 26) said, 'Uncle Henry seems to me to be a thoroughly *unreal* person. All that he says, and his manner of saying it, is pirouetting and prancing, and beating the air, very charmingly, but still once in a while you crave a strong simple note. And yet strong it certainly is too.' She was echoing her father. Her uncle, perhaps sensing her feelings, said to her 'I hate the American simplicity. I glory in the piling up of complications of every sort. If I could pronounce the name James in any different and more elborate way I should be in favour of doing it.'

2

That autumn in London James received from André Raffalovich a volume of Aubrey Beardsley's last letters, edited by Father John Gray.

I knew him a little, and he was himself to my vision touching, and extremely individual; but I hated his productions and thought them extraordinarily base – and couldn't find (perhaps didn't try enough to find!) the formula that reconciled this baseness, aesthetically, with his being so perfect a case of the artistic spirit.

Beardsley's letters disclosed this personal spirit to James. 'The amenity, the intelligence, the patience and grace and play of mind and of temper – how charming and individual an exhibition!'

James had a fairly decent winter in 1913–14. Van Wyck Brooks remembered a glimpse of the novelist at a lecture given by Georg Brandes over which Edmund Gosse presided. He had heard James lecture at Harvard; and now he saw him rise at the end of the evening and climb to the platform to salute Brandes. The young continued to come to James; and he took great pleasure in Compton Mackenzie's *Sinister Street*. He remembered young 'Monty' Compton (Compton Mackenzie was his writing name) as a boy, the son of Edward Compton the actor who had produced *The American*. There was perhaps this partiality of memory which led James to praise *Sinister Street*. He made Hugh Walpole jealous. Then the second volume came out and James had to climb down. But he continued to write affectionate letters to Mackenzie, who in his late years, like Pearsall Smith, like Hueffer, like so many others, had his hoard of cherished and embellished anecdotes to build the 'legend' of the Master.

In the spring of 1914 James showed an active interest in the plight of Robert Ross, Oscar Wilde's friend and executor. Ross had, in the years since Wilde's death, slowly rebuilt the reputation of his friend, and brought the Wilde estate from bankruptcy to stability. He was avowedly homosexual, but enjoyed the friendship of the literary world, not least of Gosse and it was with the latter that James gossiped about Ross as he had about Symonds long ago. Ross was now suing Lord Alfred Douglas for libel, a repetition as it were of the Wilde case itself, but in a new and less exercised age. Behind the trial there were old animosities and old jealousies. It was, said James, an 'infamous history' but he felt haunted by Robbie Ross's 'demoralized state'. The thing was, he wrote to Hugh, 'to try to help him to keep his head and stiffen his heart'.

Early in 1914 James went to lunch with A. B. Walkley, the drama critic of *The Times*, whose work he admired. Walkley wanted him to meet Henry Bernstein, the French dramatist. Bernstein talked to James of a new writer across the channel named Marcel Proust and of his novel *Du Côté de Chez Swann*. He promised to send the book, just published. When he didn't, James accepted a copy from Edith Wharton; he received it, acknowleged its arrival, said he could not at the moment read it. We do not know whether he did. There is no evidence save Mrs Wharton's remark that 'his letter to me shows how deeply it impressed him'. Beyond the letter saying he would read *Swann*, no other letter mentioning Proust has survived.

3

James had dispatched the manuscript of *Notes of a Son and Brother* before leaving Rye late in the fall of 1913. This left him free for other work. He had promised Bruce Richmond, the editor of *The Times Literary Supplement* an article on 'the new novel' and this he now wrote. It was so long that it appeared in two instalments – entitled 'The Younger Generation'. It dealt with the generation younger than James, but certainly not the youngest save for Hugh Walpole, Compton Mackenzie and Gilbert Canaan. It revealed the old and vigororus James, but it might be said that for the first and only time in his long critical career he had not read all the novels carefully nor surveyed the entire horizon. His most remembered lapse was his speaking of D. H. Lawrence's *Sons and Lovers* as a novel that might be mentioned 'should we wish to be *very* friendly to Mr Lawrence'. In reality the entire article seems to have been a failure in discernment if not in power. He began by wanting to say publicly why he disliked Wells and Bennett whose money-opportunism he deplored – that is their willingness to compromise art; then he found himself wanting to say something approvingly about Conrad's *Chance*, and he had at last an opportunity to praise Mrs Wharton for he had liked *Ethan Frome*, and commended *The Reef* – writing her a letter comparing it to Racine – and had been delighted by the satire of *The Custom of the Country*. Then he wanted to be nice to Hugh, in his old way, and to pat young Monty Mackenzie on the back. The mixed motives of the article made it a grab-bag of comment; the old lessons of the master are repeated, but the attack is principally on the *saturated* novel, of which Tolstoy was the supreme example, and Wells and Bennett lesser English counterparts. His image for them was that of the squeezing of the sponge dry (sometimes he changed the sponge to an orange), an image to which he often returned. Thus James brought his criticism of Wells into the open; this may have been in part due to the fact that Wells, two years earlier, in a lecture on 'The Scope of the Novel' had denied that the novel could be an aesthetic and artistic end in itself; in effect offering another version of Shaw's criticism of James in the theatre. Shortly after, James had insisted at the Royal Society of Literature that Wells be elected, saying that it was difficult to vote for other candidates so long as his particular talent was not represented. Wells, to James's surprise, declined election : he wasn't going to allow himself to be voted into the Establishment. After a private talk with Wells, James wrote to Gosse that Wells 'has cut himself loose from literature clearly – practically altogether'.

In his article James described Wells and Bennett as squeezing 'to the utmost the plump and more or less juicy orange of a particularly acquainted state'. They 'let this affirmation of energy, however directed or undirected, constitute for them the "treatment" of the theme'. Tolstoy, James argued, was 'the great illustrative master-hand on all this ground of disconnection of method from matter'. He repeated what he had said both publicly and privately, that the Russian master stood as 'a caution' and only 'execrably, pestilentially, as a model'. Just as there was no 'centre of interest' or sense of the whole in *War and Peace* so there was none in *The Old Wives' Tale* or *The Passionate Friends*. The reader was left with the simple amusement of watching the orange being squeezed.

We have already seen how deeply Conrad was disturbed by the passages devoted to him. Hugh, whose youth rather than his work was praised, felt that he had got off lightly; the other young men were pleased to have some notice, and Mrs Wharton could not but derive satisfaction at having finally had public acclaim from the man she so intensely admired. All the English novelists of the time read the article and many felt themselves ignored; the title 'younger' generation exempted Hardy, but then James had dealt with Conrad, who was certainly no longer young, and whose reputation dated from the 1890s. The Master, undisturbed, had had his say. He revised the article and gathered it in with the series of brilliant and definitive essays he had written on Balzac, Flaubert, Zola, and George Sand earlier in the century. The book was his last critical collection. He called it *Notes on Novelists*.

109

The Ivory Tower

PUBLICATION of *Notes of a Son and Brother* on 7 March 1914 was the occasion for many new tributes to Henry James and letters from old friends. All were moved by the pages in the book devoted to the memory of Minny Temple, his long-dead cousin. She had always been James's 'heroine of the scene'. He had lately re-read his own letters to his mother on the death of Milly; and he used letters she had written to John Gray, the lawyer, who had ended his career in the Harvard Law School. These were sent to him by Gray's widow. As always James retouched the letters; but his revisions were sparse. A note Harry made in his own copy of the book casts a particular light on these pages.

Everything said about [Minny] by H.J. seems to me to be as appropriate as possible to W.J. allowing for differences of sex. They were clearly chips of the same block. It is as if time and distance had enabled H.J. to see in her and to describe traits conspicuous to me in W.J. which he doesn't refer to in his allusions to his brother.

We might speculate that the love that Henry had for William – but could not offer or express because William so stubbornly would not accept it – found its expression in the book of memory: there was also in Minny something boyish, vigorous, passionate. She had been for Henry long ago cousin, brother, sister, sweetheart, all in one. She had burned herself out in the flames of her own intensities. Whatever the truths of this long-ago relation, it is clear that Minny Temple remained, as James had predicted in his 29th year, a living figure within 'the crystal walls of the past'. Now he had placed her at the very centre of his and his brother's early lives. It was true, he had said then, that he did not love her. He *adored* her – he worshipped her. She had been a Diana in the temple of his life; and he had offered his genius to her memory – and in doing so offered it also to his brother.

Such were some of the psychological complexities and ambiguities of Henry James. Henry Adams, reading the book, which James sent him promptly, had other feelings. His memory went back to the old years; his wife, Clover Hooper, had belonged to that period – and he looked across the decades with the dry pessimism of his old age. 'I've read Henry James's last bundle of memories which have reduced me to a pulp,' Adams wrote to Mrs Cameron. 'Why did we live? Was that all? ... Poor Henry James thinks it all real, I believe, and actually still lives in that dreamy, stuffy Newport and Cambridge, with papa James and Charles Norton.' Henry Adams embodied these feelings in a letter to the novelist which does not seem to have survived. James's reply, however, was an elegant and highly documentary expression of the new-found emotional energies of his old age. In spite of illness and reduced activity and much suffering, all vestiges of his old depression seem to have left him. He wanted to live; he was determined to take from life all that it would offer him.

He had received, he said, Adams's 'melancholy outpouring'. The only way to acknowledge it was to recognize 'its unmitigated blackness'.

Of course we are lone survivors, of course the past that was our lives is at the bottom of an abyss – if the abyss *has* any bottom; of course, too, there's no use talking unless one particularly *wants* to. But the purpose, almost, of my printed divagations was to show you that one *can*, strange to say, still want to – or at least can behave as if one did.

He went on to say that he found his consciousness still interesting 'under *cultivation* of the interest'. Why it yielded the interest, he did not know. He wasn't challenging it or quarrelling with it – he was encouraging it 'with a ghastly grin'.

You see I still, in presence of life (or of what you deny to be such), have reactions – as many as possible – and the book I sent you is proof of them. It's, I suppose, because I am that queer monster, the artist, an obstinate finality, an inexhaustible sensibility. Hence the reactions – appearance, memories, many things, go on playing upon it with consequence that I note and 'enjoy' (grim word!) noting. It all takes doing – and I *do*. I believe I shall do yet again – it is still an act of life.

I

Old, tired, Henry James continued to perform the acts of life and nothing showed this more than his last writings. *The Finer Grain*, his volume of tales of 1910, assembled just before his brother's death, and the novel he was trying to write, subsidized by Edith Wharton, which he called *The Ivory Tower*, contain new subjects derived from his two visits to America. The stories, nearly all set in New York, and the fragment of the novel set in Newport and Manhattan have within them recurrent themes. In effect James was saying that certain members of the American wealthy had too much wealth; that this wealth was corrupting – and corruption; and that he had been robbed of his national birthright. The theme of his tale *A Round of Visits* and of *The Ivory Tower* is of Americans who inherit great wealth only to have it stolen by other Americans. The American world was a great predatory competitive world; and

James, had he had the strength would have completed – as some critics have held – one of his finest novels. The title of *The Finer Grain*, as he explained in a memorandum he wrote for his English publisher, was supposed to suggest 'the finer grain of accessibility to suspense or curiosity, to mystification or attraction – in other words, to moving experience'. His heroes are sentient, perceptive, reflective, and engaged in 'the personal adventure'. But what the sentience reflected was an anger more fully expressed than in earlier works. A single paragraph in the story *Crapy Cornelia* contains James's vision of America :

This was clearly going to be the music of the future – that if people were but rich enough and furnished enough and fed enough, exercised and sanitated and manicured and generally advised and advertised and made 'knowing' enough, *avertis* enough, as the term appeared to be nowadays in Paris, all they had to do for civility was to take the amused ironic view of those who might be less initiated. In *his* time, when he was young or even when he was only but a little less middle-aged, the best manners had been the best kindness, and the best kindness had mostly been some art of not insisting on one's luxurious differences, of concealing rather, for common humanity, if not for common decency, a part at least of the intensity or the ferocity with which one might be 'in the know'.

The women particularly in these tales are devoid of all sympathy; fat, ugly, rich, cruel, they seem to have lost the meaning of kindness. Civilization, as he had shown in his three large novels, had many masks and it was by its masks that it could survive. What one can read above all in these final stories is a picture of the crass money side of Edith Wharton's world – in effect a sense of America's betrayal of its own original high civilization.

2

The Ivory Tower was to have been written in ten books and in the manner of *The Awkward Age* – that is each section was to have been devoted to a different character, and the whole designed to illuminate the central situation. That situation seemed as fantasy to be a continuation of *The Jolly Corner*, the question of what America did to individuals and what one 'escaped' by being in Europe. If *The Golden Bowl* enabled Henry James to return and claim his American heritage, *The Ivory Tower* questioned the worth of the heritage – implied that someone had absconded with its riches. The novel has in it no sign of James's old age save that the images are over-weighted and the prose is heavy and 'difficult', shot through with the symbolic imagery he had been cultivating ever since *The Wings of the Dove. The Ivory Tower* combines the themes of his last three novels – the American innocent, called here Graham Fielder, who, however, returns to America rather than live in Paris; the couple in love, Horton ('Haughty') Vint and Cissy Foy, like Kate Croy and Merton Densher, who cannot marry and plot to obtain the millions Fielder inherits from his uncle. In the opening scenes we have the old rivalries of James's works re-expressed in two former business partners who are both dying – of their millions – full of guilt and unforgiveness. One partner bears the Biblical name of the archetypal rival – Abel; and as in *Roderick Hudson* the Cain figure seems to be regarded as the better of the two; James gives him, indeed, the name of Betterman. Possessed of the riches of their lives, they seem adumbrations of William and Henry James at the end of time, with their intellectual and artistic capital. They are even rivals in the process of dying; Abel Gaw wants to outlive Betterman but dies of a stroke when he learns that his former friend has improved – a symbolic rehearsal of the Cain and Abel story. The great scene that survives is the interview between Betterman and Fielder in the second part of the novel, in which Fielder is judged sufficiently innocent and worthy to inherit the huge fortune – which he is not sure he wants. The stage for this interview is set by Gaw's daughter Rosanna, the Jamesian heiress now revived as an obese good-natured woman who has loved Fielder from the days of her young years in Europe. She now plays 'angel' to him as Ralph Touchett did to Isabel in *The Portrait of a Lady*.

All the Jamesian ingredients were present as James planned this novel, re-working an old theme found among his papers he had called 'The K.B. Case' – an allusion to Mrs Bronson of Venice and C.F. – probably the other Venetian of his later years, Constance Fletcher, who had some of Rosanna's rotundity. If the ingredients are familiar the background is new. The novel would have been the story of a year, like Henry's own year in America in 1904–5. From Newport it would move to New York and later to the world of Edith Wharton at Lenox. What James intended to bring into this novel was the 'money-passion', the spirit of 'ferocious acquisition'. The question was whether a life built on such gains was any life at all. Christopher Newman had been proud of his 'pile', but he had talked of thousands. James's rich now talk of millions. The central symbol of the novel is the ivory tower, an *objet d'art* in which Fielder chooses to place an unread document left him by Gaw, the betterman's rival. He had been offered a cigar case but rejected it as wrong – doubtless too symbolic of the wealth about which he has such misgivings. The ivory tower is represented as 'the most distinguished retreat' – from commerce, from sex, from all the turbulence and passion of this world. In his own way, Fielder is suggesting that the American values – the accumulation of money – are not his values; the ivory tower, or Europe, was perhaps the only way to escape the curse and guilt of wealth. In a sense therefore *The Ivory Tower* is not the pagoda of *The Golden Bowl*. The pagoda was a symbol of innocence and escape from reality; the ivory tower was a symbol of conscious withdrawal from reality looked in the face. And in *The Ivory Tower* James projected also his chorus-like Assinghams of the *Bowl*; here they would have been the Bradhams.

James's last novel was emerging as an apologia for his own life; it would have denounced with all the delicacy and subtlety of his style, the world of the American rich which he had seen, at Biltmore, at Lenox, in Washington in the great houses of New York and in the palaces at Newport: a richness so gross and devoid of the humane that he had fled back to England never to return. He had reclaimed his American heritage, but he seems to have felt it wasn't worth reclaiming. 'You seem all here so hideously rich,' says his hero.

3

James wrote Howells who urged him to return in May of 1914 for still another visit to the United States, 'I don't like to frequent the U.S. ... weigh *prosperity* against posterity ... That autumn, winter and spring (1910–11) which I spent in Cambridge and New York – well, I shall go down to my grave without having breathed to another ear what I went through with then.' And to Alice James his sister-in-law he had written a year earlier:

Dearest Alice, I could come back to America (could be carried back on a stretcher) to *die* – but never, never to live ... but when I think of how little Boston and Cambridge were of old ever *my* affair, or anything but an accident, for me, of the parental life there, to which I occasionally

and painfully and losingly sacrificed, I have a superstitious terror of seeing them at the end of time again stretch out strange individual tentacles
to draw me back and destroy me ... You see my capital – yielding all
my income, intellectual, social, associational, on the old investment of
so many years – my capital is *here*, and to let it all slide would be simply
to become bankrupt.

   The Ivory Tower re-created the old myths of Henry James's life
in what would have been a dense and powerfully conceived work.
Even in the fragment we can discern the shapes of strong highly
individualized characters, the American versions of Cain and Abel,
of Jacob and Esau, of rapacity and violence and greed. James was
drawing upon the oldest material he possessed – tales of treachery
and fraternal humiliation. And the crowning irony was that as he
worked innocently on this book, he could not know that it had been
secretly subsidized by the very kind of wealth – and treachery – he
condemned.

110

A Wreck of Belief

THE year 1914 began for Henry James with the extraction of most
of his teeth, 'the wounds, the inconvenience, the humiliations', not
to speak of the effects of the anaesthetic. He relied heavily now on
nitroglycerine tablets for his heart discomfort; he spoke frequently
of his 'desiccated antiquity'. In the midst of the dentistry, however,
he had told Henry Adams to cultivate an interest in life; and he was
vigorous enough that spring to welcome again and entertain his
niece and his youngest nephew and be highly critical of their American companions. Peggy had with her in Europe this time a young
lady he believed to have had the kind of background about which
he had written so often in his fiction. She was like Daisy Miller, a
product of the permissive vacuity of a childhood without direction.
James had pity, he said, 'for a poor young creature whose elders
and home-circle have handed her over, uncivilized, untutored, un-
advised, and unenlightened to such a fool's paradise of ignorance
and fatuity'. He was no less concerned about the boon companion of
his nephew, who was silent and unsociable, with no grace of communication and no subject but athletics – and he discoursed at great

length about the cultural environment William James had created for his young and the environment from which these other young Americans had come. They had affluence, a large measure of it, but no enlightenment.

He had seen Edith Wharton in recent weeks; the previous autumn he had found she had lost her 'harassed look'; a few weeks later he saw her as 'a figure of entire unmitigated *agitation*'. Still, she was 'so clever, powerful, and stimulating that I think one forgives her very much'. For the rest, he kept up his social life and Peggy noted the general level of his strength was better than the previous year. His date-book of the spring of 1914 shows him as active and as observant as of old. Thus on 25 March he goes to the London Zoo, with Mrs Sutro, conveyed there in her motor 'we walked about a long time to my benefit; then to tea at Mrs S's'. On 28 March he joins Lucy Clifford and Ethel Dilke in a box at the Vaudeville Theatre for 'deplorably platitudinous performance – dramatization of Arnold Bennett; drove her home and then came by apartment and had tea (5.30) with Emily Sargent. Dined with Lady Lovelace 8.15.' The next day he lunches with Owen Lankester in Upper Wimpole Street, goes to an art exhibition and pays a call on Lady Courteney. He still had his London life.

A note of 3 April in his appointment book records however,

Bad days: climax of the long effect of privation of exercise – more intense demonstration of imperative need of sacrificing *everything* to this boon ... Long resolute walk from Piccadilly Circus down to Westminster and thence all along the Embankment to the corner of Chelsea Barracks and Hospital Road. I was more than three hours – nearer four – on foot – the length of the effort was the effective benefit – and this benefit was signal. I broke the hideous spell of settled *sickness*, which had become too cruel for words – and if I haven't now learned the lesson – ! I worked in consequence well again yesterday (Friday) forenoon; but renewed my locomotion in due measure again in the afternoon. That is I called on Rhoda Broughton but walked both there and back – with better and better effect.

His niece provided him with company for his walks. They went to the cinema and to the Royal Academy where Peggy saw the Sargent portrait and teased her uncle for wearing 'exact clothes ... watch chain, waistcoat and tie, so that every eye ... was rivetted to him'. They dined at the Philip Morrells', Prime Minister Asquith being present. The uncle took Peggy and her companion to the House of

Commons for the third reading of the Home Rule Bill, the government obtaining a majority. He took Lady Ottoline, Morrell's wife, home. 'Rather historic occasion,' he noted.

The Master stayed in London into July and on the 14th he went to Lamb House. A long entry in his appointment book of 30 July begins with his trying to remember the date on which he sent Ellen Terry his one-act play of 1895; he then recalls his stay in Torquay, when he got the idea of *The Ambassadors* from Jonathan Sturges. 'Oh the full De Vere Gardens days of those years!' he writes and remembers how he began dictating to the typewriter in 1897. He then notes, with some minuteness, all his comings and goings of that summer but breaks off in the middle. There is no further entry until 4 August. On that day he scrawls: 'Everything blackened over for the time blighted by the hideous Public situation. This is (Monday) the August Bank Holiday but with horrible suspense and the worst possibilities in the air. Peggy and Aleck came down on Saturday to stay.'

I

The coming of the war was, for Henry James, 'a nightmare from which there is no waking save by sleep'. Later he would say that it 'almost killed me. I loathed so having lived on and on into anything so hideous and horrible.' The letters which he wrote during the early days of August – days of blandness and blueness at Rye – are among the most eloquent of his life. He pictured himself dipping his nose into the inkpot 'but it's as if there were no ink there and I take it out smelling gunpowder, smelling blood, as hard as it did before'. He believed civilization had collapsed totally into barbarism and that this had turned his life into a gross lie. 'I write you under the black cloud of portentous events on this side of the world, horrible, unspeakable, iniquitous things – I mean horrors of war criminally, infamously precipitated.' Thus to his old Newport friend Margaret La Farge. 'These are monstrous miseries for *us*, of our generation and age, to live into; but we wouldn't not have lived – and yet this is what we get by it. I try to think it will be *interesting* – but have only got so far as to feel it sickening.' To Edith Wharton in Paris he wrote in some anxiety, for he had had no news of her. She had been on the verge of a motor tour in Spain, with Walter Berry – 'even like another George Sand and another Chopin'. Now he wrote her (on 6 August) of 'this crash of our civilization. The only gleam in the blackness, to me, is the action and the absolute unanimity of this country.'

However, it was to the old irascible and undividedly British Rhoda Broughton, whom he had known for so many years, that he poured out his deepest anguish.

Black and hideous to me is the tragedy that gathers and I'm sick beyond cure to have lived on to see it. You and I, the ornaments of our generation should have been spared this wreck of our belief that through the long years we had seen civilization grow and the worst become impossible. The tide that bore us along was then all the while moving to *this* as its grand Niagara – yet what a blessing we didn't know it. It seems to me to *undo* everything, everything that was ours, in the most horrible retroactive way – but I avert my face from the monstrous scene.

He could not avert his face. He had always lived too close to the realities behind human illusion. He felt that the exquisite summer mocked him. The 'shining indifference' of nature chilled his heart. 'Never were desperate doings so blandly lighted up.' He had been betrayed. All that he had done, the little private adventures that he had chronicled were suddenly 'so utterly blighted by the public'. His mind went back to the other war, the Civil War, and Mr Lincoln's call to arms. He remembered the hushed crowds and the solemnity; for a while everyone seemed to walk on tip-toe. Now everything moved with extraordinary speed. James awoke each day to find the same light, the same air, the same sea and the sky, 'the most beautiful English summer conceivable'. This was 'the sole, the exquisite England, whose weight now hangs in the balance'. He had remained an American all his years. Now he began to speak of 'we' and 'us'. His imagination could not encompass the horrors. 'I go to sleep, as if I were dog-tired with action,' he wrote to Mrs Wharton, 'yet feel like the chilled *vieillards* in the old epics, infirm and helpless at home with the women, while the plains are ringing with battle.'

Mrs Wharton was in Paris when Belgium was invaded; she came over to England and visited James briefly at Rye. Peggy found 'a cleverness and insight and economy of words about her that is masterly'. She liked in particular the fact that Mrs Wharton was 'tactful and non-fatiguing' for her uncle. James felt unwell; he had a spell of illness in late August. He ate little; his nerves remained on edge. But he summoned all his strength and in September began to

speak of returning to London. He couldn't work. He found it difficult to read. He wanted to mitigate 'the huge tension and oppression' of the Sussex solitude. He described himself as living under
'the funeral spell of our murdered civilization'. He wanted to be
nearer to some source of information and contact. His old need for
action was strong; his sense of drive and power remained in spite of
his infirmities. In the days before his departure, his restlessness was
increased by the war activities in Rye; the local enlistments, the
drilling of recruits, the continual marching of men. Then Burgess
announced he was joining up. He was sturdy and athletic, a bantamweight fit for military service. His master gave him his blessing.
'It's like losing an arm or a leg,' James wrote to Mrs Wharton. She
promptly sent one of her menservants, Frederick, to help James for
the time being. James wrote to Burgess, 'I see you are going to make
a first-rate soldier and nothing could give me greater pleasure.' His
job would be kept for him; James hoped he would visit him during
his leaves. 'If it's *socks* you will throughout most want, I will keep
you supplied,' James wrote in his most maternal vein; he also kept
Burgess supplied with goodies and pocket change.

Two or three nights before James's departure from Rye the first
Belgian refugees arrived, assigned to the small Catholic congregation of the town. James had offered his Watchbell Street studio as a
gathering place. They were awaited all day, from train to train. In
the evening a sound of voices made the Master go to his door at the
top of the winding street. Over the grass-grown cobbles came the
procession of the homeless. 'It was swift and eager, in the autumn
darkness,' the Master would write, 'and under the flare of a single
lamp – with no vociferation and, but for a woman's, scarce a sound
save the shuffle of mounting feet and the thick-drawn breath of
emotion.' James saw a young mother carrying her child. He heard
'the resonance through our immemorial old street of her sobbing'.
History had reached his doorstep.

III

Soldiers

EVEN before he left Rye, James heard from Hugh. It was a brief letter and it hold him that he was leaving for Russia. Hugh had been turned down by the Army; he was helpless without his glasses. But the thought of inaction was as painful to him as to the Master. 'Think of me as I cross the North Sea,' Hugh wrote, 'I shall think of you continually.' James replied he was 'deeply moved', and said that Hugh – who was to be war correspondent on the eastern front for the *Daily Mail* – was showing 'the last magnificence of pluck, the finest strain of resolution'. James added, 'I bless and cheer and honour it for all I am worth.' From Jocelyn Persse came word almost at the same time. He had joined the Royal Fusiliers and was in a camp in Essex. The strenuous life, the English damp and cold, soon caught up with Jocelyn and he came down with pneumonia and was sent on sick leave. Desmond MacCarthy was among the early callers at Carlyle Mansions once the Master was reinstalled. He 'looked remarkably well and solid in his khaki'. He had joined the Red Cross and was leaving for France. This would give him much experience, said James, and 'can only contribute hereafter to his powers of conversation'.

'We must for dear life make our own counter-realities,' James wrote to Lucy Clifford. Having all his life declined to serve on committees, he immediately threw himself into Belgian relief in Chelsea; and when it was suggested that he visit Belgian wounded in St Bartholomew's Hospital because he could speak French to them, he went eagerly. Presently he was moving from bedside to bedside talking to the English wounded as well. 'I am so utterly and passionately enlisted,' he wrote to his nephew, 'up to my eyes and over my aged head in the greatness of our cause, that it fairly sickens me not to find every imagination not rise to it.' His date-book provides a record of constant visits and of aid to individual soldiers. 'Took three maimed and half-blind convalescent soldiers from St Bart's to tea 24 Bedford Square and delivered them home again.' The Protheros lived at No. 24. The next day he 'telephoned Dr Field inquiring about his attending to Private Percy Stone who has practically lost an eye'. He sends chocolates to St Bartholomew's. He visits St George's. He notes 'the deaf soldier in Harley Ward – John Willey. The others in the same ward with wounded arm.' He sends a pocket comb to one soldier, cigarettes to others. One soldier, a sapper of the Royal Engineers, found in James a loyal friend. On leaving the hospital he was invited to the Master's flat for meals; presently James arranged for him to have his teeth taken care of 'at very reduced military rates'. Sapper Williams had been a great runner; James liked his vitality. Friends of the Master wondered how the soldiers reacted to his subtle leisurely talk – but he seemed quite capable of entertaining and comforting them. He likened himself to Walt Whitman during the Civil War. It made him feel less 'finished and useless and doddering when I go on certain days and try to pull the conversational cart uphill for them'.

He had long ago written about the British soldier. Ever since his visit to a Civil War camp, where he had gone to see his younger brothers, he had had an image of men committed to heroism and to death. He was appalled by war as he had shown in his tale of *Owen Wingrave*, but thrilled to human endurance and strength. The sense of power and glory in James made him an admirer always of the soldier – 'such children of history' – and he said 'there is nothing, ever, that one wouldn't do for them'. He stopped soldiers on the street and astonished them by emptying his pockets of small change for them. He couldn't keep away from the windows of his flat if he heard the sound of a bugle, or a band, or the skirl of the bagpipe. Saturated reader of Napoleonic memoirs, admirer of the kind of action he himself had never had, he interrupts a letter to his nephew

to watch from my windows a great swinging body of the London Scottish, as one supposes, marching past at the briskest possible step with its long line of freshly enlisted men behind it. These are now in London, of course, impressions of every hour, or of every moment; but there is always a particular big thrill in the collective passage of the stridingly and just a bit flappingly kilted and bonneted when it isn't a question of mere parade or exercise, we have been used to seeing, but a suggestion, everything in the air so aiding, of a real piece of action, a charge of an irresistible press forward, on the field itself.

Of his visits to the hospitals he left a record in an essay written for a book edited by Edith Wharton to raise funds for refugees. It is called *The Book of the Homeless* and James's essay is entitled 'The

Long Wards'. In it one discerns the quick human sympathies James brought to the bedside. Certain observers might wonder what this super-subtle civilized man could offer the 'Tommies'; the essay shows the precise nature of the relations he established. James came to the soldiers not as a great writer or an admirable intellect of the age; the men probably didn't know who he was. What came through to them was his kindness, his warmth. He told himself that to sit and help them complain against fate was useless. 'The inmates of the long wards have no use for any imputed or derivative sentiments or reasons.' He did ask himself how these quiet, patient, enduring men, who seemed so amiable and now so helpless could have welcomed 'even for five minutes the stress of carnage?' And how could 'the murderous impulse at the highest pitch, have left so little distortion of the moral nature?' To ask himself these questions was to dismiss them. It was clear to him that the soldiers wanted a complete rest 'from the facing of generalizations'. Out of this, and in his characteristic way, James seems to have found the right human note 'of one's poor bedside practice'. The master of wit and irony simply fell back on the solace of small talk; and apparently with great success. His portly presence, quiet, authoritative, composed, conveyed almost in silence admiration without condescension, trust without question, an air of acceptance. All his life he had preached the thesis of 'living through' and of 'infinite doing'. Now he practised it in full measure. It gave him new reason for existence; and through the rest of 1914 and well into 1915, until recurrent illness slowed him up, he surrendered himself to the British soldier. His essay contains much reflection on the peace-time soldier, the figure he had found absent from the American cities during his recent visits to his homeland. Such soldiers were familiar to him from all the years of his European residence. The professional soldier was 'rooted in the European basis'. But even such reflections, he recognized, belonged 'to the abyss of our past delusion'. Now there was only one thing – human suffering. He did what he could.

He enlisted himself in the same way in the service of the particular American activity that arose in England during the early days of the war before America's entry which he would not live to see. He accepted the chairmanship of the American Volunteer Motor-Ambulance Corps in France. Richard Norton, the son of his old friend Charles Eliot Norton and a friend of Mrs Wharton, had thrown himself into this work, and James and Mrs Wharton were committed to help. James wrote a long letter to the American press on the nature of this endeavour. It was designed to be informative as an appeal for funds. The Corps was one of the pioneer enterprises in the new age of the motor; it helped change the care of the wounded; it made possible rapid transportation to hospitals and care centres. At first tentative and experimental, it grew rapidly in importance; and in Russia, Hugh Walpole, tired of inaction in Moscow, enlisted in the first hospital units on that front and saw action in this way – even while certain ladies in London gossiped fiercely and imputed to him an attempt to dodge military duty – a matter which enraged James.

His work among the Belgian refugees in Chelsea was recorded in an essay which also solicited contributions. It was first published in *The Times Literary Supplement*. His essay was a report – 'the statement of a neighbour and an observer deeply affected by the most tragic exhibition of national and civil prosperity and felicity suddenly subjected to bewildering outrage that it would have been possible to conceive'. The headquarters in Chelsea were in Crosby Hall, in the ancient suburban site of the garden of Sir Thomas More. Here was Chelsea's hospitality 'to the exiled, the broken, and the bewildered'. James joined their hours of relaxation which had the nature of a 'huge, comprehensive tea-party'. The Belgians seemed to James persons who had 'given up everything but patience'. They lived now from hour to hour. He brought to them the same qualities he took into hospitals.

2

With the pain – and resolution – of helping the wounded and the victims, James experienced the anguish of the wives and the widows. He scanned casualty lists, and had constant news of the decimation of youth. Clare Sheridan, daughter of Moreton Frewen, his neighbour at Brede and a cousin of Winston Churchill's, wrote to James of her loneliness when her husband went off to the front. James gave her his usual prescription, in a letter that spoke for his own pain as well as hers.

I am incapable of telling you not to repine and rebel, because I have so, to my cost, the imagination of all things, and because I am incapable of telling you not to feel. Feel, *feel*, I say – feel for all you're worth, and even if it half kills you, for that is the only way to live, especially to live at *this* terrible pressure, and the only way to honour and celebrate these admirable beings who are our pride and our inspiration.

There came moments, however, when the feeling got too intense for the Master. At the end of August 1915 he went to lunch with Wilfred Sheridan going 'back to front after a week's leave; he splendid and beautiful and occasion somehow such a pang – all unspeakable: 8 or 10 persons: sat between Mrs Frewen and Lady Poltimore. Afterwards at tea at Lady C's – very interesting (splendid) young *manchot* [armless] officer, Sutton.' To which he adds the words: 'They kill me!'

He died a thousand deaths with the deaths of these handsome uniformed men who dined in London one week and were dead the next. Wilfred Sheridan was killed at the front three weeks after this entry, and James couldn't pretend to offer consolation – 'who can give you anything that approaches your incomparable sense that he was yours, and you his, to the last possessed and possessing radiance of him?' He had

sight and some sound of him during an hour of that last leave just before he went off again; and what he made me then feel, and what his face seemed to say amid that cluster of relatives in which I was the sole outsider (of which too I was extraordinarily proud), is beyond all expression … I live with you in thought every step of the long way.

The first elation and tension of the war, with the seizing at any and every rumour, the quiet passing on of 'inside' information gleaned out of thin air, gave way in James to an overwhelming sense of the loss of youth – 'the destruction, on such a scale, of priceless young life, more and more reiterated, poisons and blackens one's whole view of things, and makes one ask what the end, *anywhere*, will be'. Thus to his niece in America. He was writing two months after the death of Rupert Brooke – the shining youth of his 1909 visit to Cambridge. Rupert remained in his mind, a bright vision of another time – another century! He had died of blood poisoning on a French hospital ship after serving with the Royal Naval Division. 'He isn't tragic now – he has only stopped,' James wrote to Edward Marsh, Brooke's closest friend. Of his poems he had written 'Splendid Rupert – to be the soldier that could beget them on the Muse! and lucky Muse, not less, who could have an affair with a soldier and yet feel herself not guilty of the least deviation.' He foresaw 'a wondrous romantic, heroic legend will form'. James agreed to write a preface to Rupert's posthumous book, *Letters from America*.

Closest of all perhaps, because it touched him intimately, was the army experience of his man Burgess, to whom James wrote as a father to a son, letters of the greatest simplicity and concreteness, in declarative sentences plain as his characteristic sentences were complex.

What things you are seeing, and perhaps will still more see, and what tremendous matters you will have to tell us! ... I think it wonderful for you to be able in the midst of such things to write to us at all, and we are very grateful, but want you not to worry when you can't, to leave it alone always till you can, and to believe that we always understand your difficulties, just as much as we rejoice in your news.

James added, 'my life manages in spite of the horrible sad difference the War brings with it to be so quiet and regular that I want very little waiting upon beyond what Minnie is able very devotedly and easily to do. She and Joan bear up admirably, though they miss you very much and often tell me so.'

Burgess was wounded early in his service. In mid-1915 he was back in England in a Leicester hospital with thirty shrapnel wounds, none of them serious. What was serious was that the exploding shell had deafened him, as it turned out, for life, although there was some improvement in later years, thanks to a hearing aid. 'You have clearly been very bravely through very stiff things, but have paid much less for it than you might,' James wrote him. 'I hope your hospital is a good and kind one and that they take the best care of you, but am very sorry you couldn't have been sent to London or to somewhere nearer to us here, and where we could have got to see you ... Keep up your heart – there are many so much worse.' Burgess was ultimately invalided home. Later by special dispensation he was allowed to remain in James's service.

112

Statesmen

HENRY JAMES had a last meeting with Henry Adams, his friend of so many years, in the opening weeks of the war. Adams had crossed from Paris, and remained in England until he could sail to America. Aileen Tone, his secretary-companion, a woman of distinction and beauty, remembered to the last the encounter of the two Henrys; how they threw their arms around each other, as if bridging a great chasm. James's report to Mrs Wharton was that

Henry, alas, struck me as more changed and gone than he had been reported, though still with certain flickers and *gestes* of participation, and a surviving capacity to be very well taken care of: but his way of life, in such a condition, I mean his world wandering, is all incomprehensible to me – it so quite other than any I should select in his state.

The historian and amateur of the arts had had a stroke a few years earlier. He would return to Washington and there outlive Henry James. The novelist saw other Americans in London; for he fell into the habit of periodically calling on Ambassador Walter Hines Page, and discussing with emotion America's failure to come to the aid of the Allies. He resented the continuing amenities between Berlin and Washington. And he waited eagerly for news, when Walter Berry went to Berlin on a mission. Berry was not reassuring. German morale was too high. The Fatherland was confident, arrogant. James's nephew Harry also came abroad on a Belgian relief mission and went to the Continent. He brought back to his uncle some weeks later eye-witness experiences which the latter seized upon eagerly. Finally he had continuing news from Mrs Wharton herself, her accounts of her visit to Verdun, and other fronts. He wrote to her with passion and fervour – and great admiration. 'I am too aged and too battered to do almost anything but feel.'

We get a glimpse of this in the diary of John Bailey, an English critic. 'Old Henry James asked me to come,' wrote Bailey, in his diary in October of 1914. He went on to say that James received him, 'kissing me on both cheeks when I arrived and thanking me enormously for coming. He is passionately English and says it is almost good that we were so little prepared, as it makes our moral position so splendid. He almost wept as he spoke.'

It was of such utterances that Percy Lubbock – who knew best the James of this time – wrote, when he came to edit the Master's letters. 'To all who listened to him in those days, it must have seemed that he gave us what we lacked – a voice; there was a trumpet note in it that was heard nowhere else and that alone rose to the height of the truth.'

2

Walmer Castle, in Kent, near Deal and not far from Dover, a thick-walled machicolated old fortress with embrasures twenty feet deep, was used late in 1914 and early 1915 as a halfway point to the front by the Prime Minister, Herbert H. Asquith. Pitt had lived here; Wellington had died here. The wartime leaders would congregate, with members of the Army and Navy, for conferences; at Walmer too, on week-ends, Margot Asquith, the former Margot Tennant, wife of the Prime Minister, gathered notables with the skill of an old and practised hostess. To Walmer Castle Henry James came on 16 January 1915. He was an old friend of Margot's; he had known Asquith in the 1890s before high office had come to him. He remembered the young Margot from her hunting and riding days, as one of a group of daughters of a Scottish border landlord, a Liberal baronet. Margot had heard the 'trumpet note' of James, and had lost no time in having him to lunch in recent weeks at No. 10 Downing Street. Her luncheons were famous – a gathering, very casual, of prominent figures in the London world – the world of war and the arts, of men and women whose vitality and leadership counted for so much in the national morale. The Prime Minister, coming from his morning's conferences, never knew whom he would find at table. He found again, after many years, Henry James.

In December 1914, at one such luncheon, the Master had chatted with General Sir Ian Hamilton; and it had led to his dining with Haldane, the Lord Chancellor, in the company of Ambassador Page and Winston Churchill, First Lord of the Admiralty, and his wife Clementine. There is no record of that first encounter between the 40-year-old Winston, not then the bulky bulldog of his old age, and Henry James, almost 72, who bulked much larger. Churchill was straight, athletic; and as always articulate and incisive; he was at the top of his younger form when James met him : he breathed war and action; he had wit and eloquence. James's comment after this occasion was simply that he found in the war leadership 'no illusions, no ignorances, no superficialities' – and 'deep confidence'. He seems to have been remembering some of Churchill's talk in an interview he gave a few weeks later to the New York *Times* on behalf of the American Volunteer Motor-Ambulance Corps. 'A distinguished English naval expert happened to say to me that the comparative non-production of airships in this country indicated a possible limitation of the British genius in that direction.' Then on James's asking this distinguished person why airships shouldn't be within the compass of the greatest makers of sea-ships the person had replied, 'Because the airship is essentially a bad ship, and we English can't make a bad ship well enough.'

It is possible that Churchill read this interview. For in it there was a sentence of Henry James's that seems to have lodged in his memory. 'English life,' said Henry James, 'wound up to the heroic pitch, is at present most immediately before me, and I can scarcely tell you what a privilege I feel it to share the inspiration and see further revealed the character of this decent and dauntless people.' James's rhetoric of the First World War thus seems to have made its contribution to one of the most characteristic Churchillian utterances of the Second World War.

3

'Mr James being away weekending with Mr Asquith and his daughter Elizabeth, who is decidedly cultivating him, I had a free morning,' Miss Bosanquet recorded in her diary. Both Violet Asquith, later Lady Violet Bonham-Carter and Elizabeth, then a precocious 17, but already a lively companion of her father on the political scene, liked James; and he was charmed by them. Violet was the child of Asquith's first marriage, Elizabeth was Margot's daughter. James brought with him Frederick, Mrs Wharton's man, who was still serving him. The Master was eager and curious. 'I don't do things easily nowadays,' Henry James wrote to his nephew on the day that he made the trip to Walmer Castle. 'But I thought this, in all the present conditions, almost a matter of duty, really not to be shirked.' More than 'duty', it was an occasion to assuage curiosity about the conduct of the war, the personalities involved, the social fabric in which England's leaders moved in a time of high stress. James added that 'one "hears" and "learns" on such occasions much less than one might fancy – officialdom never turns its official side outward : only, mostly, some *other* pleasant comparatively not at all thrilling side.' Still, 'the great Winston' was expected and other important guests.

The day was bright and cold. Walmer Castle was picturesque – a great terrace over the Channel – and James was thrilled to see the ships of England 'going about their business in extraordinary numbers'. On arrival he had tea with Violet Asquith. Before dinner, writing to Edith Wharton to tell her that without the aid of Frederick he would not have been able to accept this invitation, James said that

the sentiment the place makes one entertain in every way for old England is of the most acutely sympathetic, and the good kind friendly easy Asquith, with the curtain of public affairs let thickly down behind him and the footlights entirely turned off in front, doesn't do anything to make it less worth having.

James had had a bitter cold motor run around the Isle of Thanet with the Prime Minister and the actress Viola Tree. 'The car was practically open, but the friendly sight of all the swarming khaki on the roads made up for that.'

Of that week-end we know very little. There seems, however, to have been a collision between the First Lord of the Admiralty and the Master – the two most articulate men present on the occasion. Churchill, jaunty, full of his characteristic note of pride, confidence, assurance, faith, and swagger, accustomed to having the centre of the scene found Henry James at that centre. 'Winston,' said one who was present, 'was at his very worst.' He had never read Henry James; he was impatient at the respect and deference shown this old man who was so slow-spoken, even though his rhetoric was so remarkable – when he finally got it out. Everyone listened to Henry James in awe. Winston was impatient, irritable; he could not wait for the end of such long and intricate sentences. He disregarded the Master; or he interrupted him. He showed him 'no conversational consideration'. He used a great deal of slang. Some of it James must have liked, for he himself appreciated the colloquial, decorously placed between quotation marks, in his novels. Some of it, however, apparently grated on him. Churchill had piqued his curiosity; but this re-encounter of two men of personality possessed of a great sense of their dignity and power was not a happy one for the Asquiths, who were very fond of Henry James.

When James was about to leave, at the end of the week-end, he said to Violet that it had been a very interesting 'very encouraging experience to meet that young man. It had brought home to me very forcibly – very vividly – the *limitations* by which men of genius obtain their ascendancy over mankind. It,' said the Master, fumbling apparently for a bit of *argot* in the Churchill manner, 'bucks one up.'

4

He lunched again with the Prime Minister late in March of 1915 – 'on the chance of catching some gleam between the chinks – which was idiotic of me, because it's mostly in those circles that the chinks are well puttied over'. James had to content himself with the same rumours as everyone. To Mrs Henry White he wrote of the Asquiths, saying that Margot, in the setting 'appears a fairly weird fruit of time'. She was, he said, 'a voluble restless ghost'. She had acquired remarkable Asquith sons, but she looked 'as if she had lost her luggage, that of the past we originally knew her in, at a bustling railway station'. The indefatigable Margot had sent James her diaries and he read all the old gossip with great relish. He was probably being ironic, however, when he wrote her that she was 'the Balzac of diarists'. He said 'St Simon is in forty volumes – why should Margot be put in one?' Margot herself acknowledged some years later that her diaries seemed an assemblage of trivialities and gossip. James observed the amenities by telling her her diaries had created 'an admirable portrait of a lady, with no end of finish and style ... if I don't stop now, I shall be calling it a regular masterpiece'. He stopped.

He worked hard at this moment on the interview he had agreed to give to the New York *Times*. Or, as Miss Bosanquet put it in her diary,

his consent was given on condition that he might see the Copy produced. H.J. finding that it wouldn't do at all from his point of view, has spent the last four days redictating the interview to the young man who is, fortunately, a good typist. I think the idea of H.J. interviewing himself for four whole days is quite delightful!

The result, published in the *Times* of 21 March 1915, belongs in the Jamesian canon. It is doubtful whether the reporter was allowed to write a single sentence of his own. James artfully introduced sections on style, achievement, revisions in the New York Edition; but he focused mainly on the courage of England at war and the appeal for funds on behalf of the Ambulance Corps which was the main reason for the interview. Again and again the great rhetoric of valour, the cadences foreshadowing the future Churchill are striking:

'It is not for the wounded to oblige us by making us showy, but for us to let them count on our open arms and open lap as troubled children count on those of their mother.'

'We welcome any lapse of logic that may connect inward vagueness with outward zeal!'

'The horrors, the miseries, the monstrosities they are in presence of are so great, surely, as not to leave much of any other attitude over when intelligent sympathy has done its best.'

The war has used up words; they have weakened, they have deteriorated like motor car tires; they have like millions of other things, been more overstrained and knocked about and voided of the happy semblance during the last six months than in all the long ages before, and we are now confronted with a depreciation of all our terms, or, otherwise speaking, with a loss of expression through increase of limpness, that may well make us wonder what ghosts will be left to walk.

There is one passage which may have been the work of the reporter, although even here one senses Jamesian revision. This was his description of the Master:

Mr James has a mobile mouth, straight nose, a forehead which has thrust back the hair from the top of his commanding head, although it is thick at the sides over the ears, and repeats in its soft gray the colour of his kindly eyes. Before taking in these physical facts, one receives the impression of benignity and amenity not often conveyed, even by the most distinguished. And, taking advantage of this amiability, I asked if certain words just used should be followed by a dash and even boldly added: 'Are you not famous, Mr James, for the use of dashes?' 'Dash my fame!' he impatiently replied. 'And remember, please, that dogmatizing about punctuation is exactly as foolish as dogmatizing about any other form of communication with the reader.'

113

Loyalties

EARLY that summer Henry James, friend of the Prime Minister, great figure in England's literary establishment, incessant worker among the wounded and the refugees, discovered to his deep chagrin that he was considered still – officially – an alien. It was a rude shock. He had lived in England for forty years. Yet when the time came to plan a summer at Rye, he was told he would have to report to the police. Rye was a forbidden zone. Aliens – however friendly – had to have permission to go there. This gave James some troubled hours. With his inveterate logic, he felt that the situation should be rectified. The upshot of this was his writing to his nephew Harry, telling him he had decided to become a British subject. He had felt he should do this ever since the war began, but his feeling had become 'acute with the information that I can only go down to Lamb House now on the footing of an Alien under Police supervision'. It labelled him a 'technical outsider to the whole situation here, in which my affections and my loyalty are so intensely engaged'. He wanted to take the only logical step that would 'rectify a position that has become inconveniently and uncomfortably false'. He would make his civil status agree with his moral and his material status. 'Hadn't it been for the War, I should certainly have gone on as I was, taking it as the simplest and easiest and even friendliest thing; but the circumstances are utterly altered now.'

I have spent here all the best years of my life – they practically have *been* my life: about a twelvemonth hence I shall have been domiciled uninterruptedly in England for forty years, and there is not the least possibility, at my age, and in my state of health, of my ever returning to the U.S. or taking up any relation with it as a country.

He was telling Harry this simply to let him know; his mind was made up and he hoped his nephew would understand why he had taken such an important decision. In fact, if his nephew had any reserves, Henry 'should then still ask you not to launch them at me unless they should seem to you so important as to balance against my own argument, and frankly speaking, my own absolute need and passion here; which the whole experience of the past year has made quite unspeakably final'.

He did not wait for Harry's answer. He found out readily enough from his solicitor that all he needed was to apply for British citizenship, surrender his American passport, and have four persons testify – it amused him greatly – to his literacy as well as his good character. He turned to Gosse, in his exalted position as librarian of the House of Lords. And then it occurred to him that he could call in another excellent witness. Why not the Prime Minister himself? There went forth on 28 June a letter from Henry James to Herbert H. Asquith at No. 10 Downing Street:

I am venturing to trouble you with the mention of a fact of my personal situation, but I shall do so as briefly and considerately as possible. I desire to offer myself for naturalization in this country, that is, to change my status from that of American citizen to that of British subject.

He wished 'to testify at this crisis to the force of my attachment and devotion to England and to the cause for which she is fighting'. He had made up his mind. It was beyond all doubt, and brooked 'no inward denial'.

I can only testify by laying at her feet my explicit, my material and spiritual allegiance, and throwing into the scale of her fortune my all but imponderable moral weight – 'a poor thing but mine own'. Hence this respectful appeal.

Would the Prime Minister join with Edmund Gosse, in offering his testimony and bear witness to Henry James's 'apparent respectability, and to my speaking and writing English with an approach to propriety?' The Master's solicitor would wait on the Prime Minister with a paper requiring simply his signature 'the affair of a single moment'.

Prime Minister Asquith was delighted. He went beyond the act of bearing witness to asking the Home Secretary Sir John Simon to facilitate the Master's desire to become a subject of the King. Asquith, Gosse, George Prothero, editor of the *Quarterly Review*, and James's agent J. B. Pinker were the four witnesses. The application went through in record time. On 29 June he surrendered his passport. His application for citizenship contained the following statement:

Because of his having lived and worked in England for the best part of forty years, because of his attachment to the Country and his sympathy with it and its people, because of the long friendships and associations and interests he has formed there these last including the acquisition of some property: all of which things have brought to a head his desire to throw his moral weight and personal allegiance, for whatever they may be worth, into the scale of the contending nation's present and future fortune.

At 4.30 p.m. on 28 July, accompanied by his solicitor, Henry James took the oath of allegiance to King George V. *'Civis Britannicus Sum'*, he proudly announced. He added: 'I don't feel a bit different.'

2

The news was formally proclaimed by *The Times*: 'Mr Henry James. Adoption of British Nationality.' 'We are able to announce,' said the newspaper,

that Mr Henry James was granted papers of naturalization on Monday and took the oath of allegiance as a British subject. All lovers of literature in this country will welcome the decision of this writer of genius, whose works are an abiding possession of all English-speaking peoples, and they will welcome it all the more on account of the reasons which Mr James gives in his petition for naturalization.

The Master had expected the avalanche of mail that descended upon him from all parts of England – from all those friends who two years before had honoured him, and from many strangers. What he had not expected was the acute American reaction. Perhaps it was the sensitivity of some Americans before the spectacle of the European horror; the ambiguity of feeling among those who wanted to help England and France while being at the same time eager to keep the country out of the war. Certainly the gesture made by James was distorted in the United States out of all proportion. He had after all kept his American citizenship for four decades. Yet to many Americans his swearing allegiance to the English King seemed an act of disloyalty; a confirmation of the long-nurtured legend that James was 'anti-American'. Long after his death, the issue would be kept alive. James in the end simply shrugged his shoulders. It seemed to him highly irrational of a country which measured aliens by the speed with which they became naturalized Americans, to judge him so severely because he had performed the same kind of act in the country of *his* residence.

He could go and come now freely. But his life had become constricted. The 'wear and tear of discrimination', as he put it, was now beyond his endurance. He was eloquent on this subject in a letter to Edith Wharton:

I myself have no adventure of any sort equal to just hearing from you of yours – apart I mean from the unspeakable adventure of being alive in these days, which is about as much as I can undertake at any moment to be sure of. That seems to go on from day to day, though starting fresh with *aube* and getting under way in fact always then with such difficulties, such backings and tanglings and impossible adjustments ... I stagger out of my dusk to follow the path of the hours, and I *have* followed them I suppose, when I flop back to my intersolar swoon again – though with nothing whatever to show for them but that sad capacity to flop ...

He was learning to take for granted, he said, 'that I shall probably on the whole *not* die of simple sick horror – than which nothing seems to me at the same time more amazing. One aches to anguish and rages to suffocation, and one is still there to do it again, and the occasion still there to see that one does.' He lived in a world of death. Everyone is killed, he remarked, who belongs to anyone, and one was getting the habit of looking 'straight and dry-eyed, hard and arid, at those to whom they belonged'. There was a final question in the letter about Fullerton. What had become of him? He had seemed to be, even before the war, without ambition, without focus, without anything but a kind of passive continuity. 'The non-eventuation of him!' He signed the letter to Edith '*Je vous embrasse, je vous vénère.*'

114

Treacheries

ON 5 July 1915, during the period when James was awaiting British citizenship, he stopped one day at the Reform Club and was handed a book parcel which had lain there unforwarded. The book was by H. G. Wells, who for years had sent the Master everything he published. It had an elaborate title-page *Boon*, *The Mind of the Race*, *The Wild Asses of the Devil*, and *The Last Trump*, and purported to be 'a first selection from the literary remains of George Boon'. It was edited by one Reginald Bliss and there was 'An Ambiguous Introduction by H. G. Wells.' Clearly some kind of literary joke was intended. Wells said he had not read the book through 'though I have a kind of first-hand knowledge of its contents' and he added 'it seems to me an indiscreet, ill-advised book'. The preface ended with the statement that 'Bliss was Bliss and Wells is Wells. And Bliss can write all sorts of things that Wells could not do.'

The design of this soon became clear to James. It was a long and witty joke, and it poked fun at many things and named many writers by their name, not least Henry James who was indeed the very centre of the joke. In a word, Wells himself could not sign such a book; its authorship could be imputed to the demonic *gaminesque* side of him, the little boy with the pea-shooter who behind the prophet, seer, scientist–journalist–historian, was treating himself to a lark. James turned to 'Chapter the Fourth' which was entitled 'Of Art, of Literature, of Mr Henry James'. In this chapter, with more impishness than was apparent to outsiders, Wells constructed a dialogue on the novel between George Moore and Henry James: he knew James's opinion of Moore; and Hueffer was brought into the picture as well. With considerable wit, and a great deal of animus, Wells let loose all his bottled-up anger against James's essay on 'The Younger Generation' and the endless unsolicited reviews of his novels the Master had sent Wells in their private correspondence. He laughed at the concept of fiction as a 'craft'. In reality he echoed his lecture on the novel in which he had argued for the loose 'usable' novel as against the *organic* creation the Master had always espoused. James had called Wells 'cheeky' once too often, and Wells now proved his cheekiness. 'Your cheek is positively the very sign and stamp of your genius,' Henry James had once said to Wells and in half a hundred letters he had spoken of 'your sublime and heroic cheek', and exploded into 'cheeky, cheeky, cheeky' when he praised three of Wells's utopias.

This is what James read in *Boon*:

In practice James's selection becomes just omission and nothing more. He omits everything that demands digressive treatment or collateral statement. For example, he omits opinions. In all of his novels you will find no people with defined political opinions, no people with religious opinions, none with clear partisanships or with lusts or whims, none definitely up to any specific impersonal thing. There are no poor people dominated by the imperatives of Saturday night and Monday morning, no dreaming types – and don't we all more or less live dreaming? And none are ever decently forgetful. All that much of humanity he clears out before he begins his story.

In this vein, the character Boon starts to write a novel in the James manner. What ensued was an elaborate parody of *The Spoils of Poynton* interlarded with echoes from *The Turn of the Screw*. The crucial passage, which would be quoted across the years, read as follows:

The thing his novel is *about* is always there ... It is like a church lit but without a congregation to distract you, with every light and line focused on the high altar. And on the altar, very reverently placed, intensely there, is a dead kitten, an egg-shell, a bit of string ... Like his *Altar of the Dead*, with nothing to the dead at all ... For if there was they couldn't all be candles and the effect would vanish ... He splits his infinitives and fills them up with adverbial stuffing. He presses the passing colloquialism into his service. His vast paragraphs sweat and struggle; they could not sweat and elbow and struggle more if God himself was the processional meaning to which they sought to come. And all for tales of nothingness ... It is leviathan retrieving pebbles. It is a magnificent but painful hippopotamus resolved at any cost, even at the cost of its dignity, upon picking up a pea which has got into a corner of its den. Most things, it insists, are beyond it, but it can, at any rate, modestly, and with an artistic singleness of mind, pick up that pea.

I

James read these passages with bewilderment. He had always considered himself Wells's friend and their discussions of art to have been on the level of 'profession' without any thought of any kind of *ad hominem* penetration. He wrote to Wells with great simplicity, but also in pain.

I have more or less mastered your appreciation of H.J., which I have found very curious and interesting, after a fashion – though it has naturally not filled me with a fond elation. It is difficult of course for a writer to put himself *fully* in the place of another writer who finds him extraordinarily futile and void, and who is moved to publish that to the world – and I think the case isn't easier when he happens to have enjoyed the other writer enormously, from far back; because there has then grown up the habit of taking some common meeting-ground between them for granted, and the falling away of this is like the collapse of a bridge which made communication possible.

He said that 'the fact that a mind as brilliant as yours *can* resolve me into such an unmitigated mistake ... makes me greatly want to fix myself, for as long as my nerves will stand it, with such a pair of eyes ... I try for possible light to enter into the feelings of a critic for whom the deficiencies preponderate.' He couldn't keep it up, it was too difficult; he had to fall back on his sense of his 'good parts'. And the Master concluded by saying that 'my poetic and my appeal to experience' rested upon '*my* measure of fulness – of fulness of life and of the projection of it, which seems to you such an empti-ness of both'. The fine thing about the fictional form was that it opened 'such widely different windows of attention'.

Wells replied by being contrite. James had written 'so kind and frank a letter after my offences that I find it an immense embarrass-ment to reply to you'. He confessed to having set before himself a *gaminesque* ideal – he had a natural horror 'of dignity, finish, and perfection'. There was

a real and very fundamental difference in our innate and developed atti-tudes towards life and literature. To you literature like painting is an end, to me literature like architecture is a means, it has a use. Your view was, I felt, too dominant in the world of criticism and I assailed it in tones of harsh antagonism.

He confessed *Boon* was 'just wastepaper basket'. He had written it to escape from the war. Wells ended, 'I had rather be called a jour-nalist than an artist, that is the essence of it, and there was no other antagonist possible than yourself.' He had regretted a hundred times that he had not expressed 'our profound and incurable dif-ference and contrast with a better grace'. He signed himself James's 'warm if rebellious and resentful admirer, and for countless causes yours most gratefully and affectionately'.

James's answer to Wells was his last letter to that writer. It is dated 10 July 1915. He began by saying that he didn't think Wells had made out any sort of case for his bad manners. One simply didn't publish the contents of waste-baskets. He wasn't aware that his view of life and literature had as much of a following as Wells imputed to it. He believed literature lived on the individual practi-tioner. That was why he had always admired Wells. 'I live, live intensely and am fed by life, and my value, whatever it be, is in my own kind of expression of that. Art *makes* life, makes interest, makes importance,' James told Wells, adding he knew of no substitute whatever for 'the force and beauty of its process'. He rejected the idea that literature was like architecture. Both were art. He rejected the 'utility' idea of the arts.

Years later Wells in his autobiography, apparently still feeling some twinges of guilt over his behaviour, sought to justify his attack on James. In reality his reminiscences, often quoted, were a renewed attack, and revealed that the differences between the two ran deeper than doctrine. Wells had never got over his below-stairs origins; he resented James's easy acceptance of his place in the world and his aristocratic view of man-made hierarchies. Wells was in open revolt against these hierarchies. James had come to represent for Wells the sovereignty and established power of the aristocracy and no matter how genial and accepting the American was, Wells faced him with an under-edge of hostility. The American wielded his pen as if it were a sceptre; Wells's pen was a dagger, a sabre, a gun.

The autobiography tells us much about how Wells saw James. Where other writers are described – the brilliant fire in Conrad's eyes, the deportment of Shaw, the aspect of Crane – we see James only in externals. With all his comings and goings at Lamb House, Wells could paint only the formal side of the novelist, his habits and rituals, the special hats he wore for different occasions, the matching sticks, the regularity with which he dictated in his 'charming room in his beautifully walled garden' – dictated 'with a slow but not unhappy circumspection'. The picture seems drawn in malice; it is in reality a below-stairs view of a settled aristocrat – for when did aristocrats possess a single hat or a single stick? As Wells had over-dressed himself for the first night of *Guy Domville* compared with Shaw, so he singled out as formality those very objects which made James in reality look informal. Snapshots of the novelist in his peaked cap or his knickerbockers, his colourful waistcoats and his varied walking sticks convey the opposite of what Wells suggested. Wells was intent, however, on showing that James 'never scuffled with Fact'. This was true to the extent that James did not need to 'scuffle' as Wells did. James could re-imagine Fact, could remake the world in his mind and his sentience, Wells could remake it only by writing utopias.

'He saw us all as Masters or would-be Masters, little Masters and great Masters, and he was plainly sorry that *Cher Maître* was not an English expression,' Wells remembered.

One could not be in a room with him for ten minutes without realizing the importance he attached to the dignity of this art of his. I was by nature and education unsympathetic with this mental disposition. But I was disposed to regard a novel as about as much an art form as a market-place or a boulevard. It had not even been necessarily to get anywhere. You went by it on your various occasions.

Thus the fundamental dynamics of this friendship always remained the same. James had an easy acceptance of himself and the world; Wells worked hard to make the world accept him. In the end Wells would try to excuse himself by calling James 'a little treacherous to me in a natural sort of way'. Certainly there had been no treachery in James's attempt to have him elected to the Royal Society of Literature: it was Wells who had refused. But the Master had criticized his work with too much candour. The victory long after was James's. Wells's social novels have been judged at this distance obsolescent. James's novels, those which left out fact but dealt truthfully with human dilemmas, have more vogue today than they ever did.

The literary quarrel was fast forgotten by James in the announcement of his newly-acquired citizenship. The Prime Minister entertained him at dinner on the day of his naturalization. It was one of the last dinners James attended in London.

115

The Mulberry Tree

IN January of 1915 Henry James received word that the large mulberry tree in the centre of his garden at Lamb House had been toppled by a violent storm. To Mrs Dacre Vincent, a Rye friend who sent him these tidings, he answered,

He might have gone on for some time, I think, in the absence of an *inordinate* gale – but once the fury of the tempest really descended he was bound to give way, because his poor old heart was dead, his immense old trunk was hollow. He had no power to resist left when the southeaster caught him by his vast *crinière* and simply twisted his head round and round. It's very sad for he was the making of the garden – he was *it* in person.

I

James had hoped to go to Rye shortly after his naturalization in the mid-summer of 1915. But he was ill throughout August and finished with effort his preface to Rupert Brooke's *Letters from America*. The prose of that essay shows, however, little strain; it is a beautiful eulogy and was James's last piece of writing. Long before, he had stopped his work on *The Ivory Tower*. That novel was too actual; the war seemed to make it obsolete. Instead he turned to the unfinished *Sense of the Past*, which he had set aside in 1900. The story of an American walking into a remote time seemed more possible to James in the midst of casualty lists. He worked intermittently on this, but in reality half-heartedly. Its subject had always been difficult.

He did not get to Rye until 14 October, going down with Burgess, his cook Joan Anderson, and his maid, Minnie Kidd. He had loaned Lamb House during the year he had been away to various persons who needed temporary housing, and he was turning it over to still another tenant. Apparently his trip was mainly to take care of certain of his papers, for Mrs William James later said 'he burned up quantities of papers and photographs – cleared his drawers in short'. In the midst of this he developed acute symptoms and sat up for three nights breathing with difficulty. With his addiction to self-diagnosis, he treated himself for a gastric upset. But on calling in the local doctor, Ernest Skinner, he was told that there was a change in his heart rhythm – he seems to have had intermittent tachycardia or auricular fibrillation. Skinner gave him digitalis, and he was able to return to London, where Sir James Mackenzie confirmed the doctor's diagnosis and the medication.

In November James wrote to Rhoda Broughton 'I have really been miserably ill these three months, but only during the latter half of them have I emerged into a true intelligence of the source of my woe – which has been a bad heart crisis ... Bustling is at an end for me for ever now – though indeed, after all, I have had very little hand in it for many a day.' Hugh returned from Russia at this time and talked to the Master over the phone from Cornwall. 'I hear that people have been seeing you so that I hope that means that you are better,' he wrote him. James replied tenderly: 'The past year has made me feel twenty years older, and, frankly, as if my knell had rung. Still, I cultivate, I at least attempt, a brazen front. Do intensely believe that I respond clutchingly to your every grasp of me, every touch, and would so gratefully be a reconnecting link with you here.' Hugh wrote in his diary, 'delightful letter from H.J. – one of the most truly affectionate I've ever had from him'.

2

A few weeks earlier Mrs Wharton had arrived in London for a brief visit. She telephoned James one morning wanting to drive him to Qu'Acre to see Howard Sturgis. He told her he was too ill. She then asked him whether he could lend Miss Bosanquet to her for the day. 'I suppose,' Miss Bosanquet noted, 'he could hardly say he was well enough to work if he was not well enough to go to Windsor.' Excited at the prospect of getting to know Mrs Wharton better, Miss Bosanquet hastily tidied herself up and then 'made a rather flurried way' to Brook Street, to Buckland's Hotel. She found the lady novelist in a very elegant pink négligée, wearing a cap of écru lace trimmed with fur. 'Her arms,' Miss Bosanquet wrote in her diary, 'were very much displayed, coming from very beautiful frills of sleeve, and they were good arms, not either scraggy or too fleshy, but just the right plumpness and ending up in hands most beautifully manicured.' Her only complaint was that Mrs Wharton used too intense a perfume. The central heating was turned up too high for Miss Bosanquet's comfort. Mrs Wharton's face was 'squareish' and finely wrinkled; her complexion was 'browny-yellow'. She had 'good eyes and a strong mouth'.

'Of course, Miss Bosanquet,' said the Firebird, 'I didn't really want you to come here to write letters for me, but just so that we might have a quiet talk.' Miss Bosanquet, knowing the closeness of Mrs Wharton's relation to James, spoke candidly of his ever-increasing illnesses. Mrs William James and Peggy had wanted to come over during the previous summer but James had not wanted them to risk a voyage amid prowling enemy submarines and they had gone to California instead. The doctors now considered that James had a real, not a simulated, heart condition.

Miss Bosanquet confided to her diary: 'I was rather unhappily conscious all the time we were talking that I wasn't as much charmed as I ought to be. I could see the charm and I couldn't feel it – and that was so disappointing.' She decided that Mrs Wharton 'so evidently depends on fascinating people all about her, her sole effect makes one continually conscious of that'. Mrs Wharton did turn to literature once or twice, but Miss Bosanquet didn't feel like pursuing the subject.

The importance of this meeting was that Mrs Wharton established a link within the Master's household. It ministered to her need for omniscience and power. And it would enable her to act, if some emergency occurred.

116

A Terror of Consciousness

EARLY in the morning of Thursday, 2 December 1915, Henry James's maid, Minnie Kidd, came to Miss Bosanquet's flat in nearby Lawrence Street and told her that Mr James seemed to have had 'a sort of stroke'. The maid had been in the dining-room at eight-thirty and heard the Master calling. She entered his bedroom. He was lying on the floor; his left leg had given way under him. She called Burgess. Between them they got Henry James into bed; it wasn't easy – the Master was heavy. Miss Bosanquet came at once to Carlyle Mansions. James was lying in bed. He was open-eyed and calm. He had had, he told her, a stroke 'in the most approved fashion'. The most distressing thing, he said, was that in wanting to ring for his servants he had found himself fumbling with the electrical wiring of the bedlamp. He had then called for help. Mrs Wharton years later said that Howard Sturgis was told by James that his first thought as he fell was 'so it has come at last – the Distinguished Thing'. Minnie Kidd reported she heard James say, 'It's the beast in the jungle, and it's sprung.'

Dr Des Voeux arrived promptly and confirmed that it was a stroke, a slight one. The Master then dictated a cable to his nephew : 'Had slight stroke this morning. No serious symptoms. Perfect care. No suffering. Wrote Peggy yesterday.' James had written a long letter to his niece the previous day. He had recounted his recent illnesses; described life in London; complained of his sleepless nights. Peggy had told him of Frank Duveneck's being 'lionized' in Cincinnati. He wondered why Lizzie Boott's husband should be lionized at this time when his work belonged 'to such an antediluvian past'. He told Peggy of Burgess being back on an extended leave from service. Then he felt tired and ended his letter with the words 'the pen drops from my hand!'

It had indeed dropped, and for all time. Mrs William James cabled she was sailing at once; she had long ago promised her husband she would 'see Henry through when he comes to the end'. Miss Bosanquet meanwhile took charge. Having no specific instructions, she answered queries, sent daily bulletins to Mrs Wharton, and instructed the servants. She took control of James's friends who flocked to see him, flocked in such numbers that the doctor had to restrict visiting drastically.

On the second day, Dr Des Voeux announced that James had had a second stroke. The paralysis of his left side was more complete. He called in Sir James Mackenzie. They pronounced the novelist to be in grave condition, and that night Emily Sargent and her sister Mrs Ormond stayed up in the flat in case they should be wanted. Miss Bosanquet had in the meantime obtained the services of a male nurse; he proved inefficient and the doctor brought in two regular nurses. Miss Bosanquet sent a second cable to Harry James and also telegraphed Mrs Wharton. The Firebird would have come directly, but she was at Hyères. Within twenty-four hours, the patient had rallied and was calling for a thesaurus to discover the exact descriptive word for his condition. He didn't think 'paralytic' was right. He told Miss Bosanquet to write to Mrs Wharton and to Hugh Walpole. Mrs Wharton wired 'can come if advisable' but with Mrs James en route and the novelist improving, Miss Bosanquet suggested there was no need of her for the present. A week after the first stroke Miss Bosanquet noted that the Master was 'more himself'. In the interval, proofs of the Rupert Brooke preface arrived and she read them.

I

Two diaries were kept during Henry James's last illness. Miss Bosanquet's records with some minuteness the comings and goings, the daily reports of the doctors, and such talk of the Master's as she heard. Mrs William James began a diary shortly after her arrival. She wrote down certain remarks made by James. These show a distinct pattern of confusion; they reveal that he was from the first disturbed about his 'sense of place', and then, as he struggled to orient himself in the scale of his mental wanderings, he experienced a strange terror. He began to think he was mad – and that his visitors would notice he was mad.

This condition went at first unnoticed; he seemed simply to be rambling. On 10 December Miss Bosanquet recorded 'mind clouded this morning and he has lost his own unmistakeable identity – is just a simple sick man'. He was running a temperature; the doctors found he had 'embolic pneumonia' due to a clot in his lung. In this condition, James spoke to Miss Bosanquet very strongly and clearly about wanting to take Burgess to Lady Hyde's with him. He would then send Burgess back. 'Where am I?' he asked. 'What is this address?' When Miss Bosanquet told him it was 21 Carlyle Mansions, he answered 'How very curious, that's Lady Hyde's address too.' On the next day he spoke of himself as being in a strange hotel far away from London and when Mrs Charles Hunter came to see him he couldn't account for her presence in this hotel. He was delirious at moments. On 13 December he wanted to know where certain manuscripts were, he thought they had gone to Ireland. In the latter part of the day he spoke of himself as being in Cork. In the evening he asked whether the 'plumbers had carried out the alterations in the bathroom', a corollary to his having dictated to Miss Bosanquet certain paragraphs about alterations in the Tuileries. Then he spoke of 'the curious annexation of Chelsea to Cork'. He told Miss Bosanquet he felt 'the mantle of her protection was flung over him to a far greater extent than he was at all conscious of'.

Mrs William James arrived on the evening of 13 December after a stormy crossing. James seemed glad to see her. He patted her hand and said, 'I don't dare to think of what you have come through to get here.' Then he began to speak of being in California, probably because Mrs James had been there with Peggy during the preceding summer. Mrs William said to him, 'You remember Mr Bruce Porter in San Francisco. He and Peggy have made fast friends on the basis of their love of you.' The Master rejoined 'they have a pretty feeble basis'. He complained that he was constantly surrounded by women. 'The absence of the male element in my entourage is what perplexes me.' On 22 December he told one of his visitors 'this is a desperately long tunnel I see'. He held his thumb and forefinger up to form a circle, then added there was 'a gleam of blue' at the tunnel's end. On another day Mrs James brushed his hair and he said 'that ardent brushing does not mitigate my troubles'.

2

The confusion returned on 16 December when the barber came to shave him. Later James summoned Miss Bosanquet. He told her it was 'most painful and distressing' to be spoken of as if he were in London. He found it 'equally painful' that, when he asked for an account of the country and the people round, no one seemed able to give an intelligible answer. 'Even the barber who came to shave me this morning is in on the conspiracy. I had last seen him in London and when I asked him this morning if he'd been in London recently he actually said he was here now.'

After tea on this day he returned to the subject. He wanted to know whether someone could help clear up his mystification. 'Someone whom I could ask if this extraordinary state of utter dependence upon the good offices of these quite well-meaning nurses doesn't strike them as uncanny in the same way in which it strikes me.' Miss Bosanquet told him he had been ill. The mystery would resolve itself when he was stronger, and 'I tried to impress on him the idea that eating would help to make him stronger.'

'I have a curious sense,' Henry James said, 'that I'm not the bewildering puzzle to all of you that you are to me.' He returned to the absence of males in his entourage with the 'negligible exception of Burgess and the doctor'.

The next day James again said he was in Cork. His return, again and again to Cork, may have been a memory of the death of his mother. He had been in that city only once – on his journey back to England after Mary James had died. He had found Cork full of soldiers, and had not lingered.

On 21 December Miss Bosanquet came into the bedroom. Minnie Kidd was by his bed. He opened his eyes, looked towards his amanuensis, and Kidd said : 'You know who that is, don't you, sir ?' He replied. 'Oh, Miss Bosanquet.' She went beside the bed and took James's hand. He said :

'Miss Bosanquet, there were two or three things I wanted to say to you. We had some talk, you remember, two or three days ago.' Miss Bosanquet said everything was perfectly clear. He said : 'This place in which I find myself is the strangest mixture of Edinburgh and Dublin and New York and some other place that I don't know.'

Miss Bosanquet mentioned Mrs Wharton, and James asked : 'Does she seem at all aware of my state ?' Miss Bosanquet said she seemed aware. James may have been talking of his mental state; Miss Bosanquet believed he was referring to the state of his illness. His message was 'tell Mrs Wharton that I thank her very kindly for her inquiries and that at present I'm entrusting the answers to you, but that I hope very soon to get into closer relation with her.'

There seems to have been considerable strain between Mrs James and the nurses: she constantly interfered. On 22 December Miss Bosanquet noted that

he looked desperately ill – his face all drawn and wasted and unshaved, head falling right over to the paralysed side, and his body barely covered by a brownish Jaeger blanket – his feet sticking out beyond it at the bottom. He was uncomfortably propped on a variety of pillows and many-coloured cushions and each arm rested on a pillow too. If ever a man looked dying, he did.

During Christmas James suddenly became restless with what Miss Bosanquet called 'a passion for motion'. He was moved into the drawing-room and then from one chair to another. 'He was furiously angry with everyone who tried to reason with him.' In the afternoon the whole household was prostrate, 'Kidd and Burgess flat in the kitchen, the nurse hysterical in the passage and Mrs James more miserable than she has ever been before, which is saying a very great deal'.

The next day some movement seemed to have returned to James's arm and leg. Dr Des Voeux had a wheel-couch brought in and James was easily moved into the drawing-room. He asked for Miss Bosanquet. She found him looking 'a complete wreck of his former self now, and his eyes have a strained, wandering expression – they don't look intelligently at one a bit'. She gave him messages from Miss Allen and Lucy Clifford. She mentioned Mrs Clifford was reading proofs of an article and noted that his face clouded – evidently the idea of proof-reading gave him a momentary pang. On the next day he was profoundly depressed. He kept saying good-bye to each member of his household.

During the early days of January there seemed to be some improvement and on 12 January he asked if he mightn't go to Rye. Then he seems to have made the journey in his mind for he spoke to Burgess of how nice it was to be back in Lamb House. There was an increasing concern about the effect he was having on other people. He asked Burgess whether his muddled condition of mind didn't make people laugh. Mrs James intervened defensively, 'Never, Henry, no one wants to smile.' The Master fixed her with his right eye – the left eyelid was drooping because of the stroke – 'What is this voice from Boston, Massachusetts breaking in with irrelevant remarks in my conversation with Burgess?'

On another occasion he seems to have been imagining one of his plays was being produced. He asked Mrs James, 'What effect will my madness have on the house?' He also wanted to know about 'Fanny'. When he was asked if he meant Fanny Prothero he said no. Apparently he was thinking of Fanny Kemble. Then he waved to Mrs James 'not to speak before them' meaning the nurses. He indicated he wished to conceal his 'madness' from them.

3

Read in their fragmented form, these partial records of Henry James's mental confusion suggest a kind of heroic struggle to retain his grasp on reality in the midst of his death-in-life. Taken together they suggest that in some mysterious way the Master may have been living out that 'terror of consciousness' with which he had sought to endow his hero in The Sense of the Past, the unfinished novel he had been trying to complete. He had actually turned over some of its pages on the evening before his stroke. In his notes for this novel James had spoken of his hero, walking into the year 1820, with his knowledge of the future, as being 'in danger of passing for a madman'. He feels 'cut off ... and lost'. We are indeed in the presence of the uncanny when we think of James's sense of being cut off from those around him, in the grim comedy of confusing London and Cork. He was apparently living out a part of his fiction. Perhaps some of his remarks related to the continuation of his creative work on this novel; and then, in his confused memory, shuttling between the cities of his pilgrimages – the Ireland of his father and grandfather, the London, Rome, Edinburgh, of his own experience, he had to cope with the disoriented sense of being in two places at once. Memory became actual; the actual of the sickroom intruded on memory. This, in another form, was a part of the fantastic idea for The Sense of the Past – it had been designed as a novel dealing with 'the conscious and understood fusion' taking place between the hero and his ancestral self; it was as if the Jamesian character in The Jolly Corner and his alter ego were no longer distinct from one another. His original fantasy of 1900 seemed to come true now within his dispossessed imagination. He had written of 'scared and slightly modern American figures' moving against the background of three or four European environments. 'I seem to see them *going* – hurried by their fate – from one of these places to the other, in search of, in flight from, something or other.' And the danger of his being thought mad was a terror imposed on the terror of death. During his last hours he would speak of nights 'of horror and terror'. His imagination, cut loose perhaps by the paralytic stroke from temporal moorings, floated through moments of nightmare all the more ghastly for the disconnection.

117

Final and Fading Words

A STRANGE thing had occurred during the first period of his confusion, before the arrival of Mrs William James. In his delirium, when his fever was high, Henry James had wanted to write. He kept asking for paper and pencil. When he got it, his hand would make the movements of writing. Then he wanted to dictate. The typewriter was brought into the sickroom. The familiar sound pacified him. Miss Bosanquet took his dictation. 'I find the business of coming round about as important and glorious as any circumstances I have had occasion to record, by which I mean that I find them as damnable and as boring,' he dictated. He said it was 'not much better to discover within one's carcass new resources for application than to discover the absence of them; their being new doesn't somehow add to their interest but makes them stale and flat, as if one had long ago exhausted them'. Miss Bosanquet said these sentences were spoken slowly and with many pauses, as if he were making a great effort to mobilize his thoughts. 'Such is my sketchy state of mind, but I feel sure I shall discover plenty of fresh worlds to conquer' and he added 'even if I am to be cheated of the amusement of them'.

The Master's mind was disintegrating; but it still had its force and its logic. On the afternoon of Saturday, 11 December, he called once more for the typewriter and dictated words about touching 'the large old phrase into the right amplitude ... we simply shift the sweet nursling of genius from one maternal breast to the other and

the trick is played, the false note averted'. Then he exclaimed:
'Astounding little stepchild of God's astounding young stepmother!'
There followed a passage that seemed to contain a recall of the war,
but it became confused with his reading of Napoleonic memoirs.
He was back in the Paris of the Second Empire which he had known
in his boyhood: back in the Louvre. This was his dictation; sometimes Miss Bosanquet missed a word; sometimes there was discontinuity of thought:

... on this occasion moreover that, having been difficult to keep step ...
we hear of the march of history, what is remaining to that essence of
tragedy, the limp? ...
... mere patchwork transcription becomes of itself the high brave art.
We ... five miles off at the renewed affronts that we see coming for the
great, and that we know they will accept. The fault is that they had
found themselves too easily great, and the effect of that, definitely, had
been, within them, the want of long provision for it. It wasn't why they
[were] to have been so thrust into the limelight and the uproar, but why
they [were] to have known as by inspiration the trade most smothered
in experience. They go about shivering in the absence of the holy protocol – they dodder sketchily about as in the betrayal of the lack of early
advantages; and it is upon *that* they seem most to depend to give them
distinction – it is upon that, and upon the *crânerie* and the *rouerie* that
they seem most to depend for the grand air of gallantry. They pluck in
their terror handfuls of plumes from the imperial eagle, and with no
greater credit in consequence than that they face, keeping their equipoise,
the awful bloody beak that vindictive intention, during these days of
cold grey Switzerland weather on the huddled and hustled after campaigns of the first omens of defeat. Everyone looks haggard and our only
wonder is that they still succeed in 'looking' at all. It renews for us the
assurance of the part played by that element in the famous assurance
[divinity] that doth hedge a king.

During recent months James had met various Bonaparte descendants: he had seen his old Roman friend Count Primoli and Princess
Victor Napoleon of Belgium. Perhaps some recollection of this
caused him to dictate on the next day – 12 December – the sentence
'the Bonapartes have a kind of bronze distinction that extends to
their fingertips and is a great source of charm in the women'. He
went on to say 'therefore they don't have to swagger after the fact;
fortune has placed them too high and anything less would be trivial.
You can believe anything of the Queen of Naples or of the Princess
Caroline Murat.' He rang in a change: 'There have been great

families of tricksters and conjurors; so why not this one, and so pleasant withal?' Whether he was moving in consciousness from the Napoleonic family to the James family is not clear; this is suggested, however, by the sentence immediately following, as if he were dictating a passage in *Notes of a Son and Brother*: 'Our admirable father keeps up the pitch. He is the dearest of men.' Then he went back to the Napoleonic legend:

I should have liked above all things seeing our sister pulling her head through the crown; one has that confident ... and I should have had it most on the day when most would have been asked. But we jog on very well. Up to the point of the staircase where the officers do stand it couldn't be better, though I wonder at the *souffle* which so often enables me to pass.

We are back from ... but we breathe at least together and I am devotedly yours ...

The sudden transition, as if he were ending a letter, suggests that in his mental confusion Henry James was busy writing recent and old books, and also thinking of himself as dictating letters. At one moment there is a recollection of Mrs Wharton, 'We squeeze together into some motor-car or other and we so talk and talk and what comes of it?' Then another fragmentary thought, 'Yes, that is the turn of public affairs. Next statement is for all the world as if we had brought it on and had given our push and our touch to great events.'

'After luncheon,' Miss Bosanquet noted at the time (this was on 12 December),

he wanted me again and dictated, perfectly clearly and coherently two letters from Napoleon Bonaparte to one of his married sisters – I suspect they weren't original compositions, but subconscious memory – one letter about the decoration of the Louvre and the Tuileries and the other about some great opportunity being offered them which they mustn't fall below the level of. After he had finished the second letter he seemed quite satisfied not to do any more and fell into a peaceful sleep.

Actually the first letter was the Bonaparte letter, and he signed it with Napoleon's original Corsican form 'Napoleone', apparently having dictated the exact spelling he wanted. The second letter, no less Napoleonic in its sharpness of tone and military eloquence, was signed with his own name. Again his memory was mingling Napoleonic family affairs and James family affairs. It sounded as if he had gone out into the world and had conquered, and was allowing William and Alice to share in the spoils. William had been dead now almost six years; and Henry in alluding to him during his delirium spoke always of his being in some other room. Following are the letters, with Miss Bosanquet's notes of the time:

Dictation resumed at 2.10 p.m. on the same day.

The letter following originally began 'Dear and highly considered Brother and Sister' but after its conclusion, H.J. reconsidered the opening words and changed them.

Dear and most esteemed Brother and Sister,

I call your attention to the precious enclosed transcripts of plans and designs for the decoration of certain apartments of the palaces here, the Louvre and the Tuileries, which you will find addressed in detail to artists and workmen who are to take them in hand. I commit them to your earnest care till the questions relating to this important work are fully settled. When that is the case I shall require of you further zeal and further taste. For the present the course is definitely marked out and I beg you to let me know from stage to stage definitely how the scheme promises and what results it may be held to inspire. It is, you will see, of a great scope, a majesty unsurpassed by any work of the kind yet undertaken in France. Please understand I regard these plans as fully developed and as having had my last consideration and look forward to no patchings nor perversions, and with no question of modifications either economic or aesthetic. This will be the case with all further projects of your affectionate

Napoleone.

My dear Brother and Sister,

I offer you great opportunities, in exchange for the exercise of great zeal. Your position as residents in our young but so highly considered Republic at one of the most interesting minor capitals is a piece of luck which may be turned to account in the measure of your acuteness and your experience. A brilliant fortune may come to crown it and your personal merit will not diminish that harmony. But you must rise to each occasion – the one I now offer you is of no common cast, and please remember that any failure to push your advantage to the utmost will be severely judged. I have displayed you as persons of great taste and judgment. Don't leave me a sorry figure in consequence but present me rather as your fond but not infatuated relation, able and ready to back you up, your faithful Brother and Brother-in-law,

Henry James.

The remaining passages of James's dictation were taken down at various times, some in longhand by James's niece. This part comes closest to modern 'stream of consciousness' fiction for there is fragmentation and discontinuity:

> across the border
> all the pieces
> Individual souls, great of ... on which

great perfections are If one does ... in the fulfilment with the neat and pure and perfect – to the success or as he or she moves through life, following admiration unfailing ... in the highway – Problems are very sordid.

He wandered off to allude to Robert Louis Stevenson in a less fragmentary way and perhaps to Henry Adams who had visited at Vailima.

> One of the earliest of the consumers of the great globe in the interest of the attraction exercised by the great R.L.S. of those days, comes in, afterwards, a visitor at Vailima and ... there and pious antiquities to his domestic annals.

At the end, on a day of sore throat and much malaise, he dictated a cogent passage which seemed to show an awareness that he no longer could command his old coherence. 'These final and faded remarks,' he dictated, 'have some interest and some character – but this should be extracted by a highly competent person only – some such whom I don't presume to name, will furnish such last offices.' Implicit in this was still the lingering of an old curiosity, his sense that all of life, even the act of dying, had interest in it, to be discerned and recorded. The rest of the passage, however, has in it a note of despair and then of resignation:

> invoke more than one kind presence, several could help, and many would – but it all better too much left than too much done. I never dreamed of such duties as laid upon me. This sore throaty condition is the last I ever invoked for the purpose.

There would be another Napoleonic stance, some time later. In talk with Mrs William James one day he asked if his nephew Billy had friends and said he wished one of the boys had connections in England. The conversation could have occurred in a tale by Henry James:

'You are their connection with England and Europe,' Mrs William James said.

'Yes, I know, and I should say, without being fatuous, with the future.'

'With the future always. They will try to follow you.'

'Tell them *to follow, to be faithful, to take me seriously.*'

118

Over the Abyss

LORD MORLEY, later Viscount Morley of Blackburn, statesman and man of letters, had always regarded Henry James as a superficial and trivial person. To be sure, James had written one of the most successful volumes in the 'English Men of Letters Series' which Morley edited for the Macmillans – his study of Hawthorne – but he had also written on French writers and on France and Lord Morley considered his aesthetic view and concern with French novelists simply 'honest scribble-work'. Morley's subjects were grandiose – Voltaire, Rousseau, Diderot, and then he had done a large life of Gladstone. Thus it was that when Prime Minister Asquith told Morley that he was thinking of recommending James for the Order of Merit, the greatest distinction conferred by the Crown on civilians, and that James as a British subject was now eligible for this honour, held by Thomas Hardy and George Meredith, Morley opposed him. What had James done but write of the idle rich as compared with Hardy's personages? In the face of Morley's vigorous opposition, Asquith wavered. He was fond of Henry James. He knew that he was gravely ill. And the New Year's honours list was almost ready.

Edward Marsh, who had served as Winston Churchill's secretary, was now attached to the Prime Minister's office. He had known James for some years. When he read James's preface to the Rupert Brooke volume he was profoundly moved. On 18 December he wrote a long and remarkable memorandum to the Prime Minister. 'May I write a few words in the hope that the question of the Order of Merit for Henry James has not been irrevocably set aside?'

There was, he argued, little doubt of James's right to stand beside Meredith and Hardy, the only novelists admitted thus far to the Order. If they had qualities not in James, it was equally true James had qualities which they did not possess.

It has been said that the great French novelists are conscious artists, the English inspired amateurs. Henry James is the exception. No writer of his time gives the same impression of knowledge and mastery in the architectural structure of his works, and in the gradual building up of atmosphere, character, and situation.

Marsh reminded Asquith that James's 300 friends and admirers had said in presenting him with the portrait and a Golden Bowl, 'You are the writer, the master of rare and beautiful art, in whose work creation and criticism meet as they have never met before in our language.' Marsh continued:

He is sometimes blamed for dealing only with characters drawn from the hothouse life of the leisured classes, hypertrophied in intellect and emotion; but an artist should be judged not by his choice of material but by his treatment. It would be equally fair to rule out Thomas Hardy for his complete failure to represent any educated person. Henry James's shorter stories are certainly not inferior to those of any English writer. His style may be criticized as mannered, and sometimes obscure; on the other hand it is one of the most individual that has ever been evolved; it is infinitely expressive, except when it defeats itself by trying to express too much; and it rises at times to the height of beauty.

In his thorough way Marsh proceeded to descibe James's qualifications as a critic. He mentioned the prefaces to the New York Edition, 'a uniquely illuminating account of an artist's creative processes'. He then pointed to James's influence on other writers – listing Bennett, Wells, Mrs Wharton, Anne Douglas Sedgwick. He invoked Stevenson's regard for James; he mentioned Edmund Gosse. He said he was certain 'the profession of letters as a whole would warmly welcome this appointment'. There were two extraneous considerations. One was James's generous and impressive gesture of adherence to England's cause. And the other was that the United States would appreciate the compliment to an American-born writer such as James. 'I understand Lord Morley is against the proposal; but with the greatest respect for him I could wish that some opinion might be taken which would be representative of a later epoch in taste.'

The effect of this vigorous memorandum was immediate. Asquith needed just such arguments to stiffen the case for James against Morley. Two days after Marsh submitted the memorandum, a message came from Buckingham Palace, signed by the King's secretary. 'The King, acting upon your recommendation of the case, will be prepared to confer the Order of Merit upon Henry James.'

I

It was announced on New Year's day. A great pile of telegrams and letters descended on Carlyle Mansions. One was a note from George Alexander, who said that he was proud to have produced *Guy Domville* even though it had not been a success. How much of this mail Henry James saw we do not know. Lord Bryce brought the insignia of the rare order to James's bedside. The distinguished invalid seemed pleased. Minnie Kidd reported that he said to her 'turn off the light so as to spare my blushes'. Mrs James read him some of the telegrams and he said 'what curious manifestations such occasions call forth!' The occasion was muted; the novelist did not need excitement. Miss Bosanquet was a little disturbed at Mrs William James's nonchalance when word arrived from Buckingham Palace that Sir Harry Legge wanted to know when he could see Mr James to deliver a message from the King.

Things had become a little easier during the first days of the new year. Peggy after a rough wintry voyage reached her uncle's bedside. James's mind seemed clearer; he signed a power of attorney for Mrs William James to allow her to take care of all the servants and the bills. But at this time Miss Bosanquet received a jolt. She found a note written by Peggy criticizing her for having taken too much upon herself and that she had seemed to be getting pleasure 'managing things in a heartless sort of way while the faithful servants have slaved to the breaking-point'. In a letter to her oldest brother, Peggy said Miss Bosanquet had been 'getting a bit above herself'. The reality was that Mrs William did not like Miss Bosanquet's writing about Henry James's condition to Mrs Wharton – she so intensely disliked Mrs Wharton, partly from her puritanical revulsion at the adultery in *The Reef* and partly from gossip she had heard that Mrs Wharton had lovers. Peggy had told her mother Mrs Wharton's morals 'are scarcely such as to fit her to be the companion of the young and innocent'. From this time on James's amanuensis found herself more and more excluded from 21 Carlyle Mansions. Miss Bosanquet was deeply hurt and unaware that New England puritanism as well as bourgeois morality played a large role in her banishment. She noted 'it was none of my wish to be alone with the household'. She had done what she felt was her duty. She was, however, summoned when James wanted her. Otherwise there was little for her to do except occasional typing jobs. On the day in which her diary records the criticism of her work, she sets down also the message dictated by James for Edmund Gosse – 'tell Gosse that my powers of recuperation are very great and that I'm making progress toward recovery without withdrawal'.

2

There were moments when James seemed to be entirely in the past. He spoke for example of having tea at Carlyle's house with his father. There were further incidents between Miss Bosanquet and Mrs William. Miss Bosanquet asked whether she was to write to Mr Pinker about a contract and was told 'I'll see Mr Pinker myself if necessary.'

Peggy and Mrs James were distinctly hostile – 'the presumptuous secretary being put in her place and slinking out of the presence of righteousness', Theodora wrote in her diary. From then on she came daily to inquire about her employer but stayed only if asked to do a specific bit of work. Occasionally the New Englanders were more friendly. One morning Peggy said her uncle was remembering things more clearly as for instance the English clothes she was wearing. He had helped her buy them a year before. Apparently Edith Wharton sensed that all was not well, for she wrote to Miss Bosanquet asking her whether she would like to be her secretary. 'I don't think I shall,' Miss Bosanquet noted, 'it's too alarming a prospect.' She declined the offer on the ground she did not know French well enough. Actually she was proficient in the language.

In January, James's nephew, Harry arrived 'nearly white-haired, but still black-moustached. He has a tremendous chin – the most obstinate-looking jaw,' Miss Bosanquet noted. He asked her to go through the unfinished typescripts and make lists. He went to Rye and had inventories made of the furniture and the books. Mrs James gave Miss Bosanquet her cheque for her month's salary. Miss Bosanquet returned it. Mrs James, contrite, insisted that she keep it.

Intrigue surrounded the Master to the end. His sick-life was now reduced to a routine. Harry prepared himself to be James's executor. Mrs William wondered which furniture to take back to America from Lamb House. But what is most interesting, in reading her letters to her children, and her diary, is the dawning on her that Henry James was a great and important figure; that the English stood in awe of him. She had for so long accepted the idea that he was simply William's artistic brother, a kind, amiable, gentle, idiosyncratic man. In her letters this light grows and grows. Some of her letters to her sons in America are touching in their picture of the Master finally at bay:

He seems like a tired child but tranquil, comfortable, enjoying his food and the sitting on a big lounge in the window whence he can look out at the river, with the ever-creeping barges and the low-lying clouds. He thinks he is voyaging and visiting foreign cities, and sometimes he asks for his glasses and paper and imagines that he writes. And sometimes his hand moves over the counterpane as if writing. He is never impatient, or contrary or troubled about anything. He still recognizes us and likes to have us sit awhile beside him. He very especially likes Burgess – 'Burgess James' he called him yesterday. It is a touching sight to see little Burgess holding his hand and half kneeling in the chair beside him, his face very near to Henry, trying to understand the confused words Henry murmurs to him.

James thought as he watched the passing boats on the Thames that he was on a ship. When he asked for Burgess on one occasion, Mrs James said he was out doing errands. 'How extraordinary that Burgess should be leaving the ship to do errands!' he exclaimed. To Peggy he turned one day and said 'I hope your father will be in soon – he is the one person in all Rome I want to see.' And again 'I should so like to have William with me.'

The Master continued on this plateau until the last week of February. On the 23rd when Mrs William came into the sickroom he said to her 'Beloved Alice' and then told her to tell William he was leaving in two days. And then to Alice he said 'helpful creature to William and to me'. He may have been having a premonition of death. Two days later he was seriously ill. On the 24th he spoke of 'a night of horror and terror'. On the next day 'stay with me, Alice, stay with me'. He lapsed into unconsciousness on that day. On 27 February the nurse summoned Mrs William. The novelist was breathing hard and trembling. She sat beside him till the symptoms passed and he slept. His pulse and temperature were normal. He tried to speak during the day but his words were unintelligible. On 28 February he could take no nourishment. At four that afternoon the doctor said 'this is the end'. James was breathing in short gasps. He had oedema. At six he sighed – three sighing breaths, at long intervals, the last one, Mrs William James noted, 'very faint'. She wrote, 'He was gone. Not a shadow on his face, nor the contraction of a muscle.'

3

Miss Bosanquet, arriving at Carlyle Mansions that evening, met Emily Sargent in the hall and learned the news. She left a note for Mrs James and then wired Edith Wharton who wrote her a day or so later that James had been 'one of the wisest and noblest men that ever lived. We who knew him well know how great he would have been if he had never written a line.'

The long cruel dying was at an end. Howard Sturgis called it that. James's will to live had been strong and he had died with the same tenacity as he had lived. On the 29th Miss Bosanquet asked if she could be of help; she was assured that 'everything had been provided for'. There was talk of a service in Westminster Abbey; it was however not feasible and Mrs William decided in favour of a funeral in Chelsea Old Church. The body remained in Carlyle Mansions. Burgess gave his master his last shave. The coffin was brought and James was placed in it. Miss Bosanquet returned on 1 March and was taken into the drawing-room by Minnie Kidd. Henry James O.M. lay in his coffin. It was covered with a black pall and there was a white square over his face which Minnie Kidd the maid folded back. The face was bandaged to keep the jaw from falling. 'It looked very fine,' Miss Bosanquet wrote,

a great work of art in ivory wax. Perfectly peaceful, but entirely dissociated from everything that was his personality. I quite understand what Mrs James meant by speaking about the great feeling of tenderness one has for the dead body that is left behind. One feels that the spirit that inhabited it isn't there to care for it any longer.

She went back and viewed the body on the next day. The Master looked more like his living self because this time there was no bandage around his face. 'Several people who have seen the dead face are struck with the likeness to Napoleon which is certainly great.'

And so the funeral of the Master was held, in the little old Chelsea church which had seen much literary history. There came to it, in the midst of war, those who had known Henry James and cherished him – Sargent and his sister, Kipling, Gosse, swollen-eyed Goody Allen, Lucy Clifford, representatives of the Prime Minister and the war group James had met. Dickens's daughter, Mrs Perugini was there, and Howard Sturgis, the Colvins, the Pollocks, and many others including Ellen Terry. The coffin was carried in and placed in the chancel. Mrs James, Peggy, Sargent and his sister sat in the front pew; the servants sat on the opposite side. Fanny Prothero wandered in looking lost, and found herself a seat far back. Whether Persse was there, we do not know. Hugh was back in Russia; he did not get the news until some days later. The service was conventional – the lesson from I Corinthians and two hymns *For all the Saints* and *O God, our help in ages past*. But it wasn't the beautiful singing or the service so much as the emotion of the mourners, a kind of universal love that held them together for this strange lonely man from America who had lived so much and so intensely in their midst and was now gone.

Henry James had inscribed *Notes on Novelists* at the outbreak of the war to Edmund Gosse with the words 'Over the Abyss'. Gosse conveyed the emotion of the mourners who overflowed Chelsea Old Church in a letter to *The Times* on the day after the funeral.

As we stood round the shell of that incomparable brain of that noble and tender heart, it flashed across me that to generations yet unawakened to a knowledge of his value the Old Chelsea Church must for ever be the Altar of the Dead ... He was a supreme artist; but what we must remember and repeat is that he was a hero ... an English hero of whom England shall be proud.

Gosse was alluding to James's embrace of England and expression of loyalty in the time of war. A plaque honouring James and speaking of 'amenities of brave decisions' hangs on the wall of the church. Sixty years later England paid its ultimate honour by unveiling a memorial stone to James in the Poet's Corner of Westminster Abbey.

The body was cremated at Golders Green. Mrs James later took the ashes back to America. She smuggled them in; it was wartime and she took no chances. The urn was buried beside the graves of Henry's mother and sister. He had stood there in 1904 and looked at the 'Medusa Face of life' and cried *Basta! Basta!*

The will was simple. James left all his property to Mrs William James and after her to her children. Harry received Lamb House and its contents. Peggy got his insurance. The Sargent Portrait was left as promised to the National Portrait Gallery. James bestowed gifts of £100 on Jocelyn Persse, Hugh Walpole, and Lucy Clifford. All the servants were provided for. There were gifts to various nephews and nieces, children of his younger brother, but a codicil withdrew the gift from his nephew Edward Holton James, Robertson's son, because he had written an anti-royalist pamphlet which had embarrassed his uncle.

The obituaries – in newspapers filled with the war – were of great length. One newspaper inquiring into the status of James's works found that very few of the Master's novels were in print, and the late ones were expensively available in the New York Edition. James would indeed sink from sight; swallowed up by the war, his would be among the forgotten reputations of the 1920s, although an occasional subject of controversy, mainly about his expatriation. It would take time for the world to rediscover him. When the Second World War came he was, however, remembered and read, and his centenary awoke new interest in a new generation. The author of *The Portrait of a Lady* and *The Wings of the Dove*, of *The Ambassadors* and *The Golden Bowl* had sensed in his own life that somehow he would be, as he had spoken of Pater, a Figure. Unlike Pater's, his work itself gained an audience, slowly at first, until in the mid-twentieth century his books were in print in great numbers, as many as five editions in paperback of *The Ambassadors* alone. His letters were saved in quantities that would have astonished him and became expensive autographs. He became a word, an image, a symbol long after his death. He was constantly quoted – certain of his phrases reverberating beyond the grave into modernity. The secret of his enduring fame was a simple one: he had dealt exclusively with the myth of civilization; he had written about men and women in their struggle to control their emotions and passions within the forms and manners of society. He understood human motive and behaviour and was the first of the modern psychological novelists. He had carried his art into a high complexity and he had endured because he had fashioned a style. Long ago he had said that a style is a writer's passport to posterity. He had issued such a passport to himself. He had had great ambitions; he had sought power in craft and had found it; he had fashioned a trans-Atlantic myth; he had learned that artists take the chaos of life and shape it into forms that endure. 'The older civilization gave him the wonderful things he wanted: but the wonder was his own,' said G. K. Chesterton in one of the most discerning and eloquent of the tributes. 'His whole world is made out of sympathy; out of a whole network of sympathy.' To his nephews and nieces his message had been that they be kind, and kind, and kind! Younger men would find him a signpost, a guide, a vast encompassing intelligence. Ezra Pound would speak of him as a Baedeker to a Continent. Unlike Browning, his disciples formed no 'James Societies'. They simply read him and wrote about him. His centenary in 1943 found him claimed by the two great literatures of the English-speaking peoples. His influence was pervasive – the entire 'modern movement' drew upon his explorations of subjective worlds, from Joyce to Virginia Woolf. He had given his message, 'tell them to follow, to be faithful, to take me seriously'. He would be taken seriously. But the memory of his wit also remained, and of his courage. He had indeed planned a career and carried it out as a general plans his campaigns and wins his victories. His elegy of Jeffrey Aspern might have been written of himself

... at a period when our native land was nude and crude and provincial, when the famous 'atmosphere' it is supposed to lack was not even missed, when literature was lonely there and art and form almost impossible, he had found means to live and write like one of the first; to be free and general and not at all afraid; to feel, understand and express everything.

Long before he had urged young novelists to 'be generous and delicate and pursue the prize'. He had been generous; he had been delicate; and the prize for him had been always the treasure of his craft. He felt powerful because he knew that his imagination could transfigure life; and he said that the greatest freedom of man was his 'independence of thought', which enabled the artist to enjoy 'the aggression of infinite modes of being'.

He had written some years before his death an essay, *Is There a Life after Death?* If one meant physical life, he believed there was none. Death was absolute. What lived beyond life was what the creative consciousness had found and made: and only if enshrined in enduring form. Like Proust he saw that art alone retains and holds the life – the consciousness – of man long after the finders and the makers are gone. The true immortality was the immortal picture or statue, the immortal phrase whether of music or of words. This was his deepest faith. He sought beauty instead of ugliness, kindness instead of cruelty, peace instead of violence; he preferred the poetry of prose, the magic of style, the things shaped within the past given sacredness by their survival. In one of the last sentences of his essay on life after death he wrote : 'I reach beyond the laboratory brain.'

This was his final word to the new age.

New York 1950
Honolulu 1971

Index

Works by Henry James

MENTIONED IN THIS VOLUME

Novels

Tales

Plays

Collected Tales and Non-Fiction

MORE ABOUT PENGUINS
AND PELICANS

Penguinews, which appears every month, contains details of all the new books issued by Penguins as they are published. From time to time it is supplemented by *Penguins in Print*, which is our complete list of almost 5,000 titles.

A specimen copy of *Penguinews* will be sent to you free on request. Please write to Dept EP, Penguin Books Ltd, Harmondsworth, Middlesex, for your copy.

In the U.S.A.: For a complete list of books available from Penguins in the United States write to Dept CS, Penguin Books, 625 Madison Avenue, New York, New York 10022.

In Canada: For a complete list of books available from Penguins in Canada write to Penguin Books Canada Ltd, 2801 John Street, Markham, Ontario L3R 1B4.